AutoCAD Advanced Techniques

Craig W. Sharp
Walter W. Hamm

AutoCAD®
Advanced Techniques

© 1989 by Que® Corporation

All rights reserved. Printed in the United States of America. No part of this book may be used or reproduced in any form or by any means, or stored in a database or retrieval system, without prior written permission of the publisher except in the case of brief quotations embodied in critical articles and reviews. Making copies of any part of this book for any purpose other than your own personal use is a violation of United States copyright laws. For information, address Que Corporation, 11711 N. College Ave., Carmel, IN 46032.

Library of Congress Catalog No.: 89-60848

ISBN No.: 0-88022-436-3

This book is sold *as is*, without warranty of any kind, either express or implied, respecting the contents of this book, including but not limited to implied warranties for the book's quality, performance, merchantability, or fitness for any particular purpose. Neither Que Corporation nor its dealers or distributors shall be liable to the purchaser or any other person or entity with respect to any liability, loss, or damage caused or alleged to be caused directly or indirectly by this book.

93 92 91 90 89   8 7 6 5 4 3 2 1

Interpretation of the printing code: the rightmost double-digit number is the year of the book's printing; the rightmost single-digit number, the number of the book's printing. For example, a printing code of 89-4 shows that the fourth printing of the book occurred in 1989.

AutoCAD Advanced Techniques is based on Release 10 of AutoCAD.

DEDICATION

To Renee and Leo.
-C.W.S.

To Charles and Elaine.
-W.W.H.

Publishing Manager

Allen L. Wyatt, Sr.

Editors

Gail S. Burlakoff
Midge Stocker

Editorial Assistant

Ann K. Taylor

Technical Editors

Robert L. Knight
Scott D. Pesci

Index

Sherry Massey

Illustrator

Susan Moore

Cover and Book Design

Dan Armstrong

Production

Dan Armstrong   Joe Ramon
David Kline   Dennis Sheehan
Lori A. Lyons   M. Louise Shinault
Jennifer Matthews   Peter Tocco
Jon Ogle

Composed in Garamond and American Typewriter by Que Corporation

ABOUT THE AUTHORS

Craig W. Sharp

Craig W. Sharp, a registered architect in Florida and Indiana, has practiced architecture internationally for 17 years. He has been involved in the use of CAD from its early years, beginning during his education at Ball State University, where he earned a Bachelor of Architecture degree, with a minor in Urban Planning.

Craig has been using AutoCAD since Release 2.1. For three years, he has provided CAD consulting services including custom menu design, AutoLISP programming, and instruction in the use of AutoCAD and AutoCAD AEC. He can be contacted on CompuServe; his I.D. number is 73417, 2320.

Walter W. Hamm

Walter W. Hamm, of Tampa, Florida, is a registered architect practicing as a sole proprietor. He earned a Master of Arts degree in Architecture from the University of Florida.

Walter, who has used AutoCAD since Release 2.1, has practiced architecture for 13 years and has developed and implemented CAD systems in several firms. He has designed many multifamily, commercial, and residential projects in the United States and abroad, and uses AutoCAD daily in his practice.

Content Overview

Introduction 1

Part I Getting in Shape

Chapter 1   CAD Management: An Overview 9
Chapter 2   Evaluating and Developing Your CAD Habits...... 25
Chapter 3   The Basics 51
Chapter 4   Basic System Management...................... 75
Chapter 5   Software Companions........................... 93
Chapter 6   Project and Drawing Management............113
Chapter 7   Advanced Management Techniques...........143

Part II Perfecting Your Techniques

Chapter 8   The Ten Commandments—Times Three 171
Chapter 9   The Tasks At Hand 185
Chapter 10 Look, Ma—No Hands! 215
Chapter 11 The Professional Look 239
Chapter 12 AutoCAD from All Sides: 3-D 269

Part III Getting Serious

Chapter 13 AutoLISP Never Was Plain English..............297
Chapter 14 AutoLISP's Bells and Whistles..................319
Chapter 15 Advanced Presentation Techniques 353
Chapter 16 Advanced Hardware Concepts 371
Chapter 17 The Ultimate CAD-Management Tool 399

Appendix A   LSRPREP.LSP 411
Appendix B   Removing and Inserting Drawing Details 423
Appendix C   Sample Batch Files 435
Appendix D   A LISP Routine for Renaming Layers of Entities....441
Appendix E   DPLOT.LSP.......................................453
Appendix F   A Set of Job-Management Tools 465
Appendix G   Sample Menu Macros..............................517
Appendix H   Routines for Automated Drawing................525
Appendix I   ACAD.DWG Settings 543
Appendix J   Common AutoCAD Errors (and What To Do
             About Them)......................................547
Appendix K   Other Sources of Information...................553

Glossary 587
Index 591

TABLE OF CONTENTS

Introduction 1
    Who Should Use This Book 2
    How To Use This Book 2
    What Is in This Book 3
    Assumptions about the Reader 4
    What This Book Will and Won't Do 5
    Why We Wrote This Book 5

I   Getting in Shape

    What Chapter 1 Is About 8
1   **CAD Management: An Overview** 9
    CAD Management and Implementation 9
        Financial Issues 11
        Anticipated Work Flow 12
        Processes Suitable for Automation 13
        Installation Procedures 14
            Personnel 14
            Physical Workstation 16
    Drawing Management 18
    Procedures and Manuals 18
        Procedures 19
        Manuals 19
    Customization 20
    Training 20
    Data Management 21
    Summary 23

    What Chapter 2 Is About 24
2   **Evaluating and Developing Your**
       CAD Habits 25
    Comfort before Speed 26
    Your AutoCAD System 26
        Input Devices: Keyboards, Digitizers, and Mice ... 27
            Plotters 29
    Supplementary Software 30

	AutoCAD Commands You Should Know..................	31
	Macros and Menus	32
	Using DOS...	32
	Disk Drives	33
	Naming Conventions...............................	33
	Directories	35
	Utilities..	37
	A Checklist of AutoCAD Concepts	38
	A Test of AutoCAD Basics................................	39
	Develop Good Habits	42
	Avoid Bad Habits	42
	Ways You Can Learn More about AutoCAD	43
	Answers to the AutoCAD Test.............................	45
	Summary	48
	What Chapter 3 Is About................................	50
3	**The Basics**	**51**
	Start with DOS	51
	Using Directories	52
	Can You Write a Batch File?.........................	53
	The ECHO Command	54
	The PAUSE Command	55
	Replaceable Parameters...........................	55
	The GOTO Command	56
	The IF Command	56
	FOR..IN..DO......................................	59
	The SHIFT Command	59
	Does Your Hard Disk Live a Clean Life?..................	60
	Optimizers	61
	Help—I Lost a Drawing!.................................	62
	What Is the Cause?.................................	62
	Media Failure	62
	Hardware Failure	64
	Improper System Management.....................	64
	Recovering Lost Files	65
	Don't Let It Happen Again..........................	65
	Word Processors	65
	Document and Nondocument (Programming) Modes.....	66
	The Right One for the Job...........................	66
	A Little about Hardware	67
	Inside the Box—The Computer	68
	Behind the Scenes—The Monitor.....................	69
	Inside the Tablet—The Digitizer	70
	Summary	72

	What Chapter 4 Is About...	74
4	**Basic System Management**.............................	**75**
	The CONFIG.SYS File	75
	The Shell Program (COMMAND.COM).................	76
	BREAK...	77
	Buffers and Files	77
	Device Drivers..	78
	Hard Drive..	79
	Extended/Expanded Memory......................	79
	Tape Storage	79
	Keyboard..	79
	LASTDRIVE	80
	The AUTOEXEC.BAT File.....................................	80
	ECHO OFF...	81
	PATH...	81
	PROMPT..	82
	SET	82
	Memory? What Memory?	84
	Classification of Memory	84
	Expanding Your Horizons and Extending Your Goals	85
	Memory Management...	86
	Is It Working? How To Find Out	89
	OS/2 or DOS V4.0—Should I Be Concerned?.............	90
	Summary	91
	What Chapter 5 Is About...	92
5	**Software Companions**......................................	**93**
	DOS Utilities...	93
	Hard Disk Management and Backup....................	94
	Shareware and Freeware DOS Utilities	94
	Database-Management Programs	96
	dBASE	96
	Programs for Numbers	97
	Lotus 1-2-3...	98
	Draw A Graph...Impress Your Friends	98
	Project Management	99
	Watching the Clock	99
	Calculators..	101
	Multitasking Software	101
	TSR Programs...	102
	Word-Processing Software	103
	Desktop Publishing Programs.................................	104
	The Entire Software Environment	105

	It All Works Together	108
	Communications	109
	Modems and the ADESK Forum	109
	Summary	111
	What Chapter 6 Is About	112
6	**Project and Drawing Management**	**113**
	Project Management	113
	Overall Procedures	113
	Create an Office Manual	114
	File Management	114
	Drawing Management	115
	Plot Procedures	116
	Consultant Procedures	116
	General Procedures	117
	Project Conventions: If You Don't Have Any, Get Some	118
	Organize with DOS Directories	119
	Using AutoCAD Directories	120
	Loading from a Subdirectory	121
	The DOS PATH Command	122
	The DOS SET Command	125
	Two Tricky, More Complicated Methods	125
	File-Naming Conventions	127
	Backing Up Before You Go Forward	130
	Drawing Standards	131
	Limits and Setup	132
	Reusable Work	135
	Standard Notation	138
	Plotting for Success	139
	Drawing Standards Make Plotting Standards	139
	Summary	140
	What Chapter 7 Is About	142
7	**Advanced Management Techniques**	**143**
	File Management: That File Was Just Here	143
	Simple Batch-File Management: Cook Up a Batch for the Menu	144
	Other Menu Systems: Someone Else's Recipes	146
	Accessing Drawing Files: So That's What's in that Drawing	147
	Annotating Your Drawing Files	147
	Backups Revisited: Storing and Archiving Your Files	148
	Clean Backups	149

	Backing Up with LISP	150
	Drawing Management: Make Your Drawings Work for You	151
	Layer-Naming Conventions	152
	Combining Pin-registering and CAD	156
	Storing Plot Information in the Drawing	158
	Record Maintenance	162
	A LISP Routine for Tracking Drawings	162
	Create a Project Library System	164
	Automating the Process: Programs You Can Use	165
	Summary	167

II Perfecting Your Techniques

	What Chapter 8 Is About	170
8	**The Ten Commandments—Times Three**	**171**
	Buying Software and Hardware	171
	Developing Your Ideas	174
	Making Your Pieces Fit Their Puzzle	178
	Summary	182
	What Chapter 9 Is About	184
9	**The Tasks At Hand**	**185**
	Menus—The Link from Project Management to Drawing Management	185
	A Worthwhile Drawing Menu System	186
	Yours or Theirs?	187
	Assessing Your Requirements: How Do You Spend Your Time?	188
	Analyzing Your Work Flow	188
	Menus and Drawing Standards—Jack and Jill	190
	Layer Control	192
	Drawing Use	192
	Number the Drawing, Using Established Standards	193
	Standardized Insertion	193
	Variable Scales	194
	Menu Limitations	195
	How To Manipulate Your Work with Menus	195
	Section Labels	196
	Submenus	196
	Command Selection	197
	Screen- and Pull-Down Menu Commands	198

Tablet- and Button-Menu Commands	198
Icon Commands	198
Special Characters and Conventions	199
Task Menus: The Solution to Productivity	200
When To Standardize—and How Far To Go	201
Basic Tools for Standardization	202
AutoLISP	202
Blocks	203
Shapes	204
Modify Other Menu Systems To Meet Your Needs	205
Pitfalls and Standard Errors	206
Testing and Debugging Processes	206
Protection	208
Kelvination	208
Pull-Down versus Screen versus Tablet Menus	209
Macros Are Easy—Typing Isn't	210
Menu Tips and Tricks	210
Combining a Menu Library	211
Help—A Slideshow	211
Create Your Own Durable Menu	212
Summary	212

10

What Chapter 10 Is About	214
Look, Ma—No Hands!	**215**
Management from the Coffee Room	215
Script Files	216
Automated Drawing Assembly and Plotting	217
Automated Drawing	221
Shapes versus Blocks	222
The Basics—Parametrically Speaking	223
Orientation, Angles, Radians, Polar Functions	223
Are dBASE and Lotus 1-2-3 CAD Programs?	227
Importing and Exporting Data	228
Drawings, Schedules, and Charts	230
Revealing the Hidden Power of Attributes	231
Taking an Inventory of Your Drawing	234
Summary	236

11

What Chapter 11 Is About	238
The Professional Look	**239**
Lines	239
Line Weight Standards	240
How Linetypes Work	241

	Modifying and Improving Linetypes	244
	Make Your Own Linetypes	245
	Font Files	247
	How Font Files Work	248
	Modifying, Improving, and Creating Font Files	252
	Third-Party Fonts	254
	Hatch Patterns	256
	How Hatch Patterns Work	257
	Modifying, Improving, and Creating Hatch Patterns	258
	Rendering with AutoCAD	262
	Plotting	264
	Halftones	264
	Plotting Media	264
	Camera-Ready Drawings	265
	If You Plot Somewhere Else	265
	Summary	266
	What Chapter 12 Is About	268
12	**AutoCAD from All Sides: 3-D**	269
	Project Management and 3-D	269
	Draw It and Walk Around It	271
	Dos and Don'ts	272
	If You're Falling Asleep Waiting for Regens	279
	3D in Release 10 Is Really Three-dimensional	279
	Isometric, Axonometric, and Perspective Drawings	283
	AutoShade	285
	Other Shading Software	292
	At the Movies—Using AutoFlix	293
	Summary	294

III Getting Serious

	What Chapter 13 Is About	296
13	**AutoLISP Never Was Plain English**	297
	Basic AutoLISP Concepts	298
	Atoms	298
	Lists	299
	Functions	300
	What Does that LISP Term Mean?	300
	Special Characters in AutoLISP	302
	Special Conditions	304
	General Functions	305

(load <filename> <failure option>) 305
　　　(defun <routine name symbol> <argument list>
　　　　　<expressions>...) 306
　　　(setq <symbol1> <expression> <symbol2>
　　　　　<expression>...) 306
　　　(setvar <variable name> <value>) 307
　　　(command <arguments>...) 307
　　　(eval <expression>) 307
　　　(progn <expression1> <expression2>...) 308
　　Manipulating Data Types 309
　　　(angtos <angle> <mode> <precision>) 309
　　　(atof <string>) and (atoi <string>) 310
　　　(itoa <integer>) and (rtos <real> <mode>
　　　　　<precision>) 310
　　　(float <integer>) 311
　　　(strcase <string> <which case>) 311
　　　(strcat <string1> <string2> ...) 311
　　　(strlen <string>) 312
　　　(substr <string> <start> <length>) 312
　　Mathematical Functions 312
　　　(angle <pt1> <pt2>) 313
　　　(distance <pt1> <pt2>) 314
　　　pi (π) 314
　　　(polar <pt> <angle> <distance>) 314
　　　(rem <first number> <second number>) 314
　　LISP Programming Pitfalls 315
　　Summary 316

　　What Chapter 14 Is About 318
14　**AutoLISP's Bells and Whistles** 319
　　Advanced Mathematical Functions 319
　　　(trans <pt> <from> <to> <disp>) 320
　　List Manipulation 321
　　　(append <list 1> <list2>...) 321
　　　(assoc <item> <association list>) 321
　　　caar, cdar, cadr, cddr, cadar, car, cdr, etc. 322
　　　(cons <element> <list>) 323
　　　(list <expression 1> <expression 2>...) 323
　　　(length <list>) 323
　　　(member <expression> <list>) 324
　　　(nth <integer> <list>) 324
　　　(subst <newitem> <olditem> <list>) 325
　　Entity Manipulation 326

(entsel <prompt>)	326
(entnext <entity name>)	326
(entlast)	327
(handent <handle>)	327
(entdel <ename>)	328
(entget <entity name>)	328
(entmod <new entity list>)	328
(entupd <entity name>)	329
(ssget <mode> <pt1> <pt2>)	330
(sslength <selection set>)	331
(ssname <selection set> <index>)	331
(ssadd <entity name> <selection set>)	332
(ssdel <entity name> <selection set>)	332
(ssmemb <entity name> <selection set>)	332
Table Manipulation	333
(tblnext <table name> <rewind>)	333
(tblsearch <table name> <symbol> <setnext>)	334
Input/Output	334
(getangle <pt> <prompt>)	335
(getcorner <pt> <prompt>)	335
(getdist <pt> <prompt>)	336
(getenv <variable name>)	336
(getint <prompt>) and *(getreal <prompt>)*	337
(getkword <prompt>)	337
(getorient <prompt>)	337
(getpoint <pt> <prompt>)	338
(getstring <carriage return> <prompt>)	338
(getvar <variable name>)	338
(initget <mode> <string>)	339
(findfile <filename>)	340
(open <filename> <mode>)	340
(write-line <string> <file symbol>)	341
(read-line <file symbol>)	341
(close <file symbol>)	342
(menucmd <string>)	342
(prompt <string>)	342
(prin1 <expression> <file symbol>)	343
(princ <expression> <file symbol>)	343
(print <expression> <file symbol>)	343
Conditional Functions	344
(and <expression 1> <expression 2>...)	344
(cond (<test> <result>)...)	345
(equal <expression 1> <expression 2> <fuzz>)	345

           (if \<test\> \<then do\> \<else do\>) 346
           (while \<test\> \<expression1\> \<expression2\>...) 346
   AutoLISP's Limitations and Pitfalls 347
       Different System Configurations 348
       Software Conflicts—Who's on First? 349
   Summary 349

What Chapter 15 Is About 352

15   Advanced Presentation Techniques 353

   When AutoCAD Gets Fancy 353
   Can Your Client Afford It? 355
   Talk the Talk: Some New Terms 356
   From AutoCAD to Simulated Reality 359
   Video and Scanner Input and Superimposition:
       Image Capturing 362
   Video Output and Presentation: Modeling 363
   35mm Slides 365
       Homemade Slides 366
       Electronic Slides 367
   Color Printing 367
   Projectors 368
   Summary 369

What Chapter 16 Is About 370

16   Advanced Hardware Concepts 371

   A Few More Basics 371
       Hexadecimal Numbers and Bytes 372
       Buses 374
       Adapters 374
       Microprocessors and Math Coprocessors 375
       Other Chips 375
       Ports 376
       Registers and Stacks 376
       Interrupts 377
       Processor Modes 378
   Monitor and Graphics Cards 379
       Palette of Colors 380
       Display-List Processing 380
       Interlaced and Noninterlaced Display 381
       Scan Rate 382
       Assembling the Pieces 382
   Plotters 384
       Plotter Types 384

	Specifics for Comparison	385
	Expanded/Extended Memory	387
	Dip Switches	389
	RAM Disks	390
	AutoCAD's Use of Extra Memory	392
	Unique Input Devices	394
	Summary	395
	What Chapter 17 Is About	398
17	**The Ultimate Cad-management Tool**	399
	Creative CAD Management	400
	Checking the Basics	402
	Software Considerations	402
	Hardware Considerations	404
	Focusing on Specifics	405
	Finding Solutions	406
	Where To Look for More	407
	What To Do Next	408
	Summary	409
A	**LSRPREP.LSP**	411
B	**Removing and Inserting Drawing Details**	423
	Routine for Extracting Drawing Details (DTL.LSP)	423
	Routine for Inserting Drawings into Different Scale Drawings (INSDET.LSP)	428
C	**Sample Batch-file Menus**	435
	An Interactive Addition: Yes or No?	438
D	**A LISP Routine for Renaming the Layers of Entities**	441
	Creating a New Set of Layer Names (LYRTBL.LSP)	442
	Routine for Converting Entities to New Layers (CNVRT.LSP)	448
E	**DPLOT.LSP**	453
F	**A Set of Job-Management Tools**	465
	The Main Program for AutoCAD Database Manager (MAIN.PRG)	466
	A Program for Importing CDF ASCII Files from AutoCAD (JOB_IMP.PRG)	469

	A Program for Printing a Job History Report (JOB_HIST.PRG)...........................	472
	A Program that Creates Time Report Header (JOB_HEAD.PRG)...........................	475
	A Program for Creating Summaries for Job Report (JOB_SUMM.PRG)...........................	476
	Accumulated Totals Program (JOB_2A.PRG)...........	479
	A Program for Creating a Job Time and Task Report (JOB_TIME.PRG)...........................	483
	A Program for Editing Master Data (MASTER.PRG).......	487
	Program Controller File (PRO_FILE.PRG)..............	489
	Program Data File Structures......................	491
	A Material, Labor, or Equipment Schedule Generator........	492
	A Program for Importing CDF Schedule Files from AutoCAD (SCH_IMP.PRG).....................	492
	A Program for Adding Records to AutoCAD Schedule Records (SCH_ADD.PRG)...................	495
	A Program for Deleting Schedule Records (SCH_DEL.PRG)...........................	498
	A Program for Editing Schedules (SCH_EDIT.PRG).......	502
	A Program for Exporting Schedule to ASCII File (SCH_EXPT.PRG)...........................	506
	Schedule Report Header Program (SCH_HEAD.PRG).....	508
	Data-File Structure...........................	509
	Schedule Report.............................	509
	USER.LSP......................................	509
	Redefining AutoCAD's END Command for USER.LSP........	513
	Sample Reports.................................	513
	Time/Task Report............................	513
	Job History Report...........................	514
	Multiple Script Program (SCR_ALL.EXE)................	515
G	**Sample Menu Macros**............................	**517**
H	**Routines for Automated Drawing**.................	**525**
	A LISP Routine To Combine Drawings for Plot (COMBPLOT.LSP)...........................	525
	The Automated Widget Drawing (WIDGET.SCR)..........	528
	A Parametric Schedule Routine (SCHED.LSP)............	531
	A Lotus 1-2-3-generated Critical Path..................	534
	A LISP Routine for Importing Text (IMPASCII.LSP).........	541
I	**ACAD.DWG Settings**............................	**543**

J	**Common AutoCAD Errors (and What To Do About Them)**	**547**
	Common Error Messages	547
	Problems With AUTOEXEC.BAT	548
	Problems With DOS Environment Space	549
	Memory Settings	549
	SHELL Errors	550
	Tracing and Curing Errors	551
K	**Other Sources of Information**	**553**
	A Listing of Third-party Software	553
	Graphic Aids	554
	Hardware	554
	Utilities	555
	Civil Design Software	560
	Menu Systems	561
	AutoLISP Aids	564
	Facilities Management	564
	Symbols Libraries	565
	Companion Software	565
	Additional Software	566
	AutoCAD Users' Groups	567
	A Reading Resource List	581
	Books on AutoCAD	582
	Books on CAD in General	582
	General Computer Books	583
	Glossary	**587**
	Index	**591**

Acknowledgments

We would like to thank, in no particular order, the people who knowingly or unknowingly contributed to this book. If we left out anyone, we apologize...

Allen Wyatt, Gail Burlakoff, Jamie Clay, Duff Kurland, Brad Zehring, Lansing Pugh, Image Resources of Tampa, CAD Associates, Jerry Norman, Mark Vodhanel, Roger Clay, Phil Kreiker, Lowell Walmsley, John Intorcio, John Segneri, Jason Osgood, Trevor Palmer, Robert Schutz, all the members of the Autodesk Forum, the third-party vendors listed in Appendix K, and Wolfgang Amadeus Mozart.

Trademark Acknowlegments

Que Corporation has made every attempt to supply trademark information about company names, products, and services mentioned in this book. Trademarks indicated below were derived from various sources. Que Corporation cannot attest to the accuracy of this information.

1-2-3, Lotus, Symphony, and VisiCalc are registered trademarks of Lotus Development Corporation.

AEGIS and Domain are trademarks of Apollo Computer Inc.

Apple and Macintosh are registered trademarks of Apple Computer, Inc.

Ashton-Tate, dBASE II, dBASE III, and Multimate are registered trademarks, and dBASE III Plus is a trademark of Ashton-Tate Corporation.

AutoCAD, AutoCAD AEC, and AutoLISP are registered trademarks, and ACAD, ADE, ADI, Advanced User Interface, AUI, AutoFlix, AutoSolid, AutoShade, and DXF are trademarks of Autodesk, Inc.

AutoDATUM is a trademark of CADMASTER Inc.

AutoSHAPE is a trademark of CAD Systems Unlimited, Inc.

Berboulli Box is a registered trademark of Iomega Corporation.

Clipper is a trademark of Nantucket, Inc.

CompuServe Information Service is a registered trademark of CompuServe Incorporated and H&R Block, Inc.

DEC is a registered trademark of Digital Equipment Corporation.

DESQview is a trademark of Quarterdeck Office Systems.

Dr. HALO is a registered trademark of Media Cybernetics, Inc.

FASTBACK Plus is a registered trademark of Fifth Generation Systems, Inc.

IBM and OS/2 are registered trademarks, and IBM PC XT and PS/2 are trademarks of International Business Machines Corporation.

LETTEREASE is a trademark of CAD Lettering Systems, Inc.

Mace Utilities is a registered trademark of Paul Mace Software, Inc.

Microsoft Windows/386, MS-DOS, and XENIX are registered trademarks of Microsoft Corporation.

Norton Commander and Norton Utilities are trademarks of Peter Norton Computing.

PageMaker is a registered trademark of Aldus Corporation.

PC Paint is a trademark of Mouse Systems Corporation.

PC Paintbrush is a registered trademark of ZSoft Corporation.

PCTOOLS Deluxe is a trademark of Central Point Software.

PostScript is a registered trademark of Adobe Systems Incorporated.

ProKey is a trademark of RoseSoft, Inc.

Rampage is a registered mark of AST Research.

SideKick, SuperKey, Turbo C, and Turbo Pascal are registered trademarks of Borland International, Inc.

SmartKey is a trademark of Software Research Technologies.

Software Carousel is a registered trademark of SoftLogic Solutions Corporation.

Sun 3, Sun 386i, Sun 4, and SPARC are trademarks of Sun Microsystems, Inc.

SuperCalc is a registered trademark of Computer Associates International, Inc.

TOPAS and UNIX are trademarks of AT&T Company.

Ventura Publisher is a registered trademark of Ventura Software, Inc.

WordPerfect is a registered trademark, and WordPerfect Library is a trademark of WordPerfect Corporation.

WordStar is a registered trademark of MicroPro International Corporation.

Xerox is a registered trademark of Xerox Corporation.

Introduction

Chapter 1: CAD Management: An Overview
  Chapter 10: Look, Ma—No Hands!
Chapter 2: Evaluating and Developing Your CAD Habits
  Chapter 11: The Professional Look
Chapter 3: The Basics
  Chapter 12: AutoCAD from All Sides: 3-D
Chapter 4: Basic System Management
  Chapter 13: AutoLISP Never Was Plain English
Chapter 5: Software Companions
  Chapter 14: AutoLISP's Bells and Whistles
Chapter 6: Project and Drawing Management
  Chapter 15: Advanced Presentation Techniques
Chapter 7: Advanced Management Techniques
  Chapter 16: Advanced Hardware Concepts
Chapter 8: The Ten Commandments—Times Three
  Chapter 17: The Ultimate CAD-management Tool
Chapter 9: The Tasks At Hand

Introduction

Everyone knows that, as the salesperson said, "CAD will make you four times as productive...!" Well, based on what we have seen, that may be the exception rather than the rule.

Consider Walter's experience:

"I recall that first day with some horror and embarrassment. The vendor had gone, after showing me how to turn the machine on and off and how to plot. He made it look easy. Using the AutoDesk AEC master template, I drew a few lines and circles before adventurously picking ARRAY and innocently answering the prompts. The dark screen grew lighter in color and became white as the lines and circles kept repeating and arraying and repeating and arraying. Well it should be no problem—it should stop after one revolution—shouldn't it? But oh no! What had I done? It would not stop. Had I created some kind of loop? (I had heard about loops.) Drained of all composure and with my face as white as the screen, I called the vendor. This had to be the beginning of the end!?! Ah ^C! I hurriedly quit the drawing and brought up a standard AutoCAD drawing so that my employees could see the ease with which AutoCAD can display a drawing."

Fortunately for us, things got better. Many CAD users are not so lucky. The promises of CAD can be substantially different from the reality. The purpose of this book is to make that salesperson's promises come true.

We don't know anyone who became committed to CAD with the intention of doing work of the same (or poorer) quality than what could be done by hand. But we do know many CAD users who find themselves floundering and won't admit it. They won't admit that they have lost drawings, that they feel confused and frustrated by what goes on inside those beige boxes on their desks, or that they bought an expensive electrostatic dust collector called a CAD system. They won't admit that their CAD system is managing them.

Computerization is a difficult process. The key to making AutoCAD work for you is CAD management and the underlying customization of the system to suit your firm's needs. There are no shortcuts to managing CAD. It takes hard work. Period. The ideas in this book will help you manage CAD systems, CAD projects, and CAD drawings; they also will help you customize your system to your special needs.

The economic justification for introducing computers into your business is based on increased productivity and improved quality of documents. Individuals and companies that have difficulty achieving cost-effectiveness with computers and CAD often suffer from shortcomings in the administration of the project and the CAD system rather than from limitations of the software and hardware.

Who Should Use This Book

This book is for every AutoCAD user who wants to work faster, smarter, and more effectively, alone or as an AutoCAD system manager.

We wrote this book for anyone who has mastered AutoCAD itself but has not mastered system management. Something is missing—but you don't quite know what it is. We have accumulated technical tips, advanced techniques, and helpful shortcuts that can turn you into a power user and your office into a profit center.

How To Use This Book

We think that the best way to become productive with AutoCAD is to venture beyond the AutoCAD command prompt, armed with confidence, a clear understanding of what can (and can't) be done, and how much is involved in doing it. Each chapter in this book is meant to be used as a resource guide on a particular topic. This book is *not* a step-by-step tutorial, nor is it a reformatted version of the *AutoCAD Reference Manual*.

To make sure that you have a good understanding of the basics, you can read all or part of Part I, "Getting In Shape." Then you can read any chapter in Part II, "Perfecting Your Techniques," when you decide that it is time to address the chapter's topic and apply it to what you are doing. As your proficiency grows, you can go on to any chapter in Part III, "Getting Serious."

We intentionally wrote the book this way. We know that you are busy and that you want to solve a problem without having to wade through pages of material that doesn't apply to what you are doing. You'll want to keep this book on your shelf right next to the *AutoCAD Reference Manual*. You can pick it up at any time and explore an unfamiliar area of AutoCAD or refresh your memory of a specific topic.

The book is designed to help you find what you need. Preceding each chapter, you'll find an overview of the topics discussed in that chapter and two lists: one of helpful things to know before you read the chapter, the other of things you should have on hand. In each chapter, we take you on a tour of the topic, including examples and explanations that should not only fill in any gaps in your understanding of the subject but also help you envision broader possibilities. At the end of each chapter, we recommend activities to improve your skills and help you master the subject.

What Is In This Book

We divided this book into three parts. Part I, "Getting in Shape," is designed to help you make sure that your foundation in DOS and AutoCAD is sound, one that will provide you with a basis for CAD development for years to come. Chapter 1, "CAD Management: An Overview," covers the office, project, drawing, user, and system environment. Chapters 2 and 3, "Evaluating and Developing Your CAD Habits" and "The Basics," review the basic habits and abilities that make up a good foundation in CAD. Chapter 4 addresses "Basic System Management." In Chapter 5, "Software Companions," you learn how to use other software with AutoCAD to improve your management abilities. Chapter 6, "Project and Drawing Management," includes both beginning and advanced information. Chapter 7, "Advanced Management Techniques," provides some advanced system-management concepts.

In Part II, "Perfecting Your Techniques," we guide you through all the major areas of CAD customization. Chapter 8, "The Ten Commandments—Times Three," provides guidelines for staying out of trouble when you buy hardware and software, for writing your own macros and routines, and for applying your work to a larger user group. Chapter 9, "The Tasks At Hand," shows you how to design faster, more appropriate menus. Chapter 10, "Look, Ma—No Hands!" gives you instructions on how to get AutoCAD to do your work for you. In Chapter 11, "The Professional Look," you'll find ways to improve the quality of your product. If you want to implement 3-D into your services, read Chapter 12, "AutoCAD from All Sides: 3-D."

In Part III, "Getting Serious," you move on to features of AutoCAD you may not even know exist! This part of the book is sure to spark your imagination and provide you with keys for opening new doors to creativity and productivity with AutoCAD. Chapters 13, "AutoLISP Never Was Plain English," and 14, "AutoLISP's Bells and Whistles," will convince the uninitiated to use AutoLISP or, if you already do, will improve your understanding of AutoLISP. Chapter 15, "Advanced Presentation Techniques," introduces you to concepts that are on the cutting edge of CAD development. Chapter 16, "Advanced Hardware Concepts," teaches you about what it takes to make your system your best friend, rather than a mysterious stranger. Finally, Chapter 17, "The Ultimate CAD-management Tool," discusses our favorite topic—getting someone else to do your work for you.

The appendixes at the back of the book include not only a variety of code listings for specific tasks but also sample menu macros, AutoCAD drawing settings, and a list of common errors in AutoCAD and what to do about them. Also included is an appendix you can use to get information about other books and software packages, as well as a list of AutoCAD users' groups.

Assumptions About the Reader

We assume that readers of this book:

- have a DOS-based computer system. (Macintosh users and 32-bit workstation users can use most of this book; they just can't use some of the DOS techniques.)
- have a working knowledge of DOS.
- use AutoCAD in a design and/or production capacity.
- have a reasonably good understanding of AutoCAD Release 9 or 10.
- have word-processing software that can create and manipulate ASCII or nondocument text files (or can use DOS EDLIN).

What This Book Will and Won't Do

This book will give you a more complete understanding of the concepts of AutoCAD and will make you an informed generalist rather than an expert in any particular area of AutoCAD. We augment your increased and improved conceptual understanding by referring you to outside resources that you can use when and if you choose to know more about a subject. These references direct you to resources that *will* make you an expert in specific areas. The appendixes also provide detailed explanations of routines, programs, and techniques so that you can study a particular aspect of a subject at your leisure.

This book will help you become an expert at doing things your way, rather than ours.

Why We Wrote This Book

As the leading PC-based CAD package, AutoCAD has given architects, engineers, manufacturers, interior designers, landscape architects, builders, and many others a powerful tool. Advanced desktop hardware technology has brought CAD design and drafting capabilities into even the smallest businesses. We think that most AutoCAD users focus on being more productive and effective than they were with the old, hand-drawing methods when, in our opinion, the focus should be on competent, efficient system management. Speed is not the only factor involved; potential cost savings, compatibility, and the power of the database and drafting package also are important. In other words, mastering the ability to draw with AutoCAD is only the first step and has little to do with being more productive.

We wanted to collect the wide array of concepts, principles, tips, tricks, and management techniques we have developed and encountered through our experiences with AutoCAD. Our many encounters with users, dealers, and firms that have reached an "effectiveness plateau" in the use of AutoCAD made us aware of the need for this book. The only way to increase your productivity with AutoCAD to the levels you originally imagined is to understand fully the program's capabilities and use them to their best potential.

AutoCAD Advanced Techniques

We have three goals for this book:

- To enable you to use AutoCAD to its fullest capability, according to your needs.
- To help you implement effective system management.
- To provide you with an informative resource guide.

We think that the complex tasks involved in our drawing process provide us with a broad overview of the use of AutoCAD, and we keep bumping into all the nooks and crannies of the program. Although this book is based on our experience as practicing architects and AutoCAD consultants, it is not just for architects and engineers. We intentionally discuss many topics as generically as possible. Our primary interest is to help you gain insight into the dynamic range of AutoCAD as a total production system. Most of all, we want you to have fun with an exciting and challenging tool—AutoCAD.

I

Getting in Shape

What Chapter 1 Is About

This chapter discusses many of the factors that will contribute to your success as a CAD manager. These factors include the following:

- Management and implementation of CAD practices
- Drawing management
- Preplanned task management
- Customization
- Training
- Data management

This chapter discusses also the goals you need to establish, which types of projects to begin automating, your CAD system, and personnel.

Helpful Things To Know Before You Start

- General ideas about managing your projects and personnel
- A collection of problems you expect CAD to solve
- Anticipated goals in using CAD

What To Have on Hand

- A desire to make CAD productive
- The office practice and standards manuals you already use
- An outline of what you expect to achieve in the immediate future by using CAD

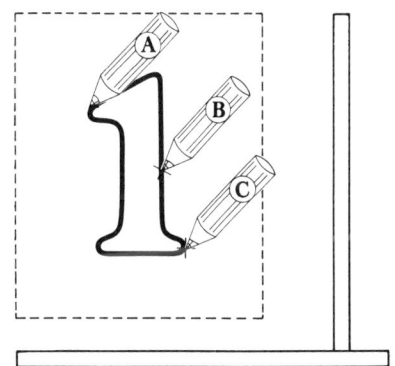

CAD Management: An Overview

If you manage, intend to manage, or want to learn how to manage a CAD installation, you aspire to be a CAD or systems manager. If you work by yourself? Surprise! You already are a CAD manager. Even if you work for someone else, you more than likely are an integral factor in the effective management of the CAD system. How well you accomplish this task, however trying it may be, determines how productive you will be with CAD.

If you think that managing people is tough, double the intensity (and some of the associated headaches) and you have CAD management. Many factors contribute to the successful implementation of a CAD system; sometimes these factors are overlooked in the rush to enter the "computing zone." This chapter discusses many factors that will contribute to your success.

CAD Management and Implementation

Good CAD management begins with understanding your goals for your CAD system. Many factors contribute to the possibility that your CAD system's performance does not or will not live up to your expectations. By establishing up-front long- and short-term goals, you assure the successful implementation of your CAD system. If you are no longer in a situation where the up-front opportunity exists, it may be time to start over.

Long-term planning goals and concerns for CAD usage are generally broad, varying in the degree of refinement. Typical management concerns might include the following:

- Financial (purchase, lease, and investment return)
- Anticipated work flow
- Projects, tasks, or processes that can be automated economically
- Installation procedures
- Personnel selection and training
- An estimate of hardware, software, and operating costs for automation
- An estimate of cost savings with automation
- An estimate of the effect of automation on company management and organization
- Improvement in the quality and accuracy of production output

Your specific management concerns may vary, depending on the type of work you do and how that work has been done in the past, but the general management priority is to make sure that the implementation of a CAD system will provide concrete, quantifiable benefits.

Fig. 1.1.

An AutoCAD drawing of management perfection.

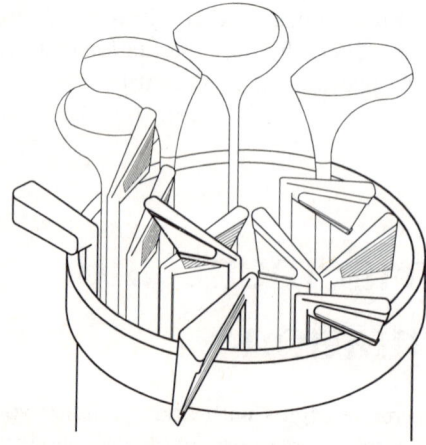

With these concerns paramount in a manager's mind, the first few days, weeks, or months of a CAD implementation can be critical. In addition, many managers find CAD unnerving because they cannot physically view the current condition of a CAD drawing. This makes it difficult, when compared to traditional methods, to judge what percentage of a drawing or project is complete, how accurate the work is, and whether the intended direction is being taken. These factors can cause trouble in the implementation of your CAD system. You must be able to continue to provide a project and progress-of-the-work overview, confident that your assessment is accurate.

Clearly, dedicated support of company management for CAD is essential. If management feels that results are not coming fast enough or resists altogether the use of computers, it can mean real trouble. If the firm expects a CAD system to solve problems that existed in company management practices before the implementation of the CAD system, things will only get worse. The implementation of CAD amplifies shortcomings in project-management practices.

Financial Issues

Financial issues range from the basic cost of the system to whom should you trust with your new electronic T square. Important issues are purchase price, lease options, payback periods, effect on billing rates, and so on. Indeed, a company must review many important financial considerations when purchasing a CAD system.

What follows is a checklist to review with your accountant; develop your own list, using this one as a guide. Even if you already have a CAD system in place, you may need to review its performance and refocus some of your original intentions.

- ❏ Training costs, initial and ongoing
- ❏ Income tax considerations
- ❏ Life span of hardware and software, both mechanically and compared to new technology
- ❏ Realistic productivity factors
- ❏ Pay and billing rates of CAD versus non-CAD personnel
- ❏ Downtime
- ❏ Maintenance costs
- ❏ Office refurnishing

Of these cost factors, the most difficult to evaluate is productivity, unless you already have an extensive history of your firm's performance with CAD. The anticipated life of the software and equipment depends on the personality of your firm, more than anything else. For example, we know that some people are still using AutoCAD releases earlier than 2.6. Considering the relatively low price of AutoCAD updates, that is fanatical dedication to cost control!

Several books, some available through book clubs, can help you evaluate these factors. We recommend *The Microcomputer CAD Manual*, published by New Riders Publishing.

Anticipated Work Flow

Whether you are interested in implementing CAD for the first time or are going to redirect an existing set of practices that has gotten off course, the timing of the development and implementation of those practices must be coordinated with upcoming projects.

The better you are able to predict your work flow, the easier it will be to begin a project on CAD. You should begin with a project that has a generous timetable, so that you have time to correct any problems that arise. A natural slack period in your business cycle is another good time to implement CAD. During these times the pressures of getting the job done are reduced. Using slow periods to improve the future performance of the firm is a good business practice. A suitable project that is expected to start three or four months from the time you begin training will give personnel adequate time to become familiar with day-to-day CAD operations before they jump in with both feet.

Company management may want to see magic after making this $20,000 investment, but CAD is not magic. Your firm may need to lessen its expectations; managers must be patient. It can take months to realize the benefits of CAD. Proper anticipation of work flow and gradual transition of the production of that work from manual to CAD methods will ensure that the magic of CAD eventually becomes the status quo. If your firm has already reached this revelation, we hope that this book was purchased as a guide to moving forward.

Processes Suitable for Automation

In most instances, start with CAD where the largest potential savings will be realized. The cost of the CAD system may be justified by automating just a few design or drafting operations. The same applies when you begin to implement new management procedures: start with the projects and tasks that will benefit most from the changes.

A personal experience illustrates how a CAD system should *not* be implemented. Walter worked as a branch manager for a firm whose senior management dictated that the first and only use of an expensive CAD system would be for a symbol library. Although symbols are needed for some drawings (like floor plans), what the senior management saw as a symbol library was a composite of every wall section imaginable. To Walter, it was almost unbearable to waste the capabilities of the CAD system this way. Finally, Walter decided to reuse some earlier drawings of a multifamily project. He drew the apartment unit plans, mirrored, copied, and rotated them into building plans and building modules for site planning. Such an infraction of company policy was not viewed kindly by senior management. Meanwhile, when the symbol library as dictated was completed, it was basically unusable because its details were designed for construction techniques in a different part of the country. This is a clear example of inappropriate and uninformed management decisions about how a CAD system should be used.

The moral of the story is that repetitive items and reusable objects—not a library of details—are the first things that should be automated. A library of electronic details will be developed, just as the manual one was, over time.

In determining what types of drawings or tasks you will select for implementation efforts, look for the following:

- Repetition of effort
- Basic components used by many people
- Standard, rather than new or unique, tasks
- The most flexible personnel to work on the task
- Level of disruption to the status quo
- Availability of help in the event of trouble
- Benefit of positive results to all concerned

In our business—architecture—floor plans are a good place to begin automation. Many AutoCAD commands—such as those for dimensioning, lines, and so on—work well with floor plans, and floor plans are used by several different disciplines—structural, mechanical, and electrical engineering. We can benefit immediately by automating plans and using them for other disciplines, as well as by starting a symbol library because we include drawings of doors, windows, and so on. Floor plans are a standard task and represent a large portion of our project work load. A wide range of our personnel can work on nearly any plan drawing, because the technical aspects of the floor plan are not project-specific. Therefore, we have the best opportunity to select the personnel we feel are best suited for the implementation of the new procedures.

The work flow in our office is affected by the type of project and the type of task we are working on. Highly detailed drawings require the coordination of effort of many of the project personnel. On the opposite end of the spectrum, drawings that have no definition whatsoever also require input from project personnel because carefully made decisions must be in place to initiate the development of the drawing.

When you implement and change CAD procedures, you must be sensitive to the status quo. You don't want everyone saying, "Here we go again!" You would rather they just happen to notice that a drawing looks better or was produced faster. This consideration, which is often overlooked, can have a major influence on whether change is accepted.

Expanding these considerations to the project level, avoid introducing new management practices on highly detailed or highly undefined projects. Prototype projects that only have to be adapted to minor unique considerations are good projects to begin developing as you establish or update your CAD procedures. Not only does the aspect of their reuse help defray the cost of implementation, but the effect of positive results will benefit everyone in the firm, as well as clients, consultants, and your banker!

Installation Procedures

If you belong to a firm that is installing a CAD system, or if you will be managing an installation for someone else, you face a formidable task. We have a few suggestions to help make the process smoother.

Personnel

Most of the firm's technical staff will be eager to learn and begin using the new technology you are introducing. This initial enthusiasm should be supported and encouraged—it can help you get everyone through the problem periods that undoubtedly await you.

Staff acceptance and support of the integration of CAD is most important. Do your best to reduce anxieties about the computer by explaining the overall picture to the staff. Make sure that you understand and discuss with your staff what the expectations, limitations, and capabilities of the CAD system will be. It is also important to note that "on-the-job" training can make employees feel as though they are in the spotlight without a clue as to what is expected of them.

The personnel involved in the implementation of the CAD system should be the same people who will be responsible for the performance of the CAD system. Eventually, all of the personnel in the firm—from the president to the junior draftsmen—should feel comfortable with the installation. Secretaries and accounting personnel are included in this group, as they frequently may interface with the system. Above all, everyone who draws must learn to use the system. We suspect that many more companies would be using CAD if the principals of the firm knew how to use CAD first. Then they would not feel that things are no longer under their control.

One way to make CAD more productive is to add a second or third shift; although this may seem to be a good solution, be aware that management and supervision problems may arise that diminish productivity gains. For multiple shifts to work, personnel have to become sensitive to the fact that others will be continuing with the work they started. This major training requirement relies on the installation of hard-and-fast office standards. The communication of the work that has been completed and the work that needs to be done from one shift to the next becomes paramount in successful multiple-shift operations. These problems can be alleviated by ensuring adequate training and communication with multiple shifts and having overlap managers who work at least two hours into the new shift.

A different approach to eliminating shift coordination problems is to make the shifts *hardware shifts*, so that each shift arrives and begins using a tool with no evidence left of what was done on that tool during the previous shift. This approach requires that projects become shift-specific. The advantage to this approach is that hardware costs are more readily offset by increased productivity. The disadvantages are that 1) the work must be such that information required to complete the work is available 24 hours a day, and 2) the task of balancing the work load becomes more complex.

Be realistic in your expectations of both personnel and the CAD system. Allow sufficient time for training and orientation before and during system implementation or procedural changes. If you are managing only yourself, make sure that you do not demand too much of your own time schedule. In all cases, taking the time for proper initialization will forestall problems in the future.

Physical Workstation

One workstation is never enough. Most firms try to ease into CAD by buying a single computer workstation, but the need for more workstations becomes evident the first time you try to produce a complete job on the computer. This becomes a major problem when you need to complete some final drawing changes and the computer is tied up plotting other drawings. In addition, it is good practice to have one station designated specifically for training (at least part time), and another for research and development, particularly if you are customizing your CAD system (preparing your own macros and menus under AutoCAD, for example).

Working conditions generally are better with CAD than they were for manual work stations. Some people, however, may develop back strain, eyestrain, headaches, or sore necks. To help correct these problems, experiment with different chairs, screens, lighting, and table heights, until an improvement is realized.

When designing or purchasing a station, consider the following:

- ❏ The desk or table must allow proper depth and width for computer hardware and paper drawings. Space for computer manuals, calculators, notepads and layout should be included. The table height should be adjustable, if the chairs are not.

- ❏ Choose a comfortable, adjustable chair with good back and arm support.

- ❏ Select furnishings and install the hardware to allow for the hand preference of the operator. Digitizers, mice, and layout space can be right or left sided.

- ❏ Provide adjustable monitors to suit individual needs.

- ❏ Place lighting and/or the workstation to reduce glare. This can be accomplished also through the use of monitor screens.

- ❏ High-resolution graphics systems and extra memory boards can increase the computer's heat output, which can affect both human and computer performance. Proper sizing of the air-handling systems is a must.

- ❏ Control smoke and dust in the work area. Neither is good for the computer or the operator.

- ❏ Computers and plotters increase the overall noise level in an office. Place the plotter in its own room, if possible.

Figure 1.2 shows one way you might set up a workstation. The effective design of a CAD office will differ from the manual drawing environment. The design will require new furniture, lighting, electrical installations, and flooring materials. A benefit of CAD is being able to select CAD stations that use less space than the nonelectronic offices used to use.

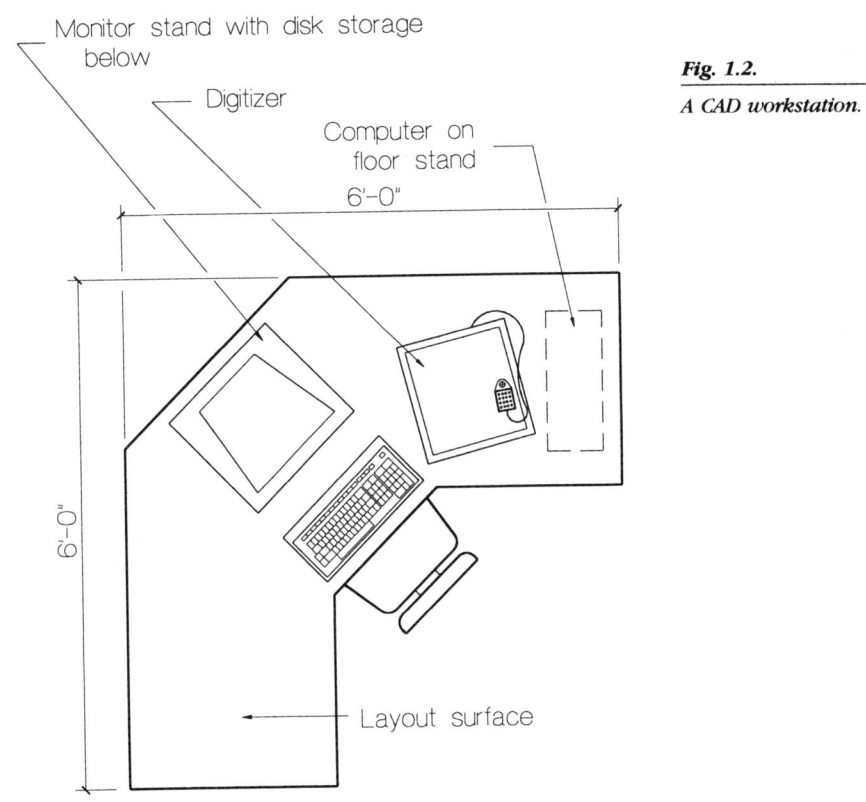

Fig. 1.2.

A CAD workstation.

Although you may not think that the design of the workstation is important, its importance will become self-evident as you continue with the everyday use of CAD.

Drawing Management

Successful drawing management is necessary to make the speed of drawing with CAD at least equal to the speed of drawing by hand. The first symptom of a drawing-management problem is more time spent on CAD drawings and related activities than was spent on hand drawings.

The task of managing the drawing files can quickly become overwhelming. It does not take long to completely fill your hard disk with old drawing files, even though the computer dealer said your hard disk would give you "plenty of room." As you read through this book, think about how you manage your files. You probably will reevaluate which files you keep, deleting those that no longer are necessary and backing up others on floppy disks for off-line storage.

We find that keeping only the most current project files on our hard disk is a good idea. You can back up any others to floppy disks, labeling all backups carefully to avoid confusing another user. Some firms place each drawing on a floppy disk and copy it to or from the hard disk as the need arises.

In Chapter 6, "Project and Drawing Management," and Chapter 7, "Advanced Management Techniques," we discuss in detail the management of the drawing process and associated files. Drawing-file management is one of the major duties with which you will become involved, and its complexity increases with the number of projects you have completed.

Procedures and Manuals

With the advent of computer-aided design, many of the old methods of doing things no longer apply. Nevertheless, many traditional problems still exist—drafting mistakes, work hours in excess of budget, poor project coordination, and missed deadlines. Additionally, CAD presents some problems of its own—drawing elements on the wrong layers, different text styles and linetypes, using outdated symbol libraries, and symbols of the wrong size.

A CAD system will not do all your work for you. Management tools are available, however, that make the work you have to do more palatable. As AutoCAD has developed over the years, more CAD-management tools have been added with each release. You can install some sophisticated aids that make your management tasks much easier by adding third-party software or software you have written yourself to the AutoCAD environment. But first you must establish what your management needs are. Two effective tools for developing a cohesive management approach are standard procedures and office manuals.

Procedures

By establishing good CAD-management techniques and procedures, you can reduce the occurrence of these problems and perhaps eliminate them altogether. AutoCAD forces you to get organized, both in the way you work and the maintenance of drawings and standards. Here are some important highlights of good practices:

- Make procedures consistent, simple, and transparent.
- Let everyone in on the design of the procedures.
- Create effective yet flexible rules and standards that promote both creativity and consistency.
- Record all procedures, both for the computer system and for the drawing and project standards.
- Review written procedures to track recurring problems.

Manuals

One of the CAD tasks that may seem unpleasant is that of developing internal manuals for your CAD system. This practice absolutely must be carried out, no matter how much you dislike doing the work. We have found it helpful to develop two separate manuals: a production manual and a project manual.

The production manual documents your drawing standards, layers, naming conventions, sheet sizes, symbol and text sizes, dimension locations, backup frequency, system sign-off procedures, security, and archival (as opposed to working or temporary) storage information. The objective is to detail a standard approach for your company's drawings. Ideally, it should appear as if all drawings from your firm were drawn by a single person.

The project manual keeps tabs on individual projects and may include such data as plotting records, changes to the drawings, block names, and production schedules. It generally serves to keep the project manager informed as to the progress of the work and the status of key personnel, deadlines, and man hours.

In Chapters 6 and 7, we show you how AutoCAD can help you prepare, maintain, and use these two manuals.

Customization

Your use of CAD reflects the character of your firm. Design firms tend to use a CAD system for the conceptual phases of a project; production firms tend to focus on drafting. An outstanding feature of AutoCAD is that it can be customized—whether via a symbol library, a menu, or a sophisticated parametric program. AutoCAD can be customized to fit your firm's needs or the specific needs of a particular project. In fact, the argument can be made that if you do not customize AutoCAD, you are not achieving full productivity.

There are two levels of AutoCAD customization. The first level involves changing the AutoCAD environment by changing AutoCAD's system variables (SETVARS, DIMVARS) and prototype-drawing settings; customizing button, screen, icon, and tablet menus; and setting up a symbols library. The second level involves making AutoCAD do some of the work for you, which requires some programming knowledge and involves writing script files and AutoLISP programs. Parts II and III of this book ("Perfecting Your Techniques" and "Getting Serious," respectively) focus on these levels of customization as they apply to proper system management.

The benefits of customizing are great leaps in productivity, speed, performance, consistency, reduction of errors, quality of designs, and creative motivation.

Training

If your firm is committed to and built around effective CAD management, training is generally quick and easy. Successful firms realize that training and education are not optional. Over the years, we have completed what we consider to be the equivalent of a master's degree in CAD and AutoCAD. We are now on our way to a doctorate. The only unusual thing about this type of doctorate is that our grade card is delivered to us in the form of enjoyment, increased productivity, and profits. Everyone in a firm, from principals downward, should have some CAD training. Even nontechnical support people can benefit the overall management of the system by understanding the conceptual aspects of the CAD system and its requirements.

Generally, four levels of training are necessary for various CAD users:

- Initial training
- Technical training
- Continuing education
- Programming

Initial training: Intended to acclimate the firm or prospective operator to the new technology (the CAD system), this type of training may be performed initially by your firm by providing relevant articles and newsletters for staff.

Technical training: At this level, the company installing your CAD system conducts courses for the operator. These courses should include introductory skills, basic graphics and text creation, and editing functions. Autodesk has a reasonably up-to-date list of authorized training centers and provides a toll-free number you can call to find out where you can go for training. We recommend some formal training, whether from one of these centers or from someone you know who has a proven track record with AutoCAD.

Continuing Education: This training may be accomplished in-house or through advanced skills courses taught by outside consultants. At a minimum, frequent review of proper command usage is essential during the first six months of operation to keep operators from using inappropriate commands for a particular task. Additional ways to obtain advanced skills are discussed in Chapter 2, "Evaluating and Developing Your CAD Habits."

Programming: This training may be achieved at one's own expense (of time and energy) or through programming classes such as those offered by Autodesk's authorized training centers. In this type of training, an operator writes, debugs, and executes user-written programs.

Data Management

Getting data into the CAD system takes as long as or longer than manual drafting methods, because the data contains potentially more information. We say *potentially* because some firms never utilize that potential. Computers make, or complete, more work in the same amount of time originally allotted for the noncomputer effort. They never get the job done sooner. The additional data that is made available is the source of increased productivity by computerization. Therefore, CAD management must include the capability to manage all data components of a CAD drawing.

AutoCAD drawing entities represent data (lines, circles, arcs, polylines, and so on). Most firms have other project data requirements that were handled entirely by other methods before CAD arrived. This collection of project data is separate from the production of drawings, and includes:

- Project specifications
- Schedules of equipment and fixtures
- Time records
- Correspondence
- Purchase orders
- Invoices
- Maintenance manuals
- Standard drawings
- Company brochures

This project data is used by the firm itself, the client, any consultants, customers, and a potentially ever-expanding group of people (building departments, for example). Any of these data types can be contributed to by AutoCAD. Project specifications and equipment and fixture schedules can be assembled automatically by a separate database program, using information extracted from AutoCAD. Time records, purchase orders, correspondence, and invoices all can be supplemented with information from AutoCAD. You can even write an AutoCAD drawing to a FAX line and send the drawing to any other FAX machine. You can create maintenance manuals by adapting the production drawings of a piece of equipment. You will be creating a library of standard drawings that will improve drawing speed. Finally, if you use desktop publishing software, you can import AutoCAD drawings into your own brochure.

The possibilities are extensive, and we discuss many of them in this book. Because you have the potential for tapping the AutoCAD database as a resource for all of this data, why not do it? All it takes is good CAD-system management and some programs that you can create or purchase. This book provides many of the resources you need to realize this potential.

Stripped to its bare bones, a CAD system is a data-management system. It follows then that CAD management is just the management of that data to produce the results expected by the users of the CAD system. Herein lies the true secret to CAD productivity. This simplification denies the complexity of the issues, but the point is that AutoCAD itself will not make you draw faster. To do real magic with a CAD system, you must master the deployment of project data.

Summary

In this chapter we discussed the foundation of a successful CAD system: effective CAD management. We reviewed the major aspects of CAD management:

- ❏ Firm management and implementation of CAD practices
- ❏ Drawing management
- ❏ Planned procedures
- ❏ Customization
- ❏ Training
- ❏ Data management

Although we can provide only guidelines for the implementation of CAD in your firm, we can help you with drawing management, planned procedures, customization, and training. This book is part of your training experience and will serve as a curriculum outline.

As you develop processes and procedures for CAD management, be sure to build upon solutions to problems. Project scheduling, work-hour accounting, and cost tracking should also be part of a CAD system operating shell and working environment (ideally with a link to the office's computerized accounting software). Solutions to problems are, after all, what the purpose of management in a competitive economic system is all about.

The next few chapters in Part I will help you evaluate your capabilities and knowledge base in the use of AutoCAD. Then we will go on to explore methods for improving the management of your CAD system.

What Chapter 2 Is About

This chapter establishes a basis from which we can begin to explore CAD management. As with any foundation, there must be a consistent body of knowledge and you must develop a set of good habits. Use this chapter to review your current understanding of AutoCAD. Here we discuss areas in which good habits are critical to the implementation of good CAD management practices. We are going to discuss a series of topics with which we expect you to be comfortable before you attempt to use the rest of this book. These topics include:

- Developing the proper attitude
- An overview of AutoCAD commands
- A checklist of things you should know
- A test to help you review your AutoCAD foundation
- Habits to develop in using your system components
- A recommended compilation of foundation basics in AutoCAD, DOS, macros, menus, plotting, and hardware
- A warning about other software you will need

Helpful Things To Know Before You Start

- Most, if not all, AutoCAD editing and drawing commands, in detail
- A cursory understanding of AutoCAD's environment variables

What To Have on Hand

- The *AutoCAD Reference Manual*
- A DOS reference guide (We recommend *MS-DOS User's Guide*, 3rd edition, and *Managing Your Hard Disk*, 2nd edition, both published by Que Corporation.)
- Manuals for your hardware components

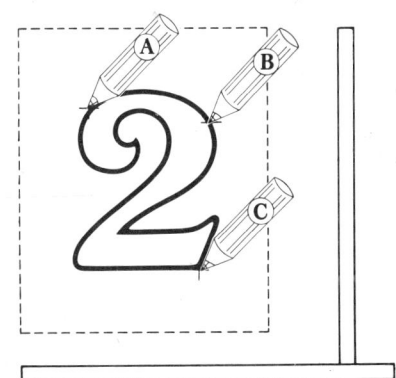

Evaluating and Developing Your CAD Habits

One of the major barriers to the development of good management practices and efficient productivity in the use of AutoCAD is a collection of practices and procedures we call "bad habits." The purpose of this chapter is to help you establish good habits and avoid or eradicate bad ones.

The flexibility of AutoCAD lets you perform any given task in more than one way. Some users learn one method and are content; they don't search out other, perhaps better, ways of doing things. We think that this attitude leads to bad habits. Because the AutoCAD manual is extensive, you probably didn't absorb everything in it the first, or even the second, time you read it. The first good habit you need to develop is the habit of continually learning about AutoCAD—referring to the manual, reading books like this one, and communicating with other AutoCAD users.

You may be wondering how there can be "bad" habits in the use of AutoCAD, as long as everything is working properly. We contend that active use of AutoCAD is based solely on the development of habits. If you don't agree, try relocating a portion of a screen or tablet menu, or renaming a command—is the difference a problem? If you are like most of us, you will have a problem. People pick up many habits in their everyday use of

AutoCAD. You must be aware of the dynamic effect these habits can have on productivity, and take the necessary steps to mold a good set of habits into your CAD procedures and techniques.

Comfort before Speed

Developing habits in your use of AutoCAD is easy. You should progress gradually from the basic AutoCAD commands to more sophisticated operations. If you go too far in one aspect of AutoCAD before you develop others, you may develop a habit that you will have to unlearn (and unlearning can be difficult). Even the most advanced users sometimes have this problem, but following the guidelines in this chapter will help you limit the possibility that it will happen to you. For example, we had to rethink completely our menu customization when we learned the full capabilities of AutoCAD's CHANGE and INSERT commands. In this case, we didn't have a "bad" habit, but we were underutilizing two important aspects of AutoCAD.

The learning process with AutoCAD is a continuing one, so keep pressing ahead. Investigate the many methods available for performing an activity, before you make one method a habit. Your speed will develop naturally and reach its greatest potential if it has been developed from a solid foundation. If you try to get into advanced practices too fast, you may have to do a lot of backtracking.

Your AutoCAD System

If you ask five different AutoCAD users, you will find five different ways of using AutoCAD. Some users have had training, others have learned by the seat of their pants, and each user has different strengths and weaknesses using a computer. In this section we discuss, in general terms, what we have found to be the best way to use the equipment available to you.

Chapter 2: Evaluating and Developing Your CAD Habits **27**

> **Hardware Basics**
>
> To run AutoCAD, you should have at least the following equipment:
>
> ❏ One of the following computers:
>
>   IBM-compatible XT, 286 AT, or 386 AT
>   Apple's Mac II, Mac IIx, or Mac IIcx
>   Apollo Domain with 68020 or 68030
>   Sun 3, 386i, or 4
>   DEC Vaxstation II/RC/GPX 2000, 3200, or 3500
>   WANG
>   NEC
>   AT&T 6300
>   Texas Instruments PC
>
> ❏ Intel 8087, 80287, or 80387 math coprocessor (applies only to IBM equipment)
>
> ❏ Hard disk drive (at least 20M)
>
> ❏ Asynchronous Communication Adapter(s)
>
> ❏ EGA monitor and graphics card
>
> ❏ Digitizer or mouse
>
> ❏ Plotter or printer plotter (or access to one)
>
> Remember that these are *absolute minimums*; your equipment may well be more advanced. Whatever equipment you have, make sure that you have the manufacturer's manuals for each piece of equipment. Review those manuals so that you basically know the location of each piece of equipment, what it does, and what maintenance it requires.

Input Devices: Keyboards, Digitizers, and Mice

In our opinion, to get the most from your AutoCAD system you need a keyboard and a digitizer for complex drawing tasks; for drawing tasks that are less complex, you need a keyboard and a mouse. If you use a mouse, you must have a graphics card with the capability of displaying Autodesk's Advanced User Interface (AUI)—pull-down menus and icons.

AutoCAD allows you to use any of these devices to enter data. Our experience indicates that a combination of typing and digitizing is the most effective way to enter data (with emphasis on typing). The fastest users can type ahead in their keyboard buffer while AutoCAD acts on previously issued commands; this will change as the processing speed of computers increases. The primary objective of any system is that the user rarely has to sit and wait for the opportunity to provide input to the computer; this objective is affected by your habits as well as the computer's processing speed. As you will see from the following discussion, users must develop a set of skills for each input device.

In the computer world, typing is an essential skill. If you can't type and you want to be effective with AutoCAD, we recommend taking a night course in typing at a local high school. It will be the most economical training investment you make and will provide you with the highest results-to-cost ratio of anything (and we mean anything) you can do to improve your abilities in using AutoCAD.

One benefit of using a keyboard is that you can type ahead of AutoCAD in your computer's 15-character keyboard buffer (or you can use a program that expands the keyboard buffer size by making a little of the computer's memory available exclusively to the keyboard). If you watch AutoCAD users who know what they are doing, you will notice a constant flow of interaction with the computer and the information around them, such as books or reference drawings. Of the available input methods, typing (if done properly) is the least tiring on the eyes and neck.

Digitizing is an effective way to enter all types of data by using a tablet menu. Some users expect a digitizer to replace any and all typing. Digitizers are useful for manipulating a library of standard drawings, entering drawing coordinates, and controlling a library of symbols and functions through the use of large macros. A multibutton digitizer can be programmed to execute AutoCAD commands or macros at the touch of a button. We have included our most frequently used commands in our multibutton cursor button menus. We think that digitizers are faster than screen menus at executing menu macros—because the graphics card is removed from the middle of the process—but we have no proof to support our observation.

On the down side, because the digitizer does not allow commands to be stacked in a buffer as the keyboard does, you have to wait for the command prompt before you can enter information. You may begin working so fast that AutoCAD misses some input because the program was not ready for it. Another disadvantage to using a digitizer is that you have to take your eyes off the screen to find a command, which can be tiring as well as slow. We don't know anyone who has memorized a digitizer menu by hand location, the way a good typist memorizes the keyboard.

A mouse is a reasonable substitute for a digitizer. Many users are more comfortable using a mouse because (like good typists) they can keep their eyes on the screen. Although using a mouse means less wear-and-tear on the neck, your eyes may get tired. With a mouse, you have less natural "feel," and you cannot trace drawings or select items from tablet menus. If you are accustomed to using a digitizer, it may take some time to get used to the fact that the cursor location for a mouse is not fixed—but practice helps.

Screen menus, icons, and dialogue boxes can be used with a digitizer or a mouse. The limited screen area available requires that selections from the screen be placed in a hierarchy (a menu tree). Complex menus can make the use of screen-activated menus an extremely tedious process. A digitizer's large selection area can provide much more immediate access to a macro. If you prefer a mouse, the AUI is the only tool currently available that will increase the selectable area of a screen. By using the techniques we discuss in Chapter 9, "The Tasks At Hand," you can improve the macro selection process for mice or digitizers.

For More Information

CADENCE. 3, no. 2 (February 1988): 17.
————.2, no. 6 (June 1987): 19.

Plotters

Do you know how to operate your plotter or printer plotter? The best source for learning how to do this is your plotter manual. (You will need information from your plotter manual when we discuss plotting in more detail in Chapter 7, "Advanced Management Techniques.") Most plotters are easy to set up and operate.

AutoCAD makes the process of plotting a drawing simple. To plot a drawing after you have altered the AutoCAD configuration to reflect your plotter and its communications port, type **PLOT** (**PRPLOT**, if you have a printer plotter) at the AutoCAD command prompt (or select Option 3 or 4 from AutoCAD's opening menu). Then answer the questions as AutoCAD prompts you for input.

We tend to answer the `What to plot?` prompt with `Display` or `Limits`. In either case, you must have established some parameters. If you select `Display`, your plot will be what is currently on the screen. If you have not used ZOOM ALL or EXTENTS, or specified a certain area to be plotted, you may not get the entire drawing plotted. If you select the `Limits` option, the origin of the plot will equal the origin of the drawing. Some third-party software packages (Autodesk's AEC, for example) do not set the full limits of your drawing; they take into consideration the plotter's inability to plot on the extreme edges of the sheet.

`Remove hidden lines? <N>` is used only for drawings that contain 3-D faces, extrusions, or meshes. Even if you have hidden the lines while editing a drawing, you must respond **Y** to this plotting prompt when you plot three-dimensional drawings; otherwise, all lines will be plotted. In order to plot with hidden lines removed, AutoCAD must do extensive calculations before plotting; for a complex drawing, the process can be time-consuming.

`Rotate the plot 90 degrees <N>` can be a paper saver if used properly on continuous roll plotters or printer plotters. If you answer **Y** and rotate a plot, the drawing will have its shorter dimension along the length of the paper roll and still fit within the width of the roll. This practice can save you from having to change paper rolls whenever you want to plot a different sheet size.

The *plot origin*, which is defaulted at 0,0, may need to be moved for your plotter's requirements.

Some plotters require that you `Plot to a file`. This option is important if your plotter or printer plotter uses a different type of data image than the one AutoCAD creates with its plot option.

Your plotter manual contains much of the information required for developing the proper plotting procedures for your needs. You should read it, from front to back, probably more than once.

Supplementary Software

If you are unfamiliar with software other than AutoCAD, you will have to become familiar with some to follow the procedures described in this book. You need to know how to use a word processor or text editor (WordStar, WordPerfect, Norton Editor, for example). To keep your system working smoothly, we recommend that you use a hard disk manager (such as Norton Commander, Norton Utilities, PC Boss, Mace, etc.) and a disk optimizer (such as Disk Optimizer, PCTOOLS Deluxe, etc.). Other kinds of commercial and public domain software may also enhance your use of AutoCAD. These software packages are discussed in more detail in other chapters of this book.

AutoCAD Commands You Should Know

Although only 20 percent of the AutoCAD commands are used 80 percent of the time, you should be familiar with *all* of the commands. As you refine your CAD installation and customize your system, you will use all of the commands (with the possible exception of 3-D commands) at some time.

AutoCAD commands have many options for how and when they are used. The most extreme example is SETVAR, which has more than 85 options in AutoCAD Release 10! Each of these options, at one time or another, could solve a particular problem for you.

Our definition of "knowing" commands has more to do with developing good habits than with an in-depth understanding of the commands. You should know what the options are and where to look for them before you begin a customization or write a LISP routine or macro. For example, Craig wrote several involved LISP routines to update blocks in his drawings. This expenditure of wasted effort on his part was due entirely to a bad habit he had developed. His AutoCAD reference manual was gathering too much dust on the shelf. All he had to do was use an option of the AutoCAD INSERT command which uses an equal sign (=). Fortunately for him, some of his other good habits helped him discover his error. Develop a good habit: fully research the commands surrounding each task you want to accomplish and then develop procedures based on that research.

Eventually, you should understand all the options available to all Auto-CAD commands. We recommend that you review each section of the *AutoCAD Reference Manual* at your leisure, making sure that you read even the sections you think you already have mastered. As you encounter each command, actively use the command in a test drawing, trying out all the options. We recommend that you not begin extensive customization of your entire system until you have completed this task because subtle differences in commands can make a big difference in performance. For example, try using the CHANGE command and the STRETCH command to join the ends of two disconnected lines. In some cases, the CHANGE command will be faster and more effective than the STRETCH command. You need to understand the proper application of these differences.

Before we discuss DOS, one AutoCAD command needs to be mentioned: AutoCAD's SH (or SHELL) command, which allows you to access the DOS commands while you work in AutoCAD. You can enter the DOS environment by typing **SH** or **SHELL** at the AutoCAD `Command:` prompt. SHELL is the more functional of the two commands because it allocates part of the computer's memory for use by DOS commands. SH works well for simple DOS commands such as TYPE, COPY, DELETE, and DIR. If you enter a DOS command at the DOS prompt presented by SH or SHELL, the command will be executed and you will be returned to the AutoCAD `Command:` prompt. By pressing Enter twice, you can repeat DOS commands. To exit the repeating DOS shell, type **EXIT**.

Note: The SH and SHELL commands are not really commands; they are requests made to AutoCAD via the ACAD.PGP file. We discuss the ACAD.PGP file in detail in Chapter 5, "Software Companions."

Macros and Menus

A *macro* is a string of commands and responses designed to reduce the input required to accomplish a task. A *menu* generally is a grouping together of macros that automate an entire series of commands. For a more detailed discussion of their use, see Chapter 9, "The Tasks At Hand." If you do not understand the concepts involved, review the sections about macros and menus in the *AutoCAD Reference Manual*. You do not need to know yet how to format the macros or how to edit a menu, but make sure that you understand how they are used in AutoCAD.

Using DOS

To operate AutoCAD effectively on a PC, you must learn a little about DOS. Because DOS does not make drawings and is largely invisible, you may tend to ignore DOS and disk management. But knowing how to manage your hard disk can save you valuable time and avoid catastrophes. To be able to work well with AutoCAD, you need to know a few areas of DOS. This section reviews the basic DOS commands. Make sure that you feel comfortable using these commands. For a more detailed discussion, we strongly suggest that you take the time to read one of the DOS manuals recommended in this book.

Disk Drives

On most PCs, the C: prompt is your hard disk. If your hard disk is partitioned, you also have a D: drive and perhaps an E: drive. Although DOS V3.3 does not require that you partition the hard disk (as did earlier versions of DOS), you still may want to partition your hard disk to keep some programs separate. AutoCAD can be directed to work in any of these drives. We strongly recommend that you use a hard disk manager. Although you can accomplish all disk-management tasks with DOS, a hard disk manager is important; because of the hard disk's storage capacity, you must manage a larger number of files.

Floppy drives generally are defined as A: for the first drive and B: for the second. Furthermore, you may have a tape backup device or other media storage devices (compact disks, for example). Whatever drives you have, make sure that you know how to access, format, and maneuver among them.

Naming Conventions

DOS directory and file names are limited to eight characters. A file name can also have a three-character extension (see table 2.1). Common extensions include .COM (which represents a program), .EXE (which represents a program), and .BAT (which represents a batch file). A *batch file* is a series of instructions received by the computer as if they were entered from the keyboard.

Table 2.1. Typical File Extensions

Extension	Meaning
.$$$	Temporary work file created by DOS or a program
.$AC	Temporary drawing file
.$RF	Current temporary working file
.ARC	File archived with a compression program
.ASC	ASCII text file
.ASM	Assembler source file
.BAK	Backup file
.BAS	Basic source code
.BAT	Batch file
.BIN	Binary file

Table 2.1. continues

Table 2.1. continued

Extension	Meaning
.BK!	WordPerfect backup data file
.BLD	Bload format for BASIC
.C	C source code
.CAL	Spreadsheet data (calculation) file
.CFG	File used by a program to store its configuration
.CHK	File recovered by CHKDSK command
.COB	Cobol source code
.COD	Object code from compilers
.COM	Executable command programs in memory image format
.DAT	Generic data files
.DBF	dBASE III database files
.DIF	Data interchange file (used by VisiCalc)
.DOC	Document files
.DRV	Device driver file
.DVP	Driver initalization for peripherals
.DWG	AutoCAD drawing file
.DXB	Drawing interchange binary file
.DXF	Drawing interchange file
.DXX	Drawing attribute extract of DXF file
.ERR	File created to store error messages
.EXE	Executable programs in relocation format
.FIL	File format
.FMT	Format specification
.FLM	AutoCAD file for AutoShade input
.FOR	Fortran source code
.H	Include file for some programming languages
.HLP	Help files
.HDX	AutoCAD help-file index
.IDX	Index file
.IGS	IGES drawing interchange file
.LIB	Library routines for some compliers
.LIN	ACAD.LIN AutoCAD linetype file
.LSP	AutoLISP file
.LST	Spooled printer plot file
.MAC	Macro file
.MAP	Program MAPs from a program linker
.MID	Master identification file

Table 2.1. continues

Chapter 2: Evaluating and Developing Your CAD Habits

Table 2.1. continued

Extension	Meaning
.MNU	AutoCAD menu file
.MNX	AutoCAD compiled menu file
.MSG	Message file
.NDX	dBASE III index file
.OBJ	Program object code from compilers
.OLD	Original version of a converted drawing file
.OVL	Program overlay files
.OVR	Program overlay files (less common)
.PAT	AutoCAD pattern file
.PAS	Pascal source code
.PB	Paradox database file
.PGP	AutoCAD program parameter file
.PLT	Spooled plot file
.PRN	Print format file
.PRP	ADI printer plotter output
.REL	CBasic relative or relocatable object files
.RND	AutoShade rendering file
.SCR	Used for script and screen format files
.SLB	AutoCAD slide library
.SLD	AutoCAD slide file
.SHP	AutoCAD shape file
.SHX	compiled AutoCAD shape file
.SYS	System files
.TMP	Temporary work files
.TST	Test file
.TXT	Text files
.VC	VisiCalc data files
.WK1	Lotus 1-2-3 Release 2 data file
.WKS	Lotus 1-2-3 Release 1A data file
.WR1	Symphony Release 1.1 data file
.WRK	Symphony Release 1.0 data file
.ZIP	Archive file created with PKZIP.EXE file compression utility

Directories

Directories are useful for keeping related files together. To view the contents of a directory, you must change to the drive and directory or subdirectory you want to view. We discuss the use of directories for CAD management in Chapters 3 and 6 ("The Basics" and "Project and Drawing Management," respectively).

To experiment with DOS commands, go through the following steps:

1. At the C: prompt, type the following drive/directory change:

    CD\ACAD

    In this command, C: is the drive, *CD* is the DOS command to change directory, and *ACAD* is the directory. (You may have AutoCAD on a drive other than C:.)

2. To see the files in the ACAD directory, type **DIR**.

3. If the files fly by too fast, type **DIR/P**. The directory will pause at each screenful of files; to go on to the next screen, press any key.

4. To view the files without the size and date for each file, type **DIR/W**. The files will be displayed across the full width of the screen.

5. To go to a subdirectory of AutoCAD, type the name for the AutoCAD directory and the name for the subdirectory:

    C: **CD\ACAD***subdirectoryname*

    or, if you are already in the ACAD directory, type:

    CD *subdirectory name*

6. To create a subdirectory of AutoCAD, make sure that you are in the root directory (C:\) or in the AutoCAD directory (C:\ACAD); type **MD**, followed by the name of the subdirectory you want to create:

    C: **ACAD**
    MD \ACAD\88004

7. To remove a directory, first delete all files in that directory. Then type **RD** and the directory name:

    DEL ACAD\88004*.*
    RD\ACAD\88004

Utilities

This section lists some useful DOS utilities commands:

FORMAT: Prepares floppy disks or hard disk for use. Be careful with this command because you can inadvertently format your hard disk or floppy disk, which removes all data from the disk. There are several options you can add to the FORMAT command; these vary somewhat between computers. The /S option transfers the hidden files and COMMAND.COM to a floppy disk so that the disk can be used to boot the system. The /V option allows you to give the disk a name, or volume label. Refer to your DOS reference guide for additional options. Do not use FORMAT on your hard disk unless you are an experienced user; many operating systems have an extremely involved procedure for formatting hard disks. For details on formatting your hard disk, consult your hardware manuals and Que's *Managing Your Hard Disk*.

CHKDSK: An acronym for check disk. Useful for determining the current disk status, total space in bytes, amount of disk space used, and amount of available RAM. The /F option writes any lost clusters to files and is important for keeping your hard disk organized. This is discussed in more detail in Chapter 3, "The Basics."

COPY: Allows you to copy files from one directory or drive to another. To use COPY, type **COPY**, followed by the name of the file you want to copy and its new file name (if it is being copied to the same drive) or destination drive (if it's being copied to a different drive). Files may be overwritten if you are not careful. Learn to use wild-card characters (* and ?), if you haven't already.

WILD CARD (* and ?): The asterisk (*) and the question mark (?) are wild cards; they represent undefined characters. For example, DEL 89????A1.DWG deletes any eight-character file that begins with *89*, ends with *A1*, and has the file extension *.DWG*. Copy A:*.* C: copies all the files on a floppy disk in drive A:\ to the C:\ drive.

DEL: Use this shortened form of delete to erase files. The file to be deleted must be specified with its full name or by using wild cards.

TYPE: Displays the specified file in ASCII format on-screen. This is best suited for small files that can be displayed on a single screen. ASCII files used by AutoCAD include line type, hatch patterns, fonts, menus, the ACAD.PGP file, and AutoLISP programs.

MORE: Allows you to view, one screen at a time, the contents of files and directories larger than the screen will display. For example:

   C:>**TYPE filename.ext** |**more**

CLS: Clears the screen.

ECHO OFF: Placed in a batch file so that you do not see the commands being executed on the screen.

PROMPT: Customizes the DOS prompt. You can customize the prompt by putting this command in your AUTOEXEC.BAT file (see Chapter 4, "Basic System Management") by typing the PROMPT command followed by several options. $P tells DOS to display the current drive and directory. $G tells DOS to display the greater-than sign. Such customization can provide valuable information, such as which directory you are in, the current date, or a computer identification name.

PATH: Placed in the AUTOEXEC.BAT or other batch files, PATH tells AutoCAD and any other programs to look for files in specified directories, regardless of what directory the search begins in. We discuss PATH in greater detail in Chapter 3, "The Basics."

RENAME: Renames an existing file. In order to use this command, type **RENAME**, the name of the file you want to rename, and new name for the file.

You need to know the proper format for each of these DOS commands. In Chapter 3, "The Basics," we discuss writing batch files to simplify DOS use.

A Checklist of AutoCAD Concepts

Before you begin structuring the management practices you intend to implement, we want you to be sure that you have a solid foundation in AutoCAD. Soon you will be confronted by the way others use the system; you need to understand the many possibilities because you will be investing a great deal of time creating management procedures.

To give you an idea of how well-rounded your overview of AutoCAD is, we have compiled a checklist of things you should have done already and a test of a smattering of AutoCAD tidbits. Our approach is not scientific. We hope that this exercise will make you think about the overall scope of and the areas you may need to work on. You should feel confident that you have walked the forest before you select a tree. Before you consider overhauling the way you (or your business) use AutoCAD, you should have completed the duties or accomplishments in the following checklist:

- ❏ I know my hardware—its capacity, maintenance procedures, and basic functioning.
- ❏ I am familiar with the contents of each page of the *AutoCAD Reference Manual*.
- ❏ I have tried every AutoCAD command at least once, making sure that I understand its use.
- ❏ I am familiar with the absolute, relative, and polar coordinate systems for angles and points.
- ❏ I know what each file type associated with AutoCAD (ACAD.PGP, ACAD.PAT, ETC.) is for.
- ❏ I understand the relationship between layers, linetypes, colors, and block insertions.
- ❏ I fully understand the relationship between drawing scale and sheet size, plotting, block insertion, hatch patterns, text size, and linetype scale.

A Test of AutoCAD Basics

The following true-false test measures, in general terms, the level of your exposure to AutoCAD commands or concepts. The first 10 questions are basic command questions, the second 10 are more advanced, and the third are aimed at someone who has programming experience with AutoLISP and menu macros. (You'll find the answers at the end of this chapter.)

These questions are in no way a scientifically developed analysis for job applicants or for grading employees. Your answers to these questions will give you an indication of your level of experience with AutoCAD.

1. BLOCK. Drawing elements used to create a block can be restored to a drawing by the OOPS command, if it is used immediately after the block is made.

2. STYLE can be used to create different types of lettering styles.

3. LAYER. One layer can have a different color and linetype from other layers.

4. ARRAY. Objects can be arrayed in a rectangular or circular pattern.

5. HATCH is used to create material patterns that can be used in an AutoCAD drawing.

6. PEDIT can turn a line into a PLINE.

7. ZOOM DYNAMIC is a way of zooming into or out of a drawing; it always causes a regeneration to occur.

8. UNDO undoes all the previous commands back to the beginning of the present editing session.

9. With LTSCALE, a smaller number increases the size of the dashes in a dashed line.

10. DTEXT. Used to visibly place text in a drawing while you type at the keyboard; if no start point is provided, DTEXT automatically starts the text line on the line below the previously created text.

11. DXFOUT can be used to export AutoCAD drawing files to another software program.

12. SETVAR is used to change all AutoCAD system variables, which affect many invisible aspects of the AutoCAD drawing environment.

13. DIMVARS are variables that affect the appearance of dimensions and the way they are used.

14. SHELL can be used to run other programs outside of AutoCAD during the current AutoCAD editing session.

15. WBLOCK can be used to purge a drawing of all unused blocks, linetypes, and lettering styles if they are not nested inside another block's definition.

16. User Coordinate System (UCS) allows the user to locate the origin point anywhere in the World Coordinate System (WCS), with the UCS axes turned and tilted.

17. Prototype drawings can be set up for drawings of different scales, sheet sizes, and with different settings for the AutoCAD environment. Prototype drawings can be used by configuring AutoCAD to select different drawings or by using the equal sign (=) when you start a new drawing.

18. ACAD.PGP allows you to execute external programs at the AutoCAD command prompt; automatically assesses a program's memory requirements before loading it.

19. Configure AutoCAD. AutoCAD has to be reconfigured if you use a different digitizer, even one of the same size.
20. Transparent commands allow you to ZOOM, PAN, REDRAW, and SET system VARiables while executing another AutoCAD command.
21. In AutoLISP, *ATOM* means "change a variable from *A*ssociative *TO Measured* dimensions."
22. Button menus can be reprogrammed to suit the user; a menu can contain numerous button-menu definitions.
23. Any word processor you use to write letters can be used to write AutoLISP routines or to modify a menu.
24. Screen and Tablet menus are interchangeable.
25. GETREAL is an AutoLISP function that allows entry of real numbers.
26. AutoLISP can write data to files, but it can't write other LISP routines or programs.
27. To load an AutoLISP program, type **(LOAD "Lisp Program Name")**.
28. **DEFUN C:** tells AutoLISP to define a function that can be executed at the AutoCAD command prompt and doesn't have to be loaded as a LISP file.
29. EXTLISP is an add-on program that increases the number of functions in AutoLISP by extending its command list.
30. LISPSTACK defines AutoLISP's temporary work area in memory during execution of a routine.

We hope that you can answer correctly 16 of the first 20 questions and 5 of the last 10. If you fall short of these numbers, work with Part I of this book; make sure that you have a good grasp of all its contents before you proceed to Part II or Part III.

More specifically, if you missed many of the first 10 questions, you need to spend more time reviewing the AutoCAD manual. If you fell short in the second 10 questions, you need to spend more time using AutoCAD and a tutorial book. If you fell short in the last 10 questions, spend more time in Part II of this book before you go on to Part III.

Develop Good Habits

Do you practice these habits? You should.

- Draw with precision. AutoCAD is so accurate that you must draw accurately. Problems will arise in area calculations, dimensioning, and reuse of drawings if lines do not intersect, join at the corners, or have the exact length they are supposed to represent.

- Save your drawing frequently, particularly if you are new to AutoCAD.

- Don't create stray points or pieces of lines scattered in your drawings (plot in color occasionally to verify that lines have not been drawn on top of lines).

- Keep backup copies of your drawings, programs, and operating system. The simplest, but not the safest, storage device is floppy disks. We suggest that you make two backup copies and keep one outside the office. (We say more about this in Chapter 6, "Project and Drawing Management.")

- If your keyboard has a numeric keypad, learn to use it. And learn to use the space bar (which is easy to find from any position) instead of the Enter key.

- Learn to accomplish the same task in a variety of ways. You will expand your knowledge and effectiveness as a side effect of this habit.

- Plan your work before you start drawing on the computer. Don't rely on AutoCAD to do all of your thinking for you. Research each task by reviewing associated commands in the *AutoCAD Reference Manual*. Ask others what they think will be the best way to get the work done.

- Keep your work space and your computer well organized and maintained.

Avoid Bad Habits

- Do not overdraw. Because you can zoom into extremely fine detail on AutoCAD, you must be aware of the scale you will use to plot the drawing—don't fill the drawing with so many details that it becomes a black blob when plotted.

❏ Extremely large drawings. Instead of cramming every bit of information into one drawing, create more drawings. Make sure that you use the PURGE command at least once a day.

❏ Do not become overly dependent on a digitizing tablet. Develop the ability to provide input effectively from any of your input devices.

❏ Soft drinks or coffee at the workstation. Spill some on a floppy disk or in your keyboard if you want to waste a great deal of time. Otherwise, drink them in a break room.

Ways You Can Learn More about AutoCAD

Nothing is free; nothing is easy. It takes hard work and dedication to make AutoCAD as productive as it can be. The only way to become proficient with AutoCAD is to take the time to learn the system and expand your knowledge of AutoCAD's capabilities. Dedicate yourself to working through some tutorials, if you haven't already done so. Those in *Mastering AutoCAD* and *Inside AutoCAD* are a good place to start, and be sure to read the *AutoCAD Reference Manual*. You can learn a great deal from completing a tutorial, even if you don't think you need to.

Additional methods of comparing and expanding your knowledge include:

❏ Become involved in users' groups. If there is not one in your area, start one. As few as three or four users can offer a surprising amount of information and tips.

❏ Attend conferences. Some of the latest technology and future developments are exhibited and talked about during conferences. There are many seminars, covering a variety of topics; they are not inexpensive, but the information distributed is invaluable. You may meet other users and vendors.

❏ Subscribe to CAD magazines. Two excellent publications that deal specifically with AutoCAD are *CADENCE* and *CADalyst*. The Memphis Chapter Users' Group publishes a newsletter full of information and tips. Every day, more magazines directed at the microcomputer user enter the marketplace.

- ❏ Purchase books and manuals. Books are available for all levels of AutoCAD users, from beginning to advanced, and also for programming in AutoLISP. Each has something to offer. An elementary AutoCAD manual may be helpful for training new users; many advanced guides offer in-depth advice on modifying and customizing the program to suit your needs.

- ❏ Don't expect too much. Many first-time AutoCAD users have unrealistic expectations. There are many benefits to using CAD. Allow time for exploring the benefits, while demanding the quality and accuracy AutoCAD can produce. It takes time to design and draft with CAD (compared to manual methods) and to establish standards and procedures that fit your needs.

- ❏ Learn one step at a time—but keep walking. The AutoCAD manual is thick and can be overwhelming. Books such as *Inside AutoCAD,* published by New Riders, provide easy-to-read tutorials and exercises that help users become productive. Keep learning ways to increase your productivity and to avoid being stranded on a productivity plateau. Make time to experiment with AutoCAD. You may not currently be interested in every AutoCAD capability, but make an effort to understand at least the basics. There may come a time when you need to use that knowledge. The ability to customize AutoCAD and use AutoLISP are welcome in any AutoCAD firm. You can use simple AutoLISP routines to make tedious chores easy, if you are able to write and implement the routines.

- ❏ Learn DOS fundamentals. You can't get around DOS. You must learn at least the fundamentals so that you can manage the files. MS-DOS V4.1 is more user-friendly than earlier versions; it is equipped with pull-down menus, so you don't have to work as much with cryptic DOS commands. Learn to structure your hard disk so that you can find project files quickly. However, because Autodesk does not yet support DOS V4.X compatibility, you have to proceed assuming the worst.

- ❏ Training. Get help if you need it, but learn by doing. Users' groups or contacts outside the firm may help you solve specific problems. Training courses provide hands-on experience and an in-depth look at how someone else works with AutoCAD.

- ❏ Don't give up. AutoCAD is not easy to learn for all users; parts of the entire AutoCAD environment are hard for everyone to learn. Keep trying. Evaluate the ideas just presented to find a way over any hurdles, and never look back.

Answers to the AutoCAD Test

Here are the answers to the questions asked earlier in this chapter, along with a brief explanation of each answer:

1. **True.** This fact is also useful for WBLOCK, which should be used instead of BLOCK when you aren't going to insert multiple copies of the block in the drawing on which you are working.

2. **False.** The STYLE command only allows you to define a lettering style using an existing shape file. The style of the letters can be modified by obliquing angles and width factors, but the creation of the style comes from the font (shape) file itself.

3. **True.** This important feature of AutoCAD is a major factor in CAD management and standard office procedures. We discuss this at length in Chapter 7, "Advanced Management Techniques."

4. **True.** You should also learn how to indicate what you want to do with the ARRAY command by pointing.

5. **True.** In Chapter 11, "The Professional Look," we discuss how you can create hatch patterns so that you can customize the look of your drawings.

6. **True.** You can also select one line, convert it to a polyline, and then use the JOIN option to add other connected lines to the pline. The added lines will adopt the polyline's width.

7. **False.** ZOOM DYNAMIC is a great tool for moving about your drawings without causing a regen. If you missed this one, try it out!

8. **True.** The only thing UNDO won't do is remove your drawing from the disk if you just started a new drawing! Be careful with this command. The placement of marks in your drawing to designate groups of UNDO objects is an important feature of the UNDO command.

9. **False.** LTSCALE is a variable used to multiply the scale of the line description in the ACAD.LIN file so that the length of the dashes is the same for each drawing. This can create problems; some alternatives are recommended in Chapter 11, "The Professional Look."

10. **True.** DTEXT is a great timesaving device. You don't have to keep entering the text height and rotation angle. You can also move the text insertion point with your cursor before you start typing. Even if the previous text is no longer on the screen, you can locate the text where you want it!

11. **True.** If you intend to investigate third-party programs or exchange files with other CAD systems, you need to become familiar with the capabilities and limitations of this command.

12. **False.** Many of the system variables are read-only. Make sure that you have reviewed in detail what is available.

13. **True.** Use of DIM VARIABLES can greatly simplify your life and improve the appearance of your drawings.

14. **True.** This will become more and more important to you as you improve your CAD management practices.

15. **True.** This is a great enhancement to the practice of archiving files, as it will save a great deal of disk space.

16. **True.** This is probably *the* major 3-D enhancement of AutoCAD Release 10. Gaining an understanding of all the systems will take time.

17. **True.** A major feature of CAD management is to have drawings configured for each type of task you complete in your everyday practice.

18. **False.** You must understand completely the program you intend to add to your ACAD.PGP file, and instruct AutoCAD how much memory to make available in each program line of the .PGP file.

19. **True.** Digitizer drivers usually are not interchangeable.

20. **True.** You should make them part of your menu system in order to save time and effort.

21. **False.** An ATOM is the most basic unit of an AutoLISP statement.

22. **True.** You could add a configuration of your buttons so that they contain OSNAP definitions, change button menus during a command, and continue the command with a variety of OSNAP options at your fingertips. We discuss this in Chapter 9, "The Tasks At Hand."

23. **False.** Word processors must have an ASCII, programming, or nondocument mode for writing menus and LISP routines.

24. **False.** Screen menus must have bracketed phrases ([ ]) for their selection to work if they contain more than one word in the macro command line.

25. **True.** This is one of the primary input commands for AutoLISP and can be used extensively in menu macros. See Chapter 13, "AutoLISP Never Was Plain English," for more information.

26. **False.** AutoLISP can write script files, AutoLISP routines, and screen menus, and then put them to use.

27. **True.** To work with AutoLISP, you must learn how to use parentheses at the AutoCAD command prompt.

28. **True.** This is a way to add your own commands to AutoCAD.

29. **False.** This welcome addition to AutoCAD Release 10 permits AutoLISP to use extended memory for working space.

30. **True.** You should have this quantity *SET* in your AUTOEXEC.BAT or ACAD.BAT file for using AutoLISP.

Summary

This chapter is intended to get you to establish the basic knowledge you need to continue improving your use of AutoCAD. AutoCAD is a sophisticated program; it takes time and effort to learn the basics. The *AutoCAD Reference Manual* is an excellent manual, but it is not a tutorial. Complement your AutoCAD learning process with information from other sources and your AutoCAD capabilities with DOS capabilities, basic hardware knowledge, other software, and good habits. We will build on this basic knowledge in Chapter 3, "The Basics," and begin putting it to use to improve your AutoCAD performance.

Recommended Accomplishments

- ❏ Establish a clear understanding of all AutoCAD commands by using a tutorial or the reference manual.
- ❏ Put all of your hardware manuals and specification sheets into a three-ring binder.
- ❏ Evaluate your AutoCAD overview with an objective viewpoint.
- ❏ Review your habits in your use of hardware and software.
- ❏ Become a reasonably capable typist.

What Chapter 3 Is About

This chapter describes the basics of computer system maintenance and use—all the things you have to do in order to manage your system outside of AutoCAD. We discuss the following topics as they pertain to CAD and project management:

- Using DOS: directories and batch files
- System management: hard disk maintenance; file maintenance and recovery
- Using a word processor in CAD management
- Hardware basics: the computer, monitor, and digitizer

Helpful Things To Know Before You Start

- How to type (at least be able to hunt and peck well)
- How AutoCAD addresses its files
- What most of the .EXE and .COM files on your disk do
- What DOS's EDLIN or a word processor can do

What To Have on Hand

- Your hardware manuals (in a three-ring binder)
- A word processor (EDLIN if there is no other choice) and the corresponding manual
- A listing of your disk directory
- Your operating system manual
- A DOS reference guide (We recommend *MS-DOS User's Guide*, 3rd edition, and *Managing Your Hard Disk*, 2nd edition, both published by Que Corporation.)

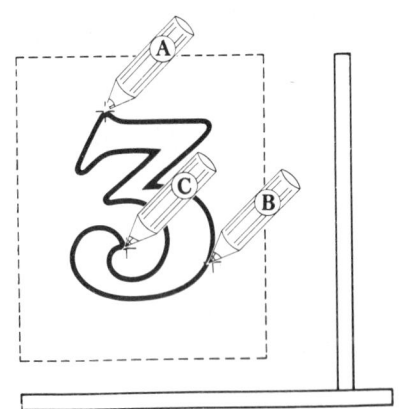

The Basics

Even if you know something about the topics in this chapter, review them with us to make sure that you have all the skills you need to proceed with the tasks outlined in this book.

We do not provide you with everything there is to know about these topics—only what you need to know for basic CAD management. Just as you need a good foundation to begin using AutoCAD effectively and efficiently, you need a good foundation in system management to manage CAD and your projects effectively. This chapter and the next provide you with that foundation.

Start with DOS

DOS is the operating system for IBM PC-compatible computers. You need to learn enough about DOS to manage files and directories, and preferably enough to create management techniques that allow others to use the system without knowing any more about DOS than what its command prompt is and how the DOS COPY command works. One of the focuses of this book is to help you automate your system so that its use is as transparent and user-friendly as possible. Automated management will also help guarantee that you receive predictable results from your system.

Using Directories

The most effective way to manage your files for AutoCAD use is through the use of directories and subdirectories. You can use program directories to keep your major programs in logical groups and to keep their associated files separate (and use job subdirectories to separate the drawings for each project). For instance, many programs come with a README.DOC file. If you were not placing your programs in separate directories, whenever you copied a new program to your hard disk you'd lose the README.DOC file from the last program you copied to your hard disk. This would happen also with SETUP.EXE files and many others. To avoid these kinds of problems, directory management is one of the first things you should learn about DOS.

If you want to know what you're doing and where you're doing it, you'll have to master a necessary evil—using DOS directories. In Chapter 4, "Basic System Management," we recommend ways to structure directories. We also discuss some programs that help you use DOS and its directories. You may be using DOS directories now, without understanding much about how they work.

Some users overdo it with directories. Here are some rules of thumb for directory usage:

- Keep programs in separate directories.

- Separate your work files by project or task.

- Put all of each program's reference files in a subdirectory unless you frequently have to back them up or will be working on them. (Some programs can't find these files even if you tell them where to look or put the directory on DOS's file-search path; you may have to put them in the program's main directory.)

- Too many subdirectories can impede the backup process and slow the operation of your computer.

Keep these concepts in mind as you start to create disk-management batch files. Batch files make abusing the directory concept easy, because everything becomes automated. See Chapter 4, "Basic System Management," for more specific ways to structure your directories for use with AutoCAD and for a discussion of programs to help you use DOS directories.

Can You Write a Batch File?

If you know how to start a program, you can write a batch file. A batch file is written almost as though you were typing directions at the DOS prompt (that's *exactly* how elementary batch files are written). Here are some things to remember about batch files:

- Batch files are executable text files, just as .EXE and .COM files are executable programs. The primary difference is that batch files contain legible ASCII text characters and the others contain machine language or assembly language. Nonetheless, writing a batch file amounts to writing a program.

- Whenever you find yourself executing the same series of DOS commands over and over, it's time to write a batch file.

- Batch files must have unique names, just like programs.

- To write a batch file, use EDLIN or a word processor. If you use a word processor, remember that you *must* use nondocument (programming) mode.

We use a batch file menu system that we created to simplify implementing programs and other menus that provide more detailed choices of activities or tasks. The batch files are all numbered so that selection is easy. The menu itself was created with DOS's extended characters, which allowed us to develop a graphic image. We discuss this system in detail in Chapter 4, "Basic System Management."

In this chapter, we discuss how to write batch files; we use some of our batch files as examples. We use a numbering system for our batch files so that the user can execute one simply by typing its number and pressing Enter.

We use our batch files to activate frequently used programs, such as AutoCAD, WordStar, and Norton Commander. Our 1.BAT file takes us from the main directory to the ACAD directory. We created 1.BAT with our ASCII editor by typing the following:

    CD\ACAD
    TYPE MENU1

This batch file changes directories (CD) to the ACAD directory and lists MENU1, which contains our AutoCAD subdirectories. That's all there is to it. Now, instead of typing the whole sequence of commands, all we have to do to access MENU1 is type **1** and press Enter. We've reduced the keystrokes from 19 to 2! Imagine what kind of efficiency you can achieve by creating batch files for more complex tasks.

Notice that we used the DOS TYPE command exactly as though we were entering it at the DOS prompt. This is true for all DOS commands. For example, if you want to access a program on a different drive, you could use this sequence in a batch file:

```
D:
CD\WS
WS
CD\
C:
TYPE MENU
```

This batch file takes you to the D: drive, changes directories again to the WordStar directory (WS), and loads WordStar. When we exit WordStar, the batch file continues, returning to the root directory (C:\) and displaying our main menu again.

The following sections describe some special batch file subcommands that you can use to make the execution of your batch files more efficient, elegant, and dynamic.

The ECHO Command

ECHO tells DOS to send to the screen whatever follows the command (on the same line) in the batch file. It also tells DOS whether you want the command lines in the batch file echoed to the screen as they are being executed. If you have on your hard disk a batch file that displays on-screen a bunch of lines you don't want to see, add the line *ECHO OFF* at the beginning of the batch file. We use the following batch file to load AutoCAD from the AutoCAD directory:

```
ECHO OFF
CLS
ACAD
ECHO OFF
CLS
TYPE MENU1
```

Notice that we start the file by turning off the ECHO and then using the DOS CLS command to clear the screen—both steps are more for appearance than for functionality. Next, the batch file loads AutoCAD. (Remember, we were already in the AutoCAD directory, thanks to the previous batch file.) When we exit AutoCAD, the balance of the batch file (still resident in the DOS environment) will be executed, once more displaying our AutoCAD-directory graphic, MENU1.

The PAUSE Command

PAUSE stops the batch processing, displays the message Press any key to continue, and waits until the user presses a key. By using PAUSE with ECHO, you can implement some rudimentary user-friendliness. For example, you could make the preceding batch file more sophisticated as follows:

```
ECHO OFF
CLS
ECHO About to begin the AutoCAD program...
ECHO Enter ^C to abort or...
PAUSE
ACAD
ECHO OFF
CLS
TYPE MENU1
```

The PAUSE command adds a couple of new twists to this batch file. First, even though we turned ECHO off, notice that we still can echo a message to the screen by using the ECHO command. Next, any batch file can be terminated by entering a ^C while it executes. DOS displays the message: Terminate Batch Job? Y or N. PAUSE completes the message by displaying Press any key to continue.

Although you may not consider it necessary to prompt users that they are about to start the AutoCAD program and give them the option to cancel the command, we find that this type of interaction helps build confidence in new users. When new users become more advanced, the original batch routine suffices.

Replaceable Parameters

If you want a batch file to work for a variety of conditions, you can use a *parameter*. The valid parameters (*%0* through *%9*) represent the words on the DOS command line, in order, with %0 representing the first word. The first word is the name of the batch file; the second and following words are *arguments* that are added after the batch file name. These arguments are fed to the batch file in place of the parameters incorporated into the batch file. Parameters are good tools to use when you want to make a batch file do more than one thing.

To use the following sample batch file, called CPY.BAT

```
ECHO OFF
COPY \ACAD\%1\*.* A:
```

the user types **CPY xxxxxxxx** at the DOS prompt (*xxxxxxxx* is the name of an AutoCAD subdirectory). Then DOS copies every file in that subdirectory to drive A:.

You can use more than one parameter in a file, as in:

```
ECHO OFF
COPY \ACAD\%1\*.%2 A:
```

To use this batch file, type **CPY 88007 DWG** at the DOS prompt. Then DOS copies all drawings from the subdirectory 88007 to the A: drive. (By using the SHIFT command, you can use as many parameters as you want. But before you can use SHIFT effectively, you'll have to learn some other commands.)

The GOTO Command

The GOTO command lets you create choices of action in your batch files. Normally, GOTO is used with a test created by the IF command (we'll talk about IF in a moment). To use the GOTO command you provide a label to which the GOTO command sends the batch file processing. A senseless but valid use of the GOTO command follows:

```
ECHO OFF
COPY \ACAD\%1\*.DWG A:
GOTO END
:END
```

In this example, the label for the GOTO command is END. Notice that the location to which GOTO sends the batch file is preceded by A:. In this case, the use of the command is redundant because the batch file was headed to the end, anyway. You'll see how to really use GOTO in just a moment, when we discuss the IF command.

The IF Command

The IF command tests to see whether a statement is true; if it is, IF completes the command that follows on the same line. If the test is not true, the rest of the line is ignored. IF tests for three conditions:

1. Whether one string equals another
2. Whether a file exists
3. The error status of a program or command request

By adding the word *NOT* after IF, you can test for the false condition instead of the true one. Let's look at some examples of these tests, using the GOTO command.

```
ECHO OFF
IF %1 == MOUSE GOTO MOUSE
IF '%1' == '' GOTO DIG
:MOUSE
MOUSE
SET ACADCFG=\ACAD\MOUSE
ACAD
GOTO END
:DIG
SET ACADCFG=\ACAD
ACAD
:END
```

This batch file tests to see whether the parameter after the batch file name is *MOUSE*. If it is, the batch file branches to the *:MOUSE* label, executes the MOUSE.COM program, sets the environment variable *ACADCFG* equal to the \ACAD\MOUSE subdirectory, and loads AutoCAD. If the parameter is blank, the batch file branches to the *:DIG* label, sets the *ACADCFG* variable equal to the \ACAD directory, and executes AutoCAD.

You should note certain things about this file:

❏ The use of == is required as part of the syntax for the IF command.

❏ DOS does not like to process null responses. The only way to test for a blank with the IF command and avoid an error message is to use apostrophes (') to enclose the parameter and the blank.

Remember that in this case IF is testing the equality of two strings. The first string is constructed of an apostrophe ('), the value of the parameter %1, and another apostrophe. The second blank string is comprised of two apostrophes (''). Therefore, if %1 is null or left blank, the IF test says "Yep—'' is equal to '','' and processes the GOTO command. This batch file will choose between a standard configuration of AutoCAD using a digitizer, and a second configuration of AutoCAD using a mouse, by testing to see whether the string mouse was typed after the batch file name.

Another use of IF tests for the existence of a file name. For example, the following batch file:

```
ECHO OFF
CLS
IF NOT EXIST \ACAD\%1\*.DWG GOTO ERROR
COPY \ACAD\%1\*.DWG A:
GOTO END
:ERROR
ECHO THE AUTOCAD SUBDIRECTORY %1 IS NOT ON DISK
ECHO OR THERE ARE NO DRAWINGS IN THE %1 SUBDIRECTORY
ECHO PLEASE TRY AGAIN BY ENTERING THE BATCH FILE NAME FOLLOWED
ECHO BY THE SUBDIRECTORY OR CHECKING TO SEE IF THE DRAWINGS ARE
ECHO THERE USING THE "DIR" BATCH FILE...
:END
```

tests to see whether the user correctly typed the subdirectory and whether there are drawings in the subdirectory. If either possibility is not true, or if the subdirectory has been removed from the disk, a prompt to the screen asks the user to check the entry or the directory of the subdirectory. Otherwise, the batch proceeds and copies the drawings as requested. Notice that, in this case, we used the NOT statement with the IF statement.

Finally, DOS returns a number greater than zero as an ERRORLEVEL if a program is exited with an error, or finds that a mistake (such as a Disk Full error) has been made in the execution of the batch file. Here is an example of the use of ERRORLEVEL:

```
ECHO OFF
CLS
CD\ACAD\ARCHIVE
ARCHIVE A %1 \ACAD\%1\*.DWG
COPY %1.ARC A:
IF ERRORLEVEL 1 GOTO ERROR
ERASE %1.ARC
CD\
ECHO ARCHIVING OF %1 COMPLETED
GOTO END
:ERROR
ECHO ARCHIVING OF %1 FAILED!!!
:END
```

By using ERRORLEVEL in this way you avoid having the %1.ARC erased if, for some reason, DOS was unable to COPY the file created by the ARCHIVE program to the A: drive.

FOR..IN..DO

The FOR..IN..DO command lets you test *FOR* a particular file or group of files *IN* a particular set and *DO* a command to each of the files. The syntax of the command is

```
FOR %%a IN <set> DO <command>
```

The *%%a* is a variable that DOS uses to hold the name of a file temporarily while the command is executed. DOS then reads the name of the next file in the specified set of files, continuing until there are no more files in the set. The set can be a list of files separated by commas or a group of files designated by wild cards. Here is an example of the use of FOR..IN..DO:

```
ECHO OFF
CLS
FOR %%a IN \ACAD\PLOT\*.DWG DO ACAD %%a PLOT
```

This batch file uses a script routine called PLOT that automatically plots a drawing and then exits AutoCAD. When AutoCAD is loaded, the PLOT script is executed on all of the drawings in the \ACAD\PLOT subdirectory, one by one.

The SHIFT Command

SHIFT is used in batch files to increase the number of available parameters for batch file use. The use of SHIFT is necessary because only nine replaceable parameters are available to batch files. For example, let's say that you are going to execute a batch file for a long list of files that you will type in following the name of the batch file. The *%0* parameter is the batch file name. The parameters that follow, *%1* through *%9*, will substitute, into the batch file for action, the next phrase at the command prompt following the batch file name. If you type more than nine file names following the batch file name, the batch file will ignore them. If you use SHIFT within the batch file, however, you can type as many file names as you want. Here is an example; if you type the following line at the DOS command prompt:

```
MOVEARC 002A1_1.DWG 002A1_2.DWG 002A1_3.DWG 002A2_1.DWG
002A3_1.DWG 002A3_2.DWG 002S1_1.DWG 002S1_2.DWG 002M1_1.DWG
002M1_2.DWG 002E1_1.DWG
```

and you have the following batch file, named MOVEARC.BAT:

```
:start
copy %1 c:\acad\archive
del %1
shift
if not %1" == " goto start
```

each of the listed files will be copied to the \ACAD\ARCHIVE subdirectory and then deleted from the current directory. (If you enter a file name with a mistake in it, the batch routine will quit also.) In this example, SHIFT causes DOS to substitute each of the file names entered at the DOS command prompt for the variable *%1*. The `if not` command tests to see whether a file was found; if it was found, the batch routine loops back to the start label. This comes in handy when you don't want to execute a batch file for all the files in a directory, because you type in the explicit name of each file.

Other techniques that are more complex and flexible can be used with batch files, such as using *command piping*, calling batch files from within batch files, and incorporating a yes/no query program. We discuss batch files further in Chapter 6, "Project and Drawing Management." If you want to create more sophisticated batch files than we present in this book, we suggest that you refer to a book like *Supercharging MS-DOS*. In our opinion, however, you would do better to consider third-party management software packages, which we also discuss in Chapter 6, rather than create more sophisticated batch files.

Does Your Hard Disk Live a Clean Life?

After our computers had been used for six months by users who didn't really know how to use them, we wondered why the computers were becoming so slow and why we did not have more space on the hard disk. We did a CHKDSK and discovered almost 100 lost clusters! (Expletive deleted!)

Lost chains and lost clusters result if the computer is shut off during its operation, possibly through power failure or a failure of the AutoCAD system (indicated by the message: `AutoCAD cannot continue-do you wish to save your drawing (Y)`).

We immediately got a disk optimizer program. By using it and the CHKDSK/F command, we cleaned up and organized the files on the hard disk.

Optimizers

When you start using AutoCAD you become a serious hard disk user. Along with this responsibility comes additional maintenance requirements that, if you have been using only floppy disks, you may never have had to think about. Some versions of DOS V3.3 include their own hard disk optimizer. If you have one, you should be using it already; if you don't have one, you should get one.

Optimizers reorganize the files and directories on a hard disk so that they are located in contiguous blocks of information. Optimizers are important because files and subdirectories are added, added to, and deleted as you use your hard disk. All of this activity causes disk fragmentation which, with time, tends to grow like a pyramid, compounding in ever increasing proportions until the performance of the hard disk begins to suffer noticeably. This deterioration in performance is due to the simple fact that the recording heads must move over larger areas in order to retrieve the data from a single file.

Disk optimization relocates the files so that the recording head movement is minimized; the hard disk works faster and is more responsive. Because disk optimization is slow and time-consuming, it is best performed when you can leave the computer unattended. You can make a batch file to automate the optimization process, which is particularly useful if your hard disk has multiple partitions.

There is some risk in hard disk optimization because the optimizer essentially rewrites the hard disk's file allocation table and relocates data clusters to new positions on the hard disk. We strongly recommend that you back up your files before you optimize your hard disk.

The size of the files you create and the frequency with which they are erased or made larger determine how often you need to optimize your hard disk. For most computers, optimization should be performed at least once a month. If you create and delete many small files, your disk will fragment more quickly than if you are manipulating large files.

> **For More Information**
>
> Berliner, Don. *Managing Your Hard Disk*, 2nd edition, Que Corporation, 1988.

Help—I Lost a Drawing!

Sooner or later, it will happen to you: you will lose a file or a drawing. You can do certain things to recover from the problem; you must do certain things to prevent it from happening again. First, we'll discuss what causes it to happen—even if you back up your work.

What Is the Cause?

There are three basic reasons you can lose or damage a file. Some you can prevent; others you can only allow for. All of them can give you nightmares. In a nutshell, the problem is caused by:

- Media failure
- Hardware failure
- Improper system management

There is no perfect solution to the problem. If your system has many users, the problem is compounded many times. In the following sections we point out some general considerations you must be aware of in order to address the problem.

Media Failure

The media on which you store your information can have defects from the factory or develop defects through mishandling. The only ways to avoid complications from defective media are to use the verify option when you use the DOS COPY command (by using the syntax *COPY/V* when you make copies of your files), and to make two copies on different media. Tape units generally are error-free because the media is sealed in a cartridge (which can create a false sense of security). To keep copies of your files, use tape units in addition to floppy disks, or use two tapes. Or you may want to consider another option—a WORM (Write Once Read Many) drive; they are becoming increasingly popular as their price declines. The most prevalent storage medium, however, is still the floppy disk.

Handling Disks

Floppy disks come as either 5 1/4-inch minifloppies or 3 1/2-inch microfloppies. Microfloppies are becoming increasingly popular because of the protection afforded by their rigid plastic jacket and because they are not only as portable as standard floppies but they also have comparable data storage capacity. Most software developers ship their programs on 5 1/4-inch disks; some offer optional shipment on microfloppies.

Physical damage is not the most common type of damage to a floppy disk. *Logical* damage—damage to a disk's directory and file allocation table (FAT) is.

A floppy disk can be read or written to more than one billion times before wear flaws it. A disk drive has a *spin life* (the amount of time it actually reads or writes information on a disk) of several years. Poor disk handling, accidental spills and contamination, bending, extreme heat, stray magnetic fields, and misplaced disks ruin more information than wear. You should be wary also of formatting lower density disks as high density disks. A floppy disk formatted for a higher capacity than was originally intended may work for a while and then suddenly produce errors.

Floppy disks are sensitive to and can be damaged by wide temperature changes or extremes. The jacket can warp and prevent the disk from spinning properly. The acceptable temperature range for floppies is from 50 to 124 degrees Fahrenheit. (Because the temperature in an automobile can be higher than 124 degrees, don't leave your floppies in the car!) The microfloppy's plastic sleeve offers better thermal protection than that of the standard floppy. Although cold does not damage disks, it can affect their use. When a disk is cold, the tracks move slightly; a read error is displayed when DOS tries to read the disk. Just let the floppy warm up to room temperature—you should be able to continue using it.

Keep disks away from magnetic fields and electric motors or appliances (all of which generate magnetic fields) or you may find that the data on your disk is in a "foreign language"! A common, albeit innocent culprit is the electric pencil sharpener. The magnetic field of an electric pencil sharpener is not strong but its frequent use and variation in strength can do the damage. Hopefully, you will be proficient enough at AutoCAD to sell your pencil sharpener along with your old drafting stations.

Hardware Failure

One of the most disastrous things that can happen in the electronic world is a hard disk failure. When your hard disk fails, you lose everything stored on the disk.

The design of the motors and heads is important in the life of a hard disk. Hard disks can damage the information on the disk platens and render useless a file or group of files. Many hard disks park their heads in a location that will not damage data on the platens when the heads are not in use. Physical shock to the computer itself can ruin a hard disk, as can air pollution. The only kind of control you can have over hard disk failure is proper file backup. If you want to know more about the construction of the hard disk so that you can buy one sensibly, *Managing Your Hard Disk* will tell you nearly everything you need to know about them.

Power loss and power surges are another cause of hardware failure. Unless you own the utility company, there is little you can do to prevent power loss. One thing you *can* do is buy a UPS (Uninterrupted Power Supply) system. Whether you want to make this rather expensive choice depends on the characteristics of the electric utility in your area.

A power surge can destroy the circuits in your computer. We happen to live in the lightning capital of the world—every spring and summer, we start thinking that it's time to buy a UPS. Single station users generally can avoid buying a UPS by using proper backup methods and a surge protector that is rated to protect the computer against a lightning strike to the building's electrical system. A power failure generally means that you lose the work you have done since your last backup. If you follow the guidelines presented in Chapter 6, you will be able to recover from many power failures before you will pay for a UPS system. On the other hand, if your system has many users, all it takes is one very badly timed failure for the UPS system to pay for itself right then and there.

Improper System Management

Most data loss results from inadvertent operations, such as formatting the wrong disk, misdirecting erase commands, and overwriting the wrong file during a copy command. This is due to poor system management; in Chapters 6 and 7, we spend a great deal of time talking about ways to correct this problem. Basically, you need to establish proper back-up procedures, use file-naming conventions, standardize directory management, and have a controlled routine for the end of the work day.

Recovering Lost Files

Several software packages can help you recover a lost file. When a file is erased, it is not removed from the hard disk. The space the file occupied is released up so that new information can be written there. Therefore, if you know that you have erased a file you need to recover, stop using that subdirectory (to be even safer, stop using the computer) until you can get a recovery program such as Norton Utilities. If you lose a drawing, a standard file-recovery program may produce a file that AutoCAD cannot use. This happens because a highly fragmented file is pieced together by the recovery program, and everything may not be as it originally was. If the file you are recovering is a text file, you can usually erase any portions that seem unusual. On the other hand, if you are recovering a drawing file, AutoCAD cannot use the file unless all the drawing data bits are exactly where they belong. AutoSAVE (by CYCO International) is a special recovery program; it can recover most of a lost drawing. We strongly suggest that you get and learn to use one or more recovery utilities—they easily pay for themselves.

Don't Let It Happen Again

The best way to prevent lost files is to have some sort of file backup procedure and use it consistently. It is also advisable to keep a comfortable amount of working space free on the floppy disk, so that when working files expand, there will still be enough room for the file to be recopied to the floppy. The amount of space needed depends on the size you estimate your final drawings will be. You can use your existing files to provide a reasonable estimate. Always keep a couple of formatted floppy disks on hand so that you don't have to stop in the middle of what you are doing to format some.

If you have had numerous problems with data and file loss, we suggest that you spend your time and energy developing the procedures outlined in Chapters 6 ("Project and Drawing Management") and 7 ("Advanced Management Techniques").

Word Processors

To modify AutoCAD, you need word-processing or editing software that will prepare ASCII files. An *ASCII file* is one that contains only the numbers, letters, and symbols that can be entered from the keyboard without the use of any special keys other than the Alt key.

EDLIN is a DOS editor that comes with your computer's disk operating system. Unfortunately, learning to use it is difficult; it requires many keystrokes and its commands are not intuitive. EDLIN does not give you full-screen editing, and cursor movement is awkward at best.

We strongly recommend that you purchase and learn to use one of the popular word-processing software programs such as WordStar, WordPerfect, or Norton Editor. WordPerfect has a major advantage—its ability to capture an AutoCAD drawing. Some excellent shareware editors are available also; they can be obtained from electronic bulletin boards or shareware catalogs. If you are uncertain about what software you want, or you want to get shareware but do not know how to start, go to a local AutoCAD users' group and ask people there what they are using and why they are using it.

Document and Nondocument (Programming) Modes

All the text editing that you will be doing in order to use and manage the AutoCAD environment requires editing in nondocument, or programming, mode. The editor you use *must* have this capability. What does that mean? Some word-processing software puts what are called *high ASCII characters* in their files for the purpose of screen display, column and paragraph formatting, and printing options such as boldface or italic. These characters make the final product look nice, but will make your programs crash. Different word-processing packages use different names for creating ASCII files. Make sure of what you are getting before you buy the software.

The Right One for the Job

All computer users have their favorite word-processing software. They choose that software based on a combination of price, features, and hardware requirements. If you can afford it, we recommend that you use two text editors: one that requires very little memory to run and therefore has somewhat limited features—we refer to it as *low overhead* software—and one that has every word-processing function you think you could ever use. You will be able to use the low overhead editor from within AutoCAD through the ACAD.PGP file. In this book we describe how you can use it to create the following:

- LISP routines
- Script files
- Attribute-extraction templates
- Hatch patterns
- Line patterns
- Minor shape file edits
- Batch files
- Test menu files

You will use your full-featured editor to create and edit large menu files. The requirements placed on your text editor vary with the task and make certain features more desirable than others. We discuss these features at length in Chapter 5, "Software Companions."

A Little about Hardware

It has often been said that "a microcomputer CAD system offers 80 percent of the capabilities of a mainframe CAD system at approximately 10 percent of the cost." AutoCAD enables you to use a wide variety of display systems and input/output devices, thereby allowing you to put together a system that suits your needs and budget. The problem with this wide range of possibilities is that you must become conversant (at least in the basics) about hardware.

Computers are not intelligent. If you look inside one, it seems terribly complex—as though it ought to be doing everything for you while you play tennis or go sailing, with little or no input from you. Unfortunately, it doesn't work that way—yet. Computers require a complex and detailed set of instructions called an *operating system*. Essentially, this is a program that directs and controls all the input and output devices. The operating system establishes a standard environment within which your applications programs work.

Input-output devices give to or receive instructions from the computer. Keyboards, mice, and digitizers are input devices. Output devices are monitors, printers, and plotters. Hard disks and floppy drives are input-output devices—they provide information to and receive information from the computer.

Work performed on the computer is done in random access memory (RAM). RAM depends on electrical power to maintain information. Information from RAM can be stored on media such as a hard disk or a floppy disk. A hard disk stores information magnetically and is a mechanical device. Although it is not easily transportable, the hard disk has a large capacity for storage and transfers data quickly, compared to a floppy disk. A floppy disk does not store much information and slows down the performance of tasks that require the disk to be read frequently, but it is removable and transportable.

Inside the Box—The Computer

Four hardware elements provide the fundamental power for your system: the central processing unit (CPU), memory, the expansion bus, and disk storage. The elements are interrelated; the CPU is designed to work with a certain amount of memory and a particular expansion bus design. The operating system is designed to access memory in a certain way and has a maximum amount of memory it can access. The design of a CPU must be sensitive to the fact that it may require the design of an entirely new operating system.

Speed of the expansion bus can constrain the speed of memory and peripherals. CPUs with wide data buses work faster than those with narrow buses. A 32-bit data bus is twice as fast as a 16-bit data bus. (*Data bits* are the number of bits moved at one time between the CPU and memory.) Because PCs depend on precise timing, a crystal clock regulates the timing of your PC's main processor and keeps it synchronized with the other components of the system. A faster clock speed usually means that a computer performs more work in the same time as a slower computer. However, some computers are faster than others running at the same clock speed due to the quality and speed of their peripheral devices. This is measured by *throughput*. Clock speed and throughput are rated in megahertz (one MHz equals one million cycles per second) and MIPS (Millions of Instructions Per Second) and currently have an effective range of 7 to 33 megahertz and 12 MIPS for PCs that are used with CAD.

CPUs vary in their capability to execute instructions. Some can execute identical instructions in less time than others, and some have additional instructions for performing tasks in a different, faster way. The main processor is an integrated circuit that controls most of these activities. The main processor constantly accesses RAM while it works. If RAM cannot keep up with the processor, *wait states* must be employed. (Zero or low wait states produce maximum speed.) The CPU waits one clock cycle for information to become available when 1 wait state is in use, for example. All the peripherals in your system must be able to synchronize with the clock speed and wait states of your CPU. A really fast CPU with no wait states for internal operations can be hampered tremendously by improperly coordinated peripherals. Ordinarily, your computer manufacturer coordinates wait-state issues. You don't have to be concerned. The quality of a system is related to how finely coordinated the peripherals are, however.

A math coprocessor shares information processing with the main processor by taking care of floating-point calculations. AutoCAD Release 9 and later requires a math coprocessor.

Special-features cards are plugged into the expansion bus of your computer to allow the CPU to communicate with your system's peripheral devices. Disk controllers, graphics cards, communication ports, internal modems, and memory expansion cards are plugged into 16- or 8-bit slots on the expansion bus. Clearly, 16-bit communication is the fastest. Unfortunately, most peripherals are 8-bit devices (and therefore work on a wide range of computers).

Communication adapters (ports) are either parallel or serial. Parallel (Centronics type) ports are just that—all data is passed in a parallel stream to the device and then back to the computer. Serial ports (RS-232 adapters) send the data in series; they can hanle a variety of error-checking and handshaking techniques. We discuss these issues in more detail in Chapter 16, "Advanced Hardware Concepts." For the time being, you should know that these parallel and serial cards allow the exchange of data between printers, modems, plotters, and mice or digitizers.

Behind the Scenes—The Monitor

What you see when you work with AutoCAD represents cooperation between your monitor (screen) and the graphics card residing in your computer. Graphics displays are complex, and their technology is changing as fast, if not faster, than that of computers. The quality of your display can have a great deal to do with the success of your use of AutoCAD. The combination of graphics cards and monitors used with AutoCAD is probably the major source of consternation among users who have ventured beyond the EGA standard. We provide a brief overview of graphics displays here; for an in-depth analysis, see Chapter 16, "Advanced Hardware Concepts."

Graphics displays are measured by their *resolution*—the number of pixels the device can display. A *pixel* is the smallest unit of light the screen can produce (the smallest unit of light containing the red, green, and blue color elements). The more pixels a graphic card and monitor can display, the higher the resolution. The Enhanced Graphics Adapter (EGA) has a standard resolution of 640 by 350 pixels. This is the minimum resolution suitable for computer-aided drafting.

The resolution of the popular EGA card (640 by 350 pixels) is barely adequate for computer-aided drafting applications. The ideal resolution is one that most nearly matches the height/width ratio of the monitor. The IBM Professional Graphics Adapter and IBM Personal System/2 monitors are close to that ratio, which is approximately 640 by 480 pixels.

Higher resolution gives smoother-looking lines and circles, and better detail. The number of pans and zooms you need to use is reduced with higher resolutions. A resolution of 800 by 600 enables you to see nearly twice the area you can see on an EGA monitor. Higher-resolution cards cost more but can save you money by reducing the amount of time required to perform redraws and regenerations. Some EGA-compatible boards offer, as an added feature, resolution of 800 by 600.

Graphics cards are available that offer even higher resolutions and added features such as hardware pans and zooms. Hardware pans and zooms are accomplished instantaneously by storing a large part of drawing display in memory or on the hard disk. This is known as *display list processing*. Some displays are capable of storing 2,000 by 2,000 pixels. The smaller the number of pixels that can be stored, the less helpful is magnification. Pixels begin to fatten after two or three magnifications. Lines appear thicker as the image is magnified and less detail is shown.

The number of displayable colors available from a graphics card varies. AutoCAD uses a maximum of 16 colors. AutoShade uses 256 colors, whereas a good paint program uses as many colors as are available. The number of colors is listed as displayable and as color palette. *Displayable colors* are those that can be displayed simultaneously on the monitor. The *color palette* is the number of colors that can be generated but cannot be displayed at the same time. Typically, a monitor will display 16 colors, but by adding memory to the graphics card you can achieve 256 colors.

Monitors come in two general types: interlaced and noninterlaced. The difference is the monitor's scan rate and the speed of the card's refresh rate. *Interlaced display* monitors have a lower scan rate and rely on long-persistence phosphors to keep the image from flickering. *Noninterlaced display* monitors are more expensive, bright, and produce more brilliant colors.

Inside the Tablet—The Digitizer

A deceptively simple-looking device sits on many CAD-station tables. It's flat and beige, perhaps with a few coffee spots, and sitting on it is a device that looks like a mouse. Not all CAD stations have one, but complex drafting environments usually do. The digitizer was originally intended to allow the user to input drawings by hand. It has been expanded to include the capability to handle command macros by sending an address to the computer. AutoCAD knows that the information is coming from the digitizer and checks to see what has been assigned to that address. AutoCAD can use as many as four menu areas and one screen area on a digitizer. If the address is in one of the menu areas, AutoCAD interprets the macro or command that is stored there by referring to the menu file. If the address is in the screen pointing area, AutoCAD receives a screen coordinate and a real coordinate, which it subsequently displays and writes as data to the drawing file.

Digitizing tablets come in various sizes—up to a full table size—the most popular of which is 12 inches square. The digitizer is a natural way to draw because the movement of the puck is translated directly into cursor movement. The puck's buttons can be programmed with your most frequently used commands, which is much faster than searching through on-screen menus.

Digitizers, like printers and plotters, have their own communication language (which is why they are connected to the computer by a serial cable). Some digitizers can emulate a mouse, which comes in handy for programs like AutoShade and Ventura Publisher.

Summary

This chapter reviewed the basic ingredients of the system environment outside of AutoCAD. Gaining proficiency in the use of the system is the first step to developing good CAD-management practices and procedures. In this chapter, we discussed the basics of the following:

- ❏ DOS use and system management
    - ■ Directory use
    - ■ Batch files
    - ■ Hard disk maintenance
    - ■ File maintenance and recovery
- ❏ Word-processor use in CAD management
- ❏ Hardware basics
    - ■ Computer
    - ■ Monitor
    - ■ Digitizer

In Chapter 4, "Basic System Management," we review how some of these basics can be applied to setting up your system for better overall system performance and AutoCAD capability.

Recommended Accomplishments

- ❏ Write some batch files to accomplish repetitive DOS commands.
- ❏ Use a disk optimizer to clean up your hard disk.
- ❏ Use a file recovery program to recover a lost file.
- ❏ Master the use of directories.
- ❏ Review the capabilities of your word processor.

What Chapter 4 Is About

After your system was up and running, you may have followed others' suggestions about ways to improve its performance—whether you understood what you were doing or not. Each system has unique capabilities that can be affected by various advanced installation and hardware considerations. In this chapter we talk about the components that determine the performance characteristics of your system. If, as you read this chapter, you decide that you need to know more about advanced hardware considerations, see Chapter 16, "Advanced Hardware Concepts." CAD management requires that you master certain elements of system management. These are summarized as follows:

- The CONFIG.SYS file
- The AUTOEXEC.BAT file
- Communications ports, graphics cards, and their drivers
- Expanded and extended memory
- Operating systems

Helpful Things To Know Before You Start

- What your system is made up of
- How to write simple batch files
- The contents of your existing CONFIG.SYS and AUTOEXEC.BAT files

What To Have on Hand

- Your three-ring binder of system-component manuals
- A variety of PC magazines
- Word-processing software
- A stopwatch or a watch with a second hand
- A DOS reference manual (We recommend *MS-DOS User's Guide*, 3rd edition, published by Que Corporation.)

Basic System Management

With an overview of the concepts in this chapter and their influence on system performance, you can make an informed adjustment to your system configuration(s) and communicate your needs to a vendor with greater definition and confidence.

The CONFIG.SYS File

Whenever the system is booted, DOS reads the CONFIG.SYS file, executes its commands, and then executes the AUTOEXEC.BAT file, if it finds one. The CONFIG.SYS file customizes your computer's BIOS (Basic Input Output System). The specific contents of the CONFIG.SYS files vary between systems; the file specifies the following for a computer system:

- Allocation of memory for the DOS environment
- Control of various devices (peripherals)
- Management of file access
- Control of various DOS default conditions

In the following sections, we discuss some of the components of the CONFIG.SYS file and explain how they work. Your system may have requirements different from those we present here, because major system manufacturers build into their BIOS the device handlers for devices provided with the system. Systems with a diversified component approach require a driver for nearly every piece of equipment included within or attached to the system.

The sample CONFIG.SYS file shown here is from one of our systems with middle-of-the-road driver requirements. A typical CONFIG.SYS file might look like this one:

```
SHELL=C:\DOS\COMMAND.COM /P/E:512
BREAK=ON
BUFFERS=20
FILES=25
DEVICE=HARDRIVE.SYS
DEVICE=REMM.SYS
DEVICE=REX.SYS 1408
DEVICE=FASTDISK.SYS/M=1408/EXTM
DEVICE=RCD.SYS
DEVICE C:\DOS\ANSI.SYS
LASTDRIVE=G
```

Now we'll look more closely at the contents of this sample file. For a more detailed analysis, consult your DOS reference manual.

The Shell Program (COMMAND.COM)

The *shell program* surrounds DOS, displays prompts and messages, and interprets commands. You never see the inner workings of DOS, only the shell program—COMMAND.COM. The standard COMMAND.COM configuration is loaded automatically, unless you use the SHELL command in your CONFIG.SYS file. A custom COMMAND.COM file is written by the authors of your particular version of DOS and contains the major resident DOS functions that you and some of your programs use for managing your system. With DOS V3.1 and later, you can use the SHELL command with COMMAND.COM optional parameters to increase the size of the DOS environment. We use this feature of the SHELL command to extend the number of directories we can have on our DOS path. For a detailed discussion of AutoCAD's use of the PATH command and your considerations for the size of your environment, see Chapter 6, "Project and Drawing Management."

BREAK

BREAK=ON tells DOS to check whether you have pressed Ctrl-C or Ctrl-Break. With the default DOS setting of BREAK=OFF, the computer checks for Ctrl-C only when the program you are running is communicating with the keyboard or the screen. Extensive disk access during long procedures will cause the computer to ignore your Ctrl-C until the procedure is finished, unless you set the BREAK command to BREAK=ON. Some operations are slower when BREAK is on, but when you don't want it on you can simply type **BREAK=OFF** at the system prompt. If you find yourself pressing Ctrl-C a number of times to get a procedure to halt processing, try setting BREAK to ON.

Buffers and Files

To improve the system's disk access performance, RAM is set aside in the form of *buffers*. By using the BUFFERS command you can specify enough buffers to retain recently used information in RAM, instead of having to access the disk (which is much slower than RAM). The syntax for the BUFFERS command is BUFFERS=nn, where *nn* is the number of buffers you want DOS to create. This number (*nn*) can range from 1 to 99. Each BUFFER reduces by 528 bytes the amount of memory available for your programs.

The number of buffers you need to create depends on three factors:

- The access speed of your hard disk
- The speed and type of your computer's RAM
- The amount and type of file access your program uses

Some 386s with high-performance hard disk controllers access information from disk with great speed. Older ATs, on the other hand, generally access RAM much faster than they access the hard drive. On a fast system, a large number of buffers may take as long to access and manage as a single, well-placed disk access. AutoCAD does a great deal of random disk work, which means that files are accessed and written to in different locations. It also means that AutoCAD requires a lot of disk head movement. We suggest that you start by setting your buffers at 20 and experimenting with AutoCAD, using different buffer settings and one of your largest drawings. As you experiment, remember that RAM available for AutoCAD decreases with each buffer you add and that AutoCAD uses RAM for paging space. If you decrease the available RAM too much, your menu access will begin to get slower and slower.

AutoCAD often accesses several files simultaneously, both for its own use in program overlays and drawing files and for users' requirements such as script files and AutoLISP functions. The FILES command establishes the number of files a program can have open at one time; its syntax is FILES=nn, where *nn* is a number from 8 to 255. Each file over 8 that you specify increases DOS's use of RAM by 39 bytes. Just as you need to experiment with BUFFERS, you need to experiment with FILES to find what number works best for your system. Your program will have to close files before it opens new ones if the FILES setting is too low, which will slow the access time of your system. Limit your FILES command only to allow for the fact that the amount of RAM available to AutoCAD and your other programs is reduced when you increase the FILES setting. Although our sample file shows a FILES setting of 25, we recommend that you start with FILES=20.

Device Drivers

Almost every device attached to your computer requires a program called a *device driver*. Device drivers, which generally have a .SYS file extension, also use RAM; how well they are written by the computer manufacturers can have a dramatic effect on the amount of RAM used and the speed of the peripheral device.

Device drivers are supplied by the peripheral manufacturer or with your operating system, depending on the device. If you buy a mouse, for example, a driver is supplied. You put the driver on your hard drive and add its name to your CONFIG.SYS file. The same is true for some graphics cards, digitizers, and printers. Each of these drivers sets specific addresses for communicating with the CPU and each other. It is important that you understand, for now, that conflicts in these addresses can occur. If you intend to use a number of devices that require drivers, make sure that you have an expert review their compatibility. For more information about drivers, see Chapter 16, "Advanced Hardware Concepts."

The sample CONFIG.SYS file lists several device drivers. If a driver is not in your root directory, its name in the CONFIG.SYS file must be preceded by the correct path. (As you can see from the sample CONFIG.SYS file, our ANSI.SYS driver is not in the root directory; it is in the DOS subdirectory.) In the following sections we discuss the devices (and associated drivers) listed in our sample CONFIG.SYS file.

Hard Drive

HARDDRIVE.SYS, which controls the hard disk, was supplied by the maker of the hard disk and disk controller on this system.

Extended/Expanded Memory

REMM.SYS, which stands for *Rampage Expanded Memory Manager*, lets DOS know that this computer has an expanded memory board installed. REX.SYS is Rampage's Extended Memory Manager driver. We discuss memory a little later in this chapter and in Chapter 16, "Advanced Hardware Concepts".

FASTDISK—Rampage's version of a RAM disk—is used in lieu of VDISK.SYS, which is DOS's disk driver.

Tape Storage

RCD.SYS controls a Bernoulli Box, which is a tape storage unit.

Keyboard

ANSI.SYS is a DOS driver that provides detailed control of the display and keyboard. The ANSI driver has many uses for customizing your screen, cursor, and character display. We discuss one use of ANSI.SYS in Chapter 7, "Advanced Management Techniques".

ANSI.SYS commands position the cursor, change colors, and clear the screen, for example. By combining ANSI.SYS commands with text, you can control the appearance of the display. With *escape* sequences, you can redefine keys on the keyboard to produce different characters, commands, or even macros. Escape sequences also let you move the cursor up, down, left, right, to a specific position. These sequences also let you save the current cursor position and restore the cursor to the saved position. You can use erase sequences to erase a line or the entire display. Attribute and mode sequences let you control the number of columns (40 and 80), graphics and color modes, and attributes such as high intensity, blinking, foreground color, and background color.

Extensive functions are available through the use of ANSI escape sequences. We feel that the amount of memory used by an abuse of ANSI.SYS (through extensive key redefinition and screen customization) is prohibitive, and better left for AutoCAD's benefit. If you need extensive screen customization, however, we suggest that you refer to a book that focuses on DOS.

LASTDRIVE

Not all computers require the use of LASTDRIVE. We have had to use this command to get some systems to recognize more than one RAM disk, because DOS defaults to a last drive of E:. Additional storage devices also may require that you set the LASTDRIVE variable. The syntax for the LASTDRIVE command is LASTDRIVE=x, where *x* is any letter of the alphabet representing the drive you want to specify as the last drive DOS will recognize. DOS uses the letter *before* the letter you specify for its last logical device designation. See Chapter 6, "Project and Drawing Management," for information about using LASTDRIVE with the SUBST command.

The AUTOEXEC.BAT File

The AUTOEXEC.BAT file is the second file the computer looks for after booting up. It lets the computer execute automatically a number of commands that would otherwise have to be entered at the DOS command prompt or by using a standard .BAT file. The only differences between the AUTOEXEC.BAT file and and other .BAT files is that the name *AUTOEXEC* is reserved by DOS for *AUTO*matic *EXEC*ution when the system is switched on.

The *AutoCAD Reference Manual* tells you to place in your AUTOEXEC.BAT file a number of SET commands and modify the PATH command. Although these are not definitive requirements of the system, we had the impression that they were (when we first started using our PCs with AutoCAD). If you intend to use your system under different configurations and for different software, you can install the appropriate drivers in the CONFIG.SYS file (making sure that they don't conflict with each other) and then set the PATH and other environment settings in each batch file that you use to start the programs. It is especially important to adjust the PATH as needed as you move around your system.

The AUTOEXEC.BAT file controls many variables that set the proper stage for the effective use of your system. These variables include, but are not limited to, the following:

- The main path of the system
- The environment for the software
- The type of system prompt you want to use
- Initialization of a program or system menu

The contents of our sample AUTOEXEC.BAT file reflect a basic system setup and are explained in the following sections.

```
ECHO OFF
PATH C:\;C:\ACAD;C:\DOS;C:\UTIL;C:\WP;E:
PROMPT=$P$G
SET ACAD=/AEC/A/D
SET ACADCFG=/ACAD
SET ACADFREERAM=24
SET LISPHEAP=40000
SET LISPSTACK=5000
SET ACADXMEM=1024,1408
SET ACADLIMEN=NONE
M
```

ECHO OFF

The ECHO OFF batch file command tells DOS not to display on-screen any of the command contents of the batch file. It serves only as a way to provide a clean screen while the batch file is running. If you want to display a message, you can do so by entering *ECHO message* into the batch file, where *message* is the text you want to display on-screen. (Refer to Chapter 3, "The Basics," for a discussion of the use of ECHO.)

PATH

The PATH command allows DOS and application programs to search the directories listed in the PATH command for files that are not in the current directory. If you use an extensive PATH command, one which requests that a number of subdirectories stay accessible at all times, you may need to make adjustments to the DOS environment. We discuss these adjustments in Chapter 6, "Project and Drawing Management."

If you use the PATH command, you don't need to type in the entire directory path to every file whenever you want your program or DOS to access the file. When DOS looks for a file, it searches each directory and subdirectory designated by the PATH command. You can reset the path from the DOS prompt or with any batch file. In this sample AUTO-EXEC.BAT file, the use of the PATH command is a general application; it does not anticipate a reassignment of the value of the path to be required. If you are using several programs in addition to AutoCAD, you may want to set the PATH in the batch file you use to start each program.

PROMPT

The PROMPT command—in this case, PROMPT=PG—accepts special codes that cause specified information to be included in the system prompt. The *PG* causes the name of the current directory to be displayed at the DOS prompt. This command has many options, which you can review in your DOS reference guide. In the sample AUTOEXEC.BAT file, the PROMPT command uses *$P* to specify display of the name of the current path (directory and subdirectories) and *$G* to specify display of a greater-than sign.

SET

The SET command assigns various quantities to a variable name. These quantities can be referred to by applications software in order to determine what considerations need to be made for the environment in which they are working. Not all programs use this DOS capability. The variables set in the sample AUTOEXEC.BAT file are for the benefit of AutoCAD. You can use SET to set any environment variable equal to any quantity, regardless of whether you will be using it. This fact is important to some new features of Extended AutoLISP (see Chapter 13, "AutoLISP Never Was Plain English").

The memory use variables are discussed in more detail later in this chapter. A brief explanation of the SET commands used in the sample AUTOEXEC.BAT file follows:

ACAD=/AEC/A/D tells AutoCAD that the directory for the library of drawings is in the subdirectory /AEC/A/D. We explain the use of this variable in Chapter 6, "Project and Drawing Management."

ACADCFG=/ACAD tells AutoCAD that the information for the configuration of AutoCAD will be in the ACAD directory. You can use different configurations of AutoCAD by changing this variable in a batch file. If you have a digitizer and a mouse, for example, you can set up the configuration of AutoCAD in two different directories. By changing this environment setting, AutoCAD can be configured automatically for the digitizer or the mouse.

ACADFREERAM tells AutoCAD how much memory to set aside for working storage area. The default amount (24,000 bytes) is indicated by SET ACADFREERAM=24 in your AUTOEXEC.BAT file. Input/Output (I/O) page space is more important than FREERAM to the performance of AutoCAD. Keep ACADFREERAM set as close to 24 as possible; the setting you need depends on your system and on the type of work you do. You can make adjustments until you receive the error message FATAL ERROR: OUT OF RAM. We suggest that you set FREERAM this way: use a copy of one of your larger drawings and reduce ACADFREERAM until you get the error message. The setting of ACADFREERAM can be tested by using AutoCAD's HIDE, TRIM, and OFFSET commands.

LISPHEAP, which is the amount of RAM set aside for use by AutoLISP, creates node space. *Node space* is the portion of memory in which the names of the functions defined by AutoLISP are stored. Because AutoLISP is a primary tool for AutoCAD customization and system management, you should include this statement, as well as the LISPSTACK statement, in your AUTOEXEC.BAT file (even if you haven't been using AutoLISP). In AutoCAD Release 10, AutoLISP can run in extended memory; AutoLISP can use extended memory for node space, thereby releasing more RAM for AutoCAD's I/O page space.

LISPSTACK is the amount of memory set aside for AutoLISP to use as temporary work space. This memory is in active use during the calculation or evaluation of AutoLISP functions. If you receive the error message LISPSTACK OVERFLOW, you need to increase the size of LISPSTACK.

The total memory allocated to LISPHEAP and LISPSTACK cannot exceed 45,000 bytes. If you have deeply nested LISP routines which require that a great number of calculations be completed and maintained in memory until a final result is found, you may have a LISPSTACK size problem. (We discuss nesting in Chapter 13, "AutoLISP Never Was Plain English.")

ACADXMEM is an AutoCAD setting for the use of extended memory; it addresses the use of extended memory.

ACADLIMEM controls memory that meets the Lotus-Intel-Microsoft (LIM) expanded-memory-management specifications. It defines the amount of workspace available in expanded memory for I/O paging.

M is the name of a batch file we use to display a batch menu. We discuss this use of batch files in Chapter 6, "Project and Drawing Management."

Memory? What Memory?

Memory is a major factor in the performance of your computer system. Unfortunately, computer memory is not like human memory—it does not retain a permanent record of anything. The computer's memory is a workspace in which information is stored and manipulated by requests made through the central processing unit (CPU). The type of CPU you have (8086, 8088, 80286, 80386) determines the range and flexibility of the types of requests your software can make.

Classification of Memory

Memory has four classification factors: type (ROM or RAM), amount, addressability (real, extended, or expanded), and construction (dynamic, static, or static column).

Read only memory (ROM), which is nonvolatile and nonchanging, is used for programs and information that should always be present in the computer. Random access memory (RAM) is volatile, changeable, and can have data written to it (stored within it) as well as read from it. RAM is used to hold the information to be manipulated and referred to by your programs.

The amount of memory, particularly RAM, is a performance resource of the computer. More RAM means more horsepower and the capability for speed, up to a point. If you have enough memory in the computer to place all of AutoCAD and all of your drawing into memory, AutoCAD's functions operate at the fastest speed available to your computer, which in turn depends on the computer's clock speed, wait states, and divide access time. The drawback to using RAM is that if your computer loses power, all information stored there is lost. To avoid that catastrophe, some computer installations use an Uninterrupted Power Supply (UPS), which provides an immediate switchover to battery power for the computers in the event of a power failure.

Memory, which is addressable in real, extended, and/or expanded modes, relates to the CPU's hardware and instruction set. Unless the capability to access extended or expanded memory is built into the structure of your software, your use of memory will be limited to a RAM disk (discussed in the next section of this chapter). AutoCAD can use expanded or extended memory automatically for I/O page space, allowing large chunks of data to be swapped for input and output from AutoCAD through the use of memory rather than the hard disk. This capability makes adding extended and expanded memory a significant improvement to your system if you are having a problem with system speed.

RAM's construction can be dynamic, static, or static column. A 286-based system can use only one type of RAM, dynamic. A 386-based computer can use all three types of RAM. The speed of RAM is critical to the speed of your system. Memory speeds range from 60 to 300 nanoseconds (billionths of a second). The type and speed of your system's memory is directly proportional to the cost of the system. If you are considering buying a system, spend some time studying the aspects of the system's memory specification.

Expanding Your Horizons and Extending Your Goals

On most DOS systems, the first 640K of RAM is *base* memory. (Some DOS systems can use 1M [1,024K] of base memory, but they are beyond the scope of this book.) Memory greater than a system's conventional memory is called *extended* or *expanded* memory, depending on how it is configured.

To address extended or expanded memory, a 286 or 386 machine must use an operating mode called *protected*, which protects programs and data from being overwritten by DOS. The 640K barrier exists only as a management limitation of DOS. Versions of DOS later than 4.0 may well overcome this limitation, making all of this information about extended memory and expanded memory unnecessary.

Extended memory is addressed in one contiguous bank of memory; it works like conventional memory, except that it is addressed by the CPU at addresses above the 1M memory location. DOS keeps a section of the memory between 640K and 1M for the management of this memory. In order to use extended memory on most 286-based computers, you have to use your system's SETUP command to let the computer know that the extra memory is available. Precisely how this works varies between systems; because we cannot predict what your system's requirements are, refer to your system manual when you are studying the configuration or addition of extended memory in your system.

Extended memory can be configured as a (very fast) disk drive known as a *RAM disk*. The management of this memory is controlled by the VDISK.SYS driver that comes with the computer's DOS. We discuss RAM disks more extensively in Chapter 16, "Advanced Hardware Concepts."

Expanded memory uses one of three kinds of management software—EMS (Expanded Memory Specification), LIM (Lotus-Intel Microsoft), or EEMS (Enhanced Expanded Memory Specification). Expanded memory is made available to programs as 16K pages mapped into a contiguous 64K area called a *page frame*.

Memory-management drivers can also cause expanded memory to be used as extended memory (emulation). We have found that in some cases, quirks in the computer system's BIOS cause AutoCAD's automatic memory-sensing capabilities to be confused by the emulation of extended memory that originally was configured as expanded memory.

Memory Management

The way you set up your machine's memory is important to the way AutoCAD functions. We recommend extended memory for everyone who either works on drawings in excess of 350K (or 250K on a slow machine) or who intends to use Release 10 of AutoCAD.

The amount of extended memory you use depends on the speed of your system and the type of work you do. If you have really large drawings or a slow system, you need enough memory to store two to two-and-one-half times the size of your largest drawing plus enough to put all of the AutoCAD Release 10 overlay and execution files in direct memory (about 2M is required if you have the full complement of AutoCAD), eliminating most of the disk access. We discuss these concepts in Chapter 16, "Advanced Hardware Concepts."

Figure 4.1 shows a map of memory for a PC. Notice the addresses of memory shown. AutoCAD, a RAM disk (VDISK.SYS), and expanded-memory managers (EMM.SYS, CEMM.SYS, QEMM.SYS, etc.) all become concerned about this memory map when you add an expanded memory card to your system. In addition, some graphics cards get into the act. Now we're talking about a real traffic jam. The more complex your system, the more intricate the management of extended or expanded memory can be. Extended AutoLISP also puts in its two cents, and will not work with some memory managers on 386s. (Autodesk is currently working on this problem, which will be fixed to some extent by the time you read this.) Finally, on some clone PCs, the BIOS is not 100-percent IBM compatible; because of the way these machines use various parts of the CPU, AutoCAD may not be able to use extended and expanded memory as advertised.

What does this all mean? You have to manage your system's memory, along with AutoCAD, its users, the drawings, billing, and everything else.

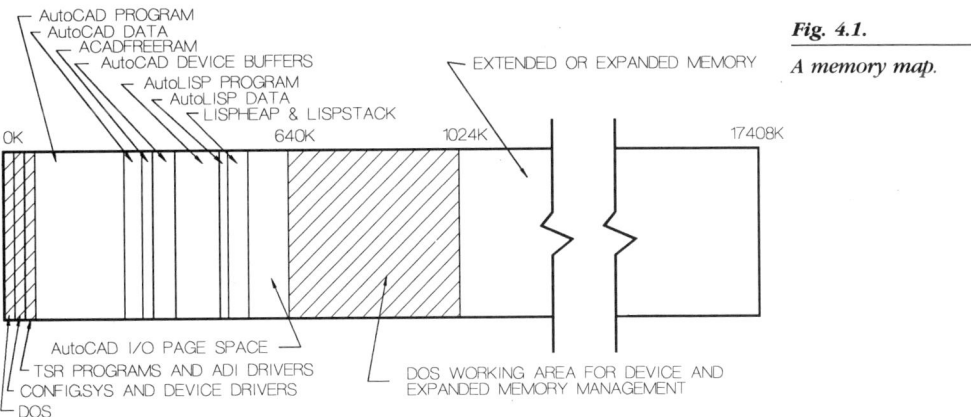

Fig. 4.1.

A memory map.

Fortunately, we may not have to worry about these management problems forever—they probably will be eliminated on new operating systems during the next few years. Meanwhile, follow these rules of thumb to set up extended and/or expanded memory:

❏ Ignore the first 1M of memory on your computer unless you are using part of your extended memory to fill in your base memory to 640K. Start thinking about extended memory from the 1024K (1M) address. All of AutoCAD's system variables that address extended memory start at this address.

❏ If you are using a version of AutoCAD earlier than Release 10, extended memory is best used as a way to enhance the display speed of larger drawings (350K on 12mHz systems and faster, 250K on slower systems). This can be accomplished by using a card with display list processing capabilities or by setting up a RAM disk and configuring AutoCAD to use the RAM disk as temporary drawing-file storage. (See Chapter 16, "Advanced Hardware Concepts.")

❏ If you are using a version of AutoCAD earlier than Release 10, extended memory used in conjunction with small drawings is best used as extended I/O page space, which helps AutoCAD read from the hard disk.

- You need to be concerned about the memory address size parameters for the AutoCAD memory environment settings only if you are going to mix memory use. For example, the statement:

    SET ACADXMEM=1024K,640K

    tells AutoCAD to start its use of extended memory at the 1M address and use only 640K of that memory. Then,

    SET ACADLIMEM=1664K,384K

    would tell AutoCAD to use another 384K of the extra memory as expanded memory, bringing the total memory used by AutoCAD to 1024K (640K + 384K). These statements must also be accompanied by the proper memory management statements in your CONFIG.SYS file. If you are concerned about a mix of memory use, read Chapter 16, "Advanced Hardware Concepts."

- If you don't have complex memory use requirements, have the extended memory board set up as extended memory by using the hardware switches on the board.

- If you are not sure how well your memory is being used and don't feel that you can change it yourself, get some help. Memory boards are expensive. To help pay for their added costs by improving the performance of the system, you have to have them set up properly.

- Anything you store in extended memory can be lost if your system loses power. A good drawing-save practice, executed on a regular basis, is always in order.

- Improper memory management can result in EREAD errors. These are provided by AutoCAD and often result in a damaged drawing, even if AutoCAD gives you the option of saving the work. EREAD errors occur because extended memory has to have a file allocation table (FAT), just as a hard disk does, that tells AutoCAD where to look for parts of drawings. If the FAT gets written over by AutoCAD because the memory boundaries are not clearly defined, portions of drawings can be lost so that AutoCAD unknowingly damages the drawings. If you have had this problem, your extended memory is not set up properly and you should seek some help in finding a solution.

Is It Working? How To Find Out

AutoCAD will sometimes, but not always, provide you with an error message stating that extended memory has been disabled. If you are not sure that AutoCAD is working effectively with your computer's memory, even though you haven't received an error message, type **status** at the AutoCAD command prompt and then press Enter. You will see a screen like that shown in figure 4.2.

```
       7 entities in test
    Limits are         X:    0'-0"   0'-9 3/4"  (Off)
                       Y:    0'-0"   0'-7 1/4"
    Drawing uses       X:    0'-0"   0'-9 3/4" **Over
                       Y:    0'-0"   0'-7 1/4" **Over
    Display shows      X:    0'-0"   0'-11 3/4"
                       Y:    0'-0"   0'-7 1/4"
    Insertion base is  X:    0'-0"   Y:   0'-0"   Z:    0'-0"
    Snap resolution is X:    0'-6"   Y:   0'-6"
    Grid spacing is    X:    2'-0"   Y:   2'-0"

    Current layer:     0
    Current color:     BYLAYER -- 7 (white)
    Current linetype: BYLAYER -- CONTINUOUS
    Current elevation:   0'-0"   thickness:    0'-0"
    Axis off  Fill on  Grid off  Ortho on  Qtext off  Snap off  Tablet off
    Object snap modes: None
    Free RAM: 10836 bytes        Free disk (dwg/temp): 2234368/1565696 bytes
    I/O page space: 90K bytes    Extended I/O page space: 512K bytes

    Command:
```

Fig. 4.2.

Status screen showing use of extended memory.

Figure 4.2 shows a status screen from one of our computers that indicates how AutoCAD is using the extended memory. We have a directory size for (dwg/temp) that shows approximately 1.5M for the temporary drawing directory; this is a RAM disk that AutoCAD is using to store the temporary drawing files. We have extended I/O page space of 512K. This gives us an exact total of 2048K—the size of extended memory on this system. You can use the STATUS command to make sure that the total amount of memory in use on your system is exactly the amount of memory available. There is one exception to this rule: you may have a graphics card that is using your extended memory for display list processing, which means that AutoCAD will not have that amount of memory for its own use.

For More Information

CADENCE 2, no. 5 (May 1987): 67.

OS/2 or DOS V4.0—Should I Be Concerned?

OS/2 is the logical successor to DOS; currently, however, it is not widely accepted in the United States. There are two principal reasons for this: the cost of implementing it effectively and the lack of popular software written for it. OS/2 is clumsy on a 286 system and does not run at all on earlier systems. Nevertheless, OS/2 offers two benefits that eventually will make DOS obsolete: multitasking power and extended RAM beyond the 640K limit. The command structure of OS/2 is similar to that of DOS and selecting commands in OS/2 is simple with the use of Presentation Manager.

DOS V4.0 does not lend itself to complex applications, either multiuser or multitasking. It does have both a pop-up menu for easier selection of commands and the ability to exceed the 32M limit placed on hard disk storage in DOS versions prior to V3.3. The problem with DOS V4.0 for AutoCAD users is that Autodesk does not yet support it.

XENIX is another operating system that may offer competition to DOS and OS/2. In five out of nine nine bench mark tests on a 386-based system, XENIX beat OS/2. However, AutoCAD probably won't be written for UNIX or XENIX on a 286 system, and the minimum hardware required for XENIX is quite different, and generally more expensive, than for DOS, because it is a processor-dependent system. XENIX can address all the memory the hardware can handle—16M for a 286, and 4,000M direct and 64,000,000M in virtual address memory. Autodesk has announced that it will release a 32-bit version of AutoCAD available for use with SCO XENIX on a 386 by the fall of 1989. This application should blow the doors off anything any of us have seen in terms of AutoCAD on a PC!

Who is going to establish the standards and alleviate the potential disasters of purchasing an operating software that is not widely used and little software is written for it? We can't say. We *can* say that it is in your best interest to follow developments in this area. The changes that result from eliminating the 640K barrier will be dynamic. Unless you have a real need to use the absolutely latest equipment on the market, you probably won't be making any serious changes until the fall of 1990 or later. If you already have a 386 system, however, take a serious look at the SCO XENIX application of AutoCAD.

Summary

In this chapter, we discussed the basic internal components of your system configuration and how it works with AutoCAD. To provide the best possible interface between your system and AutoCAD, you need a full understanding of the topics presented here.

Our discussion focused on the functions of the CONFIG.SYS and AUTOEXEC.BAT files, the use of drivers to manage peripherals, and possible configurations of memory. For specific discussions about the relationships of the CONFIG.SYS and AUTOEXEC.BAT files with AutoCAD, see Chapters 6 and 7; for specific discussions about the hardware characteristics discussed here, see Chapter 16.

Recommended Accomplishments

- ❏ Review the contents of your CONFIG.SYS file.
- ❏ Review the contents of your AUTOEXEC.BAT file.
- ❏ Review the relationship between these files and your specific hardware installation.
- ❏ Verify the use of any expanded memory you may have.

Optional Accomplishments

- ❏ Revise your system configuration in a variety of ways, and time the regeneration, redraw, and loading of your largest AutoCAD drawing with each configuration.

What Chapter 5 Is About

In this chapter, we discuss several categories of software that make dealing with DOS easier and that—directly or indirectly—enhance AutoCAD's capabilities. By *indirectly*, we mean that some of these programs can make customizing AutoCAD easier or expand the range of office tasks AutoCAD can help you with. We discuss how to integrate some of these packages conveniently into the AutoCAD environment by customizing the ACAD.PGP file, and we disclose where you can find the best AutoCAD support. We group the topics into the following categories:

- ❏ DOS utilities
- ❏ Database-management programs
- ❏ Programs for numbers
- ❏ Project-management software
- ❏ Multitasking software
- ❏ TSR (terminate-and-stay-resident) programs
- ❏ Word-processing software
- ❏ Desktop publishing
- ❏ Integration of programs
- ❏ Communications

We cannot possibly describe or even mention the entire gamut of available software, nor are we completely familiar with every program we mention here. This chapter is not a software review, nor do we claim that any of the programs mentioned is better or worse than those unmentioned. This chapter is a discussion of the wide range of tools available to AutoCAD users. Some of the software we mention is discussed in more detail elsewhere in this book. For information about where to get any of the commercially available software we mention by name, see Appendix K.

Helpful Things To Know Before You Start

- ❏ What you expect to do with programs other than CAD
- ❏ A complete overview of your office management requirements for information gathering and disbursement
- ❏ How to use the software you currently have on hand

What To Have on Hand

- ❏ A set of your software manuals

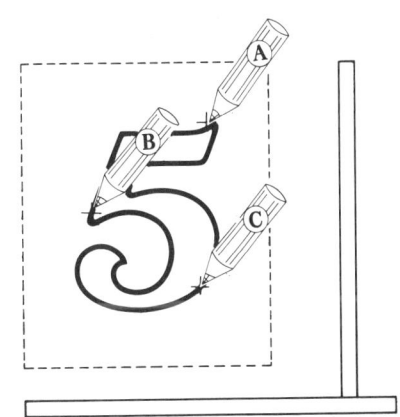

Software Companions

You may have thought your electronic T-square was a complete, self-sufficient package that would perform every task with ease. Maybe the salesperson forgot to tell you about DOS, housekeeping, and the many programs that can enhance AutoCAD's performance. Your operating system and AutoCAD are not enough to make using a computer efficient for CAD project management. You can make your work simpler by getting some additional software to complement AutoCAD.

DOS Utilities

DOS utilities, sometimes called DOS shell programs, help manage your system using DOS and generally are inexpensive. Many of them use a graphically oriented approach to file management and common DOS commands; some utility programs can execute programs from a user-defined menu. By making DOS easier to use, a DOS shell can reduce the learning curve to get a user up and running. Some shells require too much memory for proper AutoCAD performance; use a shell only when needed, and exit before you start AutoCAD. Users can access a DOS shell from AutoCAD by defining it in the ACAD.PGP file or by executing it through AutoCAD's SHELL command. We discuss the ACAD.PGP file later in this chapter.

If you have an aversion to DOS or are a system manager who needs to insulate users from DOS, you should investigate the use of DOS shells.

Norton Commander, PCTOOLS Deluxe, and many others are useful in almost any situation. New programs and updates of the older ones constantly appear on the market. General computer magazines such as *PC World*, *Personal Computing*, and *PC Week* are the best source of information and reviews on current utility programs.

Some DOS shell programs are comprehensive utility packages. We use Norton Utilities and Norton Commander as a comprehensive utility package. Norton Commander has an easy, point-and-select user interface and many hard disk management and cleanup tools as well as an extremely intuitive file-recovery program. Other available programs can move entire directory trees intact. Some other typical features include sorting by file name, text searching groups of files, finding files no matter where they are on the disk, finding strings of words or characters in groups of files, testing disks, and changing file names.

Hard Disk Management and Backup

The shareware programs PKZIP or PKPAK are useful for archiving your files. Many bulletin boards and CompuServe forums have a variety of archiving utilities that compress files and then group them into one file known as an *archive*. This is particularly important, because many of the programs available on bulletin boards come as archived files. We discuss the use of archive programs more extensively in Chapter 6, "Project and Drawing Management"; we discuss the use of CompuServe later in this chapter.

Shareware and Freeware DOS Utilities

If you have never used freeware or shareware, now is the time to start. If you join CompuServe, these programs will help you offset the cost of your link-up time.

Here is a list of DOS utility programs you may find of interest; most are on bulletin boards and/or CompuServe:

BADSEC.ARC finds bad sectors on hard or floppy disks.

BC.EXE is a simple backup utility.

COMSWT.ARC is an archived program that switches COM1 and COM2.

DKEY.ARC is a low-overhead keyboard macro processor. It is our favorite shareware program found this year.

FILL.ARC is an archived program that copies a group of files on a minimum number of floppies, filling each completely.

GLOBAL.ARC executes a DOS command, program, or .BAT file on a group of files or directories. We have not tried it for script files. (The program we use, SCR_ALL.EXE, is included in Appendix F.)

GUDLUK.ARC is a text file comparison utility.

HELP.ARC is a DOS help utility. Great for interactive batch files that always need a help option.

HIDE.ARC is a set of archived programs that can hide or unhide directories, providing you with some semblance of security, or clean up the hard disk for easy viewing. Get rid of all of your batch files and so forth so that a TREE command displays only what you need to see.

HOTKEY.ARC is cursor speed-up and run-on stopper.

KEYBUF.COM extends your keyboard buffer so that you can type farther ahead in AutoCAD. You need it only if you type faster than AutoCAD operates; if you don't need it, don't use it because it uses RAM that AutoCAD would otherwise use.

LOC.COM is a small, quick file finder (wild cards allowed).

MOVE.ARC moves files between subdirectories.

NEWKEY.ARC is a keyboard macro processor like DKEY.

NOTEPAD.COM is a small, memory-resident notepad like SideKick.

PKZIP.EXE or **PKPAK.EXE** are useful for archiving your files.

PWORD.ARC requires a password for booting.

VDL.ARC is a wild card file-deletion with file-by-file verification.

WAITEX.ARC executes programs at an appointed time and is excellent for advanced automation techniques.

WHATIS.ARC adds 60-character comments to files. (Norton's FI, part of Norton Utilities, does the same thing.)

We learned about these utilities through our use of CompuServe. Most of them came from either the Autodesk Forum (GO ADESK) or the IBM Software Forum (GO IBMSW). Many of them are available also from shareware software houses that advertise in the PC magazines. PC Software Interest Group, for example, publishes annual catalogs with updates that list a variety of freeware and shareware products; they charge a distribution fee of about $6 per PC.SIG disk. You send the shareware fees to the respective authors after you receive the disk(s).

Database-Management Programs

AutoCAD *attributes* are used primarily for creating a bill of materials or generating a schedule. The AutoCAD extracted data can take on two of the common database formats to be manipulated by another program such as an ASCII editor, word processor, spreadsheet program, or database-management program. The complexity of the database and the type of format in which you want the data reported determines which program suits your needs. If your needs grow to exceed the capacity of the program you started with, you will have wasted time and money; try to anticipate what your future needs will be.

Many third-party software packages that will format this information for you are available. AutoCAD has had a direct link of sorts to dBASE for some time and, in releases earlier than AutoCAD Release 9, included instructions for using dBASE II to generate schedules.

dBASE

Many people consider dBASE the industry standard for database management. We are not going to tell you that it is easy to learn; we *are* going to tell you that dBASE is extremely powerful and that it can accommodate almost any programming need you may have, as well as manage databases. And it has a compiler called Clipper that converts an ASCII-file program written for dBASE into a compiled program (an .EXE file) that runs faster than the ASCII file. For a discussion of how to use dBASE with AutoCAD, see Chapter 7, "Advanced Management Techniques."

We know enough about dBASE to communicate what we want to a good programmer. We also can use dBASE in ASSIST mode to create basic databases and get some sophisticated statistics, as well as to balance our checkbooks. If you want to gain command of the AutoCAD database so that you can manage all kinds of material quantity and costs, personnel and facilities, location and maintenance, and a host of other applications from the AutoCAD database, you must become familiar with dBASE III Plus. Doing so is relatively painless and will expand greatly the services you can offer over and above the creation of drawings (drafting and design).

We have an acquaintance who is not comfortable with AutoLISP, but who really knows his stuff in dBASE. He was asked to use AutoCAD to create several charts which tracked a complex construction project that contained a number of buildings. The contractor had a program that printed data for the critical-path management of each facility our acquaintance was supposed to translate into the charts. He asked the contractor to provide the data on disk, in comma-delimited format. Using dBASE III Plus, he was able to write a program that created a script file for each chart, loaded AutoCAD, created the drawing, saved it to disk, and started a new drawing. When last seen, he was sitting in the middle of a CAD room, watching his creation at work—four computers were creating the charts without one iota of human intervention. He probably created 40 charts in less than an hour! As you can see, the potential of the interface between AutoCAD and dBASE III Plus is limited only by your imagination.

For More Information
CADENCE 2, no. 11 (November 1987): 81, 117.

Programs for Numbers

Spreadsheets such as VisiCalc, SuperCalc, and Lotus 1-2-3 have features that include arithmetic, trigonometric, financial, and statistical functions, as well as graphing (bar, line, and pie graphs). Although spreadsheet programs are not as competent as a database manager at sorting a database, they can perform rudimentary sorts for the order of the information in the spreadsheet.

Some programs perform as calculators, design structures, calculate the energy usage of a building, and perform many other complex mathematical manipulations that would otherwise be done on a calculator and recorded by hand. Many of these programs provide output that AutoCAD can use to lay out automatically designs for bridges, roads, beams, or ductwork. Some of the programs are dangerous, according to some engineers, because they allow less-than-qualified users to perform calculations they don't understand. This is because the user interface is so well designed that all the user has to have is a basic understanding of the ingredients to the problem. For an extensive listing of these types of programs, ask your AutoCAD dealer for a copy of the *AutoCAD Applications Catalog*.

Lotus 1-2-3

The most popular spreadsheet program on the market is Lotus 1-2-3. It is relatively easy to use and can make calculating repetitive columns of numbers easy and fast. It can organize the numbers and characters from high to low or low to high, by date, or in alphabetical order and provide the mean or arithmetic average. You can change a few numbers, such as profit margin, and see the effect of the change on the entire picture. 1-2-3 also can draw bar, line, or pie graphs.

The spreadsheet is much more effective than AutoLISP at manipulating numbers and calculating the trigonometric, statistical, or financial mathematics you may be required to complete. Through the use of AutoLISP and the Lotus 1-2-3 command language, you can extract data from AutoCAD, have Lotus 1-2-3 load the data into a spreadsheet format, perform the calculations, and return the data to AutoCAD. This work can be completed using the ACAD.PGP file (which we discuss later in this chapter) and a set of programs developed in AutoLISP and Lotus 1-2-3.

In Florida, the energy code primarily involves a comparison of glass, wall, and floor area, and insulation against a desirable performance factor. Home designers quite feasibly could have AutoLISP export the wall, floor, and window/door areas to 1-2-3, have 1-2-3 perform the necessary calculations, and verify that the design meets the energy code. If the design failed to meet the code, the designer could edit the design and try again. Then from the finished design, AutoCAD and the printer could produce the compliance form; AutoCAD and the plotter could produce the drawings. This is just one example of how you can use Lotus 1-2-3 to perform intensive arithmetic calculations instead of having AutoCAD do the work. Lotus 1-2-3 is faster and prepares the desired report much more easily than would AutoCAD.

Draw A Graph . . . Impress Your Friends

You can import Lotus 1-2-3 graphs to AutoCAD. Preparing status-of-the-work reports in drawing format lets you post the information on a wall in a large enough format that you won't have to buy an overhead projector. This can be accomplished through the use of AutoLISP, which can create automatically a drawing from data output by Lotus 1-2-3. The MiGRAPH program will complete this task and, if you don't like what you see, will let you edit the graph by changing the data. The best use of this facility is in managing the status of your projects. We discuss this a little more in Chapter 7, "Advanced Management Techniques."

> **For More Information**
> *CADENCE* 2, no. 11 (November 1987): 71.

Project Management

Project-management (PM) software can provide more data than you could possibly want about complex tasks and projects. This data is in the format of CPM (Critical-Path Management), PERT (Project Evaluation and Review Technique), and Gantt techniques. We don't know much about the last two, other than that business school grads all know about the difference in the theories and equations used to perform the calculations for each of these methods. Some programs will even use AutoCAD to create drawings and graphs from the management software data. These programs generally are provided with the management software; if you are going to buy project-management software, check whether it comes with such a translation capability.

In our business, CPMs often are used to track construction schedules, providing milestones and work requirement estimates. We sometimes use AutoCAD to prepare CPM charts (see fig. 5.1), because everyone knows that the dates and times are going to slip constantly and end up all at the end of the project schedule. AutoCAD's editing capabilities provide flexibility that lets you prepare a CPM chart weekly if you need it.

Some project-management software packages are as complex as Auto-CAD. Each is tailored to a specific type of company. Purchasing project-management software is similar to purchasing accounting software: what works for one person may not work for the next. Before you invest, carefully review the capabilities of a particular program.

Watching the Clock

When we first got our computers, we thought an electronic calendar that let us know about appointments, kept track of anniversaries and birthdays, and managed reimbursable and tax-deductible expenses was a great idea. Then we discovered that we couldn't carry our AutoCAD workstation with us, so we forgot everything just as we did before we had computers.

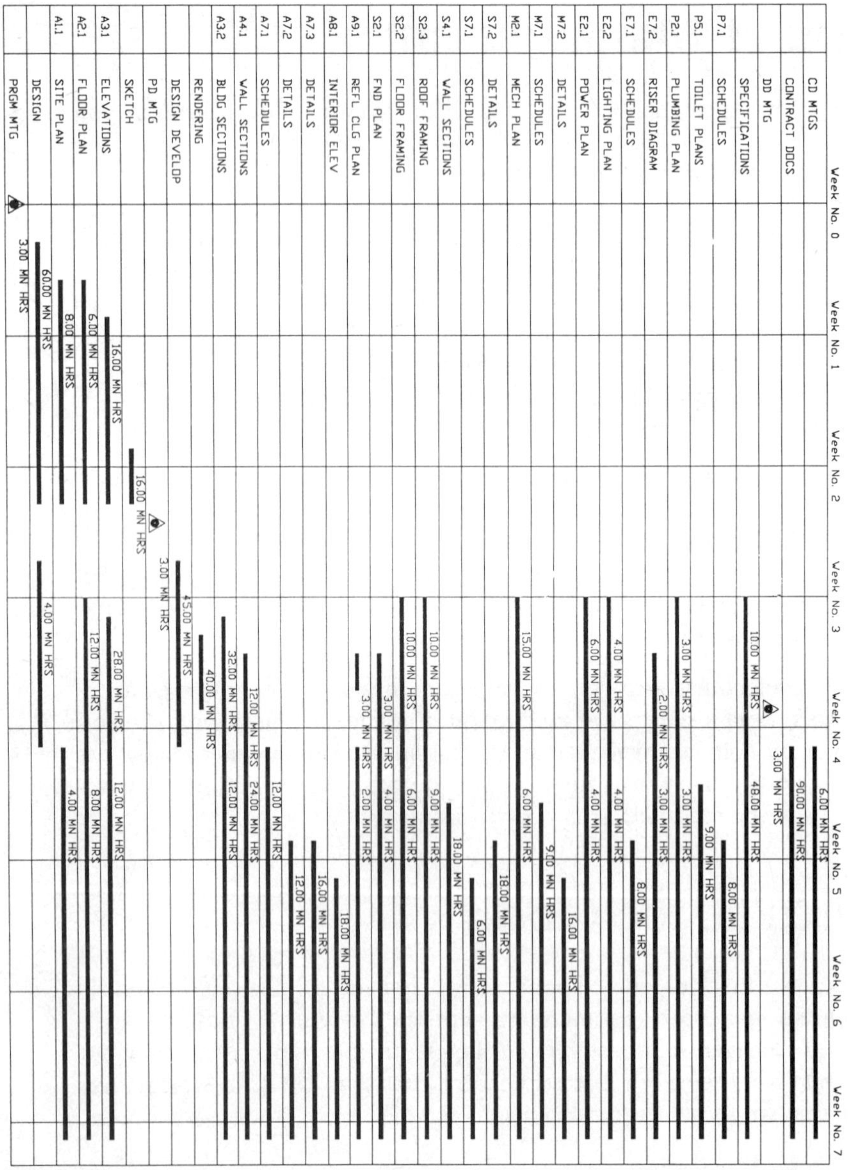

Fig. 5.1.
A sample CPM chart.

AutoCAD does keep track of time spent in the Drawing Editor. Some time-management programs can be integrated with AutoCAD so that hourly billing can be automated by combining the records of each workstation. This capability will become more important and of great use to network users; office calendars and time records that keep a large group of people working well together are valuable electronic services.

If your company is small, we suggest that you keep track of drawing time by using methods that we explain in Chapter 7, "Advanced Management Techniques." If you want an electronic calendar and expense record, you may want to check out the ones that are about the size of a hand-held calculator. (Just think—if they could be plugged into you car's odometer, you might be able to convince the IRS that you really did travel all those miles!)

CAD TIME-CARD, from HHS Software Solutions, is a TSR program that keeps track of the time you actually spend working on an AutoCAD drawing, not just the time the computer was on.

Calculators

Many people are interested in software calculators that can be used within and outside of AutoCAD. The programs of this type that we have seen are much slower to use than a hand-held calculator. We recommend that you use a hand-held calculator for basic calculations. You needed something to do with your nondigitizing hand, anyway.

Multitasking Software

Multitasking software like Windows, Desqview, Windows 386, and Carousel are actually operating systems; they can keep several programs running in the background while you work with a different one. The drawback to these programs is that they require a 386 machine to operate as effectively as is required for AutoCAD. We have been able to use our expanded memory and run AutoCAD on our 286 using Desqview, but we found that the limitations in the way AutoCAD functions weren't worth the multitasking. Not everyone agrees with us about this. The Sun Microsystems 386i, Digital Equipment VAX, and SCO XENIX 386 offer multitasking as a matter of course, due to the capability of their respective operating systems and CPUs.

The real utility of multitasking software lies in the fact that it lets you run multiple sessions of AutoCAD, edit more than one drawing at a time, and unlike DOS, it does not give memory a size limit. And you can plot while you work on drawings, or type a letter to your new client while Lotus 1-2-3 figures out what you are going to charge the client. You should become familiar with this concept, which soon will be standard practice on PCs. The primary effect it will have is that many third-party programs that work outside AutoCAD and do things that AutoCAD can do will no longer be required. Instead of using one of them, you can open another window of AutoCAD.

TSR Programs

Terminate-and-Stay-Resident (TSR) programs are loaded into RAM before other applications. They can be activated by the use of a hot key. A *hot key* is a key (or combination of keys) on your keyboard that suspends operation of the program you are working with and activates the program you want to access. Many keyboard macro, calculator, and notepad programs are TSR programs.

Keyboard macros are electronic shorthand programs, like DKEY (available as shareware), Borland's SuperKey, and Smartkey, from Software Research Technologies. Keyboard macro programs can be extremely useful to AutoCAD users because they allow high-speed entry of repetitive text and/or commands and reduce typing errors; the disadvantage is that, because they are memory-resident programs, they use some RAM.

AutoCAD leaves very little space for wasteful use of RAM. If you have a large environment because you have a long DOS PATH, and you want to increase your keyboard buffer and use keyboard macros, AutoCAD may complain. One way to work with some of these programs is to use them from the AutoCAD SHELL command; however, for those that have to be loaded before anything else, this technique won't work because you would also have to be able to remove them from memory before reentering the AutoCAD editor. In order for the keyboard macro, some time-management programs, the keyboard buffer, and screen capture programs to work, they must be resident.

We suggest that any TSR program you select have only the minimum features you require and use very little memory. For best results with AutoCAD, look for a nonresident calculator, calendar, or other utility program you might want to use to augment AutoCAD's capabilities.

Word-Processing Software

As we have mentioned repeatedly, a good text editor is invaluable for customizing AutoCAD. We consider a good word processor to be one that can create and manipulate ASCII files, loads quickly, uses little RAM, and saves and exits quickly. It should be able to save to another file name, handle large files, and merge files. Some of the popular word-processing programs include:

Program	*Tips*
❑ WordStar Professional	Select nondocument mode.
❑ WordStar 2000	Use UNFORM.FRM.
❑ WordPerfect 4.2	Save and retrieve files with F5.
❑ Microsoft Word	Save unformatted.
❑ MultiMate	Convert MultiMate file to ASCII.

We use the same program for word processing and editing programs because we already knew how to use it when we started writing script files, menus, and AutoLISP routines. We discovered that when we are doing a lot of programming and word processing at the same time, we often place control characters and formatting characters in a program file because we forget to separate the document and nondocument modes. Sometimes this mistake is impossible to detect when you look at the file; it can be totally frustrating when you can't figure out why the program won't run properly.

When we started writing more LISP routines, we realized that jumping in and out of AutoCAD would become extremely time-consuming. That is why we use Norton Editor for a word processor from within AutoCAD. Norton Editor has the major editing capabilities of the larger programs, and takes up much less memory; it just isn't as pretty. One of its important capabilities is that it can open two files at once, which is invaluable in writing LISP routines. Text-block manipulation, search and replace functions, and simple cursor movement are just as important in LISP writing as they are in menu editing.

If you write large bodies of text that are going to be imported into an AutoCAD drawing file, spell checking is a good feature to have. There are times when we include product specifications in our drawings—the amount of text involved is quite extensive.

Desktop Publishing Programs

Architects and engineers will find this area extremely useful. By using a desktop publishing program to merge AutoCAD drawings with text produced on a word processor, even the smallest firms can produce professional-quality documents such as brochures, technical manuals, and product catalogs (see fig. 5.2). In fact, the ability of some desktop publishing programs to import AutoCAD drawings reduces the duplication of effort that companies sometimes experience when one drawing serves for the product manual, another for the catalog, and another for the manufacturing drawing. A desktop publishing program that can import an AutoCAD drawing makes this a one-drawing-for-all-needs effort.

Fig. 5.2.

Sample brochure, created with Ventura Publisher and AutoCAD.

By using a program with a PostScript driver, you can generate files that many typesetters and print shops can use directly. This means that you can get the highest quality output while you do most of the work (and have most of the control). And you won't have to buy an expensive laser printer until (by using the desktop publishing program) you have to saved enough money to pay for it.

The only difference you may encounter between a drawing produced with a laser printer and a plotted drawing is that the laser-printed drawing will not show line weights. You must use polylines to create the required line weight. We used a laser printer for some of the illustrations in this book. To do that, we wrote an AutoLISP routine that converts lines by color to different-width polylines. If you are going to create drawings in AutoCAD for a laser printer you might find the routine (LSRPREP.LSP) useful. (It is in Appendix A.)

The Entire Software Environment

If you use your CAD system the way we do, you probably wish that all the programs discussed in this chapter were somehow integrated into one simple set of tools. (That was the idea at Apple Computers when they developed the Macintosh.) There are advantages and disadvantages to a fully integrated system, primarily involving the trade-off of speed to avoid memory conflicts, and lack of flexibility in program choice. Well—by using the ACAD.PGP file, you can integrate a wide range of your personally selected programs for use from within AutoCAD.

The ACAD.PGP (AutoCAD Program Parameter) file lets you tell Auto-CAD how to free up enough memory so that you can leave AutoCAD temporarily, load another program or execute a DOS command at the DOS prompt, complete any required tasks, and then return to AutoCAD. That is what happens when you execute the AutoCAD SHELL command, except that the program or command you are requesting is executed automatically. The ACAD.PGP file can include batch files, any DOS utility command except CHKDSK, and most applications programs, provided that they fit in the available memory. Be aware, however, that some programs, such as text editors, don't have any memory-management capability. If you load a large text file or data file that causes the program to exceed the allotted memory, the system will crash.

Figure 5.3 shows the structure of an ACAD.PGP file line. This structure includes a few rules about creating the ACAD.PGP file we would like to review:

Fig. 5.3.
ACAD.PGP file line structure.

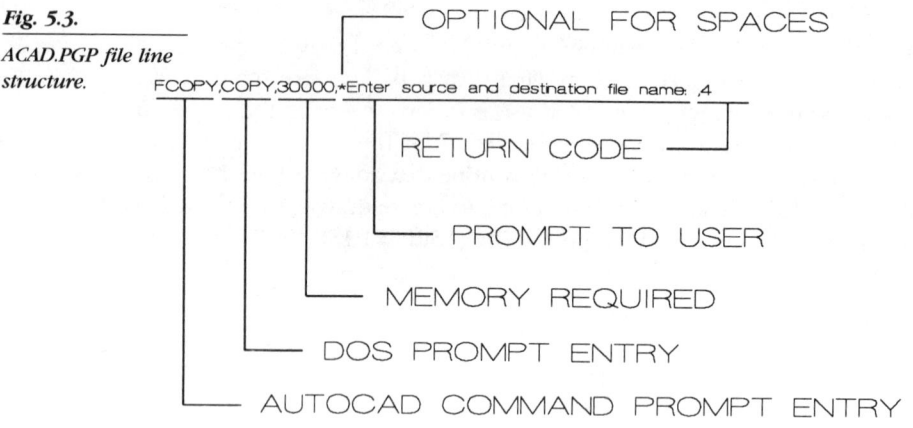

- *File Name:* The name of the command you use to exit AutoCAD temporarily and begin another program can have any name except one used as a command by AutoCAD. The command must be formatted and typed in upper- or lowercase letters at the AutoCAD command prompt, just as it appears in the ACAD.PGP file.

- *Memory Usage:* The amount of memory you tell AutoCAD to set aside should exceed by 4,000 bytes the requirements of the desired program, because 4K of DOS's COMMAND.COM will remain in memory while the program is being executed. Therefore, the minimum size for DOS V3.3 is 27K; for DOS V3.2 and earlier, minimum size is 24K. A little extra memory won't hurt anything; you can be generous until there is a problem with the size of the program you want to run. AutoCAD will let you know if there is insufficient memory to load the program.

- *User Prompts:* You can have AutoCAD optionally prompt the user with a message requesting additional information. If you leave the prompt section blank, AutoCAD will not prompt the user and will execute directly the external program or DOS command. If an asterisk is placed before the prompt message, spaces will be allowed in the user's response. This is required when you want to pass parameters to a DOS command, batch file, or other programs. Place extra spaces in the prompt to separate the user's response from the message.

❑ *Return Codes:* When the user returns to AutoCAD, certain options determine what happens next. Return code 0 is a used for dual-monitor systems or single-monitor systems if you want the text screen active. On a single-monitor system, the text screen must be active for a DOS directory command to be read. Return codes 1 and 2 are used to interface with custom AutoCAD applications that utilize .DXB (drawing exchange binary) files. Special text-editing routines use .DXB files to alter the content of the drawing with a program that is external to AutoCAD. Return code 3 is reserved and not used at this time. Use return code 4 on a single-monitor system to make the graphics screen active.

If you made a mistake in the ACAD.PGP definition, you will see error messages when you enter the AutoCAD Drawing Editor. If you made a number of errors (and don't realize it), you may enter AutoCAD several times and still get an error message, because AutoCAD looks only at the first error in the file.

You may want to add the following sample commands to your ACAD.PGP file:

1. DOS copy command:

    FCOPY,COPY,30000,
    *Enter source and destination file names: ,4ret

    Note that this is one line, although it appears as two lines in this book. (The command name COPY cannot be used because it is an AutoCAD command.)

2. DOS delete command:

    FDEL,DEL,30000,Enter file to delete: ,4ret

3. Command to list all the files in the LISP subdirectory:

    DLSP,DIR /p c:\acad\lisp*.*,30000,,0ret

    (This assumes that you are putting your LISP files in the directory `\acad\lisp`.)

4. Find Files command from the Norton Utilities:

    FF,FF,30000,*List files to find: ,0ret

5. File Information command from the Norton Utilities:

    FI,FI,27000, *file, comment, switches: ,0ret

6. Norton Commander. (We use this to do minor file editing when we are just correcting errors, which is why the memory shell is as big as it is.)

    NC,NC,150000,,4ret

7. Norton Editor. (This will allow editing of two fairly large LISP files at the same time.)

    NE,NE,150000,*Enter the name of file to edit: ,0ret

8. DOS's rename command:

    REN,REN,30000,*File to be renamed and new name: ,0ret

9. AutoCAD SLIDELIB program used to generate slide libraries for presentations and icon menus:

    **SLIDELIB,c:\acad\slidelib,50000,
    *Library name [Slide-list]: ,0ret**

Again, type this as one line, even though it appears as two lines in this book.

When you add programs to your ACAD.PGP file, keep the following things in mind:

- Sometimes the program you want to run from within AutoCAD will conflict with the port address of your drivers. For example, you may lose the use of your monitor if an interrupt conflict occurs. If you do, see whether the driver can be configured with different interrupts, reconfigure AutoCAD, and try again.

- Increase the memory reserve if the error message Program too big to fit in memory appears when you try to load the program at the AutoCAD command prompt.

- Make sure that your application will not leave you in a different drive and/or subdirectory when you want to return to AutoCAD. If it does, AutoCAD will lose the temporary files that it has open for the drawing edit and you will lose your work. It is always best to perform a SAVE before charting unknown .PGP waters.

It All Works Together

You may be able to construct an ACAD.PGP file that allows you to work from within AutoCAD for the entire gamut of your drawing tasks and as well as your customization work. Many third-party programs simply add a statement to the .PGP file and shell out to another program, so why can't you? Try using dBASE and Lotus 1-2-3 from within AutoCAD to create some automated features. Or write your own BASIC program that reads a .DXF file and creates a modified block for insertion into the drawing on which you are working. All of this can be done with a combination of AutoLISP, script files, and the ACAD.PGP file.

> **For More Information**
>
> *CADENCE* 2, no. 11 (November 1987): 103.

Communications

The age of electronics really arrived when people could complete all of their work on computers and submit their work to their clients *without ever leaving home*. You can do this by using a *modem*—which stands for MOdulation-DEModulation. A modem allows you to send and receive files in an electronic format, from different types of computers and operating systems, over the telephone line. You can trade stock, make airline reservations, or buy another computer, and many major banks are providing computer banking to customers who have modems.

External, rather than internal, modems are best for CAD workstations. You will run out of serial ports and expansion slots fast enough, and even though four COM ports are available, it has taken a long time for most software packages to become compatible with the use of all four ports. We use a switch box and an external modem. (Incidentally, our modem originally was purchased to work with a CP/M-based system; we can use it today because we bought good a one, and because it was external.)

What does this have to do with AutoCAD? Well, how about a users' group that has Autodesk employees as members and even a few of the founding fathers to look in on you once in a while?

Modems and the ADESK Forum

We think that anyone who wants to excel at using AutoCAD should be an active member of the Autodesk Forum on CompuServe. The CompuServe information service is a nationwide network of databases available to anyone with a computer, a telephone line, and a modem. Autodesk is sending out complimentary memberships with the purchase of AutoCAD—a quick way to get going and 15 minutes of free link-up time. Membership information and manuals are available also at computer stores and book stores. With either of these packets, you receive an ID number and a password (which will be changed once you become a regular member of CompuServe). Once you have signed up, all you have to do is dial a number provided by CompuServe (a local number, for most users)—and you're connected.

CompuServe's forums are divided into major topics or activities. Here is a sample of what you will see when you arrive at the Autodesk Forum (GO ADESK):

```
Autodesk

1 (L)  Leave a message
2 (R)  Read message
3 (CO) Conference mode
4 (DL) Data libraries
5 (B)  Bulletins
6 (MD) Member directory
7 (OP) User options
8 (IN) Instructions
```

The Autodesk Forum menu is fairly self-explanatory. You can leave and read messages, a feature that lets you find out what you need to know about a problem you may be having or help another member with one he or she is having. Because it is the collective knowledge of all the Autodesk Forum members, this body of information represents an unequaled AutoCAD expert. You also can join active conferences with other members in "live" communication on your screen. The data libraries contain helpful articles, programs, and third-party catalog information about AutoCAD, AutoLISP, AutoShade/AutoFlix, third-party software, and user wish lists. Many of the programs we use were found with the assistance of Autodesk Forum members.

Summary

After reading this chapter, you probably feel as though you've spent an hour at your neighborhood computer software store. We probably touched only the surface of the possibilities of AutoCAD enhancement through companion software. We reviewed the following types of software companions for AutoCAD:

- DOS utilities
- Database-management programs
- Programs for numbers
- Project-management software
- Multitasking software
- TSR (terminate-and-stay-resident) programs
- Word-processing software
- Desktop publishing programs
- Integration of programs
- Communications

Most of what we talked about was not software designed specifically for use with AutoCAD. That is a topic we cover in Chapter 17, "The Ultimate CAD-management Tool." Nevertheless, you can see how important a good command of a variety of software is to proper CAD management.

Recommended Accomplishments

- Start a wish list of the supplementary software you would like to have, and begin researching your choices.
- Find some people who will help you understand and use dBASE and Lotus 1-2-3, even if you can't afford the software just yet. This will have a major influence on development of your CAD-management practices.
- Join CompuServe and the Autodesk Forum.

Optional Accomplishments

- Make AutoCAD your system manager by adding to your ACAD.PGP file.

What Chapter 6 Is About

This chapter is about all the things you know you're supposed to do to make your computer system run effectively—but that you never get around to doing. These concepts, presented in the order you should complete them, involve three basic areas:

- ❏ Setting up CAD-management standards
- ❏ Setting up drawing standards that will work in most, if not all, cases
- ❏ Maintaining the project data

Helpful Things To Know Before You Start

You will get the most out of this chapter if you have mastered the topics covered in Chapters 2, 3, and 4 and if you already know the following:

- ❏ The basic DOS commands and how to use directories
- ❏ Generally, how you want to manage your projects (how they will be organized, who will be involved, etc.)
- ❏ A little LISP programming
- ❏ AutoCAD's LIMITS, ATTRIBUTE, and PLOT commands

What To Have on Hand

- ❏ Your plotter or printer plotter manual
- ❏ The *AutoLISP Programmer's Reference*
- ❏ The *AutoCAD Reference Manual*
- ❏ A DOS resource book or two (We recommend *MS-DOS User's Guide,* 3rd edition, published by Que Corporation, and *Supercharging MS-DOS,* published by Microsoft Press.)
- ❏ Word-processing software that can create and manipulate ASCII or nondocument text files

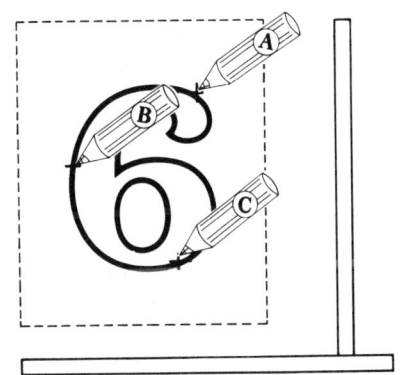

Project and Drawing Management

The ideas presented in this chapter will help you develop standards for managing your system.

Project Management

CAD can create as many project-management problems as it solves. In this chapter we discuss project management as it relates to use of AutoCAD on your hard disk, and we provide solutions to some problems you may have encountered. To make your business as efficient as possible, your overall management practices must be designed to take advantage of the dynamic tools provided by AutoCAD and related products.

Overall Procedures

Almost all of the disappointment experienced by intermediate AutoCAD users results from poor CAD management practices. Managing your business using CAD is a two-way street. You have to alter your management practices to fit the needs of the CAD system, and you have to customize the CAD system to fit your specific management needs. Overall management procedures should address and master at least three areas:

- ❏ Project management
- ❏ Drawing management
- ❏ Quality control

Each of these areas presents a multitude of issues—some that existed before CAD and some created by CAD. Problems with drawing standards, such as nonuniform symbols, text height, and so on, need to be addressed by both manual and CAD management procedures. But losing an entire drawing because of electronic malfunction or operator error is unique to CAD, and project scheduling often should include many days of plot time with CAD. On the other hand, some well-designed software coordination can eliminate the Friday afternoon time-sheet ritual. Because of the nature of CAD, quality-control drawing checks must be accomplished by reviewing progress plots. The best way to get a good overview of all of the issues is to create a procedure manual.

Create an Office Manual

Whether you're a one-man band or the manager of a large CAD system, you should create an office manual—casual or formal—of standard practices. The process of creating the manual serves as a tool, forcing you to organize your thoughts and helping you design an overall CAD-management system. If you need help developing a list of practices and standards, you may want to adapt to your specific needs the ideas detailed in the following sections. These ideas can be the basis of an outline.

Whether you base your manual on our ideas, or start from scratch, we suggest that you first create an outline for the manual and then continue reading, refining the manual as you go. As you read this chapter, make notes about ideas or problems that occur to you. Then, after you finish the chapter, review your manual to verify that you've covered all the ideas in your notes.

File Management

1. Create a file log for logging files in and out, and establish procedures for drawing editing check-outs. Make sure that two people are not editing a drawing at the same time unless it's a coordinated effort.

2. Establish disk-handling procedures.
3. Establish backup and disk-rotation procedures.
4. Establish drawing procedures that include routine saves on set time increments, or use software that automatically executes a save.
5. Set procedures for drawing directory creation, use, and elimination.
6. Establish remote drawing and data-file storage.
7. Establish procedures for special menu, shape, and font files that must accompany a drawing.
8. Review and implement the use of transmittal letters, including in-house file transfers, consultant and client transmittals, and service bureau transmittals.

Drawing Management

1. Checking the drawings by electronic or manual methods must be controlled by set procedures.
2. Implement a revision procedure which ensures that the revision is recorded in the drawing as well as in a project log, and ensures also that the proper backup files are overwritten following the approval of the revision. This is a tough one!
3. Establish a procedure to maintain a job history and drawing file log in the form of a database or by traditional hard copy methods. In other words, projects that require staged approvals must have record sets of those stages in their approved form. How you intend to maintain those records is important, since electronic media is generally alterable without detection (for example, file dates are not permanent).
4. If you intend to make revisions by hand instead of replotting the drawings, establish a procedure to ensure electronic updating also.
5. Transmittal forms should include a standard for recording the transmittal of disks. (A disk label using DOS's LABEL command would be one method.)

6. Create a drawing control sheet that records the scale, drawing location, drawing name, project name, file name, AutoCAD system variable changes from the office standard, layer additions to the office standard, text fonts loaded, line color/pen weight settings, and special comments.

7. Establish and maintain the standards discussed in this chapter and in Chapter 7.

8. Establish block-management procedures, especially for project-specific blocks, but include standard drawing updating and additions.

9. Establish project closeout procedures, both manual and CAD. These will change from existing manual practices because of the use of CAD.

Plot Procedures

1. Create a drawing plot request form that works in conjunction with the drawing control sheet. This form should include the information shown in figure 6.1.

2. Implement a plot priority request procedure that will accommodate emergencies without ruffling project managers' feathers.

Consultant Procedures

1. Establish shared database procedures for updating and editing base drawings.

2. Coordinate menu standards.

3. Coordinate block controls, such as exploding, reuse, and redefinition. Establish who is empowered to do what.

4. Maintain title block coordination.

5. Establish who is responsible for "master drawing" management.

6. Coordinate drawing standards, pen weights/colors, drawing limits, standard symbols, text fonts, and layers.

7. Share customized AutoLISP routines that affect drawing standards.

PLOT ORDER:

REQUESTED BY: DATE/TIME:
PROJECT NO: REQUIRED BY:
PROJECT NAME: P.O. NO.

MEDIA: ☐ PLOT BOND ☐ VELLUM ☐ FILM OTHER:

PENS: ☐ DISP ☐ REFILL ☐ FIBER ☐ BALL

DWG	PEN SET	FILE NAME	SCALE	PLOT TIME	COMP

	SET #1	SET #2	SET #3	SET #4
RED				
YEL				
GRN				
CYN				
BLU				
MGA				
WHT				

APPROVED:

PRINTS:

Fig. 6.1.
Sample drawing plot request form.

General Procedures

1. Establish hard disk maintenance and clean-up procedures, such as how often to run DOS CHKDSK and a disk optimization program, when to erase files (and who approves file erasure), and system-menu maintenance procedures.

2. If you have more than one shift working, establish overlap conditions.

3. Establish error-handling, system-crash, and lost-drawing procedures.

4. Create a feedback system for tracking and reporting to you problems in the management procedures you have implemented.

5. Integrate the CAD procedures with other in-house and consultant procedures.

For More Information

Architectural and Engineering Systems, February 1988, 9.
CADalyst 4, no. 2 (April 1987): 77.
———— 4, no. 6 (October/November 1987): 51.
CADENCE, October 1988, 100.
Memphis AutoCAD USER GROUP JOURNAL, April 1988, 15.
Stitt, Fred A. *Systems Drafting*. McGraw Hill, 1980: 43-58.

Project Conventions: If You Don't Have Any, Get Some

As architects, we can turn not only to a national organization that makes recommendations for numbering drawings but also to numerous professional publications that address the issue. Not all AutoCAD users are as fortunate. In the absence of guidelines from a professional organization, you need to establish some of your own. Whatever their source, the conventions you adopt have to work for all your in-house situations. They must be easily understood by anyone you work with, consult with, or use as a consultant.

Architects tend to have customized versions of these standards that reflect the complexity of their thought process rather than the intelligence of those standard practices. Computers, having no opinion on the matter, allow almost any range of complexity that you want to create. Try to resist the temptation to use all of the possibilities available with a computer when you are developing your own standards.

In this chapter, we explain how to develop your own standards, using our standards as a guide. Instead of incorporating our standards word for word, look at them conceptually and determine whether they can help you.

Your standards should manage the following areas:

- Job numbering
- Drawing names
- Layer names
- Drafting standards
- Paste-up work (standard drawings)

We have some ideas that will help you implement controls over these issues, if you don't have any in place already. If you do have controls in place, check to see whether they will work for the possibilities we discuss.

Organize with DOS Directories

Directories are the key to controlling the organization of your files on a DOS system. Effective system management depends on the proper use of these DOS directories. You can make the process so complicated that you spend all your time maintaining the system, but you don't have to.

With the advent of 120-megabyte-plus hard disks for PCs, using a hard disk can be pretty confusing. If you don't separate your files into directories and subdirectories, the list of files quickly becomes so long that you can't find anything. Using directories can do two important things for you: reduce the amount of time you spend searching for a file and protect your work from unintended erasure.

We recommend a tree structure similar to that shown in figure 6.2. Some users create a subdirectory for each drawing in a job. If your projects continue for extended periods of time and you tend to bounce from project to project and drawing to drawing, having separate individual drawing subdirectories might be a good idea for you. Caution: drawing-by-drawing subdirectories can complicate any project data manipulation you may want to do.

Properly organized directories can keep your files neat and easy to access. Keep your directories to a practical number. If you use a batch-file system to manage your disk and overdo it, you will spend a great deal of time editing batch files. On the other hand, you don't want to spend much time typing a long DOS PATH command whenever you need access to a file.

Fig. 6.2.

Sample directory tree.

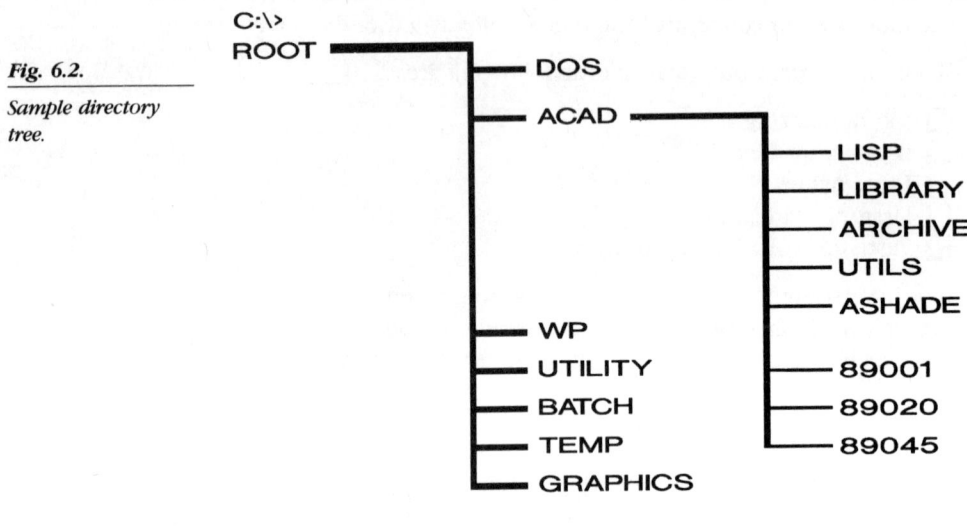

For More Information

Berliner, Don. *Managing Your Hard Disk*, 2nd edition. Que Corporation, 1988: 121-243.

Devoney, Chris. *MS-DOS User's Guide*, 3rd edition. Que Corporation, 1988: 171-219.

Using AutoCAD Directories

The DOS concept of directories is one of the hardest things to make sense of (considering how simple they look). Couple that with the way a program uses directories, and things really get confusing. But once you grasp the concept, everything falls into place. Your use of directories is the key to productivity when you work on more than one job at a time.

AutoCAD uses many files that pertain solely to the program and not necessarily to your drawing. For that reason, the sample directory tree in figure 6.2 has subdirectories that separate AutoCAD's files from your project files. It is good practice to keep your drawing files absolutely separate from AutoCAD's program files.

As you can see from figure 6.2, we name our drawing subdirectories after our job numbers. Because we don't expect to do more than 999 jobs a year, we number our projects so that the first two digits indicate the year and the last three digits, the job number. For instance, a project number of 89007 represents job number 7 in the year 1989.

This project-numbering system will always sort in the hierarchy we need, even if we use AutoLISP or other software to manipulate project or drawing data. If we want to extract the time spent on each project, for example, we want to attribute to a single job number all the time from a group of project drawings. After we extract all that data, we sort into sequence the time from all the projects, first by year and then by job number. Project 88006 will always sort before 89007, which will sort before 89008. If we didn't use this type of system, we would have to "take apart" the project number and sort the data more than once to get the results we want. We learned this technique in our preCAD days, when we used computers only for accounting. Today, we also use this numbering system with AutoCAD to keep our drawings grouped by project.

We know of three practical ways to get AutoCAD to look at different directories:

- Load AutoCAD from a drawing subdirectory
- Use the DOS PATH command
- Use the DOS SET command

In the following sections we explain these methods as we have found them to be useful, but feel free to experiment for your own requirements. There are two other ways to alter AutoCAD's use of directories but, because they are not as transparent to the user as the first three, they are less practical. For detailed discussions of these methods, consult a DOS reference book.

Loading from a Subdirectory

Loading AutoCAD from the directory you are working in is the easiest method of directory control. AutoCAD automatically uses this subdirectory as its editing directory. If you use a batch file to load AutoCAD from the directory that contains the drawing you want to work on, you won't have to remember each time how to get into the correct directory.

If you have a subdirectory called \ACAD\JOB1, for example, you can write a simple batch file that will load AutoCAD. With your word processor in program (nondocument) mode, create a file called JOB1.BAT. (For "JOB1," substitute an appropriate subdirectory name that fits your needs.) Then type the following lines into the file:

```
CLS
ECHO OFF
IF NOT EXIST \ACAD\JOB1\*.* GOTO ERROR
CD\ACAD\JOB1
\ACAD\ACAD
GOTO END
:ERROR
ECHO SUBDIRECTORY IS NOT ON DISK!
ECHO CREATE THE SUBDIRECTORY AND TRY AGAIN!
PAUSE
:END
CD\
```

After you have created the JOB1.BAT file, you can start working on JOB1—just go into the directory in which you have placed JOB1.BAT and, at the system prompt, type **JOB1**. If you forgot to create a subdirectory called \ACAD\JOB1, this batch routine proceeds to the :ERROR branch and displays the message:

```
SUBDIRECTORY IS NOT ON DISK!
CREATE THE SUBDIRECTORY AND TRY AGAIN!
```

Otherwise, it loads AutoCAD from the \ACAD directory. When you exit AutoCAD, the batch file returns you to the DOS root directory.

Be sure to include the complete path in the batch file, even if \ACAD is in the PATH= statement of your AUTOEXEC.BAT file. This is good practice; if you change your AUTOEXEC.BAT PATH= statement in the future, you won't have to edit all the batch files.

With AutoCAD loaded with your default path being your working subdirectory, all the drawing files you create or edit will be stored in the subdirectory unless you type in a different subdirectory for AutoCAD to use.

The DOS PATH Command

The DOS PATH command normally resides in your AUTOEXEC.BAT file. You can place other PATH commands in other batch files to change the file search path as you move around your hard disk. (And you can enter a PATH command at the DOS prompt, but that doesn't serve our purposes.) If you want to know how your computer file search path is currently set up, type **PATH** at the DOS prompt. You probably will see something like this:

```
PATH=C:\;C:\DOS;C:\ACAD
```

This path shows you that your computer and any software that is running search for a file or command by looking first in the computer's main (root) directory, next in the DOS subdirectory, and then in the ACAD subdirectory. The number of paths you can have is limited by the amount of space given the DOS environment in your computer's operating system configuration. The default for most systems is 160 bytes. You can increase your environment space by putting a statement in your CONFIG.SYS file. If you have DOS V3.1, that statement looks like this:

```
SHELL=C:\COMMAND.COM /P /E:62
```

If you are using DOS V3.2 or later, use this statement:

```
SHELL=C:\COMMAND.COM /P /E:1024
```

Make sure that you type the statement line correctly. If you make a mistake, your computer may lock up when you reboot. You will then have to use your DOS diskette to reboot the computer.

This line sets up a permanent installation (/P) of COMMAND.COM with an environment size (/E:) of 62 x 16 = 992 bytes or 1,024 bytes. DOS V3.1 has a maximum of 992 bytes available; versions 3.2 and later, a maximum of 32,767 bytes. You can create any size DOS environment you need, up to these maximums. Keep in mind that:

- ❏ The longer the path search, the more work the hard disk does and the slower things run.
- ❏ The more memory you designate for the environment, the less is available for AutoCAD.

We think you should include only those directories you need to access permanently. (You would exclude the job directories, for example.) Programs that you use with AutoCAD may have their own path requirements that must be included. Your primary considerations are

- ❏ Programs that require path statements
- ❏ The number of times you will type the file's path vs. deterioration of AutoCAD's performance
- ❏ Maximum DOS environment size you can have

Begin with the size shown in the sample paths shown earlier in this section (by modifying your CONFIG.SYS file and rebooting the computer). Then, at the system prompt, type a PATH command that includes all the directories you need. Be sure to type the directory or subdirectory correctly, and use semicolons to separate them. When you finish typing the line, press Enter. If you see the OUT OF ENVIRONMENT SPACE error message, decide which directories you can do without—and try again, retyping the command and your proposed path. Once you have a successful entry, modify your AUTOEXEC.BAT file to include the successful PATH command.

If you do not get the error message on your first attempt, edit your AUTOEXEC.BAT file to include the PATH command with which you were successful. Then edit your CONFIG.SYS file to reduce the size of the environment by 128 bytes. Reboot the computer, and enter the successful PATH command again. Continue editing the CONFIG.SYS file, rebooting the computer, and entering your PATH command until you get an environment error. Then add 16 bytes at a time to the environment (remember to reboot after each change) until the error message stops appearing. This process will balance your system environment size with your path requirements.

The PATH command in our AUTOEXEC.BAT file looks like this:

```
PATH=C:\;C:\ACAD;C:\ACAD\LISP;C:\ACAD\UTILITY;E:;
```

We use the \ACAD\LISP directory for our own LISP files, and the \ACAD\UTILITY directory for all our shape, slide, and miscellaneous files. AutoCAD finds all these files without our having to type the directory information whenever we want a file. The E: in our PATH command is for a RAM disk. We have this path installed in 512 bytes on our computers.

You may have to have something like C:\DOS and C:\BATCH on your path if you make extensive use of programs that use DOS commands and batch files. If you don't need the C:\DOS for anything but your batch files, we recommend placing the full file name with its path in the individual batch files.

Device drivers, terminate-and-stay-resident (TSR) programs such as Superkey or Sidekick, graphics display drivers, and ANSI.SYS, all contribute to reducing the amount of system memory available to AutoCAD. If you increase the DOS environment space too much, you will get an OUT OF RAM error message from AutoCAD. It's always best to stay as lean and quick as possible. Experiment until you find the proper balance between speed and your system's setup.

The DOS SET Command

The third way to get AutoCAD to look elsewhere is to use the DOS SET command. The statement SET AUTOCAD tells AutoCAD that it can look in a particular subdirectory for anything it can't find. In effect, this is AutoCAD's internal PATH command. If you are using a third-party menu system that has a library of drawings, you probably have to set it to a predetermined subdirectory. For example, AutoCAD's AEC Architectural requires that you use the statement:

```
SET ACAD=\AEC\A\D
```

for its library of drawings. If you are not using a third-party menu system, or if the one you use doesn't have such a requirement, we recommend that you create a subdirectory called \ACAD\DRAWINGS, put all your standard drawings in that subdirectory, and put the statement:

```
SET ACAD=\ACAD\DRAWINGS
```

in your AUTOEXEC.BAT file. Then, when you want to insert a drawing, all you have to type is the name of the drawing.

Two Tricky, More Complicated Methods

The fourth way to change AutoCAD's directory usage is a little more devious than the first three. This fourth method involves using the DOS SUBST command in your AUTOEXEC.BAT file. What this amounts to is that you assign an imaginary drive letter to a subdirectory. This method isn't as clean as the others because AutoCAD can't find a file unless you type the drive letter before the file name.

To use this technique, add the following line to your CONFIG.SYS file:

```
LASTDRIVE=x
```

The drive letter x should be one letter beyond the dummy drive, or drives, you intend to use. The first dummy drive letter should be one letter beyond all the drives (including RAM disks) on your system.

Suppose, for example, that you have drive E: as a RAM disk. You would include in the CONFIG.SYS file the command:

```
LASTDRIVE=G
```

The SUBST command that you would put in your AUTOEXEC.BAT file would look like this:

```
SUBST F: C:\ACAD\TOOLS
```

Then, while in the AutoCAD Drawing Editor, you can insert a drawing from the TOOLS subdirectory by typing **INSERT** **<RETURN>** and **F:BITONE**.

The fifth way to modify AutoCAD's directory usage is available only in AutoCAD Release 10. Release 10 uses a new LISP command called *getenv* that lets you set environment variables in your batch files and then access those definitions through LISP. For example, you can put the following statement in your AUTOEXEC.BAT file:

```
SET ACADLISP=\ACAD\LISP
```

Then, from within the Drawing Editor, you can run the LISP command:

```
(GETENV "ACADLISP")
```

which returns:

```
"\\acad\\lisp"
```

This method isn't particularly useful unless you want to maintain separate configurations of AutoCAD or separate libraries for your LISP programs and load them with menu commands. If you have LISP routines that you don't want mixed in with a someone else's set of routines, you can load your programs by using:

```
(SETQ DIR (GETENV "ACADLISP"))
```

and then:

```
(LOAD (STRCAT DIR "MYPROG"))
```

to load \ACAD\LISP\MYPROG.LSP. Typing in the latter statement at the AutoCAD command prompt whenever you want to load a program wouldn't warrant using this technique. It is no better than typing in the full directory path and file name.

The DOS ASSIGN command (refer to Chapter 3, "The Basics") should be used for redirecting AutoCAD when it searches for program files only—not when it searches for files AutoCAD will write to.

For More Information

Berliner, Don. *Managing Your Hard Disk*, 2nd edition. Que Corporation, 1988: 128-131, 237-243.

Devoney, Chris. *MS-DOS User's Guide*, 3rd edition. Que Corporation, 1988: 175-177, 199-207, 389-397.

File-Naming Conventions

Most computer users are well aware of DOS's file-naming limitations. Your imaginative use of those limitations can make a big difference in project management.

Naming conventions need to answer one simple question: One year after you name a file, will you know what the eight-character file name means?

When you create file-naming conventions, consider the following:

- The number of projects you do in a year
- The computerized billing process you have now or may have in the near future
- The number of drawings in a typical project
- How your consultants, or people for whom you consult, affect your drawings
- How you intend to keep track of your files
- Whether you use more than one drawing to create the final product

Figure 6.3 indicates one way to name a file. As you can see, this method codes a great deal of information into the name. Each part of the file name responds to a consideration in the list. Although this method may look complicated at first, it works well for us because it uses a standard already established in our field of practice (architecture). You may be able to get by with much simpler coding. Remember, however, that two years from now your data-management requirements may demand greater detail and you will want a standard that accommodates more options. If you don't allow for that possibility now, you may hate yourself later.

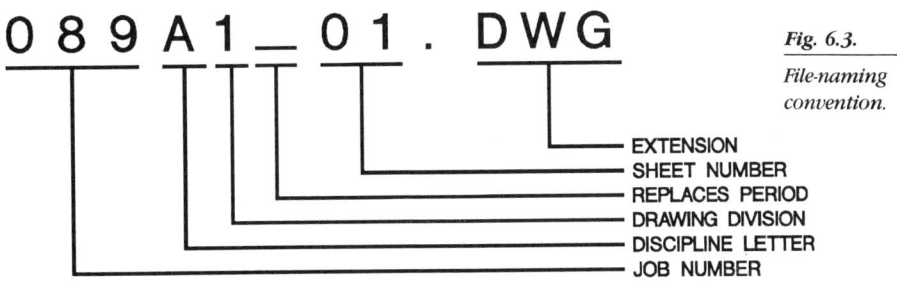

Fig. 6.3.
File-naming convention.

Let's take a detailed look at this file-naming system. First, we use the first three digits to represent the job number. As you know, our job-numbering system combines the year number and the project number. Because we seldom work on job number 88007 and job number 89007 at the same time on the same computer, we eliminate any reference to the year in our file-name description. We do, however, include the full job number in the name of the subdirectory in which we keep the job drawings, thus keeping job number 88007 and job number 89007 separated.

If we use AutoLISP or some other third-party software to extract the time from our drawings, the file name helps to associate that time with a job number. If you need the year number, the subdirectory name supplied by our directory tree can provide the necessary data.

Thanks to others, we have conventions that we use for naming our drawings (see fig. 6.4). These conventions have four important features that your system should address:

1. Who your consultants or clients are
2. What type of drawings you create
3. A flexible numbering system
4. How readily data can be sorted

All of our consultants know which drawings are theirs and readily understand how the system works. We give our consultants a self-explanatory outline that they follow for numbering their drawings. The letter designation indicates which discipline is responsible for the drawing, and the first number in any group shows what type of drawing it is (plan, elevation, section, etc.). As work progresses, we can add drawings to any section without disrupting the system and having to renumber all the drawings.

Clearly, we had to make trade-offs because of the DOS limitation of eight-character file names. For instance, we can't put the year number in a drawing's file name and we are limited to 999 job numbers in one year. We can have no more than 26 consultants and 9 drawing types—and we are limited to no more than 99 sheets of any one drawing type. Although these trade-offs have not created problems for us, they may not be acceptable to you. Chapter 7, "Advanced Management Techniques," discusses some ways to get around these limitations.

Unless you are an architect, your numbering system probably won't be as complex as ours. You may want to separate your work into categories: shop drawings, material drawings, and production drawings, for example. You may need additional drawing categories and no separate categories for consultants. You can include cost code information or revision numbers. Or you can make the file names shorter. It's up to you.

```
ARCHITECTURAL DRAWINGS
A0.1,2,3...    GENERAL
A1.1,2,3...    SITE PLANS
A2.1,2,3...    FLOOR PLANS
A3.1,2,3...    EXTERIOR ELEVATIONS, BUILDING SECTIONS
A4.1,2,3...    WALL SECTIONS
A5.1,2,3...    DETAILED PLANS
A6.1,2,3...    VERTICAL CIRCULATION, STAIRS (ELEVATORS, ESCALATORS)
A7.1,2,3...    DETAILS & SCHEDULES
A8.1,2,3...    INTERIOR ELEVATIONS
A9.1,2,3...    REFLECTED CEILING PLANS
STRUCTURAL DRAWINGS
S0.1,2,3...    GENERAL NOTES
S1.1,2,3...    SITE WORK
S2.1,2,3...    FRAMING PLANS
S3.1,2,3...    ELEVATIONS, BUILDING SECTIONS
S4.1,2,3...    WALL SECTIONS
S5.1,2,3...    DETAILED PLANS
S6.1,2,3...    VERTICAL CIRCULATION
S7.1,2,3...    DETAILS & SCHEDULES
MECHANICAL DRAWINGS
M0.1,2,3...    GENERAL NOTES
M1.1,2,3...    SITE PLANS
M2.1,2,3...    FLOOR PLANS
M3.1,2,3...    ELEVATIONS, SECTIONS
M4.1,2,3...    DETAILED SECTIONS
M5.1,2,3...    DETAILED PLANS
M6.1,2,3...    VERTICAL CIRCULATION AND CHASE DETAILS
M7.1,2,3...    DETAILS, SCHEDULES, AND DIAGRAMS
PLUMBING DRAWINGS
P0.1,2,3...    GENERAL NOTES
P1.1,2,3...    SITE PLAN
P2.1,2,3...    FLOOR PLANS
P3.1,2,3...    SECTIONS
P4.1,2,3...    DETAILED SECTIONS
P5.1,2,3...    DETAILED PLANS
P5.1,2,3...    DETAILS, SCHEDULES, AND DIAGRAMS
ELECTRICAL DRAWINGS
E0.1,2,3...    GENERAL NOTES
E1.1,2,3...    SITE PLAN
E2.1,2,3...    FLOOR PLANS
E3.1,2,3...    SECTIONS
E4.1,2,3...    DETAILED SECTIONS
E5.1,2,3...    DETAILED PLANS
E5.1,2,3...    DETAILS, SCHEDULES, AND DIAGRAMS
This system continues on for Interior Design (I), Civil
Engineering (C), Landscape plans (L), Acoustical Engineering (V),
etc.
```

Fig. 6.4.

Drawing-name industry standards.

Remember that unless the naming convention is always exactly the same, with the same information always in the same location, any database program (or LISP) that will look at these file names will take longer to run. With this naming convention, all of the drawings for a job number can be accessed by using DOS (099*.dwg), all of the architectural drawings for that job number can be accessed (099A*.dwg), all of the floor plans for that job number can be accessed (099?2*.dwg), and so forth.

For More Information

CADENCE, November 1986, 16.
Stitt, Fred A. *Systems Drafting*. McGraw Hill, 1980: 21-24.

Backing Up Before You Go Forward

Well, here it is—your favorite topic! Did you remember to back up your work? Yes, we know—you had to go home for dinner. If you've done your homework in this chapter so far, you now have a smooth-running file-naming convention and an orderly directory system. Your directory tree and file-naming conventions will save you a great deal of time when you back up your data. The trick is to automate the process so that you don't mind doing it. You can wait to get motivated; losing a hard disk and $10,000 (or more) of work is a great motivator—just ask us.

Because we know how important backing up your data is, this chapter includes a batch routine. (To use the routine, you need to be comfortable with the DOS BACKUP and RESTORE commands, so be sure to practice using these commands. If you need help, refer to your system's DOS manual and one or more other DOS references.) Or you may want to look into software (FASTBACK Plus, DSBACKUP +, PCTOOLS Deluxe, or PKPAK, for example) designed specifically for making backups.

With your new drawing subdirectory and file-naming conventions in place, backups are much easier to do. You can improve your attitude about backing up data and make the procedure a habit. All you have to do is write a simple batch file and put it either in your batch-file subdirectory or in your ACAD directory, as needed. To create a BACKUP.BAT file with your word processor, type the following lines:

```
ECHO OFF
VERIFY ON
\DOS\BACKUP C:\ACAD\%1\*.DWG A: /M
IF ERRORLEVEL =1 GOTO ERROR
:ERROR
ECHO BACKUP UNSUCCESSFUL!!!
GOTO END
:END
VERIFY OFF
```

Before you use this batch file, you need to do three things:

1. Make sure that you have enough formatted floppy disks to hold all the drawing files in the directory you are going to back up.

2. Number the disks, so that they'll be in order when you use them.

3. Remove all terminate-and-stay-resident programs from memory.

To execute the backup batch file, go to the directory in which you have stored BACKUP.BAT and type **BACKUP XXXXX**. (*XXXXX* represents the name of the drawing subdirectory you want to back up.) The batch file then copies all drawings modified since the last subdirectory backup (it even asks you to insert the next disk when one is needed). In Chapter 7, "Advanced Management Techniques," we discuss more sophisticated methods of automating the backup process.

To retrieve any of the files on which you have used BACKUP.BAT, you will have to use the DOS RESTORE command:

1. Insert in drive A: the diskette that contains your backed-up job files.

2. To restore a whole directory, go to that directory and type:

    \DOS\RESTORE/M/P A: *.DWG

    If your backups are on a tape drive or another storage device, substitute the appropriate designation for A:.

3. To restore only a specific drawing, enter the drawing name **XXXXXX.DWG** in lieu of *.DWG.

For More Information

Berliner, Don. *Managing Your Hard Disk*, 2nd edition. Que Corporation, 1988: 473-491.

Devoney, Chris. *MS-DOS User's Guide*, 3rd edition. Que Corporation, 1988: 367-388.

Drawing Standards

Drawing standards are a major concern for every drafting professional who works with a group of people. CAD systems add a number of new concepts to an already long list of considerations:

- ❏ Limits represent the drawing surface but are in "real world" sizes (in other words, 22-by-33 feet for a 24-by-36-inch sheet).
- ❏ Drawing setups must be flexible.
- ❏ Drawings need to be reusable.

- Uniformity goes beyond line weights and lettering style.
- Plotters do the drawing.

Limits and Setup

The safest and easiest way to control your drawings is to make sure that your setup routines establish limits based on your sheet size and drawing scale. If you always draw within the limits of the drawing and plot the limits, you will avoid many plot-time errors. Plotting the display will work as long as you remember to ZOOM ALL whenever you leave the drawing. If limits are properly set, however, you won't have any problems, unless you are doing something that modifies the limits in your drawings. (We can't think of a good reason to do so.)

Every AutoCAD user has a different method of setting up limits, scale, and plotting methods for drawings. This can create problems when you want to move your drawings to someone else's plotter or to have one of your consultants or clients work on your drawings without getting confused. The first place to start controlling your drawing standards is in the Setup option.

To get predictable results from any plotter and in coordination with other firms working with you, everyone has to agree on a uniform standard. Autodesk has made some assumptions about available plotting areas that will not necessarily use your plotter, or printer plotter, properly. If you select SETUP from AutoCAD's screen menu, the program establishes the limits of your drawing based on a relatively universal drawing size. This decision is more delicate than it may seem. For instance, we adjusted our ACAD Menu to maximize the available plotting area and then—later— bought a plotter with a smaller plotting area. Consequently, our title block and border were placed at the limits of the drawing and all the work we had done before we bought the plotter had to be modified to fit it.

If your plotter breaks down, you may have to have a plotting service do your work. That's when your sheet size standard becomes very impormtant: If the service's plotter has a smaller plotting area than yours, you will have to revise all of your drawings to obtain the proper plot.

Figure 6.5 shows the range of possibilities available when you work with a sheet border and title block. To use your plotter's maximum available plotting area, set up your drawing limits by obtaining the maximum size in inches shown in your plotting manual and substituting that size in the ACAD menu as follows (AEC users must modify the SETUP.MNU file).

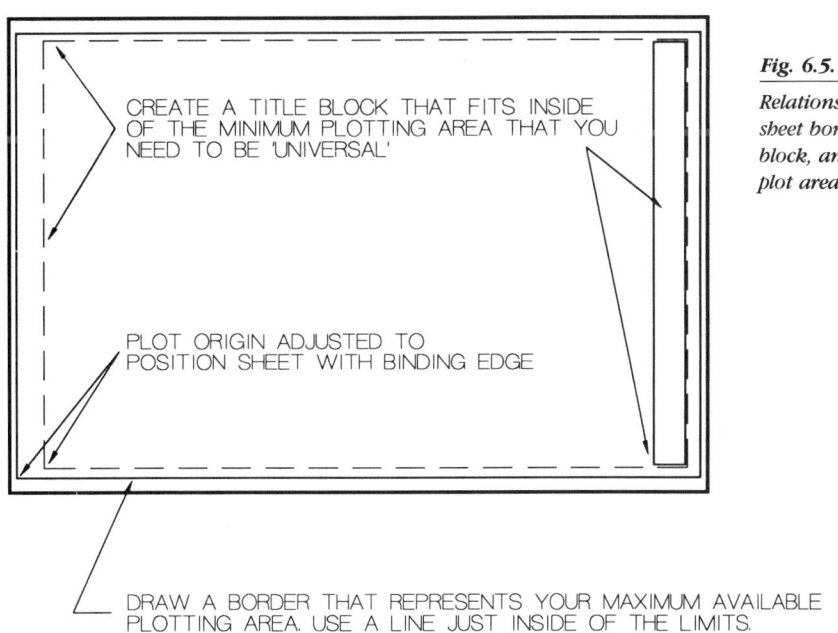

Fig. 6.5.
Relationship of the sheet border, title block, and available plot area.

1. Make a copy of your ACAD.MNU file.
2. With your word processor in nondocument mode, locate the following portion of the ACAD.MNU file:

   ```
   *ENGLISH 2

   [Horizntl]

   [ Sheet  ]
   [ Size   ]

   [A-8.5x11]11.0 8.5;
   [B- 11x17]17.0 11.0;
   [C- 22x34]34.0 22.0;
   [    18x24]24.0 18.0;

   [D- 24X36]36.0 24.0;
   [    30x42]42.0 30.0;
   [E- 36x42]42.0 36.0;
   ```

Menu continues

Menu continued

```
        [OTHER  ]0 0;

        [VERTCAL]$S=ENGVERT



        **ENGVERT 2

        [Vertical]

        [ Sheet  ]
        [ Size   ]

        [A-8.5x11]8.5 11.0;
        [B- 11x17]11.0 17.0;
        [C- 22x34]22.0 34.0;
        [    18x24]18.0 24.0;

        [D- 24X36]24.0 36.0;
        [    30x42]30.0 42.0;
        [E- 36x42]36.0 42.0;

        [OTHER  ]0 0;

        [HORZNTL]$S=ENGLISH
```

3. For each sheet size, change the numbers shown to reflect the maximum available on your plotter for each sheet size. The new sizes will be less than the original sizes. On our plotter, for example, the maximum plotting area for a horizontal D-size sheet is 35.61 x 22.66. To make the required adjustment, we would change 36.0 to 35.61 and 24.0 to 22.66.

Make the appropriate changes for all sheet sizes. Be careful not to modify any other portions of the file.

4. If you use metric units, make the same changes under the Metric Menu (which is part of the (ACAD.MNU) file.

5. When you have finished, copy the ACAD.MNU file back to your \ACAD directory.

In our opinion, the best way to go is with prebordered sheets on media suitable for plotters, if you can afford them. To ensure transportability between plotters, design your borders so that any information you place in the title block with AutoCAD will fall within the limits set up by AutoCAD. The final product will look as though you used the entire sheet, and you will never have to make adjustments.

If you have to transport to an outside plotter, create a drawing that puts information into your title block at a predetermined location. Plot this drawing and measure the variation in the plotted location from your predetermined location. Adjust the plot origin in the plot menu so that your title block and drawing information will be properly aligned. Before finalizing your setup, test your configuration on plotters at plot services and other firms. In an emergency, you don't want any surprises.

If you want the plotter to draw your borders, use a title strip only at the right end of the sheet. The title strip must fit within the AutoCAD setup limits. With this arrangement, you can draw to the very edge of the limits. When the drawing is plotted, it will look as though you used as much of the sheet as possible. If you use a continuous border around the sheet, your drawn border will have about 7/8-inch from the edge of the paper to the border, plus an additional 1/2-inch from the border to the drawing information for good appearance. The final result is that you will have lost 2 3/4 inches from your drawing sheet rather than 1 3/4 inches without a border.

Reusable Work

One of the productivity keys your computer dealer told you about was the ability to reuse previous work, thus saving hours of production time so that you can pay for all your hardware and software. We have a few ideas that will help you make this a reality instead of something that you'll "get around to."

First, set up in your drawing sheets standard divisions that translate between the sheet sizes you will be using (see fig. 6.6). All of your standard drawings should be set up on multiples of these modules. A good place to start is with an 8 1/2-inch-by-11-inch sheet. This allows you to divide a standard 24-inch-by-36-inch sheet into 3 × 3 submodules or into 3 × 2 submodules with a column for notes. You can use different standard sheet sizes, but approximating an 8 1/2-inch-by-11-inch sheet will be helpful.

You can set up a slide library and use icons to display your standards, but to do so you must use AutoCAD's advanced user interface (AUI), which is not supported by all graphics cards. For a detailed discussion of slide libraries, see Chapter 8, "The Ten Commandments—Times Three." A simpler way to keep your drawing standards available for ready reference is to plot them and put them in a three-ring binder.

Fig. 6.6.

Some ideas for standard sheet divisions.

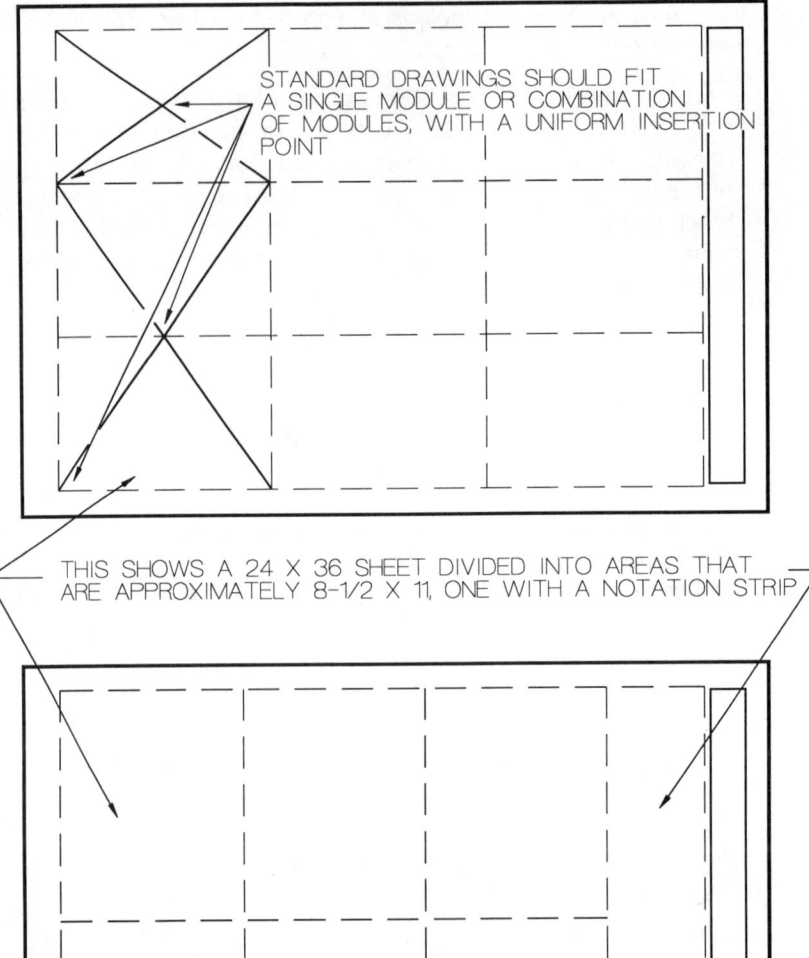

If you want to make your drawings reusable, you must consider also the following important factors:

- File-naming conventions
- Uniform insertion-point location
- Drawing title attributes
- Drawing scale

The file name for your standard drawing poses the same problems as the file names for your project drawings. You can eliminate much deciphering of the file name by using a three-ring binder for reference or by using icons or menus to insert the drawings. You will be able to see the drawing if it's in a binder or an icon, or you can provide an extended description in the menu. We suggest that you name the drawing after its location in the binder, icon, or menu, and that you subdivide the binder, icons, or menus into logical categories based on your standard drawings.

Suppose, for example, that you use standard Widgets, Digets, and Fidgets in your drawings. You could divide your binder into W, D, and F sections and name your drawing files after their page number (W-1, D-33, F-6, for example). Icons and screen menus can contain only a limited number of items. To get around this limitation, you must create several icons or screen menus, each with a coordinated name. Icon menus for the Widgets could be called IW1, IW2, and so on; the icon standard drawing numbers would be IW1-1, IW2-1, IW2-2, etc. The screen menu standard drawing numbers would be MW1-1, MW2-1, etc.

If you have many standard drawings, we recommend that you use a three-ring binder rather than icons or menu descriptions; a binder requires the least maintenance, updating, and coordination.

Each standard drawing must have the same insertion-point location. If you divide your drawing sheets into modules, the insertion point should always be in the same corner of the module. The distance from the insertion point to the drawing title or body of the drawing should be a uniform plotted distance. If you use your standard drawings in a variety of scales, you will have to adjust each drawing location after you have inserted it into the composite drawing.

If your standard drawings are to be used as independent drawings, create each standard drawing with a drawing title. When you make a block of the drawing, define the drawing name, drawing number, sheet number, scale, and other pertinent information as attributes. You then will be able to create drawing title information as it applies to each project.

Drawing scale can be a sticky problem with standard drawings. In our work, we use drawings at different scales, omitting (for smaller scale drawings) the layers that contain details. A column wrapped with brick can be used on a floor plan, for example, and then "blown up" on a detail sheet, the first use omitting a material indication for the brick. Sophisticated drawing management allows you to use the same drawing for both the plan and detail sheets. If you want to mix scale on a sheet, however, things can get complicated. Text heights can get confused, as can arrow sizes and hatching. Appendix B contains some LISP routines to help you mix scales, as well as a routine for cutting out details from drawings you already have created. We discuss this practice also in Chapter 9, "The Tasks At Hand."

> **For More Information**
>
> *CADalyst* 5, no. 1 (February 1988): 55.
> Stitt, Fred A. *Systems Drafting*. McGraw Hill, 1980: 101-116.

Standard Notation

We were trained as designers and drafters, not as typists. Many firms have developed standard sets of notes. Secretaries do the typing and drafting professionals do the drafting. The same benefits can be realized by using LISP or third-party software with AutoCAD. Text can be imported from an ASCII file and then revised for proper justification, style, height, spacing, etc. The point here is that computers with appropriate software allow one person to type the text while someone else does the drafting. In addition, you can create a note library that is already imported into AutoCAD and stored on disk as blocks of text for editing on insertion. One of the programs we use for this task is AutoWord. Furthermore, with its latest releases of AutoCAD, Autodesk is shipping LISP routines with sophisticated text-editing capabilities. A number of LISP routines with many options for managing text can be found also on CompuServe's Autodesk Forum and in *CADENCE* or *CADalyst*. You need an assortment of programs or routines that fill your specific needs.

> **For More Information**
>
> Stitt, Fred A. *Systems Drafting*. McGraw Hill, 1980: 117-135.

Plotting for Success

After all is said and done, the one really important thing about all of this work is the final result—the hard copy of your electronic drawing. This aspect of the work is easy to neglect when the bulk of the effort is done on the computer. Plotting is a high-tech science in its own right. Don't overlook this aspect of the job when you design your standard practices.

Drawing Standards Make Plotting Standards

To achieve predictable hard copy results, you must have drawing standards. Line weight and color must always be the same. The line types you use should be standardized, and the layers you turn on or off will control what you produce. And, as we mentioned earlier in this chapter, you must also set up standard sheet sizes and control your drawing limits. It's a good idea to create a specific plot-standards document. Plotting services can benefit from this information, as can you, your clients or consultants, and any coworkers. For a discussion of advanced plotting methods, see Chapter 7, "Advanced Management Techniques."

Once your limits, plot area, and plot origin are under control, focus on what lies inside the limits. The standards that most affect plotting in this case are the pen weight/line color/linetype/layer coordination. In most firms, line weight and line type standards already are set; all they have to do is add AutoCAD's color and layer requirements to their standards. If you don't have preestablished standards, most drafting manuals, published industry-wide, can provide guidelines in these areas.

You must consider also the type of plotter media and pens you intend to use. Disposable pens come in only four line weights. Reusable pens, which generally come in ten line weights, are considerably more expensive than disposable pens. Before you decide on a standard, get a catalog from your supplier and look at the possibilities. If you use a printer/plotter, you have to use polylines for line-weight considerations. Polylines, pen type, paper type, and line types all affect plotting speed. Pen manufacturers recommend speeds and pen forces for each type of pen. Many good resource articles on these topics are published in almost every issue of *Plan and Print* magazine. Other aspects that may influence your plotting-related drawing standards are discussed in Chapters 9, 11, and 16.

> **For More Information**
>
> *CADalyst* 4, no. 4 (July 1987): 40-43.
> *CADENCE*, December 1987, 100-106.
> *Plan and Print*, International Reprographic Association.

Summary

Does the work in this chapter seem overwhelming? You may be reluctant to learn and stick with these habits. Although it may seem painful at first, getting yourself on a system will save you countless hours and make you more productive. Remember that it's best to experiment with each element of this system setup until you get it working to your satisfaction. In other words, *don't install it just because it ran the first time.* The key to a well-maintained, functioning CAD office is to put all the elements together in as automated a form as possible. The system will increase your productivity, help keep you out of trouble, and let you concentrate on drawing. Who knows—you might even find yourself having fun.

Here's a summary of what you should have accomplished in this chapter. Make sure that you can complete the checklist of recommended accomplishments, because all the elements work together.

Recommended Accomplishments

- ❏ Create a structured directory tree.
- ❏ Use PATH and SET to expand AutoCAD's view of the system.
- ❏ Create a file-naming standard for drawings.
- ❏ Create an automated backup methodology.
- ❏ Standardize your limits.
- ❏ Standardize your sheets.
- ❏ Standardize your borders.
- ❏ Plot with limits.
- ❏ Create a plotting standards document.

Optional Accomplishments

- ❏ Create a standard drawing system.
- ❏ Standardize drawing notation methods.

What Chapter 7 Is About

This chapter covers the following topics:

- Managing more than one drawing at a time
- Exercising greater control over project files
- Increasing accessibility to project information
- Improving backup techniques
- Linking individual drawings with the entire project's database
- Creating project-tracking databases
- Achieving more automation

Helpful Things To Know Before You Start

You will get the most out of this chapter if you already know or understand the following:

- Advanced DOS commands and directory usage
- Standard drawing practices
- A little more LISP than Chapter 6 used
- AutoCAD LIMITS, attributes, and PLOT commands
- The topics covered in Chapters 2, 3, 4, and 6

What To Have on Hand

As you read, you should have the following references handy:

- Your plotter (or printer plotter) manual

- The *AutoLISP Programmer's Reference*

- The *AutoCAD Reference Manual*

- A DOS resource book or two (We recommend *MS-DOS User's Guide*, 3rd edition, published by Que Corporation.)

- Word-processing software that can create and manipulate ACSII or nondocument text files

- The standards manual you created while reading Chapter 6

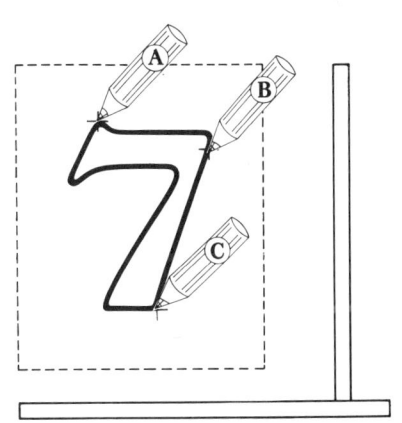

Advanced Management Techniques

This chapter develops the concepts presented in Chapter 6 into more sophisticated practices that have broader application. It includes a few LISP routines that demonstrate the importance of the concepts discussed in Chapter 6 as well as those presented here. We suggest that you try the LISP routines whether you are a LISP programmer or not. Once you see what these routines can do, you may become much more interested in the power of AutoLISP. If you are an old hand at AutoLISP, a review of these LISP routines will be sufficient to show you how the management standards we are presenting work together.

File Management: That File Was Just Here

As you increase your project-management activities, the amount of data in your files will increase. You will have to coordinate not only your drawing files but also information shared between drawings. Project data such as time expenditures, drawing history, base drawings, project notes, titles, drawing indexes, and quantities of material can be extracted and must then be kept track of.

Now that all your files are neatly organized on your hard disk, how are you going to manage this monster? For the job of managing the project drawing files and associated tasks, the DOS file-management utilities we told you about in Chapter 5 won't meet all of your needs. Fortunately, a wide range of options is available to you. In this chapter we discuss tools you can use to:

- Manage the system with simple batch files
- Manage the system with a third-party menu system
- Look at drawing files without AutoCAD

Simple Batch-File Management: Cook Up a Batch for the Menu

The most basic approach to file management is a batch-file menu system you create. This type of menu system is economical to produce and is customized to your specific requirements. It takes time to produce and maintain, however, and there are limitations to what it can do for you. We started out with this type of system and used it successfully, graduating to more complex needs as our experience increased. Creating your own menu system will help you refine your requirements for CAD management. By the time you are ready to move on to a more sophisticated system, you will have a clear understanding of what you need.

Creating a basic batch-file system is not difficult. First, create a directory called BATCH. Then write a batch file for each project. For example, 1.BAT could contain the following code:

```
CLS
ECHO OFF
CD\ACAD\89001
\ACAD\ACAD
TYPE \BATCH\MENU1
```

This batch file changes the ACAD directory to a job-number directory (89001) and loads AutoCAD. When you exit AutoCAD, a menu you will create in a file called MENU1 will be displayed.

You will have to create a batch file for each new project. Because our average project stays on disk for quite a while, we chose this method instead of typing the job number after the batch-file name. If you are constantly removing and creating directories on your hard disk, substitute the line CD\ACAD\%1 for the third line in the batch file, and name the batch file JOB.BAT. Then, whenever you want to work on a project, enter the appropriate job number by typing **JOB XXXXX** (*XXXXX* represents the job number).

Next, add batch files for loading other programs, backing up files, displaying the directory tree, finding files you need, and so on. End each of these files with a TYPE \BATCH\MENU1 line. If you have room in your DOS environment, add C:\BATCH to your path and put all your batch files in the BATCH directory. If you don't have room, or don't want to take the room, put in the root directory only the batch files associated with the opening menu. You can put all the other batch files in the BATCH directory; to load them, simply precede each file name with *\BATCH* in your batch files, such as **\BATCH\JOB1**.

Now create the MENU1 file. We suggest a format like that shown in figure 7.1; you can modify this format as you see fit. And you can add submenus by using *menu2, menu3,* etc.

To create the graphics characters in figure 7.1, you use the extended ASCII-character set. The ASCII numbers are in the range of 176–223. (For details, see the ASCII chart in the DOS book mentioned at the start of this chapter.) You can even add tones! Get creative and have fun.

Exactly how you go about doing this depends on your word processor —not all word processors accept extended characters. In WordStar, for example, you choose a character, position the cursor, and then press Alt-*xxx* (*xxx* represents the number from the extended character set). The character is displayed after you release the Alt key. Norton Commander, in edit mode, cruises right along—no problem. You may need to review basic batch-file writing to learn all the possibilities for your system and your work environment, using the DOS reference we mentioned at the beginning of this chapter. Appendix C provides specific examples of this batch-file system, including some programs that you can use to make the batch files interactive (so that the user can answer a series of questions).

Be sure to edit your AUTOEXEC.BAT file so that the last two lines are as follows:

```
CLS
TYPE \BATCH\MENU1
```

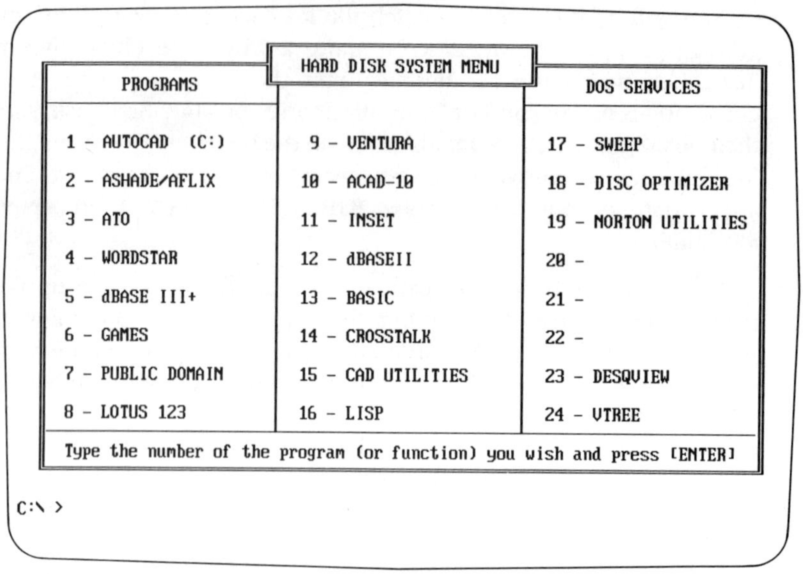

Fig. 7.1.

Standard Batch menu created with extended ASCII characters.

```
┌─────────────────────────────────────────────────────────┐
│                   HARD DISK SYSTEM MENU                 │
│      PROGRAMS                         DOS SERVICES      │
│                                                         │
│   1 - AUTOCAD  (C:)        9 - VENTURA      17 - SWEEP           │
│   2 - ASHADE/AFLIX        10 - ACAD-10      18 - DISC OPTIMIZER  │
│   3 - ATO                 11 - INSET        19 - NORTON UTILITIES│
│   4 - WORDSTAR            12 - dBASEII      20 -                 │
│   5 - dBASE III+          13 - BASIC        21 -                 │
│   6 - GAMES               14 - CROSSTALK    22 -                 │
│   7 - PUBLIC DOMAIN       15 - CAD UTILITIES 23 - DESQVIEW       │
│   8 - LOTUS 123           16 - LISP         24 - VTREE           │
│                                                         │
│   Type the number of the program (or function) you wish and press [ENTER]│
│                                                         │
│  C:\ >                                                  │
└─────────────────────────────────────────────────────────┘
```

Other Menu Systems: Someone Else's Recipes

If you have a fairly stable group of activities, we recommend that you consider using a hard disk navigation system. You can get a shareware program called Automenu, for example. The main attribute of this sophisticated batch-file system is that it keeps all your files in one directory and can combine many of them into one file. The menus displayed by Automenu are much fancier than the homemade one we showed you, and the program provides "point-and-shoot" access to menu options. Although you have to learn a small set of commands to create the Automenu files, its command language is more powerful than that provided by the DOS batch-file system. You can even incorporate passwords with this program, although it is not secure against an experienced user. If you need moderately sophisticated file management, a program like Automenu is for you. Other software packages, which we discuss later in this chapter, include menu systems as part of their capabilities.

Accessing Drawing Files: So That's What's in that Drawing

A unique requirement placed on a CAD-management system is that you must be able to view drawings. This aspect of CAD management frequently is not given the importance it merits. For proper reference to other drawings from within AutoCAD and for good file management from outside of AutoCAD, some form of visual reference to specific drawings is essential.

One way to view your drawings is to create drawing slides with AutoCAD's MSLIDE and VSLIDE commands. And by using a program supplied on the AutoCAD Support disk, you can create a slide library. If you have many small drawings and are on a tight budget, you should create slide libraries of your standard drawings as well as a library of your current project drawings. Although you will have to update these libraries, you will find that being able to view your other drawings will save you considerable time and help reduce errors in drawing coordination. In Chapter 9, "The Tasks At Hand," we show you how to use screen or icon menus to make your slides much more accessible.

We strongly recommend that you examine some of the software programs that let you view your drawings from within or outside of AutoCAD and that, if your budget allows, you choose the program that works best for you. This aspect of project management is almost a must-do because you are forced to adapt to the little window in front of your eyes instead of viewing the in-progress drawings sitting on the table next to you. Your only other choice is to run reference plots continuously. Many users seem to think that because they now use computers, a reference table is no longer needed at the CAD station. If you have the proper software, you can reduce or eliminate the need for hard copies of your reference drawings.

Annotating Your Drawing Files

For large projects and projects for which you want a history of extensive revisions, we strongly recommend that you annotate your drawing files. You can add descriptions, revision notes, or comments to your files in several ways. The simplest way is to create an attribute in your drawing and then update the attribute whenever you work on the drawing. Then, by extracting the attribute, you can create a text file that contains a continual record of your drawing activity on the project. You can write a LISP routine that automatically updates the attribute and writes the information to a file when you finish working on the drawing. We provide an example of a routine for this purpose later in this chapter.

If you want something fancier, you need Lotus 1-2-3 or dBASE. By importing into either of these packages the data extracted from your AutoCAD drawing, you can create a job-file-management database that holds an unlimited number of notes and comments about each drawing. (Appendix F includes a program that does all of these things, on a limited basis.) Lotus 1-2-3 is best used for generating simple reports about your drawing activities and man hour/deadline scheduling of projects. Use dBASE if you want a really sophisticated, customized management system. We recommend that you consult a good dBASE programmer before tackling this approach. For best results, you should have a general understanding of dBASE's capabilities and a well-rounded knowledge of AutoCAD. See Chapters 5 and 9 for more information about dBASE and 1-2-3.

Unless you are using dBASE or 1-2-3 for many other tasks in AutoCAD, we recommend attribute-extraction combined with LISP routines or another alternative—buying a software package designed specifically to manage AutoCAD drawings. The exercises in this book will prepare you for purchasing management software; these exercises help you understand what you need and what kind of customization you may require. We have yet to see the perfect management program. That's not suprising—a detailed management program would have to sacrifice flexibility or it would cost as much as AutoCAD does.

Think carefully about any file-management requirements that are particular to your needs and see whether you can live without them. If you can't, you will have to become a LISP and/or dBASE programmer or be prepared to pay someone else for those services.

Backups Revisited: Storing and Archiving Your Files

In Chapter 6 we discussed the importance of backing up your files. Several programs can help considerably with this task. From our point of view, the perfect backup program would do the following:

- ❏ Back up entire directories, or allow you to tag files for backup
- ❏ Compress files in order to save space

- ❏ Allow you to annotate files
- ❏ Collect files into an archive
- ❏ Allow you to add comments to the archive
- ❏ Keep track of the file size and the area available on the target disk, prompting for a new disk when needed
- ❏ Automatically split an archive file

PCTOOLS, FastBack, PKPAK (a shareware program), and other backup software programs compress files for archiving. By using this type of utility, you can realize a savings of at least 35 percent in disk or tape space.

Clean Backups

You can use a combination of script files and batch files to make the backup procedure even easier and cleaner. To use the following batch file, you need a program called SCR_ALL.EXE, which runs any script file on every drawing in a directory. (This program, written by Mark Vodhanel, is available from CompuServe's Autodesk Forum; its source code (in C) is included in Appendix F.)

Let's "walk through" the procedure, step by step.

1. Create under ACAD (or on its own) a subdirectory called ARCHIVE, TEMP, BACKUP, or something like that. In this example, we'll use \ACAD\ARCHIVE. Type:

   MD \ACAD\ARCHIVE

   and then press Enter.

2. Put SCR_ALL.EXE in the \ACAD\ARCHIVE subdirectory.

3. Using your text editor in nondocument mode, write a batch file (ours is called DWGBAK.BAT) in the \ACAD\ARCHIVE subdirectory. This batch file should contain the following code:

   ```
   CLS
   ECHO OFF
   CD\ACAD\ARCHIVE
   COPY \ACAD\%1\*.DWG
   SCR_ALL STRIP
   ```

   This file assumes that you have a job-number subdirectory (such as \ACAD\88099) under ACAD.

4. Write the following script file (STRIP.SCR) in the \ACAD\ARCHIVE subdirectory:

   ```
   2

   wblock (getvar "dwgname") y * quit y 0
   ```

   Be sure to leave a blank line between the *2* line and the *wblock* line, and end the file with another blank line. Be sure also to include the spaces within the text exactly as shown.

5. To start the batch file, type **DWGBAK XXXXX**, with *XXXXX* the job number or directory name that you want to back up.

The batch file first copies all of the drawing files from a job-number subdirectory and then starts a script file running with AutoCAD. The batch file uses SCR_ALL.EXE, which runs any script file on every drawing in its resident directory and can be used for any of your other script files that run on more than one drawing. In this case, the script file strips all the files in the directory of any unnecessary layers, blocks, shapes, etc. You can write batch files also to automate archiving, depending on which backup program you use.

Backing Up with LISP

As an alternative to using the batch file for backing up, you can write a LISP routine called BACKUP.LSP. The routine, which consists of the latter portion of the STRIP.SCR file, looks like this:

```
(defun c:backup () (command "wblock"
(strcat "\\acad\\archive\\" (substr (getvar "dwgname") 4) "" "*" "")))
```

At the end of the day, your \ACAD\ARCHIVE directory will be full of files ready for backup if you do one of the following:

❏ Use the BACKUP command within AutoCAD

❏ Add the BACKUP command to your CAD menus

❏ Redefine AutoCAD's END command to include the BACKUP command

One of the nice things about PKPAK and some of the other archiving programs is that they allow you to add comments not only for the archive file but also for each individual file in the archive file. Including these comments is a good idea—they will help you to remember, months later, what is in the archived drawing. You should put the archived files in a job subdirectory.

And if you keep each job on a separate disk, you can use DOS's LABEL command to create a title for the disk on which you keep the archived files. The label, which can be 11 characters long, will tell you something about the job that is stored on that disk. The only major drawback to PKPAK that we know of is that it won't prompt for another disk if the archive file exceeds the disk capacity.

Figure 7.2 shows what one of our archived files look like.

```
Searching Archive: 88005.ARC - Bayshore Conch Club - 88005

Filename      Comment                            Date       Time       CRC
--------      -------                            ----       ----       ---
005A0_0.DWG   Title sheet                        01-31-89   20:11:26   6BFB
005A0_1.DWG   Architectural Site Plan            01-20-89   15:25:30   C024
005A1_1.DWG   Overall fl pl, dr & fin sched      01-30-89   17:37:26   17AC
005A1_2.DWG   Dining rooms - house               01-30-89   17:40:58   FB3D
005A1_3.DWG   Bar and outside dining             01-30-89   17:32:00   BA57
005A1_4.DWG   Kitchen plan                       01-30-89   17:52:34   AC39
005A2_1.DWG   Elevations -S&W                    01-31-89   19:01:58   1B41
005A2_2.DWG   Elevations -N&E                    01-31-89   15:28:04   65C9
005A2_3.DWG   Existing Elevations                01-31-89   19:43:12   7B0A
005A3_1.DWG   Building Sections                  02-01-89   03:28:54   1CB1
005A3_2.DWG   Wall Sections                      02-01-89   04:49:22   7C75
005A7_1.DWG   Equipment Schedule                 01-31-89   15:48:20   6304
005A7_2.DWG   Equipment Schedule                 01-31-89   22:30:16   3065
05C101.DWG    Civil Site Plan                    11-15-88   11:45:52   4F05
3DMAIN.DWG    Main 3d drawing                    11-15-88   11:49:14   B4E7
3DPOD.DWG     gazebo 3d drawing                  11-15-88   11:50:48   B128
----          -------                            -------    ---
0016          2123757                            1083826    49%

D:\TEMP >
```

Fig. 7.2.

Commented archive file using PKPAK.

Drawing Management: Make Your Drawings Work for You

Even when they are hand drawn, drawings contain a good deal of information. With the advent of CAD systems, this information no longer is limited to graphic information. The data in an AutoCAD drawing has tremendous potential. An AutoCAD drawing can manage quantity takeoffs, strength of materials, product specifications, and such simple information as whose line is whose. The guidelines in the following sections will help you set up a flexible drawing-management system that can be adapted to any data-management requirements.

Layer-Naming Conventions

Layers are almost as much help as attributes when you want to sort your AutoCAD database. Why would you want to sort the database? Did you realize that you are constantly sorting the database if you freeze and thaw layers? In order to use AutoCAD efficiently, you need to name layers in a way that lets you know what's on them, lets you manipulate them in assorted groups, and follows any industry standards that may be available to you.

The layering system we have developed is based on an industry-standard specification system, shown in figures 7.3A and 7.3B. Your layering system should accomplish the same goals for your profession as this one does for ours. These goals follow:

- ❏ The standard naming convention is recognizable.
- ❏ Layer names are "data sortable".
- ❏ Similar layers hold similar data.
- ❏ Layer purposes are combined, wherever possible.

This numeric system corresponds to different categories of materials, called divisions, established by the Construction Specifications Institute. We can use it to do some pretty neat things. For instance, because concrete block is Division 0400, we can control our layers for concrete block by using *04??* in a layer freeze or thaw command. If we want to extract the layers prepared by our structural consultants, we designate *??2?*, which manipulates layers 0020-0029, 0120-0129, 0220-0229, etc. Even if your requirements are not this elaborate, a similar system will let you do some nifty things.

The Construction Specifications System is a five-digit system. If we wanted to designate one layer for each product-specification section, we would have a five-digit layering system—useful for quantity takeoffs, but more than we need. We did set up the system so that if we ever want to go to a five-digit layer-naming convention, we can make the conversion relatively easily through LISP, by multiplying the existing layers by 10 and adding new layers with a simple incrementing routine. Our priority—controlling the drawing information between consultants and tasks—is reflected in the way we have grouped the layer information. Many others use this system, based on their data priorities, in different ways.

You may look at this layer-naming convention and say "Hey, they're using 1,700 layers!" We don't use all the layers in every drawing. The maximum number of layers in any single drawing would be 330—and that would be an architectural drawing that contains something from every material division and uses all of the base drawing layers.

Chapter 7: Advanced Management Techniques 153

LAYERING SYSTEM CONVENTIONS- DIVISION CATEGORIES

```
'XXXX' -   DIVISION CATEGORY      0000   UNIVERSAL
'XX' -     DISCIPLINE LAYERS      0100   GENERAL
'X' -      LAYER CONTENTS         0200   SITEWORK
                                  0300   CONCRETE
DISCIPLINE LAYERS                 0400   MASONRY
                                  0500   METALS
00    BASE DRAWING                0600   WOOD & PLASTIC
10    ARCHITECTURAL               0700   THERMAL & MOISTURE PROTECTION
20    STRUCTURAL                  0800   DOORS AND WINDOWS
30    MECHANICAL                  0900   FINISHES
40    ELECTRICAL                  1000   SPECIALTIES
50    PLUMBING                    1100   EQUIPMENT
60    LANDSCAPE                   1200   FURNISHINGS
70    CIVIL                       1300   SPECIAL CONSTRUCTION
80    INTERIORS                   1400   CONVEYING SYSTEMS
90    MISC.                       1500   MECHANICAL
                                  1600   ELECTRICAL
LAYER CONTENTS:

0    ATTRIBUTES
1    ULTRA-FINE LINES
2    ULTRA-FINE PATTERN LINES
3    FINE LINES
4    FINE PATTERN LINES
5    MEDIUM LINES
6    TEXT
7    HEAVY LINES
8    SYMBOLS
9    VARIABLE
```

0000   UNIVERSAL

0000-0009	SHEET BORDER & PROJECT TITLE
0010-0019	ARCHITECT'S LOGO, TITLE, ETC.
0020-0029	STRUCTURAL ENGINEER'S LOGO, TITLE, ETC.
0030-0039	MECHANICAL ENGINEER'S LOGO, TITLE, ETC.
0040-0049	ELECTRICAL ENGINEER'S LOGO, TITLE, ETC.
0050-0059	PLUMBING ENGINEER'S LOGO, TITLE, ETC.
0060-0069	CIVIL ENGINEER'S LOGO, TITLE, ETC.
0070-0079	LANDSCAPE ARCHITECT'S LOGO, TITLE, ETC.
0080-0089	INTERIOR DESIGNER'S LOGO, TITLE, ETC.
0090-0099	MISC. CONSULTANTS

0100   GENERAL

0100-0109	KEY PLANS, DATES, MAJOR BLOCKS
0110-0119	ARCHITECTURAL SHEET TITLE AND NO.
0120-0129	STRUCTURAL SHEET TITLE AND NUMBER
0130-0139	MECHANICAL SHEET TITLE AND NUMBER
0140-0149	ELECTRICAL SHEET TITLE AND NUMBER
0150-0159	PLUMBING SHEET TITLE AND NUMBER
0160-0169	CIVIL SHEET TITLE AND NUMBER
0170-0179	LANDSCAPE SHEET TITLE AND NUMBER
0180-0189	INTERIORS SHEET TITLE AND NUMBER
0190-0199	MISC. SHEET TITLE AND NUMBER

0200   SITE WORK

0200-0209	BASE SITE DWG, BOUNDARIES, PARKING, ETC.
0210-0219	ARCHITECTURAL SITE INFORMATION
0220-0229	STRUCTURAL SITE INFORMATION
0230-0239	MECHANICAL SITE INFORMATION
0240-0249	ELECTRICAL SITE INFORMATION
0250-0259	PLUMBING SITE INFORMATION
0260-0269	CIVIL SITE INFORMATION
0270-0279	LANDSCAPE SITE INFORMATION
0280-0289	NOT USED
0290-0299	MISC. SITE INFORMATION

0300   CONCRETE

0300-0309	BASE DRAWING CONCRETE INFO
0310-0319	ARCHITECTURAL CONCRETE INFO
0320-0329	STRUCTURAL CONCRETE INFO
0330-0339	NOT USED
0340-0349	NOT USED
0350-0359	NOT USED
0360-0369	CIVIL CONCRETE INFO
0370-0379	LANDSCAPE CONCRETE INFO
0380-0389	NOT USED
0390-0399	MISC. CONCRETE INFO

0400   MASONRY

0400-0409	BASE DRAWING MASONRY INFORMATION
0410-0419	ARCHITECTURAL MASONRY INFORMATION
0420-0429	STRUCTURAL MASONRY INFORMATION
0430-0439	NOT USED
0440-0449	NOT USED
0450-0459	NOT USED
0460-0469	CIVIL MASONRY INFORMATION
0470-0479	LANDSCAPE MASONRY INFORMATION
0480-0489	NOT USED
0490-0499	MISC. MASONRY INFORMATION

0500   METALS

0500-0509	BASE DRAWING METALS INFORMATION
0510-0519	ARCHITECTURAL METALS INFORMATION
0520-0529	STRUCTURAL METALS INFORMATION
0530-0539	NOT USED
0540-0549	NOT USED
0550-0559	NOT USED
0560-0569	CIVIL METALS INFORMATION
0570-0579	LANDSCAPE METALS INFORMATION
0580-0589	NOT USED
0590-0599	MISC. METALS INFORMATION

Fig. 7.3A.

Layer-naming standards for the construction industry, using four-decimal system (continues).

Fig. 7.3B.

Layer-naming standards for the construction industry, using four-decimal system (continued).

0600	WOOD & PLASTIC		0700	THERMAL AND MOISTURE PROTECTION
0600-0609	BASE DRAWING WOOD INFORMATION		0700-0709	BASE DRAWING THERM & MOIST INFO
0610-0619	ARCHITECTURAL WOOD INFORMATION		0710-0719	ARCHITECTURAL THERM & MOIST INFO
0620-0629	STRUCTURAL WOOD INFORMATION		0720-0729	STRUCTURAL THERM & MOIST INFO
0630-0639	NOT USED		0730-0739	MECHANICAL THERM & MOIST INFO
0640-0649	NOT USED		0740-0749	NOT USED
0650-0659	NOT USED		0750-0759	PLUMBING THERM & MOIST INFORMATION
0660-0669	CIVIL WOOD INFORMATION		0760-0769	CIVIL THERM & MOIST INFORMATION
0670-0679	LANDSCAPE WOOD INFORMATION		0770-0779	NOT USED
0680-0689	INTERIORS WOOD INFORMATION		0780-0789	NOT USED
0690-0699	MISC. WOOD INFORMATION		0790-0799	MISC. THERM & MOIST INFORMATION
0800	DOORS AND WINDOWS		0900	FINISHES
0800-0809	BASE DRAWING DOOR AND WINDOW INFO		0900-0909	BASE DRAWING FINISHES INFORMATION
0810-0819	ARCHITECTURAL DOOR AND WINDOW INFO		0910-0919	ARCHITECTURAL FINISHES INFORMATION
0820-0829	NOT USED		0920-0929	NOT USED
0830-0839	NOT USED		0930-0939	NOT USED
0840-0849	NOT USED		0940-0949	NOT USED
0850-0859	NOT USED		0950-0959	NOT USED
0860-0869	NOT USED		0960-0969	NOT USED
0870-0879	NOT USED		0970-0979	NOT USED
0880-0889	INTERIORS DOOR AND WINDOW INFORMATION		0980-0989	INTERIORS FINISHES INFORMATION
0890-0899	MISC. DOOR AND WINDOW INFORMATION		0990-0999	MISC. FINISHES INFORMATION
1000	SPECIALTIES		1100	EQUIPMENT
1000-1009	BASE DRAWING SPECIALTIES INFORMATION		1101-1109	BASE DRAWING EQUIPMENT INFORMATION
1010-1019	ARCHITECTURAL SPECIALTIES INFORMATION		1110-1119	ARCHITECTURAL EQUIPMENT INFORMATION
1020-1029	STRUCTURAL SPECIALTIES INFORMATION		1120-1129	STRUCTURAL EQUIPMENT INFORMATION
1030-1039	NOT USED		1130-1139	MECHANICAL EQUIPMENT INFORMATION
1040-1049	NOT USED		1140-1149	ELECTRICAL EQUIPMENT INFORMATION
1050-1059	NOT USED		1150-1159	PLUMBING EQUIPMENT INFORMATION
1060-1069	NOT USED		1160-1169	NOT USED
1070-1079	NOT USED		1170-1179	NOT USED
1080-1089	INTERIORS SPECIALTIES INFORMATION		1180-1189	INTERIORS EQUIPMENT INFORMATION
1090-1099	MISC. SPECIALTIES INFORMATION		1190-1199	MISC. EQUIPMENT INFORMATION
1200	FURNISHINGS		1300	SPECIAL CONSTRUCTION
1200-1209	BASE DRAWING FURNISHINGS INFORMATION		1301-1309	BASE DRAWING SPECIAL CONST. INFO
1210-1219	ARCHITECTURAL FURNISHINGS INFORMATION		1310-1319	ARCHITECTURAL SPECIAL CONST. INFO
1220-1229	NOT USED		1320-1329	STRUCTURAL SPECIAL CONST. INFO
1230-1239	NOT USED		1330-1339	MECHANICAL SPECIAL CONST. INFO
1240-1249	NOT USED		1340-1349	ELECTRICAL SPECIAL CONST. INFO
1250-1259	NOT USED		1350-1359	PLUMBING SPECIAL CONST. INFO
1260-1269	NOT USED		1360-1369	NOT USED
1270-1279	NOT USED		1370-1379	NOT USED
1280-1289	INTERIORS FURNISHINGS INFORMATION		1380-1389	INTERIORS SPECIAL CONSTRUCTION INFO
1290-1299	MISC. FURNISHINGS INFORMATION		1390-1399	MISC. SPECIAL CONSTRUCTION INFO
1400	CONVEYING SYSTEMS		1500	MECHANICAL
1400-1409	BASE DRAWING CONVEYING SYSTEMS INFO		1501-1509	BASE DRAWING MECHANICAL INFO
1410-1419	ARCHITECTURAL CONVEYING SYSTEMS INFO		1510-1519	ARCHITECTURAL MECHANICAL INFO
1420-1429	STRUCTURAL CONVEYING SYSTEMS INFO		1520-1529	STRUCTURAL MECHANICAL INFO
1430-1439	MECHANICAL CONVEYING SYSTEMS INFO		1530-1539	MECHANICAL MECHANICAL INFO
1440-1449	ELECTRICAL CONVEYING SYSTEMS INFO		1540-1549	ELECTRICAL MECHANICAL INFO
1450-1459	NOT USED		1550-1559	PLUMBING MECHANICAL INFO
1460-1469	NOT USED		1560-1569	CIVIL MECHANICAL INFORMATION
1470-1479	NOT USED		1570-1579	LANDSCAPE MECHANICAL INFORMATION
1480-1489	INTERIORS CONVEYING SYSTEMS INFO		1580-1589	INTERIORS MECHANICAL INFO
1490-1499	MISC. CONVEYING SYSTEMS INFO		1590-1599	MISC. MECHANICAL INFO
1600	ELECTRICAL			
1601-1609	BASE DRAWING ELECTRICAL INFO			
1610-1619	ARCHITECTURAL ELECTRICAL INFO			
1620-1629	STRUCTURAL ELECTRICAL INFO			
1630-1639	ELECTRICAL ELECTRICAL INFO			
1640-1649	ELECTRICAL ELECTRICAL INFO			
1650-1659	PLUMBING ELECTRICAL INFO			
1660-1669	CIVIL ELECTRICAL INFORMATION			
1670-1679	LANDSCAPE ELECTRICAL INFORMATION			
1680-1689	INTERIORS ELECTRICAL INFO			
1690-1699	MISC. ELECTRICAL INFO			

If you are interested in this system, take a highlighter and mark the layers you would need to complete one of your drawings. Remember to put everything shared by everyone in division 0000 and everything shared by a base plan on each division's 00-09 layers. For example, door (0800-0809) shows up on nearly everyone's plans but is not on framing plans or reflected ceiling plans. When you finish, you may find that you use a total of about 150 layers. With this numbering system, typical users must remember the 17 divisions (already a standard in our industry) and their layer code group, such as 20. In an example of a specific case, the structural engineer (discipline layers 20-29) can work on concrete block notes and plans with layers 0400-0409 and 0420-0429—a total of 20 layers!

We can also make this system less complex. The design of the three-digit system shown in figure 7.4, for example, is a derivative of the five-digit system. This three-digit numeric system will work for many applications. Although it cannot separate the layers by consultant, it does provide a clear way to control materials designations in a project. If you don't have an industry standard like ours, you still can use this type of system for your own standard. Anyone working with you will find such a system easy to use—all you have to do is give them a list of your categories.

LAYERING SYSTEM CONVENTIONS-   DIVISION CATEGORIES -

'XXX' -   DIVISION CATEGORY
'X' -   LAYER CONTENTS

LAYER CONTENTS:

0	ATTRIBUTES	000	UNIVERSAL
1	ULTRA-FINE LINES	010	GENERAL
2	ULTRA-FINE PATTERN LINES	020	SITEWORK
3	FINE LINES	030	CONCRETE
4	FINE PATTERN LINES	040	MASONRY
5	MEDIUM LINES	050	METALS
6	TEXT	060	WOOD & PLASTIC
7	HEAVY LINES	070	THERMAL & MOISTURE PROTECTION
8	SYMBOLS	080	DOORS AND WINDOWS
9	VARIABLE	090	FINISHES
		100	SPECIALTIES
		110	EQUIPMENT
		120	FURNISHINGS
		130	SPECIAL CONSTRUCTION
		140	CONVEYING SYSTEMS
		150	MECHANICAL
		160	ELECTRICAL

Fig. 7.4.

Layer-naming standard for the construction industry, using a three-decimal system.

EXAMPLES OF DIVISION LAYERS (ALL DIVISIONS TYPICAL) -

020   SITEWORK

020   SITEWORK ATTRIBUTES
021   SITEWORK ULTRA-FINE LINES
022   SITEWORK ULTRA-FINE PATTERNED LINES
023   SITEWORK FINE LINES
024   SITEWORK FINE PATTERNED LINES
025   SITEWORK MEDIUM LINES
026   SITEWORK TEXT
027   SITEWORK HEAVY LINES
028   SITEWORK SYMBOLS
029   VARIABLE

If you are using a menu program, you may encounter some problems because most menu programs establish their own layer-naming conventions. Not only do you have to update all of your drawings to make them fully compatible with your menu system, but you also have to edit the menu system. This is reasonably simple to do using the search-and-replace feature of a word processor. However, if the menu system uses a number of protected LISP files, you are out of luck. See Appendix D for a LISP routine you can use for renaming layers.

Because AutoCAD can place objects of different color and linetype on the same layer, you can develop your layer names to include all the line information about a type of object. For example, we use dotted lines for overhead objects and solid lines for visible objects in a plan view, and we add line weights to improve the plan's readability. Some layering schemes would separate the dotted lines, the heavy lines, and the light lines onto different layers. If all of these lines designated the same part of the project, such as cabinets, you would have to maneuver three layers whenever you wanted to do something with the cabinets. With our system, all the cabinet information is on one layer.

We recommend using colors primarily for line-weight control. You can use color, to a certain degree, to indicate a change in material or a change in the type of information represented. Just remember that something as simple as changing from four to eight different pen weights for plotting can render a color scheme invalid.

If you want to use task menus or create base drawings that are combined only at editing and plotting sessions, a good layer-naming convention is a must. For a discussion of task menuing, see Chapter 9, "The Tasks At Hand."

Combining Pin-registering and CAD

CAD layering is very much like pin-registered drafting. The exception to this analogy is apparent in AutoCAD, because all floor-plan drawings, for example, don't share the same database. If you have several drawings that share a title block, a base drawing, a job title, and some general notes, you have a situation to which pin-registered drafting would apply.

We frequently have consultants who share information with our drawings (see fig. 7.5). Thanks to our layering- and file-naming conventions, we can assemble a drawing for editing. Assembling the drawing might entail inserting into the drawing we are working on 1) a title sheet, 2) a base drawing, and 3) a drawing that shows our consultants' designs. After the editing session is finished, only the work on our layers is saved.

Chapter 7: Advanced Management Techniques 157

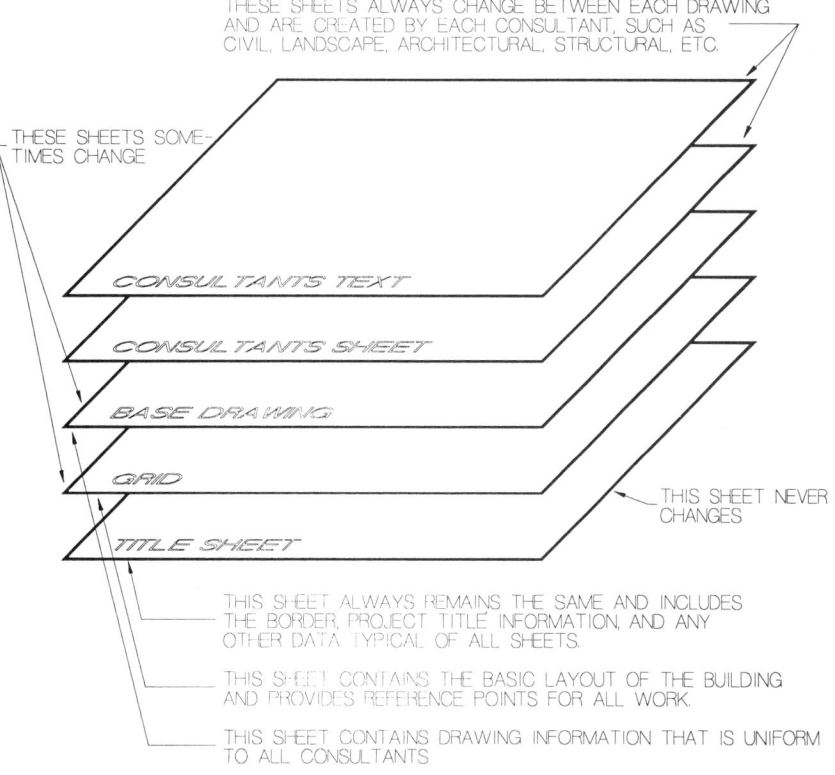

Fig. 7.5.

Assembling a drawing for editing.

In essence, this system creates a drawing database. For complex projects, this is the best way to keep drawings current. For it to work properly, however, you must use directories well and have both a predictable layering scheme and an easily controlled file-naming convention.

We create a base drawing that contains only the shared information. Then we give the drawing an appropriate title. The title *005B1_01,* for example, tells us that this is the base drawing for all 101 sheets in job number 5. Then we use a simple LISP routine to insert this base drawing into the drawing we are working on:

```
(defun c:insbase ()
(command "insert" (strcat (substr (getvar "dwgname") 1 3) "b"
  (substr (getvar "dwgname") 5)) "0.00,0.00" "" "" "")(princ))
```

A second routine asks whether we want to update the base drawing:

```
(defun c:udbase (/ rm)
(setvar "cmdecho" 0)
(initget 1 "y Y n N")
(setq yn
  (getkword "Do you want to update the base drawing? <Y or N>"))
(setq yn (strcase yn))
(if (= yn "Y")
(command "insert" (strcat (substr (getvar "dwgname") 1 3) "b"
  (substr (getvar "dwgname") 5) "=" (substr (getvar "dwgname")
  1 3) "b" (substr (getvar "dwgname") 5) ) "0.00,0.00" "" "" "")
(princ))
```

Together, these routines automate the process of updating drawings that share information. With the base drawing inserted as a block, we can access objects in the base drawing with any of the OSNAP selections without worrying about editing the base drawing.

To try out these routines, place in a job subdirectory (\ACAD\89001, for example): a drawing file named 001A1_00.DWG, a base-drawing file named 001B1_00.DWG, and these routines. If you like what you see, place the LISP routines in your \ACAD\LISP subdirectory. You load each routine from the AutoCAD command prompt by typing **(load "insbase")** and **INSBASE**; for updating, type **(load "udbase")** and then **UDBASE**.

Thanks to our standardized layer-naming convention, we can use similar LISP routines to extract or merge drawings that will include only the layers required for a specific drawing. Thus, we are able to automate the creation of drawings for our consultants to use. For further discussion of this practice, see Chapter 9, "The Tasks At Hand."

Storing Plot Information in the Drawing

If you get tired of answering all the questions in the AutoCAD plot menu, don't feel like the Lone Ranger. You can use a LISP routine to store the plot information in the drawing so that you can plot from the drawing and never have to remember the proper plot scale for your drawing or what you were supposed to change. You can use the following LISP routine to create a batch file that plots all the drawings in a plot directory. The process is almost completely automatic—you still have to make sure that there is ink in the pens, and you have to press Enter when the paper is ready. The technique for the batch file is similar to the archiving technique we discussed earlier. Appendix E, "DPLOT.LSP," contains detailed instructions for batching this routine.

Using your word processor, create the file DPLOT.LSP and then type the following lines of code *exactly* as you see them:

```
(defun c:dplot (/ ss1 ent yn e anm llc urc psc ps
                   p1 p2 p3 p4 p5 p6 p7 po pfl )
(setvar "cmdecho" 0)
(setq ss1 (ssget "X" (list (cons 0 "INSERT")(cons 2 "plotblk"))))
(if (null ss1)
    (progn
     (prompt "\nYou Must Insert Block 'Plotblk' Before Proceeding...")
     (princ))
     (setq ent (ssname ss1 0))
)
(if (/= ss1 nil)
(progn
(initget 1 "y Y n N")
(setq yn (getkword "Do You Wish To Update the Plot Parameters?
     <Y or N>:"))))
(setq yn (strcase yn)))
(if (= yn "Y")
(progn
(setq e (ssname ss1 0))
(command "ddatte" e)))
(setq yn nil)
(while ent
(setq ent (entnext ent))
(if (/= ent nil)
(progn
(setq anm (cdr (assoc 2 (entget ent))))
(if (= anm "LLC")(setq llc (cdr (assoc 1 (entget ent)))))
(if (= anm "URC")(setq urc (cdr (assoc 1 (entget ent)))))
(if (= anm "PSIZE")(setq ps (cdr (assoc 1 (entget ent)))))
(if (= anm "PSCALE")(setq psc (cdr (assoc 1 (entget ent)))))
(if (= anm "P#1")(setq p1 (cdr (assoc 1 (entget ent)))))
(if (= anm "P#2")(setq p2 (cdr (assoc 1 (entget ent)))))
(if (= anm "P#3")(setq p3 (cdr (assoc 1 (entget ent)))))
(if (= anm "P#4")(setq p4 (cdr (assoc 1 (entget ent)))))
(if (= anm "P#5")(setq p5 (cdr (assoc 1 (entget ent)))))
(if (= anm "P#6")(setq p6 (cdr (assoc 1 (entget ent)))))
```

Listing continues

Listing *continued*

```
(if (= anm "P#7")(setq p7 (cdr (assoc 1 (entget ent)))))
(if (= anm "PORIG")(setq po (cdr (assoc 1 (entget ent))))))))
(if (not (null ss1))
(progn
(setq pfl (open "dplot.scr" "w"))
  (write-line "plot" pfl)
(if (/= llc "")
(progn (write-line "w" pfl)
  (write-line llc pfl)
  (write-line urc))
  (write-line "l" pfl))
  (write-line "y" pfl)
  (write-line "y" pfl)
  (write-line p1 pfl)
  (write-line "c2" pfl)
  (write-line p2 pfl)
  (write-line "c3" pfl)
  (write-line p3 pfl)
  (write-line "c4" pfl)
  (write-line p4 pfl)
  (write-line "c5" pfl)
  (write-line p5 pfl)
  (write-line "c6" pfl)
  (write-line p6 pfl)
  (write-line "c7" pfl)
  (write-line p7 pfl)
  (write-line "x" pfl)
  (write-line "n" pfl)
  (write-line "i" pfl)
  (write-line po pfl)
  (write-line ps pfl)
  (write-line "n" pfl)
  (write-line "0.010" pfl)
  (write-line "n" pfl)
  (write-line "n" pfl)
  (write-line psc pfl)
(close pfl)
(command "script" "dplot")))
(princ))
```

In order for this routine to work, your drawing must contain a block called *plotblk*. This block must contain specific attributes, defined with AutoCAD's ATTDEF command. All of the attributes are invisible; your preferred defaults are preset values. For a detailed explanation of how to create the PLOTBLK.DWG file, see Appendix E.

Put the PLOTBLK.DWG file in your standard library subdirectory (\ACAD\DRAWINGS), and the DPLOT.LSP file in your \ACAD\LISP subdirectory. Select a practice drawing from your archives and insert PLOTBLK.DWG into the drawing. At the AutoCAD command prompt, type **(load "ACAD/LISP/dplot")**; the computer should show this response: DPLOT. If you see an error message or a number on your screen, go back and check your typing. If you receive no error message, type **DPLOT** at the AutoCAD command prompt. Again, if you receive any error messages, check your typing.

A prompt will ask whether you want to update the plot information. When you enter **Y** you will see an icon that contains your default plot values. Modify the plot values to reflect what you want to use, adjusting for the number of pens you have, and then exit the icon. Note that if you leave the Lower Left Corner and Upper Right Corner blank, the routine will plot the limits; if you fill them in, it will plot a window. You have created an automated plot-command series that leaves everything ready for you to enter the paper and start the plot. If you receive errors from the routine, check to make sure that you created all the attributes correctly, including typing the correct names (in all uppercase letters) for the attribute tags. If you like what you see and want to use the routine on all your drawings, put PLOTBLK.DWG in your setup drawing.

Most of the LISP routines we discuss in this book are detailed in the appendixes. We included DPLOT here so that we could discuss some of the things the routine does as it pertains to management. Even if you don't understand all of the AutoLISP programming at this point, you will learn something from completing this exercise. We want you to see a good example of automated project management in action. The following important aspects of this routine can apply to many project-management requirements:

- ❏ It reduces errors and standardizes an activity.
- ❏ It makes preset conditions automatic.
- ❏ It is transparent to the user.
- ❏ It works with other programs you have created (SCR_ALL.EXE).
- ❏ It uses options and error-trapping routines.

This routine searches the drawing for an invisible block that contains invisible data. If it doesn't find the block, it lets you know that you need to insert the block; then it exits the program. If it finds the proper block, the routine lets you modify the plot requirements (if you want to) and then it answers all of AutoCAD's questions about plotting automatically. This routine uses some extremely powerful AutoLISP commands that access the drawing database. For further discussion of AutoLISP, see Chapter 13, "AutoLISP Never Was Plain English."

Record Maintenance

Good project management requires proper record maintenance. Create a drawing history procedure that records when, what, who, and why certain activities occurred in relation to a drawing and a project. Milestones such as design approval, production, revisions, or as built can be recorded in the drawing file or on the disk in a project file. You should determine the information you need, and then design a program to record it. We present what we think is important; you can modify it for your use.

A LISP Routine for Tracking Drawings

If you want to keep track of the work done on your drawings, a LISP routine may do the trick. Our LISP routine writes lines to a file whenever you open a drawing. To gain information about a project or to do your billing by the hour, you can sort and use this data file with dBASE or Lotus 1-2-3. If you are using AutoCAD Release 10, you can put this routine into the S::STARTUP function so that the END command is redefined from the beginning and the user is prompted automatically for input. The best way to force this to happen in earlier releases of AutoCAD is to use a script file to load all your drawings and to run a LISP routine that redefines the END command before the command prompt is made available to the user. If you want to use this LISP routine and don't have one of the take-a-peek programs mentioned later in this chapter, make this procedure optional so that you don't have to enter data in order to just take a look at the drawing.

The following routine creates a file based on your project name or number. If you don't use a consistent numbering system, you will get a unique file for each drawing. Create the file USER.LSP containing the following:

```
(defun c:user (/ ch ctr dfl dwg usr utk hrs min pro pro2 yn rno
   co datafile)
(setvar "cmdecho" 0)
(setq dte (strcat (substr (getvar "cdate") 5 2) "/" (substr
(getvar "cdate") 7 2) "/" (substr (getvar "cdate") 3 2)))
(setq ch (substr (getvar "dwgprefix") 9 1))
(setq ctr 8)
(while (/= ch "\\")
(setq ctr (+ ctr 1))
(setq ch (substr (getvar "dwgprefix") ctr 1)))
```

```
(setq ctr (- (1- ctr) 8))
(setq dfl (substr (getvar "dwgprefix") 9 ctr))
(setq dfl (strcat dfl ".dta"))
(setq dwg (getvar "dwgname"))
(setq usr (getstring T "\nEnter Your First Initial
    and Last Name: "))
(initget 1 ("Y y N n"))
(setq yn (strcase (getkword "\nDoes this work require a revision
         number? <Y or N>: ")))
(if (= yn "Y")
  (setq rno (getint "\nEnter the revision number: ")))
(prompt "\nTask Codes Are: <Preliminary Design: PD>
    <Design Development: DD>")
(prompt "\n<Working Drawings: WD> <Contract Administration: CA>
    <Revisions: R>")
(setq utk (strcase (getstring T "\nEnter A Task Code Or
    Combination of Codes Separated by a Slash (/): ")))
(setq hrs (fix (* 24 (getvar "tdusrtimer"))))
(setq min (fix (* (rem (* 24 (getvar "tdusrtimer")) 1) 60)))
(setq pro (strcat usr ", you worked on the drawing " dwg))
(setq pro2 (strcat " performing the task(s) " utk " for "
    (itoa hrs) " hours and " (itoa min) " minutes"))
(prompt pro)(prompt "\n")
(prompt pro2)(initget 1 "Y y N n")
(setq yn (getkword "\nIs this correct <Y or N>?"))
(setq yn (strcase yn))
(if (= yn "N")
(progn (Prompt "\nTry Again: ")(load "/acad/user")(user)(princ))
(progn
(setq datafile (open dfl "a"))
(write-
line (strcat  dte "," dwg "," rno "," utk "," (itoa hrs) ","
    (itoa min) "," usr "," co ",") datafile)
(close datafile)
(command "time" "r" "")
(command "end" "y"))))
```

The preceding routine prompts you for your name and a task code. It then gives you a chance to review your reponses before writing the information to a file. Note the effective use of job subdirectories and drawing file names. To illustrate, let's use a drawing we used earlier—drawing 001A1_11, in the subdirectory \ACAD\89001. Now, when you want to end a drawing, type **(load "user")** and **USER** at the AutoCAD command prompt. The resulting file (called 89001.DTA) will contain an entry that looks like this:

```
(Today's date), 001A1_11, (your name), (a task code that you
selected), X,Y,(remarks)
```

with *X* and *Y* representing the hours and minutes you spent working on the drawing.

This LISP routine creates in the job subdirectory a data file that keeps track of every drawing for that job. If you like what you see, you can edit the task codes and redefine the END command in AutoCAD.

The routine resets the timer. If you use an old drawing in which the timer was not reset, the first line written to the file will be the total time spent in the drawing to date. This lets you start invoicing immediately from the information collected by this routine. If you want an accurate description of each task, you must use this routine whenever you work on a drawing. Even if you don't use the routine consistently, you will get an accurate accounting of the time spent in the drawings. The file, which will be in comma-delimited format, will be readable by dBASE or Lotus 1-2-3.

Create a Project Library System

If you have added to your drawing-management system all the practices we have discussed, you may find that things are starting to get a little complex. The best way to control all of this is to create a project library system.

If you use floppy disks for backups and storage, you must think carefully (*before* you set up a project library) about how many kilobytes you will need for a job. In our opinion, the best approach for temporary storage is to create disks with archive files separated into the smallest denominator necessary for your estimated job size, adding a disk for data and another for slides if we need to. We separate our archive files by drawing category (001A1_1, 001A1_2, etc.) and place each category in an archive file (this one would be called 89001A1.ARC, for example). We continue the process for all files—drawing category file 001A2_1 goes in archive file 89001A2.ARC, and so forth. We can automate the procedure by using the proper wild-card extensions with the archiving program. For example, the following line:

```
PKPAK A A:89001A1 001A1*.DWG.
```

tells the PKPAK program to add (`A`) to the archive file (`A:89001A1.ARC`) all A1 drawings of job number 001.

We recommend storing slides together on the same disks and in non-compressed mode so that you can always take a look at the entire job. At the end of the day, you can use a simple batch file to copy `*.sld` from any named or selected directory to the disk. Then, when you have finished a project, you can condense all the disks into the most compact storage you can manage.

Automating the Process: Programs You Can Use

All the file- and drawing-management concepts discussed in Chapter 6, "Project and Drawing Management," can be implemented fairly easily with shareware or commerically available programs. Each of these programs focuses on different aspects of CAD management. We have not yet found one that does everything we would like it to do. You may be able to find one or two that, when combined with your own menu system, accomplish 95 percent of the management tasks you need.

If you are really good with dBASE, you can write a program that will do everything we have discussed, customized to your requirements. (If you're not a dBASE whiz, maybe you know someone who is!) The nice thing about dBASE is that it can write custom batch files for each job and then erase the file when it has finished the task. This makes for a really clean installation. For further discussion of dBASE, see Chapter 5, "Software Companions." Remember, though, that the only way you can truly automate the system is to make sure that your standards are predictable.

A good shareware program for viewing slides inside or outside AutoCAD is Slidemanager, version 4.0, written by John Intorcio. To use Slidemanager, you need to write batch files that automate its use from your menu system. If you put the program in your ACAD.PGP file, you can shell out and have a look at your standard drawings on file to see which drawing you want to insert. You can zoom and pan around the slides and generally find your way visually around the drawings you have on disk. The great thing about Slidemanager, besides its quality, is its cost. The drawbacks are that you have to create slides of all of your drawings, and that large drawings take some time to display.

With Cyco International's AutoManager, a more sophisticated program, you don't have to create a slide in order to view the file. Like Slidemanager, AutoManager can be loaded from inside or outside AutoCAD, allows you to pan and zoom views, and has many other features that help with file maintenance. It also can be added to your ACAD.PGP file. AutoManager has utilities for copying, erasing, and renaming drawings; for displaying layers, blocks, and attributes; and many other commands for manuevering between files.

Auto-Log, from SeCAD, helps you manage projects by annotating files, providing navigational menus, and doing a multitude of other management tasks. This program not only extracts the time-management information that USER.LSP does, but also allows you to add to the project any time you spend outside the drawing editor. Auto-Log can execute the major DOS functions and create the project-data logs you need for keeping track of a project. The program can provide password protection for the system and for each project and can create AutoCAD menus of your standard library of drawings. Moreover, given its many capabilities, Auto-Log is reasonably priced. We wish it had the capability to link other programs into its framework, so that it could manage the entire system—but then we're also waiting for a direct brain that acts as a drawing input device.

We are not familiar with every program on the market, and you may find others that work as well as or better than those discussed here. These are the ones we do know about; for information about where you can get them, see Appendix K.

Summary

This chapter is really about database management. Your standards are the key to linking together the entire management system. You should spend some time making notes about shared information so that you can determine what you need to coordinate with your management system. In many respects, this chapter is a combination of all the management systems that existed in a preCAD office (time sheets, project manuals, invoicing, and drawing storage, for example) combined with good computer-management practices.

In this chapter, you learned what kinds of options are available to you and saw some examples of how those options can be implemented. Clearly, you can't buy one software package that meets all your needs. Each individual has his or her own management style and priorities, and no software package can sufficiently respond to that many variables. It is up to you, therefore, to make the effort needed to ensure competent management of your system and projects. Once you do, your productivity will improve and the quality of your work will exceed your expectations!

Recommended Accomplishments

- ❏ Create a menu system for automating directory usage.
- ❏ Create an automated backup methodology.
- ❏ Create a layering standard.
- ❏ Create a project-library system.

Optional Accomplishments

- ❏ Create a file-annotation system.
- ❏ Get a utility for viewing your drawings.
- ❏ Create an automated file-tracking system.
- ❏ Establish an automated management system.
- ❏ Automate plotting.

II

Perfecting Your Techniques

What Chapter 8 Is About

In Chapter 2, "Evaluating and Developing Your CAD Habits," we stressed the development of good habits as the proper foundation for AutoCAD use. (You may have found that you also have some bad habits to get rid of.) You should develop good habits also for all the new skills you will learn from the rest of this book. To make sure that you have a solid foundation, and as a send-off for Part II: "Perfecting Your Techniques," this chapter covers some good practices for the following areas:

- ❏ Buying software and hardware
- ❏ Putting your ideas into practice
- ❏ Making your pieces fit their puzzle

Helpful Things To Know Before You Start

- ❏ We strongly recommend that you review all the "Recommended Accomplishments" in Part I

What To Have on Hand

- ❏ An open mind

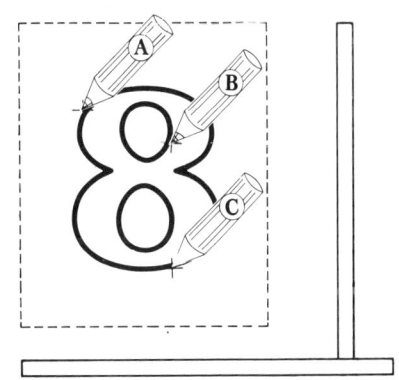

The Ten Commandments— Times Three

We know that the title of this chapter seems presumptuous, but we have learned why people have problems getting all they want out of AutoCAD. Most of the problems occur because people haven't developed the guidelines that can keep them out of trouble when they get into uncharted waters. This is normal: lack of experience is a constant companion to experimentation. We have developed a few sets of rules that should help you proceed with greater confidence.

Buying Software and Hardware

If you learn the simple rules in this section and force yourself to abide by them, you probably will stay out of trouble when you buy unknown products. Although you won't always be able to follow these rules to perfection, do your best to stick to them.

1: Don't Buy Anything Unless You've Seen It Used with AutoCAD

The safest approach is to work from the AutoCAD *Installation and Performance Guide*'s list of supported hardware. If you use supported hardware, you are sure to get help from your authorized Autodesk dealer if you have a problem. If you buy something else, you have to depend on that product's dealer or manufacturer. Get anything you can on a trial basis until you are sure it works. Autodesk does not warrant any of the software listed in the third-party catalog (available from your dealer).

2: Use Only the Complete Configuration

Do not buy anything you have seen used with AutoCAD but not configured with the other hardware and/or software you have or are buying. Be sure to check out everything with the entire configuration up and running.

3: You Get What You Pay For

For some strange reason, nobody ever seems to pay attention to those six words until there's a problem. You should negotiate with the supplier of your choice instead of shopping for the best price.

4: Speed, Durability, and Adaptability All Cost Money

Everyone is excited about 386s, 486s, display-list processing, big monitors, 33 MHz clock speeds, etc. When evaluated for adaptability (capacity, expandability, peripheral support) and speed, the life of the top-of-the-line system with AutoCAD is about 18–24 months. That, at least, has been our experience. Sure, you can use an XT—but you won't want to. Release 10 essentially overwhelms a 286 if you have large drawings. The only way you can buy the perfect system or software is if you know exactly what you are going to do with it for the next five years—and if you don't care whether everyone passes you by.

5: Buy It by Mail, Get It Serviced through Your . . .

We would be the first to suggest that you should save money. If you know exactly what you are getting into, there's no reason not to buy through the mail—except if it breaks. If you're considering buying something that generally doesn't break, like software, go ahead. But if you're thinking of buying anything else, think again.

6: Don't Finance Your Purchase with Time Savings

Computers let you work smarter and better, but not necessarily faster. Don't finance the cost of the system with "improved productivity by a factor of three." Finance it with improved quality by a factor of six.

7: Take It for a Test Drive

Because you can easily have as much money tied up in your computer system and its software as in a new car, try it before you buy it. Knowing something about the software or hardware will improve your eye when you shop.

8: Buy the Latest and Greatest, and Visit the Wilds

If you get anything on the cutting edge of the market, you're a pioneer. As a pioneer, you may get stranded in the woods and left to your own abilities. Believe us. We once sent back a graphics card: it took two-and-a-half months to get the problem resolved.

9: Clones Are Not the Real Thing

IBM compatibility is hard to measure. AutoCAD is a demanding program, especially because of the peripherals it uses. Flaws in compatibility show up in the deepest cracks of the system with AutoCAD. If you have doubts, get a full-refund compatibility guarantee. If the sales representative hesitates, do some fast back-pedaling.

10: Your Dealer Should Be Your Best Friend

You should check out your dealer completely, but even with the best of references your decision to buy still boils down to whether you trust the dealer. The dealer's knowledge about what you buy is your first, and sometimes only, resource (with the exception of the Autodesk Forum on CompuServe). AutoDesk expects you to get answers from your dealer, as do many other hardware and software manufacturers. Unless you can point to a specific problem that a manufacturer can't avoid, the manufacturer is likely to contend that your problem is someone else's fault. A good dealer can figure out which component is the real culprit.

This drawing (see fig. 8.1) was created by using AEC from Autodesk, our own custom LISP routines (including the routine for insertion of detail drawings, listed in Appendix B), and customized dimension blocks.

Developing Your Ideas

We are sure that, while working at the computer, you have had many ideas about customizing your software. If you decide to venture into customization, you may want to live by the rules in this section.

1: Keep It Simple

A truly simple solution is sheer genius. Simplicity has a beauty all its own, whether it is in programming, the design represented by your drawings, or the methods you use to create the drawings. The easiest path to simplicity is to make sure that you have stepped back from the problem and grasped the whole picture. In most problem-solving methodologies, getting the whole picture involves an evolution of the final product that is created by an ongoing investigation moving from the trees to the forest and back again to the trees. Don't be afraid to work on a problem, set it aside, and then come back to it with a fresh outlook. Some of our LISP routines have definitely improved with age.

2: Try It Out—Often, and Elsewhere

When developing advanced AutoCAD practices, the biggest problem most people have is that they fail to allow for every possibility. Only experience can help—and Murphy's law is sure to defeat even your best ideas.

Chapter 8: The Ten Commandments—Times Three

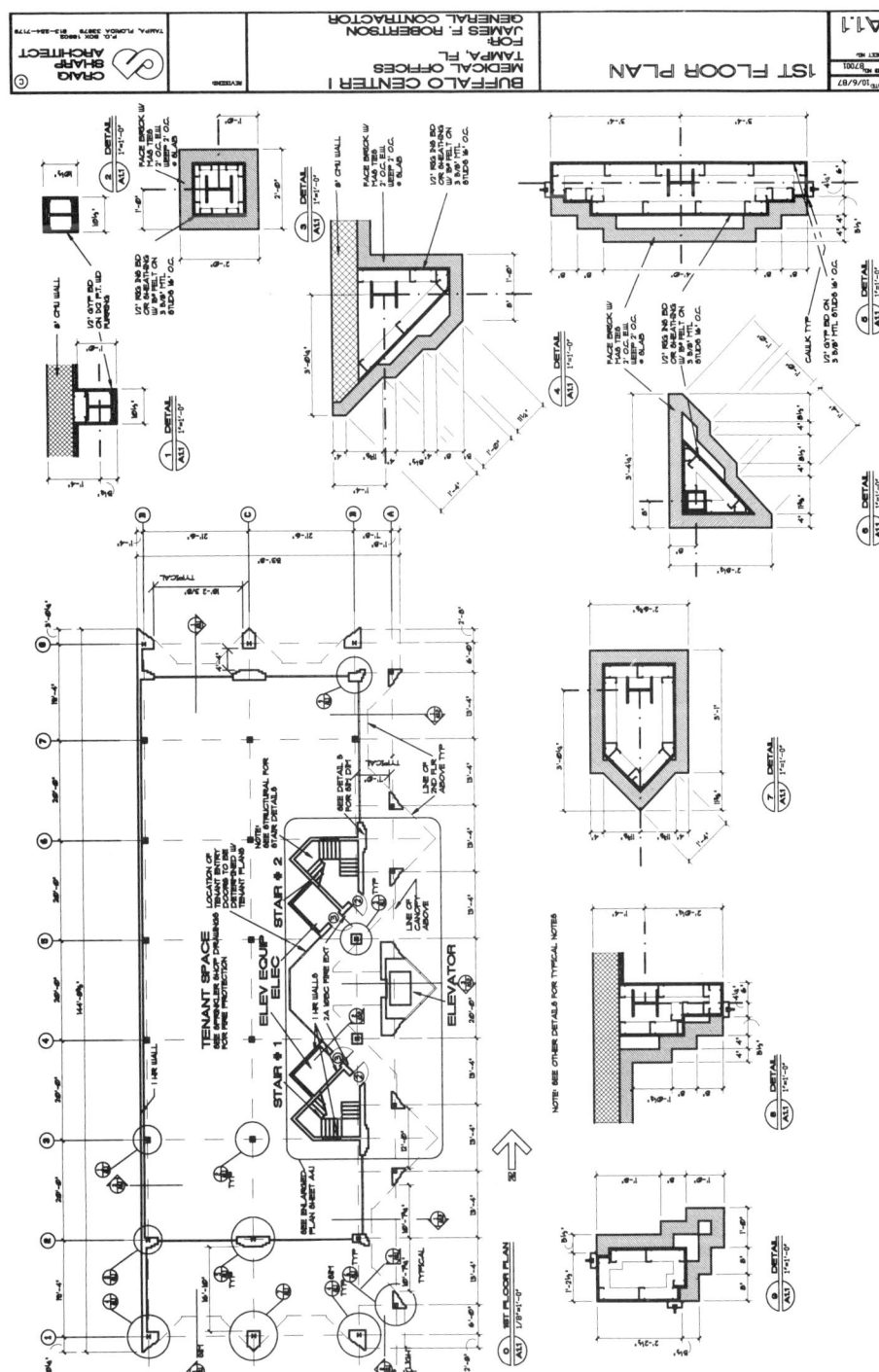

Fig. 8.1.
A sample customized drawing.

Take, for example, a LISP routine that one of us once wrote. In this routine (for creating views in a drawing), the user could move around the entire drawing without ever worrying about a regen. Terrific! But when used on a system that was not a standard EGA with a 12″ monitor, the routine was a complete failure. Further investigation revealed that you can't write one routine that works for every graphics card and every monitor.

3: Get Someone Else To Look at It

One of the most amazing things we've discovered about AutoCAD—and one of the main reasons for its success—is that everyone has a different way of doing things with the program. If you want to know whether what you are doing is going to work, try it out on other users or your local AutoCAD users' group, if you have one. *CADENCE* and *CADalyst* magazines publish up-to-date lists of users groups; the list in Appendix K is current at the time of this book's publication.

4: Do More with Less

Try to make whatever you are doing flexible enough to be used with or within something else. This is especially important for LISP routines. Instead of writing programming code that does the same thing repeatedly, you can write subroutines and call them from the program you are working on. The same is true for the drawings you create. Try to make them as universally applicable as possible—then add the unique elements later. It's better to have one really good drawing than twenty that you constantly have to sort through.

5: Try Something New Every Week

Every week, make a special effort to set aside an hour or two to try something new—whether it's a LISP routine you've been meaning to write, a new use you've heard of for an AutoCAD command, or a piece of software you've wanted to look at. After a year has gone by, you will be amazed at the number of people who consider you an expert.

6: Software Is Smart—Hardware Is Stupid

Your hardware doesn't care what you want to do with AutoCAD or third-party add-on packages. If you don't know what to look out for, you can have trouble with display devices, plotters, mice, interrupt vectors, memory, and a host of other things. If you are going to customize your system, you need to have a good understanding of your hardware. Make sure that you have *full* documentation for *all* of the parts of your hardware system.

7: Computers Make Work—They Don't Save It

Because computers provide great control of information, firms or individuals who use computers become information junkies. You will find yourself adding to a drawing detail that you would never add if you were drawing by hand. Of course, your work will also be more accurate and of higher quality. Just remember that although computers can help you work smarter and produce more work in a given amount of time, they also give you more to do. You must educate yourself, manage additional data, and keep up with the developments in an industry that has little or nothing to do with your basic job.

8: AutoCAD Is Only as Good as You Are

Most tasks in AutoCAD can be accomplished effectively in at least two, and sometimes three, ways. The best method for completing even the simplest drawing task depends entirely on the way an individual works. To perfect your technique, you must fully understand AutoCAD's capabilities and verify which way works best for you.

9: Get Tuned In and Stay Informed

Staying informed requires that you seek out sources of information. We strongly recommend that you do the following:

- ❏ Subscribe to *CADENCE*, *CADalyst*, and at least two PC magazines of your choice.
- ❏ Join the local AutoCAD users' group.
- ❏ Join CompuServe and the Autodesk Forum.
- ❏ Visit computer shows and expositions whenever you get the chance

For information about computer magazines, users' groups, and the Autodesk Forum, see Appendix K.

10: Keep It Simple

When it comes to what you can do with AutoCAD, the possibilities seem endless. We explain to our clients that we can do with AutoCAD anything we could do drawing by hand—including freehand work, if need be. The temptation is to get so involved in automating your work that you never get anything done. The best approach is to limit your efforts to those things that will really save you time, again and again. Keep in mind also that whenever a new update of your software comes out or your hardware is upgraded, you may have to redo all of your customization work.

This drawing (see fig. 8.2) was created using Autodesk's AEC menu, our own custom LISP routines and hatch pattern, and custom lettering fonts. Notice the use of the title block without a border, discussed in Chapter 6, "Project and Drawing Management."

Making Your Pieces Fit Their Puzzle

After you customize something for your own use, the next logical step is to develop it into a product that others can use. Whether your idea is a routine, a menu, a set of symbols, or some unique hatch patterns, you probably will spend a good deal of time creating it. Because your time is precious, you surely want to spend it effectively. If you think your ideas will help your friends, improve your office productivity, or sell to others, we recommend that you consider the ten points in this section.

1: Keeping It Simple Is Difficult

You may have discovered, as we have, that others are slow to accept new ideas—the usual response is, "We just don't do things that way." No matter how great your idea, it may work for only a small percentage of users because you can only suggest that others change their thinking and habits. Your approach to solving the problem must be as flexible as possible. Having both flexibility and simplicity in the same package is tremendously difficult when it comes to computers. That is why AutoCAD is such a large program.

Chapter 8: The Ten Commandments—Times Three **179**

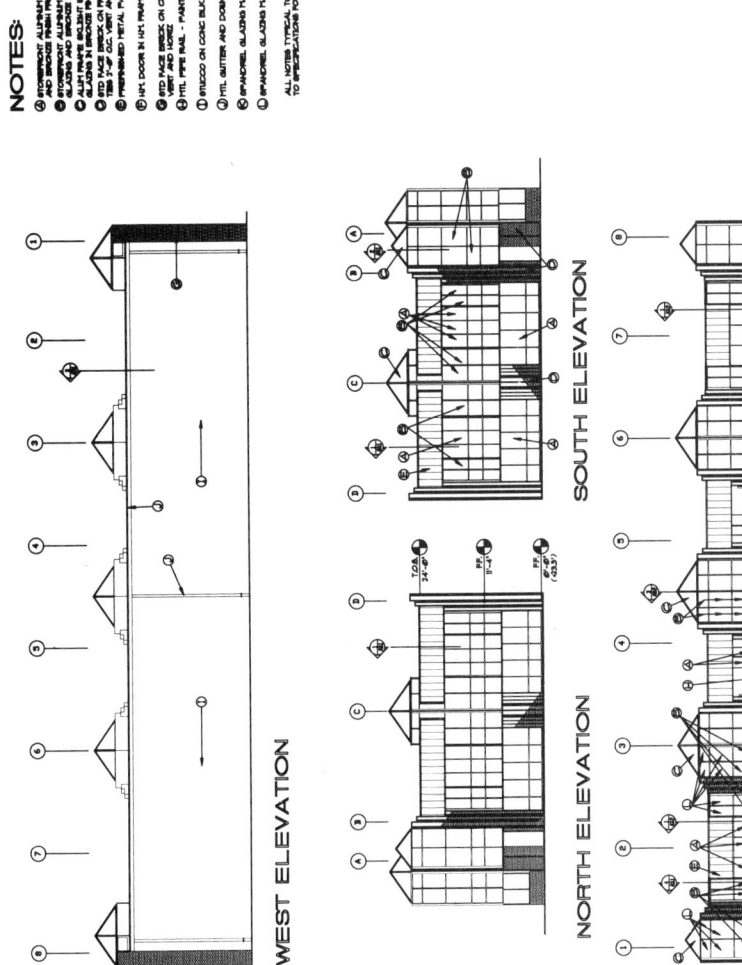

Fig. 8.2.
Another sample customized drawing.

2: Keep Up with the Joneses

Keeping tabs on the capabilities and configuration of the newest equipment and software is a full-time job. Many people have to have the latest, greatest, fastest, biggest, costliest system available. Although you may not be one of these people, suppose that an idea you want to develop has to be used by your consultants or your clients to remain compatible with your work. To ensure the viability of your idea, it will have to be tried out on their equipment. If you develop the idea for an even larger market, you will spend countless hours getting rid of the bugs in hardware compatibility.

3: Beta Is the Second Greek Letter

After you develop an idea, you have to let your friends and neighbors fool around with it. This second step—the *beta*, or test, version of your idea—is important. Even if you are just developing an idea for use within a large office, you should have a few people beta test it before you release it for general circulation.

4: Standardize Your Approach

Some people consider programming an art form. An experienced programmer can recognize the programming style of another. Over time, your programming concepts should become an extension of the way you think and the experience you have gained. Testing each as you go, develop building blocks that will serve as the foundation of your work. This practice is very important in developing menus, for example.

5: Document What You Do

Frequently, those of us who work on customizing a product tend to focus only on the immediate task—we forget about other users and don't think about the future. Your product's success depends on good documentation, both from a user's point of view and for your own future reference. The comments you use to annotate your reasons for doing things will help you not only to write documentation providing information for users but also to keep track of your ideas in case you want to use them for another project.

6: Study the Way Others Work

Before you put time and effort into creating the "greatest thing since sliced bread," spend some time observing and discussing how others accomplish the results your idea will provide. If you don't work for a large office, bring up the idea at a users' group meeting. Many people don't do this—either they are afraid that someone will steal their idea or they don't think they have the time to spend on research. If you are good enough to share your work in its final form, you can afford to share your idea with others. Sometimes even Autodesk has a hard time with this one—witness early versions of AEC.

7: If Your Idea Was Original, It Must Have Been Perfect

It is highly unlikely that you'll come up with an idea that hasn't been thought of by someone else. Your goal is to have the energy to implement the idea, and/or the insight to put it together with other ideas to create a unique concept. If you have a good library of examples of what others have done, you frequently will find something already exists that will do what you are trying to do, or is close to it. If you can improve on it, do so and use it.

8: The Eye Is Quicker than the Hand

AutoCAD accepts input from a variety of sources, almost all of which involve a user. Although you may be comfortable with only one form of input, your idea will not be readily accepted unless the user also is comfortable. Additionally, a constant method of input is often tiring to the user. For example, many menu systems rely entirely on digitizer input which, because it sets a pattern that is hard on the neck, can reduce the user's productivity. Staring at a screen all day isn't pleasant either, and some screen menu systems are very slow. Generally, the quickest form of input is usually the best. Nontypists can hunt-and-peck faster than they can digitize letters; numeric keypads also are faster than digitizers, but macros from a digitizer are fast and more readily accessible than a crowded screen or extensive typing.

9: Look at the Forest—Work on a Tree

Any application you may develop has to fit into the big picture. We are giving you a good look at AutoCAD's overall capabilities and, a chapter at a time, helping you develop specialized skills. Although you must always keep track of the overall concept and utility of AutoCAD, you don't have to be a specialist in all areas. Choose those you are good at and enjoy doing.

10: Have Fun

Because its flexibility is so challenging, AutoCAD has a group of followers who border on fanatical. AutoCAD's sensitivity to the evolution of software and hardware makes the program an ongoing and ever-expanding collection of knowledge and ideas. Truly mastering AutoCAD can be a lifelong task. This phenomenon will continue as long as computers continue to change our lives. You can use the program not only for your work but also to have fun being creative in other areas. You can send a building to the contractor over the phone lines; fax your latest tool design to the shop; create a three-dimensional mesh of a friend's face; design a postage stamp; develop presentation videotapes (including music and voice-overs) of your firm's work. There really is no end to the possibilities.

Summary

This chapter, which introduces you to Part II: "Perfecting Your Techniques," isn't intended as gospel—but should make you think about the way you look at AutoCAD. You should formulate an attitude that works hand in hand with this overview and allows you to focus on any detail with the right questions in mind. Basically, we hope you'll remember three important points:

- ❏ The best answers come from good questions.
- ❏ Increased productivity always starts with you.
- ❏ Master AutoCAD and your computer, or they will master you.

What Chapter 9 Is About

Once you have established management standards for your AutoCAD projects and drawings, you must communicate those standards to AutoCAD so that all the hard work you've put in so far is not diminished in any way. The primary tool for communicating with AutoCAD is a menu. The AutoCAD menu has evolved from a simple screen menu to include a tablet menu, a pull-down menu with icons, a complex screen-menu system, a push-button macro device, a voice-input command system, and a light pen directly to the screen. If your menu system doesn't properly communicate your needs to AutoCAD, your effective management of AutoCAD is being compromised. This chapter discusses the implementation of your AutoCAD management strategy with menus, including the following topics:

- Assessing management demands on a menu system
- Evaluating whether to write or buy your menu
- Establishing a reasonable scope for your menu system
- Using menu macros
- Dividing the work by tasks for greater speed
- Customizing someone else's work

Helpful Things To Know Before You Start

- The complete sequences involved with the fundamental AutoCAD commands
- A little LISP
- AutoCAD menu structure
- AutoCAD menu command conventions
- Your complete management standards from Chapters 6 and 7

What To Have on Hand

- The *AutoCAD Reference Manual*
- The *AutoLISP Programmer's Reference Manual*
- A printout of the AutoCAD menu and/or the menu system you currently use
- A list of your standard drawings, if any
- A great deal of patience
- A word processor capable of handling large documents

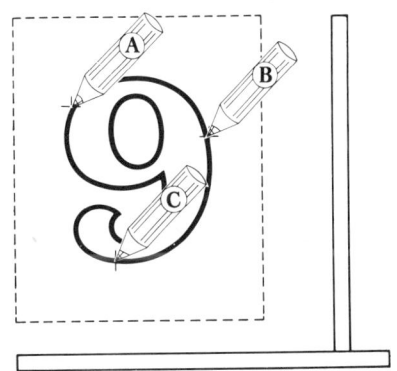

The Tasks At Hand

When you bought AutoCAD, did you realize that the budget for the system should include a custom menu? Our dealer knew little about AutoCAD AEC, but we insisted on getting it. We were lucky. We happened to know about the AEC menu system, and it fit our needs well enough that it gave us better productivity than we would have had with the stock, out-of-the-box AutoCAD. You may find that such a menu system exists for your industry.

Menus—The Link from Project Management to Drawing Management

Many books about AutoCAD focus on helping you write a custom menu for your particular application of AutoCAD. We are not going to indoctrinate you into our specific school of menu construction; in one chapter, we can't teach you to write the ultimate menu. We are going establish an approach to menus that will help you with your present setup and be flexible enough to adapt to your future needs. The fact that so many books focus on AutoCAD menu writing should give you some indication of the importance of menus in AutoCAD. If you add to that the fact that a large percentage of the software written to go with AutoCAD is menu systems, the message is clear: "The medium is the menu, and the menu is the medium," to paraphrase Marshall McLuhan. Writing menus is also a great way to learn advanced AutoCAD techniques: menus typically are based on command macros—the most basic of programming languages—and some relatively easy AutoLISP.

A Worthwhile Drawing Menu System

Almost anyone who ventures beyond the AutoCAD command prompt begins experimenting with the AutoCAD menu. We began with the Auto-CAD AEC/Architecture Menu by Archsoft/Autodesk. Convinced that we could develop better menus, we dove right in. We adapted our menus to the way we prefer to use AutoCAD, and added routines (like the one for maximizing your plotter, mentioned in Chapter 7). During those early forays into programming, we immediately discovered that everyone has an opinion about the order of priority of AutoCAD command use. And we found out that you really need to study how you use AutoCAD before you change the original AutoCAD menu.

We learned also that:

- Although third-party menu systems don't have all the answers, they are worth their authors' weight in microchips.

- AutoCAD menus and our work habits both needed improvement.

- Good menus are only as good as the standards behind them.

- The perfect menu may exist, but is not worth the effort.

Notice that we said "forays into programming"—which is just what you'll be doing, in a basic way. Don't let this intimidate you. Your ability to manipulate AutoCAD will improve, and you will be on your way toward more powerful LISP programming. If you have noticed things you would like to change about the menu you are using, there is no reason to avoid the issue. If you don't have a menu that works the way you want your AutoCAD system to be managed and used, get one. Even if you have already mastered menu customization, you probably need to revise your menu so that it works with your management and drawing standards. By sharing what we've learned, we may help you avoid some of the problems we had.

Yours or Theirs?

We have encountered many users who operate on one of two extremes: either they are unhappy with AutoCAD because it takes them much longer than they expected to do simple drawings, or they have written their own menu with a menu command for every imaginable possibility (but there is still no flow to the way they work). The first group wants to know why there isn't an AutoCAD command for automatically drawing parallel lines or inserting blocks into lines. The other group decides that the only way to pay for all the time they spent developing the menu and maintaining it with each update is to sell the menu, their services, and/or their LISP routines. As we see it, the primary force behind this situation is cost. The secondary force is the need for customization. How you relate to these two extremes will determine how you approach menu customization. If you follow the guidelines in this chapter, you will be able to respond intelligently to the dilemma of whether to customize or write menus.

Before you decide to write new menus for yourself, buy someone else's, or customize what you already have, ask yourself the following questions:

- Which is more valuable—the time I spend writing a menu or the time I spend at my occupation?
- In my work, where can I draw the line between a unique task and a standardized, repetitive drafting practice?
- How much of my management practice can I afford to have CAD dictate?
- How many different people will need to use the menu, and how long will they use it?
- How much typing do I want to do?
- Do I need to use each new update of AutoCAD?

After you finish reading this chapter you will be able to select a third-party menu system intelligently, and you'll be well on your way to customizing the menu to suit your needs.

Assessing Your Requirements: How Do You Spend Your Time?

Writing a menu takes *many* hours. Even if you are really good at it, you probably will spend at least 400 hours writing, testing, and developing an original, medium-sized menu and its associated macros. If you add to that the amount of planning you do before you write the menu, and the time it took you to become an expert—we're talking major effort.

Autodesk has done some of the work for you, at least concerning the AutoCAD commands—the AutoCAD menu comes with the top section blank, and you can add your own menu in this section. Nonetheless, we estimated that duplicating the customization efforts of the AEC architectural menu would cost us well over $10,000 in work hours. The AEC architectural menu cost us $1,000. By writing our own menu, we could have had every single drawing and detail just the way we wanted it, but we didn't think that was worth $9,000! Furthermore, we discovered that (using Autodesk's years of experience as a guide) we could fix almost anything we didn't like about the AEC menu. We don't understand why any architect would avoid purchasing a third-party menu system for AutoCAD. If menus that suit your needs are available, we urge you to look at them and allow for one in your budget. As a matter of fact, consider buying two or three and combining their best features.

We can think of only four possible reasons to write your own menu from scratch:

1. No one writes a menu for your purposes.

2. The only menus available for your purposes are not open to your customization.

3. You want to take up menu-writing as a career or hobby.

4. You are a masochist.

Analyzing Your Work Flow

If your time is better spent using AutoCAD than writing menus, you need to think about how you now work with AutoCAD (or how you plan to). One of the most important aspects of creating menus is understanding the flow of your work.

In our work, for example, we tend to do things in groups. In particular, we don't design everything in one part of the building and then move on. The original AutoCAD AEC architectural menu returned to the main menu or previous menu after nearly every menu selection from the screen or the digitizer. We changed the menu so that we could pan and zoom around a drawing, inserting standard light fixtures as we went, and we eliminated at least two menu picks for each insertion. No big deal. But—over several years—much time saved!

We frequently use OSNAP. Using the AEC menu, we generally either had to pick the row of asterisks at the top of the screen to get the OSNAP menu or select an OSNAP command from the digitizer. With some simple menu modifications, we always had an OSNAP menu on the screen when we needed it, eliminating one pick or eye movement in nearly every two or three picks.

By investing a total of about 10 hours learning how to make these two types of changes and editing the menu, we probably saved 50 hours of pick-and-read time.

In your approach to buying or customizing a menu system, you need to consider four major areas of work-flow analysis: activity assessment, project-management data requirements, ergonomics, and the hierarchy of information in your task procedures.

Begin your work-flow analysis by assessing the activities your menu must oversee. This includes the way you work as well as your own capabilities and those of your coworkers. The best way to analyze your work is to get a small tape recorder and, for a couple of weeks, talk to the recorder about what you are doing, noting what you wish you could do at the moment. If a recorder isn't practical, keep a written wish list, noting which AutoCAD command or drawing task you associate with each wish. You also need to consider the skills of the people who will use the menu. Clearly, a menu used only by great typists will be different from a menu used by nontypists. If you have a great LISP programmer in your midst, let AutoLISP do your drawing. If you use a large symbols library, your menu must be the index to that library, making everything easy to find.

If you expect much of your project management to occur through data extraction from your drawings, the menu must be designed to organize that data and extract it at logical times. Your menu has to control such behind-the-scenes activities in AutoCAD as system variables, layers, attributes, blocks, and user queries.

The ergonomics, or human engineering, aspect is extremely important. Users of a digitizer must constantly move their hands and eyes in order to operate the system; on the other hand, people who use only the screen must constantly stare at the monitor. Both situations, improperly handled, are tiring and counterproductive.

The hierarchy of the information will determine the movement through the menu. You must outline, at least in general terms, the type of information you want presented in menu form and the order in which it should be presented. Write an outline or create a drawing similar to the menu hierarchy supplied within your AutoCAD manual. At first, just try to cover the major areas. As you work on the customization, you will refine and add detail to this hierarchy.

Menus and Drawing Standards—Jack and Jill

You can customize your menus to control and implement your drawing standards. Menus can take advantage of your drawing standards by accessing layers, attributes, standard drawing components, and LISP routines. Your menu usage and drawing standards must work well together. If one is poorly done, the other will fail to meet its fullest potential.

Our layering schemes, discussed in Chapter 7, rely heavily on our menus. We find that the easiest way to help our consultants adapt to our standards is to have them use our menu system. Menus are also the easiest way to standardize an office. Essentially, you can force the user to follow your standards for text, layers, symbols, and drawing setup.

To show you a variety of drawing-standard concepts that a menu can handle, we are going to walk through the highlights of a drawing insertion. Even if you don't intend to use this type of activity, you will find that the concepts discussed in this example can apply to many applications.

Figure 9.1 represents one of our standard drawings. It has a title block, some text and dimensions, a number of different line weights, and a border. It also has some symbols nested inside the block that makes up this standard drawing. Nothing is unique about this drawing; anyone could have a detail in his or her work containing similar elements. But we want you to look more closely at the process of using this drawing.

Most people say, "OK. I pick INSERT from the menu, type the drawing name at the AutoCAD command prompt, drag this drawing into place, tell AutoCAD that x, y, z, scale factors are 1, or whatever, that the rotation angle is 0, and that's it, right?" Well—if the menu handles this insertion in the

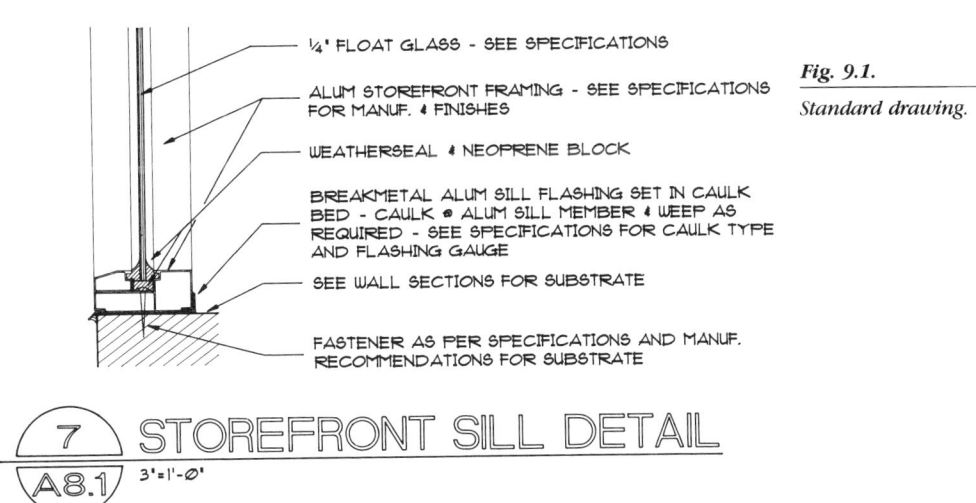

Fig. 9.1.

Standard drawing.

same way it handles a standard symbol (an electrical outlet, for example), that comment could be correct. But with a properly written menu, you could have AutoCAD do the following with this drawing:

- ❑ Control the layer that's set when the drawing is inserted
- ❑ Determine whether the drawing is a stand-alone large-scale detail or part of an assembly
- ❑ If the drawing is part of an assembly, remove such unwanted items as a border, the drawing title, and the material hatches
- ❑ If the drawing is a stand-alone detail, prompt the user for the sheet and detail numbers
- ❑ Display a standard sheet layout and request an insertion area
- ❑ Ensure that everyone uses this drawing in the same way
- ❑ Automatically set the insertion scale and fill in the drawing scale
- ❑ Allow one drawing to work for a number of different scales

If you are to accomplish all of these tasks, your drawing standards must be established before you use the menu and must remain predictable. To point out how menus and drawing standards work together, we will discuss how each of the preceding capabilities is related to the drawing standards. For specific routines to do the work, see Appendix B, "Removing and Inserting Drawing Details."

Layer Control

The layer on which a block should be inserted depends on the purpose of the block. If you want everything to remain as originally drawn if you need to explode the block, have the menu set the layer to AutoCAD's layer 0. If you want parts of the block that you drew on layer 0 to take on the properties of a different layer when the block is inserted, you have to insert the block on the required layer. You can control all of this easily with a menu macro. Just remember that the final results of the block insertion will be influenced by the way the block originally was constructed (whether the entities that make up the block were assigned their color, linetype, or layer BY BLOCK or BY LAYER, for instance).

> **For More Information**
>
> *AutoCAD Reference Manual*, Chapter 9, Sections 5.3, 7.7, 7.8, and 9.1-9.1.5.2; pp. 125, 204, 209, 243-252 Release 10.
>
> "Viewpoint." *Memphis AutoCAD User Group Journal* (May 1988): 18-19.

Drawing Use

You can use a little LISP in the menu macro to prompt the user for an answer that will determine what is going to happen to the inserted drawing. A question prompt within a menu macro would look like this:

```
(progn (initget 1 "Y y N n)(strcase(setq yn (getkword "\nDo you want+
this drawing to be a stand-alone detail? <Y or N> :")))
```

Note: The "+" at the end of the first line tells AutoCAD that, in this menu cell, the line continues to the next line. If you type this line at the AutoCAD command prompt, you don't have to use the "+." Try it if you want, and then find the value of the variable *yn* by typing **!yn** at the AutoCAD command prompt. Depending on what you typed when you answered the question, a Y or an N will be displayed. When you master the AutoLISP IF statement, you will be able to present all kinds of choices to users by incorporating a variation of this question prompt.

We used the IF statement to determine whether we wanted to explode the block, remove parts of the drawing placed on various layers, and then re-create the block for insertion. This option wouldn't be available to us if we didn't use standard layers. By using a LISP routine, we can easily remove the notes, the drawing title, the material hatches, and the dimensions from the drawing, because we used standard layers and colors when we created the inserted drawing. We don't have to have two drawings on file for every detail we want to use as 1) a stand-alone or as 2) part of a larger drawing.

Number the Drawing, Using Established Standards

If we choose to insert the drawing as a stand-alone drawing, AutoCAD can prompt us automatically for the sheet number of the drawing. To supply this information from the menus, we have to make sure that our menus include a numeric input menu and that (if we want to use a screen menu instead of a digitizer or the keyboard) the numeric menu is called by the first selection. We accomplish this by embedding the following statement in the menu macro:

    $S=NUMBERS

This statement tells AutoCAD to change to the screen menu ($S) called *numbers*. If we didn't have standard drawing-name conventions, we would have to enter the entire sheet number whenever we inserted this drawing. Instead, once we define the attributes properly, AutoCAD automatically enters the detail number (1, in this case) and the last digit or digits of the sheet number. Without the drawing-name convention A8.X, the user would have to enter the entire sheet number. If you have a complex set of drawing types and no standards, you can waste a great deal of time entering the same information again and again, writing an inordinate number of menus to provide the information to the user, waiting for screen menus to page in and out of each screen, and maintaining the menus whenever you want to do some updating. The time adds up.

Standardized Insertion

Now that you are ready to insert the drawing, you may want to control its insertion locations. If you created a standard sheet layout with the modular divisions we suggested in Chapter 6, you can automate this process by using an icon menu (if your graphics card supports it) or by displaying a slide with a screen menu on the side. Figure 9.2 shows an icon of our standard sheet. All the user has to do is select a box that represents the portion of the drawing in which he or she wants the standard placed—AutoCAD automatically inserts it. This controls the relationship between the standard drawings, and ensures that the relational placement on the sheet is the same for all of the details. For this to work properly, the insertion point of each standard drawing must be a standard.

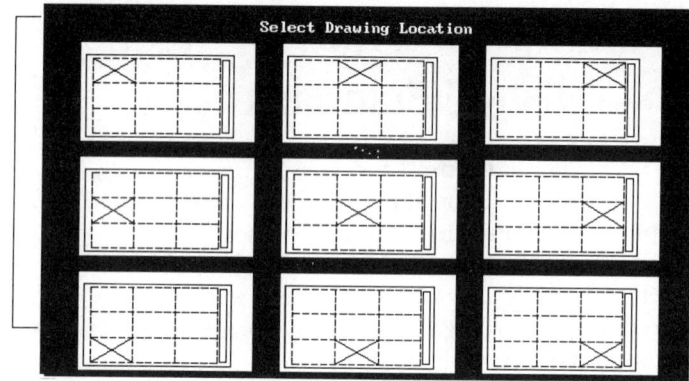

Fig. 9.2.

Icon of standard drawing sheet.

Variable Scales

By storing a scale variable when we set up any drawing, we can use that variable to set the proper scale for the insertion of a standard drawing. Furthermore, we can use the same variable for answering an attribute prompt that asks for the scale of the drawing. You should set the drawing-scale variable when you create a Drawing Setup Menu, or begin using one from another source. The drawing-scale variable can be based on a multiple of 12 (12"=1'). For example, the drawing-scale value of 1/4"=1' would be 48 (4×12/1). A scale of 1"=10' would have a drawing-scale value of 120 (10×12/1). Suppose that we create a standard drawing which we plan to use as a stand-alone drawing at the scale of 1 1/2"=1' (drawing-scale value of 2×12/3=8). In order to insert it in a drawing with a scale of 1/4"=1', we would have to use an insertion scale factor of 8/48 (or .16667). The great thing about a menu is that all of this gobbledygook required by AutoCAD is made transparent to the user. A menu macro can retrieve the scale variable and automatically make the conversion.

As you can see from this rather lengthy discussion, the simple task of inserting a drawing can solve a variety of needs when the power of a menu macro is added. If you are interested in all the detailed routines required to accomplish this specific task, see Appendix B. All of the options presented here can be applied also to other tasks. It is important to note the direct link between your drawing standards and your menu system.

Menu Limitations

Menu systems have limitations. The number of limitations is directly proportional to the size and complexity of the menu system. These limitations are as follows:

- Any menu system can be voided by typing at the keyboard.
- Each update of AutoCAD means menu-system maintenance.
- Each update of a third-party menu system means menu-system maintenance.
- Loading and paging through large menus takes time.
- Major menu editing and construction is a continual time-consumer.
- Menus reduce flexibility; every user has different priority preferences.

Although these limitations will never be eliminated entirely, later in this chapter we'll give you some recommendations for overcoming them. First, we give you the highlights of menu construction.

How To Manipulate Your Work with Menus

Menus get their power from macros. When we first started editing menu macros, we were constantly confused by problems in the macro sequence. Actually, we had a hard time understanding a simple fact: using a menu macro is exactly like typing commands at the AutoCAD command prompt, with the following exceptions:

- Section labels
- Submenus
- Command selection
- Special characters and conventions

Section Labels

Section labels divide a menu into logical parts that access different parts of the hardware system. Each section label is preceded by three asterisks, which indicate to AutoCAD that the line is a section label. The section labels are

Label	Description
***SCREEN	The area displayed as a strip of options on the right side of the monitor.
***POPn	The pull-down menus at the top of your monitor, if you have Advanced User Interface (AUI) capability. *n* designates which pull-down menu (from 1 to 10 follows).
***ICON	These menus use slides to provide graphic information for selection of a command. They require AUI compatibility.
***BUTTONS	Defines what each button on your digitizer puck will do (generally excludes the pick button).
***TABLETn	One of four menu areas (n = 1 to 4) that define a digitizer tablet area.
***AUX1	An alternate definition of the buttons on your digitizer puck, to be used with a special requirement you may have (to temporarily redefine all the buttons to OSNAP selections, for example). You can also define more button menus for this same purpose.

If you look at a printed copy of your menu, you'll see examples of how at least some of these section labels are used. Note that each section continues until another definition begins or to the end of the file.

Submenus

AutoCAD's capability to use submenus allows the program to have a large array of information available in its menus. Submenus, which generally are called from one of the main menus, usually provide detailed choices for further selection, following a general request. After picking LINE from a menu, for example, you'd want to select a line weight from a submenu; then you might want to access a submenu of OSNAP options.

A title for a submenu looks like this:

`**name`

where *name* can be a list 31 characters long (a string), using letters, numbers, hyphens, dollar signs, and underscores in any combination. Submenus are always displayed on the screen. For an EGA monitor with standard resolution, the submenu can have a maximum of 21 items for selection. If the length of a submenu is less than the maximum number of lines your monitor will display, the remaining lines of the previous menu will not be overwritten by the submenu. Suppose that you want a CANCEL option at the bottom of your screen at all times. If you make the ***SCREEN menu 21 items long, and the rest of the menus 20 items long, you won't have to put CANCEL in every submenu.

To call a submenu automatically from a menu or menu option, put a line like the following into the menu macro:

`$S=OBJECTSNAP`

By placing the preceding line into a menu macro or as a menu pick, you would call the submenu OBJECTSNAP. You should see examples of this syntax scattered throughout your menu printout.

You can also use the following lines to call submenus:

Code	Description
`$P1-$P10=xxxx`	Calls the pull-down menus named *xxxx*
`$I=xxxx`	Calls the icon menu named *xxxx*
`$B=xxxx`	Calls the button menu named *xxxx*
`$T1 - T4=xxxx`	Calls the tablet menus named *xxxx*
`$A1=xxxx`	Calls the auxiliary menu named *xxxx*
`$S=`	Calls the previously displayed screen menu, up to a total of eight previous menus. (It is supposed to be left blank after the =.)

Command Selection

There are different format (or syntax) requirements for command activation from the screen, digitizer, or pull-down menus. Each format is discussed in the following sections.

Screen- and Pull-Down Menu Commands

Use brackets ([]) to create menu options, or *picks*. In screen menus, the maximum length of a label inside brackets is 8 characters. The maximum length for a pull-down menu label is 14 characters. If you have 10 pull-down menus, you must limit their length to 8 characters each (screens are 80 characters wide). A selectable label (pick) in a menu macro looks like this:

    [LINE]^c^cLINE

Select this option to cancel whatever you are doing and start a LINE command.

Tablet- and Button-Menu Commands

There are no special requirements for selecting commands from tablet or button menus. Each *independent* line in the menu represents the next available selection for the number of choices the configuration allows. (A line is independent if it is terminated by a carriage return and does not end with a plus sign [+].) This amounts to the number of buttons on your puck or the number of rows and columns you configured your tablet to have. To help you keep track of tablet menus, you can provide labels for your tablet lines by using brackets as described in the preceding section. A tablet selection looks like this:

    [B04]^C^CLINE $S=OBJECTSNAP

We like the way Autodesk's AEC menu uses cell addresses similar to this example, which represents row B, column 04. This example starts the line command and calls a screen menu of object snaps.

Icon Commands

Icons are created with AutoCAD slides or slide libraries. The screen can be divided into 4, 9, or 16 divisions, with one slide displayed in each division. The selections are made from boxes that AutoCAD automatically places in the divisions. The number of lines in the icon menu tells AutoCAD how to divide the icon. For example, if there are four lines and four slides, the icon will be divided into four possible selections. AutoCAD will place a selection box next to the slide that is displayed. A word, such as *CANCEL* or *NEXT*, can be displayed. Here is an example of an icon menu selection:

    [std1(si)](seta pt (83,60))
    [CANCEL]^C^C

The first line displays the slide "SI" from the standard library (std1). The second line displays the word CANCEL and executes a CANCEL.

Special Characters and Conventions

Using a menu macro is similar to executing all of the commands typed at the AutoCAD command prompt, but in a batch process. We have already described three kinds of exceptions to that concept; the fourth exception is special characters. A list of these special characters and their effect follows:

- A space in the macro line has the same effect as pressing the space bar at the AutoCAD command prompt—it executes a return.

- A semicolon (;) embedded in a menu macro is the same as a return.

- A backslash (\) causes a menu macro to pause for user input. (In a button menu, the backslash causes use of the button to pass the current coordinates of the crosshairs to AutoCAD.) The pause lasts until one of the following things happens:

    - One point is selected from the digitizer.

    - A return is executed from the digitizer or keyboard.

    - A transparent command and a point or return have been selected.

    - A select command is completed. (The selection of multiple objects for use in the command, such as CHANGE, COPY, MOVE, etc.)

    - Another menu selection is completed.

- A plus sign (+) at the end of a line tells AutoCAD to continue a menu macro from one line to the next. Otherwise, the macro is terminated at the end of the first line.

- A blank line as the first line in a menu section of a pull-down menu renders the menu inactive.

- Control characters (such as ^C, for CANCEL) are entered into macros by using the caret symbol (^) followed by the appropriate character.

- To use a LISP routine in a macro, enter it as you would type it at the AutoCAD command prompt, with the required parentheses.

❏ An exclamation mark (!) entered before an AutoLISP established variable quantity returns the value of the variable as it would at the AutoCAD command prompt.

The following menu macro contains most of the special characters we just discussed. You should be able to find many examples of these conventions in your menu printout.

```
[CIRCLE]^C^C$S=OBJECTSNAP CIRCLE;\(prompt "Select center of+
circle/n") \$S=CIRCLE \(prompt "Select the method of circle+
construction/n") \$S=NUMBERS \(prompt "Enter distance or drag+
the distance\n")
```

This macro first cancels all activity, including dimensions. (Thus the use of two ^Cs.) It then brings up an Object Snap screen menu, with a space used for the return. The CIRCLE command is issued with a semicolon used for the return. A pause backslash and an AutoLISP command allow the macro to prompt the user for the center of the circle. Note the use of a plus sign (+) to continue the lines. The macro then displays a screen menu from which users can select Diameter or Radius as the method of circle creation. Finally, the macro displays a screen menu that provides the user with numbers with which he or she can enter the length of the radius or diameter.

Once you learn that customizing a menu really is simply a question of typing the commands in advance and storing them in a menu document, menu customization becomes the most readily accessible option with which you can shape AutoCAD into the design you want.

Task Menus: The Solution to Productivity

We don't know who coined the phrase *task menuing*—it is used in many third-party systems. What does it mean? If your work involves different kinds of activities, you can divide it into tasks, with a menu for each set of tasks. We divided our work into the following tasks:

1. Preliminary design and presentation site plans
2. Preliminary design and presentation floor plans
3. Preliminary design and presentation elevations
4. Preliminary design and presentation sections
5. Preliminary design and presentation 3D drawings

6. Production site plans
7. Production floor plans
8. Production elevations
9. Production sections
10. Technical review and edit
11. Revisions

A menu is associated with each of these tasks. By using the menus independently, we can adapt them to the specific needs of the tasks. This methodology has certain benefits:

- Small menus increase computer speed because they involve less memory paging.

- The user's speed increases; with less information in the menus, the user does not have to make multiple menu picks to get to a specific item.

- Menus are made up of small building blocks, which are easier to maintain, update, and edit than large, complex menus.

If you use only screen menus, or screen and pull-down menus, all you have to do in order to use task menus is automatically load other menus. If you use a digitizer, the setup process is a little more complex. You have to devise a way to have interchangeable menu templates on the tablet without having to reconfigure the tablet whenever you change menus. Slide-in or drop-in menus for this purpose are readily available from third-party developers. Creating templates on your own is best accomplished by using a durable reproduction under a clear plastic cover. You can also mount the reproductions on thin polystyrene cutouts (similar to a jigsaw puzzle for children).

When To Standardize— and How Far To Go

We've noticed that AutoCAD users tend to have a drawing standard for every situation, a LISP routine for every imaginable task, and a menu macro for all seasons. The reasons may have something to do with how spoiled we are by the truly effective use of standards (coupled with what we are paid for creating such routines), and with the hobbyist in all of us. Creating successful routines and macros can be rewarding; it gives you a sense of accomplishment in a new field (drawings are old hat to most of us). Each of us has to decide when to standardize what we're doing and when just to go do it—but we want to pass along our observations on the subject.

- ❏ If someone else has already done it and you simply need to make minor modifications, make it a standard. Many LISP routines and drawings are available (free, or for a nominal fee) in CAD magazines and on the Autodesk Forum.

- ❏ On average, it takes a single user six months of constant use of a macro or routine to recapture an hour's worth of customization effort. Some routines save a great deal of time, but the more you customize, the less time each routine will save. (This is our estimate, based on random samples taken when we researched writing our own system, and not a statistical fact.)

- ❏ Saving time is important, but so are the psychological side effects of making the work seem easier.

- ❏ Standardize wherever you want to ensure quality control or enforce standard office practices. You will reduce revision and checking time, which are just as important as actual drawing time.

As you create your custom menus, review Chapter 8, "The Ten Commandments—Times Three," to see whether your work follows the guidelines there; if not, you may find yourself bogged down in a complex and unworkable system.

Basic Tools for Standardization

AutoLISP, blocks, and shapes are the basic tools with which you can standardize images by using menus. Each of these AutoCAD features can create a standard drawing within another drawing, and each has advantages, disadvantages, and appropriate uses.

AutoLISP

AutoLISP can be used not only to automate data management but also to create drawings parametrically, with the user supplying parameters for choices the program will make during its execution. By selecting different parameters, you can modify slightly the results of a common exercise. For a fuller discussion of parametrics, see Chapter 10, "Look Ma, No Hands!"

In our work, parametrics are great for things like window, door, and cabinet elevations. In order to store on disk the multitude of sizes available, you would need a tremendous number of block drawings. Using AutoLISP to create these elevations requires the user to answer a few questions about type, height, and width; AutoLISP does the rest. It can transform each drawing into a block, if that's what you want. Because the LISP routine for cabinets uses techniques that are similar to those used for window and door elevations, by writing one routine we did most of the work for the others.

Using AutoLISP in your menus for standard drawing creation has both advantages and disadvantages. The advantages are

- ❏ Compared to shapes or blocks, AutoLISP techniques afford greater flexibility in the type of images that can be created.
- ❏ Uses minimal disk-storage space
- ❏ Drawings available ready to edit or as blocks
- ❏ Numerous similar figures available with minor modification in routine
- ❏ One menu selection location for many drawing choices

The disadvantages are

- ❏ Prohibitive routine length for large drawings results in slow loading of routines
- ❏ Slower image creation than blocks or shapes
- ❏ To work properly, correct layers must be in drawing if layers are required
- ❏ User must learn LISP programming

Blocks

Blocks are the main tool used to automate drawing-standards with menus. You create blocks by storing a library of standard drawings on disk and then inserting them with appropriate scales and rotation angles. Blocks are basic—you use standard drawing techniques to create them. The only complexity related to blocks is understanding their use of layers, linetypes, and colors. If you have problems with blocks, we recommend the suggested reading listed in this chapter's "Layer Control" section.

There are advantages to the use of blocks. They

- allow rapid image creation.
- can be inserted in either "editable" or "noneditable" form.
- can be moved and rotated when inserted, before or after final placement.
- can be viewed before you use them.
- are independent of drawing contents and layers.
- use up drawing data space only when first inserted.
- are easy to create.
- can be updated en masse.

But the use of blocks has the following disadvantages:

- Blocks use up disk space for storage.
- Many blocks are required for minor variations in design or symbol creation. If you explode a block to edit it for a minor variation, its advantages are lost.
- Each block requires a menu-selection location.

Shapes

Shapes are a special AutoCAD entity that require the use of an ASCII file that describes to AutoCAD a graphic image. The shape description is stored in a file with the extension *.SHP*. Text font files are a special type of shape file. As you can imagine, describing a drawing with a text file can be a difficult task. Fortunately, programs are available that can convert an AutoCAD drawing to a shape by automatically writing a .SHP file. Shapes are unique drawing entities with special advantages and disadvantages:

The advantages of using shapes follow:

- Shapes take up less drawing space than any of the methods available for creating a graphic image.
- Shapes are the fastest way to create images.
- Because shapes cannot be edited, they are good image-only tools.
- Shapes are easily eliminated from a plot or drawing image; you simply make the .SHP file unavailable.

The disadvantages of shapes include the following:

- ❏ They need disk storage space.
- ❏ They are difficult to create without third-party software.
- ❏ They must always accompany the drawing file in order to provide a complete drawing image.
- ❏ Numerous disadvantages for practical use in a drawing include: noneditability, images on one layer only, uniform x-y scale, no OSNAP selections, etc.

We recommend that you use AutoLISP, blocks, and shapes in conjunction with your menu system, incorporating the following simple guidelines, which are based on the advantages and disadvantages of each.

- ❏ Use AutoLISP to create drawings that have a wide variation of minor changes to a basic design or concept, and that aren't too large.
- ❏ Use blocks for most of your standard drawing insertions of any size. Always use blocks for larger drawings.
- ❏ Use shapes for uniform images that don't require editing. For example, a good use of shapes would be a shape file of your sheet title block and company logo. If you are doing a check plot and you don't want to plot the title block, just rename the shape file temporarily. (AutoCAD won't be able to find the shape.) Shapes should be used also when you need to insert one image many times.

Modify Other Menu Systems To Meet Your Needs

Whatever the size of your operation, if a third-party menu system is even moderately applicable to your needs, using it instead of starting from scratch will save you time and money. The only absolute requirement for any menu system you obtain is that it must be alterable by the user. You probably will not be able to alter parts of the system; the LISP routines, drawings, or programs written in a coded program language residing outside of AutoCAD probably will be inaccessible. Verify what cannot be changed, and then see how much of that effort you want to re-create.

Pitfalls and Standard Errors

Most menu systems come with their own ACAD.LSP file (the LISP file that AutoCAD loads upon entering the Drawing Editor). Such a file may conflict with other routines you have written: for example, functions defined in it may have names that conflict with the names of functions you have defined elsewhere, or the file may include certain AutoCAD commands redefined for its own purposes. Make sure that you understand these issues before you buy or customize a third-party menu system.

Third-party menus frequently require that you extend the DOS path. If the path requirements of these menus exceed the size of your available DOS environment, they can render inoperable other portions of your existing system. If this happens, try to blend the paths together in some way by combining LISP or DRAWING directories. As a last resort, extend your environment space and add to your DOS path, as we explained in Chapter 6.

Certain AutoLISP techniques require different settings for the environment settings LISPHEAP and LISPSTACK. These settings can easily send AutoCAD into a crash to your DOS prompt. Be sure to verify their requirements with yours. For more about LISPHEAP and LISPSTACK, review Chapter 6 and our discussion about your AUTOEXEC.BAT file.

As you start editing a new drawing, if you use a standard prototype drawing the settings may not allow the menu system to work properly. DIM settings, AutoCAD's user-definable variables USERR1–4 and USERI1–4, and the variables DRAGMODE, EXPERT, CMDECHO, LTSCALE, POPUPS, TEXTEVAL, ATTMODE, ATTDIA, and ATTREQ can all affect the way your LISP routines and menu macros operate. You should verify the conflicts between their standard setups and your standard setups and see what problems any conflicts may create for you. AutoCAD system variables are most often the location of conflicts; trying to get everything straight can be very confusing.

Testing and Debugging Processes

To test and debug your edited menu, you must first create, item by item, a test menu that replicates the environment of an existing menu. This test menu must contain the opening screen menu, a buttons menu (if required), and either a tablet menu (T1) with at least one cell or a screen submenu with at least one cell. Any submenus that you intend to call with your test cell must also be included. Because we use a tablet, our menu (TEST.MNU) looks like this:

```
***BUTTONS
$S=VIEWSET
^CREDRAW
'PAN
^O
^CBREAK $S=OSNAPB
^CLINE $S=OSNAPB
'ZOOM P
'ZOOM W
;
***SCREEN
[  TEST  ]^C^C$S=S
[  MENU  ]^C^C$S=S

[  AEC   ]^C^C(command "menu" "/aec/a/m/aec-a")

[  ACAD  ]^C^C(command "menu" "/acad/acad")
[-CANCEL-]^C^C
***TABLET1 3
[A01]
[A02]
```

When you edit menus, you need to develop good cut and paste techniques because you use your word processor to move, save, and delete large blocks of text. A printout of the menu you intend to edit or work within is a must. Make sure that the printout is current and has numbered pages. Photocopy the pages you are going to edit and mark them up, indicating which submenus you will need to import into your test menu. When you have the new macro working, install it into your main menu and delete it from your test menu.

If you intend to write several menu macros and/or completely revise an existing menu, use the test menu to try out each macro and then, when you have the macro working, write it to a file of its own.

You will need to create a menu outline that shows the tree of submenus, including the names you intend to use. Develop each menu "family" into a tree on its own sheet of paper (refer to the menu tree in your AutoCAD manual for helpful hints).

When you have a complete tree of macros working, insert each of them into your test menu and give them a whirl. Continue this process until you have written a complete menu section. Assemble the menu section into a second test menu with an appropriate name, such as TAB1TEST.MNU. Try it in the Drawing Editor and, if it works, go on to the next menu section. Finally, after all the sections are complete, combine them into the total menu file.

If you have the luxury of two word processors—one that is large in memory requirements and another that is lean—the test menu approach lets you edit the test menu from within AutoCAD using the smaller editor. You then can reload the test menu with the same name every time. AutoCAD will recompile the menu for you. This is another reason we suggest test menus—the time needed to recompile them is greatly reduced.

Protection

The LISP routines provided with our copy of Autodesk's AutoCAD AEC/Architectural menu system are not fully accessible because of a protection scheme involving the program PROTECT.EXE. We can at least add our own resident routines to the ACAD.LSP file, which became accessible in AEC Release 2.0/9.0. If Autodesk had left its LISP routines unprotected, we would have been able to use portions of their work (for our own purposes only) and we could have made corrections to obvious errors in their routines.

We understand that Autodesk protects its routines to keep unknowing users from inadvertently changing the program and to keep others from using the Autodesk code to create routines for sale. By writing our own macros, we can completely eliminate Autodesk's from the menu. And with the open ACAD.LSP file, we can use Autodesk's resident LISP routines so that our macros work in a similar fashion to theirs. Recently, many third-party LISP programmers have been asking for copies of PROTECT.EXE from the Autodesk Forum. We understand the complexity of the issues concerning copyrights and pirating. We also understand the problems created by encrypting programs and the resulting conflicts with customization requirements. Nonetheless, we wish to alert you to this situation, because it can create major roadblocks to your expected use of a third-party menu system or set of LISP routines.

Kelvination

Kelvination is a process whereby a program (available on the Autodesk Forum) changes the name of all AutoLISP variables to semicoded names up to four characters long. This process also removes all unnecessary spaces, comments, and returns from the file, thereby creating a smaller and somewhat faster-loading routine. You can recognize a kelvinated routine by its apparently random variable names, lack of spaces, and the fact that the routine is all on one line. (To decipher what you see, you must be an advanced programmer.) If you write LISP routines, we recommend that you use kelvination on your active routines (for efficiency) and that you keep the source code of your routines in a source-code library.

Pull-Down versus Screen versus Tablet Menus

When you select a menu location, you need to consider three questions:

- What type of hardware is available?
- How is the system set up?
- What are the ergonomics?

In our opinion, AutoCAD Release 10 is so complex that you need a combination of the screen menus and at least one of the two other choices. This means that you must have an AUI-compatible graphics card or a digitizing tablet. If your computer is fast, a mouse and the AUI will be sufficient. Slower computers cannot take proper advantage of full-blown AUI pull-down menus, icons, and dynamic displays unless the menu system is very simple.

If you work on complex drawings, executing complex tasks, you probably need a large menu system. If you like using a mouse, you need the AUI. Your system should be set up so that it is independent of either the AUI or the digitizer; in other words, it should work using either just the AUI or just the digitizer, in combination with the screen menu.

As for ergonomics, our monitors are up on milk crates—literally! This reduces the strain on the neck but increases the eye movement between our digitizers and screen. (One of us is content, but the other now uses the screen and keyboard almost exclusively.) Keep in mind that the amount of movement between devices affects the user's speed. You can write menus so that tasks are grouped together and most of the work for a particular task is completed in one area.

Macros Are Easy—Typing Isn't

Typing is the fastest way to enter single commands at the AutoCAD prompt. But because menu macros combine several commands into one activity, they are easier to use (even if you like to type). A macro probably will catch you within three commands, no matter how fast you type, because of the size of your keyboard buffer. A good CAD operator uses the keyboard to select almost all commands. Although all of these commands usually are available on the digitizer and screen menus, the process of finding them on the digitizer or paging to them on screen is too slow for a good typist. What does this mean to your menus? In most cases, single commands are best placed on a pull-down menu or a digitizer for immediate selection without "paging" through a hierarchy of selections to find them. But to improve speed you should promote use of the keyboard for simple commands.

You can get a utility program that extends your keyboard's capability. Such a program increases the size of the keyboard buffer so that you can type ahead while you wait for AutoCAD to catch up. It also allows you to create keyboard macros by reassigning parts of your keyboard so that two keystrokes will issue an entire line of commands to AutoCAD. These keyboard enhancements may reduce the number of simple macros you need in your menus. Our favorite, DKEY, uses less memory than any other we have found; its capabilities are basic but more than suitable for use with AutoCAD. One of us uses DKEY for OSNAP selections; the other, for keyboard macros. DKEY is available as shareware on the Autodesk Forum; for another source for DKEY, see Appendix K.

Menu Tips and Tricks

To give you an idea of the wide range of customization possibilities, this section includes a few additional tips for working with menus. *CADENCE* and *CADalyst* are another good resource.

Combining a Menu Library

The easiest way to switch between menus is to use a little LISP and a submenu in each menu that lets the user choose among all the menus. For example, you could use the following routine:

```
[PLAN ]^C^C(command "menu"  "/acad/menus/plan")
```

to load the menu PLAN.MNU from the subdirectory \ACAD\MENUS.

If you use task menus, you can create a set of script files that selects automatically the menu you want. You should combine the script file with a batch file so that you can name both the drawing and the task. To create a file 010A1_1 for preliminary plan work, we use the following files:

PRELPLAN.SCR

```
1

MENU "/ACAD/MENUS/PRELPLAN"
```

PRELPLAN.BAT

```
ECHO OFF
\ACAD\ACAD %1 PRELPLAN
CD\
```

Then, to start the preliminary floor plan 010A1_1, we simply type **PREPLAN 010A1_1** at the DOS prompt in the job-number subdirectory.

Help—A Slideshow

If your office is large you may want to create a help menu that displays slides or uses icons, and use it for walking users through the menu you have created as well as the office standards. You could even create a complete help menu system with the commands in their usual locations but which displays slides whenever a selection is made. Put this help system on the computer used by the newest person in the office so that users who have already learned the system do not lose the disk space required for the help.

Create Your Own Durable Menu

To create a durable version of your menu system, you need some very thin polystyrene. Use it to make interchangeable menus that fit under the main AutoCAD template in the open window area. Using a craft blade, score the polystyrene and then fold it along the scoring. It will snap easily along the score. By making a master panel the same size as the AutoCAD template, and snapping out insert panels the same size as the transparent portion of the AutoCAD template, you can create interchangeable menu templates that maintain a flat surface. With spray photomount, you can glue to the inserts various task-menu drawings you create; the AutoCAD template will protect them. If you create an entire template from scratch, find someone to laminate your menu in plastic.

Summary

You now have a broad view of the capabilities of AutoCAD's menu system. We did not intend to take you step by step through the writing of a menu because AutoCAD must be customized to fit your needs. If you have trouble writing menus, we recommend that you get a copy of *Customizing AutoCAD*, 2nd edition, by J. Smith and R. Gesner, published by New Riders Publishing. By doing some of the exercises in the book, you can learn by trial and error how to write menus. You really need to be able to write menus in order to manage projects and drawings properly. We do not think that anyone should operate AutoCAD with a stock, out-of-the-box menu system. We recommend that you customize someone else's menu system (even the original AutoCAD menu) instead of writing your own from scratch.

For More Information

CADENCE 1, no. 6 (December 1986): 13.
———2, no. 6 (June 1987): 23.
———2, no. 11 (November 1987): 23.
———3, no. 1 (January 1988): 21.
———3, no. 2 (February 1988): 17.

Recommended Accomplishments

- ❑ Coordinate a customized menu to your project and drawing standards.
- ❑ Learn to use menu macros.
- ❑ Set a reasonable scope for your system.
- ❑ Customize a menu system that suits your needs.

Optional Accomplishments

- ❑ Develop a task menu system.
- ❑ Develop keyboard macros.
- ❑ Create your own tablet menu templates.
- ❑ Write script and batch files to set up menu use.

What Chapter 10 Is About

In this chapter we present the basic concepts of several automation tools and give you some examples of what can be done. You don't have to learn dBASE III Plus right now, but you may want to when you see what it can do.

Helpful Things To Know Before You Start

- AutoCAD script file conventions
- A moderate amount of AutoLISP
- A moderate amount of geometry and trigonometry
- dBASE III Plus capabilities, in general
- Lotus 1-2-3 capabilities, in general

What To Have on Hand

- The *AutoCAD Reference Manual*

- The *AutoLISP Programmer's Reference*

- A good dBASE III Plus reference book. (We recommend Que's *dBASE III Plus Handbook*, 2nd edition.)

- A good Lotus 1-2-3 reference book. (We recommend Que's *Using 1-2-3*, Special Edition.)

- Word-processing software that can create and manipulate ACSII or nondocument text files

Look, Ma—No Hands!

Chapter 7, "Advanced Management Techniques," touched briefly on how to let your drawings work for you. Then, in Chapter 9, "The Tasks At Hand," we discussed how to combine multiple activities into a single menu selection by using macros with menus. You can automate repetitive tasks on an even larger scale by using AutoCAD script files, AutoLISP, and external programs such as Lotus 1-2-3 and dBASE. As we explained in Chapter 5, you can even automate an entire drawing. Enlisting the help of script files, AutoLISP, or an external program to achieve automation ensures uniformity in your work and saves time, two of CAD management's primary goals.

Management from the Coffee Room

Do you ever daydream, "If only AutoCAD could do this by itself, I could go home" or "Since AutoCAD has all of this macro capability, why can't it do this too?" Well, Chapter 4 gave you a glimpse of the possibilities. The automation of AutoCAD is one of its most wide open and least explored avenues of productivity. Computer equipment is best used if it works for you 24 hours a day, 7 days a week. When combined with some powerful, friendly software, AutoCAD can extend your computer's workday without putting bags under your eyes. Script files are one of the primary tools for automating AutoCAD—and they aren't hard to write.

Script Files

The AutoCAD reference manual includes a brief section on scripts. At first, that brevity led us to overlook the real capacity of scripts. Many programs use scripts, which are similar to batch files. A *script* is an ASCII file that contains a line-by-line set of instructions for AutoCAD to follow. Scripts can be loaded from inside or outside AutoCAD. The AutoCAD manual notes that scripts are good tools for running demonstration slide shows at trade shows. They do more important work for us.

Use your word processor in nondocument or ASCII mode to create a script file. To write a script file, you need to have complete knowledge of the command sequence for each AutoCAD command you include. Use blank spaces as returns or data field separators, the way AutoCAD does. Scripts differ from menu macros: using a script is *exactly* like typing at the AutoCAD command prompt; scripts use none of the special characters required by menu macros. When you name the file, use the extension *.SCR*.

To load a script file from within AutoCAD, enter the following at the AutoCAD command prompt:

Command: **SCRIPT** Script file <default>: <name>

where *name* is the file name (without the .SCR extension) of the script you want to run; you must provide this file name.

To load a script file from outside AutoCAD, enter the following at the DOS prompt:

ACAD <default drawing> <script file>

where *default drawing* is the name of the drawing on which you want to use the script file and *script file* is the name of the script file you want to use. (Note that file extensions are not used in this entry.)

Say, for example, that you like to use different drawing setups for different tasks. Assuming that you have configured AutoCAD to use a prototype drawing, you could create a set of script files that will insert a second drawing which will add any necessary blocks and layers for a unique task.

This scenario would be especially useful if you were using different menus for different tasks, as discussed in Chapter 9. To start the drawing session, you would enter the following command at the DOS prompt:

ACAD 005_ED1 PRELIM

This command would start a preliminary drawing for job 5, environmental development sheet 1. The script file for the task would look like this:

```
1
<blank line>
INSERT PRELIM 0,0 1 1 0
<blank line>
```

The first line of the script tells AutoCAD to create a new drawing. The effect of the second line, which is blank, is the same as pressing Enter; it tells AutoCAD to use the default file name *005_ED1* for the new drawing. This default name comes from your entry at the DOS prompt that loaded AutoCAD and the script file. The INSERT command in the script file uses spaces as returns between the information the script file is providing to AutoCAD. As you can see, the drawing PRELIM is being inserted at 0,0 with an x and y scale factor of 1 and a rotation angle of 0. The blank last line completes the INSERT command. The use of script files in this manner is a powerful tool that lets you define secondary configurations of your drawing environment. A simple example of the use of this technique is the use of one set of layers for a floor plan and a different set of layers for a site plan. Duplication of unnecessary layers would be eliminated by using different drawing insertions.

Script files are extremely flexible. With a good batch-file menu system, you can make the entire operation of script files transparent to the user. With a LISP routine, you can change the preliminary drawing to make it suitable for completion as a final drawing. A script file can even call LISP routines that write script files and then run the script from within Auto-CAD. By implementing these simple concepts, you may be able to establish an AutoCAD system in which the user encounters only menus to create certain drawings. In the following sections, we'll show you some examples of what can be done.

Automated Drawing Assembly and Plotting

In Chapter 7, we showed you a LISP routine that enables you to store plot information inside an AutoCAD drawing. That routine writes its own script file and then executes the script, which plots the drawing. When the script file finishes execution, it returns to the LISP file, which returns the AutoCAD command prompt to the screen. We can expand on this concept a little further, adding some interesting capabilities.

On more than one occasion we have advised AutoCAD users to separate a drawing into parts. A drawing can be so large that the time it takes for a REDRAW, much less a REGEN, is prohibitive. Such a drawing often doesn't fit on a 1.2M floppy disk. You can make this scheme even simpler by automating the assembly of the smaller drawings into the large drawing, and then plotting it. To do so, you combine blocks with attributes, a LISP routine, and a script file or two. Here's what you do.

First, create a script file called COMBPLOT.SCR:

```
2

(load "/acad/lisp/combplot")
COMBPLOT
(load "/acad/lisp/dplot")
DPLOT
QUIT Y
0
```

This script file loads a ghost drawing, which is just an electronic sheet that eventually will contain all parts of the drawing. At first, all it contains are some attributes that describe which drawings will be needed and where they will be located. Then the script file will load a LISP routine called COMBPLOT.LSP, which will find out where to insert each drawing. Finally, the script file executes DPLOT.LSP, our ol' faithful routine from Chapter 7.

Next, create the file COMBPLOT.LSP:

```
(defun c:combplot (/ ss1 e ent ent2 anm anm2 dnm ipt)
(setq ss1 (ssget "X" (list (cons 0 "INSERT")(cons 2 "INSBLK"))))
(if (not (equal ss1 nil))
 (progn
 (setq ndx 0)
 (repeat (sslength ss1)
  (setq e (ssname ss1 ndx))
  (setq ent (entnext e))
  (setq ent2 (entnext ent))
  (setq anm (cdr (assoc 2 (entget ent))))
  (setq anm2 (cdr (assoc 2 (entget ent2))))
   (if (equal anm "DNAME")(setq dnm (cdr (assoc 1 (entget ent))))
       (setq ipt (cdr (assoc 1 (entget ent)))))
```

```
     (if (equal anm2 "DNAME")(setq dnm (cdr (assoc 1 (entget ent2))))
         (setq ipt (cdr (assoc 1 (entget ent2))))))
   (command "insert" dnm ipt "" "" "")
   (setq ndx (1+ ndx)))
       (prompt "\nNo INSBLK's were found in this drawing...")
     )(princ))
```

This routine looks for all INSBLK blocks in the drawing, extracts from them the name of the drawing and its insertion point, and then automatically inserts all the drawings specified in the ghost, or master, drawing. (See Appendix H for a detailed discussion of COMBPLOT.LSP.)

To create the block INSBLK, do the following exercise within AutoCAD:

Prompt:	`Command:`
Response:	Type **ATTDEF** and press Enter.
Prompt:	`Attribute modes -- Invisible:N Constant:N Verify:N Preset:N` `Enter (ICVP) to change, RETURN when done:`
Response:	Type **I** and press Enter.
Prompt:	`Attribute modes -- Invisible:Y Constant:N Verify:N Preset:N`
Response:	Press Enter.
Prompt:	`Attribute tag:`
Response:	Type **DNAME** and press Enter.
Prompt:	`Attribute Prompt:`
Response:	Type **Enter the name of the drawing to be inserted:**
Prompt:	`Default Attribute Value:`
Response:	Press Enter.
Prompt:	`Start point or Align/Center/Fit/Middle/Right/Style:`
Response:	Pick a point on your screen.
Prompt:	`Command:`
Response:	Press Enter.
Prompt:	`Attribute modes -- Invisible:Y Constant:N Verify:N Preset:Y`
Response:	Press Enter.
Prompt:	`Attribute tag:`
Response:	Type **INSPT** and press Enter.
Prompt:	`Attribute Prompt:`
Response:	Type **Enter the coordinates of the drawing insertion point:**
Prompt:	`Default Attribute Value:`
Response:	Press Enter.

Prompt:	Start point or Align/Center/Fit/Middle/Right/Style:
Response:	Press Enter.
Prompt:	Command:
Response:	Type **WBLOCK**
Prompt:	File Name:
Response:	Type **INSBLK**
Prompt:	Block Name:
Response:	Press Enter.
Prompt:	Insertion Point:
Response:	Pick a point on your screen.
Prompt:	Select Objects:
Response:	Type **(Select the two attributes you just created)**
Prompt:	Select Objects:
Response:	Press Enter.

Place the block INSBLK in your symbols library directory or a drawing directory on your path.

Figure 10.1, an example of the way we use COMBPLOT.LSP, illustrates one scheme of a ghost drawing. When you create the ghost drawing, insert the block INSBLK of each drawing you want included in the final drawing. Insert also the block PLOTBLK from Chapter 7.

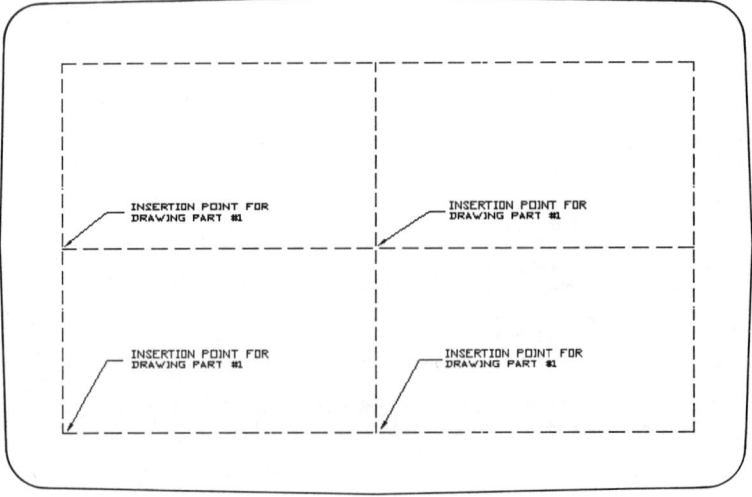

Fig. 10.1.

Using a sheet for COMBPLOT.LSP. Different overlays can all be inserted at 0,0, similar to pin registering.

You now have a set of tools that will assemble your drawing, plot it, and then quit the drawing without storing the assembled drawing as a whole. Before you use COMBPLOT.SCR, however, make sure that you have enough disk space available for the assembled drawing.

If you want to use the drawing database approach described in Chapter 7, you can insert the base drawing and each consultant's overlays into the ghost drawing, all at insertion point 0,0. This amounts to a CAD system of overlay drafting. This technique may be the most appropriate if you work with large drawings. It will save you a great deal of disk space by eliminating drawings that contain duplicate data. It's also a good idea to have your consultants provide you with drawings that contain only their design works; then you can use these drawings, together with a base drawing, for plotting.

Automated Drawing

Script files can be used to draw automatically all of the entities AutoCAD can draw. If you are not comfortable with LISP programming but have an automated drawing task, script files will provide you with a tool for automating the process. Suppose that you have a diagram which shows a standard widget configuration and that all you need to enter are a text description of the parts, a serial number for the main component, and a customer name. You can write a script file that creates a standard drawing and prompts the user for text input.

Take a look at figure 10.2, a drawing of our widget, with part numbers and a title block. This drawing won't exist until we run the WIDGET script. The script file sets the units and limits, and creates the layers we want to use in the drawing. Then it draws the lines, circles, and arcs on the different layers (as required for line weight) and inserts the appropriate text in the proper locations. Finally, it uses some simple LISP prompts and `getstrings` to place the part numbers, date, and customer name where they belong.

A draftsperson would look at this and say, "Why not use a block with attributes?" If you want a nontechnical salesperson to create the widget drawing, using a script file will enable you to expand this concept by using dBASE III Plus. The salesperson simply enters the part numbers, date, and customer name at a screen menu; dBASE III Plus can append the script file with the proper responses and call AutoCAD to create the drawing. We will get to that type of use of dBASE III Plus a little later in this chapter. If you want to see the WIDGET script, you'll find it in Appendix H, "Routines for Automated Drawing."

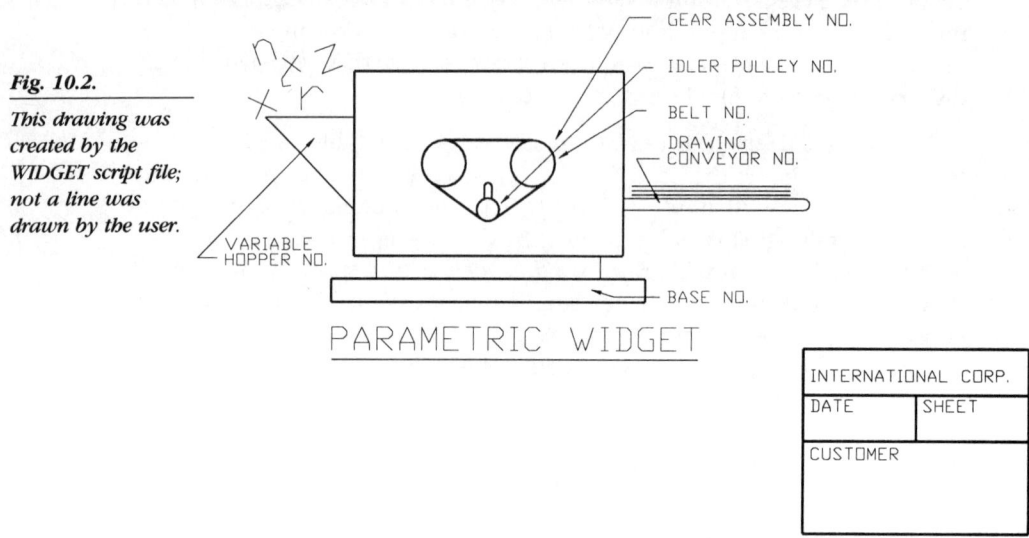

Fig. 10.2.
This drawing was created by the WIDGET script file; not a line was drawn by the user.

Shapes versus Blocks

We discussed the advantages of shapes and blocks in Chapter 9. The use of shapes and blocks affects automated drawing also. The speed of shapes in automated drawing and the simple data structure they have within drawing files makes them very appealing alternatives to blocks. Blocks, on the other hand, provide data you can use for many other purposes we talk about. You must decide which method to use.

Complex shapes are difficult to create in text form. There is a program called AutoShapes that will create shape files from a drawing. Although we haven't used the program, it purports to accomplish the task equal to creating the shape "by hand." If you are automating a drawing with many objects of the same definition, you definitely should consider using shapes. You can get a program that will take site information, for example, and create an AutoCAD drawing with the data from the field. If there are many different types of trees on a site, you can accelerate creation speed and reduce the size of the site drawing by using shapes as the tree symbols. We don't think that simple shapes such as trees are beyond practical application even if the shape file is hand written.

If you use blocks in automated drawings, your use of file-naming conventions is very important. When you are writing LISP routines and script files, the location of any particular block must be predictable. The blocks you use must be part of your standard library or in the job subdirectory. If you don't use your drawing name and directory conventions, the results of your automated process will be unpredictable. When you create automated drawing processes, you will quickly discover the gaps in predictability of your standards.

The Basics—Parametrically Speaking

As we mentioned in Chapter 9, parametrics mean using parameters to create a drawing from a standard geometric description of the drawing. A parameter supplied from an outside source tells AutoCAD what adjustments it needs to make in the drawing it will create. In many ways, script files are similar to a parametric routine. The difference is that the parameter you choose selects which script file to execute, and a parametric routine has the ability to adapt internally to outside input. AutoLISP is the main arena for the performance of parametrics in AutoCAD.

Parametrics, one of the main ingredients of automated drawing, use techniques familiar to designers and draftspeople with a background in geometry and trigonometry; they also require the use of many AutoCAD entities, such as lines, arcs, and circles. Although we will discuss the required AutoLISP commands in detail in Chapters 13 and 14, we present here the concepts that make up parametric routines while automating drawings as examples.

Orientation, Angles, Radians, Polar Functions

When you learned to use AutoCAD, you encountered many new concepts about axes, orientation, cartesian coordinates, planes, angles, and general geometric construction because drawing by hand gives an approximation and a graphic image of what will be produced, whereas AutoCAD draws precisely. A side effect of this precision is that you can extract from or input to your drawings extremely predictable elements of the design. Parametrics rely heavily on AutoCAD's accuracy and specific requirements. Parametrics consist of the following ingredients:

- Mathematical formulas
- Reference points and reference angles

- AutoCAD drawing and editing commands
- A little geometry and trigonometry
- User-supplied input

What is simple to do in the AutoCAD Drawing Editor is more complex when you use AutoLISP. Mathematical formulas are used in parametrics to calculate the location of various points in the drawing, based on the coordinates used by AutoCAD; all points are set in x, y, and z coordinates. This creates some tricky situations. Suppose, for example, that you want to add 4 inches to a line that has an endpoint with the coordinates 6.0,5.0,0.0. You have to be able to add a simple number like 4 to the complex set of numbers 6.0,5.0,0.0 that AutoCAD stores as a point location. What really has to happen is that you add 4 units in the direction of a specified angle.

Mathematical formulas typically create numbers called reals. AutoLISP is always concerned about the type of data it is receiving. Typically, the results of your AutoLISP machinations will be a real, an integer, or a string. A *real* is a number that has precision (a decimal point followed by a certain number of decimal places). An *integer* is a number (like 4) that will be evaluated as a mathematical quantity. A *string* is a fixed set of characters that have only a literal value. Although strings can include numbers, letters, and symbols, they are known to AutoLISP strictly as a set of characters. When executing mathematical formulas, you have to be sure which of these quantities you are dealing with.

You use a reference point in parametrics just as you do in AutoCAD. A parametric routine uses this reference point to calculate distances from and to a new location, to rotate objects about, or as a point at which to place objects in the drawing. Reference points can be entered by the user, from a database, or as a fixed point that never changes, such as the center of the current view. Almost everything you do in parametrics will use a reference point.

A reference angle is the angle at which you want to create or move objects from a reference point. It can be obtained from user input or by the angle of existing objects in the drawing. Angles in AutoLISP are expressed in radians for purposes of calculating positions and new coordinates. Radians are expressed as portions of the value of π. Two radians equal 360 degrees around a circle; therefore, 360 degrees equals 2 times 3.14159, or 6.28318 π radians.

All AutoCAD drawing and editing commands are at your disposal in AutoLISP. Getting used to writing the command and your response without the opportunity to read the command prompts from AutoCAD just takes practice. (We found ourselves omitting the extra return after the LAYER command, for example.) To execute various drawing commands, create them in AutoLISP as if you didn't have a pointing device and you had to type in all the required information. The exception to this rule is that you can act on or draw to an existing entity provided that you have bound that entity to a variable. For example, if you have the user select an entity and you use the AutoLISP command SETQ to bind that entity to the variable *e*, you could use the AutoLISP command (command "erase" e "") to erase that object. You could also draw to its endpoint, and so on.

To use parametrics, you need to know a little trigonometry in addition to the geometric functions that you already know from using AutoCAD (perpendicular, tangent, quadrant, etc.). AutoLISP has built-in trignometric functions. Understanding the sine, cosine, and tangent functions will help you complete some of the more complex tasks.

Parametrics include user input. In fact, most of the parameters for the execution of the routine come from the user. AutoLISP provides several functions for gaining or reading input. In addition, you can create a data file that automatically provides the parameters to AutoLISP. This data file can be used in specialized instances when the only choice to be made is simple—selecting which part number or model number has to be drawn, for example. Additional parameters corresponding to the selected part can be retrieved from the data file, if they don't change at any time.

Now we want you to draw parametrically. The following routine (SCHED.LSP) draws a schedule in which the user can select the number of rows and columns and the row and column spacings:

```
(defun sched (/ row rsp col pt scf row1 bor1 csp tp2 pt3 pt4
              pt5 pt6 pt7 pt8 nu)
 (setq row
    (getint "\nEnter the number of rows that you want: "))
 (setq rsp
    (getdist "\Enter the spacing between the rows in inches: "))
 (setq col
    (getint "\nEnter the number of columns that you want: "))
 (setq pt
   (getpoint "\nSelect the upper
     left corner of the schedule location: "))
 (setq scf (getvar "ltscale"))
 (setq rsp (* scf rsp))
 (setq row1 (* rsp row))
 (setq bor1 (+ row1 (* scf 0.5)))
 (setq pt2 (polar pt (* 1.5 pi) row1))
 (command "line" pt pt2 "")
```

Listing continues

Listing *continued*

```
(setq nu (- col (1- col)))
(repeat col
(prompt "Enter the spacing for column ")
   (princ nu)(prompt " in inches: ")
(setq csp (* scf (getdist)))
(setq pt2 (polar pt2 (* 2.0 pi) csp))
(setq pt3 (polar pt2 (* 0.5 pi) row1))
(command "line" pt2 pt3 "")
(setq nu (1+ nu)))
(setq pt4 (polar pt (* 1.5 pi) row1))
(command "line" pt pt3 "")
(command "array" "l" "" "r" (1+ row) "1" (- rsp))
(setq pt5 (polar pt (* 0.5 pi) (* scf 0.0625)))
(setq pt6 (polar pt (* 0.5 pi) (- borl row1)))
(setq pt7 (polar pt3 (* 0.5 pi) (* scf 0.0625)))
(setq pt8 (polar pt3 (* 0.5 pi) (- borl row1)))
(command "line" pt5 pt6 pt8 pt7 pt5 "")
(setq pt4 (polar pt4 (* 1.25 pi) (* scf  0.0625)))
(setq pt (polar pt4 (* 0.5 pi) (+ borl (* scf 0.125))))
(setq pt2 (polar pt2 (* 1.75 pi) (* scf 0.0625)))
(setq pt3 (polar pt2 (* 0.5 pi) (+ borl (* scf 0.125))))
(command "line" pt pt4 pt2 pt3 pt "")
(princ))
```

See Appendix H for a line-by-line explanation of SCHED.LSP. This routine contains many redundancies and can be made to run faster; we present it in this form for clarity. Even if you don't use schedules of information in your work, try this routine so that you can see the potential for parametrics. Figure 10.3 shows what you should end up with.

For More Information

CADENCE, January 1989, 54-56, 57-61, 66-70, 75-90.

Gesner, R., and Smith, J. *Inside AutoLISP, Release 10*. New Riders Publishing, 1989.

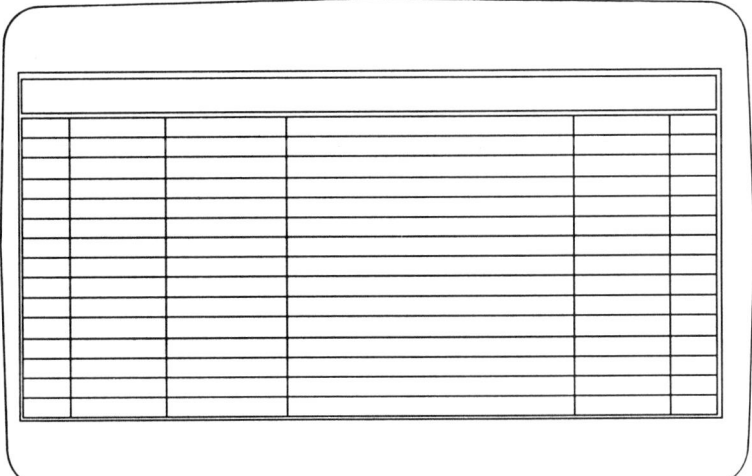

Fig. 10.3.
A schedule box created by SCHED.LSP.

Are dBASE and Lotus 1-2-3 CAD Programs?

For AutoCAD to be a truly powerful tool, it should have a spreadsheet and a database manager bundled with it. It doesn't. Nevertheless, AutoCAD can communicate very well with Lotus 1-2-3 and dBASE—two of the most popular programs available. Most people think that AutoCAD, as a drafting package, has about all the muscle it needs. As a management package, however, AutoCAD leaves a lot to be desired. As we explained in Chapter 7, you can use dBASE to help manage your projects and drawings (and just about anything else on the computer). We have discussed all sorts of options for project and drawing-file management. And we have looked at ways to make AutoCAD drawings manage themselves. What could possibly be left, you ask? What's left is data management.

Each AutoCAD drawing contains a wealth of information. That information can be used to create new drawings, to make changes to an existing drawing without using the Drawing Editor per se, to provide quantity take offs, to locate and track personnel and equipment in a large company or plant, or to create schedules of doors, windows, and plumbing or electrical fixtures. Creating schedules and putting together specifications are two ugly jobs that someone in our office has to do. If you have to do them too, why not let dBASE handle them accurately and automatically? If you want to maintain an organizational chart or a project schedule, you can use Lotus 1-2-3 to maneuver the data and AutoCAD to draw it.

Most AutoCAD users do not want to become AutoCAD, AutoLISP, dBASE, and Lotus 1-2-3 experts all at the same time. Thanks to the wide availability of commercial and public domain software written to complement Auto-CAD, you may not need to become expert at any of them. It is important, however, that you understand their capabilities (both as separate programs and when used together). This knowledge will help you evaluate a third-party package or determine whether you need to do some customization. A good rule of thumb in making decisions is that any task you want to automate with a combination of dBASE, Lotus, AutoLISP, and AutoCAD should be repetitive, important, and done often.

Importing and Exporting Data

AutoCAD can export information in a variety of ways (see table 10.1). We find the SDF and CDF formats the easiest and most useful for our purposes.

Table 10.1. Formats for Exporting Data

Format	Meaning
CDF	Delimited Format; consists of a series of data fields separated (delimited) by commas
SDF	Space Delimited Format; consists of a series of data fields separated by spaces
DXF	Drawing Interchange Format; uses ASCII characters to list all the drawing-data information AutoLISP needs in order to manipulate drawings
IGES	International Graphic Exchange Standard; used primarily to trade files between AutoCAD and other graphics and drawing programs
DXB	Drawing Interchange Binary; uses AutoCAD's ADI plotter option. (Release 10 has also added a binary option to the DXF output file.)

We normally need files with an ASCII format, which provides text we can read. Binary files, which are smaller and therefore faster in transfer speed than ASCII files, can be used by sophisticated programs. The extent of their decimal-place output makes binary files more accurate than ASCII files in their representation of the AutoCAD drawing.

You can extract an entire drawing file from AutoCAD in DXF or DXB format; attributes can be extracted in CDF, SDF, and DXF file format.

AutoCAD can import DXB, DXF, and (using AutoLISP) ASCII files. Lotus and dBASE can import and export SDF and CDF files, which are special forms of an ASCII file, as well as ASCII files. With all of the options available, programmers can choose what best fills their needs.

We primarily use the DXF, CDF, and SDF formats because they are ASCII files. We will provide you with the highlights of these types of files so that you know what kind of data is available in each. Before looking at different interchange formats, however, you need to understand data files.

A data file contains records, fields, and delimiters. A *delimiter* is a symbol that separates a data file into logical groups of information. Common delimiters are periods, commas, spaces, and returns. Some database managers use combinations of delimiters. A *field* is a collection of data between delimiters; fields can be mathematical or alphabetical. A data *record* is a complete group of associated fields. An example of a simple data record is one address in your address book; each part of the address (name, street, town, state, ZIP code, and telephone number) is a data field. In a data file, these fields might be separated by commas, the data delimiters.

Attributes extracted from a drawing might look like this in CDF format:

```
P-1,LAVATORY,AM-STD,64.8006,WHITE,,
P-2,LAVATORY,AM-STD,64.8006,WHITE,,
P-3,TOILET,AM-STD,60.4008,WHITE,HDCP,
P-4,TOILET,AM-STD,60.4002,WHITE,,
```

or like this in SDF format:

```
P-1    LAVATORY    AM-STD    64.8006    WHITE
P-2    LAVATORY    AM-STD    64.8006    WHITE
P-3    TOILET      AM-STD    60.4008    WHITE    HDCP
P-4    TOILET      AM-STD    60.4002    WHITE
```

In DXF format, attributes might look like this:

```
0
INSERT
  8
FMSPEC
 66
     1
  2
AU017T1
 10
152.307799
 20
190.786369
 41
12.0
 42
12.0
 43
12.0
  0
ATTRIB
  8
0
  1
-
  2
FCOST
 70
     1
  0
EOF
```

Clearly, the DXF output is a little more complex. It is essentially what you would see if you looked at the data with AutoLISP. This listing provides, among other things, the layer the attribute is on, the text height, the insertion-point x and y coordinates, the attribute tag, and the attribute's value. We discuss this in this chapter's "Revealing the Hidden Power of Attributes" section.

Drawings, Schedules, and Charts

If you have a dot-matrix printer and a pen plotter, the best graphic image comes from the pen plotter, right? If you are creating management charts, project schedules, or critical path charts on dBASE or Lotus 1-2-3 and want the graphic output to look a little better, why not use AutoCAD to create the drawing? Both dBASE and Lotus 1-2-3 can output SDF and CDF files. You can create a parametric LISP routine that reads the file output from your database manager and parametrically creates a drawing. By editing the drawing after the basic graphic information is included by LISP, you can create a graphic presentation far beyond the capabilities of dBASE or Lotus

1-2-3. (See Appendix H for a routine that creates a critical-path chart from a Lotus 1-2-3 file; you can adjust the routine for your own use and for project management.)

There probably are numerous other opportunities for using dBASE and Lotus 1-2-3 with AutoCAD that we haven't even considered. We are interested primarily in using the programs together for management. Because we are graphics-oriented, we don't tend to think in terms of database management. That is why we have shown you how to create schedules and charts from data created outside of AutoCAD by other programs, with a graphic representation of the data as the final goal.

Another kind of program that uses externally generated data in the creation of an AutoCAD drawing is called a *parametric engine*. From data provided by the user, parametric engines create drawings that test, modify, and draw standard configurations of a design. These programs primarily use AutoCAD's DXF and DXB formats. Some of these programs take field data and generate a database that creates a drawing for AutoCAD. Using them, we can survey a site or building, record the information in a field computer, and produce a graphic image of the existing conditions. These programs eliminate the tedious process of converting the field data into a drawing. You will find examples of this type of program in Appendix K.

Although having all those bells and whistles would be nice, we have to stick with what we can do for ourselves. From AutoCAD's point of view, the primary tool for item-by-item data extraction and data management is an ATTRIBUTE.

Revealing the Hidden Power of Attributes

In Chapter 7, we used some attributes with AutoLISP. But unless you were entering the LISP commands one at a time, you couldn't see how an attribute is listed in the AutoCAD database. What would you find if you looked at the PLOTBLK block in an AutoCAD drawing? To find out, retrieve the block data from the database by entering at the command prompt the following:

```
(setq ss1 (ssget "x" (list (cons 0 "INSERT")
   (cons 2 "PLOTBLK"))))
```

When AutoLISP returns <Selection Set: 1>, type this:

(setq e (ssname ss1 0))

AutoLISP returns <Entity Name: 60000014>, or something similar. Next, you type:

(entget e)

and AutoLISP returns something like this:

```
((-1 . <Entity Name: 60000014>) (0 . "INSERT") (8 . "0")
(66 . 1) (2 . "PLOTBLK") (10 . 805.668900 376.237200)
(41 . 1.0000) (42 . 1.000000) (50 . 0.000000) (43 . 1.000000)
(70 . 0) (71 . 0)(44 . 0.000000) (45 . 0.000000))
```

Now type:

(setq e (entnext e))

AutoLISP returns <Entity Name: 60000028>.

Type **(entget e)**. AutoLISP returns:

```
((-1 . <Entity Name: 60000028>) (0 . "ATTRIB") (8 . "0")
(10 . 850.157100 376.936900) (40 . 0.200000) (1 . "") (2 . "LLC")
(70 . 9) (73 . 0) (50 . 0.000000) (41 . 1.000000) (51 . 0.000000)
(7 . "HL") (71 . 0) (72 . 0) (11 0.000000 0.000000))
```

What does all of this mean? We will explain a little about the output from AutoLISP in this chapter. If you need an explanation of the LISP statements, see the detailed description of DPLOT.LSP in Appendix E.

What you see first in each AutoLISP response is an entity name, which AutoCAD uses to keep track of the drawing data in the database; this is not a permanent name, but a location in the database. The next output is a list (prepared by AutoLISP) of the information contained in this data record; enclosed within each pair of parentheses is a *dotted pair*—a special data type used by AutoCAD. Each *dotted pair* consists of a *group code* and a value. The group codes shown in the preceding interchange are listed in table 10.2. Additional group codes are created when they are required for a more specialized attribute creation. A complete listing of group codes for all entities can be found in Appendix C of the *AutoCAD Reference Manual*.

Table 10.2. Attribute and Block Group Codes

Code	Indicates
−1	Entity name (record number)
0	Entity type ("INSERT" for block; "ATTRIB" for attribute)
8	Layer
66	Attributes follow flag
2	Block name or attribute tag
10	Origin or insertion point
41	X scale factor or attribute text width factor
42	Y scale factor
50	Rotation angle
43	Z scale factor
70	Column count for minsert
71	Row count for minsert
44	Column spacing for minsert
45	Row spacing for minsert
1	Attribute value
70	Attribute flag
73	Field length
51	Attribute text obliquing angle
7	Attribute text style
71	Text generation flag
11	Centered insertion X Y coordinate

The data list for a block with many attributes would be much longer than the example for the PLOTBLK block, and each attribute would have a group code set accompanying its definition list. For purposes of attribute extraction, we are most interested in the Block Name or Attribute Tag (group code 2) and the Attribute Value (group code 1). These two codes are some of the group codes AutoCAD extracts when you use the AutoCAD command ATTEXT. AutoCAD needs to know the name, size, and type of the data field you are going to extract.

You give AutoCAD this information by creating a template file in which each line contains information about one field of the data you want extracted. You can obtain all of the listed group code information for a BLOCK or ATTRIBUTE using DXFOUT, but for ATTRIBUTES, only their "tag" and "value" may be extracted using ATTEXT. The field-extraction instructions in the template file give AutoCAD the name of the field, its width in characters, and its numerical precision, if applicable. The order in which fields are written to the file does not have to match the order in which you created the attributes in the block. Be sure to avoid including fields or attribute tags that do not exist. A template file looks like this:

```
BL:NAME      C008000
MARK         C00600
MODEL_NO     C010000
VENDOR       C025000
DESC         C025000
REMARKS      C025000
COST         N010002
```

This template file tells AutoCAD to extract all of the blocks with the attributes MARK, MODEL_NO, VENDOR, DESC, REMARKS, and COST. If you create in your drawing several different objects with the same attribute tag names but different block names, you will get a listing of all of those blocks in the drawing. If you don't want this to happen, be sure either to give different names to all your attributes or place the blocks on different layers for each type of object so that you can sort them by layer.

The codes to the right of the attributes and the block name in the template file consist of the following:

1. A field type identifier that tells AutoCAD to write the field as a number (N) or a string of characters (C)

2. Three digits that tell AutoCAD what size to make each field (008 means that the field is to be 8 characters long)

3. Three digits that tell AutoCAD how many decimal places the field will have

In the sample template file, the only numeric field is COST. It has a decimal flag of two decimal places so that (using dBASE or Lotus 1-2-3) we can readily sum the cost of all of the fixtures in the drawing.

Taking an Inventory of Your Drawing

If you create a block that contains the information listed in the sample template file, you can insert that block into your drawing for all types of fixtures or equipment. When you execute the AutoCAD command ATTEXT, you have to tell AutoCAD whether you want a space-delimited file (SDF), a comma-delimited file (CDF), or a drawing-interchange file (DIF). You also have to tell AutoCAD which template file to use for the extraction. You could call the template file FIXTURE.TXT. Appendix F includes a sample dBASE III Plus program that will list this information to a printer, as well as a sample dBASE III Plus program and LISP routine that will import a list of fixtures into your drawing. If you combine this with the parametric LISP routine presented earlier in this chapter, you have an automatic schedule generator. If you don't want to learn dBASE III Plus, we recommend that you find another AutoCAD user who does use dBASE III Plus and that you make data management a joint effort.

Note: We have excluded the COST field for the dBASE program. If you want to use the program "as is" in the appendix, do not include this attribute in your template file or the block.

For More Information

Jones, F. and Martin, L. *The AutoCAD Database Book*. Ventana Press, 1987.

Summary

This chapter was for those of us who don't like to work. We have introduced concepts that should make you want to learn AutoLISP and dBASE or Lotus 1-2-3 so that you can relax and watch AutoCAD do your work for you. Remember that any repetitive task can be automated. Menu macros provide some automation, but the ultimate in automation is hands-free production.

You learned that the most basic parametric tool is a script file. We also discussed the primary AutoLISP tools that allow parametric automation of drawings through LISP routines. Finally, we described how to manage drawing data with database managers such as dBASE and Lotus 1-2-3. Even if you don't intend to do all of these things yourself, a basic understanding of the concepts will make you more effective and informed when it comes to drawing-file and project management. We recommend that you use the automation tools described in this chapter, even if you don't develop them yourself.

Recommended Accomplishments

- ❏ Try at least one script-file automation.
- ❏ Try at least one parametric LISP routine.

Optional Accomplishments

- ❏ Create a project critical path in Lotus 1-2-3.
- ❏ Do an inventory of your drawing in dBASE III Plus.
- ❏ Create an automated fixture schedule.

What Chapter 11 Is About

In our profession, one complaint we hear is that AutoCAD doesn't provide the character and graphic appeal of hand-drawn techniques. We have developed several customization techniques for our AutoCAD setup; our macros have vastly improved the appearance of our drawings, compared to those produced with out-of-the-box AutoCAD. Detailing a drawing in AutoCAD takes longer than it does by hand unless the process is at least partially automated. The real trick for us was to keep everyone from spending hours of drafting time making drawings pretty. In this chapter, items that affect the appearance of a drawing are grouped as follows:

- Line weight and type
- Text appearance and style
- Hatch patterns
- Rendering
- Drawing techniques, symbols, and drafting standards

What You Should Know Before You Start

- What your symbols and drafting standards are
- Some AutoLISP
- AutoCAD's SNAP, HATCH, LINETYPE, TEXT, and PLINE commands (a complete overview)

What To Have on Hand

- The *AutoCAD Reference Manual*
- The *AutoLISP Programmer's Reference*
- Word-processing software that can create and manipulate ASCII or nondocument text files
- A magnified photocopy of your favorite hand-drafted lettering style, with the letters about one inch high

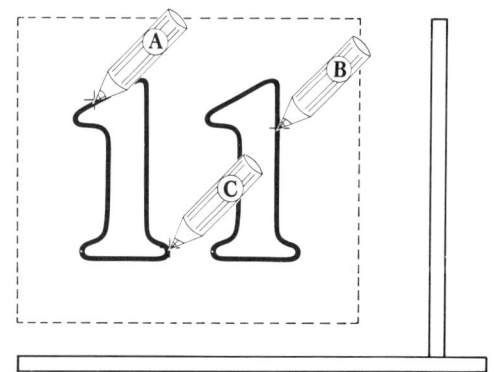

The Professional Look

You can use AutoCAD to produce practically anything you can do by hand. You can use a PLINE extended through random vertices with a spline curve to create the appearance of freehand lines. If you want to whip or snap the intersections of outside corners, you can write a LISP routine to do it. Create blocks that use SKETCH to represent people and plants with a hand-drawn appearance. If you don't like the memory consumption of freehand drawings, use a *shape* to put them in the drawing. The possibilities are limited only by your imagination, computer memory, and drawing/plotting time.

We don't intend to make AutoCAD invisible. We like the fact that people recognize our drawings as CAD-generated. We also like being asked how we achieve the quality of appearance of our drawings. This chapter provides techniques that will help you achieve a custom appearance in your drawings; it reviews all the concepts involved so that you can evaluate what degree of customization you want to undertake or purchase.

Lines

When you were drawing by hand, line types and weights eventually became an automatic function of your well-trained hand. Similarly, you have to train your AutoCAD system to use the proper line weight and linetype. To control linetypes in AutoCAD, you must make sure that your setup routine sets the appropriate scale to the variable LTSCALE. This factor is similar to the drawing-scale requirements discussed in Chapter 6 (for example, 1/4″ =1′ would require a LTSCALE setting of 48).

Line Weight Standards

We mentioned in Chapter 6, "Project and Drawing Management," that your drawing standards should include line weights. We also pointed out that the best way to control line weights is through the color of the line and a menu macro that sets the layer and/or color before drawing the line, circle, arc, etc. You can also use polylines if you don't have the luxury of a pen plotter.

There is no good way to guarantee that your menu system will not be circumvented by a fast typist. You could redefine all your ARC, CIRCLE, LINE, POLYGON, ELLIPSE, and PLINE commands so that layers or colors would be preset, but this is far more confusing than instructing users to limit keyboard entry to editing commands only. You can, however, add to your ACAD.LSP file some commands that will help.

For color, add this routine to your ACAD.LSP file:

```
(defun c:lhvy () (progn (command "color" "7")
   (command "line" pause)(princ)))
```

When you enter **LHVY** at the AutoCAD command prompt, the color will be changed to color 7, and a line will be started. You can create routines like this for medium heavy, medium, fine, and extra fine, etc. You can do this also for arcs (defun c:ahvy), circles (chvy), etc. The only drawback to this scheme is that the color remains set by the last command you use. This may conflict with your menu macros, causing unexpected results. You would have to set COLOR BYLAYER with any affected macros to be sure that you have control of the situation. Less harmful and almost as effective is this routine:

```
(defun c:lhvy () (progn (command "layer" "s" "heavy" ""
   "")(command "line" pause)(princ)))
```

where the layer name *heavy* should be changed to reflect your drawing standards. This routine draws a line on the layer *heavy*.

If you need to use polylines, try this routine:

```
(defun c:lhvy (/ wf) (progn (setq wf (getvar "ltscale"))
(command "pline" pause "w" (/ wf 48)
   (/ wf 48) pause))(princ)))
```

In this routine, we used a line width of 1/48-inch as a heavy line. This is the equivalent of a line 1-inch wide at the scale of 1/4″ =1′.

You can, of course, combine the LAYER and the COLOR settings in each routine.

How Linetypes Work

Linetypes are easy to set up for your own requirements. The following factors apply to linetype design:

- The LTSCALE setting of your drawing
- The linetype definition, pen action, and dash spacing
- The linetype alignment
- The PLOT scale versus the LTSCALE setting

AutoCAD linetypes are limited to dots and dashes of varying lengths. Linetypes are stored in a file with a .LIN file extension. (The file that comes with ACAD is called ACAD.LIN.) If you LOAD a linetype from a file into the Drawing Editor, it uses the setting of the variable LTSCALE to determine the spacing of the linetypes. By *spacing*, we mean the distance between the dashes and dots. The original spacing is set in the linetype file. It is set in terms of drawing units. In other words, if the spacing is set to 1 in the linetype file, and you load the linetype into a drawing with an LTSCALE setting of 48, the spacing between the dashes or dots will be 48 inches, which is 1 inch in real size in a 1/4″ =1′ drawing.

A linetype definition includes a linetype name, an optional description, an alignment code, a dash-length specification, and a pen-up/pen-down specification. Dash lengths are specified as positive numbers, a length specification of 0 is a dot, and pen-up specifications are specified as negative numbers.

Figure 11.1 shows the relationship between the appearance of the linetype and the linetype definition. The complete entry in the ACAD.LIN file would look like this:

```
*3EACH, - - -... - - -
A,.5,-.25,.5,-.25,.5,-.25,0,-.25,0,-.25,0,-.25
```

The name of the linetype is *3EACH*. To make an explanatory comment, place a comma after the linetype name and then include the definition. Our example uses a quasi-graphic image of the linetype as the description. The combined length of the linetype name and comment cannot be more than 47 characters long. The second line includes an alignment factor (A) and

Fig. 11.1.

Example of a linetype and its definition.

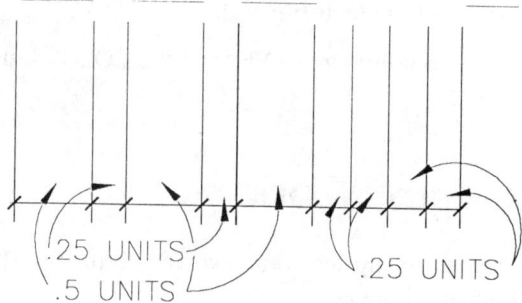

the dash, dot, and spacing sizes, separated by commas. Our example begins with a dash .5 drawing units long, separated by a pen-up space of .25 drawing units. This is followed by 2 more dashes and spaces of the same size. Next follows a series of 3 dots (0) each separated by a pen-up space of .25 drawing units. Notice that the pattern is repetitious and therefore has to end with a pen-up space. The linetype definition cannot contain more than 12 dash-length specifications and cannot be longer than one 80-character line.

AutoCAD apparently was designed to include in its linetype definition a capability to have different alignments established. Currently, the only type of alignment available is A alignment, which has to be included with every linetype definition. Figure 11.2 indicates the effect of this alignment on linetype 3EACH; the illustration is from a drawing with an LTSCALE of 48. Because the A alignment ensures that all lines start and end with at least half of the first dash definition, all linetypes must begin with a value of 0 or greater. Clearly, we have a problem with our sample linetype when the length of the line is less than 144 inches (the total of all the line types and spaces, multiplied by 48).

We don't believe that there is a universal scale factor you can apply to all linetypes and end up with a working solution without having to create an unwieldy list of lines. We expect our lines to have a graphic appearance that is not tied directly to the drawing scale. For example, a spacing of .5 units in a 1/4″ =1′ drawing is 24 inches and 1/2-inch in real size. The same spacing in a 1/8-inch scale drawing is 48 inches and 1/2-inch in real size. The appearance of a 48-inch line in a 1/8-inch scale drawing does not have

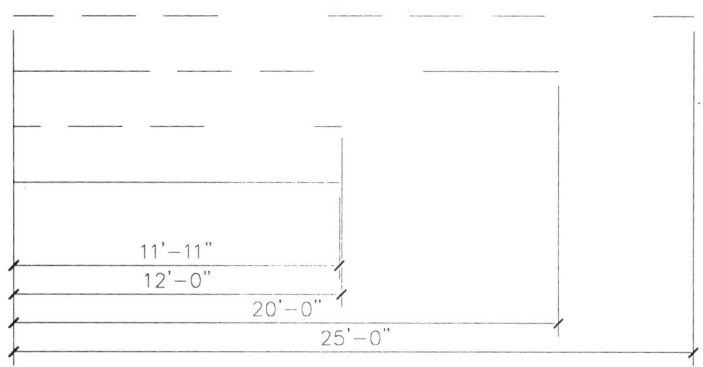

Fig. 11.2.
The effect of "A" alignment on linetype 3EACH.

the same graphic relationship to the drawing as a 24-inch line in a 1/4-inch scale drawing. We want our lines to be similar in *graphic* relationship.

If all our drawings were prepared at 1/4-inch and then plotted at 1/8-inch, the graphic relationship between lines would not be a problem, but the text would be half the proper size. The simplest solution we have found is to create a .LIN file for each typical drawing scale and define (or redefine) all linetypes in a drawing by using AutoCAD's LINETYPE command as follows:

Prompt:	`Command:`
Response:	Type **LINETYPE** and press Enter.
Prompt:	`?/Create/Load/Set:`
Response:	Type **LOAD** and press Enter.
Prompt:	`Linetype(s) to load:`
Response:	Type * and press Enter.
Prompt:	`File to search <default>:`
Response:	Type **48**
Prompt:	`Linetype (name) is already loaded. Reload it? <Y>:`
Response:	Answer **Y** to any duplicate linetypes.

This routine loads the file 48.LIN (which contains the linetype definitions for your drawing) with an LTSCALE of 48. It also redefines any linetypes that existed in the drawing. If you intend to change the scale of the drawings in which you use this technique, you should not retain the same line definitions. To create your own linetypes, all you need is your text editor (word processor) in nondocument mode. (You can do this from within AutoCAD, but we find it cumbersome.)

Modifying and Improving Linetypes

The standard ACAD.LIN file contains the following lines:

```
*DASHED,__ __ __ __ __ __ __ __ __ __ __ __ __ __ __
A,.5,-.25
*HIDDEN,_ _ _ _ _ _ _ _ _ _ _ _ _ _ _ _ _ _ _ _ _
A,.25,-.125
*CENTER,____ _ ____ _ ____ _ ____ _ ____ _ ____ _ ___ _
A,1.25,-.25,.25,-.25
*PHANTOM,_____ _ _ _____ _ _ _____ _ _ _____ _ _ _____
A,1.25,-.25,.25,-.25,.25,-.25
*DOT,.............................................
A,Ø,-.25
*DASHDOT,__ . __ . __ . __ . __ . __ . __ . __ . __ . _
A,.5,-.25,Ø,-.25
*BORDER,__ __ . __ __ . __ __ . __ __ . __ __ . __ __
A,.5,-.25,.5,-.25,Ø,-.25
*DIVIDE,__ . . __ . . __ . . __ . . __ . . __
A,.5,-.25,Ø,-.25,Ø,-.25
```

If we assume an LTSCALE setting of 48, the longest line segment in the ACAD.LIN file is 60 units—or, in a 1/4-inch scale drawing, a real length of 1 1/4 inches. The shortest line segment is 1/8-inch in real length (6 units). These linetypes with an LTSCALE of 48 will work fine for our purposes, but we need to add a few longer versions of these lines. To do that, take the standard ACAD.LIN file, leave the spaces the same, and increase the length of the dashes. This is what we added to the file:

```
*GRID,_____ _ _____
A,2.5,-.25,.25,-.25
*PROPERTY,_____ . _____
A,4,-.25,Ø,-.25
```

As you can see, modifying the existing file in order to add linetypes you may need is fairly easy. Furthermore, you can review each of these linetypes and include redefinitions in other files for different LTSCALE settings.

If you have a word processor that you can run from within AutoCAD, you can create and experiment with .LIN files this way:

1. Copy your ACAD.LIN file to a file called TEST.LIN.

2. Start a new drawing and select the drawing scale that will provide the LTSCALE setting you want.

3. If there is a linetype that is similar to what you want in the TEST.LIN file, draw one line with it.

4. Shell out to your word processor and open the file TEST.LIN, using the command that you placed in your ACAD.PGP file (discussed in Chapter 5).

5. Write a line with a linetype name you can remember easily, and (by looking at the existing linetypes) create the definition line with your best estimate of the spacing you want.

6. Save the file, exit the word processor, and load the linetype from the TEST.LIN file.

7. Create a line of sufficient length to repeat the pattern a few times. If you don't like what you see, shell out to your word processor again and create another linetype with the same name (followed by the number *1*). Try the procedure again—load the new linetype and draw a line. Repeat the process until you think you have what you need. Then try the final linetype definition with lines of varying lengths.

If you don't have a word processor that you can run from within AutoCAD, and you can't use DOS's EDLIN, create and experiment with .LIN files this way:

1. Copy your ACAD.LIN file to a file called TEST.LIN.

2. Create several trial linetype definitions in the TEST.LIN file. Do your best to cover the possibilities, estimating the spacing you need. The more linetypes you create, the better you will be able to estimate the spacing you need.

3. Reenter AutoCAD and load the new linetypes from the file TEST.LIN. Repeat these steps until you create the linetype you want.

Make Your Own Linetypes

Because AutoCAD uses only specific dash and space lengths, the linetype you want may not be available through standard AutoCAD tools. We have a technique that lets us insert letters or blocks into a line at selected locations. This technique uses the following LINS.LSP file to break and insert one or more letters or a block:

```
(defun c:lins (/ ans el e pt1 pt2 pt3 pt4 pt5 ang ll insc ins ltl)
  (setvar "cmdecho" 0)
  (initget 1 "B b T t")
```

Listing continues

Listing *continued*

```
(setq ans (strcase (getkword "\nInsert a block <B> or text <T>? <B or T>: ")))
(setvar "osmode" 512)
(setq el (entsel "\nSelect the insertion point on a line <near>: "))
(setvar "osmode" 0)
(setq e (car el)
      pt1 (cdr (assoc 10 (entget e)))
      pt2 (cdr (assoc 11 (entget e)))
      ang (angle pt1 pt2)
      pt3 (cadr el)
      ll (distance pt1 pt2)
      insc (* (getvar "ltscale") 0.125))
(if
 (and (> ang (* 0.5 pi))(<= ang pi))
  (setq ang (- ang (* 0.5 pi))))
(if
 (and (>= ang pi)(<= ang (* 1.5 pi)))
  (setq ang (- ang pi)))
(if
 (and (= ans "B")
      (> ll insc))
  (progn
   (setq ins (getstring "\nEnter the name of the block to insert: "))
   (setq pt4 (polar pt3 (angle pt1 pt2) (* insc 0.6))
         pt5 (polar pt3 (+ (angle pt1 pt2) pi) (* insc 0.6)))
   (command "BREAK" pt3 "f" pt4 pt5)
   (command "INSERT" ins pt3 insc "" (angtos ang 1))
   )
  )
(if (and (= ans "B")(< ll insc))
 (progn
      (prompt "\nThe selected line is too short for the insertion!")
      (princ)))
(if
 (= ans "T")
 (progn
  (setq lt (getstring "\nEnter the text to insert: ")
        ltl (* (1+ (strlen lt)) (* insc 0.5)))
   (if
    (> ll ltl)
    (progn
    (setq pt4 (polar pt3 (angle pt1 pt2) ltl)
          pt5 (polar pt3 (+ (angle pt1 pt2) pi) ltl))
    (command "BREAK" pt3 "f" pt4 pt5)
    (command "TEXT" "m" pt3 insc (angtos ang 0) lt))
    (progn
    (prompt "\nThe selected line is too short for the insertion!")
    (princ)))))
(princ))
```

This routine allows you to insert text or a block into a line. It doesn't have error protection if you type the wrong block name, and assumes that you have LTSCALE set for your drawing requirements. It does test for the required line length to complete the insertion. Figure 11.3 shows samples of lines that can be created with LINS.LSP.

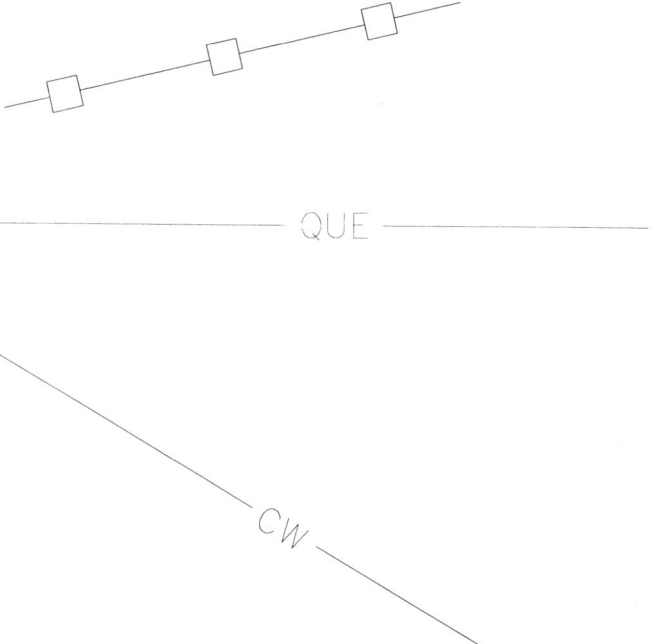

Fig. 11.3.
Lines created with
LINS.LSP.

If you want a more sophisticated line-creation routine, we recommend a third-party program such as Michael Slinn's CLINE II or CLINE III. These routines allow you to define a block of your choice and insert it into a line, and they help you to create custom linetypes. CLINE III works for irregular polylines, arcs, and circles. Figure 11.4 shows examples of what you can do with CLINE.

Font Files

The first thing anyone notices that distinguishes a CAD drawing from one that's hand-drawn is the lettering. Inklines are inklines, but consistent lettering is a major focus of any drawing technique, CAD or otherwise. Whether or not you intend it to, the quality of your lettering reflects, in a subtle way, the quality of your work. When we were able to get our lettering to look exactly the way we wanted it, we had made major progress toward professional-quality CAD drafting. Although you may not agree, we believe that good quality lettering does more than make your work attractive.

Fig. 11.4.

Lines and figures created with CLINE.

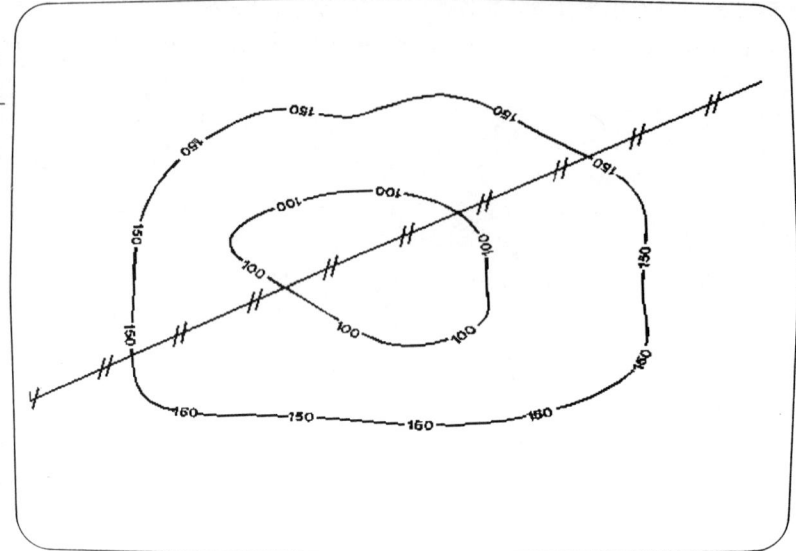

The following factors are important in a CAD lettering font:

- ❏ Regeneration and redraw speed
- ❏ Proper spacing and/or kerning
- ❏ Legibility
- ❏ Economy of space usage
- ❏ Style or appearance

We will give you the tools you need to modify any existing font files or create new ones, so that you can achieve the effects you want with your lettering styles. We also will show you how to create your own, if you have the time and energy. When you understand how a font file works, creating your own is not difficult—but the debugging required is time consuming.

How Font Files Work

A text font is a special type of shape file that includes the following items:

- ❏ Vector direction instructions
- ❏ Special codes (pen instruction sets)
- ❏ A character description
- ❏ A font description

AutoCAD text fonts are stored in .SHP and .SHX files. We focus here on the .SHP files. (AutoCAD creates .SHX files, which are compiled files, from .SHP files; the compiled files load into the drawing faster.) The .SHP file is the source file, the ASCII representation of what AutoCAD uses to represent the text in the drawings. AutoCAD does not use regular text fonts; it uses a collection of line and arc vectors to create the text in graphic form. Although this is helpful in terms of pen plotters, it can hinder your movement around a drawing—processing all those tiny vectors takes time. All those tiny vectors are exactly what you have to manipulate in order to work with .SHP files; they also have a direct impact on the five factors we think are important about CAD lettering fonts.

Figure 11.5 shows a line description of an uppercase *A*, a grid imposed over the uppercase *A*, and a vector diagram. The *A* is from the AutoCAD simplex font file SIMPLEX.SHP.

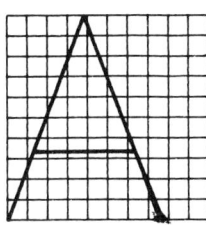
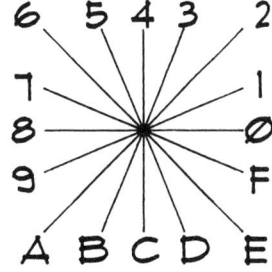

Fig. 11.5.

Uppercase A from SIMPLEX.SHP font file.

Each number and letter in the vector diagram is a code representing a vector direction. There are 16 vector directions. AutoCAD has to receive the vector direction in a single-digit format. The vector designations 1-9 and A-F are hexadecimal representations of the decimal numbers 1-15. This vector diagram represents the direction in which AutoCAD tells the plotter pen to move, on or above the paper.

Let's focus on one quadrant of the diagram and see how this system works. For purposes of this discussion, think of each line in the grid over the diagram as equal to 1/2 unit. The center of the diagram is the starting position of the pen. If we tell the pen to move along the vector 0, the pen will move 1 unit to the right. If we tell the pen to move along the vector 1, the pen will move 1 unit to the right and 1/2 unit up. Vector 2 will move the pen 1 unit to the right and 1 unit up, and so on for all 16 vectors. Notice that the vector lengths are not all the same, but that the pen always ends up on the grid.

AutoCAD has an additional 14 codes which increase the capabilities of the instruction set that controls the pen movement:

Code	Meaning
000	End of shape definition
001	Pen down
002	Pen up
003	Divide vector lengths by next byte
004	Multiply vector lengths by next byte
005	Put current pen location into stack
006	Get pen location from stack
007	Draw subshape number given by next byte
008	X,y displacement given by next two bytes
009	Multiple x,y displacements, terminated by 0,0
00A	Octant arc defined by next five bytes
00B	Fractional arc defined by next five bytes
00C	Arc defined by x,y displacement and bulge
00D	Multiple bulge-specified arcs
00E	Process next command only if vertical text style

Each character in a font file is described by a combination of vector codes and instruction codes. Each of these character definitions is preceded by a line that tells AutoCAD what the definition is supposed to create. Font files use ASCII character numbers to keep track of the definitions; that is how AutoCAD knows that a key on your keyboard is supposed to become a particular collection of drawing vectors in your drawing.

Look again at the uppercase *A* description:

```
*65,27,uca
2,14,8,(-8,-21),1,8,(8,21),8,(8,-21),2,8,(-13,7),1,0A0,2,8,
(9,-7),14,8,(-14,-10),0
```

Each description begins with an asterisk. In this character's description, the asterisk is followed by the number 65 (the ASCII character number for *A*). Following the ASCII number and a comma is a number that tells AutoCAD how many instructions follow in the description, in this case 27. (This number is extremely important, especially if you intend to modify a font file. The best way to keep track of what the number should be is to count the commas in the character-definition instructions.) The first line ends with an optional character name, in this case *uca*. (Note that this [*uca*] should have at least one lowercase character—otherwise, AutoCAD will think it is a command in Hex.)

Now we get to the fun part. The following table lists a partial translation of the instructions that follow the character description. We find it necessary to make such a translation for each character we analyze—we don't spend all our time writing font files, and need this step-by-step analysis to keep track of what is going on. In just a moment, we'll share a timesaving trick with you.

Code	Translation
2	Pen up
14	Move pen 1 unit in direction of vector 4
8	Next comes an x,y displacement to move pen
(-8,-21)	Move pen minus 8 x units and minus 21 y units
1	Pen down (finally!)
8	More x,y displacement
(8,21)	Draw diagonal line to point 8 x units over and 21 y units up
2	Pen up
8	More x,y displacement
(-13,7)	Move pen -13 x units and 7 y units
1	Pen down
0A0	Draw line 10 units to right

and so forth, until AutoCAD reaches 0, which is the end of the definition.

Although the instruction codes are listed in three digits, only one of those digits is used in the shape definition. (We don't know why.) You can use three digits if doing so helps you keep track of things; the AutoCAD's compilation of the .SHP file will remain the same size.

If you look again at figure 11.4, you'll notice that this translation matches the actual drawing of the *A*.

With all these instructions needed just to draw an *A*, you can see why text takes up so much computer memory and why AutoCAD uses a shape file to create fonts. On the other hand, if AutoCAD treated each letter as a block, you would never get any work done, except for inserting and moving text blocks.

The most basic font files use a series of lines to create an arc. Lines display and plot faster in most plotters. If you want high-quality lettering, however, you need to study the AutoCAD manual's description of instruction codes (called *special codes* by Autodesk). Herein lies the crux of the problem with font files. The speed of the font is inversely proportional to its graphic quality. However, a well-written font file of complex characters that uses pen movement judiciously and incorporates the most efficient instruction codes will have the same speed as a poorly written basic font file.

The last required part of a font file is its opening description. This description, which is required for all font files, always starts with a character number of 0, as in the following example:

```
*0,4,helv
16,8,0,0
```

These lines are the opening description for a font file named *helv*. Note that even this first line contains a number (4) which tells AutoCAD how many commas to look for.

The second line is of particular interest. The first number, *16*, tells AutoCAD that the font will be a maximum of 16 units above the text baseline. The second number, *8*, tells AutoCAD that the text will extend a maximum of 8 units below the text baseline. These characters are the *scale factor* of the font; they are important in designing and modifying the font, as we will demonstrate in a moment.

The next digit (0) is the modes description for the font. When this digit is 0, no vertical text definitions may be included; if this digit is a 2, vertical font descriptions are included. The last 0 signifies the end of the description.

Note that a carriage return for this font must be at least 24—and preferably 25 or 26—units high, so that text doesn't overwrite itself when it continues on the next line. The carriage return, which is defined as the ASCII number 10, moves the pen down the expressed number of units. It would look like this:

```
*10, ,cr
2,8,(0,-26),0
```

Modifying, Improving, and Creating Font Files

You may need to modify a font file for one or more of the following reasons:

- ❏ To correct character spacing or placement errors
- ❏ To create a monospaced font complementary to your standard font
- ❏ To add necessary characters
- ❏ To modify the appearance of characters

When you want to modify or create a font file, follow this simple set of procedures:

1. Determine the character height by adding the total units above and below the text baseline (found in the first line of the font file). If you are creating your own font file, 16, 20, or 25 units work for the distance above the baseline in moderately complex fonts; if you intend to provide lowercase letters, use 1/3 to 1/2 of those units for the distance below the line. (Commas and the "tail" on a Q require only 2 to 3 units.)

2. Start a drawing. Use full scale and a large sheet if you are going to examine or create an entire font file. If you are worried about only a few characters, a small sheet will suffice. Create a one-inch by one-inch box containing a grid equal to the number of units the font has above the baseline. Add an appropriate number of squares below the baseline. COPY or ARRAY this box grid as required to accommodate all the characters you intend to work with.

3. Starting at the left end of the baseline, insert into the grid one character of the font file you want to modify. When you have inserted all the characters, plot the drawing. If you aren't modifying an existing file, plot the drawing of the grids. You can use them to lay out your characters.

4. With your drawing of the characters on hand and your word processor in nondocument mode, open the font file. If you need to, refer to a DOS reference book for the ASCII character numbers and write the appropriate number below each character in your drawing.

Figure 11.6 shows a few of our standard text font characters; you can see the standard file as well as the monospaced file we created. To create the monospaced file, we had to determine the width, in units, of the widest character and then modify all the other characters to match the maximum required width. Our font file also contains fraction characters; we created them by using instruction codes 007, 003 and 004 to scale existing characters into the fraction definition.

When you have decided what the character description should say, save the file. Start AutoCAD and use the opening menu's compiling option to compile your new shape file. Edit your existing text-grid drawing. If it already contained text, you will be able to see the results of your .SHP-file editing. If you are creating a new font file, we recommend working on one character at a time. Compare your new character with the photocopy of

Fig. 11.6.

Comparison of standard and monospaced font.

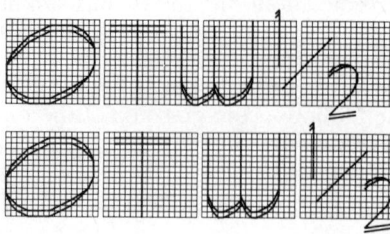

THIS IS OUR STANDARD FONT. NOTICE THAT THE SPACING IS NOT UNIFORM BETWEEN THE LETTERS

THIS IS OUR MONO-SPACED FONT. NOTICE THAT THE SPACING IS UNIFORM BETWEEN THE LETTERS

your favorite hand-drawn letter. Draw a one-inch by one-inch grid over the photocopied letter and use it as a guideline.

AutoCAD can reference shape numbers above the standard ASCII character number 128 by using *%%nnn*, where *nnn* is a number from 129 to 256. If your computer system allows it, you can access these numbers also by typing **<Alt>nnn**. If you want to, you can create unique characters for the character numbers from 129 to 256. These characters can even be standard symbols!

When you create or modify a font file, make sure that you consider the ramifications of your work on your drawing speed as well as on appearance. Generally, the larger the file, the slower the font. Carefully analyze the pen movement as you are reviewing or creating each character. Make sure that you have selected the best way to get the image you want, being as concise in instructions and pen movement as you can. Remember that you are looking at the font at a magnification that will rarely, if ever, actually be seen. The legibility of the spacing and pen strokes you will be using can be evaluated only from an actual plot.

Third-Party Fonts

Many third-party text font packages are available. If you buy one of these packages and a .SHP file is not included, find out whether one is available. The .SHX file is the coded version of the shape file; it cannot be converted to a .SHP file without special utilities.

We are familiar with CAD LETTEREASE lettering software. That's right—*software*. Not only does CAD LETTEREASE have some very refined text fonts, it also has letter-manipulation capabilities that border on desktop publishing and could satisfy a signmaker. We used CAD LETTEREASE for the job sign shown in figure 11.7. One of desktop publishing's important features is the capability of *kerning* text—text can be justified by spreading

Chapter 11: The Professional Look **255**

the spacing evenly across a fixed line length (as it is in this book). The height of the text is unchanged; only the spacing between letters is adjusted. Although this is often a desired effect when you want uniform left and right margins, the appearance of the text becomes more important. CAD LETTEREASE can kern all of its own fonts and a few AutoCAD text fonts.

Fig. 11.7.

Sign created with AutoCAD and Letterease.

The quality of these letters goes far beyond that of the standard fonts supplied with AutoCAD. If you have high-quality text requirements, you definitely should consider a third-party package. Writing one of these high-definition font files would take many hours.

> **For More Information**
>
> *CADENCE*, 2, no. 12 (December 1987): 87.
>
> Smith, J., and Gesner, R. *Customizing AutoCAD*, 2nd Edition. New Riders Publishing, 1988: 7-1 through 7-29.

Hatch Patterns

Hatch patterns consist of families of line patterns. Now that you know how to create linetypes, you are well on your way to writing your own hatch patterns. Hatch patterns are especially important to those of us who work in the construction industry. They are a great help when we need to show different materials graphically. We use them also to enhance our AutoCAD presentation drawings, or *renderings* (a sample of which appears later in this chapter—see fig. 11.13). Using hatch patterns can greatly reduce the memory available to you for drawing, however, and misusing them can hinder productivity. The following rules for using hatch patterns should help you stay out of trouble:

- Remember that hatch patterns are only a graphic representation.
- When you design a hatch pattern, remember to balance its complexity against its scale and use.
- Maintain a standard scale relationship between patterns, wherever possible.
- Use aligned elements wherever possible.

AutoCAD hatch patterns can contain only line segments. And because hatch patterns react negatively to an extremely random set of lines or dots, the appearance of your hatch pattern is limited. On the other hand, we have seen someone spend two hours drawing cedar shakes on an elevation; if those two hours had been spent creating a hatch pattern, think of the time saved the next time a drawing needed cedar shakes!

As a rule of thumb, if your hatch pattern requirements are simple, create your own; if your needs are complex, investigate what you can buy.

How Hatch Patterns Work

Understanding how hatch patterns work will help you evaluate the effort required to create them. Hatch patterns have the following ingredients:

- Pen-up, pen-down, dash-length, and offset coding
- Alignment origin tied to the AutoCAD snap origin
- Creation angle as well as installed angle
- Ability to create blocks or individual lines
- Boundary

AutoCAD accesses hatch patterns in the ACAD.PAT file. This file contains all pattern descriptions. Keep in mind that you will be adding to, rather than creating, this file. A hatch pattern definition looks like this:

```
*blk,masonry-type surface
0, 0,0, 0,.5
90, 0,0, 0,1, .5,-.5
90, .5,0, 0,1, -.5,.5
```

The first line is the name of the hatch pattern, *blk* in this case. The definition begins with an asterisk, followed by a hatch pattern name and then a description. Each of the next lines describes one of the line patterns that make up the entire hatch pattern. Each of these one-line pattern descriptions follows the format:

```
Angle, X-origin,Y-origin, X-offset,Y-offset, dash-1,dash-2
```

The dash specifications are optional; they are required only for dashed lines. The spaces preceding each pair of figures are required.

The pattern shown in figure 11.8 has a group of three lines. Line #1 has an angle of 0, an x and y origin of 0,0, an x offset of 0, a y offset of .5; it is a continuous line. The next line (#2) has an angle of 90 degrees, an x and y origin of 0,0, an x offset of 0, a y offset of 1; it starts with a pen-down dash (a positive number) of .5, followed by a pen-up dash (a negative number) of .5. Line #3 is similar to #2, except that it has an x origin of .5, and reverses the dash-dot sequence. We use this basic pattern as a material indication in our construction drawings. For presentation purposes, we have another pattern that shows all the mortar joints; we don't mind the extra drawing overhead in a presentation drawing because presentation drawings do not include all the technical information needed in a construction drawing.

258 Part II: Perfecting Your Techniques

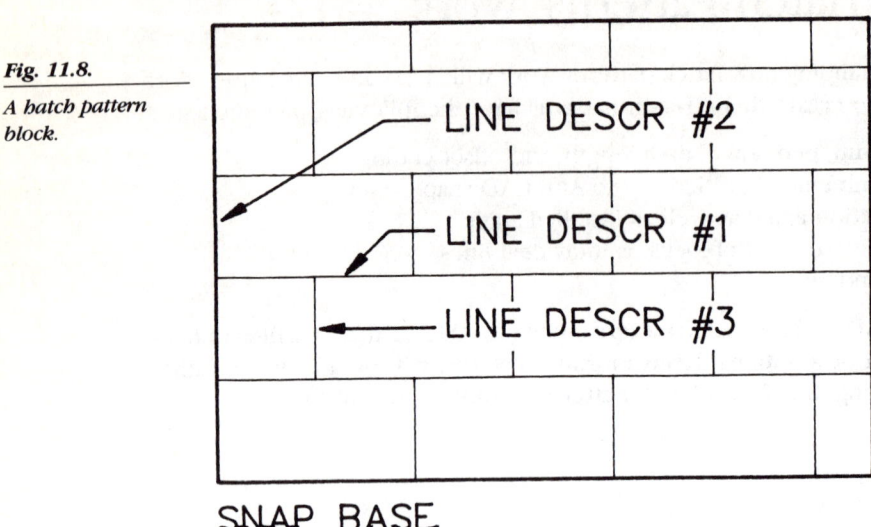

Fig. 11.8.

A hatch pattern block.

Once you understand the configuration of the definition line, the transition to writing basic hatch patterns is relatively simple. More complex patterns may require some rather involved mathematical calculations; fortunately, AutoCAD can help.

Modifying, Improving, and Creating Hatch Patterns

If you want to write your own hatch patterns and add them to the ACAD.PAT file, you should use AutoCAD to help you create patterns. If you need hatch patterns but don't want to write them, you can buy completed patterns or use a program like Hatch-Maker. Using a technique similar to the one we are going to recommend, Hatch-Maker automates the creation of hatch patterns. The great thing about the program is that all you have to do is draw the pattern; you don't have to calculate or type it.

We have purchased many hatch patterns and customized them so that they look more the way we want them to. There is a limit to the amount of memory AutoCAD will dedicate to the importation and creation of a hatch pattern. We have heard that about 75 complex line definitions is the maximum. Such a complex pattern is beyond the scope of this book.

The procedure we recommend for creating or modifying hatch patterns is similar to the font-creation technique we described earlier in this chapter. Here are the steps to follow:

1. Create a new drawing and set your AutoCAD UNITS to decimal units, with a decimal extension of 4. Create a series of 1 × 1 boxes. The number of boxes you need depends entirely on the complexity of the hatch pattern. We recommend that you limit your requirements to a 5 × 5 grid so that your lines or dots will repeat themselves within 5 units of their origin.

2. Set your snap spacing to 0.10 inches, effectively dividing each 1 × 1 box into 100 little boxes.

3. Create a drawing of the desired hatch pattern (making sure that you do your best to keep things under control and aligned). The snap setting will help you accomplish this. You may be surprised at how complex the pattern can appear with just a few well-planned objects.

4. Use AutoCAD to measure the origins, x,y offsets, and dash lengths. Make a note of these measurements.

5. Create the hatch pattern in the ACAD.LIN file, using the figures you got from AutoCAD. Try out the pattern in a new drawing and see what happens.

To illustrate this procedure, we will create a cobblestone hatch pattern and show you the technique in drawings.

Figure 11.9 shows the first line pattern required for the cobblestone hatch pattern. Its line description is

```
90, .05,.1, 0,-0.5, .3,-.2
```

Notice that we use only four boxes for this layout, and that we have the snap increment set to 0.05.

The next required line pattern (see fig. 11.10) uses all the possibilities of a line pattern description. The line description of this line pattern is

```
45, .55,.4, .3536,.3536, .0707,-.6364
```

The two line patterns shown in figure 11.11 are similar, but not quite equal. Their line descriptions are

```
0, .1,.95, 0,0, .4,-.1, .35,-.15,
0, .05,.1, 0,0, .4,-.1, .35,-.15,
```

Fig. 11.9.

First line pattern for cobblestone hatch pattern.

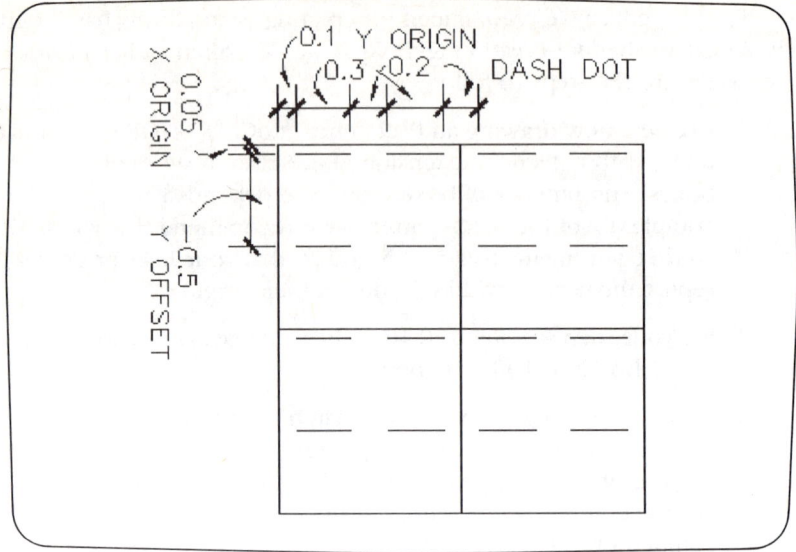

Fig. 11.10.

Second line pattern for cobblestone hatch pattern.

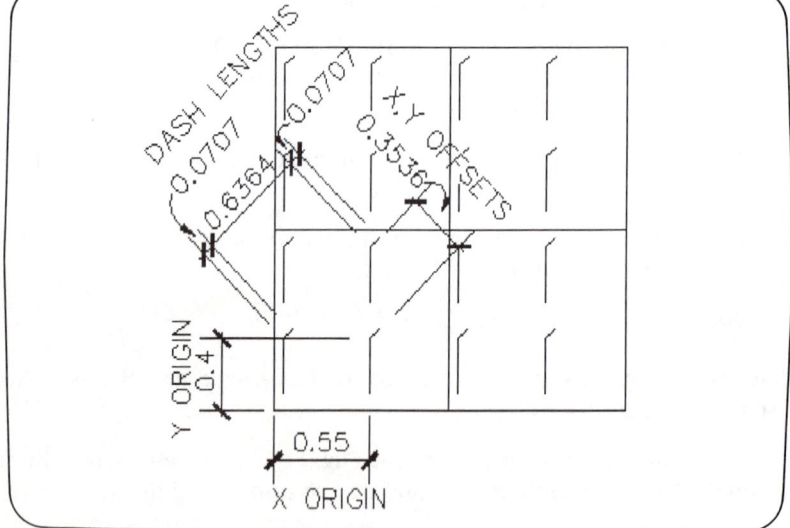

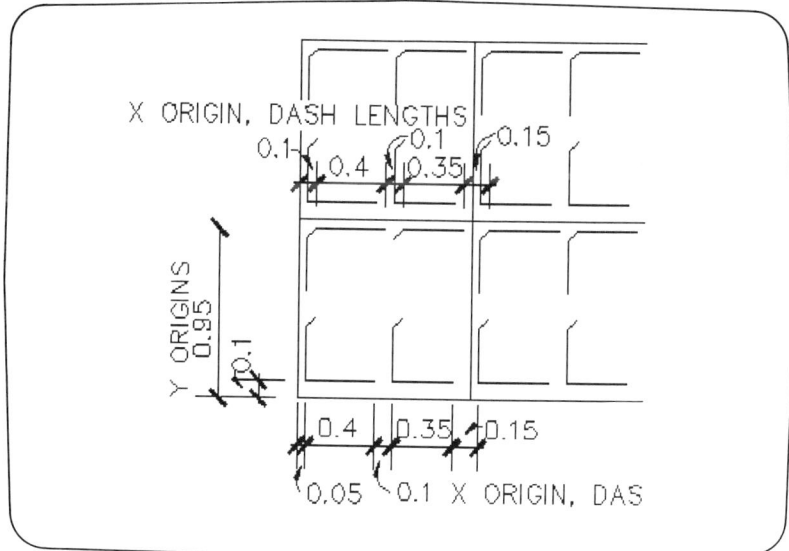

Fig. 11.11.
Two more line patterns.

Figure 11.12 shows the complete pattern.

Fig. 11.12.
Complete hatch pattern for cobblestones.

Each line description was established by going through the same procedure. If you have a word processor that you can access from within AutoCAD, you can shell out of AutoCAD as you determine each line description, and write the hatch pattern a line at a time. Otherwise, make sure that you take accurate notes when you record the line pattern information.

> **For More Information**
>
> Smith, J., and Gesner, R. *Customizing AutoCAD*, 2nd Edition. New Riders Publishing, 1988: 8-1 through 8-23.

Rendering with AutoCAD

We have developed several tools that we use for presentation drawings in AutoCAD. Your requirements may differ, but you should prepare a similar set of components if you do presentation work. This is what we have:

- A set of rendering hatch patterns, including textures, shading, and stipples
- A set of presentation standard blocks with a corresponding set of blocks to convert the drawing to a construction document
- A set of presentation text fonts, symbols, and titles
- A task menu for doing presentation drawings

We used the presentation toolbox to prepare the rendered elevation shown in figure 11.13. To create this drawing, we used our own customized version of Autodesk's AEC menu system, the Automaster menu system from AUTOEASE, the Hatch-Maker hatch pattern program from Cantec Software Systems, our own custom AutoLISP routines, and some custom plotting work courtesy of Blueprints Now, in Sarasota, Florida. Converting this drawing to a construction drawing was easy.

Although using CAD for presentation work is debatable, we think it has appropriate applications. The most important part of doing presentation drawings on CAD is making sure that you coordinate them with the balance of the work that is to be completed on the computer.

Many third-party menu systems include libraries of presentation graphics for architects, landscape architects, and interior designers. We strongly recommend that you conduct an intensive search of the third-party marketplace before you elect to create your own patterns, blocks, and fonts.

Chapter 11: The Professional Look

Fig. 11.13.
A sample rendering; everything about the drawing is custom.

Plotting

Because the final product of your efforts with AutoCAD usually is prepared by a plotter, we want to share with you a few tips about professional-quality plotting.

Halftones

In addition to varying line weight, graphic media use what is called a *screen* that varies in percentage of black dots and white space, creating a range of gray tones. Since most plotters uses ink pens, AutoCAD users can achieve this effect only by adding a camera to the process of creating the final drawings. You can also plot screened lines if you own, or know someone who owns, a laser or electrostatic plotter.

We have simulated halftones by using felt-tip pens or a mixture of violet and black ink. To try this, prepare a test sheet and experiment with plots of various felt-tip pens and your blueprint paper/machine combination. Another way to get a gray line from a blueprint machine is to mix black and violet ink in varying proportions. This can be very effective if you use background drawings in your work.

A note of caution: Because the halftone technique is extremely sensitive to print speed, the results of this practice can be unpredictable if you use a blueprint house to print your work—unless you make special arrangements. You need to establish an acceptable speed with the blueprint company, always use the same plot media, and every time you give the company a print job be sure to specify the speed at which you want the prints made.

Plotting Media

Many papers, films, and synthetics work in a plotter. Most supply houses will give you a sample set of their products to try. All pen manufacturers and many media manufacturers publish guidelines that tell the proper pen/media combination. You should become knowledgeable about these materials as they apply to your specific requirements. The options are extensive. You should settle on a media standard to ensure the professional quality of your drawings.

We have used some interesting paper and felt-tip pen combinations, including a lightly textured brown paper with dark brown felt-tips, and a heavy stock, varnish finish white sheet with black felt-tips. (The latter produces a drawing that looks almost like a photograph.) Now if we can just get felt-tip pens in seven line weights!

Camera-Ready Drawings

Because CAD drawings can be completed in color and plotted by layer, you can produce drawings of awesome quality by combining CAD and a camera. We have seen construction drawings prepared in color with this technique. Although we haven't tried it yet, we will as soon as a project that would benefit from it comes along.

To use this technique, you would plot drawings that correspond to the layering system described in Chapter 7, "Advanced Management Techniques," plotting the base drawing separately from the work of any consultants and using different colored ink to plot various materials or trades in different colors. Then take the drawings to a print shop, where they will be assembled using a camera. For example, the base drawing can be printed in halftones as a background drawing, with all the electrical conduit in blue. Have the completed drawings printed, using an offset printer, and you have a set of drawings that look as though they are part of a magazine or book! Such drawings are more than legible at half the size of the standard sheet size used for hand-drawn documents. For large projects, this process can be of great benefit and little, if any, extra cost.

If you want to use this technique, talk with a printer about the required procedures. If the printer doesn't know anything about CAD, make sure that you explain your capabilities. The printer will be able to suggest ways to prepare your drawings that will benefit both of you. Keep in mind that because your work must be copied by a camera, it will be reduced and then expanded again, which makes your use of line weights and text height extremely important.

If You Plot Somewhere Else . . .

If you have someone else do your plotting, you should not only have a plot standard form (described in Chapter 6, "Project and Drawing Management") but you also may need to have a standards directory on the plot service's computer. The plot service will need a copy of any custom .SHP files you create, because these files are loaded into the drawing only at edit or plot time. Be sure to give your shape files names that are completely different from AutoCAD's file names. And remember that if you make any revisions to your shape files, you need to update the plot service's files as well.

Summary

Everyone has a different opinion as to what "The Professional Look" is. Accommodating these different opinions is the second major component of AutoCAD customization, following closely behind increased productivity. In other words, it's a matter of style.

This chapter presented the basic concepts behind creating your own style in AutoCAD by using a variety of line, text, hatch pattern, and plotting techniques. These areas of AutoCAD are limited only by your imagination. For example, you can create a brick pattern with a shadowed look by combining two hatch patterns with different line weights; all you have to do is take apart your standard brick hatch pattern and create two new patterns on the fly, for just one drawing. You can make a block out of a line of text and then insert the block with varying x and y scale factors to see whether you prefer the appearance of this text to that of the standard font. If you do, create a text style with the appropriate width factor and revise the font file's space character so that you'll have the proper spacing between words. An entire book could be written about the topics discussed in this chapter —but *you* would be the best author. Mastering these techniques will give you a growing sense of pride and identity in your work.

Recommended Accomplishments

- ❏ Create your own linetype.
- ❏ Modify a text font file.
- ❏ Create a simple hatch pattern.

Optional Accomplishments

- ❏ Create your own font style.
- ❏ Create a complete set of presentation tools.

Chapter 11: The Professional Look

What Chapter 12 Is About

In this chapter we discuss our experience with the following aspects of using 3-D:

- Project management and 3-D, compared to 2-D
- Construction and display of three-dimensional drawings
- Methods of improving display speed
- Improvements in AutoCAD Release 10 3-D
- Types of three-dimensional representations
- AutoShade
- Third-party shading packages
- AutoFlix

This chapter is not a tutorial about drawing in 3-D with AutoCAD. It is a discussion of ways to integrate three-dimensional work into the overall scheme of things, using effective tools and techniques to make working in 3-D as efficient as possible.

What You Should Know Before You Start

- AutoCAD's 3-D LINE, 3-D FACE, and VIEWPOINT commands
- AutoCAD point filters
- AutoCAD Release 10 coordinate systems, if you will be using Release 10
- AutoCAD Release 10 viewports

What To Have on Hand

- The *AutoCAD Reference Manual*
- The AutoShade (or other shading program) manual, if you use a shading program
- The AutoFlix manual, if you have AutoFlix
- A simple three-dimensional drawing you created in AutoCAD

AutoCAD from All Sides: 3-D

Not everyone cares about three-dimensional representation of a design. For those who do care, the three-dimensional capabilities of Auto-CAD Release 10 are a dramatic improvement over those in Release 9. We were reasonably successful at creating three-dimensional drawings with Release 9, and we used AutoShade and AutoFlix successfully with those drawings. Release 10 has made the process of creating three-dimensional drawings much easier by providing more powerful display tools and increasing the three-dimensional capability of the AutoCAD commands. As you prepare three-dimensional drawings, you must consider several things; in order to use these drawings as an effective tool, you will need to make a few adjustments.

Project Management and 3-D

The first thing users discover about three-dimensional CAD drawings is that drawing a three-dimensional representation of their design is considerably faster done by hand than using CAD; and while they continue to work on other aspects of the project, someone else can build a three-dimensional model of the design. These factors have a direct bearing on measuring the impact of three-dimensional CAD on a project schedule, man-hour budget, and on record maintenance. Most of three-dimensional CAD's impact on these elements of project management is negative, unless the budget is developed to include three-dimensional CAD design and presentations. One possible exception is the preparation of relatively simple designs; the benefits of accurate three-dimensional representations outweigh the minimal impact on project production time and costs.

So why should you use 3-D in your design work on AutoCAD? We occasionally develop a three-dimensional component to a project for the following reasons:

- ❏ The client cannot visualize the final design product without being able to look at the design from all angles, inside and out.
- ❏ The project is complicated enough to merit verifying the design with 3-D.
- ❏ The project is simple or contains many duplications that will facilitate a three-dimensional presentation with a minimum expenditure of man-hours.
- ❏ The client wants a realistic-looking image of the design in its surroundings.
- ❏ Believing that things will get better and faster, we want to keep up with three-dimensional drawing techniques so that we won't lag too far behind the forefront.
- ❏ A number of three-dimensional comparisons of a variation on the concept of the design are required.
- ❏ We can afford to have some fun and use the results as a sales and promotional tool.

When you integrate three-dimensional design work into CAD management, a few requirements not needed for general production work apply. These requirements are

- ❏ The designers must be CAD users.
- ❏ The computer system must be relatively fast for complex designs and three-dimensional presentation work. (In our opinion, for a reasonable response-time from AutoCAD, you need a 16MHz 386 with a minimum of 4M extended memory while you do complex three-dimensional drawings.)
- ❏ A drawing file maintenance system that separates the preliminary three-dimensional design work from the final production work must be developed.

- ❏ A menu system dedicated to three-dimensional drawing in presentation form must be developed.
- ❏ A set of standard symbols that are three-dimensional versions of your existing standard symbols must be created, as well as a corresponding LISP routine to convert the drawing from 3-D to 2-D.
- ❏ For high-quality presentations, special equipment and software or services must be purchased from a third party.

With all these strings attached, 3-D may not seem worth the effort. But we predict that the most extensive development of CAD systems during the next few years will be in three-dimensional representation. Sooner or later, three-dimensional work will become the de facto standard. It is in your best interests, then, to stay informed.

We have found that designers who are good at visualizing things in three-dimensions find it easier to use AutoCAD in 3-D than those who do not. In our opinion, AutoCAD users are assumed to be extremely three-dimensionally oriented. As the user base expands, we anticipate that the interface between 3-D and 2-D will become more transparent. Creating three-dimensional designs will be easier to do; you won't have to know as much about the relationship of coordinate systems, vectors, viewpoints, and the two-dimensional representations of all those things. With these considerations in mind, we are going to discuss what we consider the best way to create three-dimensional objects with AutoCAD.

Draw It and Walk Around It

The most critical aspect of successful, efficient three-dimensional drawing is the display of the work. In releases of AutoCAD earlier than Release 10, you must constantly transpose the viewpoint of the drawing, creating a regeneration with each view change. We have found some practices that help reduce the impact of this viewpoint regeneration on the time required to create the drawing. These procedures involve not only the way you draw but also how you access the display of the drawing. Because of the size and variety of the objects we represent, our projects—buildings—create probably the most extreme circumstances for using 3-D. If you are working on smaller, less complex objects, you may not need to implement everything we suggest. We recommend that you develop the following management practices:

- Begin to think of drawing in 3-D as though you are building a model of the object from balsa wood or plastic. Three-dimensional CAD drawings are total representations of the object you are drawing—*in one drawing*. Traditional design methods created a check of three-dimensional design by the development of the plan, elevations, and sections of the object.

- Preplanning of the CAD work is a must. Determine how many objects can be represented by three-dimensional blocks, and draw the blocks in separate drawings. The coordination of the insertion point is critical. We generally use a common plane to most of the elements in the drawing, such as a floor plane, to define the insertion points.

- Your 3-D menu should contain extensive display-manipulation macros. Create standard views to work from and a macro that allows users easily to create and save views for future reference. An icon menu with a representation of available preset views is an excellent tool.

The development of these techniques and tools depends entirely on how you use the system and what you are drawing. You cannot rely on a third-party menu system to provide you with exactly what you need, nor can we develop something that will fit your needs precisely. The precision of the development also is important, because each tool or practice may save you a regeneration of the drawing whenever it is used. That precision amounts to tremendous time savings.

With Release 10 of AutoCAD, you can view an object from multiple viewports—you can see the object being created in space. Nevertheless, developing standard viewport configurations for each of your drawing scenarios is still a good idea.

Dos and Don'ts

Speed is a major issue when you work with three-dimensions. The effort required to create a three-dimensional drawing is something most of us are not used to, and the display requirements add further complications to the procedure. The only thing you can count on for speed, other than the clock speed of your computer, is your drawing technique. We have developed some successful methods for creating a three-dimensional drawing. These methods are based primarily on our experience building nonelectronic models of our work, although we have added a few AutoCAD-dependent considerations to the list.

Chapter 12: AutoCAD from All Sides: 3-D **273**

Figures 12.1a through 12.1g illustrate the steps we use to create basic three-dimensional elements. As you develop the three-dimensional elements of a drawing, imagine that you are cutting out pieces on a plane (work surface). If an element is tilted in space, develop the objects on the work surface by using a horizontal and vertical component of the actual line or face. After you have developed the element, use the MOVE command and the .XY and .Z filters to "glue" the object in place. When you are comfortable with three-dimensional drawings, you can begin to move your working surface to different elevations in the drawing.

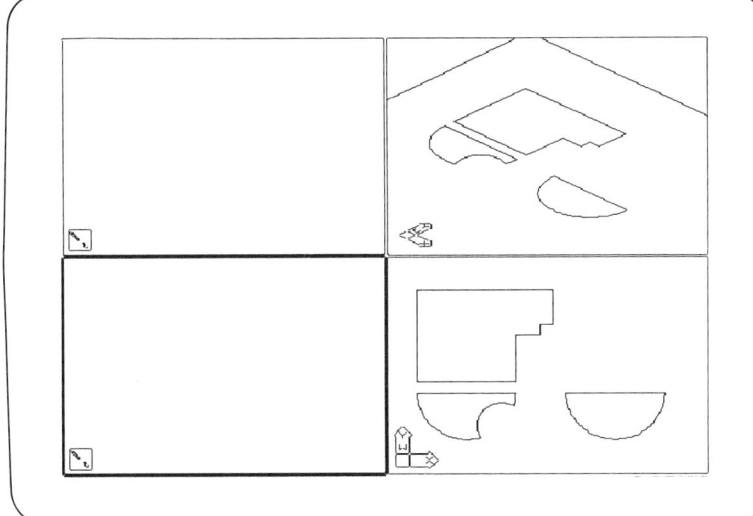

Fig. 12.1a.

Draw a plan view of each portion of the object you will create in 3-D.

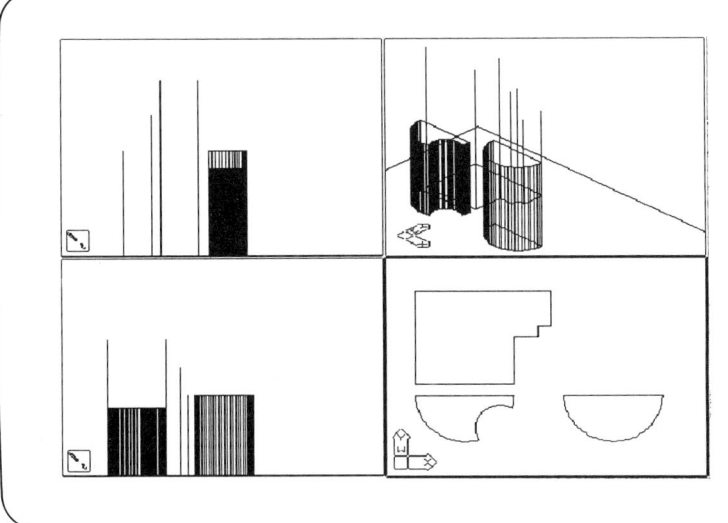

Fig. 12.1b.

Using .xy endpoints and filters, and z distances, create the vertical components. (If you have Release 10, you can use the front, side, and rear UCSs.)

Fig. 12.1c.

Put different components on separate layers and freeze the layers containing components you don't want to work on. Copy plan elements and create extrusions to refine 3-D volumes.

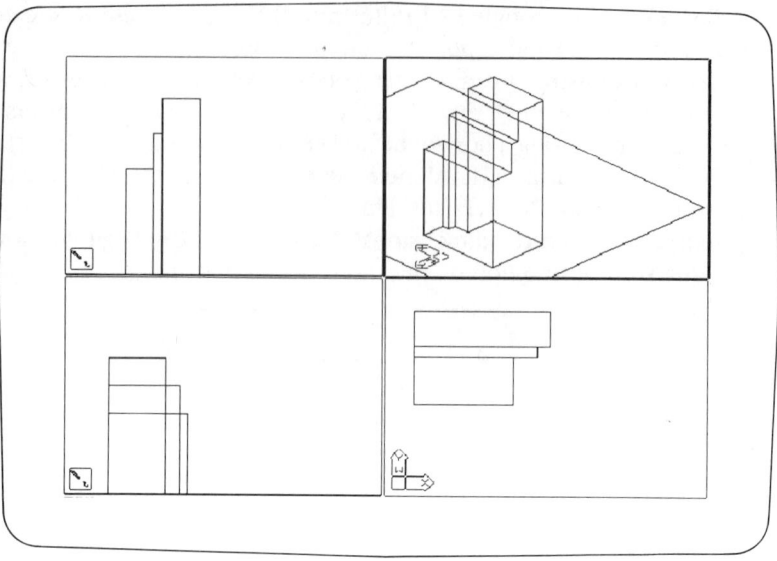

Fig. 12.1d.

Put different components on separate layers and freeze the layers containing components you don't want to work on. Copy plan elements and create extrusions to refine 3-D volumes.

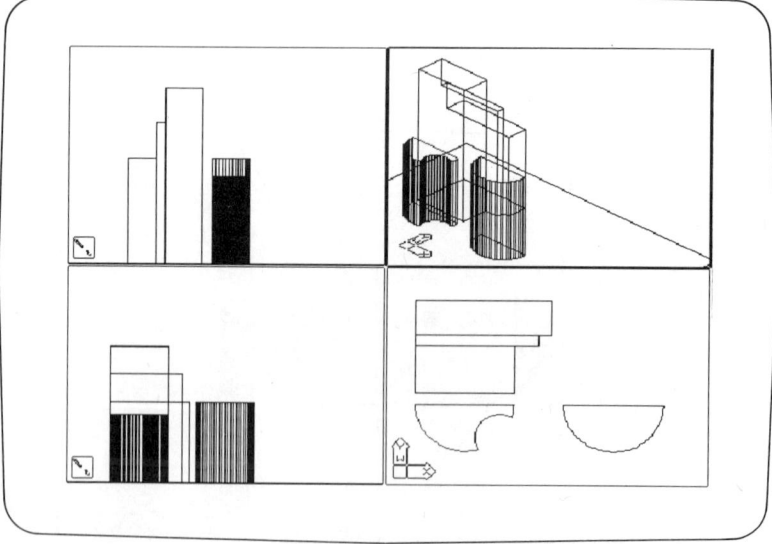

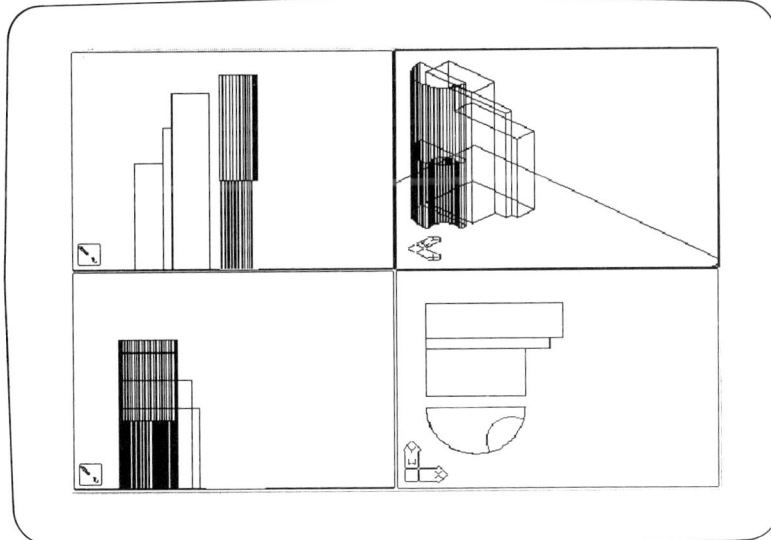

Fig. 12.1e.

Move elements to their proper elevation.

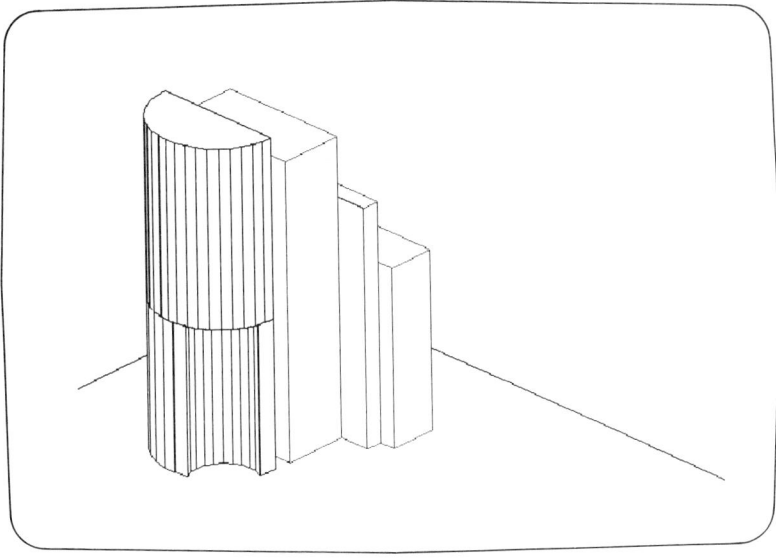

Fig. 12.1f.

Create 3-D faces on a separate layer, as required. Freeze all layers except the original construction layer, erase all construction lines, and thaw all layers.

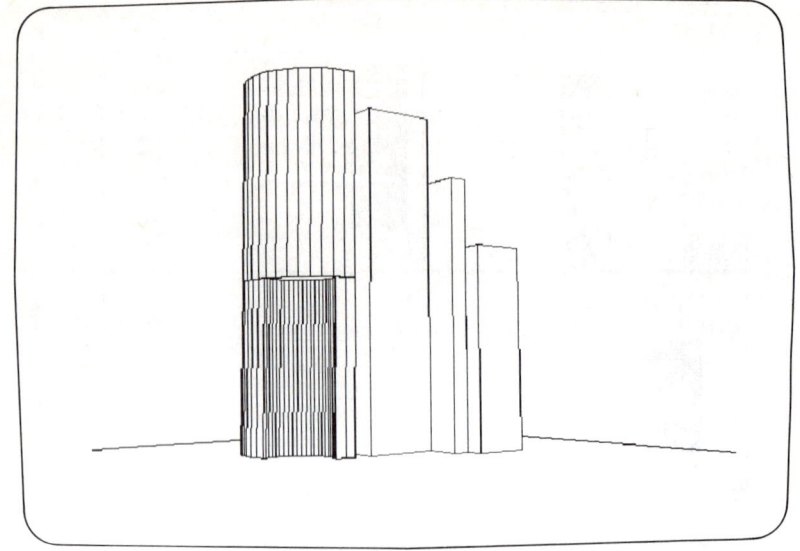

Fig. 12.1g.

This DVIEW, when plotted with hidden lines, will serve nicely as a layout drawing for a perspective study for one of our designs.

Release 10 of AutoCAD provides the additional capability of tilting and rotating your working surface. This technique is like cutting the components out of balsa wood or chipboard on a working surface, except that you won't slice your finger!

The Release 9 menus did not include a 3-D menu that allowed automatic selection of .XYZ filters or 3-D faces and lines. To correct that deficiency, we added the following screen menu to our menu system. (AutoCAD Release 10 includes a similar menu.) Our screen menu, called "3D," in this case, looks like this:

```
**3D 3

[ 3dline ]^c^c3dline;
[ 3dface ]^c^c3dface;

[ endpt  ]end;

[ midpt  ]mid;

[ .xy end].xy;ENd;
[ .z  end ].z;ENd;
[ .xy mid].xy;MId;
[ .z  mid ].z;MId;




[ cancel ]^C^C$s=s
```

For more information about creating screen menus, refer to Chapter 9, "The Tasks At Hand."

Figure 12.2 shows the use of extrusions and 3DFACES. Extrusions of objects are much easier to create and control than 3DFACES. If you want to create a hole in a surface, however, you have to use 3DFACES. The trick to using 3DFACES is that the pick order of the surface endpoints determines the flow of the work. Proper point selection will allow you to lace up a plane with 3DFACES. Putting 3DFACES on complex surfaces is similar to creating a papier-maché surface; you have to paste up the surface.

Fig. 12.2.

Drawing of an old dog using new tricks.

Figure 12.3 shows examples of what you can do with the 3-D LISP routines supplied with AutoCAD Release 9. Master the use of AutoCAD's 3-D LISP routines; they can save a great deal of drawing time. This set of routines, which comes with AutoCAD Release 9, became a set of commands in Release 10.

The routines/commands follow:

- 3DARRAY
- 3DCIRC
- 3DLISP (CONE, TORUS, SPHERE, DISH, WEDGE, BOX)
- 3DMESH
- EDGESURF
- PSURF

Fig. 12.3.

Wire-frame drawing created with some of the AutoCAD 3-D component routines.

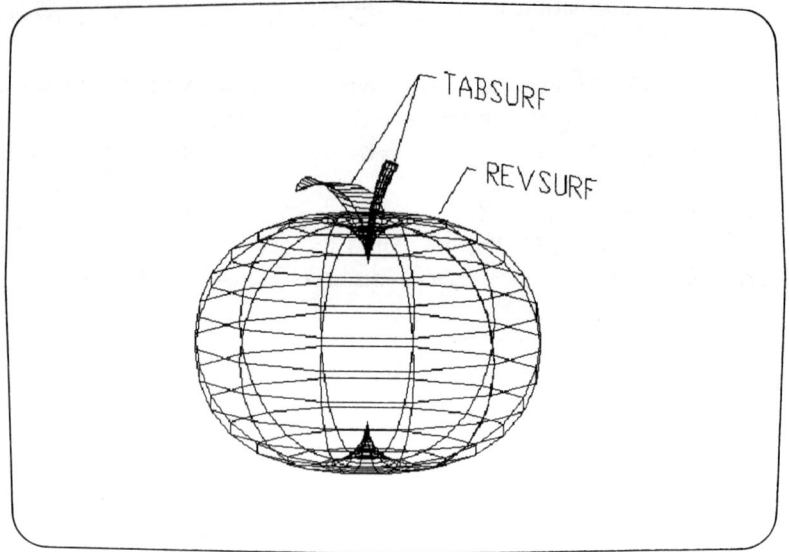

- PYRAMID
- REVSURF
- RULESURF
- TABSURF
- TUBE

To speed up regenerations, keep the VIEWRES settings at low numbers and the FILLMODE off until you are completing the final aspects of the drawing.

Establish the following views as standard views; using the VPOINT command and the VIEW S option, put these standard views somewhere on your menu system:

View	Coordinates
FRONT	0,-1,0
LSIDE	-1,0,0
RSIDE	1,0,0
REAR	0,1,0
3D	-1,-1,.5
PLAN	0,0,1

You will be able to draw in the PLAN and 3D views only in Release 9 of AutoCAD. The balance of the views will allow you to check the **progress** of your work. The 3D view must be adjusted for each sheet size and **drawing** scale that you are using. You can experiment with the 3D view to create more options for your specific needs. In Release 10, you will be able to draw from all of those views. In addition, Release 10 has corresponding User Coordinate System macros that provide settings for most of these views. We will discuss this further in a moment.

If You're Falling Asleep Waiting for Regens

The process of three-dimensional drawing may create prohibitive time constraints, even when you have the best intentions. If you have to do three-dimensional drawings, a display-list-processing graphics card is probably the best solution to the problem. Display-list processors use extended memory or the hard disk to store an image of the drawing for faster access to screen regeneration. This means that each graphics card manufacturer must write a driver for communication between the graphics card and AutoCAD. The complexity of the driver requirements for AutoCAD Release 10 has caused a delay in the development of compatible display-list processing cards; use of Release 10's three-dimensional capabilities has therefore been slow to develop. For further discussion of display-list processing, see Chapter 16, "Advanced Hardware Concepts."

> **For More Information**
> *CADENCE*, 3, no. 4 (April 1988): 19, 93.

3D in Release 10 Is Really Three-dimensional

The difference between AutoCAD Release 9 and Release 10 is that every object you draw in Release 10 has a Z coordinate. That sounds simple, doesn't it? To facilitate that fact, however, things got very involved and the program was extensively rewritten. The best part of the changes that were made is the addition of *viewports*. Now you can see your drawing from four different views simultaneously.

In general, everything you do using the Release 9 commands is sensitive to (and somewhat altered by) the current User Coordinate System, the fact that all objects have a Z value, and the extrusion thickness and extrusion direction for the objects involved. You can find more efficient ways to draw in three dimensions with AutoCAD Release 10 than you could with Release 9. And if you don't fully understand the changes involved, you inadvertently can create objects you did not intend to create. At the back of the *AutoCAD Reference Manual* for Release 10 (pp. 422-426, in our copy) you will find information about changes in Release 10. We strongly recommend that you review this information, making sure that you understand all the ramifications involved.

To draw in three dimensions in Release 10, you should set up the six standard views listed earlier in this chapter. AutoCAD Release 10 allows you to draw in any of these views and zoom in on the three-dimensional (3D) view without causing a regeneration. (The same requirements for the different sheet sizes for each view that we discussed earlier apply also for Release 10.) The views will be most useful if the object fills the sheet almost completely. Save these views as part of your standard prototype drawing.

You should configure several different viewport setups, naming each with a logical name and then using the VIEWPORT S command to save the names.

In addition to a single viewport standard, we use some other viewport configurations. For example, we use the three-viewport standard shown in figure 12.4 for plan work. The lower left port is used as an overall view of the entire drawing; the upper left port, as a detail work area; and the right port, for larger area work. You can use all of the standard transparent commands in each port, and you can make any port active during a DRAW or EDIT command. If you have a graphics card with display-list processing, it may have a bird's-eye view option. With such an option you can use the lower left port for different purposes than we do—for a second detail area, perhaps.

We use the four-viewport configuration shown in figure 12.5 for three-dimensional work. We use the lower left port for our standard FRONT view, the upper left port for the LSIDE or RSIDE standard view, the lower right port for the PLAN view standard, and the upper right port for the 3D view standard. Again, you can use transparent commands and change viewports as you actively draw or edit a three-dimensional object.

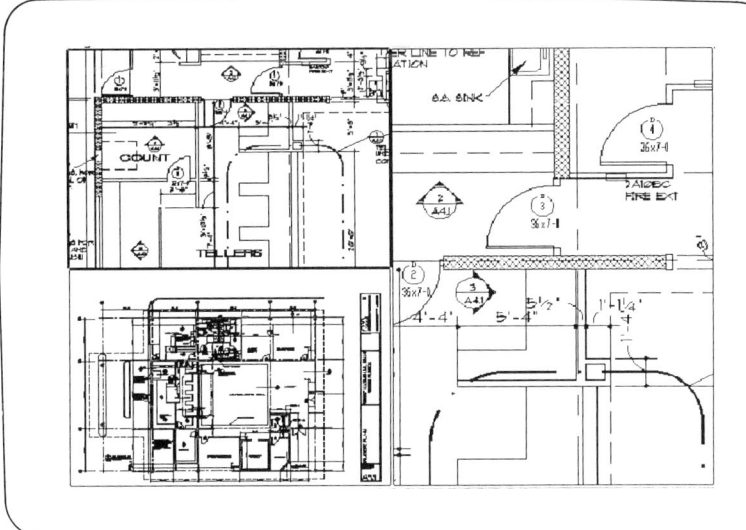

Fig. 12.4.

Three-viewport standard for plan work.

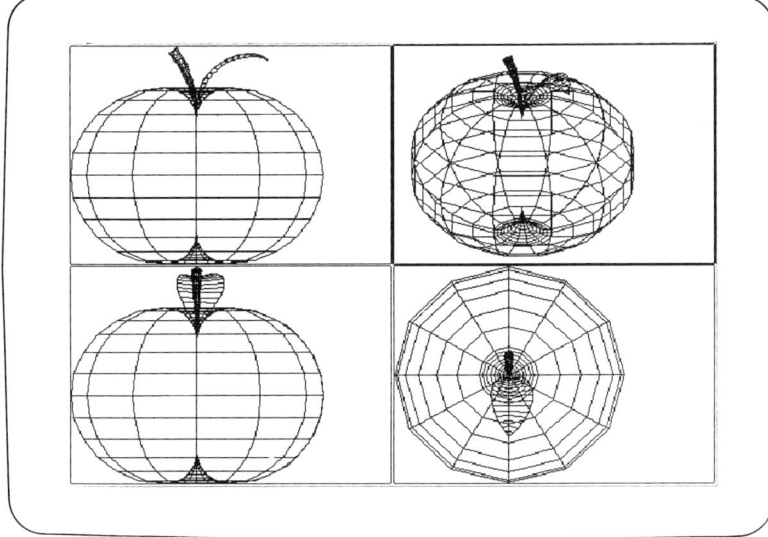

Fig. 12.5.

Four-viewport standard for 3-D work.

SAVE standard UCS configurations so that you can switch easily from drawing on the PLAN, LSIDE, RSIDE, FRONT, and REAR of the object. As you create an object, be sure to save additional UCSs that have logical names such as SROOF or BRACFACE so that you will be able to select the appropriate UCS. Here are the standard UCS names and their required settings:

Name	Setting
PLAN	Current UCS as world (WCS)
FRONT	Rotate X axis 90 degrees from WCS
LSIDE	Rotate Y axis −90 degrees and X axis 90 degrees from WCS
RSIDE	Rotate Y axis 90 degrees and X axis 90 degrees from WCS
REAR	Rotate Y axis 180 degrees and X axis 90 degrees from WCS

Note that each saved UCS is set *from* the WCS. If you don't return to the WCS between SAVEs, you must adjust for the Y-axis rotation based on the order in which you create the saved UCSs. You should save a corresponding UCS to the viewport configuration of your prototype drawing. If you use AutoCAD Release 10 for more than three-dimensional work, you will have to save a variety of prototype drawings, one for each viewport configuration you use. To use these prototype drawings, all you have to do is begin a new drawing by entering *NEWDRAWING*=**PROTO3D**, for example.

Remember that each viewport is independent of the others and that settings, regenerations, redraws, and highlighting will be unique to each viewport. To avoid redraws in each viewport, learn to work with the following system variables set in this way:

System Variable	Setting
AXISMODE	0
GRIDMODE	0 for all viewports
UCSICON	0 for all viewports
UCDFOLLOW	0 for all viewports

Because slide icons are difficult to see in small windows, use DVIEW only in single-viewport mode. (If you have a large monitor, you may be able to work always in multiple viewports.) DVIEW always causes a regeneration of the drawing. If you are working with complex drawings, we recommend that you refrain from using DVIEW—use your saved views instead. Changing views also causes a regeneration in three-dimensional work. However, you should be able to select appropriate views for a series of tasks instead of using DVIEW for each activity. If you are working on a design that will be viewed in perspective (as a presentation), DVIEW will help you visualize what the final results will be when you are using AutoShade or other third-party packages.

Isometric, Axonometric, and Perspective Drawings

If you are required to produce isometric or axonometric drawings, you can achieve some interesting results by using 3-D instead of drawing in 2-D and then representing your drawings as quasi-3-D.

The isometric drawing shown in figure 12.6 is really a hidden three-dimensional drawing from the proper viewpoint. The advantage to creating isometric drawings in 3-D is that you can create an isometric drawing from all faces of the object by creating the drawing in true 3-D and setting the proper viewpoint as 1,1,1, for example, to create a 45-degree isometric of the object's front, right side, and top. Then you can plot the drawing while hiding the lines. This technique will save you time by taking advantage of the real three-dimensional qualities of the drawing in preparing the major components of the work. (In other words, you draw one object and create plan, elevation, isometric, and perspective drawings all from the same object.)

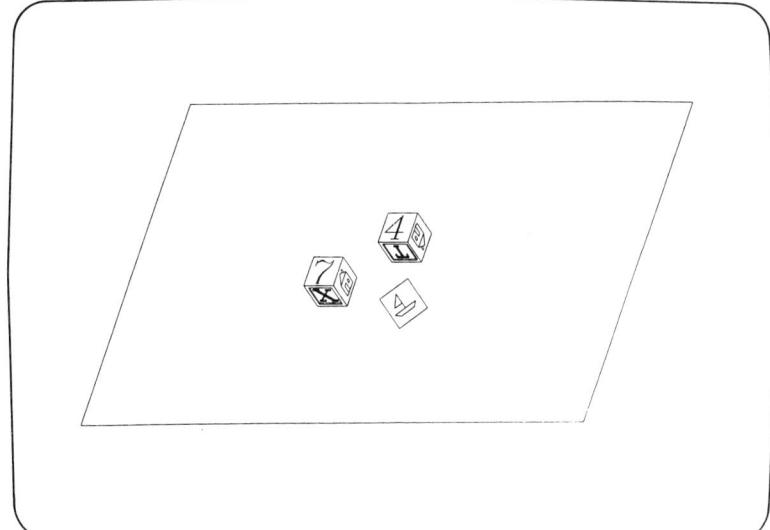

Fig. 12.6.

All of these isometric views were created using the same drawing copied to different rotations, from a 45-degree viewpoint, and then plotted with hidden lines removed.

The imitation axonometric drawing shown in figure 12.7 was created from a three-dimensional drawing by using the appropriate viewpoint. Axonometric drawings are a little trickier than isometric drawings. You can use three-dimensional drawings to create axonometric drawings, but you have to predetermine the projection angle you want to achieve and create a skewed extrusion. The skew of the extrusion will be the projection angle. Then, by combining the skewed extrusion with a viewpoint of 0,0,1, you can create an axonometric image.

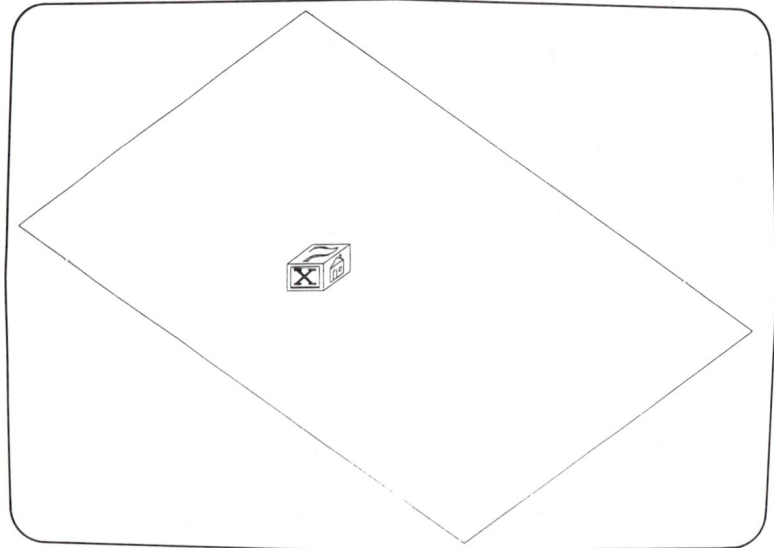

Fig. 12.7.

This axonometric is actually a 3-D drawing with the proper amount of skew to its extrusion.

You can use DVIEW's DISTANCE option to display your designs in perspective. First, you must use the POint option to set the TArget and CAmera locations. The target can be placed either inside the object (thereby creating a one- or two-point perspective) or beyond the object (creating a two-point perspective). Then, using a line of sight rubber band or the coordinates of the camera, you place the camera. Perspective mode is turned off automatically as you move the target and camera. We find that the best way to set target and camera locations is to enter the coordinates by using .XY filters and typing a Z coordinate while we are in a plan view of the drawing. When we like the target and camera positions, we jot them down so that we can use them later with AutoShade. (We discuss AutoShade in the next section of this chapter.)

Figure 12.8 shows DVIEW used as a perspective device. We suggest that you use your own camera and target icons in the drawing until just before you create the final image. Third-party packages that create perspective views are available, as are techniques that you can use to create a plot of a perspective drawing.

Fig. 12.8.
A perspective drawing, created using the HIDE option of DVIEW.

AutoShade

AutoShade is an economical Autodesk product for creating shaded images of your three-dimensional drawings. This program, which uses light sources and camera locations to represent a color-filled solid picture of your three-dimensional drawings, also points out your mistakes. AutoShade's use as a presentation tool is limited, however, unless the presentation is made on your computer. Clearly, the gray-shaded images in the following figures are much less dynamic than those same images displayed on a color monitor!

When we first started using AutoShade, we thought of it as architects would—in terms of the sun, shadows, and so on. Thinking of the program in this way caused a warp in our learning curve—causing delays in our first presentations. We have learned to think of the exterior of a shaded object as though we were taking pictures in a photo studio, placing either general illumination or point-source illumination around the object. When we are inside the object, we start thinking in terms of lights in a building, with one exception. Without some very detailed controls, the lights placed in AutoShade have infinite power and light all surfaces in every room—except the sides of an object that are not illuminated by the light source. A shadow is cast on those sides, which causes unpredictable results that can be overcome only through AutoShade's advanced user features.

Part II: Perfecting Your Techniques

We will use figures 12.9a through 12.9f (shaded versions of figure 12.3) to illustrate the variety of problems you may encounter using AutoShade. If you are using AutoShade in a complex building walk-through, studying the relatively simple object in these figures will show you that you need to analyze each scene to obtain predictable results.

Figure 12.9a was created with out-of-the-box AutoShade, average settings, and one direct light source.

Fig. 12.9a.
Stock out-of-the-box AutoShade settings with one light source.

Figure 12.9b shows a change in several factors. First, we reduced the intensity of the light source to 0.5. (The *intensity* of the light is simply how bright the light is.) Then we included a specular factor of 0.5 to give the image a slight reflective quality. The *specular* component sets the range of contrast for the light reflected from the object. We also set the diffuse light to 0.3 and the ambient light to 0.3. The *diffuse* light setting controls the way the surface of the object diffuses the reflected light, whereas the *ambient* light is the general illumination of the object from outside sources. As you can see, by reducing the ambient factor from the default, which was 0.7, to 0.3, we gave our apple a darker dark side.

Fig. 12.9b.

Lowering the intensity, setting a specular component, and lowering ambient light.

The only change we made for figure 12.9c was to reduce the ambient light to 0.1, thereby creating a more intense contrast to the overall appearance of our apple. This was what we wanted, but we also wanted the apple to look as though it were sitting on another surface—one that would reflect light up on the bottom of the apple.

Fig. 12.9c.

A further reduction in ambient light.

In figure 12.9d, we added a point light source to the bottom of the apple and set the intensity of this light source to 0.5 so that it has less impact than the direct light source, which has been set back to an intensity of 1.0. We think this is an improvement over the image in figure 12.9c. Now we want to take a look at the image with the light source on the other side and a little more around to the front of the view.

Fig. 12.9d.

A change in lighting to two lights, one below and one to the left.

Figure 12.9e shows the apple with a direct light that shines more on the front of the apple and a light below the apple with an intensity of 0.3. We're getting closer to the image we had in mind, but we need to soften the look a little.

Fig. 12.9e.
Moving one light from left to right, and lowering its intensity.

Figure 12.9f shows an increase in the diffuse factor to 0.5 and an increase in the specular factor to 0.7. We think that this image approximates what an apple looks like. After this exercise, we can go back to the AutoCAD drawing and, by using the REVSURF command again, change the apple's surface so that it has more facets. But in order to do this, we have to erase the apple body and keep the original polyline that created the shape of the apple. Then, to add the number of faces that we want for the final product, we must increase the settings for the system variables SURFTAB1 and SURFTAB2. The modified drawing will have more realistic lighting gradations on the surface, but AutoShade will take much longer to process it. Since we have an image that is close to what we want, however, we can be satisfied that our time won't be wasted.

Fig. 12.9f.

By increasing the diffuse and specular factors, we end up with what we were after.

If you want to produce shaded versions of your design and if your drawings will be somewhat more complex than an apple, you must be prepared for this type of time and effort—intensified by a factor of 10!

The image we used for figure 12.8, for example, is just one part of a restaurant we designed. The entire design, fully shaded, took about three days to produce. It had many repetitive elements, and we let the computers run overnight (while we watched football at home). Even with that efficiency, the result of those three days was 10 images—and we used Auto-Shade's *fast* shade option. If we had used the *full* shade option, which would have looked much better on our 256-color high-resolution monitor, chances are we would still be waiting for the computer to finish enough frames (60 frames, actually) to create a one-minute movie of the project. Are we suggesting that you give up? Nope. Not yet. In the next two sections, we'll tell you about two more solutions that may make things go better.

Other Shading Software

You can create shaded images with several other third-party programs that work with AutoCAD .DXF files. As you might expect, the capabilities of these programs vary in proportion to their price. BIGD, a shading program with the added capability of casting shadows to its shaded perspectives, is an example of a third-party package that compares to AutoShade. You should review the third-party packages to see which ones fit your needs. We recommend having at least one of the more economical packages if you intend to do three-dimensional presentations. You will need it to preview what you are going to do, even if you intend to send your presentation out.

There are companies that can provide you with shaded images in the form of videotapes, color prints (from a laser, electrostatic, or thermal printer), and 35mm slides. All you have to do is give them your 3-D AutoCAD file. (We discuss these options in more detail in Chapter 15, "Advanced Presentation Techniques.") If we want to provide this type of service to a client, we can do so with much more panache and economy of effort by using one of these outside companies because they use equipment and software that is much faster than our PCs.

At the Movies—Using AutoFlix

AutoFlix, an Autodesk product that can make a movie of your three-dimensional drawing, is intended for use with graphics cards that are 100-percent EGA-compatible; it will not work on any monitor that is not or cannot emulate EGA. AutoFlix takes special advantage of the EGA standard and compresses the files used to create the movie. AutoFlix can create three types of movies: it can animate objects, do a walk-through, and produce an interactive movie (the user controls his or her view of the what's in the movie).

AutoFlix depends on a motion path to create any of these types of movies. The motion path is created by using the AutoFlix LISP routine to place the path in the drawing after you have set up the drawing for use with AutoShade. AutoFlix accomplishes a walk-through, for example, by placing the camera along a motion path at intervals of movement that you specify. Once the path is set, the routine writes a script file (.SCR) and a movie file (.MVI) that automatically create (from AutoShade) the required rendering files and compile them into a movie file.

If you know something about music, you can use AutoFlix to create a musical score for your movie. In addition, you can include slides created by AutoCAD as informational stops along the way. And AutoFlix can use either fast-shaded or full-shaded images from AutoShade; this feature has a major impact on the time it takes to create a movie.

As we noted earlier in our discussion of AutoShade, you must spend a certain amount of time making sure that the lights, cameras, and action are all set up before you can be sure that you'll get what you expect. If you intend to do a movie of one of your projects, creating scenes that very generally approximate the movie you want is a good idea. When you are happy with the lighting and the views, let AutoFlix do the work for you. You may have to let your computer run for an entire weekend to create a movie. (If you get overly ambitious, it might take a week.) Make sure that you have enough disk space for the .RND files that AutoShade will produce. The possibilities for creating movies are extensive—they are limited only by your imagination. We suggest that you view a demonstration of the movies that come with AutoFlix so that you can see the possibilities. You may find that the EGA resolution makes you want to make more realistic movies— in which case, be sure to read Chapter 15.

Summary

We don't want you to expect miracles from the three-dimensional capabilities of AutoCAD and the available shading programs. They may be effective design tools that you can use to enhance your design presentations and the accuracy of your work. They may suffice entirely for the type of presentation you require. The important point is that you need to be familiar with three-dimensional drawings and make an effort to keep in touch with what is going on, because sooner or later 3-D will be the industry standard.

The concepts related to the following topics were reviewed in this chapter:

- ❏ Project management and 3-D (versus 2-D)
- ❏ Construction and display of three-dimensional drawings
- ❏ The dos and don'ts of 3-D
- ❏ Some ways to improve display speed
- ❏ Improvements in Release 10's 3-D
- ❏ Types of three-dimensional representations
- ❏ AutoShade
- ❏ Third-party shading packages
- ❏ AutoFlix

The only way to really learn how to draw in 3-D is to practice, practice, practice. The current methods for constructing 3-D drawings are even more extensive than the choices you have for 2-D, and Autodesk undoubtedly will continue to improve and develop AutoCAD's 3-D capabilities.

Recommended Accomplishments

- ❏ Create a set of 3-D standard menus, views, coordinate systems, and viewports.
- ❏ Using the techniques we showed you, create a wire-frame three-dimensional drawing.

Optional Accomplishments

- ❏ Shade a three-dimensional drawing.
- ❏ Make a movie.

III

Getting Serious

What Chapter 13 Is About

After you finish reading this chapter (and possibly the next), you should be able to begin writing simple AutoLISP routines. Then you can study and practice until you attain whatever level of AutoLISP competency you need.

We never thought that AutoLISP was plain English; the light bulbs started turning on only after we had worked with and programmed in AutoLISP for quite a while. Maybe that's because we were not computer-literate until we trained ourselves, and we had never been programmers. LISP programming may be easy for you. If it isn't, read on. We believe that our experiences will make the process easier for you.

In this chapter, we first we divide AutoLISP into its basic components. Then we discuss how each of its major commands (built-in functions) works. This chapter focuses on the "nuts and bolts" of AutoLISP, which can be categorized as follows:

- ❏ General functions
- ❏ Manipulation of data types
- ❏ Mathematical functions

Our focus in this chapter is on the functions we consider necessary for CAD management; AutoLISP's self-explained functions are mentioned in general terms only. You'll learn about the "bells and whistles" of AutoLISP in the next chapter, Chapter 14.

Helpful Things To Know Before You Start

- ❏ How to use all AutoCAD commands
- ❏ A little bit of LISP
- ❏ How to use the text editor effectively

What To Have on Hand

- ❏ The *AutoCAD Reference Manual*
- ❏ The *AutoLISP Programmer's Reference*
- ❏ Word-processing software that can create and manipulate ASCII or nondocument text files
- ❏ A couple of your favorite LISP routines
- ❏ A couple of LISP routines you don't understand

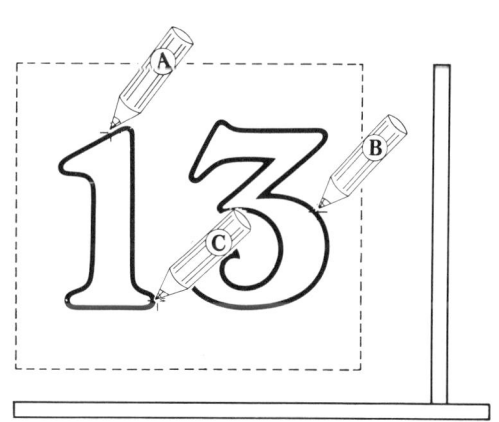

AutoLISP Never Was Plain English

AutoLISP is the primary tool for advanced AutoCAD customization. Without LISP, menu macros can accomplish basic customization and mold AutoCAD command procedures into a semblance of the way you work. AutoLISP not only can do all that but also can define new commands and manage larger groups of data. Most important of all—AutoLISP can use the flexibility of variables. Don't ask yourself *whether* you should learn AutoLISP. Just ask yourself "How much AutoLISP programming should I be able to do?"

We have seen what serious LISP programmers can do, and are happy to leave the job to them. Although we are not advanced LISP programmers, we do understand most of the concepts of AutoLISP and are able to write enough routines to solve most of our problems within AutoCAD. And we can make AutoLISP do a few things outside of AutoCAD. In our opinion, CAD managers should be able to work with AutoLISP at the level we do. All AutoCAD users can benefit from the basic capabilities of LISP.

Armed with this attitude, we wrote this chapter to show you how most of AutoLISP's major components work. We do not drag you through the process of writing a routine. Why not? Because each programmer has her or his own style of writing routines. Your programming style depends on your level of proficiency in LISP, the way the problem is conceptualized, and the way you think (logic processes). These differences in style proved a major stumbling block as we learned to use LISP from articles and books. We had to learn not only LISP but also how the programmer approached a specific problem. To show your our style of approaching a problem, which may differ from how you would do it, we annotated our LISP routines in the appendixes.

Basic AutoLISP Concepts

Both directly and indirectly, AutoLISP makes AutoCAD the CAD program of choice. Why? Because AutoLISP is the tool that ultimately customizes AutoCAD to fill your needs, and the major tool used by the "third-parties" who provide economical AutoCAD options and add-ons. AutoLISP is an extremely flexible programming language that is well suited to CAD tasks. To make AutoCAD do specifically what you need it to do, you will use AutoLISP—either someone else's programming or your own. If you want excellent productivity, you must understand AutoLISP.

LISP (which stands for *LISt Processing*) is a programming language developed specifically for its cut-and-paste capability, easy interactive response to the user, and relatively easy manipulation of all data types. AutoLISP is a subset of Common LISP, with some added functions specific to AutoCAD. Some commands are used differently in AutoLISP than in Common LISP. Nonetheless, Autodesk recommends that you get books on LISP such as *LISP*, 2nd edition, by Winston and Horn, and *Looking at LISP*, by Tony Hasemer. We recommend that you include the study of AutoLISP in a weekly regimen of reading about all aspects of AutoCAD. You will find sections on AutoLISP in the CAD magazines (*CADENCE* and *CADalyst*) as well as in almost every book written about AutoCAD.

Before looking at AutoLISP's specific capabilities, you need to understand the three basic components found in any routine: atoms, lists, and functions.

Atoms

Atoms are the building blocks of any LISP routine. An *atom*, the most elementary component of a routine, can be any word, phrase, number, or symbol listed in the routine (except special characters). Atoms can have a value or meaning assigned to them, or simply stand alone as data. Things get tricky with atoms only when you are learning about all of the types of atoms and what they will and won't do for you. For instance, the following line:

```
(setq yourname "FRANK")
```

is made up of three atoms. AutoLISP assigns the string value *FRANK* to the variable *yourname* with the function *setq*. It was simple until we started talking about functions, strings, and variables, right?

Lists

A *list* is a collection of one or more atoms enclosed within parentheses. Lists are the component from which LISP got its name. The LISP interpreter (the part of the program that evaluates all the routines) can understand lists in various ways, depending on how the lists are formatted. Lists are tricky only when you start learning how to format them. Consider the following line:

```
(This is a list)
```

which is a list of four atoms: *This*, *is*, *a*, and *list*. The previous group of atoms (changing your name to Frank) is a list also.

Lists can be nested inside lists. Nesting is the reason AutoLISP seems difficult to read (and the reason irreverent users call LISP *Lost In Stupid Parentheses*). The following nested list of atoms:

```
(jack jill (up hill (bucket water)) (fell down))
```

contains two individual atoms, two sublists, and a sub-sublist. Note that the sub-sublist (bucket water) contains two atoms, *bucket* and *water*. This sub-sublist is contained within the sublist (up hill (bucket water)), which also contains the two atoms *up* and *hill*. The complete list is formed by combining the second sublist (fell down) with the first sublist (up hill (bucket water)) and the atoms *jack* and *jill*.

Now pay attention—this is important! LISP interprets lists from the most nested list outward. In the preceding example, AutoLISP would first evaluate *bucket* and *water*, then *up* and *hill* and *fell* and *down*, and finally *jack* and *jill*. AutoLISP processes lists faster if they are nested as deeply as possible. Most of the routines in this book are moderately nested so that you can read them easily.

Parentheses are the key to formatting an AutoLISP routine. Lists in which the number of opening parentheses is not the same as the number of closing parentheses confuse AutoLISP. The way you nest lists inside your routine tells AutoLISP what action to take on which group of items. If you aren't careful, Jack fetches a dry bucket because Jill drank all the water, and nobody ever finds out that they fell down the hill.

Functions

Functions are AutoLISP commands that cause a list to become an executable list rather than a bunch of phrases and symbols. Calling a function a *command* isn't technically correct; we use the analogy because it is similar to the AutoCAD command concept. Without functions, lists remain lists of data; and they are called *lists* by AutoLISP when they are evaluated. The AutoLISP interpreter recognizes and performs certain internal functions, and AutoLISP also lets you define new functions. You don't have to know all of AutoLISP's built-in functions at first, but you will have to know how to define a function. (We'll get to that a little later in this chapter.)

In the following example of a built-in AutoLISP function statement:

`(strcat "Jack" "and" "Jill")`

the AutoLISP function is `strcat`. AutoLISP functions always return a result to the interpreter, which decides whether to store, display, act on, or send the result to AutoCAD. This example would return *"Jack and Jill"*.

A *defined function* looks like this:

`(defun practice (/...`

where *practice* is the name of the function.

The format of all of AutoLISP's built-in functions is generally the same, conceptually, with minor variations for each logical group of functions. Our discussion of AutoLISP's built-in functions divides them into logical groups based on their general purposes instead of listing them alphabetically. Before we start that discussion, we review some basic definitions and a set of special characters that affect your use of AutoLISP.

What Does that LISP Term Mean?

To benefit from our discussion of LISP, you need to know the basic definitions of the following terms:

Routine. A complete action, such as a defined function. Often used interchangeably with *subroutine* as a matter of convenience.

Subroutine. A collection, within a routine, of activities that provide specific results to the overall routine.

Program. A routine, or collection of routines, that provides a specific task to the user, regardless of whether input is required. It is the executable form of a routine. The terms *routine* and *program* frequently are used interchangeably.

List. The format of all LISP programming. Also, a set of data (data type) with no value other than the words and symbols contained in the list. For example, LISP will maintain a list of numbers strictly as a list and cannot perform calculations with those numbers unless you change their data type from *list* to something else.

Symbol. Any character (except the special characters described in the following section of this chapter) used to define a variable in LISP.

Variable. A symbol that can be assigned a changeable value.

Bind or *Bound to*. When a value is assigned to a variable, the value is *bound to* that variable. Variables also can be assigned to each other, *binding* them together.

Entity. Any specifically defined item in AutoCAD's drawing database, such as a line, arc, circle, ellipse, block, polyline, shape, or trace.

Group code. Each entity in an AutoCAD drawing is stored in the database as a list. The list contains a series of group codes that are always the same code number for the same bit of information about the entity. For example, the sublist containing the layer name the entity is on is group code 8. The list of group codes is extensive; it continues to grow with each new release of AutoCAD. For an in-depth discussion of group codes, refer to your *AutoCAD Reference Manual*.

Data type. Any of the recognized types or classifications of data in LISP (list, real, integer, string, etc.)

String. A specific group of characters, normally enclosed within quotation marks, that represents a nonoperable word value. (In other words, any collection of any type of characters, except the special characters.) A string remains a string and can be read as a set of characters only if you change its data type from a string to a list, a real, or an integer. For example, "1011" can be a string or a number used in an equation, depending on the data type to which it has been assigned. Strings can be of any length unless they are assigned as a constant. The length of a *constant string* is limited to 100 characters.

Integer. A nondecimal-precisioned number that can have a positive or negative value between −32768 and +32767.

Real. A decimal-precisioned number that can have a positive or negative value. When returning values to AutoCAD, AutoLISP normally uses a precision of 6 places to the right of the decimal point. Reals are stored in double-precision floating-point format with at least 14 digits of precision.

File descriptor. The value of a variable bound to a file that is either read or written to outside the Drawing Editor.

Subrs. AutoLISP's built-in functions.

Nil. The not-true or nothing value of symbols in LISP. Note that a symbol bound to zero (0) is not equal to nil. A nil list looks like an empty set of parentheses ( ). *Nil* is also a built-in function of AutoLISP. For housekeeping purposes, a variable that no longer is to be used should have the value of nil. Most routines are designed to return a value of nil to indicate that they have completed all their tasks.

T. The opposite of nil. Generally used in evaluating options in LISP, so that LISP can decide whether something is *T* or *nil* (and then decide what to do about it).

Expression. The formatting of a list into a functional statement, or expression, for AutoLISP to evaluate.

Argument. A condition of an expression. Arguments supply additional constraints to functions in AutoLISP. For example, many AutoLISP functions can have an integer supplied as an argument that tells AutoLISP how many decimal places to use in its calculations.

Null. Generally, a string that contains no characters. The null string "" is used by certain functions in AutoLISP to execute a return in an AutoCAD command sequence. The effect of using this null string in AutoCAD is the same as that of pressing the space bar.

Element. The most basic atom or set of atoms AutoLISP will act upon or evaluate.

Loop. An activity set up by a conditional test that continues to repeat the activity until the test is met or fails, whichever is required by the program.

Recursive. A function or loop that continues through a specified number of repetitions until the number has been met or reduced to zero, whichever is required by the program.

Special Characters in AutoLISP

AutoLISP reserves certain characters for special uses. Avoid using these characters for any reason other than their special use. The special characters for math functions are

+ – = < > / = ~   * /

The math functions are clearly explained in *AutoLISP Programmer's Reference*.

The other special characters:

( ) . ' " ;

merit fuller discussion. Any of them terminates a symbol name or a numeric constant; a space or an end-of-line character has that effect also.

Parentheses are the list separators (delimiters) for AutoLISP. AutoLISP will let you know if you don't have an equal number of right and left parentheses when you execute a LISP routine. If there are too many right parentheses, AutoLISP displays the error message extra right paren. If there are too few right parentheses, AutoLISP will tell you how many are missing by giving you the message n> (where *n* is a number describing how many parentheses are missing). Normally, adding the required parentheses will correct the problem and return you to AutoCAD. If that doesn't work, you probably have omitted a closing quotation mark from a string, thereby causing AutoLISP to include as part of the string everything that follows the opening quotation mark. To get out of this situation, you need to type " followed by *n* right parentheses. At first, you will spend a great deal of time checking whether you have the correct number (and placement) of parentheses and whether all your strings are closed.

Periods are used as decimal points and to create *dotted pairs*. Dotted pairs, which are special types of lists used for describing entities, are discussed later in this chapter.

An apostrophe (sometimes referred to as a single quotation mark) is used in AutoLISP the same way the built-in function *quote* is used.

Quotation marks (") are used to denote a string data type; they tell AutoLISP that the characters between them are a string.

A semicolon (;) allows the writer of a routine to put into the routine comments that have no effect on AutoLISP. The semicolon tells AutoLISP to ignore whatever follows until an end-of-line symbols is encountered.

Within literal strings (characters enclosed in quotation marks) backslashes are used to denote control characters. The characters currently recognized by AutoLISP for Release 10 of AutoCAD follow:

Character	*Meaning*
\\	Backslash character
\e	Escape character
\n	New line
\r	Return (Enter)

Character	Meaning
\t	Tab
\nnn	The character with octal code *nnn* (ASCII character number)

Note that if the directory and subdirectory are required to find a file, filename entries throughout AutoLISP must be strings that appear in one of the following forms:

`"\\directory\\subdirectory\\filename"`

or

`"/directory/subdirectory/filename"`

Because AutoLISP does not recognize any path you may have established in DOS, you have to specify all directories except the current directory.

Special Conditions

The following special conditions affect the way the LISP interpreter evaluates what it encounters:

- ❏ Integers, reals, strings, file pointers, and subrs evaluate to their own value. If AutoLISP evaluates an integer, such as 1, the value 1 will be returned to AutoCAD or to the next AutoLISP function.

- ❏ Symbols evaluate to the value to which they currently are bound.

- ❏ Lists are evaluated according to their first element. If the first element evaluates to a list, AutoLISP assumes that the list is a function definition; the rest of that list is evaluated as arguments to the defined function. If the first element is evaluated as a built-in function, AutoLISP evaluates the remainder of the list in accordance with the built-in function's capabilities.

- ❏ Expressions can span multiple lines. Only the completion of the list ends that part of the evaluation.

- ❏ Multiple spaces are equivalent to a single space. Routines contain indentations only to clarify the way they work; this is called *pretty printing*.

- ❏ The only functions for which AutoLISP is case-sensitive (where whether you use upper- or lowercase letters matters) are the *X* as part of the `ssget` function's filters and the matching of strings as equals. If you want, you can type the built-in function `setq` as **sEtQ**.

❏ Real numbers must have a number preceding the decimal point (for example, 0.7 not .7).

General Functions

The following functions do not fall into any specific category; they apply to all of the other categories.

```
(load <filename> <failure option>)
```

Description: This function loads any LISP routine into the current drawing session. `load` puts an AutoLISP routine into memory and returns the name of the defined function (`defun`). An optional action can be taken if AutoLISP does not find the file as requested by *filename. Filename* must be a string that includes the path for the search, if necessary, but does not include the file extension .LSP.

Usage: This function is used from the AutoCAD command prompt to load any individual LISP routine not included in your ACAD.LSP file. After the file has been loaded, you execute the routine by entering in parentheses the name of the routine, unless the routine was defined as a `C:XXX` function (see `defun`), in which case you type it in at the AutoCAD command prompt. You can use the `load` function also within another routine to load a separate AutoLISP routine and execute it from within the active routine. The following pairs of commands have the effects noted:

Function	*Effect*
`(load "dplot.lsp")`	Returns DPLOT
`(dplot)`	Executes DPLOT.LSP
`(load "dplot.lsp")`	Returns C:DPLOT
DPLOT	Executes DPLOT.LSP
`(load "dplot")`	Returns DPLOT
`(dplot)`	Executes DPLOT.LSP

The first example assumes that the routine starts its definition (`defun dplot ( /....` The second example assumes that the routine starts its definition (`defun c:dplot ( /....` The third example shows DPLOT.LSP loaded and executed from within another routine.

```
(defun <routine name symbol> <argument list> <expressions>...)
```

Description: Defun defines a function with the name *routine name symbol*, followed by arguments that describe whether any arguments will be provided, externally or internally, to the program. Once executed, defun allows the named routine to be loaded; upon execution, AutoLISP evaluates *expressions*. None of the elements listed in this defun format is optional. If no arguments are to be supplied, a nil list *( )* must be included.

Usage: Used to define the named AutoLISP functions that you will develop, defun has three formats. They look like this:

```
(defun dplot (/ v1 v2 v3)...

(defun c:dplot (/ v1 v2 v3)...

(defun S::STARTUP ()...
```

The first format creates a function (dplot) that defines local variables *v1*, *v2*, and *v3*.

The second format is the similar to the first, with one important difference: it defines a function that can be executed directly from the AutoCAD command prompt if you type **DPLOT**.

The final format, new in AutoLISP for Release 10 of AutoCAD, is a special defun that is placed in the ACAD.LSP file. When a new drawing session is started and AutoLISP loads the ACAD.LSP file, the expressions in the S::STARTUP function will be executed automatically.

If you do not understand defun, we recommend that you review the extensive discussion about it in the *AutoLISP Programmer's Reference* before you read further in this chapter.

```
(setq <symbol1> <expression> <symbol2> <expression>...)
```

Description: This function makes a list into a variable to which a symbol is assigned. setq takes the symbol *symbol1* and binds the results of whatever *expression* creates. In this book, we use setq with each assignment of a symbol name; this is not really necessary, but makes the program easier to read. When you feel comfortable with AutoLISP, you can save a little processing time by assigning your symbols en masse, like this:

```
(setq a "Q" b "U" c "E")
```

which is the same as:

```
(setq a "Q")
(setq b "U")
(setq c "E")
```

Usage: You will use Setq throughout your LISP routines. *Be sure to avoid naming symbols after AutoLISP functions!* For example, (setq angle (...)) is definitely a "no-no."

(setvar <variable name> <value>)

Description: This function retrieves an AutoCAD variable that is not read-only and that changes its *value*.

Usage: setvar is AutoLISP's way of changing the AutoCAD drawing environment. For example, if you don't want to watch all the activities of your LISP routines, add the following at the beginning of all of your routines, once you have them working properly:

   (setvar "CMDECHO" 0)

This line turns off the AutoCAD variable cmdecho so that the LISP routine commands are not echoed to the text screen.

(command <arguments>...)

Description: This function executes any AutoCAD command as if you had typed it at the AutoCAD command prompt. You can use strings for keyboard entries and symbols for values, in any combination, provided that the sequence is correct for the AutoCAD command. We have had some really strange results when we have entered an extra return as an argument to the command function. You can issue a ^C also by using the format (command "").

Usage: You will use this function throughout your AutoLISP routines. It will look something like this:

   (command "circle" pt1 pause)

In this example, the symbol pt1 is passed to the AutoCAD CIRCLE command for the center of the circle; a special function, pause, causes AutoLISP to wait for user input, allowing the user to drag the circle's radius.

(eval <expression>)

Description: This function, which returns the result of *eval*uating any LISP expression, can be used to evaluate symbols or function applications within AutoLISP.

Usage: Use `eval` as a shortcut for executing LISP functions. Suppose, for example, that you want to collect a set of numbers as a list so that you can count how many items you've collected and total the list as a *real*. You can enter the following:

(setq numlist '(+ 1 26 4 8 5 15))
(eval numlist)

which returns 59.0.

This function evaluates the list as if the actual contents of the list would be instructing LISP to execute a function. You can use `eval` to build a list that, based on choices made by the user, executes an AutoCAD command:

```
(setq do '(command "erase" "L"))
(eval do)
```

These two functions would cause AutoLISP to execute an `erase last` command.

`(progn <expression1> <expression2>...)`

Description: The `progn` function evaluates each *expression* in order of its position following `progn`.

Usage: Use this function to combine a number of expressions when only one expression is expected, or in menus when you want a number of LISP expressions to continue without effecting a return. Progn is used often in *if* expressions because the `if` function expects only an either/or choice of one expression each. Here is an example of how `progn` can be used in a menu:

```
[CIRCLE R ]^C^C$S=NUMBERS (progn (setq r +
(getreal "\nEnter Circle Radius: ") (command "circle" pause r))+
$S=
```

The use of `progn` allows the menu macro to incorporate both the `setq` and the command functions without interrupting the LISP process.

You can use `progn` also when you type AutoLISP functions at the AutoCAD command prompt for trial and error; by doing so, you can execute more than one function at a time.

Manipulating Data Types

A number of built-in functions are used to manipulate and evaluate the different data types in AutoLISP. These functions are very important because one activity may not be able to use the results of another activity. The AutoCAD variables for the date and time, for example, are provided by AutoCAD to AutoLISP as real numbers. You may want to convert the results of calculations in which these variables are used to a string that can be read as text by another program. Frequently, a problem with an AutoLISP routine occurs simply because you are trying to complete an operation on the wrong data type.

The main built-in functions for manipulating data types follow:

```
(angtos <angle> <mode> <precision>)
```

Description: This function converts an angle that is a real number expressed in radians to a string. You can select the mode by using an integer as follows:

Integer	Mode
0	Degrees
1	Degrees/minutes/seconds
2	Grads
3	Radians
4	Surveyor's units

Precision sets the number of decimal places you want returned in the string. (If you need a refresher on radians, refer to Chapter 10.)

Although `angtos` accepts a negative number (an angle expressed in a clockwise direction), that number is converted to a positive number which corresponds to the angle expressed in a counterclockwise direction. Consider the following examples:

Function	Effect
(angtos 1.570796 1 4)	Returns "90d0'0"".
(angtos -1.570796 1 4)	Returns "270d0'0"".

Usage: To dimension an angle in AutoCAD and provide a text note that expresses the angle in your choice of formats, you must convert the data to a string. Normally, the angle required for the `angtos` function is provided by the AutoLISP function `angle`. The same is true for passing a rotation angle, such as a block rotation angle or an angle for text rotation, to an AutoCAD command.

angtos is especially important in parametric routines (refer to Chapter 10). If you intend to supply the angle to angtos, remember to put a zero before any decimal points in any radians that are less than one. The following example, which assumes that you have a symbol ang bound to a value in radians:

```
(command "insert" "widget" pause "1" "1" (angtos ang))
```

inserts the block widget, pausing for an insertion point, at an x and y scale of 1 and at a rotation angle equal to the variable ang. In this case, angtos automatically converts the radians to the default unit settings in your drawing, rather than to any mode or precision you supply as arguments to the angtos function.

(atof <string>) and (atoi <string>)

Description: The atof (*ASCII to floating*) function converts a string to a real number. The atoi (*ASCII to integer*) function converts a string to an integer. atof always adds decimal points and zeros following a string such as "3" (3.0); atoi always drops any numbers following decimal places in strings such as "3.1" (3).

Usage: You may want to extract numbers from a text format so that you can use them in a mathematical calculation, or you may need a user response both as a string and as a real or integer. Instead of assigning two different variables or requesting the same input twice, you can use one of these functions, like this:

Function	Effect
(atof "19.3")	Returns 19.300000
(atoi "19.3")	Returns 19

(itoa <integer>) and (rtos <real> <mode> <precision>)

Description: The itoa function (*integer to ASCII*) converts an integer to a string. The rtos function (*real to ASCII*) converts a real to a string.

Usage: Similar to atoi and atof. You probably will use rtos, which converts AutoLISP reals into strings formatted in accordance AutoCAD unit settings. rtos is one of the best ways to supply a dimension to an AutoCAD command. Strings are used when you want to emulate data that is entered from the keyboard.

```
(float <integer>)
```

Description: This function converts an integer into a real number as follows:

Function	Effect
`(float 7)`	Returns 7.0

Usage: Suppose that a variable is bound to an integer which the user enters (for example, as in reply to the prompt How many spaces do you want?). If you want to use this number as a counter in a recursive loop, it must remain an integer; if, additionally, you want to multiply a distance by the number of spaces, the number must be a real. Float performs the conversion and you can either bind the value to a new variable or use float to perform a temporary conversion of the integer without binding it to anything.

```
(strcase <string> <which case>)
```

Description: This function converts a string to uppercase letters if <*which case*> does not exist or is nil; if <*which case*> is *T*, the string is converted to lowercase letters.

Usage: We use strcase primarily to make sure that user input is always in uppercase letters when we want to test whether user input matches a particular string. This conversion must be done because AutoLISP evaluates "CAT" as equal to "CAT" and "Cat" as unequal to "CAT", as follows:

Function	Effect
`(strcase "Cat")`	Returns "CAT"
`(strcase "cAt" T)`	Returns "cat"

```
(strcat <string1> <string2> ...)
```

Description: Strcat combines any number of strings into one string.

Usage: Use strcat to combine a collection of strings into file names, block names, dates, drawing titles, etc. This is how it works:

Function	Effect
`(strcat "Q" "U" "E")`	Returns "QUE"

All inputs to strcat must be strings; they can be other LISP expressions that evaluate to strings or symbols that are strings.

```
(strlen <string>)
```

Description: This function returns the length of the *string* atom.

Usage: This function can be used with `strcat` and `substr` to cut and paste strings (see `substr`, which follows).

```
(substr <string> <start> <length>)
```

Description: Substr retrieves a *substr*ing of *string*, starting from the location *start* and continuing to the end of the string (unless length is specified, in which case `substr` counts the length of the substring equal to *length*, including the starting character). The first character of the string is the character *1*.

Usage: Used as described in the function `strlen`, like this:

```
(setq a "5days")
(setq b "18days")
(setq c "24days")
(strcat (substr a 1 (- (strlen a) 4)) ", "
        (substr b 1 (- (strlen b) 4)) ", and"
        (substr c 1 (- (strlen c) 4)) " "
        (substr c (- strlen c) 3)))
```

and returns "5, 18, and 24 days".

In this example, we trimmed the four constant characters *days* from the end of the strings by using (- (`strlen x`) 4), which subtracts 4 from the length of string *x*, providing the resulting integer to the function `substr` as the length of the substring to be extracted. All but the last substring started with the first character; to calculate the starting position of the last substring, we then used `strlen`.

Mathematical Functions

AutoLISP's basic mathematical functions are self-explanatory. Just remember that the order of their format is *do this to this with this*. For example, the function (- 10 4) subtracts 4 from 10; the function (/ 10 4) divides 10 by 4. AutoLISP also has trigonometric functions that you may find useful in parametric programming.

The following are special types of mathematical functions.

```
(angle <pt1> <pt2>)
```

Description: This function returns (in radians) the angle of a line that would project between pt1 and pt2. The values of the points can be in two or three dimensions. The points, which can be obtained in several ways, can be supplied either as a symbol or a list. If the points are in three dimensions and you are using AutoCAD Release 10, the angle is supplied as if viewed from the current construction plane (Release 10's *user coordinate system*).

Usage: This function, when used in conjunction with angtos, is of considerable value in parametric programming. Symbols calculated as points can be supplied to the angle function; the value returned can be used to create new objects or to control the rotation angle of AutoCAD's commands and entities. Remember that the angle is from pt1 to pt2. In order to avoid getting upside-down text and insertions, use angle carefully, making sure that the angle is in the desired range. We used the angle function in Chapter 11 as follows:

```
(setq ang (angle pt1 pt2)
 (if
  (and (> ang (* 0.5 pi))(<= ang pi))
    (setq ang (+ ang pi)))
 (if
  (and (>= ang pi)(<= ang (* 1.5 pi)))
(setq ang (- ang pi)))
```

This routine sets the variable ang to the value of the angle between two previously defined variables (*pt1* and *pt2*). It then tests to see whether the angle (*ang*) is greater than 90 degrees (1/2 pi radians) and less than or equal to 180 degrees (pi radians). If it is, AutoLISP sets the value of ang to the original value of the angle plus 180 degrees; if it isn't, nothing happens.

The routine tests also to see whether the angle ang is greater than or equal to 180 degrees (pi radians) and less than or equal to 270 degrees (1 1/2 pi radians). If it is, AutoLISP sets the value of ang to the original angle minus 180 degrees; if is isn't, nothing happens.

This set of tests ensures that the value of ang, used for the text rotation angle, will always place the text at the angle you want, regardless of the order in which *pt1* and *pt2* are selected. The text rotation will always be between 0 and 90 degrees or 270 and 360 degrees.

```
(distance <pt1> <pt2>)
```

Description: This function returns the distance between two points as a real. The points can be provided either as the actual point description in real numbers or as symbols bound to a point.

Usage: This function, which is very useful for parametric routines that require the calculation of new points from existing points or lines, can be used in conjunction with the functions `polar` or `rtos` to provide a distance for calculation or a string for dimensional notation, respectively. In Chapter 11, we used `distance` in the LINS.LSP routine to calculate the length of a line; we needed to make sure that an insertion of text or a block would not be longer than the length of the line.

pi (π)

Description: Pi is not a function. It is the constant of π to be used in mathematical calculations.

```
(polar <pt> <angle> <distance>)
```

Description: The `polar` function returns the coordinates of a new point at a *distance* and *angle* from the original point *pt*. In AutoCAD Release 10, `polar` returns a three-dimensional point, although the angle will be input to the function with respect to the current user coordinate system. This fact can wreak havoc with routines written for earlier versions of AutoCAD. The relationship between the two points will almost always be a different angle as the user coordinate systems change.

Usage: In our opinion, `polar` is one of the greatest little functions in AutoLISP. It is used extensively in parametric programming. In Chapter 10, we used it this way:

```
(setq pt2 (polar pt (* 1.5 pi) row1))
```

This line creates a new point (*pt2*) at an angle of 270 degrees and a distance of *row1* from the original point (*pt*). In our example, the user selects the original point (*pt*). We used the symbol *row1* to contain the value of a calculated row length, based on the number of rows required.

```
(rem <first number> <second number>)
```

Description: rem divides the *first number* by the *second number* and returns the remainder.

Usage: rem is used frequently to round off real numbers. To ensure that the result of dividing one number by another is rounded up to the next largest number, use rem to test the remainder of the division. Depending on the value of the remainder, leave the results as they are or round them.

LISP Programming Pitfalls

When you start programming in LISP, you probably will get mired down in managing parentheses. The following suggestions will help with your basic routines:

- Check for typing errors.

- Count the parentheses, using plus for left and minus for right. You should end up with 0. If you don't like to count, find a program that will count for you.

- Try each part of your routine, a line at a time, in AutoCAD. Jot down what worked or, if you have a low overhead text editor, shell out of AutoCAD and add the line to a file. Return to AutoCAD and try the next line. You can also enter the longer programs at the command prompt. Don't worry if a an $n>$ symbol shows that you have n right parentheses to add. Stop typing at a logical point (after a right parenthesis), check your typing, and press Enter. This will allow you to catch your mistakes.

- When you test routines, start them with

    (defun testprog ()....

    Then, by typing an exclamation point (!) at the command prompt, you will be able to retrieve the values bound to your symbols. You can do this because you haven't assigned the variables to a local value (see the *AutoLISP Programmer's Reference*, pp. 34-35).

- Develop a standardized approach to naming your symbols. Try to give them short names (so that your routines will run fast and use as little memory as possible). Try also to use abbreviations of what a symbol is describing.

Some parts of AutoLISP quickly become clear; others take longer to grasp.

Summary

This chapter reviewed AutoLISP functions and concepts that generally apply to basic routine writing. We thought it best to give you a stopping point so that you could let what you have learned so far sink in before you advance to the "bells and whistles." Make sure that you understand the information in this chapter before you proceed. Chapter 14 contains some additional information about AutoLISP that you may need in order to solve simple customization problems.

We have discussed the following groups of AutoLISP concepts, which start you toward improving the quality of your menu macros:

- General functions
- Manipulating data types
- Mathematical functions

When you are ready, proceed to Chapter 14 and find out what you can really do with AutoLISP.

Recommended Tasks

- Review your favorite LISP routines in conjunction with reading this chapter.
- If you have a third-party menu system, look at the way LISP is used in the macros.
- Fool around with the concepts in this chapter by typing them in at the AutoCAD command prompt.

Optional Tasks

- Proceed to Chapter 14.

What Chapter 14 Is About

The bells and whistles of AutoLISP include:

- Advanced mathematical functions
- List manipulation
- Entity manipulation
- Table manipulation
- Input/output
- Conditional functions

Consistent with our philosophy that you really need to know only what is necessary to get the job done, this chapter does not include advanced functions that we don't consider necessary for CAD management. It focuses directly on functions you can put to work right away.

What You Should Know Before You Start

- Concepts from Chapter 13
- Effective use of a text editor

What To Have on Hand

- The *AutoCAD Reference Manual*
- The *AutoLISP Programmer's Reference*
- Word-processing software that can create and manipulate ASCII or nondocument text files

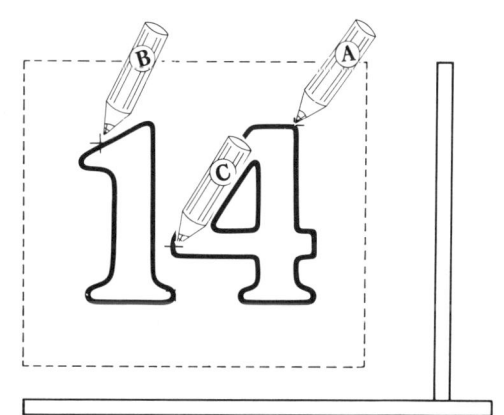

AutoLISP's Bells and Whistles

Using the information presented in Chapter 13, "AutoLISP Never Was Plain English," and a few concepts from this chapter, you can probably create with LISP almost any macro you need to use in AutoCAD. If you want to manipulate larger groups of data or accomplish major management tasks, however, you will need to become familiar with all of the concepts presented in this chapter.

If you do not have a firm grasp of the concepts presented in Chapter 13, we recommend that you reread the chapter. We started using the concepts presented in this chapter before we really had a grasp on the nuts and bolts. You can benefit from our experience—don't do it the way we did. Take your time.

Advanced Mathematical Functions

In our opinion, only one mathematical function falls into the advanced category (unless you have never used trigonometry).

```
(trans <pt> <from> <to> <disp>)
```

Description: This new function, added in AutoCAD Release 10, translates a point from one coordinate system to another. *Pt* can be a point with 3-D coordinates, or it can be used as a displacement value. *From* is a value representing the starting coordinate system; *to* is a value representing the final coordinate system. If *disp* has a value, *pt* is used as the coordinates of a 3-D point. If *disp* is nil or doesn't exist, *pt* is used as a vector. AutoCAD's MOVE and COPY commands work in much the same way. If you select a point as the base point of displacement and then press Enter, AutoCAD will use the values of that point to calculate the displacement for the MOVE or COPY.

From and *to* can be any of the following:

- An integer code of *0* for the World Coordinate System, *1* for the User Coordinate System, or *2* for the Display Coordinate System of the current viewport.

- An entity name, as returned by AutoLISP. The Entity Coordinate System can be matched by using this option.

- A 3-D extrusion direction (a list of 3 reals).

Trans can convert 2-D points to 3-D points, depending on your specification of the *from* coordinate system. If the *from* is the WCS (World Coordinate System), the Z value becomes 0.0; if the *from* is the UCS (User Coordinate System), the Z value is set to the current elevation; if the *from* is the ECS (Entity Coordinate System), the Z value is 0.0; and if the *from* is the DCS (Display Coordinate System), the Z value is projected to the current construction plane (a combination of the xy plane of the UCS with the current elevation).

Usage: Trans is the main AutoLISP tool for keeping 3-D objects interrelated in AutoCAD Release 10. Using `trans` to its fullest extent is advanced, and beyond the scope of this book. We are interested in the use of `trans` because of its capability to convert a selected point to the proper ECS and 2-D lines to a 3-D coordinate system. In AutoCAD Release 10, all lines are 3-D. If you have selected an entity and you want to connect a line from a point on that entity to a point in a different UCS during a parametric routine, use `trans`. Use `trans` also to convert standard drawings so that they are fully compatible with AutoCAD Release 10.

This is what a `trans` statement does:

```
(setq npt (trans pt e 1))
```

Suppose that you assigned the center of a circle to the symbol *pt*. Let's assume that you are now working in a different UCS than the UCS that is coplanar to the circle, and you want to draw a line from a point in the current UCS that corresponds to the center of the circle in the current UCS. This use of `trans` binds the desired 3-D point to the variable *npt*.

List Manipulation

Lists are a really big thing with AutoLISP (after all, the language got its name from them). You can access large amounts of data through lists, find data that is tied to a key (artificially, according to the order of the list), and create new sentences with lists. We have seen AutoLISP used so that it actually talks back to the user by manipulating lists in a quasiartificial-intelligence routine.

You need to be able to manipulate lists for many of the AutoLISP functions you will want to write. Here are the functions you need to do this:

```
(append <list 1> <list2>...)
```

Description: The append function will combine any number of lists into one list. Remember that the elements append uses must be lists.

Usage: This function is used to create data lists from a group of data lists. If, through different processes in a routine you end up with two or more separate lists, you can use append to combine them into one list. For example, the following line:

```
(append '(flush concealed) '(laminate #4530))
```

returns

```
(flush concealed laminate #4530)
```

You might use this code to create the description of a cabinet from a previously selected constant of *flush* doors with *concealed* hinges, a currently selected *laminate* finish, and a model number of *#4530*.

```
(assoc <item> <association list>)
```

Description: The assoc function uses a special type of list, called an *association list*, to return a value that is associated with a key *item*. An association list, which is actually a list of two element (atom) sublists, looks like this:

```
((cup coffee) (glass drink) (bowl soup) (plate salad))
```

By using the `assoc` function, this association list can provide AutoLISP with information that is tied to a key item. For example, if you bound this list to the symbol *cupboard*, you could use the function as

    (assoc cup cupboard)

which returns

    coffee

Or you could use it as

    (assoc bowl cupboard)

which returns

    soup

Usage: Throughout this book, you will see `assoc` used with entity descriptions because entity descriptions are stored as association lists in AutoCAD. To find specific information about an entity, you must use some AutoLISP functions to return the entity's association list, and then use a group code to access the specific information you want. (We will discuss this later in this chapter.)

You also can build association lists and sort data by *key*, either from a file outside the AutoCAD editor or from within AutoCAD. Suppose, for example, that you want to select a piece of equipment from a list of choices and you don't want to have to remember the fan size, the voltage rating, the wire size, the unit size, etc. Once AutoLISP knows which piece of equipment you want information about, the information can be retrieved from a file in which association lists are included with each equipment name.

`caar, cdar ,cadr, cddr, cadar, car, cdr, etc.`

Description: These functions are list readers; they are explained clearly in the *AutoLISP Programmer's Reference*. The tricky thing to remember is the difference between `car` and `cdr`. We can't figure out why they are named this way, but we keep them straight by remembering that the *A* list is the best and is therefore the first element of the list (`car`) and the *D* list is the dregs of the list (`cdr`). All of the other concatenations are translated by reading them. For example, `caar` is the A list of the A list, or the first element of the first sublist; `cadr` is the A list of the dregs of the list, or the first element of the rest of the list, and so on.

Usage: These functions are used to construct (from parts of other points) new points in parametric routines, and to retrieve parts of dotted pairs. For example, if you have an entity-description association list and you want to find the layer it is on, use the following:

```
(setq lay (cdr (assoc 8 e)))
```

where *e* is an association list you retrieve through one of AutoLISP's entity manipulators, and *8* is the group code for the entity's layer. This binds the value of the layer the entity is on with the variable symbol *lay*. *(assoc 8 e)* might return something like *(8 . "LIGHT")*, so that *layer* would be bound to the string *"LIGHT"*.

```
(cons <element> <list>)
```

Description: This function adds new first elements (atoms or lists) to an existing list. It also creates new dotted pairs from two atoms.

Usage: We use cons primarily to create dotted pairs for searching entity descriptions. For example:

```
(list (cons 0 "INSERT") (cons 8 "LIGHT"))
```

returns

```
((0 . "INSERT") (8 . "LIGHT"))
```

This result can be used, along with other AutoLISP functions, to search for a block that is inserted on layer *light*.

```
(list <expression 1> <expression 2>...)
```

Description: This function creates a list from any number of expressions. The expressions can be atoms or lists, which is what differentiates this function from append. (Append can only combine lists.)

Usage: We use list primarily to construct point descriptions for use with parametrics or AutoCAD commands. It is used also to create lists of dotted pairs to use as filters for selection-set searches, using *ssget* (which we discuss later in this chapter). For an example of this use, see the preceding discussion of cons.

An example of point construction follows:

```
(setq pt3 (list (car pt1) (cdr pt2)))
```

If *pt1* is bound to the value *(1.0 2.5 4.5)*, and *pt2* is bound to the value *(1.0 3.0 4.5)*, this use of list will return a new point, *pt3 (1.0 3.0 4.5)*.

```
(length <list>)
```

Description: The length function returns an integer that is the number of elements in a list. Sublists are counted as one element each.

Usage: Length can be used with other AutoLISP functions to *count* recursively through a list and extract one element at a time. This is handy when you are reading data from a list. (We will show you how to do this when we discuss *nth*.)

```
(member <expression> <list>)
```

Description: This function searches the named *list* and determines whether *expression* is a member of the named list. If it is, the function returns the *expression* and the remainder of the list following the expression; otherwise, *nil* is returned.

Usage: If you create a list in the order of largest to smallest, or broadest scope to smallest scope, member will allow you to prune a list based on the size of the search or group of information you want to obtain.

We use the function primarily, however, to see whether an expression is part of a list. If the expression is not part of the list, we can add it to the list or go to another list.

This is how the function works. The following code:

```
(setq day (list '(monday tuesday wednesday thursday friday
    saturday sunday)))
(setq tgif (member 'friday day))
```

returns

```
(friday saturday sunday)
```

Therefore:

```
(if (member friday tgif)(prompt "Go home!"))
```

The preceding example binds the days of the week to the list *day* and binds the symbol *tgif* to the list *(friday saturday sunday)*. It then uses the AutoLISP function `if` (which we will soon explain) to test whether *friday* is a member of the list *tgif*. If it is, AutoLISP prints the message `"Go home!"` on the screen.

```
(nth <integer> <list>)
```

Description: This function returns the element of a named *list* that is selected by the value of *integer*. If the integer is 5, the fifth element of the list is returned. If the integer is higher than the length of the list, *nil* is returned.

Usage: If nth is used in conjunction with length and a recursive loop, each element of a list can be extracted, as in the following example:

    (setq ctr (length day))
    (setq daynum (1- ctr))
    (repeat ctr (princ (nth daynum day))(setq daynum (1- daynum)))

This loop is set up by using the repeat function and a variable, *ctr*, that is set to the length of the list *day*. A second variable, *daynum*, is set to the length of the list *day* minus one. The loop is repeated a number of times equal to the length of the list *day*; the nth function counts through the list *day* and prints the contents of that list, one element at a time. This is accomplished by setting the value of *daynum* to one less, each time the loop is repeated. Zero is a valid quantity for *daynum* because the first element of the list is element zero; that is why we started with *daynum* as one less than the value of *ctr*. You will find that the first element is the zero element in a great number of lists and data groups in AutoCAD.

    (subst <newitem> <olditem> <list>)

Description: Subst replaces *olditem* with *newitem* in the named list. *Olditem* and *newitem* can be a single list or a sublist.

Usage: We use subst to modify entity description lists (discussed in the next group of functions). It is used also to update a list of data. Here is an example:

    (setq lib '(a b c d e))

returns

    (a b c d e)

and then

    (subst 'f 'a lib)

returns

    ('f 'b 'c 'd 'e)

This set of functions sets the list *lib* to *a b c d e*. Then subst substitutes *f* for *a* in the list *lib*.

Entity Manipulation

You can use AutoLISP to modify the characteristics of an entity without using the AutoCAD commands. LISP also can submit existing entities to AutoCAD commands for editing. The specific functions listed in this section are designed for this purpose.

`(entsel <prompt>)`

Description: This function requests the user to select an entity from the screen; the entity can be selected by AutoLISP if a point on the entity is known. An optional prompt can tell the user what the selection is to include. If no prompt is supplied, AutoLISP defaults to the `Select object:` prompt. This function returns the entity name and the point by which the entity was selected.

Usage: Simultaneously selecting an entity and the point by which it was selected can be useful if the point of selection will be used later. (If the point of selection will not be used later, we recommend that you use *ssget*.) Here is an example of `entsel`:

```
(setq e (entsel "Select the object for rotation <midpt>: "))
(setq en (car e))
(setq rp (cdr e))
```

This sample code provides the information necessary to ROTATE the entity *en* around the point *rp*, with some additional functions from AutoLISP tagging along. In this example it is assumed that object snap has been set previously to midpoint. The line

```
(setq en (car e))
```

returns the entity name (something like °Entity name: 60000001<), and the function `(setq rp (cdr e))` returns the point at which the selection was made—something like (2.10 2.20 0.0). Notice that we are binding a symbol to an entity name. This allows AutoLISP to tell AutoCAD exactly which entity it is altering. **CAUTION:** Entity names are valid only for the current drawing session; they change whenever you exit and reenter the Drawing Editor.

`(entnext <entity name>)`

Description: This function selects the entity following the entity defined by *entity name* in the database. To provide *entity name*, a symbol is bound to an entity name that has been retrieved by AutoLISP.

Usage: Entnext is used for working through the AutoCAD database from a predetermined starting point. Clearly, you will want to limit the size of the database so that you don't have to go through the entire drawing one entity at a time. Fortunately, AutoLISP has the capability to limit the size of the searched database by using selection sets. To use entnext, use the following format:

    (entnext e)

where *e* has previously been set to an entity name. This function returns the entity name of the next entity in the database.

`(entlast)`

Description: Entlast returns the entity name of the last entity in the database.

Usage: If you add an entity to the database by using AutoLISP, and you want to continue working with the entity, entlast will retrieve the entity name for you so that you can supply the entity name to a function or AutoCAD command, as in the following example:

    (command "insert" "ablock" pause 1 1 pause)
    (command "explode" (entlast))

These two functions insert a block, which can be dragged into place and rotated if DRAGMODE is set to 2. After the block has been inserted in the desired location at the desired rotation, entlast is used to select the block for exploding.

`(handent <handle>)`

Description: Handent, a new function added with AutoCAD Release 10, establishes a permanent index key for each entity in the database. The value of *handle* remains the same for an entity through all editing sessions and is retired if the entity is deleted from the database. Even then, the entity remains available via its handle until the end of the drawing session. Handles are part of a dotted pair with group code 5. Handent will return the *current* entity name of the entity with the *handle* string used as the argument to handent.

Usage: Entity handles are used primarily to retain the identity of groups of data from one drawing session to the next (a nonblock block, more or less). A group of entity handles can be written to a file as a list and retrieved later for manipulation. Entity handles also can provide information for quantity takeoffs and eliminate the need for attributes for every entity that is to be included in the quantity.

```
(entdel <ename>)
```

Description: Entdel removes from the database the entity with the name *ename*. The deleted entity can be restored to the database by using entdel again.

Usage: We once used entdel in a routine that finds all the entities on a particular layer of the drawing and erases only those entities. Instead of collecting all of the entities into a selection set and then using ERASE on them as a group, you can use this function for immediate action as the routine steps through the database. Entdel generally makes a routine faster when used as the response to a comparison, instead of retaining a large set of chosen entities for later action. The format for this function is simple:

```
(entdel e)
```

where *e* is bound to the name of the entity to be removed.

```
(entget <entity name>)
```

Description: This function returns a list of the description data for the entity specified by *entity name*. This list is an association list of dotted pairs. The entities' qualities can then be extracted and manipulated using the functions assoc and cdr. Appendix C of the *AutoCAD Reference Manual* has a complete listing of the group codes for entities.

Usage: The entget function is the primary vehicle for accessing the drawing database for the purpose of cataloging or modifying entities. The procedure for using entget follows:

```
(setq en (entlast))
(setq e (entget en))
(setq lay (cdr (assoc 8 e)))
```

The preceding sequence binds the entity's name (in this case the last entity) to the symbol *en*. Then the association list of the entity description is bound to the symbol *e* with entget. Finally, the name of the layer the entity is on is extracted (using cdr and assoc) and bound to the symbol *lay*. This same procedure can be used to extract the entity type, the endpoints, insertion point, the text height, etc., simply by changing the group code number to the appropriate association.

```
(entmod <new entity list>)
```

Description: The entmod function is passed a new association list that contains any changes made to the entities's group code associations. This function modifies the entity's description in the database.

Usage: We use `entmod` primarily to make changes in an automated fashion to existing entities in the AutoCAD database. Using `entmod`, all of the properties you can affect with the AutoCAD CHANGE command can be modified with a well-designed LISP routine, including text content, text height, circle diameters, endpoints, layers, color, linetypes, etc. The following continues the example we began in our explanation of `entget`:

```
(setq en (entlast))
(setq e (entget en))
(setq e (subst (list (cons 8 "LIGHT")) (assoc 8 e) e))
(entmod e)
```

Instead of extracting the layer name, we have reassigned *e* to a new list by using the function `subst`. This substitutes a new dotted pair, *8 . LIGHT*, for the existing part of the entity description associated with group code 8. `Entmod` then changes the database by replacing the entire association list in the database. This function changes the layer of the entity to layer *light*, no matter what layer it was on originally.

Notice that `entmod` replaces the entire list, not just part of it. You can change everything you see in the list and even add some items by constructing a new list using `list`. For example, you could change all the lines in a drawing to circles. You can do this because the objects you see displayed on-screen are simply AutoCAD's representation of the entities' association list.

We recommend that you try the examples under `entget` and `entmod` by typing each line, with the parentheses included, at the AutoCAD command prompt. Don't worry—you won't hurt anything if you make a mistake. Start a test drawing, draw a line on layer *0*, and make sure that you have a layer named *light* in the drawing. If layer *light* is a different color, you will notice that the line doesn't change color. This brings us to the next function.

`(entupd <entity name>)`

Description: This function is used to update the screen image of the entity named by *entity name*, as supplied to `entupd`. Remember that the entity name is a symbol that is bound to the entity name.

Usage: The purpose of this function is to save time. Instead of updating a complex set of changes, or a complex entity, as each change is made to the association list, `entupd` allows AutoLISP to wait until all the changes are made before refreshing the screen image. The following lines complete the example used in our explanation of `entmod`:

```
(setq en (entlast))
(setq e (entget en))
(setq e (subst (list (cons 8 "LIGHT")) (assoc 8 e) e))
(entmod e)
(entupd e)
```

Now the line will change colors to match the characteristics of layer *light* (assuming that *color* is set BYLAYER in the drawing).

(ssget <mode> <pt1> <pt2>)

Description: This is AutoLISP's version of AutoCAD's SELECT command, with a few added wrinkles. Ssget can be used without the mode or point settings, in which case it works like the standard selection process in AutoCAD. You can select a mode for using the selection, such as *W* or *C*, in which case you can also provide *pt1* and *pt2* for automatically selecting the window or crossing points. You can use modes *P* or *L*, for previous and last; or you can use mode *X*, which sets up a filter list of entity types. *Ssget* selects only main entities, excluding block attributes and polyline vertices. Refer to the *AutoLISP Programmer's Reference* for a detailed explanation of ssget formats.

The *AutoLISP Programmer's Reference* also contains a listing of the filter options. Take a moment to look at them. These filter options include the entity type, block name, linetype name, text style, layer name, elevation, thickness, color number, blocks with attributes, and 3-D extrusion vector. You can build a selection set with any combination of these filters. The filters must be a list of dotted pairs. *Note:* All mode options must be specified in uppercase letters; this is one of the few times AutoLISP is case-sensitive.

Ssget returns a selection set name, such as <Selection Set 1>.

Usage: Ssget allows AutoLISP to manipulate groups of entities, just as you do in AutoCAD. We use ssget primarily to extract attribute information and to filter groups of entities we want to modify as a group. You can use ssget also to supply a selection set to an AutoCAD command, if the command will accept *last* as an entity selection. Here are some examples:

```
(setq ss1 (ssget "X" (list (cons 0 "INSERT")
          (cons 2 "PLOTBLK"))))
```

and

```
(command "erase" ss1 "")
```

These functions use `ssget` to find all blocks (group code Ø "INSERT") with the name *PLOTBLK* (group code 2 "PLOTBLK") and binds them to the symbol *ss1*. The next line erases the selection set. If you combine `ssget` with a few other AutoLISP commands, you can use the `entmod` group to change the characteristics of the entities in the selection set. Keep reading.

`(sslength <selection set>)`

Description: `Sslength` returns the number of main entities in a selection set. You must supply it with a symbol bound to a selection set name that has been retrieved by `ssget`.

Usage: This function is used to count through a selection set so that you can act on each entity in the set. Entity numbers in the selection set start with zero and continue to the `sslength` of the set, minus one. Confusing? You bet! Our guess is that the reason for this is that zero is not equal to nil—if you want to know the length of a set, you get one number, but if you want to count through a set until you have completely exhausted its contents, you get another number, proceeding to zero for AutoLISP to receive a nil reply. Here is an example:

   `(sslength ss1)`

returns an integer representing the length of *ss1*.

`(ssname <selection set> <index>)`

Description: The `ssname` function returns the entity name of entity number *index* in the selection set named by the symbol bound to the selection set name.

Usage: You use this function to extract entities from the selection set so that you can act on their association list or read their vertices or attribute values. You have to be a little careful here. If the entities in the set don't have subentities of attributes or vertices, you retrieve each entity name using `ssname`. If you are manipulating a selection set of blocks and want to read their attributes, you have to use `ssname` to retrieve the block name and then use `entnext` to retrieve each subentity. The same is true for polyline vertices. Here is an example of this function:

   `(setq e (ssname ss1 Ø))`

This returns the name of the first entity in the selection set bound to the symbol *ss1*, and binds the name to the symbol *e*.

```
(ssadd <entity name> <selection set>)
```

Description: Ssadd, used by itself, creates a new selection set with no members. If *entity name* is provided, the selection set includes the entity designated by the entity name. If both the entity name and a *selection set* name are provided, a new selection set in which the named entity is added to the old set is created.

Usage: Suppose that you want to make a modification to each entity in the set, and that based on a characteristic of the entity, you then want to move some entities and leave the rest alone. Instead of reaccessing the database, you can perform the test while you modify the entities; then you can create a new selection set from those that pass the test. This function works as follows:

```
(setq ss2 (ssadd))
(ssadd e ss2)
```

This creates a selection set with a name bound to the symbol *ss2*, and then adds the entity *e* to the set.

```
(ssdel <entity name> <selection set>)
```

Description: This function removes *entity name* from *selection set*.

Usage: If you intend to perform a test on entities you are modifying, and if you are sure that most of the entities in the set will pass the test, use `ssdel`. It will work faster than creating a new set. The format is simple:

```
(ssdel e ss2)
```

This deletes the entity (with the entity name bound to the symbol *e*) from the selection set (with the selection set name bound to the symbol *ss2*).

```
(ssmemb <entity name> <selection set>)
```

Description: Ssmemb tests to see whether the named entity is a member of the named selection set, returning *T* if it is, *nil* if it isn't.

Usage: If you are comparing two selection sets to determine whether an entity is a member of each, `ssmemb` is the function that will perform the test. During the use of ssget, AutoLISP checks this for you, so that you don't need to use `ssmemb` when actively building a selection set. The format of `ssmemb` follows:

```
(ssmemb e ss2)
```

This tests to see whether the entity name bound to symbol *e* is included in the selection-set name bound to symbol *ss2*. This would return nil, because we just removed it in `ssdel`.

Table Manipulation

The AutoCAD drawing file contains a set of tables that describe the layers, linetypes, views, text styles, blocks, user coordinate system, and viewports. This is part of the database environment and, with the exception of the blocks table, does not include reference to specific entities. The tables are used to verify the conditions loaded into the drawing when it is at rest, with the exception of shapes. We don't know why shapes are excluded, since the text-style table sets up the conditions for loading text-font shape files. Valid names of tables are *"LAYER", "LTYPE", "VIEW", "STYLE", "BLOCK", "UCS",* and *"VPORT".*

```
(tblnext <table name> <rewind>)
```

Description: This function searches the drawing symbols table for the table named by *table name*, which must be one of the valid names mentioned above. *Rewind* tells AutoLISP to start at the top of the specified table if it is included as a *T*. If *rewind* is not included (is nil), each use of tblnext will proceed to the next entry in the table, until there are no more table entries. Tblnext returns a list of dotted pairs that you can read but cannot modify. The *block* table includes a dotted pair that has a group code of –2. This allows you to use entget and entnext to read the block information and its attributes. You cannot modify this information using *entmod*, which is why the *ssget* function was created.

Usage: If you are going to run LISP routines that must make sure that various layers, text styles, linetypes, etc. are loaded, you need to verify the content of the drawing tables with tblnext. We have used tblnext also to retrieve text style data, for example, so that we can use LISP to create a floppy disk containing all the text styles in a drawing. This is most helpful when we are going to plot outside our office on a service bureau's plotter. The following example of tblnext:

```
(tlbnext "layer" T)
```

accesses the first layer entry in the layer table and might return:

```
((0 . "LAYER")(2 . "0")(70 . 0)(62 . 1)(6 . "CONTINUOUS"))
```

This function returned the association list from the layers table of the first layer in the drawing—layer *0* (group code *2*). The function also reveals that the layer is thawed (group code *70* is set to *1* if it's frozen), the layer color is red (group code *62*), and the linetype is continuous (group code *6*).

```
(tblsearch <table name> <symbol> <setnext>)
```

Description: Tblsearch finds the *symbol* in the table *table name* and, if *setnext* is T, sets the search to the item that follows the symbol in the table. If *setnext* is nil, only the association list for *symbol* is returned.

Usage: `Tblsearch` should be used in lieu of `tblnext` when you do not need to know the entire contents of a table. We have used `tblsearch` to read information about a text style so we can modify all the selected text entities in a drawing to a different text style. The format to use:

```
(tblsearch "STYLE" "STANDARD")
```

returns an association list containing everything you need to know about the standard text style.

Try entering the sample line of code at the AutoCAD command prompt, and examine the output. Notice that all parts of the listing are important to the definition of the text style. If you have different styles in your drawing, do the same for them and compare the differences, especially if you have different obliquing angles and width factors. If you don't have a variety of styles, create some and look at them with `tblsearch`, noting the differences between them.

Input/Output

AutoLISP has several functions for gaining input and providing output. In this section, we cover the fundamental functions used for this purpose:

```
(getwhatever <prompt>)
(getwhatever <pt> <prompt>)
(getwhatever <variable name>)
```

Description: This is AutoLISP's primary group of functions for getting information from the user. They give your AutoLISP routines the look and feel of AutoCAD. Although we discuss how each is used, this description encompasses most of them. Minor discrepancies will be noted in each "Usage" discussion. The variety of AutoLISP getfunctions is due to the type of information that is required. Each of these getfunctions specifies the type of information AutoCAD is receiving. These functions are primarily for user input; they do not accept input from another AutoLISP expression.

Some of the getfunctions have an optional *prompt*, so that you (the programmer) can tell users what format their information should take. The *prompt*, which must be enclosed in quotation marks, can include also the special characters described in Chapter 13. You can review these special characters also in the *AutoLISP Programmer's Reference*, under the explanation of the *prompt* function. We typically use the "\n" enclosed in quotation marks, so that a new line is started. If there is no prompt, AutoLISP waits for user input without indicating what is happening. We therefore advise you to specify a prompt either within or before the get-functions that use prompts.

Other AutoLISP getfunctions have an optional *pt* input so that you can include a base point from which the getfunction projects a rubber band to the crosshairs. This shows users what their reference point should be. If there is no specified *pt*, the getfunction allows users to select one or enter one from the keyboard.

The final major format of getfunctions is a *variable name* which represents a string that is one of the AutoCAD variables. Retrieving these variables tells your program the current status of any of the accessible variables. All you have to do is supply your choice of variables in quotation marks.

Now let's look at how to use each of these functions.

```
(getangle <pt> <prompt>)
```

Usage: This function returns an angle, expressed in radians, to AutoLISP. The user can select two points to show AutoCAD the angle, or you (the programmer) can provide one of the points in AutoLISP as a reference point for the user. This is a powerful parametric tool; it is used to create lines, insert blocks, and realign text, among other things. Here is an example of its use:

```
(setq ang (getangle "\nIndicate a reference point and the
          angle of rotation: ")
```

This function sets the symbol *ang* to the value of a reference angle in radians, allowing the user to show AutoLISP the rotation angle.

```
(getcorner <pt> <prompt>)
```

Usage: This function works well for parametric and "show" corner routines for drawing rectangles. The *pt* is not optional; it must be supplied in AutoLISP. You should use a prompt with this function, as it has little use within AutoLISP. Its primary purpose is to allow users to visualize the rectangle they will create by dragging a box to the second point. This is an example:

```
(setq pt2 (getcorner pt1
"\nIndicate the opposite corner of the rectangle: "))
```

This routine prompts the user for input of a second corner drawn from the point assigned to the variable *pt1*, which AutoLISP can use to construct a rectangle by using `car` and `cdr` with *pt1* and *pt2* to construct *pt3* and *pt4*. An example is

```
(setq pt3 (cons (car pt1) (cdr pt2)))
```

`(getdist <pt> <prompt>)`

Usage: Both *pt* and *prompt* are optional. This function returns a real, no matter how the drawing units are set or how the user provides the input. It is used internally by AutoLISP to measure distances between variables that are bound to a point description; it is used also to obtain a requested distance from the user with a point supplied by AutoLISP as the starting point, or with no point and strictly a distance. We use this function extensively in parametric routines. Here is an example from the SCHED.LSP program in Chapter 10:

```
(prompt "Enter the spacing for column ")
    (princ nu)(prompt " in inches: ") (setq csp (* scf (getdist)))
```

In this example, we created a prompt outside the `getdist` function to facilitate the insertion of the variable *nu* into the prompt. (We will get to the use of `prompt` and `princ` in just a moment.) This function uses `getdist` to have the user type in the distance from the keyboard (or supply it from a menu). It sets the column spacing, *csp*, to a user-supplied distance of inches, and multiplies the distance by a scale factor, *scf*, so that the distance in inches is adjusted to the drawing-scale factor and the column spacing is always set in real inches.

`(getenv <variable name>)`

Usage: This allows AutoLISP to read automatically the ACAD directory from the system environment variable ACAD. It eliminates creating a false configuration variable in the ACAD.LSP file to tell AutoLISP where to look for files. This is especially useful for the environment variable ACADCFG. You can adjust your routines to the directory to which ACADCFG is set, so that they will accommodate the different configurations you may have, as in the following example:

```
(setq dry (getenv "ACADCFG"))
(command "menu" (strcat dry "/menu1"))
```

This function is a new feature of AutoCAD Release 10. In this example, the ACADCFG directory is combined with a menu name to load a menu required for that particular configuration. If you have a mouse and a digitizing tablet, for example, there is no sense using the digitizing tablet menu for the mouse, even though the screen menus may be the same. The size of the mouse menu may be much smaller in total bytes, thus saving you a great deal of paging time.

`(getint <prompt>)` and `(getreal <prompt>)`

Usage: These two functions use an optional prompt to retrieve their corresponding data types from the user. They are used to avoid any conversion that may be required by your routine in order to instigate other actions properly. Their usage is straightforward:

`(setq nu (getint "\nHow many widgets do you want to insert?: "))`

or

`(setq thk (getreal "\nEnter the thickness <e.g. 0.18>: "))`

These two examples set the number symbol *nu* to an integer (5, for example) and the thickness symbol *thk* to a real (1.25, for example).

`(getkword <prompt>)`

Usage: This function is a lifesaver for interactive routines in which you want to control the reply options and then have the routine react to the reply. This function is used in conjunction with `initget`, which sets a list of valid responses prior to the use of the getkword function. Here is how we used it in LINS.LSP:

```
(initget 1 "B b T t")
(setq ans (strcase
    (getkword "\nInsert a block <B> or text <T>? <B or T>: ")))
```

This prompts the user for a *B* or *T* reply. `Initget` makes sure that this is what you get. (We discuss the use of `initget` later in this chapter.) We use *strcase* in this routine to make sure that we have an uppercase reply.

`(getorient <prompt>)`

Usage: `Getorient` is the same as `getangle`, with one exception. If the user has changed the direction of zero degrees (normally to the right) or the direction in which increasing angles rotate (normally counterclockwise), `getangle` will get confused when providing absolute angles (such as North). `Getangle` adjusts for the direction of rotation (ANGDIR). `Getorient` adjusts for both the direction of rotation and the location of zero degrees (UNITS or ANGBASE).

If you want to drag a block into a drawing and rotate it a certain number of degrees, use `getangle` (rotation amount). To orient an object, such as text or property lines, use `getorient`. AutoLISP will return the angle in radians.

`(getpoint <pt> <prompt>)`

Usage: We use `getpoint` in parametric routines to establish a user-selected starting point or an insertion point that will be input to the routine. Getpoint accepts an optional *pt* that will be used as a starting point for the function, and provides a rubber band to the crosshairs. Getpoint always returns a list that represents a point. We used getpoint in SCHED.LSP in the following way:

```
(setq pt
  (getpoint "\nSelect the upper left corner of the schedule
      location: "))
```

As you can see, getpoint binds the variable *pt* to the starting location of the schedule.

`(getstring <carriage return> <prompt>)`

Usage: Getstring retrieves a string from user input, up to a maximum of 132 characters. If the optional *carriage return* is *T*, getstring allows the user to reply with spaces; in other words, it disables AutoCAD's default space bar function as a carriage return. Getstring supports an optional prompt for the information requested. Here is an example:

```
(setq nm (getstring T "\nEnter your first and last name, then
      press <ENTER>: "))
```

The symbol *nm* is bound to a user's first and last name, in this case, by *getstring*. Notice that we have included *T* to enable the use of spaces in the reply string.

`(getvar <variable name>)`

Usage: This function retrieves any of the AutoCAD drawing variables that can be read or set in AutoCAD. The `getvar` function is a primary AutoLISP tool; it ensures that the LISP routine is well coordinated with the drawing environment. We use it in our automated archiving routines to capture the drawing name; we also use it to retrieve LTSCALE to set the drawing scale. It should be used with every AutoLISP routine that resets a particular environment variable to store the original setting so that everything can be returned to its preroutine status when the routine is finished.

We recommend that you write a routine that captures all the pertinent settings you want maintained, and that you make it part of your ACAD.LSP file. Then you can call this function and capture all the important environment variables. Then write another routine that resets all the variables, and execute it at the end of the routine. Your routine might look like this:

```
(setq clay (getvar "CLAYER")
      apt  (getvar "APERTURE")
      blp  (getvar "BLIPMODE")
      hlt  (getvar "HIGHLIGHT")
      os   (getvar "OSMODE")
      snp  (getvar "SNAPMODE"))
```

The preceding routine returns the values of the variables and binds them to the symbols. The following routine resets everything:

```
(command "LAYER" "s" clay "")
(setvar "APERTURE" apt)
(setvar "BLIPMODE" blp)
```

You should become familiar with all the system variables in AutoCAD. You will be amazed at how much information is available.

`(initget <mode> <string>)`

Usage: This function sets limitations on the type of data that all the getfunctions (except `getenv`, `getvar`, and `getstring`) can receive. The mode setting is optional; it governs the restrictions. The *AutoLISP Programmer's Reference* includes a chart that lists how these restrictions apply to each function. *String* is an optional string that describes the allowable match the routine expects to receive from the user. The *modes* to be used with `initget` are

Number	Meaning
1	Disallow the input of nothing (in other words, Enter only).
2	Disallow zero.
4	Disallow negative numbers.
8	Do not check limits and ignore LIMCHECK.
16	Return 3-D points rather than 2-D.
32	Use dashed lines for rubber band or box.

The modes are additive, so that you can enforce any combination of them. For example, the value of 7 would enforce modes 1, 2, and 4. If the string is not matched as requested or the conditions of the modes are not met, initget prompts the user to try again. (For an example of the way we use initget, see our description of getkword.)

(findfile <filename>)

Description: Findfile searches the ACAD path for a file *filename* in the following order:

1. Current directory
2. Directory containing the current drawing
3. Directory named by the SET ACAD = environment variable
4. Directory containing the AutoCAD program files

Filename must include the file's name and file extension, if any. If a directory is included with the file name, findfile will search only the specified directory. If the file isn't found, findfile returns nil.

Usage: This function, which is new with AutoCAD Release 10, lets AutoLISP function more like AutoCAD does. It serves as a test to make sure that a file is available, and can be used with a conditional statement to prompt users to try again and/or to provide an error message. We use it to test for other LISP routines we want to load with the current routine, blocks for insertion, and data files. Here is an example:

```
(setq fil
(getstring "Enter the name of the standard block you wish to
    insert: "))
(setq fil? (findfile fil))
(if (= fil? nil)(prompt "ERROR: Block requested not found.")
(command "INSERT" fil pause 1 1 pause))
```

This sequence sets the symbol *fil* to a user-supplied block name, which is returned as a string. Findfile checks the ACAD path for the standard block drawing; if the drawing is not found, findfile sets the variable *fil?* to nil. The if test (which we will discuss soon) either advises the user that the block doesn't exist or inserts the block. A proficient programmer can add to this concept a loop that lets the user try again, instead of just exiting the program.

(open <filename> <mode>)

Description: This function opens a file *filename* in the *mode* requested. Because the function sets a file pointer, not an actual variable that AutoLISP recognizes, open must always be bound to a symbol before the file is acted on, and the symbol must be used to reference the file. Valid *modes* are r, which opens for reading if the file is found; w, which opens for writing whether or not the file is found; and a, which opens for appending whether or not the file is found. Note that w will overwrite an existing file.

Usage: This function allows AutoLISP to write to disk. Writing to disk can be done in various ways, but usually involves writing a script file or saving data outside AutoCAD. We used this function in DPLOT.LSP. The following line:

```
(setq pfl (open "dplot.scr" "w"))
```

opens a script file (DPLOT.SCR) for writing and binds the file pointer (<*File #nnn*>) to the variable *pfl*.

`(write-line <string> <file symbol>)`

Description: Write-line writes a *string* to the screen or, if the optional *file symbol* is supplied, to a file. The line written to the screen includes quotation marks; the line written to file does not.

Usage: We use `write-line` primarily to write data to a file. The data can be a string or a variable. The following sequence from DPLOT.LSP:

```
(setq pfl (open "dplot.scr" "w"))
(write-line "plot" pfl)
...
(write-line p1 pfl)
```

uses `write-line` to write the string *"plot"* and the symbol *p1* to the file DPLOT.SCR. Notice that *p1* is a symbol. This symbol must be bound to a string; otherwise, an error message will result.

`(read-line <file symbol>)`

Description: Read-line, the counterpart of `write-line`, reads a line from the keyboard (or from the file bound to the *file symbol*, if it is provided). Read-line returns a string until it reaches the end of the file, at which time it returns nil.

Usage: Read-line is AutoLISP's primary tool for gaining data from a file on disk. You must be careful when you use this function, because `read-line` always returns a string. For example, if you want to obtain a real number to use as a distance out of a file, you will have to use the function `atof`. In an example of `read-line` usage, the following line:

```
(setq nxtl (atof (read-line lnfl)))
```

binds to a real number the symbol *nxtl* (which represents *next length*) via `atof` by reading a line from the file LENGTH.DTA, which we bound to the symbol *lnfl*.

```
(close <file symbol>)
```

Description: This function closes any file AutoLISP has opened and requires that a symbol bound to a valid file pointer be provided.

Usage: Close must be included in every routine in which you open a file. Here is an example from DPLOT.LSP:

```
(setq pfl (open "dplot.scr" "w"))
(write-line "plot" pfl)
...
(write-line p1 pfl)
...
(setq pfl (close pfl))
```

Close is used to close the file *pfl* and bind the variable *pfl* back to nil, which was bound to DPLOT.SCR.

```
(menucmd <string>)
```

Description: This function changes menu subpages from within the current menu. The *string* must be the name of a valid menu page from the active menu, preceded by the appropriate letter designating its category of page type: screen (S), button (B), icon (I), pull-down (P1-P10), tablet (T1-T4), and auxiliary (A1) menus.

Usage: We use menucmd during LISP routines to bring up (for users who do not like to type) screen menus that will provide predetermined responses to queries for input, object snap use, and character input. In the following lines:

```
(menucmd "S=OSNAP")
(command "line" pause pause)
```

menucmd changes the screen menu to the AutoCAD object snap menu so that the user can select object snap options without having to use the keyboard while he or she is drawing a line.

```
(prompt <string>)
```

Description: This function displays the *string* in the screen's prompt area, returning nil.

Usage: We use prompt for two general problems. First, if we want to advise the user that something is going on during a long procedure, we use prompt to display messages such as "Please wait...information being processed" and "Processing complete...proceeding to next step".

Second, we use prompt for screen status-line formatting. For example, if we are using one of the getfunctions and need a rather long message for informational purposes, we may want to put the message on more than one line and include the value of a symbol in the message. In this case, we use the prompt function outside the getfunction, and do not use the get-function's prompt area. In the following example from SCHED.LSP:

```
(prompt "Enter the spacing for column ")(princ nu)
     (prompt " in inches: ")
(setq csp (* scf (getdist)))
```

prompt is used twice, on either side of princ (princ is the next function discussed) so that the value of the symbol *nu* is included in the prompt as a variable.

```
(prin1 <expression> <file symbol>)
(princ <expression> <file symbol>)
(print <expression> <file symbol>)
```

Description: Each of these functions prints *expression* to the screen and to the optional file designated by *file symbol*. All of these functions will print any expression, or the value of the symbol included as *expression*. (The differences occur only in the printing format.)

Prin1 prints the expression without a space or newline. It also precedes special characters in strings with a slash (\), such as \n for ASCII character 10. The only difference between princ and prin1 is that the former does not modify special characters. Print differs from prin1 by printing a newline before an expression and inserting a space after an expression.

Usage: We use princ or prin1 to exit a routine quietly. By using these functions, we eliminate the nil response that comes from all other LISP functions that have completed their evaluation. You will see that in many of our routines (princ) is the last statement before the closing right parenthesis.

The following sample file was created by using write-line, print, princ, and prin1, in that order. Each command used the string *"QUE"*, symbol *t1* bound to the string *"QUE"*, and symbol *t2* bound to (char 10), which is a return.

```
QUE         (write-line "QUE" fi)
QUE            (write-line t1 fi)
               (write-line t2 fi)


"QUE" QUE"QUE"   (print "QUE" fi)(princ "QUE" fi)(prin1 "QUE" fi)
"QUE" QUE"QUE"   (print t1 fi)(princ t1 fi)(prin1 t1 fi)
"\n"             (print t2 fi)(princ t2 fi)
"\n"             (prin1 t1 fi)
```

Study the example carefully. The first and second lines, written by `write-line`, contain no quotation marks and included a carriage return when they were written. In the third line, `write-line` wrote a carriage return to the file; the line after that was created by the `write-line` carriage return. The fifth line is blank also, because `print` began with a carriage return and then printed *"QUE"* and a space. `Princ` printed the string without the quotation marks. Then `prin1` printed the string with the quotation marks and no spaces or returns. The sixth line was printed with the same sequence. (Note that the only reason there *is* a sixth line is that the sequence begins with a `print`.) The last series is most interesting. `print` started a new line, printed the special character for a return, and then a space (which we can't see). Then `princ` executed a return. Finally, `prin1` wrote the special character only.

Try this exercise and then open the file for reading. Using `read-line`, read each line of the file and notice the results. Each line is a string, even the blank line with a return. In order to write data files for use in outside programs or files for AutoLISP's use, you need to understand the `prinx` choices and `write-line`.

Conditional Functions

Conditional functions, perhaps the most important functions, are tests. Thanks to them, AutoLISP makes decisions, seems intelligent, and interacts with users in a productive way. Conditional functions operate on the response of evaluation of an expression as *T* or *nil*. Because each of these functions tests for the condition in a different way, you should learn to use all of them.

(and <expression 1> <expression 2>...)

Description: This function checks each of the expressions that follow it. If any of them evaluates to nil, the function returns nil; if all of them evaluate to T, the function returns T.

Usage: To make sure that everything is all right with a group of expressions before you continue with a procedure, use and to do the test. Such a test looks like the following line:

(and t1 t2 (= t1 t2))

which checks to see whether *t1* and *t2* are bound to something other than nil and whether they are equal to each other. If all these conditions are met, and returns *T*.

```
(cond (<test> <result>)...)
```

Description: The cond function accepts any number of lists as arguments. It evaluates the first item in each list (*test*); if the test is found to be *T*, cond evaluates the second item in each list (*result*). If no *result* is supplied, the value of the *test* is returned. If more than one test is true, the last result is returned.

Usage: Use cond when you are looking at more than one possibility, with each possibility providing a unique result. If all you are testing for is that any of the possibilities are true before executing the expression, use if (discussed later in this section).

Cond makes for very efficient programming. You will notice that some of the routines in this book use a number of if tests; in some instances, we could have combined the if tests into cond functions—the program would run better, but you would have a harder time following it. Here is an example:

```
(cond
(= mn "Model1")(command "insert" "Model1" pause "1" "1"
   "Ø"))
(= mn "Model2")(command "insert" "Model2" pause "1" "1"
   "Ø"))
(= mn "Model3")(prompt "\This model is not yet ready for
   production."))
```

This example tests for a user-supplied string that was bound to symbol *mn*, and then executes the appropriate response by either inserting the correct block or prompting the user that it's not ready yet. If you are building LISP routines and menus, and expect to update the use of the routines as well as the products you are managing, this example will let you work ahead of the actual status of the products. You can use cond also to test for more diversified conditions, even determining which LISP routine to load. This function is invaluable.

```
(equal <expression 1> <expression 2> <fuzz>)
```

Description: The equal function tests to see whether *expression 1* and *expression 2* evaluate to the same value. *Fuzz* (added to the function with AutoCAD Release 10) is intended to round numbers achieved by different calculation methods. *Fuzz* is a real number that equals the amount of discrepancy you will consider "same as."

Usage: We use equal primarily for its *fuzz* feature, and when we want to compare lists. (Otherwise, we would use =.) An example of the use of equal follows:

```
(setq alst '(a b c d))
(setq blst '(a f r t))
```

then

```
(equal (car alst) (car blst))
```

returns *T*.

This example works also for symbols assigned to numbers. The test often is used for a `cond` function or an `if` function.

```
(if <test> <then do> <else do>)
```

Description: The `if` function conditionally evaluates the *test* expression. If the test evaluates to *T*, the *then do* expression is evaluated; if the test evaluates to nil, the optional *else do* expression is evaluated. If the *else do* expression is nonexistent and the test evaluates to nil, `if` returns nil.

Usage: We use the `if` statement when a choice between two options should be made or when choosing whether to complete one option depends on the status of a symbol. In this example (from LINS.LSP):

```
(if
  (and (= ans "B")(> ll insc))
    (progn...
```

`if` tests two conditions: whether the symbol *ans* equals the string B, and whether the value of the symbol *ll* is greater than the value of the symbol *insc*. If both conditions are true, *and* returns *T* and AutoLISP begins evaluating the statements that follow `progn`. Note that `progn` is necessary to contain a series of expressions within the `then do` side of the decision.

```
(while <test> <expression1> <expression2>...)
```

Description: This is a conditional loop in AutoLISP. `While` evaluates the *test* and then evaluates all expressions within the `while` loop, after which it again evaluates the *test*. This loop continues until the test expression becomes nil. This function returns the most recent value of the last expression.

Usage: We use the `while` loop in a variety of circumstances; most of the time, we use it with one of two loop generators. We either test to see whether a symbol has become nil or test to see whether a symbol used as a counter has reached a specified integer value. The `while` loop, in these cases as well as others, must include an activity that operates on the test expression. Here is an example of a loop using a counter:

```
(setq ofs 1)
(setq ctr rno)
(while (>= rno 0)
(command "offset" ofs pause)
(setq ofs (1+ ofs))
(setq ctr (1- ctr))
```

This set of instructions assigns the value of 1 to the symbol `ofs`, and the value of the symbol `ctr` to the value of a symbol `rno`. The `while` loop will be executed as long as the value of `rno` is greater than or equal to zero. Execution consists of the AutoCAD command OFFSET, with the offset distance set to the variable *ofs*, and a pause for the user to select an object to offset. Then the offset distance (`ofs`) is increased by one and the counter (`ctr`) is decreased by one. When the counter reaches minus one, the `while` loop is finished. The same thing can be accomplished with the `repeat` function. All you have to do is substitute the line (`repeat ctr` for the line (`while (>= rno 0`.

In another example:

```
(while ent
(setq ent (entnext ent))
(setq lay (car (assoc 8 (entget ent)))))...
```

this `while` loop executes as long as there are entities in the database, counting through the entities with `entnext`.

AutoLISP's Limitations and Pitfalls

AutoLISP can do almost anything you might want to do in AutoCAD—its principal limitation is the speed at which it runs within AutoCAD. AutoCAD can do many functions faster than LISP. For example, if you don't have really specific attribute names, AutoLISP has to peruse the entire database to extract attributes; in this instance, AutoCAD's ATTEXT command works much better, and dBASE would quickly find what you need. The same is true if you have many extractions to do. As you develop experience with AutoLISP, you can estimate whether AutoLISP is faster than a .DXF extraction and the use of dBASE. The speed of AutoLISP depends primarily on your specific way of doing things and the requirements you have when you get to larger tasks—it is a judgment call.

Because an AutoLISP routine is faster than doing each step from the keyboard in AutoCAD, if you don't know of a program that will accomplish what you want, you can write an AutoLISP routine. Do it for the fun of it. We have written routines that we thought would take hours—and had them working in one hour. We have also tackled what we thought were simple problems—only to have them take four hours, with bugs everywhere. Your AutoLISP routine will pay for itself if it works and if time you spend creating it is within reason. An added benefit of writing a routine is that doing so makes you better qualified to write the next one.

With AutoLISP routines that will be used on more than one system, many little pitfalls can drive you crazy. Some of these pitfalls are due to the system hardware; others are due to the software on the system. AutoLISP is not overly sensitive to these kinds of issues, but you may encounter more than you bargained for. Nothing beats testing and debugging by other users on other systems before you pronounce a routine finished. AutoCAD users' groups and CompuServe's Autodesk Forum are good sources for bug testing. In the following sections, we discuss briefly a couple of major problem areas.

Different System Configurations

We have had some crashes of AutoLISP because of the settings of LISPHEAP and LISPSTACK. Recently, for example, 2.0/9.0 AEC required a change in these settings that we didn't anticipate. Our system crashed when we installed 2.0/9.0 AEC because we had not rewritten the AUTOEXEC.BAT file and changed the settings as required, even though the changes were plainly displayed in the manual and on-screen during the installation process. (Who ever reads any of that stuff?) With the addition of Extended AutoLISP to AutoCAD Release 10, users with expanded memory no longer have to worry about LISPHEAP. What's the point? Even if you were to give instructions to everyone who uses a routine, users might still mess up the works and blame it on you. Before you write a large routine, try to determine your range of requirements.

Different graphics cards, monitors, tablets (as opposed to mice), and plotters may render your routine worthless. Even if you only write routines for yourself and think that you have everything you need, you don't. Remember that you are likely to change your system configuration over time as your needs change. Try to write your routines so that they are not hardware-dependent, or so that they include options for a variety of configurations.

Software Conflicts—Who's on First?

Anyone who uses a third-party menu system may have an ACAD.LSP file that sets variable names which conflict with the ones you choose. You can view these names, to a certain extent, by typing **!ATOMLIST** at the start of a new drawing. You probably will not be able to make changes to third-party designs, system variables, and macros without gumming up the works. Therefore, your routines must be written to avoid rocking the boat by interfering with the way your system operates.

Summary

We did not cover all of the AutoLISP functions in Chapter 13, "AutoLISP Never Was Plain English," and this chapter. Nor did we discuss conceptually or provide examples of all possible ways to use the functions. We did present the AutoLISP functions and their concepts in a way that should get you started using AutoLISP to increase productivity and improve CAD management. When you finish this chapter, we recommend that you purchase a book such as Smith and Gesner's *Inside AutoLISP* (New Riders Publishing) or *AutoLISP in Plain English* (Ventana Press).

In this chapter we discussed the following aspects of AutoLISP concepts:

- Advanced mathematical functions
- List manipulation
- Entity manipulation
- Table manipulation
- Input/output
- Conditional functions

When you begin writing larger routines, our organization of LISP functions into logical groups should be helpful. Once you recognize what you are doing—manipulating data, manipulating entities, or looking for a conditional function—you will be able to find the function you need, along with any other options that might apply, under the appropriate category.

Recommended Accomplishments

- ❑ Using this chapter, analyze LISP routines you don't understand. Annotate the routines and work until you figure out everything in them.
- ❑ Write a LISP routine that draws a rectangle with one point selected by the user.
- ❑ Write a LISP routine using a `while` loop.
- ❑ Write a LISP routine that saves information from your drawing variables to a file.

Optional Accomplishments

- ❑ Write a LISP routine that combines SCHED.LSP (from Chapter 10) and imports text aligned with the schedule. Have the routine automatically number the lines.
- ❑ Create an entire drawing using LISP only.

What Chapter 15 Is About

If you have any interest in 3-D work, you need to keep informed of developments in AutoCAD's 3-D capabilities. If you want to create three-dimensional presentations, having a service company do the work for you is a good idea, but you still need to understand the basics involved. This chapter describes the presentation alternatives available with AutoCAD and what you need to know in order to communicate intelligently with a software or hardware sales representative or with a service bureau representative. We discuss the following topics:

- AutoCAD's 3-D component
- When it makes sense to use the capability
- Video input and superimposition
- Video output and presentation
- 35mm slides
- Color printing
- Projectors

Helpful Things To Know Before You Start

- Basic AutoCAD 3-D commands and concepts
- Your design presentation requirements, budgets, and cost history
- The capabilities of your display device and display adapter

What To Have on Hand

- *AutoCAD Reference Manual*
- Your 3-D software package manual
- Your best imagined 3-D presentation, or a videotape of one
- Any cameras you want to experiment with (video or 35mm)

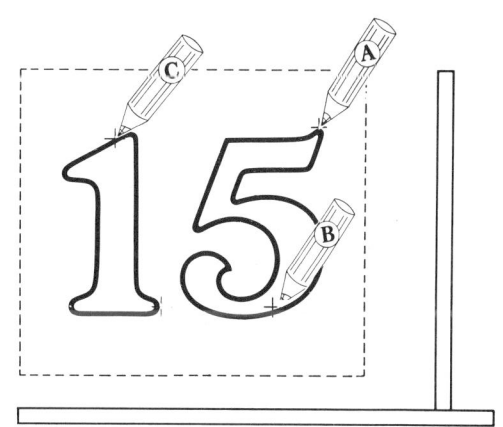

Advanced Presentation Techniques

Although this chapter may be out of date by the time you read it, the information we present will provide you with a good foundation for exploring the use of 3-D. The information in this chapter will make it easier for you to stay informed about developments in 3-D technology, even if you are not ready to use it. For more information about advanced presentation techniques, see the recommended reading list at the end of this chapter.

When AutoCAD Gets Fancy

When you see a CAD program running in a computer store, what you see probably is a three-dimensional presentation. Most dealers use such presentations as a major sales tool. If you ask enough questions, a sales representative may tell you that some of these presentations were created on expensive equipment with some add-on 3-D modules that are not included in the advertised price of the software. Many firms and individuals purchase the CAD package anyway, because they are interested in the other capabilities of the software. Nonetheless, the three-dimensional presentation still lurks in the back of our minds, right?

Advances in the realm of three-dimensional CAD are being made almost monthly. Everyone is on the band wagon, including Autodesk. In fact, while we were writing this book, Autodesk announced that they will be developing a three-dimensional interface comparable to the Renderman interface developed by Pixar Corporation. Although no details were provided, we predict that this interface will provide access to an add-on package that costs almost as much as (or perhaps more than) the full-blown ADE-3 AutoCAD. We also anticipate that the interface will allow you to create real-time movies or drawings that are almost photorealistic. The only question will be how big and fast your computer must be to make it work. With the advent of the 486 in sight, you may be surprised how soon you can be doing slick animation in photorealism at your desktop.

AutoCAD has had the capability to represent objects in three dimensions since AutoCAD Release 2.6. Release 10 adds 3-D dynamics to all of AutoCAD's commands, and now defines all entities in 3-D. If you try to present the raw content of an AutoCAD drawing three-dimensionally to nontechnical viewers, they probably will think that it's a color drawing of spaghetti. AutoCAD's wire frames are difficult for even informed viewers to visualize, much less clients. You can, of course, have AutoCAD HIDE the hidden lines for a screen image or for a plot, from any view or in perspective. But on complex drawings, the HIDE command takes a considerable amount of time. If we were going wait a long time for AutoCAD to perform a HIDE, we asked ourselves "why not get AutoCAD to do the drawing in color with the solids filled in, or in final rendered form?" We came up with two approaches.

First, we have had for some time a program that creates a perspective drawing from an AutoCAD .DXF file, which we then plot and use for the layout drawing of our hand-rendered presentation. Now that AutoCAD Release 10 does that for us, we can eliminate a few steps in the process and save some time. When the design changes, however, we still have to start over and create a new hand-drawn perspective rendering. In addition, we almost always present initially more than one concept. Then we present a refinement of one of those initial concepts, after which we present the final design. We need at least four good sketches and one final rendering.

Second, Autodesk came out with AutoShade as an answer to the request for an economical presentation tool. As architects, we don't find that AutoShade meets our standards for final presentation work. It does, however, serve some useful purposes in verifying our design in three dimensions and does fine for our preliminary presentation of multiple concepts to our client.

Can Your Client Afford It?

We used to base decisions about doing renderings in-house or shipping them out on whether we could make a profit on the in-house work, considering what the client would pay for the service. When designers first started using CAD, one of the questions often discussed was whether you could get a client to pay more for CAD and whether you should bill differently for computer time than for non-computer time. Today, that practice probably exists only in unique situations. The cost of using CAD for production work has come down, whereas reliability has increased. Now you can use CAD for a cost at least equal to that of doing the work manually—and the quality of the CAD work is better. In some cases, CAD has made the effort more profitable at the same billing rates. Many clients now expect their work to be done on a CAD system as a matter of course.

In our opinion, three-dimensional presentations are going through the same transition that two-dimensional CAD went through a few years ago. Most of the evolution of three-dimensional CAD from "an interesting curiosity" to "no big deal" is hardware-dependent. Sooner or later, clients will expect to see either photorealistic views of your design or a walk-through that is almost as real as being there. Considering the current technology, not every project can support the effort required for a three-dimensional presentation.

Service bureaus that can produce three-dimensional renderings from your AutoCAD drawings can create photoreal images of your designs, placed in their natural surroundings, for about the same cost as a professional illustrator. Variations of an image can be created for less than a variation prepared by hand, which would have to be a new illustration.

Because movies of walk-arounds, walk-throughs, and kinetic motion are still time-consuming and rely heavily on computing power, they can be quite expensive. However, some projects will be understood—and thus sold to your client—only through this type of presentation. If you can incorporate the presentation into your client's promotional needs for the project or product, some of the costs of preparing the presentation can be defrayed, thereby making the cost more in line with your client's budget—in some cases, less than what would have been spent for nonelectronic images. For example, we can sell a three-dimensional presentation to some clients by saying, "What if you used a videotape (with music and a voiceover) that you could send to a potential lessee in your new office building. This videotape would take them on a tour of the building before it is even built!" or "What if your sales reps could send an animated video of the widget to potential volume buyers?"

Why should you jump through all these hoops? If your competition doesn't offer this service, you will look better to potential clients who may need it, even if they don't want to buy it right now.

Talk the Talk: Some New Terms

Before we talk more about three-dimensional presentations, we would like you to become familiar with some new buzz words. As you continue to learn about three-dimensional presentations, these words will become part of the already absurd vocabulary you are developing by working with CAD. The terms in this section range from the most basic to the more advanced.

Three-dimensional *modeling* can apply to two different applications of a single concept. You can model your design in 3-D, which means that the computer helps you simulate the appearance and qualities of your design. The computer can also model automatically, by using various mathematical equations, the characteristics of light, a surface, a texture, a motion, or a span of time. Both types of model usually are constructed by the use of algorithms, which are mathematical formulas developed by software designers. The better the quality of the algorithm, the faster and more realistic the model. Using artificial intelligence, developers are now creating models that will allow computer-generated images to "understand" what they are supposed to do and modify themselves; one example of this sort of modeling would be a boat moving through water and developing a wake—without the illustrator instructing the image to create a wake.

A *vector* stores (in one data type) information about an object's direction, speed, and position. This is similar to any discussion of vectors you ever heard in physics, math, or structural design classes. Vectors provide information that is independent of the resolution of a screen, camera, or printer. Because AutoCAD stores the drawing data in a vector format, a wide range of output devices can be used, regardless of variations in resolution. The disadvantage of using vectors is that all devices which use dots to create an image must convert the image from vectors to rasters in order to create the image properly.

Raster images are images of electrons cast on a screen. The display of a raster image amounts to an electron code striking the surface of the device as a dot or pixel. The fully shaded images you see in a 3-D program are created by rasters. The advantage of raster imaging is that it is easy (and therefore inexpensive) to manipulate and has greater speed of reproduction than a vector image. The disadvantage is that the best resolution you will get of a raster image depends on the resolution of the output device. If you zoom in on a raster image, you can see each pixel in the image. This creates problems for AutoCAD users, who are accustomed to extremely specific intersections and endpoints. To render a raster image with a paint program, AutoCAD users must develop a representative flair rather than eight-decimal-place accuracy.

Ray tracing represents the capability of a computer to reproduce the activity and characteristics of light on any type and color of surface; reflections in water, an eye, or a mirror are accurately modeled by ray tracing. This technique produces extremely lifelike images. Ray tracing is the most sophisticated imaging technique currently in use for graphic images. It is also the most expensive in terms of computing equipment, time, and complexity. The calculations for even one frame of a movie using ray tracing can take days on a mainframe computer (months, on a PC).

Normal, a mathematical term meaning *perpendicular to*, is used to describe and manipulate the direction a 3-D face is "pointing to." In other words, if you draw a vector from one of the faces in your drawing in a direction perpendicular to that face, you have described the *normal* direction of that face.

Fractals are used to create a specific type of modeling, called *procedural modeling*. Fractals were discovered by Benoit Mandlebrot in 1980, according to the information provided with AutoShade. If you have a copy of AutoShade, you can view some fractal displays by selecting `Mandlebrot` from the Files menu and then selecting the scene you want to see. Fractals can estimate what a surface should look like at different levels of detail and from different angles and distances. If you are moving around a landscape, fractals create a texture based on the program's comprehension of where the view is taken from and a set of rules about the image that is to be created. This creates a more random appearance than a strictly mathematical model—hence the name *procedural model*.

Revolved figures are created by turning a two-dimensional figure about an axis. This is done by REVSURF in AutoCAD Release 10 (by R-SURF in Release 9).

Sweeps are created by a set of calculations made by a computer that move a two-dimensional line, circle, or polygon through space along a predefined, nonlinear path. A *torus*, one of the shapes available with AutoCAD Release 9 or Release 10, is a circle placed on a circular sweep.

Blends are created by averaging the position of a line, circle, or polygon from one predefined position to another in a series of evenly incremented steps. This is similar what you may have done as a child—moving stick figures by drawing a series of pictures on a pad and then flipping through the pictures, creating a movie-like effect.

Lambert shading, the simplest form of shading, is used by AutoShade to create shaded images in which each face of the surface is shaded, based on its position *normal* to the light source.

Gouraud shading, the next step beyond Lambert shading, creates smooth objects by interpolating the shading between each face. You can present a smooth ball by using Gouraud shading. Each face has the light calculated at its edges; the color is mixed in between the maximum and minimum range of the colors on the face, with the appropriate amount of change from light to dark.

Phong shading is used to add an appearance of hardness to the shading. It is also used to create more realistic images than the Lambert or Gouraud shading techniques. This is accomplished by calculating the effect of light on small portions of each face instead of by averaging the amount of light throughout the model, from face to face. The amount of detail to be calculated is set initially by the illustrator. Then the faceted image of the object is recalculated into the resolution selected, with a representation of the light characteristics determined for each part of the faces. As you can imagine, the computing power required to complete this task is considerable.

Some graphics programs include the capability of casting a shadow, or shadows, based on the object and multiple light sources. *Shadow casting* currently is done with algorithms. You can imagine what happens when a computer that has just calculated all the light characteristics of an object, based on light sources, is asked to calculate what shadow is cast and to reconfigure the surface accordingly. You can take a little vacation while you wait for the results, unless you want the most basic of images.

In *mapping*, an image that is used to paste up an object is captured or modeled. You can think of the process as creating a collage with photos, except that you map the particular technique onto the three-dimensional surface. There are four types of mapping: texture, transparency, reflection, and bump. *Textures* are simply a collection of pixel dots of colors that repeat themselves over and over. *Transparencies* are mapped by the amount of image allowed to show through from under the map. *Reflection* mapping maps other objects from the model onto a surface, with varying degrees of transparency and stretching of the image; mirror maps can be trimmed to fit the object onto which they are mapped. *Bump* maps capture a repetitive textured surface and map it to an object. Economical programs that use mapping techniques cannot adjust the map to the perspective of the image, and have difficulty trimming the map to meet curved surfaces.

Tweening is a three-dimensional blend/sweep. An object is placed in different locations in space, rotated and tilted as desired, and its motion between those key positions is calculated. From those calculations, images that animate the movement of the object are created.

From AutoCAD to Simulated Reality

When you want to really wow and zow 'em with a three-dimensional image, you are going to be faced with the fact that your drawing has to leave the AutoCAD environment. Before you determine which rendering environment you will use for the initial AutoCAD drawing, you need to verify and determine, from careful analysis, the following:

- The final type of image you want
- The degree of realism you want
- How many copies you want of this image
- How much time and money you want to invest
- The number of times you plan to alter the image
- The resolution you want for the final image
- What the service bureaus or dealers in your area can offer

If you want to create a three-dimensional image in AutoCAD and have it rendered in another program for presentation purposes, make sure that the third-party software will accept the format of your drawing. You can render either two- or three-dimensional images of your AutoCAD drawing. You can create those images with everything from an economical screen-capture-and-paint program, such as Dr. Halo or EGA Paint, to sophisticated mainframe programs. We won't take the time to discuss all possible formats, but we will tell you that a conversion process *must* occur. This process involves creating the required database from an AutoCAD .DXF file (typically) or from an AutoCAD IGES file. Whenever a conversion is done, the potential for lost or misdefined information exists. We suggest that you have one of your three-dimensional drawings developed into an image before you begin to rely on the technique or service bureau for a critical presentation. In this test drawing, be sure to include blocks, polylines, and anything else you might need in your final three-dimensional drawing.

Some programs have difficulty maintaining scale or detail relationships between drawings that are being combined. Take the time to sit down with the software or service bureau you intend to work with and create an image that represents a standard of what you expect to be doing. You may find that you can do things in AutoCAD to help create the final image. For example, if you intend to combine images, be sure to place in each drawing reference objects that are common to all the drawings and images. (Don't worry—these reference objects can be painted out or edited out later.) Remember that you probably know more about AutoCAD and its capabilities than does a software sales representative or service bureau; do your best to find a mutual solution to the problem.

The image in figure 15.1 was created using AT&T's TOPAS imaging software and several component drawings. Some of the objects were created in AutoCAD (Jamie Clay's X-29, for example) and others were created using the Promodeler and Supershade.

The hardware coordination effort for the techniques we discuss in the following sections is quite technical and can be extremely complex. We are going to try to make you an imaging hardware expert in three easy lessons. We discuss some of the concepts involved, so that you can better understand what is going on. Keep in mind that the hardware and software required for this type of work are part of another industry—one in which you would have to be as proficient as you are in AutoCAD if you were to invest in a system.

A PC-based system for advanced presentation techniques should include the following pieces:

- A 20mHz (minimum) 386 computer with a math coprocessor (33mHz, if you can afford it)
- High-resolution monitor capable of a display rate as low as 15kHz; graphics card with 1–4M of memory
- Video monitor
- Videotape deck with frame-by-frame editing
- Videotape deck controller board
- Genlocking device (Places all hardware and images on the same scan rate and recording mode)
- A color scanner and/or an RGB camera
- Minimum of 2M expanded memory (probably 8M)
- 35mm slide processor and interface board

Chapter 15: Advanced Presentation Techniques

Fig. 15.1.
The objects in this image are not real beyond their electronic image on a hard disk.

- The following software:
  - CAD conversion
  - Image capturing
  - A modeler
  - A renderer or shader
  - An animator

This list of the main pieces needed for an advanced presentation gives you an idea of what's involved in the process. Evaluating each piece requires considerable study.

Video and Scanner Input and Superimposition: Image Capturing

In seconds, two-dimensional images that can be used in conjunction with your AutoCAD drawing can be captured by a video camera or a color scanning device. If a video camera is used, an RGB video camera produces a better image than an NTSC video camera (which is what most home video cameras are). The NTSC (National Television Standards Committee) standard is what televisions use for color images; an RGB camera creates a digital coding of red, green, and blue colors. A color scanning device is like an electronic photocopier; the image goes to your computer instead of to a piece of paper. Cameras are somewhat less convenient to use than scanners, but can provide higher resolution for fewer dollars invested.

The captured images can be textures you want to use for mapping, the site for a building, the automobile on which the spoilers you designed belong, or the restaurant in which you'll put the furniture. Many software developers have captured a wide variety of images and are selling them as image libraries. For example, we have seen a package that allows homeowners to see their front yards landscaped before one blade of grass is turned. Furthermore, if you want only a two-dimensional rendering of your AutoCAD drawing, you can capture the AutoCAD drawing itself, after completing a HIDE (the status line, screen menu, and so on will be edited out of the drawing).

Coordinating captured images with the AutoCAD drawing can be tricky. Since the final product will be two-dimensional, proper perspective requires very careful calculation. If you are going to use a photograph, you should measure your camera's location (in real space) with respect to the object you are photographing. Then you can locate the camera and the target point in the AutoCAD drawing in the same position you used to take the photograph. If you are using close-up photography, be sure to allow for lens distortion by experimenting with the images. Take more than one photograph from different distances. Another option is to capture an image from a single frame of videotape. If you use a video camera to photograph the object, you can walk around and collect a tremendous variety of views, since videos take 30 frames a second.

Video Output and Presentation: Modeling

Some modeling software packages do a much better job of creating certain three-dimensional images than AutoCAD can. Using texture, bump mapping, and some of the basic modeling techniques, a three-dimensional site plan can be developed by mapping the AutoCAD 3-D mesh that creates a site topographical model. Creating three-dimensional landscape images in AutoCAD takes a great deal of time (and bytes); with the modeling packages, the free-form shapes are easy to handle, but drawing the object or building itself is often much easier in AutoCAD. The resulting images can be much more dynamic than a two-dimensional captured image. The AutoCAD three-dimensional model can be mapped with textures, bumps, reflections, and transparencies to create an almost photoreal walk-through of the building or a single frame of a three-dimensional model that can be used as a rendering.

The three-dimensional walk-through created in AutoCAD can be output to a videotape. The process sounds simple but is actually quite involved, in both technique and hardware. For competent animation control, you need a videotape deck with frame-by-frame editing capability. This deck requires a controller card in the computer. In addition, all of the monitors and the video input camera must be able to be genlocked, so that their image-generation rate is uniform. After you have finished creating the images with the imaging software and have completed the animation sequence, you output the movie to the videotape deck, one frame at a time. It takes 30 frames to make 1 second of images, or 1,800 frames to make 1 minute of tape. In our business, a frame can easily amount to 50,000 to 150,000 bytes! (They actually are larger, but the imaging software compresses them.) If we want a 5-minute movie, we're talking 900,000,000 (that's almost a billion, folks) bytes of drawing information. That's why animated architectural presentations are best left to super-minicomputers or mainframes. Smaller, less complicated products can be animated on a fast 386.

To create a movie of your project with near-realistic imaging, you probably will work closely with a service bureau that will prepare the images for you. If you want explicit control over the final production, expect to spend a lot of time at the service bureau watching a technician prepare your movie. You should spend some time initially learning the capabilities of the software from the service bureau personnel. This will help you determine what you want to see in the animation sequence. The less you know about what is going on, the more you will rely on the service bureau to do the work. Only you can decide what is appropriate for your design, and you probably will have a pretty good idea of what you want the presentation to look like. If you understand the capabilities of the software and develop a good rapport with the service bureau, you are less likely to be disappointed in the final results.

The process of creating video output for presentation generally includes several steps, or stages. The first major effort is the conversion of your three-dimensional AutoCAD drawing into a format acceptable to the imaging software. You must verify that all the pieces are in the right places. The imaging software will convert some of your AutoCAD primitives (faces, lines, meshes, etc.) into the primitives it uses. In this process, the software may become confused, but the modeling program of the imaging package should be able to make the required corrections without a problem. Nevertheless, you should review your design carefully with the service bureau technician to ensure that everything is in its proper place.

In the modeling stage, you define your image in terms of texture and reflection mapping, lighting, color, transparency, and anything else the software is capable of. The range of possibilities is changing rapidly, since imaging programs are evolving just as AutoCAD is. As we write, for example, some of the latest releases of software can plot the sun in relation to the project or object, and can track shadows in correct relationship to time and season. If you want to incorporate specific materials, bring a photograph from an advertisement or promotional brochure—the technician can map it onto any surface in or on your model.

At this point, take time to study the image. This image will be used for the entire movie. You can stop at this point and have the image output from different positions to a printer or 35mm slide. Compared to making a movie, this choice is a much more economical way of producing near photoreal images of your design. At this stage, the service bureau should be able to give you an accurate estimate of what a movie will cost, based on your description of the motion path and the length of time you want the movie to last.

To proceed to a movie, you will develop a script with the technician, using a storyboard to display a group of images that represent critical positions on the screen in the movie. When you and the technician have agreed on the storyboard, you will proceed to a form of a stop-action movie that displays the critical positions in sequence. You will become aware of the time and distance relationship in your AutoCAD drawing during this procedure. If you approach the project at a snail's pace because you want a great view of the outside, and then move through the interior at something more than a leisurely stroll, the time-space sequence of the animation will seem out of sync. While you are developing the stop-action movie, the technician can tell the software how many frames to place between critical steps. Make sure that you are aware of the real-scale distance you are traveling in the sequence. You are the only person who fully understands the scale of your design. The final outcome of the animation sequence depends heavily on your awareness of space and time.

Finally, the computer takes over, creating the animation frames. At this stage, you can go back to your office and start another project—or take a vacation. It may be days before the movie is finished.

From the imaging procedure you will have an impressive still image or an animated movie that, in and of itself, will impress your client. We have found that any difficulty we have getting clients excited about a design is connected directly to their understanding of the final product. Of course, the presentation of such a clearly-defined product also raises the possibility that clients will reject designs they previously had considered acceptable.

35mm Slides

There are two ways to obtain 35mm slides of your AutoCAD drawings: you can set up a camera and take a picture of the image displayed on your monitor, or you can have a 35mm slide made electronically. We will give you some pointers about each method. You should work from AutoCAD slides to create these images, so that you don't have to wait for a regeneration whenever you change images.

Homemade Slides

For a presentation, you can take reasonably good slides of your work that effectively duplicate a script-file presentation from within AutoCAD. To do so, you need the following equipment:

- A 35mm SLR camera
- A tripod
- A telephoto lens (70mm to 200mm)
- E-6 ASA 200 slide film
- Cable release or electronic shutter release
- A light meter (optional)

To take a slide of your drawing, follow these steps:

1. Mount the camera on the tripod so that the film plane (focal plane) of the camera is perpendicular to your monitor screen. Adjust the view and position of the camera using your telephoto lens. (The telephoto lens reduces the effect of screen curvature.) If you have a flat-screen monitor, you can use a standard 50mm lens.

2. Use 200 ASA film to keep the grain of the slide to a minimum. Use E-6 film for two-hour processing, unless you always get your work done ahead of time!

3. Turn the lights down very low; turn them off entirely if you have an electronic shutter. Make sure that there is no reflection in your monitor from the camera's point of view. If, for some reason, you find it necessary to experiment with the shutter speed, use a shutter speed slower than 1/8 second in order to avoid capturing the refresh rate of your monitor, which normally is 60 cycles per second.

4. Set the contrast and brightness of your monitor to the appearance you want the slide to have.

5. Set the f-stop to f5.6, and make sure that you have a sharp focus. Shoot one picture at each f-stop, from f1.2 to f11. After you have developed a few rolls of film, you will be able to narrow this bracketing range. Remember that most lenses have an f-stop that provides the sharpest focus for that lens. In addition to making sure that you have no color shift due to over- or underexposure, watch for the sharpest-looking picture and set up the f-stop corresponding to that slide as your target f-stop.

Electronic Slides

You can make 35mm slides by having a service bureau transfer the drawing electronically to a photo processor. These slides can vary in resolution from 2,000 to 8,000 lines; a typical system will provide 4,000 lines, which is very good for drawings. To capture a photoreal image, you need at least 4,000 lines. (A photograph is about 10,000 lines in resolution.) Slides can be created either by a video-driven process, which depends on the resolution of your monitor, or by a digital process that does not depend on resolution.

The photo processor contains a 35mm camera and its own CPU. After the transfer of data is complete and the photo processor takes over, placing the image on the film, your computer is free to return to other tasks. Photo processors are amazing pieces of electronic equipment. Take a look inside one, and you will see what we mean. All we care about is that somehow our electronic image is transferred to the slide film, which we take to a photo lab and have developed just like any other film. You can use this process to capture your drawing images (AutoCAD slide files) as well as the images made using the imaging software.

Some of the renderings you can achieve by using this process in conjunction with a professional modeling and shading package are awesome, and compare in cost to what you would pay to have a professional illustrator manually prepare a rendering. Moreover, with this process you know for a fact that the rendering represents your design precisely. In both cases the final quality depends on the illustrator. The other interesting aspect of this approach is that you can achieve several different renditions of your design, all in photoreal quality, for much less than a complete set of manually prepared illustrations.

Color Printing

The service bureau can output your image to a color printer that has a resolution of 300 to 400 dots per inch and an almost infinite array of colors. This process can produce multiple full-color, hand-held copies of your design quite economically, with each print prepared in a matter of minutes. Some of these printers use ink; others melt plastic pellets. They provide a better image than a color copy machine and are more than sufficient for many applications. AutoShade will provide a Postscript output as well as output to a Hewlett Packard paintjet. The professional modeling packages create drawings or images that can be done justice only by high resolution and a multitude of colors, however.

Projectors

Three types of projectors can send your images directly from your computer to a large screen. They are

- *Large CRT monitors:* these monitors have a big-screen TV look, are fairly economical, and can be moved around your offices. They work under a variety of lighting conditions, but have poor resolution.

- *Display projectors:* good ones have three lenses (one each for red, green, and blue). They have reasonably good resolution, a flexible kilohertz range for coordination with your graphics card, and they will display on large screens. They are also pretty expensive. We saw one at a recent seminar and were impressed with the presenter's ability to work with his computer and a microphone to give a presentation to a large group.

- *LCD panels:* using an overhead projector, these liquid display panels project your computer image onto a large wall screen. Although they work only in black-and-white and have low resolution, they are extremely portable and relatively inexpensive.

Summary

This chapter covered the basics of advanced presentation techniques for AutoCAD—probably the hottest field going right now, and one that will continue to change constantly. We find the field very exciting—in our opinion, it will revolutionize the way professionals present their designs to their clients. It also lends itself to the exciting prospect that designers may be able to expand their services to include, directly from the design effort, extremely professional promotional tools for their clients.

We introduced you to the following concepts in this chapter:

- AutoCAD's 3-D capability and when using it makes sense
- Video input and superimposition (image capturing)
- Video output and presentation (modeling)
- 35mm slides
- Color printing
- Projectors

As you may have noticed, we are proponents of using service bureaus for most, if not all, of your work in these areas. Large firms may find that buying imaging software and creating their own images may be worthwhile as an intermediate step. Service bureaus generally are better equipped to keep up with the new technology in this field, at least until the dust settles. We know of no other aspect of CAD more exciting than advanced presentation techniques—we think that you should follow the developments in this area very closely.

For More Information
CADENCE, May, June, October 1987.
————, March, April, July, November, December 1988.

Recommended Accomplishments

- Compile a list of the service bureaus in your area.
- Visit an imaging facility and become familiar with its procedures and products.

What Chapter 16 Is About

In some of the preceding chapters, we have discussed briefly many of the hardware devices you probably are using in your system right now. The basic factors that determine the complexity of your hardware needs are the stage of your development in AutoCAD and the demands of what you use AutoCAD for. Even if you are content with the speed and capabilities of your current hardware, a new update of AutoCAD may force you to modify or improve your system's capabilities. When this happens, you will need to know more about the components of your system than what they are called and where they are in the computer or on your desk.

In this chapter, we expand on the hardware descriptions provided in Chapters 2, 3, and 4. We also discuss some new equipment in the marketplace that can improve your system's capabilities and make it easier to use. We present information about the following devices:

- Monitors and graphics cards
- Plotters
- Expanded/extended memory
- Unique input devices

We certainly are not going to make you an expert about any of these devices, but we want to give you enough information so that you will know what questions to ask.

Helpful Things To Know Before You Start

- Hardware information discussed in Chapters 2, 3, and 4

What To Have on Hand

- Your three-ring binder of hardware manuals
- Advertisements for hardware that interests you

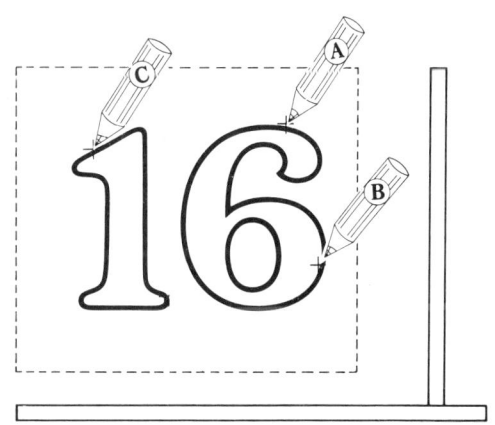

Advanced Hardware Concepts

As you become more involved with AutoCAD, you will find that you become more involved with hardware. AutoCAD is a demanding program that requires more expertise on peripheral use than almost any other program in the PC marketplace. Each new update of AutoCAD places greater demands on your peripherals. Sooner or later, you will encounter a problem, want to change your system configuration, or need to add faster or more flexible equipment. Can you discuss your hardware needs intelligently with your computer dealer?

A Few More Basics

Before we discuss each component of the system, you need to understand a bit more than we have explained so far about the way the system works. We'll define and then tell you something about the following topics:

- ❏ Hexadecimals and bytes
- ❏ Buses (not the ones you ride in)
- ❏ Adapters
- ❏ Microprocessors and math coprocessors
- ❏ Other chips
- ❏ Ports

371

- Registers and stacks
- Interrupts
- Processor modes

You may not need to understand these concepts right now, except to satisfy your own curiosity. If you develop problems with your computer or with devices and their integration with AutoCAD, you undoubtedly will learn about many of these topics as you search for solutions.

Hexadecimal Numbers and Bytes

When we first started using computers, we didn't think learning about hexadecimal numbers was particularly important. Everyone told us it wasn't. If you have tried (or are going to try) to write an AutoCAD font file, you discovered otherwise. Here comes a "Hexadecimal in Plain English" quickie course.

First, you need to know that all computers start counting at 0. Zero is not *nothing* to a computer. The word for *nothing* is *null*. You may know already that computers work on a system of *binary numbers*—a numerical system based on two numbers: 0 and 1. In fact, this is where the term *bit* (for *b*inary dig*it*) comes from. The 0 and 1 represent *off* and *on* to your computer. Eight bits collected together make up a *byte*. A *word* is two bytes, or 16 bits, put together.

Most measurement systems in the world are decimal systems. The word *decimal* derives from the Greek word for 10. The decimal system is not the numbers from 1 to 10; it is the numbers from 0 to 9, which means that the system is based on 10 numerals. Stop here until you are sure you understand what we just said. (Hint: the number 10 is made up of a 1 in the 10s place and a 0 in the 1s place.)

The *hexadecimal* system works just like the decimal system, except that it has a base of 16 unique characters instead of 10 unique characters. Table 16.1 shows a comparison of the hexadecimal and decimal systems.

Table 16.1. Hexadecimal and Decimal Systems

Hexadecimal	Decimal
0	0
1	1
2	2
3	3
4	4
5	5
6	6
7	7
8	8
9	9
A	10
B	11
C	12
D	13
E	14
F	15

The hexadecimal system follows the same logic we described for the number 10: the hexadecimal number 1F translates to 1 in the 16s place and 15 in the 1s place. If you add the two together (16 + 15) you get 31 in the decimal system. Memory addresses and system interrupts are expressed in hexadecimal numbers. You won't need to be able to calculate hexadecimal numbers to decimal numbers, but you need to recognize the concept. The conversion to decimal numbers always seems necessary so that you know what is going on. You need to understand approximately where the computer is talking about. If you had learned the hexadecimal system first, you would need to translate to the decimal system to understand it. Consider the numbers in table 16.2.

Table 16.2. Translating Hexadecimal to Decimal

Hexadecimal	Decimal
1	1 (1)
10	16 (16 × 1)
100	256 (16 × 16)
1000	4,096 (16 × 16 × 16)
10000	65,536 (16 × 16 × 16 × 16)

If you use your grade school math, the hexadecimal number F0000 is 15 in the 65,536s place (decimal number 983,040). To calculate the decimal value of more complex hexadecimal numbers, you must add the value from each of the "places" together.

Similarly, you can translate a number from binary to hexadecimal. It works the same way, using places. You won't need to perform this translation, however, unless you intend to read machine language—the most basic values communicated to the computer.

Buses

The *bus*, or data bus in your computer, is simply the path on which information travels around your computer's community of devices. The bus on a 286 AT is made up of 98 data lines. These lines are used for a variety of purposes. When you plug a card into an expansion slot, you are connecting the card to the data bus, and thereby to the CPU and other devices connected to the computer. An expansion slot connects your device to all 98 lines if the device is a 16-bit peripheral, and to 62 of these lines if the device is an 8-bit peripheral. The 98 lines are divided into 5 lines for different voltages, 3 for grounding, 16 for data, and 28 for addresses, with the balance for handling interrupt requests, busy and ready signals, and information identity. *Addresses* can be memory addresses or port addresses. Each data transfer carries an address along with the 16 bits of data. *Interrupt requests* let the CPU know what part of your computer is asking for information.

Adapters

The success of the PC family has been based on the concept of adapters. An adapter adapts a peripheral to your computer. Every device that is hooked up to your computer communicates with the computer via an adapter. Some adapter boards have the device they control included on the board or card, such as an internal modem. (We discuss modems later in this chapter.) Multiadapter boards contain all types of functions, from clocks and serial ports to extra memory. Many of the topics we discuss in this chapter will help you understand the options for an adapter and its device.

Microprocessors and Math Coprocessors

The primary chip in your computer is the microprocessor itself. In addition, there are math coprocessors, which let the microprocessor know they are present (usually because they are riding the back of the microprocessor) and several other chips.

Microprocessors perform the four basic math functions (addition, subtraction, division, multiplication), manipulating binary code to do almost everything your computer does. In addition, the microprocessors have a built-in set of instructions. They can do tests, repeats, and conditional branches (just like AutoLISP).

The microprocessor adds a data bit, called a *flag*, based on the results of the test it performs. For example, if the microprocessor flags part of a data word with 0, the result of the test was that the objects compared were equal. This flag directs the course of the next operation. If a conditional branch is performed, the flag may instruct the conditional branch to select a course of action or to perform a loop (in AutoLISP, the `if` and `while` functions). The repeat instruction set controls the type of repetition performed, such as repeating one command many times or repeating a set of instructions several times.

The math coprocessor contains a specific instruction set that has to do with math functions only. This instruction set is designed to make arithmetically complex tasks operate much faster. Its use has a dynamic effect on programs that rely on math-intensive exercises, which is why AutoCAD uses a math coprocessor. The math coprocessor receives off-loaded instructions from the microprocessor, but only if the program running at the time knows how to use the coprocessor. Because not all programs do, the speed of some programs may not be affected. The math chip does all of its calculations in 10-byte floating-point precision, which adds accuracy to the calculations (essential for AutoCAD). The math coprocessor also has special built-in constants: 0, 1, pi, and four other functions for working with logarithms. (We forgot about logarithms right after we passed that part of our college careers.)

Other Chips

The clock generator chip creates the basic timing cycle of the computer. The pulse of the clock chip is set by a quartz crystal, which the clock chip divides into slower segments as needed by various devices in the computer. This is where your clock speed is defined. The programmable timer chip works with the clock chip to create specific event timing by dividing the clock chip signal based on a request from software (which is why it's called programmable).

Bus controller chips function as a plant manager for your computer, ensuring that information moves smoothly through the bus. Some devices can communicate directly with the computer's memory. This communication is handled by a DMA (Direct Memory Access) controller. Interrupts are managed by the interrupt controller, which keeps the requests in order and holds them pending the opportunity to contact the device to which they are directed. Other controller chips usually are included on the adapter boards used with the peripherals, such as video controllers, disk controllers, etc. There also are other types of important chips, such as memory chips, but we have described the basic ones you may come across in your computing travels.

Ports

Ports are the microprocessor's windows on the world. Any part of the computer community is given a port number. The microprocessor uses that port number to communicate with any of the community members. For example, the graphics device, the keyboard, and the serial ports all have port addresses which you may have come across as you set up drivers for AutoCAD. These addresses are set up by the computer manufacturer and managed and accessed by the computer's BIOS (Basic Input/Output System). An address can be a port if it provides a "gateway" for access to a device.

Registers and Stacks

The microprocessor uses *registers* and *stacks* to keep track of what it is doing. There are three types of registers: general purpose, segment, and offset.

The *general purpose registers*, designated AX, BX, CX, and DX, are used as a work pad for programs and the microprocessor; they hold numbers that are used when the computer performs calculations.

The *segment registers* are used to gain access to a segment of memory. The Code Segment register (CS) points to a program's location in memory. The Data Segment register (DS) points to data the applications program is using. The Extra Segment register (ES) is used to point to an additional segment of RAM, typically a secondary data segment. Finally, the Segment Stack register (SS) points to a stack in memory.

The *offset registers* point to specific bytes of information and are used with the segment registers to manage RAM. The Instruction Pointer (IP) register is the microprocessor's bookmark in the program that is running. The Stack Pointer and Base Pointer registers (SP and BP respectively) help manage the efforts in progress that are stored in the stack. The Source Index and Destination Index registers (SI and DI) are used to move large amounts of data around the computer. The Flag register holds the flags that advise the application programs of the current status of the computer, the status of the results of calculations, and whether the microprocessor is listening.

Stacks are used by the microprocessor to temporarily store results that the microprocessor has in progress while it accomplishes other tasks. The term *stack* implies exactly how the stack area works: the most recent results are stacked on the previous results, and the results have to be removed from the stack in reverse order of how they were placed there.

Interrupts

Interrupts are the key to the flexibility of a computer. They allow the computer to stop what it is doing, respond to a request the user makes, and then return to what it was doing. This capability created the need for stacks. When the microprocessor is interrupted, it must set aside, temporarily, what it is doing. It puts this work in the stack.

Basically, there are three types of interrupts—hardware, software, and processing.

Hardware interrupts allow the connected devices to get the microprocessor's attention. For example, the keyboard uses the keyboard interrupt for every character that is sent to the screen and to memory.

Applications programs use *software interrupts* to request a service from the system's BIOS. If you want to print a file from a program or plot a drawing, the task is accomplished by the use of a software interrupt.

Processing interrupts are generated by the microprocessor when it runs into something it doesn't understand. This is what creates the error messages you receive from the system BIOS. Some interrupts are defined by the standard of the IBM PC; others, by the version of DOS used on your computer. This is one of the major areas where compatibility becomes a problem.

Every interrupt is given an interrupt number. Stored in a table at the beginning of the computer's RAM, this number tells the interrupt requester where to find the interrupt handler. The *interrupt handler* is a routine designed specifically to handle the requirements of the interrupt. It is similar to a subroutine in a program.

Interrupts reside in the computer's built-in ROM-BIOS programs, in the operating system (DOS), and in applications programs. An applications program can write its own interrupt handler and bypass the system-resident handler; this is sometimes done for special sequences of events or to try to obtain greater compatibility between the computer and the software.

Processor Modes

What finally sent personal computers into the next level of computerdom and qualified them as a serious force in the CAD world was the development of the 80286 microprocessor and its newer relatives, the 80386 and the 80486. The key to this development was the capability of the 286 to run in real and protected modes.

Real mode allows an 80286 to run in a mode compatible with its predecessors, the 8086 and 8088 families (8-bit and 16-bit processors, respectively). Even in real mode, the design of the 80286 allows it to run much faster than an 8086.

Protected mode allows the 80286 to execute the following:

1. Protection, which allows more than one program to run at the same time but stay within its boundaries (the program stays within the boundaries of something, but there's no indication what those boundaries belong to).

2. Multitasking, which allows the microprocessor to execute different tasks for the concurrently running programs

3. Extended memory, which allows the 286 to address up to 16M of memory

4. Virtual memory, which allows the 286 to simulate to a program the availability of one gigabyte of memory. (Virtual memory uses a portion of the hard disk as memory.)

Monitor and Graphics Cards

Monitors and graphics cards are important when you are working on or presenting drawings. You need to see what you're doing, of course, but the quality of what you see is even more important. Before we talk about this quality, we'll give you an idea of how what you see is linked to the data in your computer. Before you continue reading, please review the terms in the "Talk the Talk" section of Chapter 15.

Assuming that your computer has 1M of memory on its main board, the image you see on your screen is controlled by data stored in the 384K of memory above the 640K portion of your main memory (the memory between the 640K address and the 1M address). This 384K of memory does not govern the quality of the image you see; it controls the link of the screen data to the program you are using and to the devices that provide input to that screen.

The quality of what you see depends on the *display adapter* or graphics card. The number of colors, the resolution, and the speed at which an image is created on the screen are governed by the memory and controllers on the display adapter. AutoCAD, and other CAD programs, had to develop dynamic ways to display complex images on the monitor to get around the limitation of DOS's display capability in system RAM. High-performance graphics cards take that solution one step farther.

A monitor can operate in two basic modes: graphics and text modes. Graphics modes are subdivided according to the number of colors and the resolution of the screen: black-and-white, monochrome, Hercules (high-resolution monochrome), CGA, EGA, VGA, and PGA. Each kind of adapter uses various resolution characteristics and numbers of colors (or shades of gray); these are set by the software or by a graphics driver. Text mode allows the placement of predefined characters (the ASCII set) to the screen, which is divided into rows (25 or 40) and columns (80) of data cells. The display adapter translates the binary code into a character. There is also a video attribute code for each cell of the monitor. This code is for color, highlighting, underlining, or other attributes of the displayed character.

We discuss these modes so that you will understand the differences in AutoCAD's use of the text screen and the graphics screen when you flip screens on a single-monitor system. If you have a dual-monitor system, you won't have to worry about pixels being for graphics and character bits being for text.

In graphics mode, the only data required is the color of the pixel. (In text mode, two kinds of data are required: a data bit and an attribute bit.) This sounds deceptively simple, but if you are shopping for an advanced system graphics card, the information involved is formidable. The following sections cover certain graphics card buzz words with which you should be familiar.

Palette of Colors

Many cards state that they have a *palette* of 64 colors or of 512 colors: they can describe that number of colors to pixels on the screen. More important to you is the number of colors that can be displayed; this number depends on the amount of display memory on the board and the desired resolution. Colors that can be displayed are related to the number of bits required to define the range of colors. For example, 6 bits will define 64 colors (2 to the sixth power). If you want a resolution of 640 × 350, the palette memory required to address 64 colors at this resolution is 6 × 640 × 350, or 1,344,000 bits (168,000 bytes). This is why an EGA graphics card has a palette memory of 256K; the display memory on the card also has 256K if it is going to display 16 colors. This memory is divided up into 4-bit planes of 64K each. Each of these planes receives 1 bit from the palette memory that is sent to the monitor; this amounts to 2 (for 1 bit) to the fourth power (since it's a 4-bit plane), or 16, colors. This is an simplified explanation of what happens on these cards.

Display-List Processing

Display-list processing is a relatively recent development in the graphics-display industry and one that has significantly influenced the popularity of AutoCAD. The only way a CAD program can display a complex drawing in a reasonably short period of time is by developing a display list. Essentially, a *display list* is a database of the vectors that make up the image displayed on the screen. Also called a *virtual screen*, the display list excludes all the other stuff (such as group codes, entity handles, etc.) that you use to manipulate and retrieve data from your drawing and uses a vector description, known as a *raster*, to create the screen image. AutoCAD (versions 2.6 and later) creates its own display list, which you can store in a RAM disk (this is discussed later in the chapter).

An important development in the use of high-performance cards with AutoCAD is that AutoCAD Release 10 recognizes whether your graphics card has its own display-list processor. In earlier releases of AutoCAD, high-performance cards told the program that everything was normal in the display of the drawing, with not much going on other than the addition of an entity here and there, and an occasional erasure. What *really* was happening was a number of pans, zooms, and view changes; AutoCAD didn't know that the image was being processed by the graphics card.

Graphics cards had to have their own pan and zoom commands, called *hardware pans and zooms*. Some cards complete the zooms by using a technique called *pixel magnification*. This technique creates a very fast zoom, since the amount of calculation required is minimal compared to a true hardware zoom, which maintains the image at its original resolution. Pixel magnification is similar to using ZOOM dynamic in AutoCAD. If you do detailed work, you would not want to use pixel magnification for your display-list zooming.

Some graphics cards put the memory for storing their image on the hard disk, just as stock AutoCAD does. Some graphics cards put the display list in expanded memory. The fastest cards put the display list in memory on the card itself. Why? Because doing so eliminates the need to access your DOS BIOS and the bus on which the data is exchanged. This is especially important in AutoCAD Release 10 if you want to use Extended LISP because, as this book is being written, you cannot use all of the expanded memory managers available in the marketplace in conjunction with Extended LISP and its use of extended memory. If a graphics card uses its own expanded memory and memory manager, AutoLISP never knows the graphics card is using expanded memory.

Interlaced and Noninterlaced Display

This section has nothing to do with your grandmother's knitting, although the concepts may be similar. High-performance graphics cards use either interlaced display or noninterlaced display techniques to keep the image on your screen updated, or refreshed. Why does the screen need updating? Well, for one thing, the electron that hits the screen to create the image doesn't stay glued there. But the main reason for updating is that, in order to ensure that it keeps up with what you're doing, the graphics card must sample the database you are manipulating. The type of screen refreshing used depends on the image you want, the resolution expected, and how much the user can pay for the monitor and card.

Interlaced images are created by using long-persistence phosphors, which make the electrons stay on the screen a relatively long time. The screen-refresh rate for interlaced images is 30kHz and less. The entire screen is redisplayed over a ghost of the previous image. Without the ghost, the image would flicker and make the screen hard to use. The ghost creates a trailing effect when objects, or the cursor, are moved on the screen. Both the odd and even bits of the pixel data are brought to the screen at the same time, interlaced together and with the ghost image of the previous cycle. The primary use of lower scan rate (interlaced) monitors is for video output, which must be in the neighborhood of 17kHz.

Noninterlaced images operate at speeds of 45 to 60kHz because the image is replaced in two passes of the odd and even pixel bits. This creates a brighter and more finely detailed image than an interlaced image.

Scan Rate

The resolution of the screen, combined with the type of image creation (interlaced or noninterlaced), stipulates the required horizontal *scan rate* of the screen. The refresh rate mentioned in the preceding discussion of interlaced and noninterlaced displays is the scan rate. (Displays also have a vertical frequency of 60kHz, which you should not confuse with the horizontal scan rate.) The horizontal scan rate must accelerate as the resolution increases, because it has more pixels to address in the same amount of time. If it didn't, the screen would start to flicker. Clearly, faster scan rates mean more money.

The multisync monitors were created as a way to allow a variety of cards, and thereby resolutions, to work with them. Scan rates are important because you need to make sure that the card you may be considering will work with your monitor (or the monitor you'd like to have).

Assembling the Pieces

Before you buy a graphics card, make sure that the card you are considering will work with the monitor you have or are planning to buy. Some monitors work only with limited scan rates. Multisync monitors, on the other hand, are designed to work with a variety of graphics cards. Most large-screen, high-resolution monitors work only with graphics cards and software designed specifically for them.

Most high-performance graphics cards must have their own fairly complicated software to communicate with AutoCAD and your PC; this is similar to the communications software required for two computers to exchange information over a telephone line via a modem. The complexity of these cards is beyond the scope of this book, but we do have some guidelines for you, some things you should watch out for if you want to improve your graphics images:

- ❏ The specification sheets that come with advanced graphics cards are so complex that trying to interpret them is entirely too difficult, even for most sales representatives. Instead, try out a drawing that represents your standard work on a system equipped with the card in which you are interested.

- ❏ The software that comes with the graphics card (drivers, and so forth) is as important as the card itself. To keep up with AutoCAD and have your monitor available for use, you may have to get a driver update with every release of AutoCAD. Find out how long it took the manufacturer to prepare the current driver and whether the manufacturer provides free driver updates for the life of your card.

- ❏ In today's computer hardware market, the life of your card may be two years or less, depending on how up-to-date you like to keep your system.

- ❏ All of the warnings we gave you in Chapter 8 apply.

Because advanced graphics cards have their own software requirements, you must consider that this software will have bugs—you have a new kind of bug to worry about. Choosing a monitor and graphics card is difficult; we have no pat answers. One of our systems uses an EGA clone; it has been working with AutoCAD since we bought it and been compatible the minute that each new AutoCAD release came out. There is a certain merit to that, although we are sure that Autodesk will eventually phase the EGA out of compatibility with AutoCAD. The selection of a high-performance monitor/graphics card must be coordinated with your long-range plans and use of AutoCAD. (We discuss one particular high-performance card in Appendix K because its software is dynamic enough to make it a third-party software developer worth considering.)

For More Information

CADENCE. 2, no. 4 (April 1987): 15.

Plotters

Plotters are the tool most of us use to create the final product of our efforts. Unfortunately, we all get enraptured with what we see on the screen and with the performance of the computer, and forget what we are trying to do. We are trying to communicate with a drawing on a piece of paper, and the plotter puts it there. If you take your plotter for granted, wait until it breaks down in the middle of a deadline push. In the following sections, we review some of the important things you should know about plotters (beyond their drawing speed).

Plotter Types

There are three kinds of plotters: laser plotters, electrostatic plotters, and pen plotters. We don't know much about laser plotters, mainly because of their cost. Their technology is similar laser printers and they are fast, providing excellent line quality. We have noticed that they do not function the same as pen plotters; therefore, experimentation is necessary so that you gain enough knowledge to be able to predict the outcome of a plot. We found, for example, that the plot of a hatch-patterned area produced interruptions in the lines that bounded the hatched area. Exploding the hatches solved the problem. Laser plotters can produce great looking halftones for "special effects" in your plots.

Electrostatic plotters are expensive also, but their prices have been coming down. They use an electrostatic charge on a specially coated paper to create an image—single- or multiple-color—with toner, similar to the production of a photocopy. They also are very fast, but don't always provide the same quality as a pen plotter. Electrostatic plotters can create a plot resolution of 400 dots per inch, which is more than sufficient in most cases. The most important thing we can tell you about these plotters, within our limited experience, is to make sure before you buy one (or agree to have a service use on your project) that it can produce pen weights. Be sure to compare a plot from your drawings using alternative plotters. Many electrostatic plotters require the AutoCAD drawing to be translated to a raster image that allows the plotter to create line weights before the drawing can be plotted. Most electrostatic plotters now come with drivers that work directly with AutoCAD, and Autodesk has added to AutoCAD a driver for the Hewlett Packard electrostatic plotter. Electrostatic plotters, like laser plotters, can plot halftones (which we use to create background drawings).

We, like most AutoCAD users, are most familiar with pen plotters. Pen plotters can have one of two types of motor: a stepper motor or a servo motor. *Stepper motors* step between specific positions that are determined by electrical pulses; they are noisier, slower, and less expensive than servo motors. *Servo motors* move smoothly over their range of positions according to preset voltage levels.

Pen plotters can be flatbeds or rollerbeds. *Flatbed plotters* (except for wall-mounted models) take up more space and use two motors to create the required pen movement by varying the speed and position of each motor. Paper loading is very convenient and the paper does not move during plotting. Many flatbed plotters can plot the entire surface of the paper. One problem with flatbed plotters is that the quality of the surface on which the paper rests has direct bearing on the quality of the plot, and people tend to use available flat surfaces for anything (your plotter's bed may be somebody's lunch table!). *Rollerbed plotters*, which require less space than flatbed plotters, use rubber pinch wheels to hold the paper on a grit roller. They also use two motors to create pen movement by speed and position variation. The paper has to move for the plot, creating potential for errors.

The paper size you use may be the major factor in your decision about which type of plotter to select. Some plotters can use any size paper; others use only preset sizes. Check this information carefully before you buy a plotter. We were sold a plotter that didn't use our standard sheet sizes in the larger sheet categories, and we didn't realize it until we did our first big job on AutoCAD. We had to purchase a new platen for one of the plotter so that we could get the correct sheet size settings.

Specifics for Comparison

Consider the following capabilities of a pen plotter before you invest in one:

- ❏ *Plot area:* Some plotters can plot a larger portion of the same size sheet than others. E size plotters usually can plot a larger area of a D size sheet than D size plotters can; this is due to the pinch rollers used to hold the paper. Verify the maximum plot area for each sheet size from the plot specifications.

- ❏ *Resolution:* The smallest increment a plotter can address with the pen is the plotter's resolution. Typical resolutions are .001 inch, which is required to produce smooth circles and diagonal lines. Verify the hardware resolution of the plotter for pen movement, and the software resolution for maximum plot sizes that are capable of matching the hardware resolution.

- ❏ *Emulation:* Plotters use plotter languages as standard communication protocols between AutoCAD and the plotter. The two main standards are HPGL (Hewlett-Packard Graphic Language), which is recognized by nearly any software package, and DM/PL (Digital Microprocessor/Plotting Language), from Houston Instruments. Some plotters can plot primitives, such as circles, ellipses, and the like. AutoCAD, for purposes of universal application, does not take advantage of these capabilities. Plotter manufacturers have responded by writing drivers that improve the capability of their plotter, and its speed, over the standard driver supplied by Autodesk. Your plotter should emulate one of these languages, preferably HPGL.

- ❏ *Speed:* Overall plotting speed is the result of the speed of your computer (AutoCAD's conversion of drawings to vectors); the speed at which the plotter accepts data, changes pens, and moves the pens; and the capability of the driver that runs the plotter. In many instances, minor variations in the pen speed of the plotter result in little change in the overall plot time. Pen speed is a function of the pen type and the plot media more than of the capability of the plotter. You should verify the pen speed recommended by the pen manufacturer and then run the plotter at that speed to compare it with others. Pen acceleration can have a dramatic effect; if you have a great deal of text in your drawing, or if the drawings are highly detailed, the acceleration speed of the pen will have an effect on plot time. *Acceleration speed* is the time it takes the pen to get up to full speed. In addition, the speed at which the pen moves when it is up can have an effect on plot speed. Finally, to reduce wear on the pen, the pen must be dampened when it strikes the surface.

- ❏ *Plot buffers:* The amount of available memory on the plotter affects how fast the AutoCAD Drawing Editor returns to use. A large buffer can store the entire plot in memory, so that you can go back to work on your drawings (or start another plot) much sooner. We used the Seleris PC plot buffer (made by Western Automation) while we were writing this book; it is a well-crafted memory card that uses an expansion slot in the computer, can have 0.5M to 2.5M on-board, and is expandable (with a piggyback card) to a maximum of 8.5M. The great thing about this type of plotter buffer is that if you have more than one plotter, or if you change plotters, you always have the plotter buffer in your computer; you don't have to buy a buffer for each plotter. The plots are still subject to your computer's processing speed, and the Seleris PC requires a TSR driver that uses from 3,300 to 10,000 bytes, depending on what you have in the plot queue it lets you set up. It lets you select the order of plots and have the plots paused for paper changes or run continuously (for roll-feed plotters). We recommend the use of a plot buffer, as an expansion board in your computer or installed in your plotter, but only for multipen plotters.

Plotters can easily cost as much as $10,000, which is as much as a CAD station. This fact alone means that selecting a plotter and establishing a set of procedures for its maintenance require your serious attention.

> **For More Information**
> *CADENCE.* 2, no. 12 (December 1987): 85.

Expanded/Extended Memory

The use of expanded/extended memory is becoming a standard practice for people with 8086, 8088, 80286, and 80386 computers who use Auto-CAD with large drawings. These concepts exist only because of the DOS limitation of 640K of conventional memory. OS 2-386 and SCO Xenix-386 systems, among others, eliminate the concept of expanded/extended memory.

Understanding the use of extended/expanded memory was difficult for us. We have a manual, second only in size to the AutoCAD manual among our CAD materials, that tells us how to use our memory cards. And many other people who don't know how to use the memory are happy to give advice. We are interested only in how it benefits our use of AutoCAD, which involves some specific configurations of AutoCAD and the memory board.

If you have extended/expanded memory, you may be wondering what the best possible configuration is for you. We can't give you any specifics, but we can give you some guidelines that will help maximize your use of extended/expanded memory with AutoCAD. In addition to following the guidelines presented here, make sure that you read Chapter 4, "Basic System Management." In the suggestions that follow, we lump the two types of memory into the catch-all phrase "extra memory," to reduce the wear and tear on your eyes:

- ❏ AutoCAD stores the virtual screen of your drawing in temporary files on the hard disk. If you have a medium to slow speed hard disk (slower than 28ms) and work on drawings 250K and larger in size, extra memory should be used as extended memory and set up as a RAM disk for storage of temporary drawing files. A rule of thumb for extra memory capacities is 2.5 times the size of your largest drawing, but depends on the length of your editing session and the number of zooms and pans you execute. This practice is, in effect, improving AutoCAD's display-list processing speed.

- ❏ AutoCAD can use extended or expanded memory as I/O page space. This helps process large menus quickly, because the recently used pages of the menu are swapped into and out of memory, rather than onto and off of the hard disk. It seems to us that this functions better when the extra memory is configured as expanded memory (since 16K pages of data are swapped at one time), but we may be imagining things.

- ❏ AutoLISP, with the advent of Release 10, can use extended memory for executing routines. Autodesk recommends that a minimum of 512K be set aside for this purpose, but we have seen less used.

- ❏ The AutoCAD overlay (.OVL) and execution (.EXE) files can be placed in extra memory on a RAM disk. This improves the computer's access speed to the different parts of the AutoCAD program. If AutoCAD were placed into contiguous memory, all at once, it would exceed your computer's 640K limit. Thus, AutoCAD uses a procedure that allows portions of the program to be selected for executing different tasks. This requires a number of hard disk accesses to be made by AutoCAD. If the program files are in extended memory, access time is considerably less than if they are on a hard disk.

- ❏ Some operating systems don't tell AutoCAD enough about the condition of extended and expanded memory. You *must* verify that the AutoCAD STATUS command screen shows memory configurations that match your intentions. This will show up as temp drawing directory size and extended I/O page space. If AutoCAD doesn't recognize the boundaries you set up for the different uses of your memory, it will overwrite the file allocation table of a RAM disk. When this happens, AutoCAD can no longer find the files stored in your RAM disk—and it crashes. When it tries to save the drawing file, it saves a fragmented file that can't be used again by AutoCAD, even though AutoCAD offers to save the file for you.

❏ If you are unsure about the fastest use of your extra memory, get a stopwatch and try a series of SAME, REDRAW, and REGEN commands using a script file. This series should represent your standard efforts in a drawing session with an average-size drawing.

Dip Switches

No, this doesn't mean changing from cool ranch to jalapeño! Most memory cards have switches that allow you to set the memory configuration on the cards themselves. Half of our extra memory manual is dedicated to this proposition. Three factors determine whether you need to change the dip switches:

❏ Whether you use extended or expanded memory
❏ The capabilities of your computer's operating system
❏ How you want to divide the memory

Your computer's operating system can be configured to recognize extended memory in chunks of memory that vary in size. Some computers may allow you to step your memory only in 512K segments; others may allow you to define the memory in increments as small as 16K segments. Most extra memory boards use drivers to manage the memory on them and to create RAM disks. These drivers allow the board to be configured entirely as expanded memory; then they configure a portion of that memory so that it works like extended memory and a RAM disk. If your operating system handles the interrupts for this configuration properly, AutoCAD should have no problem recognizing the expanded memory and the RAM disk boundaries. If it doesn't, or if you intend to use Extended AutoLISP with AutoCAD Release 10, you will have to configure the board with the dip switches, bypassing the memory-management software. Before you make any final decisions, ask your AutoCAD dealer to verify with Autodesk whether Extended AutoLISP will work with your expanded memory manager. The memory manager must be 100 percent compatible with the VCPI (Virtual Control Program Interface) standard for memory management.

Our extra memory board lets us use dip switches to set up part of it as extended memory and the rest as expanded memory. We had no problem with this until we started working with AutoCAD Release 10. Extended AutoLISP currently does not work properly with all expanded memory software (although we hope Autodesk will remedy this problem). If you are working with Extended AutoLISP and AutoCAD Release 10, we recommend that you configure your extra memory entirely as extended memory, using the switches on the board.

Note: Many users will insist that they benefit tremendously from the use of expanded memory. In tasks other than AutoCAD usages, this may be absolutely true. What we are saying is that if you use LISP extensively and your expanded memory manager is not compatible with Extended AutoLISP, the advantages of extended memory and Extended AutoLISP far outweigh the availability of expanded memory.

If your system has 512K or 640K of conventional memory, it may already be using part of the extra memory to fill in the rest of the main board memory up to 1M. (Remember that all extra memory is addressed starting at 1M.) If you have a graphics card with display-list processing, your memory card may be used for the display-list storage and therefore not be available for normal AutoCAD usage.

RAM Disks

You can use the DOS VDISK utility to set up your extended memory (or part of it) as a RAM disk (also called a *virtual disk*). (If you have not set the dip switches to accommodate extended memory, you will have to use the memory-board manufacturer's software to create a RAM disk.) To use VDISK, place the appropriate version of the following line in your CONFIG.SYS file:

```
DEVICE=\DOS\VDISK.SYS 1024K 256 16 /E:
```

You can adjust the line to suit your needs. For example, if you have the VDISK utility in a different directory than \DOS, use the correct path for your directory structure.

Following the VDISK.SYS file name in the command line, the next item designates the size of the RAM disk in kilobytes; you can specify any or all of your extended memory.

The next number, *256*, is the sector size, in bytes; you can use 128, 256, or 512 for the sector size. The DOS default is 128 bytes; if you intend to use 128 bytes, omit this number from the command line.

The sector size is followed in the command line by the number of allowable directory entries. Because AutoCAD doesn't open many temporary files, 16 directory entries is probably enough for your RAM disk; 64 is the default if you omit this statement. We suggest that you experiment to see whether your system benefits from changing the sector size and number of allowable directory entries.

The last item in the command line, /E, tells VDISK to place the RAM disk in extended memory. Remember that you have to reboot the system to create the RAM disk.

Depending on the types and number of other drives your system has, DOS will automatically give the RAM disk a drive name, such as E: or F:. You may have to increase the allocation for LASTDRIVE in your CONFIG.SYS file. Check your DOS manual.

To use the RAM disk as temporary drawing storage, you must reconfigure AutoCAD. Using selection 8 from the AutoCAD reconfiguration menu, enter the drive letter for your RAM disk when AutoCAD asks you where to place the temporary drawing files, and save the configuration changes. (The AutoCAD default is DRAWING, which is the directory where your current drawing is stored.) Start a test drawing and use the STATUS command to see whether AutoCAD recognizes the RAM disk. If AutoCAD does recognize the RAM disk, the temp-dwg directory size is very close to the size you designated for the RAM disk. (The difference in size is the file allocation table reserved by DOS.)

You can use the RAM disk to hold the AutoCAD program and overlay files, so that the running program does not have to access your hard drive repeatedly. How large your RAM disk needs to be for this depends on which AutoCAD extensions you have purchased (ADE-1, ADE-2, or ADE-3). We use ADE-3 and have been able to put all of our overlay files in a 768K RAM disk. To do this, you also have to place the ACAD.CFG file on the RAM disk, add to the AUTOEXEC.BAT file the statement SET ACADCFG=E: (where *E:* is the RAM disk drive designation), and make sure that E: is on your computer's PATH. You also need to write an ACAD.BAT file that copies the AutoCAD overlay files and the ACAD.CFG file from a subdirectory that we call ACAD\RAMD to the RAM disk before you start AutoCAD. Such an ACAD.BAT file looks like this (although you may have other lines in the file as well):

```
ECHO OFF
CD\ACAD\RAMD
COPY/V *.OVL E:
COPY/V ACAD.CFG E:
CD\ACAD
ACAD
```

All of the overlay files and the configuration file (ACAD.CFG) must be moved from the \ACAD subdirectory to a new subdirectory \ACAD\RAMD; this keeps AutoCAD from using the first files it finds in the \ACAD directory instead of the ones you want it to find on the RAM disk. Many users find that AutoCAD Release 10 is best used by placing all of these files plus the ACAD.EXE file on a RAM disk.

You can add more RAM disks if you have more memory. DOS will assign drive letters automatically to your RAM disks. Because the temp drawing files are always changing in size, you should not put any other files on a RAM disk with them. You may want to set up one RAM disk for temporary drawings, one RAM disk for the AutoCAD overlay files, and another for the ACAD.EXE file and your menu files.

AutoCAD's Use of Extra Memory

If you are going to divide your extra memory into more than one use, you must use the SET statements for ACADLIMEM, ACADXMEM, or LISPXMEM in your AUTOEXEC.BAT or ACAD.BAT file (only if you have AutoCAD Release 10). These statements define for AutoCAD the boundaries of the memory use of your extra memory. If you use a memory manager to set up your extra memory and your RAM disk, you must make sure that AutoCAD recognizes their use properly. Things can get pretty complex if AutoCAD doesn't know what is going on with one or more of the memory managers. To simplify our discussion, we are going to assume that AutoCAD doesn't know anything about how your memory is configured. Once you know how to set up everything manually, you can try the automatic setup procedure, in which AutoCAD recognizes everything, and build from there.

Suppose that you have a total of 2,048K of extra memory and want to set it up as a RAM disk of 1,536K and an expanded I/O page space of 512K. (Remember, as of this writing Extended AutoLISP doesn't like some expanded memory managers.) In general, here is what to do, step by step (your board may vary slightly):

1. Set the dip switches on the board so that your extra memory board knows how many bytes are to be used for conventional and extended memory. In this case, assuming that you already have 1M of memory on your system's main memory board, set the switches for 1,536K.

2. Set the dip switches on the board to tell your extra memory board how many bytes of conventional memory already are installed on your computer—in this case, 1,024K. If you have less

than 1M of conventional memory, configure the board to fill in that memory up to 1,024K and set these switches accordingly. This setting must match the settings of your computer that are established with its dip switches and the setup program that came with your computer.

3. Reboot your computer, run the system's setup program, and tell your computer how many bytes you set in Step 1.

4. Execute the setup program that comes with your extra memory card to set up 512K of expanded (paged) memory; do not use settings about extended (non-paged) memory. This is the primary difference between physical and software settings. You are setting the dip switches physically on your extra memory board instead of using the management software that comes with the board. Save the configuration and exit the program. At this time, the program should let you know that it is adding statements to your CONFIG.SYS file.

5. Verify that your extra memory setup program added an EMM.SYS-type file to your CONFIG.SYS file; the name of this file will vary according to the manufacturer of the board. Add the appropriate DEVICE=VDISK.SYS statement to your CONFIG.SYS file, establishing the RAM disk size as 1,536K.

6. Edit your AUTOEXEC.BAT or ACAD.BAT file to include the following statements:

   ```
   SET ACADXMEM=NONE
   SET ACADLIMEM=2560K,512K
   ```

   These two lines give AutoCAD the specific starting location and size of the extended memory (ACADXMEM) and expanded memory (ACADLIMEM). Notice that we have the extended memory set to NONE. This ensures that AutoCAD, if it doesn't know we are using VDISK, will not use any of the extended memory. We then tell AutoCAD that it can use 512K of expanded memory, starting at the memory location of 2,560K. This location was established by adding the starting location of extra memory (1,024K) to the size of the RAM disk (1,536K). We have found that this is the safest way to use a RAM disk.

7. Reboot the computer and start AutoCAD. If you don't get an `extended memory disabled` message, you probably have set it up correctly. If you do get the error message, go back through the steps and check your figures and your typing. Configure AutoCAD to place the temp drawings on the RAM disk, and check

everything with the AutoCAD STATUS command. You should see that the `temp-dwg` directory has about 1,536K in it and that there is 512K of expanded I/O page space.

If you are going to use Extended AutoLISP with AutoCAD Release 10, you probably should configure all of your extra memory as extended memory; all you have to do is set the starting location above the total of conventional memory and your RAM disks with LISPXMEM (in the same way you used ACADLIMEM in Step 6 of the preceding directions) and delete the ACADXMEM and ACALIMEM statements from your AUTOEXEC.BAT file.

We think the best memory setup would include two RAM disks—one for temporary drawing files and one for all the .OVL files, the ACAD.EXE file, the ACAD.CFG file, and your menu file—512K for Extended AutoLISP, and 512K for extended I/O page space. *Caution:* temp drawing files are always changing size—do not put any other files on the RAM disk with them.

Unique Input Devices

While we were writing this book, we were loaned a device called VoiceMate (marketed by CaddLINK Corporation) that includes a headset, an expansion card, and memory-resident software that allows as many as 64 commands to be recorded and retrieved by using a hotkey and speaking clearly. You can even connect your telephone into the headset and use it to talk on the phone. Similar devices are available from other companies. The installation of these devices is fairly involved because you have to train the software to recognize your voice. We assume that each user must have an individualized set of voice templates, although we didn't test this theory.

We have read that these systems must be retrained for changes in the individual's voice from day to day, but we had no such trouble, even when one of us had a cold. These devices signal the maturation of the CAD marketplace, and we expect to see other time- and effort-saving devices appear for the benefit of CAD users. The VoiceMate not only has an application for time savings and ease of use but also can help physically-challenged users who want to become more effective CAD operators.

Another unusual and useful device we have heard about is a miniature monitor, suspended before your eyes, that creates the illusion that the monitor is 24 to 36 inches away. With the use of voice input and this type of monitor, we can imagine a CAD helmet that contains the computer, hard disk, monitor, and input device!

Those of you who *really* hate to type might want to check out a product made by Communication Intelligence Corporation. With this product, the Proficient AutoCAD Enhancer, users can handwrite AutoCAD and third-party commands by using a stylus on a digitizer. This system also adds an interface card to your computer.

Summary

In this chapter we reviewed advanced techniques in hardware management for the following:

- Monitors and graphics cards
- Plotters
- Expanded/extended memory
- Unique input devices

If you want to learn about hard disks, which are just as involved as graphics cards, we recommend *Managing Your Hard Disk*, 2nd edition, published by Que Corporation. You should expand your study to modems and serial adapters, if you are going to use the Autodesk Forum on CompuServe, and laser printers, which may serve many of you as printers/plotters. Many PC magazines contain reviews of these products and offer up-to-date information about the newest technological innovations.

Even more important, keep in touch with developments in computer hardware technology so that you can be planning your next system. Hardware updates are just as much a part of CAD management as are software developments, and they require careful financial and wish list planning.

For More Information

CADENCE 2, no. 7 (July 1988): 53.
———. 2, no. 12 (December 1988): 123.

Recommended Accomplishments

- ❏ Review a set of current PC and CAD magazines and note the hardware advertisements that you are curious about or don't understand. Call the listed telephone number or contact a dealer and learn about each of them, making sure that your questions are answered.

- ❏ Review the capabilities and configuration of your system, making sure that you understand why it was configured as it is and what the effect of any changes you make will be.

Optional Accomplishments

- ❏ Reconfigure your extra memory in a number of different ways, and check the results with a stopwatch and a script file.

What Chapter 17 Is About

This chapter provides pointers about using all you've learned from this book in harmony with what others are doing. We wrote to several third-party vendors, telling them about this book and asking them to send us literature, software or hardware samples, demos, and anything else they thought appropriate. We wanted a random sample of products to help us analyze:

- What's required for coordinating AutoCAD with add-ons
- The approach vendors take to help make their products understandable and easily implemented
- The information you can get before you buy a product
- A general sense of the products' quality, support, and the concepts of available software and hardware

We have already discussed some of these products. We neither review their quality nor represent that we like, dislike, warrant, or fully understand their capabilities. To share what we have learned and observed, we will discuss:

- Getting someone else to do it
- Checking the basics
- Determining your standards
- Getting the setup working to your satisfaction
- Focusing on new specifics
- Where to look for more; who you can call, write, or ask
- What to do next

While you review these topics, consider your management procedures and practices and how they may be affected by the conditions outlined in this chapter.

Helpful Things To Know Before You Start

- Installation procedures of your third-party products
- Contents of your CONFIG.SYS, AUTOEXEC.BAT, and ACAD.PGP
- Which third-party tools you are considering

What To Have on Hand

- Manuals for third-party products you already have
- Promotional literature for products under consideration
- Your office procedures manual
- Three-ring binder of your system hardware manuals

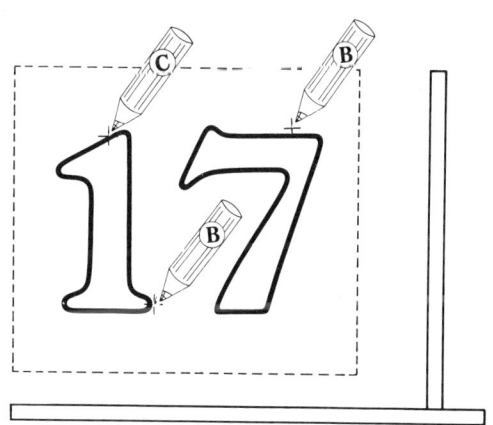

The Ultimate CAD-management Tool

Everyone is guilty of it at different times, and more than once: the independent, pioneering attitude that makes us good CAD users and talented designers or drafters stomps all over our common sense. As we wrote this book, we had quite a few conversations that began with, "Well, I don't agree because I've always done it this way..."

Almost all CAD users who enjoy what they do have some "computer hacker" in their blood. The Zen of AutoCAD maintenance, however, is the proper balance of do-it-yourselfism and the already-completed work of someone else that is close enough to what you need. One of the primary reasons that AutoCAD is the most popular PC CAD program is the amount of support it enjoys from third-party vendors, magazines, books, and user groups. To be an expert in CAD management, you must develop the proper relationship between your management practices and the collective genius of those outside resources. In our opinion, we've just described the "Ultimate CAD-management Tool: Effective Resource Implementation," or "The Tom Sawyer School of Management."

Creative CAD Management

A certain amount of the customization that you do should be from scratch, so that you can learn by doing it. Nevertheless, when you really get tuned in to what is available from outside sources, you probably will scrap most of what you did on your own. We did. Our intent is to help you understand what can be done to improve upon what someone else has probably done already. Outside sources (magazines, books, third-party software and hardware, the Autodesk Forum on CompuServe, AutoCAD users' groups, and BBSs dedicated to AutoCAD or product support) are your avenue to profitability in management efforts and true creativity.

Profitability in management efforts is generally thought of as making workers effective by investing in a management effort. In CAD management, an operations manager develops custom tools and overall procedures for the benefit of system users and the firm; the operations manager's time is considered overhead. If you are your own system's manager, think of the time you spend doing anything other than production on your system as overhead. We consider profitability in management getting the desired results from your system in the quickest, most effective way possible. Ninety-five of 100 times, profitable CAD management means wholesale adoption or minor customization of someone else's product. The other five times are when no one has developed a product that even remotely meets your specific needs so you have to create your own.

True creativity in CAD management does not necessarily mean originating a concept; it means using in a different way what others have created, or assembling pieces of what others have done into a new product. For us, creativity means what you spend your time doing after you complete what you *must* do. We did create original LISP routines for this book, to avoid infringing on anyone else's copyright (since we are offering them for resale). If we hadn't been going to use the routines in this book, however, we could have obtained someone else's routines that would have done work similar to, and most of the time better than, ours. If you use any of the LISP routines in this book without considering how you can make them more effective for your specific needs, we have failed to accomplish what we set out to do.

The following steps will get you started in the footsteps of our patriarch, Mr. Sawyer:

- ❑ Develop an indexed library of sample LISP routines, articles, promotional literature, and sample menu macros. If you are a dBASE whiz, or know one, develop a keyword database so that you can keep track of what you've collected.

- More often than not, you can piece together what you want by combining parts of various routines, menus, and the like. All you have to do is compare the cost of buying several products and putting them together with the cost of writing your own additions to the best product that you selected from all those choices.
- Join CompuServe, subscribe to magazines, and join a users' group.
- Develop friends and acquaintances who enjoy doing what you don't, and vice versa. You can trade AutoCAD tools that you both have developed.
- Keep a current wish list of what you need, with a priority rating next to each item.

We are amazed at the quality and variety of products available to supplement AutoCAD. Prices range from $5.00 to $12,000.00, and high-quality products are available throughout the spectrum. We have not examined every available product, but we have talked with many developers. This kind of commitment to AutoCAD from the marketplace reinforces our decision to focus our own development energy on AutoCAD.

To catalog our third-party information, we use the categories of available products listed in table 17.1. Many products provide more than one of these capabilities and work with AutoCAD in many ways. You should begin to keep samples of advertising and brochures in your personal third-party reference library.

Table 17.1. Categories of Third-party Product Information

Category	Includes
Graphic Aids	Products for creating enhanced graphic representations of AutoCAD drawings
Hardware	
Utilities	Helpful products that do the nice little things we soon can't live without
Civil Design Software	Has its own category due to the specialized nature of its needs and the fact that there are many non-AutoCAD resident programs

Table 17.1. continues

Table 17.1. *continued*

Category	Includes
Menu Systems	Work within AutoCAD for Civil, Structural, Landscape, HVAC, Electric, Piping, Electronic, etc. applications
AutoLISP Aids	Tools for programming with AutoLISP
Facilities Management	Miscellaneous
Symbols Libraries	Sets of drawings for use with AutoCAD
Companion Software	Software designed to enhance the use of AutoCAD

The extent of this list suggests that the potential for disaster is as great as the potential for success. Any of the products we received was workable on its own. That's not the problem. The problem is that if you are already using some third-party products, you may find a new addition to be entirely incompatible. One cannot expect every vendor to allow for the capabilities of every other. Individual users have to use their own investigative powers to limit potential problems.

Checking the Basics

There are a few things you should ask about third-party software and hardware that can help ward off potential conflicts. If you don't feel expert enough to evaluate the products yourself, be sure to point out to the vendor what you know about your system, and ask the vendor to verify the conditions surrounding the key issues in the following lists.

Software Considerations

❏ Does it modify my CONFIG.SYS file by adding a driver or other system file? If so, does it affect my extra memory, buffers, files, interrupts, or available RAM? Does it require any special DOS drivers, such as ANSI.SYS?

- ❏ Does it require changes to my AUTOEXEC.BAT file? If so, does it affect the existing statements, the path, or my DOS environment size?
- ❏ Does it have particular requirements for my directory tree or the drive on which I am using AutoCAD? If so, does it work with what I have, or can it be customized?
- ❏ How much space does it take on my disk and/or in RAM?
- ❏ Is it memory resident? Does it have hotkeys, and do any of my other programs use the same ones? Can the hotkeys be changed?
- ❏ Does it modify my ACAD.PGP, ACAD.LIN, or ACAD.PAT file? If so, are the modifications compatible with the terminology I have in them already?
- ❏ Does it have its own ACAD.LSP file? If so, can it be edited? If it can't be edited, can I call it something else? Is its ATOMLIST compatible with mine?
- ❏ Does it have a menu? If so, does it add itself to the AutoCAD menu automatically? What if I'm using someone else's menu? Does it require that I have AUI compatibility?
- ❏ Does it modify any of the AutoCAD system variables? If it does, do those modifications conflict with my existing settings? Does it require its own prototype drawing?
- ❏ If it has a symbols library, is it compatible in file names to the one that I already have? Is my symbols library directory in conflict with its SET ACAD= requirements? Are all file names unique?
- ❏ Is it compatible with my operating system?
- ❏ What parts of it can't I customize?
- ❏ Is it directly compatible with AutoCAD, or does it require a translation program or AutoCAD .DXB or .DXF file?
- ❏ Does it require me to alter my standard procedures or standard drawings?
- ❏ What hardware does it support? Is emulation of hardware through special drivers okay?
- ❏ Is it compatible with the other software I might use with it? (This is especially important for TSRs.)

- ❏ Is an informative demo available?
- ❏ What do the manuals look like?
- ❏ Who can you call at the company for high tech help?

These items should be checked, in addition to the normal software purchase requirements (copy protection, updates, etc.).

Hardware Considerations

In addition to the software purchase considerations just listed, if you are considering a hardware purchase, check the items on the following list:

- ❏ Does it require a driver written by a company other than Autodesk? If so, have their updates been timely? Do they charge for updates?
- ❏ Does it require that I change any configurations of other hardware or my computer?
- ❏ Is it compatible with my operating system?
- ❏ Does the product have uses other than for AutoCAD?
- ❏ What hardware interrupt address does it use, if any?
- ❏ Does Autodesk list it as a supported device?
- ❏ Does the guy who sells it use AutoCAD?
- ❏ If it uses cables, adapter cards, or drivers, will it work on other systems or networks?
- ❏ If it breaks, do I get a loaner? If I get a loaner, will it be the same thing or a temporary substitute? If it's a substitute, is it compatible with AutoCAD and my system?
- ❏ Does it have a TSR software companion? If it does, do I have room for it in RAM?
- ❏ If it uses an expansion slot, will I need the slot later for something else?
- ❏ Can I install it, or will I need help?
- ❏ Is it on the cutting edge of the technology? (If it is too new or too old—older than two years—it may cause problems.)

Warranties, support and service, the company behind it, and many other concerns enter into the decision to purchase a hardware product. We have listed the considerations that have to do specifically with AutoCAD. How you use your system, the costs of the software or hardware, and the immediate versus long-term returns will always be a concern, but we have found that if the preceding questions are not properly answered, trouble is ahead more times than not. If you really think you need a particular product but are unsure of the source you are getting it from, write a questionnaire, have the supplier answer it in writing and sign it. If the supplier refuses to do this, do not buy the product.

Focusing on Specifics

Specification sheets and magazine reviews are the worst traps basic users can fall into when considering new products: we don't understand half the stuff they put on the spec sheets, and the reviewer isn't going to have to use the product for the next three years. There are no industry standards for comparing software or hardware. For example, if a magazine uses AutoCAD as one of the programs used for evaluating the speed of PCs it reviews, the evaluations of PCs are not actually equivalent; the capabilities of the hard disk, the graphics card, the bus speed, whether the PC uses memory caching, and a host of other factors can change the test results dramatically.

The most reliable way to evaluate a product is to ask others who use the product in a fashion similar to the way you plan to use it. If you can get them to do it, have them answer a questionnaire. Then, armed with an informed set of basics, your own questionnaire, and Chapter 8 of this book, go to a dealer.

If, after you have done your homework, asked all the right questions and gotten mostly right answers, you find that something doesn't seem to be working quite the way you thought it would—don't panic. At least 7 times out of 10 you have left out one important step or have not considered a minor bit of tweaking you could do to make things operate as they should. Two times out of 10 there will be a minor or mid-sized problem due to an unanticipated conflict with another part of your system or software. Finally, 1 time out of 10 you will have to return it and try to get your money back.

The best resource for information about any product, after your dealer, is the Autodesk Forum. Someone on the Autodesk Forum, either a dealer or a user, is likely to have encountered the exact problem you are trying to resolve. There may not be anyone in your area who has the same equipment you do, but the Autodesk Forum has members from all over the world, and usually one of them can help.

Finding Solutions

Next to our workstation we keep a little notebook in which we jot down ideas about LISP routines, macros, or companion software we would like to develop or buy. We also do a lot of window shopping at computer stores and in magazines. When you are ready to tackle a new, specific problem, here are some steps to follow to arrive at a solution:

1. Write down exactly what the product must do, as well as what would be nice "if it did."

2. See whether Autodesk Forum members, your local users' group, and a dealer or two can add to your list or recommend a solution.

3. Prepare a chart that lets you rate what is important to you, on a scale from 1 to 10, for each possible solution. If it is something you can assess, add a factor for time expended and time saved. If you can combine two or more products to get what you want, rate the combination. Make sure that you also evaluate the product's impact on your management standards and procedures.

4. Review your keyword index of clippings and brochures for solutions you may have forgotten. You will be amazed at how many times someone else has already done it!

5. Send a letter describing the results of your preliminary review to the potential candidates, and ask whether they would like to comment.

6. Get demos of the candidates, if they are available. We have received some excellent software demos. Many of them cost little or nothing. You may be able to work a deal for a credit if you return the demo. The amount of information in a demo is obviously correlated to the cost of the product, and demos come in various forms, including videotape.

Once you have decided on a solution, don't go down with the ship if you find that you've made a mistake. Go back to Option 2.

As we mentioned earlier in this book, when we were working with AutoCAD Release 9 we wanted to develop a sophisticated program that automatically set up views in our drawings. Using transparent zooms and pans, we almost never did a regen. Once we had developed the basic routine, after spending at least 20 hours trying to write a better routine and getting answers from Autodesk, we found that we would have to write a separate routine for each display card that had a different resolution, and for each monitor size. Not long after that, AutoCAD Release 10 came on the market, with viewports, effectively eliminating the need for the routine. This is a prime example of a solution we pursued that just wasn't worth the effort; we should have quit while we were ahead.

Where To Look for More

If you feel you need a wider range of options, we'll pass on some fine print about where we told you to look for help. Here are some ideas:

- Magazines
  - Advertisers' reader service cards
  - Toll-free numbers in the advertisements
  - Classified ads for consultants and service bureaus
  - Write to the author(s) of an applicable article in care of the magazine
- Autodesk
  - The data libraries in the Autodesk Forum on CompuServe have files that list the contents of each data library. Download them to your computer and print them for reference.
  - The current edition of the *AutoCAD Applications Catalog*, which is available from your AutoCAD dealer
  - The annual AEC Expo (usually held in early summer)

If you make a serious attempt at becoming informed about a product, you may find that developers or manufacturers will be happy to spend time discussing with you things that their dealers couldn't or didn't answer. Don't expect to get any help from them, but if you are nice on the phone or in a letter, you may be pleasantly surprised. Keep in mind that you aren't the only responsibility developers and manufacturers have to take care of; contact them only if you are thoroughly discouraged by the dealer. Autodesk, in particular, will rarely help you over the telephone or in writing. The best approach is to use the Autodesk Forum on CompuServe; even then, it may not be Autodesk that has the answer to your question.

Throughout this book we have casually mentioned various hardware and software manufacturers. Appendix K lists those manufacturers, with their addresses, a point of contact, and a brief description of their product(s) or services. Feel free to contact these companies, and tell them we sent you.

What To Do Next

One of the hardest tasks for CAD managers is predicting what is coming in the future. This can have a dynamic influence on the management procedures put in practice, the hardware purchased, and the software selected to work side by side with AutoCAD. One of the best ways to develop a feel for trends is to keep reading current publications and use the Autodesk Forum frequently. At the same time, of course, you have to commit to taking a stand and implementing your CAD-management ideas. There will never be a time when this industry stops changing; you have to learn to make decisions based on what you know now and what you can anticipate of the future.

Use a chapter or two of this book to prepare you for developing a solution to a management problem, and then review the options for creating a solution to the problem, as presented in this chapter. If you take this approach, your efforts will seldom be wasted. Furthermore, once you develop the momentum, the task will seem less overwhelming than it may right now. All you have to do is get started, and the fastest way to get started is to use everyone else's efforts.

Summary

This chapter discussed the last of the CAD-management concepts we review in this book. We think it fitting that the chapter represents such a wide array of options, since that is the reality of AutoCAD. Third-party products can help you refine the principles we have presented in this book, simply because they let you see how someone else does things. We hope this chapter and this book have served as a springboard from which you will explore the entire spectrum of CAD management, and the real power of AutoCAD.

Recommended Accomplishments

❑ Take a break after reading this book!

❑ Make a wish list of what you want to achieve in customizing your system and implementing CAD-management practices, based on what you learned in this book. Try to put the list in the order in which tasks will need to be completed.

❑ Get started right after your break.

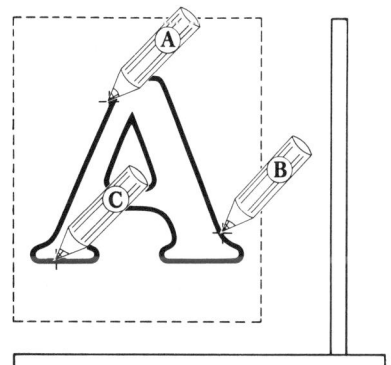

LSRPREP.LSP

L SRPREP.LSP is the LISP routine mentioned in Chapter 5. Because this routine has not been tested for AutoCAD Release 10 three-dimensional drawings, it may not work in Release 10 in all cases.

LSRPREP.LSP converts all nonblocked objects in a drawing to polylines with widths that match the American standard rapidograph pen sizes (from 4 ×0 to 2 1/2), based on the color of the object. You can edit the pens and colors under the function swd as needed. This routine requires that you have the AutoCAD variable LTSCALE set to the drawing scale.

What follows is the complete listing of the file's contents; after the listing, we go through the routine section by section, explaining its contents. Read Chapter 13, "AutoCAD Never Was Plain English," before you try to decipher the LSRPREP.LSP routine. Remember that the spaces used for indentation are for legibility only; they are not necessary for the routine to run properly.

```
(defun group ()
  (setvar "cmdecho" 1)
  (setvar "highlight" 0)
  (setq lin (ssget "X" (list (cons 0 "LINE")))
        ar (ssget "X" (list (cons 0 "ARC")))
        cir (ssget "X" (list (cons 0 "CIRCLE")))
        pli (ssget "X" (list (cons 0 "POLYLINE")))))
(princ))
```

Listing continues

Listing continued

```
(defun swd ()
    (setq unclr (cdr (assoc 62 (entget e))))
    (if (/= unclr nil)(setq clr unclr)(setq clr (cdr (assoc 62
              (tblsearch "layer" (cdr (assoc 8 (entget e))))))))
(cond ((or (= clr 15)(= clr 7))(setq plw 0.0276))   ;pen #2-1/2
      ((or (= clr 14)(= clr 6))(setq plw 0.0236))   ;pen #2
      ((or (= clr 13)(= clr 5))(setq plw 0.0197))   ;pen #1
      ((or (= clr 12)(= clr 4))(setq plw 0.0138))   ;pen #0
      ((or (= clr 11)(= clr 3))(setq plw 0.0118))   ;pen #00
      ((or (= clr 10)(= clr 2))(setq plw 0.0098))   ;pen #3x0
      ((or (= clr 9)(= clr 1))(setq plw 0.0071)))   ;pen #4x0
    (setq plw (* plw (getvar "ltscale"))))
)

(defun lincon (/ linl ctr e unclr plw)
  (prompt "\nCONVERTING LINES...")
  (setq linl (sslength lin)
        ctr 0)
  (repeat linl
    (setq e (ssname lin ctr))
    (swd)
    (command "pedit" e "y" "w" plw "")
    (setq ctr (1+ ctr)
          unclr nil
          clr nil))
(princ))

(defun pcon  (/ plil ctr e unclr clr plw)
    (prompt "\nCONVERTING PLINES...")
    (setq plil (sslength pli)
          ctr 0)
    (repeat plil
      (setq e (ssname pli ctr))
      (swd)
      (command "pedit" e "w" plw "")
      (setq ctr (1+ ctr)
            unclr nil
            clr nil))
(princ))

(defun circon (/ cirl ctr e cntr rad unclr clr plw)
    (prompt "\nCONVERTING CIRCLES...")
    (setq cirl (sslength cir)
          ctr 0)
    (repeat cirl
      (setq e (ssname cir ctr))
```

```
                        cntr (cdr (assoc 10 (entget e)))
                        rad (cdr (assoc 40 (entget e))))
        (swd)
        (command "layer" "s" (cdr (assoc 8 (entget e))) "")
        (command "color" clr)
      (command "pline" (polar cntr 0.0 rad) "w" plw "" "arc" "r" rad
                  (polar cntr pi rad) (polar cntr (* 2 pi) rad) "")
        (command "erase" e "")
        (setq ctr (1+ ctr)
              unclr nil
              clr nil))
  (command "color" "bylayer")
  (princ))

(defun arcon (/ arl ctr e cntr rad ep1 ep2 plw clr unclr)
       (prompt "\nCONVERTING ARCS...")
       (setq arl (sslength ar)
             ctr 0)
       (repeat arl
          (setq e (ssname ar ctr)
                cntr (cdr (assoc 10 (entget e)))
                rad (cdr (assoc 40 (entget e))))
          (setq ep1 (polar cntr (cdr (assoc 50 (entget e))) rad)
                ep2 (polar cntr (cdr (assoc 51 (entget e))) rad))
        (swd)
        (command "layer" "s" (cdr (assoc 8 (entget e))) "")
        (command "color" clr)
        (command "pline" ep1 "w" plw "" "arc" "r" rad
                  ep2 "")
        (command "erase" e "")
        (setq ctr (1+ ctr)
              unclr nil
              clr nil))
  (command "color" "bylayer")
  (princ))

(defun lsrprep (/ pli ar cir lin)
   (prompt "\nWORKING...")
   (group)
    (if pli (pcon))
    (if ar (arcon))
    (if cir (circon))
    (if lin (lincon))
  (setvar "highlight" 1)
  (command "redraw")
  (prompt "CONVERSION COMPLETE")
  (princ))
```

To start the routine, type **(load "lsrprep")** and then **(lsrprep)** at the AutoCAD command prompt.

Note: The easiest way to study the following description of the routine is to photocopy the complete listing and keep it handy as you read the description. Do this also for the AutoLISP routines explained in the other appendixes.

In order to reduce the amount of code that AutoLISP is required to manipulate at any one time, this routine is written in a simple fashion and uses separate function definitions for each task in the routine.

The first function collects the data that will be used by the balance of the routines in the file:

```
(defun group ()
```

This line defines the function group and sets no local variables. We don't define local variables, which normally are placed after a slash (/) enclosed within the parentheses that follow group, because we want to use them in other defined functions; the only way we can make them retain their value is to make them global. This function is going to obtain groups of like objects in the drawing and place them into defined sets of entities.

The two lines:

```
(setvar "cmdecho" 0)
(setvar "highlight" 0)
```

set the AutoCAD variables *cmdecho* and *highlight* to an off condition. This speeds execution of the routine and keeps the screen a little clearer.

A series of setq functions:

```
(setq lin (ssget "X" (list (cons 0 "LINE")))
      ar (ssget "X" (list (cons 0 "ARC")))
      cir (ssget "X" (list (cons 0 "CIRCLE")))
          pli (ssget "X" (list (cons 0 "POLYLINE")))))
```

assigns four variables (*lin*, *ar*, *cir*, and *pli*) to selection sets using the function ssget.

The "X" designation following ssget establishes a filter for sorting the drawing entities. In this case, we have set up filters for the group code 0, which is the code for the entity name. As you can see, we have selected four groups—lines, arcs, circles, and polylines.

We use cons to construct a dotted pair from the integer 0 and the string LINE, for example. Notice that the strings are enclosed in quotation marks so that the AutoLISP routine does not seek a variable *LINE* and fail. We use list to create a list from the dotted pair. This is required because AutoCAD stores this information as a list. For example, AutoLISP searches the database and looks at all of the entities. If it finds a database that has a list (0 . ARC) in its description, it adds that entity to a group (selection set) that is bound to the variable *arc*. This use of setq is faster than repeating setq for each of the variables, but you must be careful to use parentheses correctly.

The next line is

(princ))

Princ, when called with no arguments, prints nothing to the screen. This suppresses the normal activity of AutoLISP, which is to return a nil to the screen after completing the routine. The extra closing parenthesis on this line ends the defun statement.

The next function (swd) sets the width for the polylines to the American standard sizes, and is used by each routine in the file. So that we don't have to type it in for each function and AutoLISP doesn't have to read it four times, we define it in its own routine:

(defun swd ()

The preceding line defines the function swd for setting the width of the polylines that will be created by the program. Notice that we used global variables again.

Now comes a pair of statements that allow for unique color assignments to each entity and choose the layer color if no unique color assignment exists:

(setq unclr (cdr (assoc 62 (entget e))))
(if (/= unclr nil)(setq clr unclr)(setq clr (cdr (assoc 62
    (tblsearch "layer" (cdr (assoc 8 (entget e)))))))))

First, we set the variable *unclr* to the value of the group code 62 of an entity that is bound to the variable *e*. This is accomplished by using the entget function to obtain a list of the entity's description. Then we use assoc to find what is associated with the group code 62; this will be a dotted pair list. An example of such a list is (62 . 1), which tells you that the entity has a unique color of red (1) assigned to it. Because we don't care about the group code, we use cdr to extract the 1 from the dotted pair. If the entity received its color "bylayer", group code 62 won't be there, and AutoLISP will set unclr to nil.

The if statement says, "IF the variable *unclr* is not equal to nil, then set the variable *clr* equal to the value of *unclr* that we found in the last statement. On the other hand, if it is equal to nil, then set the variable *clr* to the value of the color for the layer the entity is on."

By using `tblsearch`, we accomplish the second part of the `if` statement. We tell AutoLISP to check the drawing header tables and find out the color of the layer that the entity bound to the variable *e* is on. Notice that the layer in the drawing table uses the same group code, 62, as the entity does to record the color of the layer. The group code 8 for the entity *e* is the name of the layer the entity is on. Because it is a dotted pair, just as the color would have been, we have to jump through the same hoops with assoc.

```
(cond ((or (= clr 15)(= clr 7))(setq plw 0.0276))   ;pen #2-1/2
      ((or (= clr 14)(= clr 6))(setq plw 0.0236))   ;pen #2
      ((or (= clr 13)(= clr 5))(setq plw 0.0197))   ;pen #1
      ((or (= clr 12)(= clr 4))(setq plw 0.0138))   ;pen #0
      ((or (= clr 11)(= clr 3))(setq plw 0.0118))   ;pen #00
      ((or (= clr 10)(= clr 2))(setq plw 0.0098))   ;pen #3×0
      ((or (= clr 9)(= clr 1))(setq plw 0.0071)))   ;pen #4×0
```

Now that we know what the color is and have bound it to the variable *clr*, we need to choose the pen weight to which we want to set the polyline width. We chose to use only seven pen weights and to put them in order of the color numbers, based on the EGA standard.

We simplified a lot of testing by using the cond statement and saying, "If any of these things is true, set the variable *plw* to one of these values." AutoLISP looks at the statements within the first nest of parentheses to see if the statement is true. The first line asks whether the variable *clr* equals one of two numbers, 15 or 7. Each of the following lines repeats the process for varying pen weights.

We set this up because we are going to use colors 9 through 15 just as we use the colors 1 through 7. We choose not to use 8 because it is black (and we use a black background for our drawings). If cond finds one of the "or" situations to be true, it sets the variable *plw* to the desired pen size in inches. *Note:* pen #3 would be 0.0315, pen #3-1/2 would be 0.0395, and pen #4 would be 0.0472.

The statement:

```
(setq plw (* plw (getvar "ltscale")))
)
```

resets the polyline-width variable *plw* to an adjusted value for the drawing scale. This routine requires that the AutoCAD LTSCALE system variable be set to the drawing scale. Most setup LISP routines do this, but you need to check to make sure that yours does. Notice that we don't use `princ` in this case because we will be calling this subroutine from within another routine. As usual, the last parenthesis closes the `defun` statement.

The next function is the program function that converts all of the lines in the drawing to polylines:

```
(defun lincon (/ linl clr ctr e unclr plw)
```

This statement defines the line conversion function `lincon`. We now use local variables after the slash (/) so that when this routine finishes, these variables will be set to nil. By doing this, we can use the same variables for each subroutine in the program. This is especially important for the variables *plw* and *unclr*.

The line:

```
(prompt "\nCONVERTING LINES...")
```

sends a prompt to the screen so that the user knows the routine is running; it is a nice touch for the professional look, but serves no programming purpose.

In the next two lines:

```
(setq linl (sslength lin)
      ctr 0)
```

the function sets the variable *linl* to the length of the selection set *lin* by using `sslength`, and then sets the variable *ctr* to zero. These two variables are used to control a loop and to count through each entity in the selection set.

The repeating loop, `(repeat linl`, uses the variable *linl* as the number of times to repeat the loop. Because we are going to act on every member of the selection set, we will repeat the loop the same number of times as the length of the selection set.

```
(setq e (ssname lin ctr))
```

The function `ssname` retrieves the list that is the name of the entity whose position in the selection set *lin* is the same as the current value of *ctr*. As you will see, we increment *ctr* in a later step so that we don't have to repeat this request for the first, second, third, and every other entity—for example, `(ssname lin 0)`, `(ssname lin 1)`, etc. Notice that the first entity in the group is entity number zero, which is why we started with *ctr* set to zero.

`(swd)` executes the defined function swd that we discussed previously.

By using the command function:

```
(command "pedit" e "y" "w" plw "")
```

we are able to execute the AutoCAD PEDIT command on the entity bound to the variable *e*. Since we are using PEDIT on lines, AutoCAD tells us that the line is not a polyline and asks whether we want to turn it into one. We respond with the string "y" and specify that we want to edit the width of the newly-created polyline by responding with the string w. When PEDIT asks us for a new width for all segments, we respond with the variable *plw* which is the polyline width as determined by the color of the entity and the drawing scale from the function swd. The empty quotation marks ("") in the routine have the same function as the space bar pressed at the command prompt; they execute a return to end the PEDIT command. (This is much simpler than converting the ASCII character for *return* and printing it to the AutoCAD command prompt.)

The following four lines:

```
(setq ctr (1+ ctr)
      unclr nil
      clr nil))
(princ))
```

set the variable *ctr* to one more than its previous value, *unclr* to nil, and *clr* to nil. We had to do this so that the next loop of the repeat loop would not get confused when it found that both *clr* and *unclr* had values, one obtained from the previous loop and one from the current loop. Notice that the double parentheses following the last nil close the repeat loop, and that we again close the function with princ.

The next function converts existing polylines into polylines with the proper width, whether they are ellipses, polygons, donuts, or standard polylines:

```
(defun pcon  (/ plil ctr e unclr clr plw)
    (prompt "\nCONVERTING PLINES...")
    (setq plil (sslength pli)
          ctr 0)
    (repeat plil
      (setq e (ssname pli ctr))
      (swd)
      (command "pedit" e "w" plw "")
        (setq ctr (1+ ctr)
              unclr nil
              clr nil))
(princ))
```

This function works the same as `lincon`, except that the PEDIT command doesn't require that we provide a *yes* answer.

The next function converts circles to polyarcs:

```
(defun circon (/ cirl ctr e cntr rad unclr clr plw)
    (prompt "\nCONVERTING CIRCLES...")
    (setq cirl (sslength cir)
          ctr 0)
    (repeat cirl
        (setq e (ssname cir ctr)
```

This section works the same as the previous two functions, `lincon` and `pcon`.

In the next two lines:

```
cntr (cdr (assoc 10 (entget e)))
rad (cdr (assoc 40 (entget e))))
```

the functions set the variable *cntr* to the center of the circle, which is the last part of the dotted pair associated with group code 10; they also set the variable *rad* to the radius of the circle which is associated with group code 40. This works exactly like the similar functions in swd, except that different group codes are used.

Next,

`(swd)`

executes the function swd each time the repeat loop makes a pass.

The line

`(command "layer" "s" (cdr (assoc 8 (entget e))) "")`

uses the AutoCAD LAYER command to set the layer equal to the layer associated with group code 8 of the circle we are about to convert.

`(command "color" clr)` sets the AutoCAD color setting equal to the color of the object or layer as found by the function swd. (We explain later why we had to do this.)

The following set of functions:

```
(command "pline" (polar cntr 0.0 rad) "w" plw "" "arc" "r" rad
         (polar cntr pi rad) (polar cntr (* 2 pi) rad) "")
```

draws a polyarc, starting at zero degrees from the center of the circle (*cntr*), a distance equal to the radius (*rad*). This is accomplished by using the `polar` function to find the 0 quadrant of the circle by using 0.0 radians.

We set the width of the polyline as we did before and then use the PLINE command to specify that we want an arc drawn using a radius equal to the variable *rad*. The PLINE command causes AutoCAD to prompt us for the endpoint of the arc, and we provide the 180 degree quadrant of the circle by using the `polar` function again, except that we supply pi radians as the angle from the center of the circle. Finally, we provide another endpoint, again using `polar` and 2 pi radians as the angle, finishing the PLINE command with "". What we are doing is drawing a new pair of arcs right on top of the existing circle.

Now we use the AutoCAD ERASE command to get rid of the circle that was bound to the variable *e*:

```
(command "erase" e "")
```

In the next three lines, the functions work the same as before:

```
(setq ctr (1+ ctr)
    unclr nil
    clr nil))
```

Notice that the repeat loop is closed after the nil.

To reset the drawing color to *bylayer* after all the work is done, and exit the routine quietly with `princ`, we used the following two lines:

```
(command "color" "bylayer")
(princ))
```

The next function converts the arcs in the drawing in a similar fashion to the function `circon`:

```
(defun arcon (/ arl ctr e cntr rad ep1 ep2 plw clr unclr)
    (prompt "\nCONVERTING ARCS...")
    (setq arl (sslength ar)
        ctr 0)
    (repeat arl
      (setq e (ssname ar ctr)
          cntr (cdr (assoc 10 (entget e)))
          rad (cdr (assoc 40 (entget e))))
```

The preceding section contains elements we've already explained, but the following lines:

```
        (setq ep1 (polar cntr (cdr (assoc 50 (entget e))) rad)
            ep2 (polar cntr (cdr (assoc 51 (entget e))) rad))
```

contain new elements. These two lines set the variables *ep1* and *ep2* to the endpoints of the arc, which are part of the dotted pair associated with group codes 50 and 51. We establish these endpoints in a counterclockwise fashion, so that the polyarc behaves itself.

```
(swd)
(command "layer" "s" (cdr (assoc 8 (entget e))) "")
(command "color" clr)
```

The preceding section contains elements we've already explained, but the following lines contain new elements. The line:

```
(command "pline" ep1 "w" plw "" "arc" "r" rad ep2 "")
```

draws a polyarc in the same manner as the circle except that we use the endpoints that are bound to the variables *ep1* and *ep2*.

We have already explained the elements in the following section:

```
(command "erase" e "")
(setq ctr (1+ ctr)
      unclr nil
      clr nil))
(command "color" "bylayer")
(princ))
```

The next function is the main program that executes everything we have talked about so far.

```
(defun lsrprep (/ pli ar cir lin)
```

This is the definition of the function lsrprep. Notice that we now make the variables *pli, ar, cir,* and *lin* local variables. We do this so that the selection sets to which they are bound will be returned to nil. AutoLISP allows only six selection sets to be open at one time.

This prompt:

```
(prompt "\nWORKING...")
```

lets users know that they have started something; it is displayed while group and swd are running.

Next, (group) executes the group function.

The if statements:

```
(if pli (pcon))
(if ar (arcon))
(if cir (circon))
(if lin (lincon))
```

execute each function only if there is a selection set bound to the variables.

The functions in the final four lines:

```
(setvar "highlight" 1)
(command "redraw")
(prompt "CONVERSION COMPLETE")
(princ))
```

return everything to normal and let users know that the program is finished.

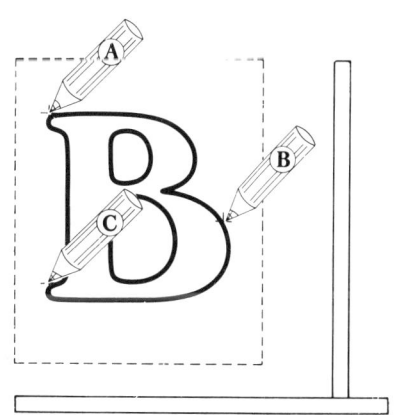

Removing and Inserting Drawing Details

This appendix contains two LISP routines. The first, DTL.LSP, is useful for extracting a portion of a drawing. The second, INSDET.LSP, can be used to insert a drawing (from disk) within the current drawing. The use of these routines is discussed in Chapter 9, "The Tasks At Hand."

Routine for Extracting Drawing Details (DTL.LSP)

DTL.LSP, a routine for cutting out drawing details, was provided to us courtesy of Lowell Walmsley of Robert McNeel & Associates, 1310 Ward St., Suite 200, Seattle, WA 98109.

McNeel and Associates, an AutoCAD dealer that creates custom routines and menus for customers, does not warrant this routine in any way. We think that it is a well done bit of work. It is free for you to use, but not for you to sell.

DTL.LSP extracts a section of a drawing for a detail. Lines, arcs, and circles are trimmed to the box boundary. Polylines and equal scale blocks are exploded one level in the detail before trimming.

DTL.LSP asks for two corners which define a rectangle to be extracted from a drawing to form a detail. It then asks for a new point for the first corner. This is a point at which to locate the corner of the detail being created. Next you are asked for a scale factor—a ratio of size in the original drawing to size of the new detail. For example, to make the detail a 2x enlargement, you would use 2.

The routine then copies to the new location all entities that cross the specified rectangle, and scales them. Blocks and polylines are exploded one level and a new selection set of entities in the detail is made. The routine then calculates what is inside and outside of the rectangular area for the new detail and trims off the excess.

Neither polylines in blocks nor nested blocks are exploded, because including such activities slows execution. Although execution time is not too bad if a few entities are selected for the detail, you can easily bog it down with large groups of information.

The points used for trimming entities are

Entity	Trimming point
Line	Endpoints
Arc	Endpoints and quadrant points
Circle	Quadrant points

Other types of entities are copied out to the detail, but ignored in the trimming. Remember that AutoLISP interprets lines preceded by semicolons as comment lines, until it encounters a return.

```
(defun val (x e) (cdr (assoc x e)))
(defun enttype (e) (cdr (assoc 0 e)))
(defun entname (e) (cdr (assoc -1 e)))
(setq >90 (/ pi 2) >270 (* 3 (/ pi 2)))
;==============================================================
; Find the 'endpoints ' of the LINES, ARCS, & CIRCLES in ss
;    that are outside a rectangle described by the opposite
;    corners pll and pur and submits them to the command function.
;--------------------------------------------------------------
(defun osends (ss pll pur / z eps)
   (ends ss)       ;this puts the 'endpoints' in a list, eps
   (foreach z eps     ;this checks if they are outside the rectangle
     (if (or (< (caadr z) (car pll))
         (< (cadadr z) (cadr pll))
         (> (caadr z) (car pur))
         (> (cadadr z) (cadr pur))
       )
       (command z)
     )
   )
)
```

```
;----------------------------------------------------------------
; Finds the 'endpoints' of LINES, ARCS, & CIRCLES in ss.
; 'Endpoints' are:
;   LINES:    endpoints
;   ARCS:     endpoints and quadrant points
;   CIRCLES:  quadrant points
; The endpoint lists are consed into the list eps (global).
;----------------------------------------------------------------
(defun ends (ss / i ent cen)
  (setq len (sslength ss) i 0)   ;get number of entities
  (while (< i len)               ;loop thru them
    (setq ent (entget (ssname ss i))) ;get assoc list
    (cond         ;Check for LINES, ARCS, & CIRCLES and cons
          ; the appropriate points into eps.
          ;Other entity types are ignored.
          ;LINES
      ((= (enttype ent) "LINE")
        (setq eps (cons (list (entname ent)
          (val 10 ent)) eps))
        (setq eps (cons (list (entname ent)
          (val 11 ent)) eps)) )
        ;ARCS
      ((= (enttype ent) "ARC")
        (setq cen (val 10 ent))
        (setq eps (cons
          (list (entname ent)
            (polar cen 0 (val 40 ent))) eps))
        (setq eps (cons
          (list (entname ent)
            (polar cen >90 (val 40 ent))) eps))
        (setq eps (cons
          (list (entname ent)
            (polar cen pi (val 40 ent))) eps))
        (setq eps (cons
          (list (entname ent)
            (polar cen >270 (val 40 ent))) eps))
        (setq eps (cons
          (list (entname ent)
            (polar cen (val 50 ent) (val 40 ent))) eps))
        (setq eps (cons
          (list (entname ent)
            (polar cen (val 51 ent) (val 40 ent))) eps))
        (setq eps (cons
          (list (entname ent)
            (osnap (polar cen (val 51 ent)
              (val 40 ent)) "mid")) eps)) )
        ;CIRCLES
      ((= (enttype ent) "CIRCLE")
        (setq cen (val 10 ent))
        (setq eps (cons
          (list (entname ent)
            (polar cen 0 (val 40 ent))) eps))
```

Listing continues

Listing continued

```
          (setq eps (cons
            (list (entname ent)
            (polar cen >90 (val 40 ent))) eps))
          (setq eps (cons
            (list (entname ent)
            (polar cen pi (val 40 ent))) eps))
          (setq eps (cons
            (list (entname ent)
            (polar cen >270 (val 40 ent))) eps)) )
     )
     (setq i (1+ i))     ;Next entity
   )
)
;-----------------------------------------------------------------
;Explodes all p-lines in selection set s
;-----------------------------------------------------------------
(defun exp_pl (s / i len ent)
  (setq i 0 len (sslength s))
  (while (< i len)
    (setq ent (entget (ssname s i)))
    (cond
      ((= (enttype ent) "POLYLINE")
        (command "explode" (entname ent))
      )
      ((= (enttype ent) "INSERT")
        (if (= (val 41 ent) (val 42 ent)
            (val 43 ent))   ;check equal scale
          (command "explode" (entname ent))
        )
      )
    )
    (setq i (+ 1 i))
  )
)
;-----------------------------------------------------------------
;erases parts of exploded p-lines that are outside target area
;-----------------------------------------------------------------
(defun era_xtra (e)
  (setq ssx (ssadd))
  (while (setq e (entnext e))
    (if (not (ssmemb e ss))
      (ssadd e ssx)
    )
  )
  (command "erase" ssx "")
)
;-----------------------------------------------------------------
; Gets the geometry and calls routines to do the trimming.
;-----------------------------------------------------------------
(defun c:dtl (/ px py pxx pyy xs ss b ssx)
  (setvar "cmdecho" 0)
  (if (and
```

```
          ;This defines a rectangle to be copied out to a detail
    (setq px (getpoint "\nFirst corner: "))
    (setq py (getcorner px "\nOther corner: "))
          ;This is the position of the lower left corner of the detail
    (setq pxx (getpoint px "\nNew first corner position: "))
          ;This is a size adjust factor for scaling the detail
    (setq xs (getreal "\nScale factor for detail: ")) )
    (progn
       ;copy out the stuff selected
(command "copy" "c" px py "" px pxx)
(command "pline" px (list (car px) (cadr py)) ;draw an outline
     py (list (car py) (cadr px)) "c")          ; of the base area.
          ;these are the new entities that may need trimming.
(setq ss (ssget "c" pxx (polar pxx (angle px py)
      (distance px py))))
          ;first explode p-lines because if you trim them, you
          ; get too many new entities to deal with.
          ; (could do blocks too)
(setq last (entlast)) ;save end of database
(exp_pl ss) ;this explodes them
  ;then get all the new parts into ss
(setq ss (ssget "c" pxx (polar pxx (angle px py)
      (distance px py))))
          ;and erase ones that are clear outside rectangle
(era_xtra last)
(command "scale" ss "" pxx xs)       ;Scale the detail
          ;new other corner point of detail
(setq pyy (polar pxx (angle px py) (* xs (distance px py))))
(command "pline" pxx (list (car pxx) (cadr pyy))  ;Box around
    pyy (list (car pyy) (cadr pxx)) "c")          ;the detail
(command "trim" (setq b (entlast)) "")  ;Last P-line is cutting edge
(osends ss pxx pyy)    ;This finds ends that are outside the box
            ; and trims them.
(command "")       ;Terminate trim
(redraw b)
    )
  )
(setvar "cmdecho" 1)
(princ)
)
```

Copyright 1988 Robert McNeel & Assoc., 1310 Ward St., Seattle, WA, 98109

Note: When you type your own copy of this routine you can omit the comments that follow the semicolons (;). The routine will still work just fine.

Routine for Inserting Drawings into Different Scale Drawings (INSDET.LSP)

The INSDET.LSP program inserts a drawing from the directory you tell AutoLISP to search. If the requested drawing is not found, the routine exits, telling you that the drawing was not found. INSDET.LSP works only for drawings that are on disk outside the drawing file. It will insert blocks already contained in a drawing, provided that there is a file for them on disk. INSDET.LSP works for both reduction and magnification of the inserted drawing and includes an option for adjusting text size. The default size (1/8-inch actual plotted size) works best for magnification only.

This routine requires some calculation for scale conversion. The knowledge of what scale was used to create the inserted drawing is required; the AutoCAD variable LTSCALE must be set to the drawing scale.

This routine was written for use with AutoCAD Release 9. If you are using AutoCAD Release 10, review the comments in the program listing to verify changes you must make; do not run the routine in AutoCAD Release 10 without making these changes.

The contents of INSDET.LSP follow:

```
(defun insdet (/ xsc psc insc tht nh blk tht?
         ip yn sst sstl ctr xts e nts e2 dm ftst p1 p2)
  (setvar "cmdecho" 0)
  (setq xsc (getvar "ltscale"))
  (cond ((= xsc 600.0)(setq psc "1 in.=50 ft."))
        ((= xsc 480.0)(setq psc "1 in.=40 ft."))
        ((= xsc 360.0)(setq psc "1 in.=30 ft."))
        ((= xsc 240.0)(setq psc "1 in.=20 ft."))
        ((= xsc 192.0)(setq psc "1/16 in.=1 ft."))
        ((= xsc 96.0)(setq psc "1/8 in.=1 ft."))
        ((= xsc 48.0)(setq psc "1/4 in.=1 ft."))
        ((= xsc 24.0)(setq psc "1/2 in.=1 ft."))
        ((= xsc 16.0)(setq psc "3/4 in.=1 ft."))
        ((= xsc 12.0)(setq psc "1 in.=1 ft."))
        ((= xsc 4.0)(setq psc "3 in.=1 ft."))
        ((= xsc 2.0)(setq psc "6 in.=1 ft."))
        ((= xsc 1.0)(setq psc "Full Scale"))
        (xsc (setq psc (strcat (rtos (/ 12.0 xsc)) " in.=1
            ft."))));close cond
```

Appendix B: Removing and Inserting Drawing Details

```
(textscr)
(prompt "\nThe existing drawing scale is ")
(princ psc)
(prompt "...")
(prompt "\nEnter the scale factor to increase or decrease the")
(setq insc (getreal "\ninserted drawing by...: "))
(initget 1 "Y y N n")
(setq tht? (strcase
   (getkword "\nDo you wish to change the text height?
      <Y or N>: ")))
(if (= tht? "Y")
  (progn
   (initget 6)
   (setq tht
     (getdist "\nEnter the desired actual plot height for the
        lettering <1/8>: "))
   (if (= tht nil)(setq tht 0.125));close if
   (setq nh (* tht xsc))))
(prompt "\nUsing forward slashes </>, please carefully")
(prompt "\nenter the drawing you wish to insert, including the")
(setq blk (getkword "\ndirectory and subdirectory,
    as required: "))
(findfile blk)
(if (/= ftst nil);if #1
(progn ;progn #1
(graphscr)
(setq ip (getpoint "\nSelect insertion point: "))
(setvar "highlight" 0)
(setq dm (getvar "dragmode"))
(setvar "dragmode" 0)
(command "insert" blk ip insc "" "")
(initget 1 "y Y n N")
(setq yn (strcase (getkword "\nIs this location O.K.?
    <Y or N>: ")))
(while (= yn "N") ;while #1
  (prompt "\nMove the block to the desired location...")
  (command "move" "l" "" (cdr (assoc 10 (entget entlast))) pause)
  (initget 1 "y Y n N")
  (setq yn (strcase (getkword "\nIs this location O.K.? <Y or
      N>: "))));close while #1
(command "explode" "l")
(if (= tht? "Y");if #2
  (progn ;progn #2
  (prompt "\nPlace a window around the ENTIRE inserted
      drawing...")
  (setq p1 (getpoint "\nFirst corner: "))
  (setq p2 (getcorner p1 "\nSecond corner: "))
  (setq sst (ssget "w" p1 p2))
  (setq sstl (sslength sst)
     ctr 0)
```

Listing continues

Listing continued

```
      (repeat sstl ;repeat #1
      (setq e (ssname sst ctr))
      (if (= "TEXT" (cdr (assoc 0 (entget e)))) ;if #3
                (progn ;progn #3
                        (setq xts (assoc 40 (entget e)))
                        (setq nts (cons (car xts) nh))
                        (setq e2 (subst nts xts (entget e)))
                        (entmod e2)));close progn #3 & if #3
        (setq ctr (1+ ctr))))));close repeat #1, progn #2, if #2
);close progn #1
(progn (prompt "\nDrawing ")(princ blk)(prompt " not
found.")));close progn & if #1
(setq ftst nil)
(setvar "highlight" 1)
(setvar "dragmode" dm)
(princ));close defun

;You can eliminate the following routine if you have AutoCAD
;Release 10.
;You must execute the STRCAT function as shown below in the
;FINDFILE function above, however, as: (setq ftst (findfile
;(strcat blk ".dwg")

(defun findfile (z / fil)
  (setq fil (open (strcat z ".dwg") "r"))
  (setq ftst fil)
  (close fil))
```

Now comes the commented listing of INSDET.LSP (for additional comments that apply to the techniques we use, see Appendix C, "Sample Batch Files."

The statements:

```
(defun insdet (/ xsc psc insc tht nh blk tht?
        ip yn sst sstl ctr xts e nts e2 dm ftst p1 p2)
  (setvar "cmdecho" 0)
  (setq xsc (getvar "ltscale"))
```

set up the function for inserting details, turn off the AutoCAD variable CMDECHO so that the program runs cleanly, and retrieve the variable LTSCALE (which we use to confirm the drawing scale).

The conditional statement:

```
(cond ((= xsc 600.0)(setq psc "1 in.=50 ft."))
      ((= xsc 480.0)(setq psc "1 in.=40 ft."))
      ((= xsc 360.0)(setq psc "1 in.=30 ft."))
      ((= xsc 240.0)(setq psc "1 in.=20 ft."))
      ((= xsc 192.0)(setq psc "1/16 in.=1 ft."))
```

```
((= xsc 96.0)(setq psc "1/8 in.=1 ft."))
((= xsc 48.0)(setq psc "1/4 in.=1 ft."))
((= xsc 24.0)(setq psc "1/2 in.=1 ft."))
((= xsc 16.0)(setq psc "3/4 in.=1 ft."))
((= xsc 12.0)(setq psc "1 in.=1 ft."))
((= xsc 4.0)(setq psc "3 in.=1 ft."))
((= xsc 2.0)(setq psc "6 in.=1 ft."))
((= xsc 1.0)(setq psc "Full Scale"))
(xsc (setq psc (strcat (rtos (/ 12.0 xsc)) " in.=1 ft."))))
```

is used to translate the variable bound to LTSCALE into standard drawing scales. Notice that we do not use quotation marks (") or apostrophes (') in our strings. The last line says to the cond function, "If you can't match any of the previous settings for LTSCALE, just set the string to the value of LTSCALE divided by 12."

The functions:

```
(textscr)
(prompt "\nThe existing drawing scale is ")
(princ psc)
(prompt "...")
(prompt "\nEnter the scale factor to increase or decrease the")
(setq insc (getreal "\ninserted drawing by...: "))
```

flip the screen (on a single-screen monitor system) to the text screen, tell the user what the existing drawing scale is, and then ask for the scale factor with which the user wants to insert the drawing.

The following statements:

```
(initget 1 "Y y N n")
(setq tht? (strcase
  (getkword "\nDo you wish to change the text height? <Y or
    N>: ")))
(if (= tht? "Y")
  (progn
  (initget 6)
  (setq tht
    (getdist "\nEnter the desired actual plot height for the
      lettering <1/8>: "))
  (if (= tht nil)(setq tht 0.125))
  (setq nh (* tht xsc))))
```

use initget to establish what the acceptable user responses will be. Users are asked whether they want to change the text height and what plot height they want for the text. Notice that we have used a default value of 1/8 inch for the text height; we have told AutoLISP, "If the user doesn't answer, make the text height 1/8 inch (.0125)." To make sure that the text height is adjusted correctly for the drawing scale, the routine multiplies the requested height by the existing drawing scale and binds it to the variable *nh* (for *new height*).

In the next group of statements:

```
(prompt "\nUsing forward slashes </>, please carefully")
(prompt "\nenter the drawing you wish to insert, including the")
(setq blk (getkword "\ndirectory and subdirectory, as required: "))
(findfile blk)
(if (/= ftst nil)
(progn
(graphscr)
(setq ip (getpoint "\nSelect insertion point: "))
```

users are prompted for a file with a path name, formatted for AutoLISP's use, after which the function `findfile` (new to AutoCAD Release 10) is executed on the variable *blk*. (Because we wrote this routine for AutoCAD Release 9, be sure to read the comments in the program listing in order to verify the changes you need to make.) The remaining lines test whether the file was found, after which they flip to the graphics screen (as though you had pressed F1) and, by using `getpoint`, prompt for an insertion point.

This series of functions:

```
(setvar "highlight" 0)
(setq dm (getvar "dragmode"))
(setvar "dragmode" 0)
(command "insert" blk ip insc "" "")
(initget 1 "y Y n N")
(setq yn (strcase (getkword "\nIs this location O.K.? <Y or N>: ")))
(while (= yn "N")
  (prompt "\nMove the block to the desired location...")
  (command "move" "l" "" (cdr (assoc 10 (entget entlast))) pause)
  (initget 1 "y Y n N")
  (setq yn (strcase (getkword "\nIs this location O.K.? <Y or N>: "))))
(command "explode" "l")
```

turns off highlighting and dragmode and inserts the drawing. A while loop is used to allow users to move the drawing around before the routine explodes the drawing for edit. This is accomplished by moving the block using the insertion point (group code 10) of the last entity in the drawing, which is the block just inserted.

Then, by requesting a window around the entire drawing, the following functions gather a selection set:

```
(if (= tht? "Y")
  (progn
  (prompt "\nPlace a window around the ENTIRE inserted drawing...")
  (setq p1 (getpoint "\nFirst corner: "))
  (setq p2 (getcorner p1 "\nSecond corner: "))
  (setq sst (ssget "w" p1 p2))
```

Notice that the `if` statement checks first to make sure that the user wanted to change the text height.

The standard way of sorting through the selection set follows, except that this time we are looking for text:

```
(setq sstl (sslength sst)
      ctr 0)
(repeat sstl
(setq e (ssname sst ctr))
(if (= "TEXT" (cdr (assoc 0 (entget e))))
```

This is something new:

```
(progn
(setq xts (assoc 40 (entget e)))
(setq nts (cons (car xts) nh))
(setq e2 (subst nts xts (entget e)))
(entmod e2)))
(setq ctr (1+ ctr)))))
)
```

The variable *xts* is bound to the existing list, which is associated with the group code 40 of the text entity currently bound to *e*. (This is the existing text size.) The variable *nts* is bound to a construction of the group code 40 and the new value for the text height (*nh*). Then, using the new text height list and the function `subst`, a new entity list is created by substituting the new text size (*nts*) for the existing text size (*xts*) in the list retrieved by entget. The function entmod then replaces the old entity list in the database with the new one. Finally, the counter is incremented to the next value.

The following lines are the second half of the first `if` statement with which we started this whole mess:

```
(progn (prompt "\nDrawing ")(princ blk)(prompt " not found.")))
(setq ftst nil)
(setvar "highlight" 1)
(setvar "dragmode" dm)
(princ))
```

If the value for *ftst* were `nil`, AutoLISP would tell the user that it was unable to find the file.

As we mentioned earlier, the next function is for use with releases of AutoCAD prior to AutoCAD Release 10:

```
(defun findfile (z / fil)
  (setq fil (open (strcat z ".dwg") "r"))
  (setq ftst fil)
  (close fil))
```

This simple routine checks to see whether a file exists. Then, by replacing the value for *z* with whatever is entered following the function name findfile, the routine opens the file that is provided to it globally. In this case, we used (findfile blk). We had to add the file extension in this location so that we could use the variable *blk* for the INSERT command in the routine. You can use this routine for many different programs.

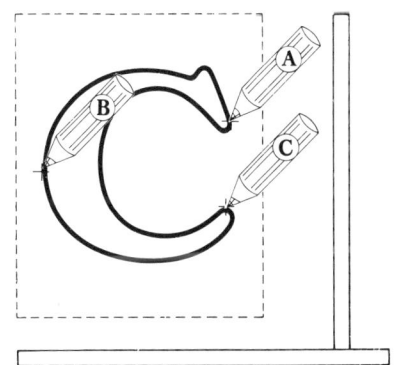

Sample Batch Files

This appendix contains some sample batch files you can use for reference as you develop your own batch-file management system. You should not copy these files exactly as you see them, because your system will require some variation. If you don't understand the contents of these files, review Chapters 3 ("The Basics"), 4 ("Basic System Management"), and 5 ("Project and Drawing Management").

Here is an AUTOEXEC.BAT file:

```
ECHO OFF
PATH C:\;C:\BATCH;C:\ACAD;E:;C:\AEC\A\L;C:\ACAD\UTILTY
SET LISPHEAP=40000
SET LISPSTACK=5000
PROMPT $P $G $S
SET ACADFREERAM=24
SET ACAD=C:\AEC\A\D
SET ACADXMEM=2560k,512k
SET ACADLIMEM=NONE
SET SHADEPAGEDIR=E:
CLS
\BATCH\M
```

The parts of this file that are pertinent to the batch file system are the PATH command and the last line. Notice that the directory BATCH is on the path in this file; this is required if you want to keep your batch files in a separate directory. Keeping batch files in a separate directory is a good idea;

doing so makes your other directories easier to read and simplifies batch-file maintenance. The BATCH directory must be on the path so that DOS can find the file you request when you type the file name at the DOS prompt; otherwise, the file you request must be in the directory you are currently using.

The contents of M.BAT follow:

```
ECHO OFF
CLS
PATH C:\;C:\BATCH;C:\ACAD;E:;C:\AEC\A\L;C:\ACAD\UTILTY
TYPE \BATCH\MENU
```

This file displays on-screen the image of the hard disk system menu. This image creates the visual directory to a series of numbered batch files that must be entered at the DOS prompt. Notice that even though the BATCH directory is on the DOS path, we provide the directory in the call for M.BAT. This makes the batch files run faster, since the order of DOS's file search is eliminated and DOS goes directly to the BATCH directory. M.BAT is used also to restore the path from other activities that require a change in the path.

The following batch file changes the path so that the batch files in the \ACAD\BATCH subdirectory, rather than those in the BATCH subdirectory, are used.

```
ECHO OFF
CLS
CD\ACAD
\ACAD\UTILITY\DK
\ACAD\UTILITY\DKEY \ACAD\UTILITY\ACAD.KEY
PATH C:\;C:\ACAD;C:\ACAD\BATCH\E:;C:\AEC\A\L;C:\ACAD\UTILTY
TYPE \ACAD\BATCH\MENU1
```

By changing the path in this way, the same numbers can be used in the \ACAD subdirectory. After changing the path, the batch file displays the AutoCAD directory menu, MENU1.

The following batch file loads AutoCAD and then redisplays the AutoCAD directory menu:

```
CLS
ACAD
TYPE \ACAD\BATCH\MENU1
```

Figure C.1 shows what MENU1 might look like. This menu manages projects in AutoCAD's domain of the hard disk.

Appendix C: Sample Batch Files

```
┌─────────────────────────────────────────────────────────────┐
│                    ┌──── AUTOCAD/AEC MENU ────┐             │
│       PROJECTS     │                          │  UTILITIES  │
│                                                             │
│   1 - ACAD            9                       17            │
│                                                             │
│   2 - STANDARDS      10                       18            │
│                                                             │
│   3 - PRELIMINARY    11                       19 - LISP     │
│                                                             │
│   4 - 88052          12                       20 - JOB DTA MGR │
│       Golden gate pt.                                       │
│   5 - 89001          13                       21 - CREATE NEW JOB │
│       1st Nat. Bank                                         │
│   6 - 89003          14                       22 - BACK-UP JOB FILES │
│       Sun City Rest                                         │
│   7 - 88025          15                       23 - FILE MAINTENANCE │
│       Conch Club                                            │
│   8 - EXIT TO MAIN MENU   16 - JOB NO. DIR    24 - LIST JOB DWGS │
│                                                             │
│   Type the number of the program (or function) you wish and press [ENTER] │
│                                                             │
│ C:\ACAD>                                                    │
└─────────────────────────────────────────────────────────────┘
```

Fig. C.1.

A sample AutoCAD batch-file menu.

These projects are activated by using a batch file like 4.BAT, which follows:

CLS
ECHO OFF
CD\ACAD\88002
\ACAD\ACAD
CD\ACAD
TYPE \ACAD\BATCH\MENU1

The 4.BAT batch file changes the current directory to the job number subdirectory (88002) and starts AutoCAD. When the editing session is over, the batch file sends DOS back to the ACAD directory and redisplays the AutoCAD menu. All of the batch files used for accessing projects are similar to this one.

The next batch file (8.BAT) returns the main directory to the screen:

CLS
ECHO OFF
CD\
\BATCH\M

Notice that this batch file resets the path to the original DOS path and executes the M.BAT file, which displays the original menu. M.BAT is used here (rather than TYPE \BATCH\MENU) to ensure that the screen is cleared from any batch file or program's previous activity. Using M.BAT in this way is more economical than typing in the TYPE command for every batch file on the disk. We also use the M.BAT file to restore the correct path for overall system requirements.

An Interactive Addition: Yes or No?

You can use this machine language program to allow your batch files to request a response from the user and then, based on that response, branch to different options. If you have DEBUG.EXE on your disk drive, type the following lines (*exactly* as you see them) to create GETKEY.COM. (You can ignore what your computer shows on this screen; this list indicates only what you should type.)

```
debug
a 100
mov ah,8
int 21
cmp al,0
jne 10c
mov ah,8
int 21
mov ah,4c
int 21
<ENTER>
u 100 10f
```

When you do this, the following lines should appear on your screen:

```
25AA:0100  B408        MOV    AH,08
25AA:0102  CD21        INT    21
25AA:0104  3C00        CMP    AL,00
25AA:0106  7504        JNZ    010C
25AA:0108  B408        MOV    AH,08
25AA:010A  CD21        INT    21
25AA:010C  B44C        MOV    AH,4C
25AA:010E  CD21        INT    21
-_
```

Although the first four characters on each line may differ on your computer, make sure that the rest of each line matches exactly. If the match is not exact, start the procedure again.

If what appears on your screen agrees with the preceding lines, use the following keystrokes to save the program you just entered in the file called GETKEY.COM and return to the DOS prompt.

```
r cx
10
n getkey.com
w
q
```

Prior to entering the last character (*q*), you should have seen a message indicating Writing 0010 bytes.

The GETKEY.COM program waits for a key to be pressed and then returns (to your batch file) the ASCII value of that key. This value is returned as an errorlevel that can be checked in your batch file with the ERRORLEVEL command. When you use the IF command in a batch file, you can test this errorlevel to control what you want the batch file to do.

The IF command tests for an errorlevel equal to or greater than the errorlevel supplied to the command in the batch file. This means that you should always test for a key that has a lower errorlevel than the one for which you are currently testing. Here is an example of how to test for a *Y* or *N* response:

```
ECHO OFF
CLS
ECHO Do you want to format the disk in A: ?
:START
GETKEY
IF ERRORLEVEL 90 GOTO MSG
IF ERROLEVEL 89 GOTO Y
IF ERROLEVEL 79 GOTO MSG
IF ERRORLEVEL 78 GOTO END
:MSG
ECHO 'Y' or 'N', please...
GOTO START
:Y
FORMAT A:
:END
```

The errorlevel tests in this program test, in descending order, the key pressed. If any key pressed has an ASCII value equal to or greater than 90, the first test transfers control to the line labeled MSG. This, in turn, echoes an error message and transfers control back to the part of the batch file that gets a keypress.

If the errorlevel is 89 (which corresponds to *Y*), the batch file goes to the line labeled Y. If the errorlevel is greater than 78 but less than 89, control is again transferred to the line labeled MSG. If the errorlevel is 78 (which corresponds to *N*), control is transferred to the line labeled END and the batch file ends. If the errorlevel is less than any of the preceding tests, control falls through to the MSG portion of the file.

There are numerous uses for this type of application, and you can test for any key or group of keys, provided that you test from the largest number to the smallest. The DOS reference books we recommend throughout this book contain ASCII code tables, which you definitely will find useful when working with GETKEY.

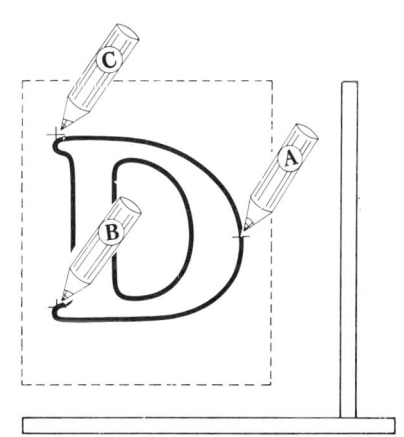

A Routine for Renaming the Layers of Entities

If you are going to create your own layering system, it's unlikely that the one you are using will match what you end up with. The two programs in this appendix allow you to convert an existing layer scheme to a new one. Because executing the conversion routine on a large drawing takes some time, you should make the conversions during off-hours.

Follow the steps listed here to create a new drawing to match your new menu system. (You should not use them more than once on any drawing because they won't do any good the second time around.) Some of the old layers will be retained if they pertain to entities nested in blocks. The layering scheme described in Chapter 7 ("Advanced Management Techniques") will still work after a conversion is done.

1. Create a prototype drawing that contains all the layers you want to use. If you are using a task menu system, you may have several prototype drawings, each with different layers. That's okay. Do not use an existing prototype drawing. You will have to set up all the linetypes, text fonts, and system variables from scratch. To save time, you can create a standard prototype that is common to each of your task prototypes and then use this standard prototype to start creating the task prototype drawings.

441

2. Execute LYRTBL.LSP on any existing drawings. If you have not created any custom layers from your old prototype, you will have to run it on your old prototype drawing only. LYRTBL.LSP will prompt you to substitute a new layer name for each existing layer name; it will ask also for a color for the new layers. Before you proceed with this routine, develop a list similar to that shown in figure 7.3 or 7.4 (refer to Chapter 7, "Advanced Management Techniques"). LYRTBL.LSP creates a data file called LYRTBL.DTA. You will need a copy of this data file in any drawing subdirectory in which you intend to convert drawings.

3. After you have created LYRTBL.DTA, you must use the CNVRT.LSP routine. CNVRT.LSP changes all the existing entities in your drawing to the new layer name that corresponds to your old layer name. The routine does not change the color of any entities to which colors were assigned uniquely.

If you or someone you know can program with dBASE III Plus, you will find that using dBASE and a .DFX file makes this process much faster. These routines are provided for your convenience, but if you are going to do a serious amount of conversion, we recommend that you establish what your layer standards are going to be and use the AutoCAD commands DXFOUT and DXFIN to create the new drawings.

Creating a New Set of Layer Names (LYRTBL.LSP)

The listing of the LYRTBL.LSP routine follows:

```
(defun lyrtbl (/ lnm fil nlnm yn lclr lylr lltyp)
  (textscr)
  (prompt "\nThis routine will ask you for a new name for every")
  (prompt "\nlayer in your drawing and store it in the file ")
  (prompt "\nLYRTBL.DTA for use by the routine CNVLYR.LSP.")
  (prompt "\n\n")
  (prompt "\nYou should have a chart of the names that you wish")
  (prompt "\nto convert the existing layers to, along with their")
  (prompt "\ncolor. You will be asked both a new layer name and")
  (prompt "\na new color, which must be input in numeric form.")
  (prompt "\nThe linetypes will remain the same.")
  (prompt "\n\n")
  (initget 1 "y Y n N")
  (setq yn (strcase (getkword "\nDo you wish to proceed? <Y or N>: ")))
  (if (= yn "Y")
```

Appendix D: A Routine for Renaming Layers of Entities

```
    (progn
    (setq lnm (assoc 2 (tblnext "layer" t)))
    (setq lyrl (tblnext "layer"))
    (setq lnm (assoc 2 lyrl))
    (setq lltyp (assoc 6 lyrl))
    (setq lclr (assoc 62 lyrl))
    (setq fil (open "lyrtbl.dta" "w"))
    (while lyrl
     (prompt "\nWhat do you wish to rename the layer ")
     (princ (cdr lnm))
     (setq nlnm (cons 8 (getstring " to?: ")))
     (prompt "\nWhat color do you want this layer to be? <")
     (princ (itoa (abs (cdr lclr))))
     (initget 6)
     (setq uclr (getint ">: "))
     (if (/= uclr nil)
        (setq lclr (cons 62 uclr)))
     (prompt "\nThe new layer name is ")
     (princ (cdr nlnm))
     (prompt " and the new color is ")
     (princ (itoa (abs (cdr lclr))))
     (initget 1 "y Y n N")
     (setq yn (strcase (getkword ".\n Is this O.K.? <Y or N>: ")))
     (while (= yn "N")
      (setq nlnm (cons 8 (getstring "The new layer name is?: ")))
      (setq lclr (cons 62 (getint "The new color is?: ")))
      (prompt "\nThe new layer name is ")
      (princ (cdr nlnm))
      (prompt "\n and the new color is ")
      (princ (cdr lclr))
      (initget 1 "y Y n N")
      (setq yn (strcase (getkword ".\nIs this O.K.? <Y or N>: "))))
     (prin1 (list lnm nlnm lltyp lclr) fil)
     (princ (chr 10) fil)
     (setq lyrl (tblnext "layer"))
     (setq lnm (assoc 2 lyrl))
     (setq lltyp (assoc 6 lyrl))
     (setq lclr (assoc 62 lyrl))
    )
    (prin1 (list (cons 2 "END") (cons 6 "END") (cons 8 "END")
              (cons 62 "END")) fil)
    (setq fil (close fil)) (graphscr)))
(princ))
```

Now let's look at each part of the routine in some detail. The following lines define the layer table function and flip the screen to the text screen so that the message can be displayed.

```
(defun lyrtbl (/ lnm fil nlnm yn lclr lylr lltyp)
  (textscr)
  (prompt "\nThis routine will ask you for a new name for every")
  (prompt "\nlayer in your drawing and store it in the file ")
```

Code continues

Code continued
```
(prompt "\nLYRTBL.DTA for use by the routine CNVLYR.LSP.")
(prompt "\n\n")
(prompt "\nYou should have a chart of the names that you wish")
(prompt "\nto convert the existing layers to, along with their")
(prompt "\ncolor. You will be asked both a new layer name and")
(prompt "\na new color, which must be input in numeric form.")
(prompt "\nThe linetypes will remain the same.")
(prompt "\n\n")
(initget 1 "y Y n N")
(setq yn (strcase (getkword "\nDo you wish to proceed?
    <Y or N>: ")))
(if (= yn "Y")
```

Using `initget` to force an answer (bit code 1) and requiring that answer to be either y Y n N, we use `getkword` to retrieve the user's response; to make sure that it is an uppercase letter, we use `strcase`. The `if` function tests for a *Y* response and then either cancels the program or proceeds with the execution.

Following the `if` statement, you must use `progn` if there is more than one expression so that the `if` statement will consider all of the functions that follow the `progn` to be one expression:

```
(progn
 (setq lnm (assoc 2 (tblnext "layer" t)))
   (setq lyrl (tblnext "layer"))
```

If you don't use the `progn` in this case, AutoLISP gets very confused. If all of the expressions that follow the true side of the `if` statement fit between a pair of parentheses, you do not have to use `progn`.

The next statement uses `tblnext` to search the drawing tables for the first layer in the layer section by using the `t` option and a `"layer"` string. The `t` option sets the table pointer to the top of the table. The first layer is always layer zero (0) in the table. Because we cannot change its use or its name, we use `tblnext "layer"` to proceed immediately to the next table entry; we bind that list to the variable *lyrl* so that we have a layer list that contains, among other things, the layer name and the layer color.

Note: Because we didn't need to use the layer 0, we could have entered the first statement as (`tblnext "layer" t`) without using `assoc`. We left it this way so that it would help us debug the program (and you should leave it this way, too—at least until you have the program working).

The next three lines extract the layer name (group code 2 of the table list), binding it to the variable *lnm*; the linetype (group code 6), binding it to the variable *lltyp*; and the layer color (group code 62 of the table list), binding it to the variable *lclr*.

```
(setq lnm (assoc 2 lyrl))
(setq lltyp (assoc 6 lyrl))
(setq lclr (assoc 62 lyrl))
```

Notice that we use assoc all by itself, without cdr, because we want to obtain the entire dotted pair, such as (2 . "LIGHT") or (62 . 1) from the list.

Next, to open the file LYRTBL.DTA for writing and bind the file pointer name to the variable *fil*, we use the following line:

```
(setq fil (open "lyrtbl.dta" "w"))
```

The only way to access a file in AutoLISP is to bind a variable to the file with the open statement. Other options for the open statement are discussed in Chapter 14, "AutoLISP's Bells and Whistles."

In the next series of statements:

```
(while lyrl
      (prompt "\nWhat do you wish to rename the layer ")
      (princ (cdr lnm))
      (setq nlnm (cons 8 (getstring " to?: "))))
```

we use the while statement to say, "As long as there is the variable *lyrl* and it isn't *nil*, do this." That's why we used the variable *lyrl* earlier. *Lyrl* has a value, even though we won't use it until after the while statement. Next, the user is asked for a new name for the layer that is bound to the variable *lnm*. Since *lnm* is a dotted pair, we had to extract the second part of the pair by using cdr, which obtains the string that is the layer name. Then, to create a dotted pair that will be the new layer name, we use cons to create the dotted pair of group code 8 and the string supplied by the user. This is bound to the variable *nlnm*, which is the new layer name.

The following lines involve some string and integer gymnastics:

```
(prompt "\nWhat color do you want this layer to be? <")
(princ (itoa (abs (cdr lclr)))))
(initget 6)
(setq uclr (getint ">: "))
```

In order to display the existing layer color (which is bound to *lclr*) as a default choice, we have to do two things. First, if the layer is frozen, the color could be a negative number. To avoid confusing the user, we want to convert (to a positive number) the number that is the second part of a dotted pair. To do so, we use the function abs.

Having converted the layer color to its absolute value, we then have to convert it back to a string so that we can display it with the rest of the prompt string. (This is accomplished by the function `itoa`.) Next, we use `initget` to ensure that we obtain a positive number and a nonzero value (there is no color 0). This is done by adding together the `initget` bit flag options of 2 and 4. Then, using `getint`, we bind the user-selected color (as an integer) to the variable *uclr*. Notice that the default color, as the original color, is displayed with the prompt. If the user presses Enter, the program response will be an empty string.

The next `if` statement says that if the variable *uclr* is not bound to an empty string, then set the layer color (*lclr*) to a dotted pair of the group code 62 and the user-selected color.

```
(if (/= uclr nil)
   (setq lclr (cons 62 uclr)))
```

Since there are no options to the "false" side of this `if` statement, the value of *lclr* remains unchanged and the value of *uclr* (an empty string) is ignored.

The next prompts tell the user what he or she has selected as the values of *nlnm*, the new layer name, and *lclr*, the new layer color:

```
(prompt "\nThe new layer name is ")
(princ (cdr nlnm))
(prompt " and the new color is ")
(princ (itoa (abs (cdr lclr))))
```

after which, by using `initget` and `strcase` in the usual manner, the program asks whether these values are correct:

```
(initget 1 "y Y n N")
(setq yn (strcase (getword ".\n Is this O.K.? <Y or N>: ")))
```

Now comes a fairly large chunk of code:

```
(while (= yn "N")
(setq nlnm (cons 8 (getstring "The new layer name is?: ")))
(setq lclr (cons 62 (getint "The new color is?: ")))
(prompt "\nThe new layer name is ")
(princ (cdr nlnm))
(prompt "\n and the new color is ")
(princ (cdr lclr))
(initget 1 "y Y n N")
(setq yn (strcase (getword ".\nIs this O.K.? <Y or N>:     "))))
```

that says, "If the answer was *N* or *n*, ask the user the same questions and make sure that the answer is accurate. As long as the user answers *N* or *n*, AutoLISP will keep showing what was entered and checking to see whether that answer is okay. Initget will let users out of the loop only if they answer *Y* or *y*; pressing any other key (except *n*) creates an AutoLISP prompt stating that it was an improper response.

The next line writes to the data file a list of the existing layer name (*lnm*), the new layer name (*nlnm*), the linetype (*lltyp*), and the layer color (*lclr*).

```
(prin1 (list lnm nlnm lltyp lclr) fil)
(princ (chr 10) fil)
```

As you can see, we use the function prin1. The line placed in the file will look something like this:

```
((2 . "LIGHT") (8 . "0010") (6 . "CONTINUOUS") (62 . 1))
```

The princ prints a return following the line just written to the file.

The next section of code resets the values of *lnm*, *lltyp*, and *lclr* to the next existing layer in the drawing, and then returns to the top of the while loop.

```
(setq lyr1 (tblnext "layer"))
(setq lnm (assoc 2 lyr1))
(setq lltyp (assoc 6 lyr1))
(setq lclr (assoc 62 lyr1))
)
```

This next line writes a final line in the file to set all of the group code dotted pairs equal to the string *"END"*:

```
(prin1 (list (cons 2 "END") (cons 6 "END") (cons 8 "END")
       (cons 62 "END")) fil)
```

This allows us to anticipate the end of the file when we read it for the next routine, which will change the drawing entities to the new layers.

Finally, these functions:

```
    (setq fil (close fil)) (graphscr)))
(princ))
```

close the data file opened at the start of the routine, flip the screen back to the graphics screen, and use princ to exit the program quietly.

Routine for Converting Entities to New Layers (CNVRT.LSP)

The following routine converts entities to new layers:

```
(defun addlyr (/ rfil lnm lclr lnl lltyp)
   (prompt "\nReading layers from LYRTBL.DTA...")
   (setq rfil (open "lyrtbl.dta" "r"))
   (if rfil
      (progn
      (prompt "\nAdding layers to drawing...")
      (while (setq lnl (read-line rfil))
       (setq lnl (read lnl))
       (setq lnm (cdr (assoc 8 lnl)))
       (setq lclr (cdr (assoc 62 lnl)))
       (setq lltyp (cdr (assoc 6 lnl)))
         (if lnm
           (command "layer" "n" lnm "ltype" lltyp lnm "c" lclr lnm ""))
       ))
      (progn
         (prompt "\nThe file LYRTBL.DTA was not found...")
         (prompt "\nPlease run the LYRTBL routine first.")))
(setq rfil (close rfil))(prompt "\nLayer addition complete.")
(princ))

(defun cnvent (/ rfil ln nlyr olyr lins linl e e2)
   (setq rfil (open "lyrtbl.dta" "r"))
 (while  (setq ln (read-line rfil))
    (setq ln (read ln))
    (if ln
     (progn
     (setq nlyr (assoc 8 ln))
     (setq olyr (assoc 2 ln))
     (if (not (equal (cdr olyr) "Ø"))
      (progn
      (setq lins (ssget "x" (list (cons 8 (cdr olyr)))))
      (if lins
       (progn
       (setq linl (sslength lins)
          ctr Ø)
       (repeat linl
       (setq e (ssname lins ctr))
       (setq e2 (subst nlyr (cons 8 (cdr olyr)) (entget e)))
       (entmod e2)
       (setq ctr (1+ ctr)))))))))
(setq ctr Ø))
(setq rfil (close rfil))
(prompt "\nDrawing conversion complete.")
(princ))
```

```
(defun cnvrt ()
  (setvar "cmdecho" Ø)
  (command "layer" "off" "*" "y" "")
  (addlyr)
  (prompt "\nConverting drawing entities to new layers...")
  (cnvent)
  (command "layer" "on" "*" "")
  (princ))
```

The CNVRT.LSP routine is made up of three subroutines and a main routine.

This subroutine adds the new layers to the drawing:

```
(defun addlyr (/ rfil lnm lclr lnl lltyp)
  (prompt "\nReading layers from LYRTBL.DTA...")
  (setq rfil (open "lyrtbl.dta" "r"))
```

It tells the user that it is reading the layers, and it opens the data file for reading as a reference file.

Before proceeding with the program, this `if` test:

```
(if rfil
  (progn
  (prompt "\nAdding layers to drawing...")
```

makes sure that AutoLISP was able to find the data file.

Then the `setq`s read the first line of the file and set up the required string of data.

```
      (setq lnm (cdr (assoc 8 lnl)))
      (setq lclr (cdr (assoc 62 lnl)))
      (setq lltyp (cdr (assoc 6 lnl)))
        (if lnm
          (command "layer" "n" lnm "ltype" lltyp lnm "c" lclr lnm ""))
      ))
```

The `if` statement says, "If the variable *lnm* was found, execute the Auto-CAD LAYER command, making a new layer (*"n"*) named whatever is bound to *lnm*, setting a color (*"c"*) and linetype (*"ltype"*) of whatever is bound to *lclr* and *lltyp* to the layer bound to *lnm*. This returns to the beginning of the while loop until the *"END"* dotted pairs are found.

```
    (progn
      (prompt "\nThe file LYRTBL.DTA was not found...")
      (prompt "\nPlease run the LYRTBL routine first.")))
(setq rfil (close rfil))(prompt "\nLayer addition complete.")
(princ))
```

This subroutine concludes with the false side of the `if` command; if the test was false, a message that the data file was not found is displayed. The file is closed and users are told that the layers have been added to the drawing.

The following lines are similar to the beginning of the `addlyr` function:

```
(defun cnvent (/ rfil ln nlyr olyr lins linl e e2)
   (setq rfil (open "lyrtbl.dta" "r"))
(while  (setq ln (read-line rfil))
   (setq ln (read ln))
```

The next code segment:

```
(if ln
 (progn
 (setq nlyr (assoc 8 ln))
 (setq olyr (assoc 2 ln))
```

sets the new layer to the dotted pair that is associated by group code 8 in the data file line bound to *ln*. It does the same thing for the old layer (*olyr*), which is designated by group code 2.

This `if` function:

```
(if (not (equal (cdr olyr) "Ø"))
 (progn
```

checks that the old layer name is not equal to 0 or to the new layer name. And there's our old friend progn again.

Then the line:

```
(setq lins (ssget "x" (list (cons 8 (cdr olyr)))))
```

sets the entities in the drawing that are on the layer named by the variable *olyr* to a selection set bound to the variable *lins*.

Our standard selection set repeat loop is

```
(if lins
 (progn
 (setq linl (sslength lins)
       ctr Ø)
 (repeat linl
 (setq e (ssname lins ctr))
```

which we discussed in Appendix B.

These two lines set the variable *e2* to a list in which all the components are the same as the list for the entity bound to the symbol *e*, except that by using `subst` we replace the dotted pair bound to the old layer name (group code 8 in the entity list) with the *nlyr* variable dotted pair.

```
(setq e2 (subst nlyr (cons 8 (cdr olyr)) (entget e)))
(entmod e2)
```

Notice that, because the old layer name was paired with group code 2 in the tables section, we had to construct a new dotted pair for the old layer name and the group code 8.

The repeat loop resets the counter so that the next entity in the selection set can be found:

```
        (setq ctr (1+ ctr)))))))))
(setq ctr 0))
(setq rfil (close rfil))
(prompt "\nDrawing conversion complete.")
(princ))
```

We had to set the counter to 0 outside of the repeat loop, in case we found entities on the layer 0 that avoided the loop.

The next routine is the one that drives the program. It sets `cmdecho` off and turns off all the layers, including the current one:

```
(defun cnvrt ()
  (setvar "cmdecho" 0)
  (command "layer" "off" "*" "y" "")
  (addlyr)
  (prompt "\nConverting drawing entities to new layers...")
  (cnvent)
  (command "layer" "on" "*" "")
  (princ))
```

Because a redraw is executed whenever a new layer is added, turning off the layers allows the routine to work faster. Finally, the layers are turned back on. This is necessary because some objects within nested blocks remain on the old layers. Otherwise, as each object is placed on the new layer, it becomes visible.

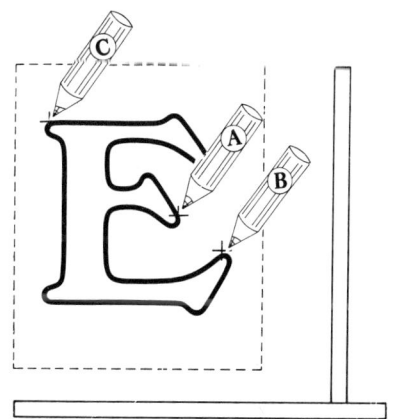

DPLOT.LSP

In this appendix we take a more detailed look at DPLOT.LSP (first presented in Chapter 7, "Advanced Management Techniques"). First, let's look again at a listing of the program:

```
(defun c:dplot (/ ss1 ent yn e anm llc urc psc ps
                   p1 p2 p3 p4 p5 p6 p7 po pfl )
(setvar "cmdecho" 0)
(setq ss1 (ssget "X" (list (cons 0 "INSERT")(cons 2 "plotblk"))))
(if (null ss1)
    (progn
    (prompt "\nYou Must Insert Block 'Plotblk' Before Proceeding...")
    (princ))
    (setq ent (ssname ss1 0))
)
(if (/= ss1 nil)
(progn
(initget 1 "y Y n N")
(setq yn (getkword "Do You Wish To Update the Plot Parameters?
    <Y or N>:"))))
(setq yn (strcase yn)))
(if (= yn "Y")
(progn
(setq e (ssname ss1 0))
(command "ddatte" e)))
(setq yn nil)
(while ent
(setq ent (entnext ent))
(if (/= ent nil)
(progn
```

Listing continues

Listing continued

```
(setq anm (cdr (assoc 2 (entget ent))))
(if (= anm "LLC")(setq llc (cdr (assoc 1 (entget ent)))))
(if (= anm "URC")(setq urc (cdr (assoc 1 (entget ent)))))
(if (= anm "PSIZE")(setq ps (cdr (assoc 1 (entget ent)))))
(if (= anm "PSCALE")(setq psc (cdr (assoc 1 (entget ent)))))
(if (= anm "P#1")(setq p1 (cdr (assoc 1 (entget ent)))))
(if (= anm "P#2")(setq p2 (cdr (assoc 1 (entget ent)))))
(if (= anm "P#3")(setq p3 (cdr (assoc 1 (entget ent)))))
(if (= anm "P#4")(setq p4 (cdr (assoc 1 (entget ent)))))
(if (= anm "P#5")(setq p5 (cdr (assoc 1 (entget ent)))))
(if (= anm "P#6")(setq p6 (cdr (assoc 1 (entget ent)))))
(if (= anm "P#7")(setq p7 (cdr (assoc 1 (entget ent)))))
(if (= anm "PORIG")(setq po (cdr (assoc 1 (entget ent))))))))
(if (not (null ss1))
(progn
(setq pfl (open "dplot.scr" "w"))
  (write-line "plot" pfl)
(if (/= llc "")
(progn (write-line "w" pfl)
  (write-line llc pfl)
  (write-line urc))
  (write-line "l" pfl))
  (write-line "y" pfl)
  (write-line "y" pfl)
  (write-line p1 pfl)
  (write-line "c2" pfl)
  (write-line p2 pfl)
  (write-line "c3" pfl)
  (write-line p3 pfl)
  (write-line "c4" pfl)
  (write-line p4 pfl)
  (write-line "c5" pfl)
  (write-line p5 pfl)
  (write-line "c6" pfl)
  (write-line p6 pfl)
  (write-line "c7" pfl)
  (write-line p7 pfl)
  (write-line "x" pfl)
  (write-line "n" pfl)
  (write-line "i" pfl)
  (write-line po pfl)
  (write-line ps pfl)
  (write-line "n" pfl)
  (write-line "0.010" pfl)
  (write-line "n" pfl)
  (write-line "n" pfl)
  (write-line psc pfl)
(close pfl)
(command "script" "dplot")))
(princ))
```

Appendix E: DPLOT.LSP

What follows is a detailed explanation of each portion of this routine. The first function:

```
(defun c:dplot (/ ss1 ent yn e anm llc urc psc ps
                    p1 p2 p3 p4 p5 p6 p7 po pfl )
(setvar "cmdecho" 0)
(setq ss1 (ssget "X" (list (cons 0 "INSERT")(cons 2 "plotblk"))))
```

can be called from the AutoCAD command prompt because we preceded the function name with `c:`. The selection set found here uses two filters to find what it is looking for. First, it looks for a block (`"INSERT"`) and then it looks for for a block named `"plotblk"`. The proper use of this routine inserts only one `plotblk` in the drawing, but the routine works just as well with more than one `plotblk`.

This `if` test checks to make sure the selection set is not null:

```
(if (null ss1)
    (progn
    (prompt "\nYou Must Insert Block 'Plotblk' Before Proceeding...")
    (princ))
    (setq ent (ssname ss1 0))
)
```

If it is null, a message is displayed advising the user to insert the block used by this routine to store information for the plot. If the selection set is not null, the first entity in the selection set is bound to the variable *ent*. This will be the block `plotblk`.

After checking that the selection set was not nil, the standard Yes/No query is used again:

```
(if (/= ss1 nil)
(progn
(initget 1 "y Y n N")
(setq yn (getkword "Do You Wish To Update the Plot Parameters?
     <Y or N>:"))))
(setq yn (strcase yn)))
(if (= yn "Y")
(progn
```

The variable *e* is assigned to the block, and the AutoCAD command DDATE is used to view the existing attributes of the block `plotblk`:

```
(setq e (ssname ss1 0))
(command "ddatte" e)))
```

The use of DDATE restricts this routine to AutoCAD Release 9 and later. To make this routine work for earlier releases of AutoCAD, you must use entnext to retrieve each of the attributes; users must enter the new values manually or leave them the same. Portions of LYRTBL.LSP (see Appendix D) will help you with this type of procedure.

The following functions retrieve the next entity in the selection set, following the block name:

```
(setq yn nil)
(while ent
(setq ent (entnext ent))
(if (/= ent nil)
(progn
```

in this case, the attributes assigned to `plotblk`. If `plotblk` had no attributes, this use of the function `entnext` would be inappropriate. The `if` statement, however, makes sure that the next entity was found. The `while` loop continues as long as attributes are found. If your drawing contains multiple insertions of `plotblk`, the plot variables may get confused when the next entity is another `plotblk`. If you expect a problem with this, test for a 0 group code of a *sequend*, or sequence end; it will mark the end of the attributes section.

The next chunk of code sets the value of *anm* to the name of the entity that was found, and sets a series of tests for the value of *anm*:

```
(setq anm (cdr (assoc 2 (entget ent))))
(if (= anm "LLC")(setq llc (cdr (assoc 1 (entget ent)))))
(if (= anm "URC")(setq urc (cdr (assoc 1 (entget ent)))))
(if (= anm "PSIZE")(setq ps (cdr (assoc 1 (entget ent)))))
(if (= anm "PSCALE")(setq psc (cdr (assoc 1 (entget ent)))))
(if (= anm "P#1")(setq p1 (cdr (assoc 1 (entget ent)))))
(if (= anm "P#2")(setq p2 (cdr (assoc 1 (entget ent)))))
(if (= anm "P#3")(setq p3 (cdr (assoc 1 (entget ent)))))
(if (= anm "P#4")(setq p4 (cdr (assoc 1 (entget ent)))))
(if (= anm "P#5")(setq p5 (cdr (assoc 1 (entget ent)))))
(if (= anm "P#6")(setq p6 (cdr (assoc 1 (entget ent)))))
(if (= anm "P#7")(setq p7 (cdr (assoc 1 (entget ent)))))
(if (= anm "PORIG")(setq po (cdr (assoc 1 (entget ent)))))))))
```

If the value is found that matches the string as shown, the appropriate variable is set to the contents of the attribute (group code 1). Alternatively, a `cond` function could be used here.

This set of functions writes a file that will become a script file for plotting the drawing:

```
(if (not (null ss1))
(progn
(setq pfl (open "dplot.scr" "w"))
  (write-line "plot" pfl)
```

```
(if (/= llc "")
(progn (write-line "w" pfl)
  (write-line llc pfl)
  (write-line urc))
  (write-line "l" pfl))
  (write-line "y" pfl)
  (write-line "y" pfl)
  (write-line p1 pfl)
  (write-line "c2" pfl)
  (write-line p2 pfl)
  (write-line "c3" pfl)
  (write-line p3 pfl)
  (write-line "c4" pfl)
  (write-line p4 pfl)
  (write-line "c5" pfl)
  (write-line p5 pfl)
  (write-line "c6" pfl)
  (write-line p6 pfl)
  (write-line "c7" pfl)
  (write-line p7 pfl)
  (write-line "x" pfl)
  (write-line "n" pfl)
  (write-line "i" pfl)
  (write-line po pfl)
  (write-line ps pfl)
  (write-line "n" pfl)
  (write-line "0.010" pfl)
  (write-line "n" pfl)
  (write-line "n" pfl)
  (write-line psc pfl)
(close pfl)
```

In order to understand this sequence, you should review the plot procedure in the *AutoCAD Reference Manual*. You will be able to see that strings are written to various portions of the file to answer plot-time questions and that variables are written that contain the value of the attributes from `plotblk`. This is how the plot information is stored in your drawing.

Next, this command runs a script file from the file created by AutoLISP:

```
(command "script" "dplot")))
(princ))
```

The script file does the plotting.

This routine (which is for AutoCAD Release 9 and later releases) must be accompanied by a block (called *plotblk*) in your drawing. This block must contain the following attributes, using the AutoCAD ATTDEF command. Make all of the attributes invisible, with your preferred defaults as preset values. Do this by typing the following at the AutoCAD command prompt:

Prompt: Command:
Response: Type **ATTDEF** and press Enter.

Prompt: Attribute modes -- Invisible:N Constant:N Verify:N Preset:N
Response: Press Enter.

Prompt: Enter (ICVP) to change, RETURN when done:
Response: Type **I** and press Enter.

Prompt: Enter (ICVP) to change, RETURN when done:
Response: Type **P** and press Enter.

Prompt: Attribute modes -- Invisible:Y Constant:N Verify:N Preset:Y
Response: Press Enter.

Prompt: Attribute tag:
Response: Type **LLC** and press Enter.

Prompt: Attribute Prompt:
Response: Type **Lower Left Plot Corner (Optional):**

Prompt: Default Attribute Value:
Response: Press Enter.

Prompt: Start point or Align/Center/Fit/Middle/Right/Style:
Response: Pick a point on your screen.

Prompt: Command:
Response: Press Enter.

Prompt: Attribute modes -- Invisible:Y Constant:N Verify:N Preset:Y
Response: Press Enter.

Prompt: Attribute tag:
Response: Type **URC** and press Enter.

Prompt: Attribute Prompt:
Response: Type **Upper Right Plot Corner (Optional):**

Prompt:	`Default Attribute Value:`
Response:	Press Enter.
Prompt:	`Start point or Align/Center/Fit/Middle/Right/` `Style:`
Response:	Press Enter.
Prompt:	`Command:`
Response:	Press Enter.
Prompt:	`Attribute modes -- Invisible:Y Constant:N` `Verify:N Preset:Y`
Response:	Press Enter.
Prompt:	`Attribute tag:`
Response:	Type **P#1** and press Enter.
Prompt:	`Attribute Prompt:`
Response:	Type **Pen For Color 1:**
Prompt:	`Default Attribute Value:`
Response:	Type **1** and press Enter.
Prompt:	`Start point or Align/Center/Fit/Middle/Right/` `Style:`
Response:	Press Enter.
Prompt:	`Command:`
Response:	Press Enter.
Prompt:	`Attribute modes -- Invisible:Y Constant:N` `Verify:N Preset:Y`
Response:	Press Enter.
Prompt:	`Attribute tag:`
Response:	Type **P#2** and press Enter.
Prompt:	`Attribute Prompt:`
Response:	Type **Pen For Color 2:**
Prompt:	`Default Attribute Value:`
Response:	Type **2** and press Enter.
Prompt:	`Start point or Align/Center/Fit/Middle/Right/` `Style:`
Response:	Press Enter.
Prompt:	`Command:`
Response:	Press Enter.

Routine continues

Routine *continued*

Prompt: `Attribute modes -- Invisible:Y Constant:N Verify:N Preset:Y`
Response: Press Enter.

Prompt: `Attribute tag:`
Response: Type **P#3** and press Enter.

Prompt: `Attribute Prompt:`
Response: Type **Pen For Color 3:**

Prompt: `Default Attribute Value:`
Response: Type **3** and press Enter.

Prompt: `Start point or Align/Center/Fit/Middle/Right/Style:`
Response: Press Enter.

Prompt: `Command:`
Response: Press Enter.

Prompt: `Attribute modes -- Invisible:Y Constant:N Verify:N Preset:Y`
Response: Press Enter.

Prompt: `Attribute tag:`
Response: Type **P#4** and press Enter.

Prompt: `Attribute Prompt:`
Response: Type **Pen For Color 4:**

Prompt: `Default Attribute Value:`
Response: Type **4** and press Enter.

Prompt: `Start point or Align/Center/Fit/Middle/Right/Style:`
Response: Press Enter.

Prompt: `Command:`
Response: Press Enter.

Prompt: `Attribute modes -- Invisible:Y Constant:N Verify:N Preset:Y`
Response: Press Enter.

Prompt: `Attribute tag:`
Response: Type **P#5** and press Enter.

Prompt: `Attribute Prompt:`
Response: Type **Pen For Color 5:**

Prompt:	`Default Attribute Value:`
Response:	Type **5** and press Enter.
Prompt:	`Start point or Align/Center/Fit/Middle/Right/` `Style:`
Response:	Press Enter.
Prompt:	`Command:`
Response:	Press Enter.
Prompt:	`Attribute modes -- Invisible:Y Constant:N` `Verify:N Preset:Y`
Response:	Press Enter.
Prompt:	`Attribute tag:`
Response:	Type **P#6** and press Enter.
Prompt:	`Attribute Prompt:`
Response:	Type **Pen For Color 6:**
Prompt:	`Default Attribute Value:`
Response:	Type **6** and press Enter.
Prompt:	`Start point or Align/Center/Fit/Middle/Right/` `Style:`
Response:	Press Enter.
Prompt:	`Command:`
Response:	Press Enter.
Prompt:	`Attribute modes -- Invisible:Y Constant:N` `Verify:N Preset:Y`
Response:	Press Enter.
Prompt:	`Attribute tag:`
Response:	Type **P#7** and press Enter.
Prompt:	`Attribute Prompt:`
Response:	Type **Pen For Color 7:**
Prompt:	`Default Attribute Value:`
Response:	Type **7** and press Enter.
Prompt:	`Start point or Align/Center/Fit/Middle/Right/` `Style:`
Response:	Press Enter.
Prompt:	`Command:`
Response:	Press Enter.

Routine continues

Routine *continued*

Prompt: `Attribute modes -- Invisible:Y Constant:N Verify:N Preset:Y`
Response: Press Enter.

Prompt: `Attribute tag:`
Response: Type **PSCALE** and press Enter.

Prompt: `Attribute Prompt:`
Response: Type **Plot Scale:**

Prompt: `Default Attribute Value:`
Response: Type **1\4″=1′** (or your most used scale) and press Enter.

Prompt: `Start point or Align/Center/Fit/Middle/Right/Style:`
Response: Press Enter twice.

Prompt: `Command:`
Response: Press Enter.

Prompt: `Attribute modes -- Invisible:Y Constant:N Verify:N Preset:Y`
Response: Press Enter.

Prompt: `Attribute tag:`
Response: Type **PSIZE** and press Enter.

Prompt: `Attribute Prompt:`
Response: Type **Paper Size:**

Prompt: `Default Attribute Value:`
Response: Type **D** and press Enter.

Prompt: `Start point or Align/Center/Fit/Middle/Right/Style:`
Response: Press Enter twice.

Prompt: `Command:`
Response: Press Enter.

Prompt: `Attribute modes -- Invisible:Y Constant:N Verify:N Preset:Y`
Response: Press Enter.

Prompt: `Attribute tag:`
Response: Type **PORIG** and press Enter

Prompt: `Attribute Prompt:`
Response: Type **Plot Origin:**

Prompt:	`Default Attribute Value:`
Response:	Type **0.00,0.00** and press Enter.
Prompt:	`Start point or Align/Center/Fit/Middle/Right/ Style:`
Response:	Press Enter.
Prompt:	`Command:`
Response:	Type **Wblock** and press Enter.
Prompt:	`File name (or ?):`
Response:	Type **PLOTBLK**
Prompt:	`Block name:`
Response:	Press Enter.
Prompt:	`Insertion base point:`
Response:	Pick a point among the attributes you just defined.
Prompt:	`Select Objects:`
Response:	Type **W**, select all the attributes with a window, and press Enter.

NOTE: *This routine is for AutoCAD Release 9 and later.*

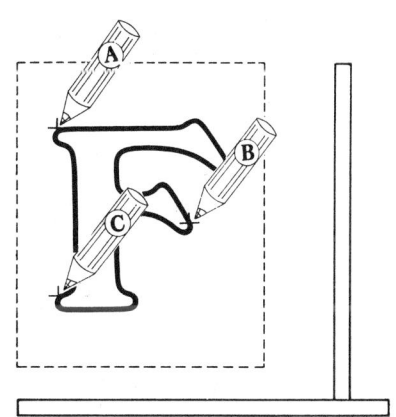

A Set of Job-Management Tools

The following programs were created by a friend of ours, Jeff Kensinger. Jeff has his own consulting business and writes custom dBASE and Clipper applications. If you would like copies of these programs for use in electronic form (so that you don't have to do all the typing) send a check for $25.00 to Jeff Kensinger, Kensinger Consulting, P.O. Box 1841, Tampa, FL 33601. Please indicate the format in which you want the disk. If you prefer, just give Jeff your CompuServe ID number and he can upload the program for you. If you need any customized or specialized routines, feel free to contact Jeff.

Figure F.1 shows the screen menu under which these programs operate. These programs allow you to use the LISP routine from Chapter 7 to extract from your drawings the data that will provide a wealth of information about your projects. If you have dBASE III, all you have to do is type the programs in an ASCII file, using the program name for the file name. You can omit the comments when you type the programs.

Fig. F.1.
Menu for project database manager.

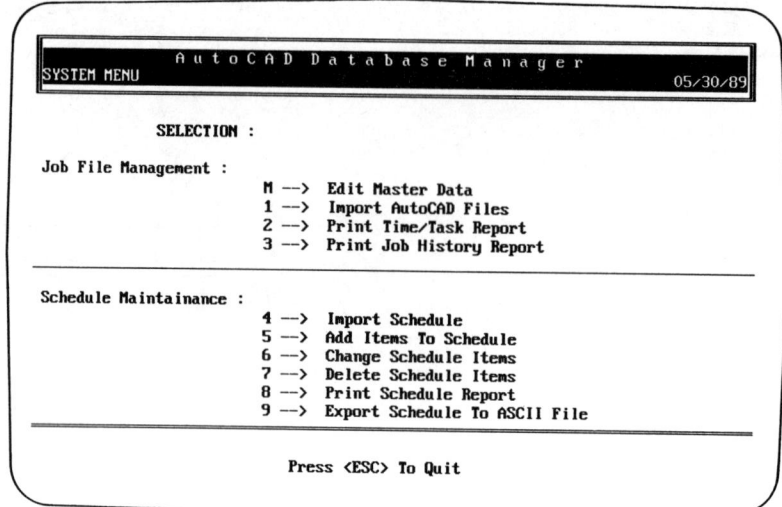

The Main Program for AutoCAD Database Manager (MAIN.PRG)

```
*******************************************************************
* Program      : MAIN.PRG
* Function     : Main menu for AutoCAD Database Manager
* Programmer   : J.Kensinger
* Last Update  : 03/20/89
*******************************************************************

CLEAR
SET SAFETY OFF
SET TALK OFF
SET BELL OFF
SET DELIMITER OFF
SET DELETE ON
SET PROCEDURE TO PRO_FILE

PUBLIC m_inkey


*------*
* Menu *
*------*
```

Appendix F: A Set of Job-Management Tools

```
DO WHILE .T.

    SET COLOR TO GR+/N
    CLEAR
    @  1, 0 TO 4,79 DOUBLE
    SET COLOR TO N/W
    @  2, 1 SAY REPL(" ",78)
    @  2,16 SAY "A u t o C A D   D a t a b a s e   M a n a g e r"
    SET COLOR TO N/W
    @  3, 1 SAY REPL(" ",78)
    @  3, 1 SAY "SYSTEM MENU"
    @  3,71 SAY DATE()

    SET COLOR TO W+/N,W+/N
    @  6,14 SAY "SELECTION : "
    SET COLOR TO R+
    @  8, 1 SAY "Job File Management : "
    SET COLOR TO GR+/N
    @  9,26 SAY "M -->   Edit Master Data"
    @ 10,26 SAY "1 -->   Import AutoCAD Files"
    @ 11,26 SAY "2 -->   Print Time/Task Report"
    @ 12,26 SAY "3 -->   Print Job History Report"

    SET COLOR TO GR+
    @ 13, 0 SAY REPLICATE( '_',80)

    SET COLOR TO R+/N
    @ 15, 1 SAY "Schedule Maintenance : "

    SET COLOR TO GR+/N
    @ 16,26 SAY "4 -->   Import Schedule"
    @ 17,26 SAY "5 -->   Add Items To Schedule"
    @ 18,26 SAY "6 -->   Change Schedule Items"
    @ 19,26 SAY "7 -->   Delete Schedule Items"
    @ 20,26 SAY "8 -->   Print Schedule Report"
    @ 21,26 SAY "9 -->   Export Schedule To ASCII File"

    @ 22,0 TO 22,79 DOUBLE
    SET COLOR TO W+
    @ 24,29 SAY "Press <   > To Quit"
    SET COLOR TO R+
    @ 24,36 SAY "ESC"
```

MAIN.PRG continues

MAIN.PRG *continued*

```
*--------------*
* Get Response *
*--------------*

STORE "*" TO key
SET CONFIRM OFF

DO WHILE .NOT. key $ " M123456789"      && Valid choices
    STORE " " TO key
    @ 6,26 GET key PICTURE "!"
           READ
ENDDO
SET CONFIRM ON

*--------*
* Action *
*--------*

DO CASE
    CASE READKEY() = 12 .OR. key = " "
        EXIT
    CASE key = "M"
        DO MASTER
    CASE key = "1"
        DO JOB_IMP
    CASE key = "2"
        DO JOB_TIME
    CASE key = "3"
        DO JOB_HIST
    CASE key = "4"
        DO SCH_IMP
    CASE key = "5"
        DO SCH_ADD
    CASE key = "6"
        DO SCH_EDIT
    CASE key = "7"
        DO SCH_DEL
    CASE key = "8"
        DO SCH_REPT
```

```
        CASE key = "9"
             DO SCH_EXPT
     ENDCASE

ENDDO

RELEASE ALL
CLOSE ALL
CLEAR
```

A Program for Importing CDF ASCII Files from AutoCAD (JOB_IMP.PRG)

This program imports the file created by the USER.LSP routine from Chapter 7.

```
****************************************************************
* Program     : JOB_IMP.PRG
* Function    : Import CDF ASCII files from AutoCAD
* Programmer  : J.Kensinger
* Last Update : 03/16/89
****************************************************************

*---------------*
* Paint Screen  *
*---------------*

SET COLOR TO N/W
@  3, 1 SAY REPL(" ",78)
@  3, 1 SAY "IMPORT DATA FILES"
@  3,71 SAY DATE()
SET COLOR TO GR+/N,W/N
@  5, 0 CLEAR

*-----------------*
* Get Job Number  *
*-----------------*
```

JOB_IMP.PRG continues

JOB_IMP.PRG *continued*

```
SELECT A
USE MASTER

DO WHILE .T.
   STORE MASTER->job TO m_job
   SET COLOR TO W+/N,W+/N
   @ 12,10 SAY "What is the job number :"
   @ 24,18 SAY "Enter Job Number to Import / <   > To Cancel"
   SET COLOR TO R
   @ 24,48 SAY "ESC"
   SET COLOR TO W+/N,N/W+
   @ 12,35 GET m_job PICTURE "!!!!!"
         READ


   *--------*
   * Exit ? *
   *--------*

   IF READKEY() = 12         && ESC Pressed
      RELEASE ALL
      RETURN
   ENDIF

   CLEAR GETS

   *-----------------*
   * Build File Name *
   *-----------------*

   m_file = TRIM(Master->job_path) + TRIM(m_job) +".DTA"

   *-------------------------*
   * Verify that file exists *
   *-------------------------*

   IF .NOT. FILE(m_file)
      STORE "Unable to locate " + m_file TO message
      DO Message
      LOOP
   ENDIF
```

```
    @ 12, Ø
    @ 12, 8 SAY "Importing " + m_file
    @ 16, Ø

    *---------------------*
    * Store job in Master *
    *---------------------*

    REPLACE Master->job WITH m_job
    USE

    EXIT
ENDDO

*----------------*
* Open Job File *
*----------------*

SELECT A
USE JOBFILE
ZAP

*--------*
* Append *
*--------*

SET TALK ON
APPEND FROM &m_file DELIMITED

*---------------------------------*
* Convert ASCII Date To Dbase Date *
*---------------------------------*

@ 14, Ø CLEAR
@ 14, 8 SAY "Converting dates."
@ 16, Ø

GO TOP
REPLACE date WITH CTOD(ascii_date) WHILE .NOT. EOF()
SET TALK OFF
USE
```

JOB_IMP.PRG continues

JOB_IMP.PRG *continued*

```
STORE "Process Complete" TO message
DO Message

CLOSE DATA
RELEASE ALL
RETURN
```

A Program for Printing a Job History Report (JOB_HIST.PRG)

This program creates a job history.

```
*******************************************************************
* Program    : JOB_HIST.PRG
* Function   : Print job history report
* Programmer : J.Kensinger
* Last Update : 03/16/89
*******************************************************************

*-----------------------------*
* Get Current Job From Master *
*-----------------------------*

SELECT A
USE MASTER
STORE TRIM(job) TO sys_job
USE

*---------------*
* Paint Screen  *
*---------------*

SET COLOR TO N/W
@  3, 1 SAY REPL(" ",78)
@  3, 1 SAY "JOB HISTORY REPORT"
@  3,71 SAY DATE()
SET COLOR TO GR+/N,W/N
@  5, 0 CLEAR
```

```
@  8,10 SAY "This report lists all available information for the "
@  9,10 SAY "job most recently imported from AutoCAD."

SET COLOR TO R+
@ 11,10 SAY "Current job : " + sys_job

SET COLOR TO W+/N,N/W+
@ 13,10 SAY "Continue (Y/N) ? "

DO Wait_key

IF UPPER(CHR(m_inkey)) <> "Y"
   RELEASE ALL
   RETURN
ENDIF


*----------------*
* Open Job File *
*----------------*

SELECT A
USE JOBFILE

IF EOF()
   STORE "No records in Jobfile - Verify Import" TO message
   DO Message
   RELEASE ALL
   RETURN
ENDIF

*-----------*
* SORT Data *
*-----------*

@ 14, 0
@ 14,10 SAY "Sorting - Please Wait....."
SELECT Jobfile
SET TALK ON
@ 16, 0
SORT ON drawing_no,task,user,date TO JOBSORT
SET TALK OFF
```

JOB_HIST.PRG continues

JOB_HIST.PRG *continued*

```
SELECT A
USE JOBSORT

*---------------*
* Print Report *
*---------------*

@ 14, Ø CLEAR
@ 14,1Ø SAY "Printing - Please Wait....."

SET PRINT ON
SET DEVICE TO PRINT
STORE 66 TO xpos
STORE .T. TO first
STORE .F. TO summary
STORE "Job History Report" TO title

DO WHILE .NOT. EOF( )

    *-------------------*
    * Check top of form *
    *-------------------*

    IF xpos > 55
       IF first
          first = .F.
       ELSE
          EJECT
       ENDIF
       DO JOB_HEAD
    ENDIF

    *------------------*
    * Print line items *
    *------------------*

    @  xpos, 1 SAY date
    @  xpos,12 SAY drawing_no
    @  xpos,23 SAY revision
    @  xpos,29 SAY task
    @  xpos,38 SAY time
    @  xpos,47 SAY user
```

```
        xpos = xpos + 1

     IF comment <> SPACE(50)
        @ xpos,12 SAY comment
        xpos = xpos + 1
     ENDIF

     SKIP

ENDDO

*------------*
* End report *
*------------*

EJECT
SET PRINT OFF
SET DEVICE TO SCREEN

STORE "Report Finished" TO message
@ 14, 0 CLEAR
DO Message

CLOSE DATA
RELEASE ALL
RETURN
```

Program that Creates Time Report Header (JOB_HEAD.PRG)

This program creates a header for the time report.

```
***************************************************************
* PROCEDURE NAME : JOB_HEAD.PRG
* FUNCTION       : Header for time/task report.
* PROGRAMMER     : J.Kensinger
* LAST UPDATE    : 03/20/89
***************************************************************
```

JOB_HEAD.PRG continues

JOB_HEAD.PRG continued

```
@ 1, 1 SAY title
@ 1,62 SAY "Your Company Name"
@ 2,71 SAY DATE()
@ 3, 1 SAY "Job : " + sys_job
@ 3,71 SAY TIME()
@ 4, 0 SAY REPLICATE("-",79)

IF summary
   @ 5, 0 SAY "                    JOB SUMMARY"
   @ 6, 0 SAY "======================================="
 ELSE
   @ 5, 0 SAY "   Date       Drawing    Rev   Task     Time ;
               User"
   @ 6, 0 SAY " --------    --------    ---   ------   ----- ;
               ------------------------"
ENDIF

xpos = 7

RETURN
```

Program for Creating Summaries for Job Report (JOB_SUMM.PRG)

This program creates for the time report a summary of the hourly totals by task, user, and drawing.

```
*********************************************************************
* Program      : JOB_SUMM.PRG
* Function     : Print task,drawing,user summary for time/task report
* Programmer   : J.Kensinger
* Last Update  : 03/20/89
*********************************************************************

*--------------------*
* Print Task Summary *
*--------------------*
```

```
summary = .T.
EJECT
DO JOB_HEAD

xpos = xpos + 1
@ xpos, 1 SAY " Task                        Total Time"
xpos = xpos + 1
@ xpos, 1 SAY "------                       ----------"
xpos = xpos + 1

SELECT Taskfile
GO TOP
DO WHILE .NOT. EOF()

   @ xpos, 1 SAY task
   @ xpos,32 SAY INT(time/6Ø) PICTURE "###"
   @ xpos,35 SAY ":"
   @ xpos,36 SAY MOD(time,6Ø) PICTURE "##"

   SKIP
   xpos = xpos + 1

ENDDO

*-----------------------*
* Print Drawing Summary *
*-----------------------*

xpos = xpos + 2
@ xpos, 1 SAY "Drawing No.                 Total Time"
xpos = xpos + 1
@ xpos, 1 SAY "-----------                 ----------"
xpos = xpos + 1

SELECT Drawfile
GO TOP
DO WHILE .NOT. EOF()

   @ xpos, 1 SAY drawing_no
   @ xpos,32 SAY INT(time/6Ø) PICTURE "###"
   @ xpos,35 SAY ":"
   @ xpos,36 SAY MOD(time,6Ø) PICTURE "##"
```

JOB_SUMM.PRG continues

JOB_SUMM.PRG continued

```
   SKIP
   xpos = xpos + 1

ENDDO


*--------------------*
* Print User Summary *
*--------------------*

xpos = xpos + 2
@ xpos, 1 SAY "            User            Total Time"
xpos = xpos + 1
@ xpos, 1 SAY "------------------------    ----------"
xpos = xpos + 1

SELECT Userfile
GO TOP
DO WHILE .NOT. EOF()

   @ xpos, 1 SAY user
   @ xpos,32 SAY INT(time/60) PICTURE "###"
   @ xpos,35 SAY ":"
   @ xpos,36 SAY MOD(time,60) PICTURE "##"

   SKIP
   xpos = xpos + 1

ENDDO


*--------------------*
* Print Grand Total  *
*--------------------*

xpos = xpos + 2
@ xpos, 1 SAY "Job total to date"
@ xpos,32 SAY INT(t_total/60) PICTURE "###"
@ xpos,35 SAY ":"
@ xpos,36 SAY MOD(t_total,60) PICTURE "##"
xpos = xpos + 1
@ xpos, 0 SAY "======================================"

RETURN
```

Accumulated Totals Program (JOB_2A.PRG)

This program creates temporary databases for totals accumulation.

```
*****************************************************************
* Program     : JOB_2A.PRG
* Function    : Creates databases to accumulate totals for task,
*               drawing number and user.
* Programmer  : J.Kensinger
* Last Update : 03/16/89
*****************************************************************

SET UNIQUE ON

*----------------------*
* Create task database *
* Index Jobfile on task *
*----------------------*

SELECT Jobfile

INDEX ON task TO Jobtask
SET INDEX TO Jobtask

*--------------------*
* Open Task Database *
*--------------------*

SELECT B
USE Taskfile
ZAP

*---------------------*
* Build Task Database *
*---------------------*

SELECT Jobfile
GO TOP
```

JOB_2A.PRG continues

JOB_2A.PRG continued

```
DO WHILE .NOT. EOF()

   SELECT Taskfile
   APPEND BLANK
   REPLACE Taskfile->task WITH Jobfile->task

   SELECT Jobfile
   SKIP

ENDDO


*----------------*
* Index Taskfile *
*----------------*

SELECT Taskfile
INDEX ON task TO Taskndx
SET INDEX TO Taskndx


*-------------------------*
* Create drawing database *
* Index Jobfile on drawing *
*-------------------------*

SELECT Jobfile

INDEX ON drawing_no TO Jobdraw
SET INDEX TO Jobdraw


*----------------------*
* Open Drawing Database *
*----------------------*

SELECT C
USE Drawfile
ZAP


*------------------------*
* Build Drawing Database *
*------------------------*
```

```
SELECT JOBFILE
GO TOP

DO WHILE .NOT. EOF()

   SELECT Drawfile
   APPEND BLANK
   REPLACE Drawfile->drawing_no WITH Jobfile->drawing_no

   SELECT Jobfile
   SKIP

ENDDO

*----------------*
* Index Drawfile *
*----------------*

SELECT Drawfile
INDEX ON drawing_no TO Drawndx
SET INDEX TO Drawndx


*-----------------------*
* Create User database  *
* Index Jobfile on user *
*-----------------------*

SELECT Jobfile

INDEX ON user TO Jobuser
SET INDEX TO Jobuser

*--------------------*
* Open User Database *
*--------------------*

SELECT D
USE Userfile
ZAP
```

JOB_2A.PRG continues

JOB_2A.PRG continued

```
*---------------------*
* Build User Database *
*---------------------*

SELECT JOBFILE
GO TOP

DO WHILE .NOT. EOF()

   SELECT Userfile
   APPEND BLANK
   REPLACE Userfile->user WITH Jobfile->user

   SELECT Jobfile
   SKIP

ENDDO

*-----------------*
* Index Userfile  *
*-----------------*

SELECT Userfile
INDEX ON user TO Userndx
SET INDEX TO Userndx

SET UNIQUE OFF

SELECT Jobfile
SET INDEX TO

RETURN
```

Program for Creating a Job Time and Task Report (JOB_TIME.PRG)

This program creates the job time and task report.

```
******************************************************************
* Program     : JOB_TIME.PRG
* Function    : Print Time & Task Report
* Programmer  : J.Kensinger
* Last Update : 03/16/89
******************************************************************

*-----------------------------*
* Get Current Job From Master *
*-----------------------------*

SELECT A
USE MASTER
STORE TRIM(job) TO sys_job
USE

*--------------*
* Paint Screen *
*--------------*

SET COLOR TO N/W
@ 3, 1 SAY REPL(" ",78)
@ 3, 1 SAY "TIME/TASK REPORT"
@ 3,71 SAY DATE()
SET COLOR TO GR+/N,W/N
@ 5, 0 CLEAR

@ 8,10 SAY "This report lists time and task information for the "
@ 9,10 SAY "job most recently imported from AutoCAD."

SET COLOR TO R+
@ 11,10 SAY "Current job : " + sys_job

SET COLOR TO W+/N,N/W+
@ 13,10 SAY "Continue (Y/N) ? "

DO Wait_key

IF UPPER(CHR(m_inkey)) <> "Y"
   RELEASE ALL
   RETURN
ENDIF
```

JOB_TIME.PRG continues

JOB_TIME.PRG *continued*

```
*---------------*
* Open Job File *
*---------------*

SELECT A
USE JOBFILE

IF EOF()
   STORE "No records in Jobfile - Verify Import" TO message
   DO Message
   RELEASE ALL
   RETURN
ENDIF

*---------------------*
* Create Databases to *
* accumulate totals.  *
*---------------------*

@ 13, 0 CLEAR
@ 14,10 SAY "Creating Temporary files....."

DO JOB_TEMP

*-----------*
* SORT Data *
*-----------*

@ 14, 0
@ 14,10 SAY "Sorting - Please Wait....."
SELECT Jobfile
SET TALK ON
@ 16, 0
SORT ON date,drawing_no,user TO JOBSORT
SET TALK OFF

SELECT A
USE JOBSORT

*--------------*
* Print Report *
*--------------*

@ 14, 0 CLEAR
@ 14,10 SAY "Printing - Please Wait....."
```

Appendix F: A Set of Job-Management Tools

```
SET PRINT ON
SET DEVICE TO PRINT
STORE 66 TO xpos
STORE .T. TO first
STORE Ø TO t_task,t_draw,t_user,t_total,min
STORE .F. TO error,summary
STORE "Time/Task Report" TO title

DO WHILE .NOT. EOF()

   *------------------*
   * Check top of form *
   *------------------*

   IF xpos > 55
      IF first
         first = .F.
      ELSE
         EJECT
      ENDIF
      DO JOB_HEAD
   ENDIF

   *------------------*
   * Print line items *
   *------------------*

   @ xpos, 1 SAY date
   @ xpos,12 SAY drawing_no
   @ xpos,23 SAY revision
   @ xpos,29 SAY task
   @ xpos,38 SAY time
   @ xpos,47 SAY user

   xpos = xpos + 1

   *------------------*
   * Accumulate totals *
   *------------------*

   min = VAL(time) * 6Ø + VAL(SUBSTR(time,4))    && Convert time to minutes
   t_total = t_total + min
```

JOB_TIME.PRG continues

JOB_TIME.PRG continued

```
   SELECT Taskfile
   SEEK(Jobsort->task)
   IF FOUND()
      REPLACE Taskfile->time WITH Taskfile->time + min
    ELSE
      STORE .T. TO error
   ENDIF

   SELECT Drawfile
   SEEK(Jobsort->drawing_no)
   IF FOUND()
      REPLACE Drawfile->time WITH Drawfile->time + min
    ELSE
      STORE .T. TO error
   ENDIF

   SELECT Userfile
   SEEK(Jobsort->user)
   IF FOUND()
      REPLACE Userfile->time WITH Userfile->time + min
    ELSE
      STORE .T. TO error
   ENDIF

   SELECT Jobsort
   SKIP

ENDDO

*---------------*
* Print Summary *
*---------------*

DO JOB_SUMM

*------------*
* End report *
*------------*

EJECT
SET PRINT OFF
SET DEVICE TO SCREEN

IF error
   STORE "Errors detected accumulating totals" TO message
 ELSE
   STORE "Report Finished" TO message
ENDIF
```

```
@ 14, Ø CLEAR
DO Message

CLOSE DATA
RELEASE ALL
RETURN
```

Program for Editing Master Data (MASTER.PRG)

This program lets you edit your data after it has been created by USER.LSP.

```
**************************************************************
* PROCEDURE NAME : MASTER.PRG
* FUNCTION       : Edit master data
* PROGRAMMER     : J.Kensinger
* LAST UPDATE    : Ø3/23/89
**************************************************************

SELECT A
USE MASTER

SET COLOR TO N/W
@  3, 1 SAY REPL(" ",78)
@  3, 1 SAY "EDIT MASTER DATA"
@  3,71 SAY DATE()
SET COLOR TO W+/N,W/N


*------------*
* Main Loop  *
*------------*

DO WHILE .T.

    *---------------*
    * Paint Screen  *
    *---------------*
```

JOB_MASTER.PRG continues

JOB_MASTER.PRG continued

```
SET COLOR TO GR+/N

@  6, 0 CLEAR

@  7,10   SAY "Company Name      :"
@  8,10   SAY "Current Job       :"
@  9,10   SAY "Job Path          :"
@ 10,10   SAY "Current Schedule  :"
@ 11,10   SAY "Schedule Path     :"

SET COLOR TO W+
@ 24,26 SAY "Enter Data / <   > To Cancel"
SET COLOR TO R+
@ 24,40 SAY "ESC"

SET COLOR TO W+/N,N/W

@  7,32  GET coname
@  8,32  GET job
@  9,32  GET job_path
@ 10,32  GET schedule
@ 11,32  GET sch_path
         READ

*--------------*
* ESC pressed *
*--------------*

IF READKEY() = 12
   STORE .T. TO finished
   EXIT
ENDIF

*------------*
* Finished ? *
*------------*
```

```
   @ 24, 0
   @ 24,10 SAY "Any further changes? (Y/N): "
   STORE " " TO change
   DO WHILE .NOT. change $ "YN"
      STORE "N" TO change
      @ 24,38 GET change PICTURE "!"
            READ
   ENDDO

   @ 24, 0 CLEAR

   IF change = "N"
      EXIT
   ENDIF

ENDDO

CLOSE DATA
RELEASE ALL
RETURN
```

Program Controller File (PRO_FILE.PRG)

This is a controller file for the program.

```
***************************************************************
* Program     : PRO_FILE.PRG
* Function    : Procedure file
* Programmer  : J.Kensinger
* Last Update : 03/16/89
***************************************************************


*-------------->
* Procedure  : MESSAGE
* Function   : Display message and wait for response.
*-------------->
```

PRO_FILE.PRG continues

PRO_FILE.PRG *continued*

```
PROCEDURE Message

SET CONSOLE OFF
SET CONFIRM OFF
@ 24, 0
@ 24, 0 SAY message
@ 24,53 SAY "Press Any Key To Continue"
STORE " " TO key
@ 24,79 GET key
        READ
CLEAR GETS
SET CONFIRM ON
SET CONSOLE ON
@ 24, 0
RETURN


*--------------->
* Procedure   : WAIT_KEY
* Function    : Wait for response from keyboard.
*--------------->

PROCEDURE Wait_key

CLEAR TYPE
m_inkey = 0
DO WHILE m_inkey = 0
   m_inkey = inkey()
   IF m_inkey # 0
      EXIT
   ENDIF
ENDDO
RETURN
```

Program Data File Structures

Using the dBASE CREATE command, you must create the following database structures to accompany this program:

Structure: `Taskfile.dbf`

Field	Field Name	Type	Width	Dec
001	Task	Character	6	
002	Time	Numeric	5	

Structure: `Drawfile.dbf`

Field	Field Name	Type	Width	Dec
001	Drawing_no	Character	8	
002	Time	Numeric	5	

Structure: `Userfile.dbf`

Field	Field Name	Type	Width	Dec
001	User	Character	25	
002	Time	Numeric	5	

Structure: `Jobfile.dbf`

Field	Field Name	Type	Width	Dec
001	User	Character	25	
002	Drawing_no	Character	8	
003	Ascii_date	Character	8	
004	Task	Character	6	
005	Time	Character	5	
007	Comment	Character	50	
008	Date	Date	8	

Structure: `Master.dbf`

Field	Field Name	Type	Width	Dec
001	Coname	Character	45	
002	Job	Character	5	
003	Job_path	Character	20	
004	Schedule	Character	12	
005	Sch_path	Character	20	

A Material, Labor, or Equipment Schedule Generator

The following group of programs takes data exported from a set of attributes and places it in columns. We have developed generic titles for these columns, which you can expand on as needed. The file created by these programs can be sent to your printer or imported back into AutoCAD via AutoWord or a LISP routine for text importation (supplied on the AutoCAD Release 10 support disk). You must create a template for the attribute extraction; this template must match the data-file structure listed with this program.

A Program for Importing CDF Schedule Files from AutoCAD (SCH_IMP.PRG)

This program imports the ASCII files created by AutoCAD's ATTEXT command.

```
*********************************************************************
* Program     : SCH_IMP.PRG
* Function    : Import CDF schedule files from AutoCAD
* Programmer  : J.Kensinger
* Last Update : 03/20/89
*********************************************************************

*---------------*
* Paint Screen  *
*---------------*

SET COLOR TO N/W
@  3, 1 SAY REPL(" ",78)
@  3, 1 SAY "IMPORT SCHEDULE FILES"
@  3,71 SAY DATE()
SET COLOR TO GR+/N,W/N
@  5, 0 CLEAR

*---------------*
* Get Schedule  *
*---------------*
```

Appendix F: A Set of Job-Management Tools

```
SELECT A
USE MASTER

DO WHILE .T.
   STORE TRIM(MASTER->sch_path) + TRIM(MASTER->schedule) TO m_file
   SET COLOR TO W+/N,W+/N
   @ 12,10 SAY "What is the schedule :"
   @ 24,18 SAY "Enter Schedule to Import / <   > To Cancel"
   SET COLOR TO R
   @ 24,46 SAY "ESC"
   SET COLOR TO W+/N,N/W+
   @ 12,33 GET m_file  PICTURE "@!"
         READ

   *--------*
   * Exit ? *
   *--------*

   IF READKEY() = 12         && ESC Pressed
      RELEASE ALL
      RETURN
   ENDIF

   CLEAR GETS

   *-------------------------*
   * Verify that file exists *
   *-------------------------*

   IF .NOT. FILE(m_file)
      STORE "Unable to locate " + m_file TO message
      DO Message
      LOOP
   ENDIF

   @ 12, 0
   @ 12, 8 SAY "Importing " + m_file
   @ 16, 0

   EXIT
ENDDO
```

SCH_IMP.PRG continues

SCH_IMP.PRG *continued*

```
*--------------------*
* Open Schedule File *
*--------------------*

SELECT A
USE SCHFILE
ZAP


*--------*
* Append *
*--------*

SET TALK ON
APPEND FROM &m_file DELIMITED


*-------*
* Index *
*-------*

@ 14, 0 CLEAR
@ 14, 8 SAY "Indexing...."
@ 16, 0

INDEX ON MARK TO Mark

SET TALK OFF
USE

STORE "Process Complete" TO message
DO Message

CLOSE DATA
RELEASE ALL
RETURN
```

A Program for Adding Records to AutoCAD Schedule Records (SCH_ADD.PRG)

This program adds bill of material or schedule records to the records you extracted from AutoCAD.

```
****************************************************************************
* PROGRAM NAME   : SCH_ADD.PRG
* FUNCTION       : Add Bill of Material Records
* PROGRAMMER     : J.Kensinger
* LAST UPDATE    : 03/20/89
****************************************************************************

*------------*
* Open Files *
*------------*

SELECT A
USE MASTER
STORE TRIM(schedule) TO sys_sched
USE

SELECT A
USE SCHFILE
SET INDEX TO Mark            && SCHFILE indexed on mark TO Mark.ndx

*--------------*
* Paint Screen *
*--------------*

SET COLOR TO N/W
@  3, 1 SAY REPL(" ",78)
@  3, 1 SAY "ADD ITEMS TO SCHEDULE"
@  3,71 SAY DATE()
SET COLOR TO W+/N,W/N
@  5, 0 CLEAR
@  6, 0 SAY "Current Schedule : " + sys_sched
SET COLOR TO GR+/N

@ 10,10 SAY "         Mark : "
@ 11,10 SAY "Model Number : "
@ 12,10 SAY "Manufacturer : "
@ 13,10 SAY " Description : "
@ 14,10 SAY "      Remarks : "
```

SCH_ADD.PRG continues

SCH_ADD.PRG *continued*

```
*-------------------*
* Main Program Loop *
*-------------------*

CLEAR TYPE
STORE .F. TO finished
DO WHILE .NOT. finished

   *---------------------*
   * Add/Edit New Record *
   *---------------------*

   STORE "  -  "          TO m_mark
   STORE SPACE(10)        TO m_model_no
   STORE SPACE(25)        TO m_vendor
   STORE SPACE(25)        TO m_desc
   STORE SPACE(25)        TO m_remarks
   @ 8,26 CLEAR

   *----------------*
   * Add/Edit Loop *
   *----------------*

   STORE .F. TO  done
   DO WHILE .NOT. done

      SET COLOR TO W+
      @ 24, 0
      @ 24,23 SAY "Enter data or press <   > to Cancel"
      SET COLOR TO R+
      @ 24,44 SAY "ESC"

      *----------*
      * Get Data *
      *----------*

      SET CONFIRM ON
      SET COLOR TO W+/N,N/W
      @ 10,26 GET m_mark      PICTURE "!!-###"
      @ 11,26 GET m_model_no
      @ 12,26 GET m_vendor
      @ 13,26 GET m_desc
      @ 14,26 GET m_remarks
            READ

      SET CONFIRM OFF
      CLEAR GETS
```

```
*-------------*
* ESC pressed *
*-------------*

IF READKEY() = 12
   STORE .T. TO finished
   EXIT
ENDIF

IF m_mark = "   -   "
   LOOP
ENDIF

*-------------*
* Duplicate ? *
*-------------*

SELECT A
SEEK(m_mark)
IF FOUND()
   STORE "Mark : " + m_mark + " currently in file" TO message
   DO Message
   LOOP
ENDIF

*--------*
* Save ? *
*--------*

@ 24, 0
@ 24,15 SAY "Add record to file ? (Y/N)"

STORE "*" TO option
DO WHILE .NOT. option $ "YN"
   STORE "Y" TO option
   @ 24,42 GET option PICTURE "!"
        READ
ENDDO

*------*
* Edit *
*------*

IF option = "N"
   LOOP
ENDIF
```

SCH_ADD.PRG continues

SCH_ADD.PRG continued

```
*-------------*
* ESC pressed *
*-------------*

IF READKEY() = 12
   STORE .T. TO finished
   EXIT
ENDIF

*-------------*
* Update Files *
*-------------*

APPEND BLANK
REPLACE mark WITH m_mark,model_no WITH m_model_no,;
        vendor WITH m_vendor,desc WITH m_desc,remarks WITH m_remarks

STORE .T. TO done

   ENDDO                          && done

ENDDO                             && finished

CLOSE DATA
RETURN
```

A Program for Deleting Schedule Records (SCH_DEL.PRG)

Use this program to delete records from the schedule.

```
**********************************************************************
* PROGRAM NAME    : SCH_DEL.PRG
* FUNCTION        : Edit schedules
* PROGRAMMER      : J.Kensinger
* LAST UPDATE     : 03/17/89
**********************************************************************

*-------------*
* Open Files *
*-------------*
```

```
SELECT A
USE MASTER
STORE TRIM(schedule) TO sys_sched
USE

SELECT A
USE SCHFILE
SET INDEX TO Mark            && SCHFILE indexed on mark TO Mark.ndx

*--------------*
* Paint Screen *
*--------------*

SET COLOR TO N/W
@  3, 1 SAY REPL(" ",78)
@  3, 1 SAY "DELETE SCHEDULE RECORDS"
@  3,71 SAY DATE()
SET COLOR TO W+/N,W/N
@  5, Ø CLEAR
@  6, Ø SAY "Current Schedule : " + sys_sched
SET COLOR TO GR+/N

@ 1Ø,1Ø SAY "         Mark : "
@ 11,1Ø SAY "Model Number : "
@ 12,1Ø SAY "Manufacturer : "
@ 13,1Ø SAY " Description : "
@ 14,1Ø SAY "      Remarks : "

*-------------------*
* Main Program Loop *
*-------------------*

CLEAR TYPE
STORE .F. TO finished
DO WHILE .NOT. finished

    *---------------*
    * Select record *
    *---------------*

    @  8,26 CLEAR
```

SCH_DEL.PRG continues

SCH_DEL.PRG *continued*

```
    SET COLOR TO W+
    @ 24, Ø
    @ 24,23 SAY "Enter data or press <   > to Cancel"
    SET COLOR TO R+
    @ 24,44 SAY "ESC"
    SET COLOR TO W+/N,N/W

    STORE "  -   " TO m_mark
    DO WHILE .T.
       @ 1Ø,26 GET m_mark PICTURE "!!-###"
             READ

       *-------------*
       * ESC Pressed *
       *-------------*

       IF READKEY() = 12
          RELEASE ALL
          CLOSE DATA
          RETURN
       ENDIF

       IF m_mark = "  -   "
          LOOP
       ENDIF

       *---------------*
       * Locate Record *
       *---------------*

       SEEK(m_mark)
       IF FOUND()
          EXIT
       ENDIF

       STORE "Mark : " + m_mark + " not on file" TO message
       DO Message
    ENDDO

    *----------------*
    * Display Record *
    *----------------*
```

```
            SET COLOR TO W+/N,N/W+
            @ 10,26 SAY mark
            @ 11,26 SAY model_no
            @ 12,26 SAY vendor
            @ 13,26 SAY desc
            @ 14,26 SAY remarks


            *----------------*
            * Confirm Delete *
            *----------------*

            @ 20, 0 CLEAR
            @ 24, 1 SAY "OK To DELETE this record ? (Y/N)"

            DO wait_key

            IF UPPER(CHR(m_inkey)) = "Y"
               DELETE
                @ 24, 1 SAY "Record Deleted - Press any key to continue..."
             ELSE
                @ 24, 1 SAY "Record Saved - Press any key to continue..."
            ENDIF

            DO wait_key
            @ 24, 0
            CLEAR GETS
            LOOP

         ENDDO                              && finished

         CLOSE DATA
         RETURN
```

Program for Editing Schedules (SCH_EDIT.PRG)

Use this program for editing records.

```
*************************************************************************
* PROGRAM NAME    : SCH_EDIT.PRG
* FUNCTION        : Edit schedules
* PROGRAMMER      : J.Kensinger
* LAST UPDATE     : 03/20/89
*************************************************************************

*------------*
* Open Files *
*------------*

SELECT A
USE MASTER
STORE TRIM(schedule) TO sys_sched
USE

SELECT A
USE SCHFILE
SET INDEX TO Mark              && SCHFILE indexed on mark TO Mark.ndx

*--------------*
* Paint Screen *
*--------------*

SET COLOR TO N/W
@  3, 1 SAY REPL(" ",78)
@  3, 1 SAY "EDIT SCHEDULE"
@  3,71 SAY DATE()
SET COLOR TO W+/N,W/N
@  5, 0 CLEAR
@  6, 0 SAY "Current Schedule : " + sys_sched
SET COLOR TO GR+/N

@ 10,10 SAY "        Mark : "
@ 11,10 SAY "Model Number : "
@ 12,10 SAY "Manufacturer : "
@ 13,10 SAY " Description : "
@ 14,10 SAY "     Remarks : "

*-------------------*
* Main Program Loop *
*-------------------*
```

```
CLEAR TYPE
STORE .F. TO finished
DO WHILE .NOT. finished

   *---------------*
   * Select record *
   *---------------*

   @ 8,26 CLEAR

   SET COLOR TO W+
   @ 24, 0
   @ 24,23 SAY "Enter data or press <   > to Cancel"
   SET COLOR TO R+
   @ 24,44 SAY "ESC"
   SET COLOR TO W+/N,N/W

   STORE "   -   " TO m_mark
   DO WHILE .T.
      @ 10,26 GET m_mark PICTURE "!!-###"
            READ

      *-------------*
      * ESC Pressed *
      *-------------*

      IF READKEY() = 12
         RELEASE ALL
         CLOSE DATA
         RETURN
      ENDIF

      IF m_mark = "   -   "
         LOOP
      ENDIF

      *---------------*
      * Locate Record *
      *---------------*

      SEEK(m_mark)
      IF FOUND()
         EXIT
      ENDIF

      STORE "Mark : " + m_mark + " not on file" TO message
      DO Message
   ENDDO
```

SCH_EDIT.PRG continues

SCH_EDIT.PRG *continued*

```
*-------------*
* Edit Record *
*-------------*

STORE model_no       TO m_model_no
STORE vendor         TO m_vendor
STORE desc           TO m_desc
STORE remarks        TO m_remarks

STORE .F. TO done
DO WHILE .NOT. done

   SET COLOR TO W+
   @ 24, 0
   @ 24,23 SAY "Edit data or press <   > to Cancel"
   SET COLOR TO R+
   @ 24,43 SAY "ESC"

   *----------*
   * Get Data *
   *----------*

   SET CONFIRM ON
   SET COLOR TO W+/N,N/W+
   @ 10,26 GET m_mark
   @ 11,26 GET m_model_no
   @ 12,26 GET m_vendor
   @ 13,26 GET m_desc
   @ 14,26 GET m_remarks
         READ

   SET CONFIRM OFF
   CLEAR GETS

   *--------------*
   * ESC pressed *
   *--------------*

   IF READKEY() = 12
      STORE .T. TO finished
      EXIT
   ENDIF

   *--------*
   * Save ? *
   *--------*
```

```
            @ 24, Ø
            @ 24,15 SAY "Return record to file ? (Y/N)"

            STORE "*" TO option
            DO WHILE .NOT. option $ "YN"
               STORE "Y" TO option
               @ 24,45 GET option PICTURE "!"
                    READ
            ENDDO

            *------*
            * Edit *
            *------*

            IF option = "N"
               LOOP
            ENDIF


            *-------------*
            * ESC pressed *
            *-------------*

            IF READKEY() = 12
               STORE .T. TO finished
               EXIT
            ENDIF


            *--------------*
            * Update Files *
            *--------------*

            REPLACE mark WITH m_mark,model_no WITH m_model_no,;
                    vendor WITH m_vendor,desc WITH m_desc,remarks WITH m_remarks


            STORE .T. TO done

      ENDDO                          && done

      ENDDO                          && finished

      CLOSE DATA
      RETURN
```

Program for Exporting Schedule to ASCII File (SCH_EXPT.PRG)

This program exports the schedule to an ASCII file.

```
**************************************************************************
* Program      : SCH_EXPT.PRG
* Function     : Export schedule to ASCII file
* Programmer   : J.Kensinger
* Last Update  : 03/20/89
**************************************************************************

*----------------------------*
* Get Current Job From Master *
*----------------------------*

SELECT A
USE MASTER
STORE TRIM(schedule) TO sys_sch
STORE TRIM(sch_path) TO sys_path
USE

*--------------*
* Paint Screen *
*--------------*

SET COLOR TO N/W
@  3, 1 SAY REPL(" ",78)
@  3, 1 SAY "EXPORT SCHEDULE"
@  3,71 SAY DATE()
SET COLOR TO GR+/N,W/N
@  5, 0 CLEAR

@  8,10 SAY "This will write the current schedule into a comma delimited"
@  9,10 SAY "ASCII file for importing into AutoCAD."

SET COLOR TO R+
@ 11,10 SAY "Current schedule : " + sys_sch

SET COLOR TO W+/N,N/W+
@ 13,10 SAY "Continue (Y/N) ? "

DO Wait_key

IF UPPER(CHR(m_inkey)) <> "Y"
   RELEASE ALL
   RETURN
ENDIF
```

Appendix F: A Set of Job-Management Tools

```
*---------------*
* Get File Name *
*---------------*

@ 11, Ø CLEAR

DO WHILE .T.
   STORE SPACE(3Ø) TO out_file
   SET COLOR TO W+/N,W+/N
   @ 12,1Ø SAY "What is the output file name :"
   @ 24,19 SAY "Enter Outout File Name / <    > To Cancel"
   SET COLOR TO R
   @ 24,45 SAY "ESC"
   SET COLOR TO W+/N,N/W+
   @ 12,41 GET out_file PICTURE "@!"
         READ

   *-------*
   * ESC ? *
   *-------*

   IF READKEY() = 12         && ESC Pressed
      RELEASE ALL
      RETURN
   ENDIF

   CLEAR GETS
   EXIT

ENDDO

*-----------*
* Open File *
*-----------*

SELECT A
USE SCHFILE

IF EOF()
   STORE "No records in file - Verify Import" TO message
   DO Message
   RELEASE ALL
   RETURN
ENDIF

*--------*
* EXPORT *
*--------*
```

SCH_EXPT.PRG continues

SCH_EXPT.PRG continued

```
@ 12, 0
@ 12,10 SAY "Exporting to " + out_file
SET TALK ON
@ 14, 0
COPY TO &out_file SDF
SET TALK OFF

STORE "Process Complete" TO message
DO Message

CLOSE DATA
RELEASE ALL
RETURN
```

Schedule Report Header Program (SCH_HEAD.PRG)

This program creates the header for the schedule report.

```
*************************************************************
* PROCEDURE NAME : SCH_HEAD.PRG
* FUNCTION       : Header for schedule report
* PROGRAMMER     : J.Kensinger
* LAST UPDATE    : 03/17/89
*************************************************************

@ 1, 1 SAY "Schedule Report"
@ 1,62 SAY "Your Company Name"
@ 2,71 SAY DATE()
@ 3, 1 SAY "Schedule : " + sys_sch
@ 3,71 SAY TIME()
@ 4, 0 SAY REPLICATE("-",79)

@ 5, 0 SAY "Mark #   Model No.        Manufacturer        ;
         Description"
@ 6, 0 SAY "------   ----------       ------------------------ ;
         ------------------------"

xpos = 7

RETURN
```

Data-File Structure

Using the dBASE III CREATE command, you must create the following data-file structure for this program.

Structure: Schfile.dbf

Field	Field Name	Type	Width	Dec
001	Mark	Character	6	
002	Model_no	Character	10	
003	Vendor	Character	25	
004	Desc	Character	25	

Schedule Report

This is what your schedule report will look like if you print it or import it back into your AutoCAD drawing:

```
MARK    MODEL NO    VENDOR          DESC.       REMARKS
-----------------------------------------------------------
AA-1    1111        ABC Corp        widget      green
AA-2    Model 23    Jaks supply     wadget      red
AA-3    86-475      Maks supply     wudget      black
AA-4    89-808      TESTERS, INC.   wedget      yellow
AA-5    448887      Hominu          wo          purple
```

USER.LSP

This program, discussed in Chapter 7, creates data from your drawing activities for the dBASE programs to use. We have made certain choices about the type of information you may need to manage your projects. A coordinated effort of customizing this routine and other dBASE programs in this appendix will yield a program that can provide you with all the information you need to manage your CAD projects.

```
(defun c:user (/ ch ctr dfl dwg usr utk hrs min pro pro2 yn rno
   co datafile)
(setvar "cmdecho" 0)
(setq dte (strcat (substr (getvar "cdate") 5 2) "/" (substr
(getvar "cdate") 7 2) "/" (substr (getvar "cdate") 3 2)))
```

USER.LSP continues

USER_LSP *continued*

```
(setq ch (substr (getvar "dwgprefix") 9 1))
(setq ctr 8)
(while (/= ch "\\")
(setq ctr (+ ctr 1))
(setq ch (substr (getvar "dwgprefix") ctr 1)))
(setq ctr (- (1- ctr) 8))
(setq dfl (substr (getvar "dwgprefix") 9 ctr))
(setq dfl (strcat dfl ".dta"))
(setq dwg (getvar "dwgname"))
(setq usr (getstring T "\nEnter Your First Initial
    and Last Name: "))
(initget 1 ("Y y N n"))
(setq yn (strcase (getkword "\nDoes this work require a revision
         number? <Y or N>: ")))
(if (= yn "Y")
  (setq rno (getint "\nEnter the revision number: ")))
(prompt "\nTask Codes Are: <Preliminary Design: PD>
    <Design Development: DD>")
(prompt "\n<Working Drawings: WD> <Contract Administration: CA>
    <Revisions: R>")
(setq utk (strcase (getstring T "\nEnter A Task Code Or
    Combination of Codes Separated by a Slash (/): ")))
(setq hrs (fix (* 24 (getvar "tdusrtimer"))))
(setq min (fix (* (rem (* 24 (getvar "tdusrtimer")) 1) 60)))
(setq pro (strcat usr ", you worked on the drawing " dwg))
(setq pro2 (strcat " performing the task(s) " utk " for "
    (itoa hrs) " hours and " (itoa min) " minutes"))
(prompt pro)(prompt "\n")
(prompt pro2)(initget 1 "Y y N n")
(setq yn (getkword "\nIs this correct <Y or N>?"))
(setq yn (strcase yn))
(if (= yn "N")
(progn (Prompt "\nTry Again: ")(load "/acad/user")(user)(princ))
(progn
(setq datafile (open dfl "a"))
(write-line (strcat dte "," dwg "," rno "," utk "," (itoa hrs) ","
    (itoa min) "," usr "," co ",") datafile)
(close datafile)
(command "time" "r" "")
(command "end" "y"))))
```

The commented listing follows. The first two lines:

```
(defun c:user (/ ch ctr dfl dwg usr utk hrs min pro pro2 yn rno
    co datafile)
(setvar "cmdecho" 0)
```

start the program and turn off the ECHO command.

Next, this routine divides the AutoCAD *cdate* variable into an mm/dd/yy format by using the `substr` function to get pieces of the string, and binds the string to the variable *dte*.

```
(setq dte (strcat (substr (getvar "cdate") 5 2) "/" (substr
(getvar "cdate") 7 2) "/" (substr (getvar "cdate") 3 2)))
```

This sequence finds the slash (\) character in the AutoCAD *"dwgprefix"* variable and sets the counter to its position in the *"dwgprefix"* string:

```
(setq ch (substr (getvar "dwgprefix") 9 1))
(setq ctr 8)
(while (/= ch "\\")
(setq ctr (+ ctr 1))
(setq ch (substr (getvar "dwgprefix") ctr 1)))
(setq ctr (- (1- ctr) 8))
(setq dfl (substr (getvar "dwgprefix") 9 ctr))
(setq dfl (strcat dfl ".dta"))
```

Then we set the variable *dfl* to the substring of AutoCAD's *dwgprefix* variable, thereby deleting the subdirectory from the drawing file name. Because we know that the drawing file name cannot be longer than eight characters, we start by looking at the ninth character and move to the end of the string.

These prompts get from the user the different information required by the dBASE program:

```
(setq dwg (getvar "dwgname"))
(setq usr (getstring T "\nEnter Your First Initial
    and Last Name: "))
(initget 1 ("Y y N n"))
(setq yn (strcase (getkword "\nDoes this work require a revision
        number? <Y or N>: ")))
(if (= yn "Y")
  (setq rno (getint "\nEnter the revision number: ")))
(prompt "\nTask Codes Are: <Preliminary Design: PD>
    <Design Development: DD>")
(prompt "\n<Working Drawings: WD> <Contract Administration: CA>
    <Revisions: R>")
(setq utk (strcase (getstring T "\nEnter A Task Code Or
    Combination of Codes Separated by a Slash (/): ")))
(setq co (getstring T "\nEnter any comments that you wish to
    include: "))
```

You may want to modify the prompts, especially the drawing task codes. Notice that the *co* variable `getstring` function uses a *T* to allow spaces to be entered into the prompt.

These two lines:

```
(setq hrs (fix (* 24 (getvar "tdusrtimer"))))
(setq min (fix (* (rem (* 24 (getvar "tdusrtimer")) 1) 60)))
```

retrieve the AutoCAD variable *tdusrtimer* and use `fix` to round the results to provide actual hours and minutes. The `rem` function retrieves the remainder of the hours multiplication and converts it to minutes.

The following chunk of code is a different way to work with the combination of variables and strings. We set the strings/variables combinations to variables and then use those variables to create the prompt:

```
(setq pro (strcat usr ", you worked on the drawing " dwg))
(setq pro2 (strcat " performing the task(s) " utk " for "
    (itoa hrs) " hours and " (itoa min) " minutes"))
(prompt pro)(prompt "\n")
(prompt pro2)(initget 1 "Y y N n")
(setq yn (getkword "\nIs this correct <Y or N>?"))
(setq yn (strcase yn))
(if (= yn "N")
(progn (Prompt "\nTry Again: ")(load "/acad/
user")(user)(princ))
```

You will see other examples in which we use combinations of `prompts` and `princs`. With a string as chopped up as this one, the variable route is the way to go. We then test to see whether the responses are correct; if they aren't, you must exit the program and start again.

The following lines write the variables to the data file and reset the timer. Because they are on the false side of the `if` test, they are used only if everything is correct. Finally, the LISP routine ends the drawing.

```
(progn
(setq datafile (open dfl "a"))
(write-line (strcat  dte "," dwg "," rno "," utk "," (itoa hrs) ","
    (itoa min) "," usr "," co ",") datafile)
(close datafile)
(command "time" "r" "")
(command "end" "y"))))
```

Redefining AutoCAD's END Command for USER.LSP

If you want to record the activities in a drawing, and force them to happen, you must redefine the AutoCAD END command, as follows:

Prompt: `Command:`
Type: **UNDEFINE**

Prompt: `Command name:`
Type: **END**

Then name your USER.LSP routine `C:END` at the `(defun` location. Additionally, you have to change the last line of USER.LSP to read

`(command ".end" "y"))))`

adding the period (.) before the END command.

You can make this part of the `s::startup` section of your ACAD LISP file if you are using AutoCAD Release 10, or you can create a script file that starts your drawings and executes the UNDEFINE command as shown, then loads your END.LSP routine.

Sample Reports

Here are some examples of the reports you will get when you use a form of the USER.LSP routine and the dBASE programs listed in this appendix.

Time/Task Report

```
Time/Task Report                           Craig Sharp Architects
                                                       03/06/89
Job : 89002                                            09:30:05
-----------------------------------------------------------------
   Date      Drawing     Rev    Task    Time         User
 --------   --------     ---   -----   -----   --------------------
 01/20/89    02A1_1             PD     06:40   C. Sharp
 02/20/89    02A1_2             PD     05:30   C. Sharp
```

Time/Task Report continues

Time/Task Report continued

```
02/21/89      02A2_1            PD      08:15     C. Sharp
03/01/89      02A1_1            PD      01:35     C. Sharp
03/01/89      02A1_2            PD      01:20     C. Sharp
03/01/89      02A2_1            PD      00:30     C. Sharp


Time/Task Report                       Craig Sharp Architects
                                                     03/06/89
Job : 89002                                          09:30:05
-----------------------------------------------------------------
                  Job Summary
=========================================
  Task                        Total Time
  ----                        ----------
  PD                             23:50

  Drawing No.                 Total Time
  -----------                 ----------
  02A1_1                          8:15
  02A1_2                          6:50
  02A2_1                          8:45

  User                        Total Time
  --------------------------  ----------
  C. Sharp                       23:50

  Job total to date              23:50
```

Job History Report

```
Job History Report                     Craig Sharp Architects
                                                     03/06/89
Job : 89002                                          09:30:05
-----------------------------------------------------------------
  Date     Drawing    Rev   Task   Time      User
  ----     -------    ---   ----   ----      ----
  01/20/89  02A1_1           PD    06:40    C. Sharp
            COMMENTS: First floor plan - preliminary
  02/20/89  02A1_2           PD    05:30    C. Sharp
            COMMENTS: Second floor plan - preliminary
  02/21/89  02A2_1           PD    08:15    C. Sharp
            COMMENTS: Preliminary elevations
```

```
03/01/89    02A1_1              PD    01:35    C. Sharp
            COMMENTS: Adjusted upon client review #1
03/01/89    02A1_2              PD    01:20    C. Sharp
            COMMENTS: Adjusted upon client review #1
03/01/89    02A2_1              PD    00:30    C. Sharp
            COMMENTS; Adjusted upon client review #1
```

As you can see, these reports will become quite lengthy for large, long-lasting jobs. To keep them manageable, you need to break them down into phases of the work.

Multiple Script Program (SCR_ALL.EXE)

This program was provided by Mark Vodhanel, a member of the Autodesk Forum. Special thanks go to Mark for allowing us to publish it. Because it is written in C, you will have to find someone who has a C compiler (if you don't have one).

This program, called SCR_ALL.EXE, allows you to run a script file on multiple drawings in a directory. Because AutoCAD does not accept file name extensions, you normally would have to type the first part of the file name. This program reads all the drawings in a directory, drops the file extension, and then feeds the file name to the script file.

```c
/* For the Microsoft C Compiler, version 5.1 */
/* Compile using the 'CP:xxxx' linking*/
/* option to control memory usage */

#include "standard.inc"

char drive[1];
char dir[1];
char fname[9];
char ext[5];
```

SCR_ALL.EXE continues

SCR_ALL.EXE continued

```c
main(cmd_l, cmd_s)
int cmd_l;
char *cmd_s[];
{
struct find_t c_file;

        /* check for no command line parameter */
        if (cmd_l == 1)
                {
                cputs ("Correct Usage:   SCR_ALL <Script name>");
                exit (1);
                }

        /* get the first '.dwg' file */
        _dos_findfirst ("*.dwg", _A_NORMAL, &c_file);

        /* separate the file name components - ACAD will not /*
        /* allow the extension */
        _splitpath (c_file.name, drive, dir, fname, ext);

        /* have ACAD run the specified script /*
        /* file on this first file */
        spawnlp (P_WAIT, "acad", "spawnlp", fname, cmd_s[1], NULL);

        /* do the rest of the drawing files in the directory */
        while(_dos_findnext(&c_file) == 0)
                {
                _splitpath (c_file.name, drive, dir, fname, ext);
                spawnlp (P_WAIT, "acad", "spawnlp", fname, cmd_s[1], NULL);
                }

}
```

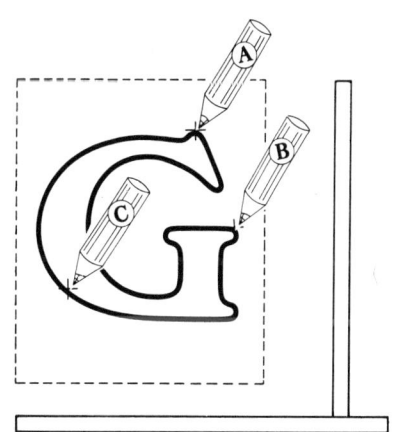

Sample Menu Macros

The menu entries in this appendix are examples of the way we handle our standard drawings. They relate, in particular, to details of glass storefronts and can be inserted as a detail or as an assembly in a larger overall drawing. When they are inserted as an assembly, we have to remove the detailed material indications and the notes, dimensions, etc. that are included in the detail drawing. This is one instance in which layer-naming standards not only can add tremendous power to automating your work but also can make your LISP routines run more efficiently.

These menus are not presented here in the order in which they are placed in our menu file. Rather, we present them in the order in which they are used in the selection process. We discuss each menu as if you are inserting the detail into one of your drawings. You may need to review Chapter 13, "AutoLISP Never Was Plain English," to understand some of the LISP statements used in these macros.

SILLS 3 is a menu of the types of window sill details we maintain as standards. We don't have a standard for every possibility (you probably don't either). Instead, we have standards of details we use frequently, and we create everything else from scratch. To keep this aspect of our work simple, we have a menu system set up for manipulating standard drawings only; we keep it out of the way during our other drawing practices.

```
**SILLS 3
[SILL TYP]

[-ASSMBL-]
[STOREFRT]^C^C$S=ASMSTFSL
[WOOD CSM]^C^C$S=ASMWDCSL
[WOOD DH  ]^C^C$S=ASMWDHSL
[ALUM AWN]^C^C$S=ASMALASL
[ALUM SLD]^C^C$S=ASMALSSL
[ALUM DH  ]^C^C$S=ASMALHSL

[-STD-DT-]
[STOREFRT]^C^C$S=STDSTFSL
[WOOD CSM]^C^C$S=STDWDCSL
[WOOD DH  ]^C^C$S=STDWDHSL
[ALUM AWN]^C^C$S=STDALASL
[ALUM SLD]^C^C$S=STDALSSL
[ALUM DH  ]^C^C$S=STDALHSL

[ CANCEL  ]^C^C$S=
```

As you can see, this is a submenu called SILLS. From this submenu, we can select which type of sill we want to use. In this example, we are interested in the storefront sills. We are inserting the standard drawing (refer to Chapter 9, fig. 9.1).

The SILLS menu offers two options. The first is for the purpose of using our standard drawing as part of an assembly. The second is to use the drawing as a standard detail. We can insert this drawing into a variety of scale drawings and add notes later. Since the scale is almost always smaller than the scale at which we create our details, we have to remove the notes, dimensions, and material indications so that the drawing looks like more than an ink blob on the sheet amidst properly prepared line work.

It is still a bonus to be able to use the detail drawing for all occasions. We do that by manipulating our layer standards and by using a LISP routine.

The following menu appears after we select [STOREFRT] from the SILLS submenu. The command line following the bracketed menu selection includes two ^Cs to make sure we can cancel out of anything, including a dimension command, and then switches us to the ASMSTFSL sub-submenu, which is the assembly storefront sill menu. The [CANCEL] selection returns us to the previous menu by using the menu selection $S= with no menu called.

```
**ASMSTFSL 3
[STOREFRT]
[ASSMBLY ]
[ SILLS   ]
```

```
[STRFNT 4]^C^CLAYER S 0810 (setq x "081021") +
((chkload "/acad/lisp/asmins")(asmins x))
[STRFNT 6]^C^CLAYER S 0810 (setq x "081022") +
((chkload "/acad/lisp/asmins")(asmins x))

[ST INT 4]^C^CLAYER S 0810 (setq x "081031") +
((chkload "/acad/lisp/asmins")(asmins x))
[ST INT 6]^C^CLAYER S 0810 (setq x "081032") +
((chkload "/acad/lisp/asmins")(asmins x))

[ST UPR 6]^C^CLAYER S 0810;; (setq x "081041") +
((chkload "/acad/lisp/asmins")(asmins x))
[ST UPR 8]^C^CLAYER S 0810 (setq x "081042") +
((chkload "/acad/lisp/asmins")(asmins x))

[SILL MNU]^C^C$S=SILLS

[  HELP  ]^C^CVSLIDE SILLHELP(STFRNT)

[ CANCEL ]^C^C$S=
```

If you select [STRFNT 4], the menu macro sets the layer to *0810*, the layer our layering standard uses for doors and windows. Then it binds the variable *x* to the name of the standard block, in this case *081031*. (The block-naming standard used the insertion layer as the first portion of its name. We can use that number to set the insertion layer from a LISP routine (by capturing the first four numbers), we can sort the standard blocks by our standard layering divisions, and we can sort the drawings by number from lowest to highest.) The macro then uses a LISP routine we wrote to check whether a LISP routine we are about to use has been loaded. The checking routine looks like this:

```
(defun chkload (fx)
  (cond ((null (eval (read fx))) (prompt "\nLoading ")(princ fx)
        (load fx)))
  (setq fx nil))
```

This routine simply checks whether a LISP routine's name evaluates to null. If it does, the routine loads the desired LISP routine; if it doesn't, there is no need to load the routine twice.

The next statement, (asmins), is a LISP routine that inserts our standard drawings and removes the unwanted information so that the drawing can be used in an assembly. This routine relies heavily on our layering standards and does not work without them. It looks like this:

```
(defun asmins (stdblk)
  (setvar "cmdecho" Ø)
  (setvar "highlight" Ø)
  (initget 1 "Y y N n")
  (setq yn (strcase (getkword "\nHave you previously inserted
    this assembly? <Y or N>: ")))
  (if (equal yn "N")
  (progn
  (setq e (entlast))
  (prompt "\nSelect temporary insertion point: ")
  (command "insert" stdblk pause 1 1 Ø "" "")
  (setq eb (entlast))
  (command "explode" eb)
  (setq asm (ssadd))
  (setq asme (ssadd))
  (prompt "\nGathering items to be removed...")
  (while (setq e (entnext e))
    (setq scod (substr (cdr (assoc 8 (entget e))) 4))
    (if (or (equal scod "Ø") (equal scod "6")
      (equal scod "8") (equal scod "9"))
      (ssadd e asme)(ssadd e asm)))
  (command "erase" asme "")
  (command "redraw")
  (prompt "\nSelect assembly insertion point: \n")
  (command "block" stdblk "y" pause asm "")
  (command "insert" stdblk pause 1 1 Ø))
  (command "insert" stdblk pause 1 1 Ø))
  (setvar "highlight" 1)
  (princ))
```

First, the user is asked whether he or she has previously inserted the standard block in the drawing. If the standard block has already been inserted, the new block is inserted as a response to a "false" reply from the **if** test. If the standard block has not been inserted, the routine selects the last entity in the drawing, inserts the standard drawing, and explodes it. Then two sets of entities are created. Those we want to keep are placed in a selection set called *asm*; those we want to erase are placed in the set *asme*.

This routine looks at all the entities that follow the entity that was the last one in the drawing prior to their insertion. It analyzes the layer they are on. You may recall that in our layering standard (explained in Chapter 7, "Advanced Management Techniques"), all entities on the layers XXX0 are attributes or blocks, all entities on the layers XXX6 are text entities, all entities on the layers XXX8 are symbols, and all entities on the layers XXX9 are miscellaneous. In this case, we put the material indications on the miscellaneous layers. Therefore, whether the entities were drawn on layer 0626 or 0976 does not matter. We know that they are text entities and will have to be removed. By using the function substr, we can look at the fourth number in the layer name associated with any entity and see whether we want to erase that entity. Notice that both the number of digits and the layer use are important as standards. This digit is bound to a set code, variable *scod*. We then evaluate whether the set code is part of the elimination set or the retention set.

Finally, the entities we kept are reassembled into a block; users are allowed to relocate the block as they choose, even selecting the block's insertion point before doing so. This routine works in a number of macros because we designed it to be used with a global variable *x*. We can assign a value to *x* in the menu selection that is the block name that we want to insert. Or we can use the routine with the syntax (asmins "081021").

Next, we'll look at the menu used for inserting standard details on our standard sheet layout. We prepare these details at a scale of either 3″=1′-0″ or 1 1/2″=1′-0″. In this case, the menus we are using are for the 3-inch scale details on a 24″ by 36″ drawing sheet.

```
**STDSTFSL 3
[STOREFRT]
[STD.DET.]
[ SILLS  ]

[STRFNT 4]^C^CLAYER S 0810;;(SETQ STDBLK "081020") $I=SS $I=*
[STRFNT 6]^C^CLAYER S 0810;;(SETQ STDBLK "081022") $I=SS $I=*

[ST INT 4]^C^CLAYER S 0810;;(SETQ STDBLK "081031") $I=SS $I=*
[ST INT 6]^C^CLAYER S 0810;;(SETQ STDBLK "081032") $I=SS $I=*

[ST UPR 6]^C^CLAYER S 0810;;(SETQ STDBLK "081041") $I=SS $I=*
[ST UPR 8]^C^CLAYER S 0810;;(SETQ STDBLK "081042") $I=SS $I=*

[SILL MNU]^C^C$S=SILLS

[  HELP  ]^C^CVSLIDE SILLHELP(STFRNT)


[ CANCEL ]^C^C$S=
```

This menu sets the layer for insertion of the standard drawing, names the standard drawing, and displays an icon menu. The icon displayed is our standard sheet layout (refer to fig. 9.2). If you work with a variety of sheet sizes on a regular basis, you will have to create menus like this for each sheet size.

The icon menu that is accessed by the macro statements $I=SS $I=* follows:

```
***icon
**ss
[Select Drawing Location]
[ss(ss7)](setq dno 7 PT "2.9,60.5") +
(setq sno (strcase (strcat (substr (getvar "dwgname") 4 2) "." +
(substr (getvar "dwgname") 7)))) +
(command "insert" stdblk pt "1" "1" "0" dno sno)
[ss(ss8)](setq dno 8 PT "2.9,31.08") +
(setq sno (strcase (strcat (substr (getvar "dwgname") 4 2) "." +
(substr (getvar "dwgname") 7)))) +
(command "insert" stdblk pt "1" "1" "0" dno sno)
[ss(ss9)](setq dno 9 PT "2.9,1.7") +
(setq sno (strcase (strcat (substr (getvar "dwgname") 4 2) "." +
(substr (getvar "dwgname") 7)))) +
(command "insert" stdblk pt "1" "1" "0" dno sno)
[ss(ss4)](setq dno 4 PT "45.34,60.5") +
(setq sno (strcase (strcat (substr (getvar "dwgname") 4 2) "." +
(substr (getvar "dwgname") 7)))) +
(command "insert" stdblk pt "1" "1" "0" dno sno)
[ss(ss5)](setq dno 5 PT "45.34,31.08") +
(setq sno (strcase (strcat (substr (getvar "dwgname") 4 2) "." +
(substr (getvar "dwgname") 7)))) +
(command "insert" stdblk pt "1" "1" "0" dno sno)
[ss(ss6)](setq dno 6 PT "45.34,1.7") +
(setq sno (strcase (strcat (substr (getvar "dwgname") 4 2) "." +
(substr (getvar "dwgname") 7)))) +
(command "insert" stdblk pt "1" "1" "0" dno sno)
[ss(ss1)](setq dno 1 PT "87.76,60.5") +
(setq sno (strcase (strcat (substr (getvar "dwgname") 4 2) "." +
(substr (getvar "dwgname") 7)))) +
(command "insert" stdblk pt "1" "1" "0" dno sno)
[ss(ss2)](setq dno 2 PT "87.76,31.08") +
(setq sno (strcase (strcat (substr (getvar "dwgname") 4 2) "." +
(substr (getvar "dwgname") 7)))) +
(command "insert" stdblk pt "1" "1" "0" dno sno)
[ss(ss3)](setq dno 3 PT "87.76,1.7") +
(setq sno (strcase (strcat (substr (getvar "dwgname") 4 2) "." +
(substr (getvar "dwgname") 7)))) +
(command "insert" stdblk pt "1" "1" "0" dno sno)
```

We will describe one selection of this icon menu in detail, but first we want to make sure that you understand the order of things in this menu. Most people number things from left to right and then from top to bottom; AutoCAD numbers the icons in an icon slide from top to bottom and then from left to right.

Furthermore, we use a drawing standard that starts the detail numbers from the uppermost right corner and numbers them from top to bottom and right to left. We do this so that the left side of a sheet is filled last, as a convenience to the builders who are constantly referring to our plans. We would never be able to keep this organized without the menus we use: we have numbered the icon slides to correspond with the detail number placement in the drawing. AutoCAD, however, still requires that we start from the upper left and number from top to bottom first. That is why things may look a little confusing at first.

In the menu, a LISP macro binds the variable *dno* to the drawing number that will be used as an attribute in the detail drawing title. Next, the macro sets the variable *PT* to a predetermined location in the drawing. As we have already mentioned, this is based on a 3-inch scale and a 24″ by 36″ sheet. The next variable, *sno*, is the sheet number that will be used in the detail title. Because we have a sheet-numbering standard, we can extract predictable results from the AutoCAD variable *dwgname*. We have to do a little juggling to overcome the fact that DOS does not allow a period in the file name—we have to take apart the drawing-name string. In this case, Auto-CAD stores this string as `001A8_1` (from which we want to obtain only the string `A8.1`). We know from our standard that we will always want to start with the fourth character of the string and obtain two characters, substitute a period, and obtain the balance of the characters in the string, starting with character number seven. This explains the numbers you see included in the `substr` functions. Finally, the standard drawing is inserted at the location determined by *PT*, with a scale factor of 1, and a rotation angle of 0. The variables *dno* and *sno* are used to reply to the attribute prompts that occur when the block is inserted. The automation of the insertion point, the detail number, and the sheet number relies on our drawing standards.

We would like to direct your attention to another important technique we use in our standards menus. Notice the [HELP] line in the screen menus. This displays a slide that provides information about the standard drawing the user is about to access with the menu. We use Help slides in two areas: 1) to steer new users through a firm's set of office standards and 2) to explain occasionally used techniques or drawings.

Also, our menus take advantage of drawings we have prepared for a project prior to the current work. Even though these drawings may be used infrequently, they can be stored on a network file server or large hard disk for retrieval. An accompanying Help slide ensures their utility long after they were created. With a little help from AutoLISP, directories of drawings and slides can be read and placed on the screen. We'll leave that up to our next book or your own research and development, however, because those AutoLISP commands are extremely advanced and hardware dependent.

At this point, you may want to review figures 9.1 and 9.2 again.

We described these macros to show you the importance and the dynamics of drawing standards. You may not need the complexity of this example, but you should consider these aspects of your standards as you develop them.

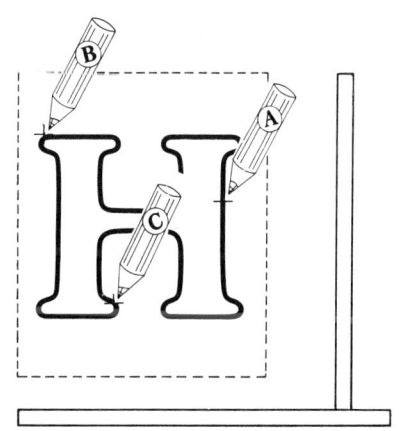

Routines for Automated Drawing

The routines in this appendix are related to Chapter 10, "Look, Ma—No Hands!" Use them to automate your drawing.

A LISP Routine To Combine Drawings for Plot (COMBPLOT.LSP)

This routine was written so that the order in which the attributes of the block INSBLK were created didn't matter. We know that each block has two attributes: the insertion point and the drawing name to insert. You can use this routine to insert a consultant's layers over a base drawing, or to insert quadrants or halves of drawings, so that they become manageable in size. Here is the routine in its entirety:

```
(defun c:combplot (/ ss1 e ent ent2 anm anm2 dnm ipt)
(setq ss1 (ssget "X" (list (cons 0 "INSERT")(cons 2 "INSBLK"))))
(if (not (equal ss1 nil))
 (progn
 (setq ndx 0)
```

Routine continues

Routine continued

```
(repeat (sslength ss1)
 (setq e (ssname ss1 ndx))
 (setq ent (entnext e))
 (setq ent2 (entnext ent))
 (setq anm (cdr (assoc 2 (entget ent))))
 (setq anm2 (cdr (assoc 2 (entget ent2))))
  (if (equal anm "DNAME")(setq dnm (cdr (assoc 1 (entget ent))))
      (setq ipt (cdr (assoc 1 (entget ent)))))
  (if (equal anm2 "DNAME")(setq dnm (cdr (assoc 1 (entget ent2))))
      (setq ipt (cdr (assoc 1 (entget ent2)))))
(command "insert" dnm ipt "" "" "")
(setq ndx (1+ ndx)))
    (prompt "\nNo INSBLK's were found in this drawing...")
  )(princ))
```

Here is a listed discussion of COMBPLOT. These two lines:

```
(defun c:combplot (/ ss1 ndx e ent ent2 anm anm2 dnm ipt)
(setq ss1 (ssget "X" (list (cons 0 "INSERT")(cons 2 "INSBLK"))))
```

set up the function `combplot` as a function that can be executed from the command prompt by using `c:` and then binding to the variable *ss1* all of the blocks in the drawing that are named *INSBLK*. This is accomplished by using the function `ssget` with a filter. The "use filter" flag is the `"X"` designation following `ssget`. The filter is *cons*tructed with a `list` that will look like ((0 . "INSERT")(2 . "INSBLK")) when the `list` function is completed. This list, which is a portion of the description of the INSBLK in the drawing, is found as a "match" by `ssget`.

This group of functions binds the variable *ndx* to 0:

```
(setq ndx (1- (sslength ss1)))
(if (not (equal ss1 nil))
(progn
(setq ndx 0)
(repeat (sslength ss1)
```

This happens because the first entity in a selection set is the "0" entity. We happen to know that this length is two, in this case, so we could have set this up as a fixed quantity. We wanted to use this to help illustrate certain LISP techniques, however, so we made LISP determine the length without our assistance. The `if` statement makes sure that we found a selection set by saying to LISP "If *ss1* is not nil, then go ahead with the following, and if it is nil, skip the first part and do the second part (display an error message)." Next, the `repeat` function will loop through the statements that are included within its parentheses as many times as the length of the selection set is.

These three statements:

```
(setq e (ssname ss1 ndx))
(setq ent (entnext e))
(setq ent2 (entnext ent))
```

find the entity in the selection set that corresponds in its location in the set to the value of ndx. The next two statements find the two entities in the database that follow immediately after the entity we just retrieved from the selection set. In this case, we retrieved only blocks in the selection set. The entities that follow the blocks in the database are the attributes we are looking for, so we bind them to ent and ent2.

The next two statements:

```
(setq anm (cdr (assoc 2 (entget ent))))
(setq anm2 (cdr (assoc 2 (entget ent2))))
```

bind the string associated with the group code 2 of the attributes to anm and anm2, respectively. Entget retrieves the list that describes each entity whose name is bound to ent and ent2. Assoc 2 retrieves the list that is the dotted pair of the group code 2 in the entity's list. Cdr retrieves the last part of the dotted pair, in this case a string that is the attribute tag in INSBLK.

These two if statements:

```
(if (equal anm "DNAME")(setq dnm (cdr (assoc 1 (entget ent))))
    (setq ipt (cdr (assoc 1 (entget ent))))))
(if (equal anm2 "DNAME")(setq dnm (cdr (assoc 1 (entget ent2))))
    (setq ipt (cdr (assoc 1 (entget ent2))))))
```

say to LISP "If the name of the attribute tag is DNAME, then set the variable *dnm* to the value of the second part of the dotted pair that is the association group 1 in the entity list. If it isn't, then set the variable *ipt* to the second half of the dotted pair that is the association group 1 in the entity's list." Group 1 codes for attributes are their attribute value. These two if statements make it possible for the attributes to be placed in the block INSBLK in any order. Since there are only two of them, we can assume that one or the other has the information we are looking for and let the if statement sort out which is which.

The statements:

```
    (command "insert" dnm ipt "" "" "")
(setq ndx (1+ ndx))))
```

conclude the repeat statement. The first one inserts the drawing depicted by INSBLK. The second one increments the *ndx* variable by 1, so that we will move on to the next entity in the set. Remember that the use of ""s in the LISP statement has the same effect as pressing the Enter key.

This is the other half of the first `if` statement:

```
(prompt "\nNo INSBLKs were found in this drawing...")
     )(princ))
```

If no selection set was found, the error message is displayed by `prompt`. Finally, `princ` exits the routine quietly.

The Automated Widget Drawing (WIDGET.SCR)

You should type in this script file exactly as you see it, including the blank lines. The script ends with a simple LISP routine that saves a series of user inputs and then, using those inputs, executes AutoCAD commands. You can use this technique to develop simple parametric LISP routines to do anything that is repeated often in a drawing, or as a drawing in its entirety. Script files are easy to write but require a complete knowledge of AutoCAD commands. In fact, script files will let you know just how much you don't know about AutoCAD because you have to account for every keystroke of the command input. The blank lines are used to add returns to commands that must end with an explicit return. Here is the WIDGET.SCR file:

```
LAYER S HEAVY

LINE 48,72 48,120 120,120 120,72 C
LINE 168,0 168,48 228,48 228,0 C
LINE 168,36 228,36

LINE 168,24 228,24

LINE 198,24 198,36

LINE 68.675,91.125 82.25,81.5

LINE 72,102 96,102

LINE 85.75,81.5 99.375,91.25
```

```
LAYER S MEDIUM

LINE 42,60 42,66 126,66 126,60 C
CIRCLE 72,96 6
CIRCLE 96,96 6
CIRCLE 84,84 3
LINE 85,86.875 85,90

LINE 83,86.875 83,90

ARC 85,90 E 83,90 R 1
LAYER S LIGHT

LINE 110,66 110,72

LINE 54,66 54,72

LINE 120,84 168,84

LINE 120,87 168,87

ARC 168,84 E 168,87 R 1.5
LINE 48,108 24,108 48,84

LINE 122,88 164,88

LINE 122,90 164,90

LINE 122,89 164,89

LAYER S TEXT

TEXT 22.625,121.5 9 19D47 '36" n
TEXT 25,117.675 9 323D45 '10" t
TEXT 39.25,119.375 9 19D47 '36" z
TEXT 27.75,109.675 9 110D34 '29" x
TEXT 33.675,110 9 0 r
TEXT 42,47 6 0 PARAMETRIC WIDGET
LINE 42,45 140,45

TEXT 170,39.5 3 0 INTERNATIONAL CORP
TEXT 170,32 3 0 DATE
TEXT 200,32 3 0 SHEET
```

Code continues

Code continued

```
TEXT 170,19 3 0 CUSTOMER
TEXT 9.375,71.5 3 0 VARIABLE
TEXT 130,99.875 3 0 DRAWING
(defun gtxt ()
(setq bano (getstring "\nEnter Base No.: "))
(setq bano (strcat "BASE NO. " bano))
(setq cno (getstring "\nEnter Conveyor No.: "))
(setq cno (strcat "CONVEYOR NO. " cno))
(setq beno (getstring "\nEnter Belt No: "))
(setq beno (strcat "BELT NO. " beno))
(setq ipno (getstring "\nEnter Idler Pulley No: "))
(setq ipno (strcat "IDLER PULLEY NO. " ipno))
(setq gano (getstring "\nEnter Gear Assembly No.: "))
(setq gano (strcat "GEAR ASSEMBLY NO. " gano))
(setq hno (getstring "Enter Hopper No.: "))
(setq hno (strcat "HOPPER NO. " hno))
(setq date (getstring "Enter the date: "))
(setq sheet (getstring "Enter the Sheet No.: "))
(setq cust (getstring "Enter the Customer's name: "))
(command "DIM1" "LEA" "87.75,85.75" "125.25,121.125"
   "127.875,121.125" "" ipno)
(command "DIM1" "LEA" "99.125,90.375"
   "123.125,79" "129.675,79" "" beno)
(command "DIM1" "LEA" "102.25,102.375"
   "121.25,134" "127.25,134" "" gano)
(command "DIM1" "LEA" "129.75,86"
   "127.5,97.375" "129.675,97.375" "" cno)
(command "DIM1" "LEA" "111.75,63.25"
   "117.75,61.375" "129.375,61.375" "" bano)
(command "DIM1" "LEA" "37.125,102.375"
   "3.675,68.875" "9,69" "" hno)
(command "TEXT" "172,27.5" 3 0 date)
(command "TEXT" "202,27.5" 3 0 sheet)
(command "TEXT" "172,12" 3 0 cust)
(princ))
(gtxt)
```

Note: The preceding lines that begin with (command *and end with* xxno) *should be typed on one line in the script file; they are shown here on two lines in order to fit the code within the margins of the book.*

A Parametric Schedule Routine (SCHED.LSP)

This routine should be combined with the text-importing routine (included with your Release 10 disks) or with the one we include later in this appendix to create drawing schedules. Here is SCHED.LSP:

```
(defun sched (/ row rsp col pt scf row1 bor1 csp tp2 pt3 pt4
              pt 5 pt6 pt7 pt8 nu)
(setq row
    (getint "\nEnter the number of rows that you want: "))
(setq rsp
    (getdist "\Enter the spacing between the rows in inches: "))
(setq col
    (getint "\nEnter the number of columns that you want: "))
(setq pt
  (getpoint "\nSelect the upper
    left corner of the schedule location: "))
(setq scf (getvar "ltscale"))
(setq rsp (* scf rsp))
(setq row1 (* rsp row))
(setq bor1 (+ row1 (* scf 0.5)))
(setq pt2 (polar pt (* 1.5 pi) row1))
(command "line" pt pt2 "")
(setq nu (- col (1- col)))
(repeat col
(prompt "Enter the spacing for column ")
    (princ nu)(prompt " in inches: ")
(setq csp (* scf (getdist)))
(setq pt2 (polar pt2 (* 2.0 pi) csp))
(setq pt3 (polar pt2 (* 0.5 pi) row1))
(command "line" pt2 pt3 "")
(setq nu (1+ nu)))
(setq pt4 (polar pt (* 1.5 pi) row1))
(command "line" pt pt3 "")
(command "array" "l" "" "r" (1+ row) "1" (- rsp))
(setq pt5 (polar pt (* 0.5 pi) (* scf 0.0625)))
(setq pt6 (polar pt (* 0.5 pi) (- bor1 row1)))
(setq pt7 (polar pt3 (* 0.5 pi) (* scf 0.0625)))
(setq pt8 (polar pt3 (* 0.5 pi) (- bor1 row1)))
(command "line" pt5 pt6 pt8 pt7 pt5 "")
(setq pt4 (polar pt4 (* 1.25 pi) (* scf  0.0625)))
```

Code continues

Code continued

```
(setq pt (polar pt4 (* 0.5 pi) (+ borl (* scf 0.125))))
(setq pt2 (polar pt2 (* 1.75 pi) (* scf 0.0625)))
(setq pt3 (polar pt2 (* 0.5 pi) (+ borl (* scf 0.125))))
(command "line" pt pt4 pt2 pt3 pt "")
(princ))
```

Here is the detailed discussion of SCHED.LSP. If you need help with some of the LISP conventions, refer to Chapter 13.

```
(defun sched (/ off row rsp col pt scf row1 borl csp tp2 pt3 pt4
              pt 5 pt6 pt7 pt8 nu)
  (setq row
    (getint "\nEnter the number of rows that you want: "))
  (setq rsp
    (getdist "\Enter the spacing between the rows in inches: "))
  (setq col
    (getint "\nEnter the number of columns that you want: "))
  (setq pt
   (getpoint "\nSelect the upper left
      corner of the schedule location: "))
```

These lines set up the function definition and represent the parametric input that is required prior to the actual execution of the routine. The user is prompted for the number of rows, the row spacing, the number of columns, and the starting point of the schedule drawing. Each of these is bound to a variable using getint when we want an integer, and getdist when we want a real number that AutoLISP can use for calculating new points. Getpoint allows the user to pick a point on the screen. To make this program more user friendly, you could add prompts that check to see whether the input is correct. Examples of these prompts can be found in the LISP routines included in Appendix D, CONVLYR.LSP and LYRTBL.LSP. We don't use them because it is less efficient to constantly answer prompts than it is to erase an occasional mistake and redo it. If you are going to create large schedules, however, some error recovery is in order.

```
(setq scf (getvar "ltscale"))
(setq rsp (* scf rsp))
(setq row1 (* rsp row))
(setq borl (+ row1 (* scf 0.5)))
```

These statements set the scale factor of the routine to the value of the AutoCAD variable LTSCALE, and then adjust the row spacing (rsp), the row length (rowl), and the border length (borl) to the scale factor. This is necessary because we are going to use the actual spacing rather than the scaled spacing of the lines. (In other words, 1/4" instead of 12" @ 1/4"=1'.) Note that we are setting the border to be a distance of 1/2 the scale factor beyond the row length. This will always provide us with a title area at the top of the schedule that is 1/2" high.

```
(setq pt2 (polar pt (* 1.5 pi) rowl))
(command "line" pt pt2 "")
```

These two functions establish a new point, pt2, which is the distance of the row length, rowl from the starting point pt at an angle of 270 degrees from the starting point using the polar function. A line is then drawn from the starting point to the new point using the command function. Notice that the line command must be terminated with a return ("").

```
(setq nu 1)
(repeat col
(prompt "Enter the spacing for column ")
  (princ nu)(prompt " in inches: ")
(setq csp (* scf (getdist)))
```

Next, the variable *nu* is bound to the first column, or 1. Then, a repeat loop is started that will repeat equal to the number of columns there will be in the schedule. The user is then prompted for the spacing of the first column and that spacing is bound to csp. Again, we adjust the column spacing to the scale factor.

```
(setq pt2 (polar pt2 0 csp))
(setq pt3 (polar pt2 (* 0.5 pi) rowl))
(command "line" pt2 pt3 "")
(setq nu (1+ nu)))
```

The first location of pt2 is moved at a distance of the column spacing and zero degrees to a new location using polar. A new point, pt3 is established at 90 degrees from the adjusted pt2 location and a distance of the row length, and a line is drawn from pt2 to pt3. The value of nu is incremented by 1, and the repeat loop starts again, until the spacing for all of the columns has been entered and lines have been drawn for each column.

```
(setq pt4 (polar pt (* 1.5 pi) rowl))
(command "line" pt pt3 "")
(command "array" "l" "" "r" (1+ row) "1" (- rsp))
```

These functions store pt4, a point we will use later, as the bottom left corner of the schedule, by using polar and setting the new point a distance equal to the row length and at an angle of 270 degrees from pt. Next, a line is drawn from point pt to point pt3. Then the line that was just drawn is arrayed as a rectangular array ("r") with rows of 1 greater than the required number of rows (a standard array practice) and 1 column at a distance of a negative row spacing distance, since we're working from top to bottom.

```
(setq pt5 (polar pt (* 0.5 pi) (* scf 0.0625)))
(setq pt6 (polar pt (* 0.5 pi) (- borl rowl)))
(setq pt7 (polar pt3 (* 0 (setq pt8 (polar pt3 (* 0.5 pi) (- borl rowl)))
(command "line" pt5 pt6 pt8 pt7 pt5 "")
(setq pt4 (polar pt4 (* 1.25 pi) (* scf  0.0625)))
(setq pt (polar pt4 (* 0.5 pi) (+ borl (* scf 0.125))))
(setq pt2 (polar pt2 (* 1.75 pi) (* scf 0.0625)))
(setq pt3 (polar pt2 (* 0.5 pi) (+ borl (* scf 0.125))))
(command "line" pt pt4 pt2 pt3 pt "")
(princ))
```

These functions draw the title box (a set of lines that are continual around the title area) and the border (a set of lines that are continual around the title area and rows and columns combined). The border is 1/16" (0.0625) outside the rows and columns. We would like to remind you that when creating these kinds of parametric routines, you must place a leading *0* in front of any decimal point. This was a constant source of consternation to us when we first started writing LISP routines.

A Lotus 1-2-3-generated Critical Path

The advantage of using Lotus 1-2-3 for this type of task is that the constantly changing data is easily manipulated by Lotus. Lotus is to numerical arrays as AutoCAD is to drafting. Rather than doing the calculations by hand and editing the last critical path you drew by hand, why not use Lotus 1-2-3 to make the changes and AutoLISP to automatically create the drawing? Figure H.1 shows a sample of the 1-2-3 output.

Figure H.1 shows the sheet layout we used to create a project schedule and estimated man hour/task outline for the project. The format of the layout isn't important, but the output from Lotus 1-2-3 is. The data file must have columns that correspond to the LISP routine. You can change the output format, but you must also modify the routine. Figure H.2 shows what the data file looks like.

Appendix H: Routines for Automated Drawing

	A	B	C	D	E	F	G	H	I	J	K	L	M	N	O	P	Q
1	DWG NO	TASK OR DWG	PHASE	EST MAN HOURS	EST START DATE	REQ'D FINISH DATE	REQ'D MAN DAYS	PHASE	EST MAN HOURS	EST START DATE	REQ'D FINISH DATE	REQ'D MAN DAYS	PHASE	EST MAN HOURS	EST START DATE	REQ'D FINISH DATE	REQ'D MAN DAYS
3		PRGM MTG	PD	3.00	02/02/89	02/02/89	0.38										
4		DESIGN	PD	60.00	02/04/89	02/18/89	7.50										
5	A1.1	SITE PLAN	PD	8.00	02/06/89	02/18/89	1.00						CD	4.00	03/03/89	03/24/89	0.50
6	A2.1	FLOOR PLAN	PD	6.00	02/08/89	02/18/89	2.00						CD	8.00	03/03/89	03/24/89	1.00
7	A3.1	ELEVATIONS	PD	16.00	02/15/89	02/18/89	2.00						CD	12.00	03/03/89	03/24/89	1.50
8		SKETCH	PD	16.00	02/19/89	02/19/89	0.38										
9		PD MTG	PD	3.00													
11		DESIGN DEVELOP															
12		RENDERING						DD	45.00	02/21/89	03/03/89	5.63	CD	12.00	03/03/89	03/24/89	1.50
13	A3.2	BLDG SECTIONS						DD	40.00	02/25/89	03/01/89	5.00	CD	24.00	03/03/89	03/24/89	3.00
14	A4.1	WALL SECTIONS						DD	32.00	02/24/89	03/03/89	4.00	CD	12.00	03/03/89	03/24/89	1.50
15	A7.1	SCHEDULES						DD	12.00	02/26/89	03/03/89	1.50	CD	12.00	03/03/89	03/24/89	1.50
16	A7.2	DETAILS											CD	16.00	03/08/89	03/24/89	2.00
17	A7.3	DETAILS											CD	18.00	03/08/89	03/24/89	2.25
18	A8.1	INTERIOR ELEV						DD	3.00	03/10/89	03/03/89	0.38	CD	2.00	03/03/89	03/24/89	2.25
19	A9.1	REFL CLG PLAN						DD	18.00	02/23/89	03/03/89	1.25	CD	8.00	03/03/89	03/24/89	8.50
20	S2.1	FND PLAN						DD	18.00	02/23/89	03/03/89	1.25	CD	6.00	03/03/89	03/24/89	0.75
21	S2.2	FLOOR FRAMING											CD	9.00	03/03/89	03/24/89	1.13
22	S2.3	ROOF FRAMING											CD	18.00	03/06/89	03/24/89	2.25
23	S4.1	WALL SECTIONS											CD	18.00	03/08/89	03/24/89	0.75
24	S7.1	SCHEDULES						DD	15.00			1.88	CD	18.00	03/08/89	03/24/89	2.25
25	S7.2	DETAILS											CD	6.00	03/06/89	03/24/89	0.75
26	M7.1	MECH PLAN											CD	9.00	03/06/89	03/24/89	1.13
27	M7.2	SCHEDULES						DD	6.00	02/23/89	03/03/89	0.75	CD	16.00	03/10/89	03/24/89	2.00
28	E2.1	DETAILS						DD	4.00	02/23/89	03/03/89	0.50	CD	4.00	03/03/89	03/24/89	0.50
29	E2.2	POWER PLAN											CD	8.00	03/03/89	03/24/89	1.00
30	E7.1	LIGHTING PLAN						DD	2.00	02/26/89	03/03/89	0.25	CD	8.00	03/03/89	03/24/89	1.00
31	P2.1	RISER DIAGRAM						DD	3.00	02/23/89	03/03/89	0.38	CD	3.00	03/03/89	03/24/89	0.38
32	P5.1	PLUMBING PLAN											CD	8.00	03/05/89	03/24/89	1.13
33	P7.1	TOILET PLANS						DD	10.00	02/23/89	03/03/89	1.25	CD	8.00	03/03/89	03/24/89	1.00
34		SCHEDULES						DD	3.00	03/01/89	03/03/89	0.38	CD	48.00	03/03/89	03/24/89	6.00
35		SPECIFICATIONS															
36		DD MTG											CD	90.00	03/08/89	03/24/89	11.25
37		CONTRACT DOCS											CD	6.00	03/03/89	03/24/89	0.75
38		CD MTGS															
39		TOTALS		112.00			14.00		242.00			30.25		395.00			53.38

	A	B	C	D	E	F	G	H	I	J
	DWG NO	TASK OR DWG	PD HRS	DD HRS	CD HRS	PD PHASE DURATION FROM START 02/02/89	DD PHASE DURATION FROM START 02/21/89	CD PHASE DURATION FROM START 03/03/89		
		PRGM MTG	3.00	0.00	0.00	0.00	0.00	0.00		
		DESIGN	60.00	4.00	0.00	2.00	19.00	0.00		
	A1.1	SITE PLAN	8.00	12.00	8.00	4.00	8.00	21.00		
	A2.1	FLOOR PLAN	6.00	28.00	8.00	4.00	21.00	21.00		
	A3.1	ELEVATIONS	16.00	0.00	12.00	6.00	22.00	0.00		
		SKETCH	16.00	0.00	0.00	13.00	0.00	0.00		
		PD MTG	3.00	0.00	0.00	17.00	0.00	0.00		

Fig. H.1.

Sample sheet layout.

Fig. H.2.
Sample data file.

Task								
PRGM MTG	3.00	0.00	0.00	0.00	0.00	0.00	0.00	0.00
DESIGN	60.00	4.00	0.00	0.00	0.00	0.00	0.00	0.00
A1.1 SITE PLAN	0.00	0.00	4.00	0.00	0.00	19.00	10.00	21.00
A2.1 FLOOR PLAN	6.00	12.00	8.00	2.00	14.00	21.00	8.00	21.00
A3.1 ELEVATIONS	16.00	28.00	12.00	4.00	12.00	22.00	7.00	21.00
SKETCH	16.00	0.00	0.00	6.00	10.00	0.00	0.00	0.00
PD MTG	3.00	0.00	0.00	13.00	3.00	0.00	0.00	0.00
DESIGN DEVELOP	0.00	45.00	0.00	17.00	0.00	0.00	10.00	0.00
RENDERING	0.00	40.00	0.00	0.00	0.00	19.00	4.00	0.00
A3.2 BLDG SECTIONS	0.00	32.00	12.00	0.00	0.00	23.00	0.00	21.00
A4.1 WALL SECTIONS	0.00	12.00	24.00	0.00	12.00	22.00	7.00	21.00
A7.1 SCHEDULES	0.00	0.00	12.00	0.00	12.00	24.00	5.00	21.00
A7.2 DETAILS	0.00	0.00	12.00	0.00	0.00	0.00	0.00	16.00
A7.3 DETAILS	0.00	0.00	16.00	0.00	0.00	0.00	0.00	34.00
A8.1 INTERIOR ELEV	0.00	0.00	18.00	0.00	0.00	0.00	0.00	36.00
A9.1 REFL CLG PLAN	0.00	3.00	2.00	0.00	0.00	24.00	4.00	29.00
S2.1 FND PLAN	0.00	3.00	4.00	0.00	0.00	24.00	2.00	29.00
S2.2 FLOOR FRAMING	0.00	10.00	6.00	0.00	0.00	21.00	5.00	29.00
S2.3 ROOF FRAMING	0.00	10.00	9.00	0.00	0.00	21.00	8.00	29.00
S4.1 WALL SECTIONS	0.00	0.00	18.00	0.00	0.00	0.00	8.00	32.00
S7.1 SCHEDULES	0.00	0.00	6.00	0.00	0.00	0.00	0.00	36.00
S7.2 DETAILS	0.00	0.00	18.00	0.00	0.00	0.00	0.00	34.00
M2.1 MECH PLAN	0.00	15.00	6.00	0.00	0.00	21.00	8.00	29.00
M7.1 SCHEDULES	0.00	0.00	9.00	0.00	0.00	0.00	0.00	32.00
M7.2 DETAILS	0.00	0.00	16.00	0.00	0.00	0.00	0.00	36.00
E2.1 POWER PLAN	0.00	6.00	4.00	0.00	0.00	21.00	8.00	29.00
E2.2 LIGHTING PLAN	0.00	4.00	8.00	0.00	0.00	21.00	8.00	29.00
E7.1 SCHEDULES	0.00	0.00	3.00	0.00	0.00	0.00	5.00	34.00
E7.2 RISER DIAGRAM	0.00	2.00	3.00	0.00	0.00	24.00	8.00	29.00
P2.1 PLUMBING PLAN	0.00	3.00	9.00	0.00	0.00	21.00	8.00	29.00
P5.1 TOILET PLANS	0.00	0.00	0.00	0.00	0.00	0.00	0.00	31.00
P7.1 SCHEDULES	0.00	0.00	8.00	0.00	0.00	0.00	0.00	34.00
SPECIFICATIONS	0.00	10.00	48.00	0.00	0.00	21.00	8.00	29.00
DD MTG	0.00	3.00	0.00	0.00	0.00	27.00	0.00	0.00
CONTRACT DOCS	0.00	0.00	90.00	0.00	0.00	0.00	0.00	29.00
CD MTGS	0.00	0.00	6.00	0.00	0.00	0.00	0.00	29.00

The data file in figure H.2 has the following field length format:

Drawing Number:	4
Task/Drawing name:	15
Preliminary Design hours:	8
Design Development hours:	9
Construction Document hours:	9
Days from start for Prelim Design:	9
Days from start for Design Devel.:	9
Days from start for Constr Docs.:	9
Task Duration for Prelim Design:	9
Task Duration for Design Develop:	9
Task Duration for Constr Docs:	9

You will notice, when reviewing the CPM.LSP routine that the use of substr in the file corresponds with these field lengths. Figure H.3 shows a chart of the preceding data prepared by CPM.LSP.

There are a few conditions for using the CPM.LSP routine. First, the drawing must be set up at full scale. Second, you must have the layers LIGHT, MEDIUM, and TEXT in the drawings. Finally, you must have created a block that represents a target for one day or for important milestones. The target should be no larger than 1/4" in any dimension. You can also add other information to the drawing if you choose, and alter the way the information is presented to suit your needs. Just be sure that you coordinate the data file and the LISP routine accordingly.

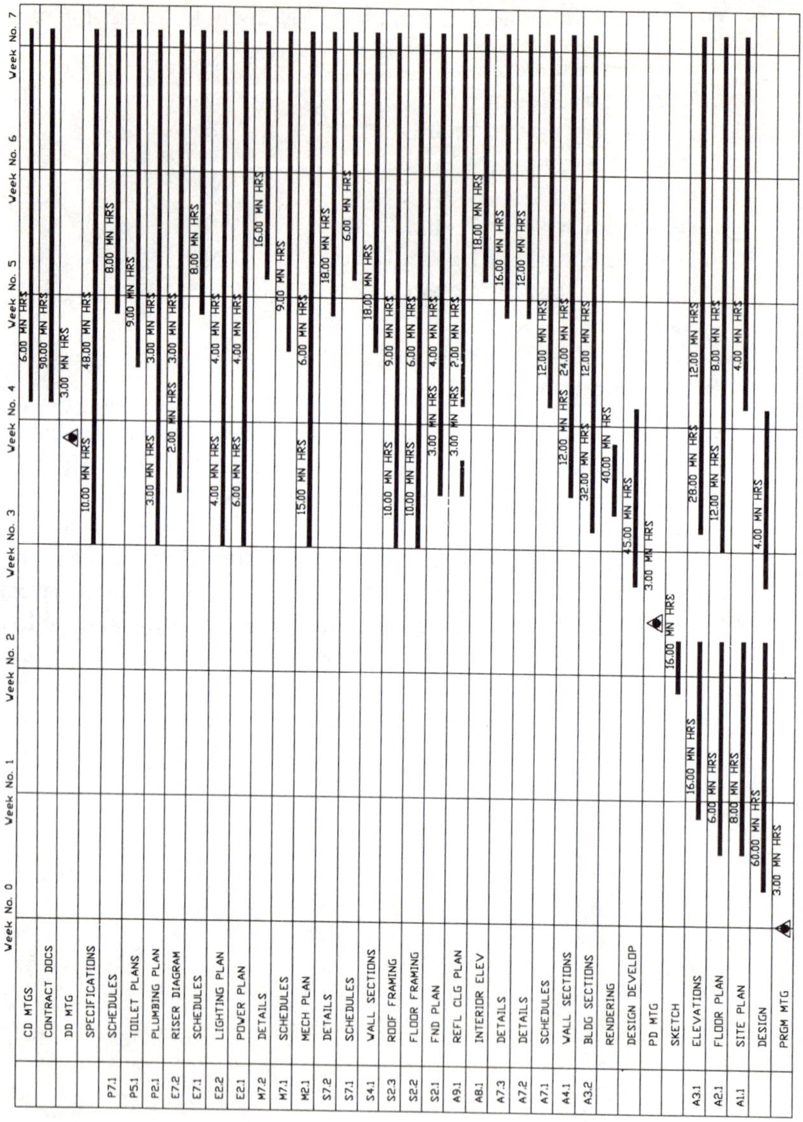

538 AutoCAD Advanced Techniques

Fig. H.3.

Sample CPM chart.

Appendix H: Routines for Automated Drawing

Here is CPM.LSP:

```lisp
(defun track (x y z)
    (setq lp 0)
    (if (not (equal (atof x) 0.00))
      (progn
        (setq pt1 (polar sp 0 (* 0.25 (atof y))))
        (if (not (equal (atof z) 0.00))
            (progn
            (setq pt2 (polar pt1 0 (* 0.25 (atof z))))
            (command "layer" "s" "medium" "")
            (command "pline" pt1 "w" 0.0625 "" pt2 "")
             (if (> (car pt2) lp)
                (setq lp (car pt2))))
              (progn
              (command "layer" "s" "medium" "")
              (command "insert" "target" pt1 "1" "1" "0")))
        (command "layer" "s" "text" "")
        (command "text" (polar pt1 (* 0.25 pi) 0.10) "0.10" ""
           (strcat x " MN HRS"))))
)

(defun chart (/ intst dfil yd dnm tsk pdhr ddhr cdhr
      pdfs pdur ddfs ddur cdfs    cdur sp pt1 pt2 ctr lp wkno wkc)
  (if (tblsearch "block" "TARGET")
   (progn
   (setvar "cmdecho" 0)
   (setvar "highlight" 0)
   (setq dfil (open "cpm.dta" "r"))
   (command "layer" "s" "medium" "")
   (setq yd 0.5)
   (setq ctr 0)
  (while (setq dlin (read-line dfil))
      (setq sp (list 0.5 yd))
      (setq dnm (substr dlin 1 4)
            tsk (substr dlin 5 15)
            pdhr (substr dlin 20 8)
            ddhr (substr dlin 28 9)
            cdhr (substr dlin 37 9)
            pdfs (substr dlin 46 9)
            pdur (substr dlin 55 9)
            ddfs (substr dlin 64 9)
            ddur (substr dlin 73 9)
            cdfs (substr dlin 82 9)
            cdur (substr dlin 91 9))
      (command "layer" "s" "text" "")
      (command "text" (polar sp (* 1.5 pi) 0.05) "0.10" "" dnm)
```

Listing continues

Listing continued

```
        (setq sp (list 1.25 yd))
        (command "text" (polar sp (* 1.5 pi) 0.05) "0.10" "" tsk)
        (setq sp (list 3.0 yd))
        (track pdhr pdfs pdur)
        (track ddhr ddfs ddur)
        (track cdhr cdfs cdur)
        (setq yd (+ yd 0.3125))
        (setq ctr (1+ ctr)))
    (setq dfil (close dfil))
    (command "layer" "s" "light" "")
    (command "line" (list 0.34375 0.375)
      (list (+ lp 0.34375) 0.375) "")
    (command "array" "l" "" "r" (1+ ctr) "1" 0.3125)
    (command "line" (list 0.34375 0.375)
      (polar (list 0.34375 0.375) (* 0.5 pi) (* ctr 0.3125)) "")
    (command "line" (list 1.0 0.375)
      (polar (list 1.0 0.375) (* 0.5 pi) (* ctr 0.3125)) "")
    (command "line" (list 3.0 0.375)
      (polar (list 3.0 0.375) (* 0.5 pi) (* ctr 0.3125)) "")
    (setq wkc (/ (- lp 3.0) 1.75))
    (command "array" "l" "" "r" "1" (1+ (fix wkc)) 1.75)
    (setq wkno 0)
    (command "layer" "s" "text" "")
    (repeat (1+ (fix wkc))
      (command "text" "c" (polar (list (+ 3.0 (* wkno 1.75)) 0.375)
        (* 0.5 pi) (+ (* ctr 0.3125) 0.0625)) "0.10" ""
          (strcat "Week No. " (itoa wkno)))
        (setq wkno (1+ wkno)))
    (command "layer" "s" "light" "")
    (command "line" (list (+ lp 0.34375) 0.375)
      (polar (list (+ lp 0.34375) 0.375) (* 0.5 pi) (* ctr 0.3125))
        ""))
(prompt "\nYou must insert block
    TARGET before starting this routine..."))
(setvar "highlight" 1)
(princ))
```

A LISP Routine for Importing Text

This routine is a really basic example of importing text into a drawing. There are more sophisticated routines on the Autodesk Forum, and there are commercially available programs that allow you a much greater degree of definition for parameters to do the importing. The routine follows:

```
(defun impasci (/ sty asfu pt ht lsp afil lin)
   (setvar "cmdecho" 0)
   (setvar "highlight" 0)
   (setq sty
    (getstring "\nEnter the text style that you want to use: ")
   (if (tblsearch "style" sty)
     (progn
      (graphscr)
      (setq asfi (getstring "\nEnter file name to import: "))
      (setq pt (getpoint "\nSelect text insertion point: "))
      (setq ht (getreal "\nEnter text height: "))
      (setq lsp (getreal "\nEnter the line to line spacing: "))
      (if (setq afil (open asfi) "r")
        (progn
         (while (setq lin (read-line afil))
           (command "text" "s" sty pt ht "0" lin)
           (setq pt (polar pt (* 1.5 pi) lsp)))
         (setq afil (close afil)))
        (progn
         (prompt "\nFile ")
         (princ asfi)
         (prompt " not found."))))
     (progn
      (prompt "\nThe style ")
      (princ sty)
      (prompt " was not found.")))
   (setvar "highlight" 1)
   (princ))
```

This very basic routine gets the job done, provided that you are reading an ASCII file from the current drawing directory. We included this one to show you how simple it can really be.

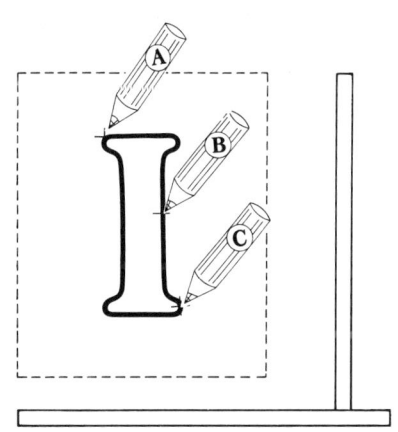

ACAD.DWG Settings

Listed in this appendix are the standard ACAD.DWG settings for stock, out-of-the-box AutoCAD Release 10. When the settings we use differ from the standard settings, we show our settings enclosed in brackets ([ ]).

Setting	Description
Aperture	10 pixels [4 pixels]
Attributes	Visibility controlled individually, entry of values during INSERT permitted (using prompts rather than dialogue boxes.) [We use the dialogue boxes, because we use default attributes.]
Axis	Off, spacing (0.0, 0.0)
Base	Insertion base point (0.0, 0.0, 0.0)
Blipmode	On [Off]
Chamfer	Distance 0.0
Color	Entity color "BYLAYER"
Coordinate display	Updated on point entry
DIM variables	DIMALT Off DIMALTD 2 DIMALTF 25.40 DIMAPOST (none) DIMASO On [Off – we don't like them]

Setting	Description	
	DIMASZ	0.18 [0.01]
	DIMBLK	(none)[ARROW or TICK]
	DIMBLK1	(none)
	DIMBLK2	(none)
	DIMCEN	0.09
	DIMDLE	0.00
	DIMDLI	0.38
	DIMEXE	0.18
	DIMEXO	0.0625
	DIMLFAC	1.00
	DIMLIM	Off
	DIMPOST	(none)
	DIMRND	0.00
	DIMSAH	Off
	DIMSCALE	1.00
	DIMSE1	Off [On]
	DIMSE2	Off
	DIMSHO	Off
	DIMSOXD	Off [On]
	DIMTAD	Off [On]
	DIMTIH	On [Off]
	DIMTIX	Off [On]
	DIMTM	0.00
	DIMTOH	On [Off]
	DIMTOFL	Off [On]
	DIMTOL	Off
	DIMTP	0.00
	DIMTSZ	0.00
	DIMTVP	0.00
	DIMTXT	0.18 [0.125]
	DIMZIN	0 [3]
DRAGMODE	AUTO	
ELEV	Elevation 0.0, thickness 0.0	
FILL	On [Off]	
FILLET	Radius 0.0	
FLATLAND	0	
GRID	Off, spacing (0.0,0.0)	
HANDLES	Off	

Appendix I: ACAD.DWG Settings

Setting	Description
HIGHLIGHTING	Enabled
ISOPLANE	Left
LAYER	Current/only layer is "0", on, with color 7 (white) and linetype "CONTINUOUS"
LIMITS	Off, drawing limits (0.0,0.0) to (12.0,9.0)
LINETYPE	Entity linetype "BYLAYER", only loaded linetype is "CONTINUOUS"
LTSCALE	1.0
MENU	"acad" [setup]
MIRROR	1 (Text mirrored like other entities) [0]
OBJECT SELECTION	Pick box size 3 pixels
ORTHO	Off
OSNAP	None
PLINE	Line-width 0.0
POINT	DISPLAY MODE 0, SIZE 0.00
QTEXT	Off
RENENAUTO	On [Off]
SKETCH	Record increment 0.10, producing lines
SNAP	Off, spacing (1.0,1.0) [6.0,6.0]
SNAP/GRID	Standard style, base point (0.0,0.0), rotation 0.0 degrees
SPLINE CURVES	Frame off, segments 8, spline type = cubic
STYLE	Only defined text style is "standard", using font file "txt", with variable height, width factor 1.0, horizontal orientation and no special modes. [HANDLETTERING STYLE TEXT]
SURFACES	6 tabulation in M and N directions, 6 segments for smoothing in U and V directions, smooth surface type = Bexier
TABLET	Off

Setting	Description
TEXT	Style "standard", height 0.20, rotation 0.0 degrees [HANDLETTERING STYLE, height 0, rotation 0.0]
TRACE	Width 0.05
UCS	Current UCS same as World, origin @ world (0,0,0), auto plan view off, coordinate system icon on (at origin)
UNITS (LINEAR)	Decimal, 4 decimal places [ARCHITECTURAL]
UNITS (ANGULAR)	Decimal degrees, 0 decimal places, angle 0 direction is to the right, angles increase counterclockwise [nnDnn'nn"]
VIEWING MODES	One active viewport, plan view, perspective off, target point (0,0,0), front and back clipping off, lens length 50mm, twist angle 0.0, fast zoom on, circle zoom percent 100 worldview 0 [zoom percent 2000]
ZOOM	To drawing limit

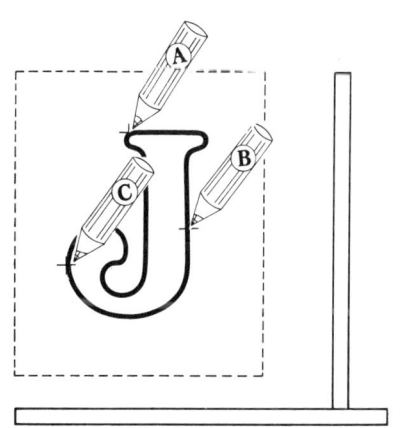

Common AutoCAD Errors (and What To Do About Them)

As any AutoCAD user knows, the road to productivity is fraught with errors. This may seem a sad commentary on the learning process, but it is nonetheless true that experience (good and bad) is the best teacher. In this appendix we have included a few common errors you may encounter as you use AutoCAD. The list is by no means complete.

A Few Common Error Messages

The only indication that your CONFIG.SYS settings are not working properly may be the following error messages:

```
Bad or missing FILENAME
```

DOS cannot find the file as it is specified. Check your typing and the path you have indicated in the CONFIG.SYS file. In order to see the error messages from your CONFIG.SYS file, you will have to disable your AUTO-EXEC.BAT file by renaming it temporarily.

```
Unrecognized command in CONFIG.SYS
```
Check your typing. Either you made a syntax error, or your version of DOS does not support the configuration command. You can also try to print the error messages by pressing Ctrl-PrtSc (PrintScreen) as soon as DOS starts reading the CONFIG.SYS file.

Problems With AUTOEXEC.BAT

AUTOEXEC.BAT errors are difficult to diagnose; the following list includes some possible remedies/tests.

- Isolate errors by temporarily editing your AUTOEXEC.BAT file by placing a colon and a space (:) at the beginning of each line, one line at a time. If your AUTOEXEC.BAT file includes ECHO=OFF, you may also need to change it to ECHO=ON.

- Echo to the printer while booting, to see what is happening. Press Ctrl-PrtSc.

- Make sure that all environment settings, including PROMPT and PATH, precede any TSR programs.

- Check the PATH command in your AUTOEXEC.BAT file for completeness and syntax.

- APPEND (DOS V3.3 or later) works like PATH to allow programs to find their support files in other directories. Use APPEND cautiously; if you're not careful, you can easily send to the wrong directory a file that is to be saved from a program editing session.

- SET environment errors are often impossible to detect, except for the fact that your program won't work. Type **SET** to see your current settings. If a setting is truncated or missing, you probably are out of environment space. Increase the environment space by adjusting your CONFIG.SYS file (refer to Chapter 4, "Basic System Management").

- If the execution of your AUTOEXEC.BAT file seems incomplete, it may be executing another .BAT file within itself. The result of nested batch files is that the second one takes over and discontinues the first one. With DOS V3.3 and later you can use COMMAND /C NAME or CALL NAME to nest batch files, where NAME is the name of the nested .BAT file.

❑ If memory is limited, insert in the AUTOEXEC.BAT file the following temporary lines to check your available memory:

CHKDSK
PAUSE

Once you determine which command is using what and how much, you can decide what to sacrifice. You must reboot to see the effects.

❑ If you use TSRs and are experiencing lockups, suspect the TSR. The cause may be hard to pin down, but TSRs do strange things to AutoCAD. Disable each TSR individually by using a color in front of the line that loads it within your AUTOEXEC.BAT. Then reboot and test.

Problems With DOS Environment Space

When your PATH command exceeds the amount of environment space allocated, you get the following error message:

```
Out of environment space
```

You may also discover this error when a program fails to execute, AutoLISP does not load, or a standard block insertion does not find the proper drawing.

To determine how much environment space you need, refer to Chapter 4.

Memory Settings

AutoCAD's memory usage is influenced by the DOS environment settings. You can find out more about AutoCAD's memory usage by referring to the *AutoCAD Installation and Performance Guide*. AutoCAD's STATUS command shows several memory values:

```
Free RAM: 11536 bytes
Free disk: 11890234 bytes
I/O page space: 119k bytes
Extended I/O page space: 536k bytes
```

(Note that these are examples; the values may vary.) *Free RAM* is the unused portion of RAM in which AutoCAD can operate. *I/O page space* is RAM used by AutoCAD to page data into and out of active memory.

If you are using extended memory and sometimes get unexplained crashes, you may have a memory conflict between programs or you may be using memory-management software that AutoCAD does not recognize. In the latter instance, you might be using a VDISK and have a crash that creates a drawing you can't use, accompanied by an EREAD error message. This message indicates that AutoCAD has written over the file allocation table and cannot find parts of your drawing. Check to see whether any programs other than AutoCAD are using the extended memory or whether you have an address port conflict.

Even if you do not encounter crashes, you may want to examine how your memory is being used. If you are using 2M or more of extended or expanded memory, you may need to restrict AutoCAD's use of it; AutoCAD uses 16 bytes of free RAM to manage each kilobyte of Extended I/O page space.

SHELL Errors

You may get some strange results if you use SHELL to change directories from inside AutoCAD: New drawings will not default to the new directory, and AutoCAD may lose track of support files and temporary drawing files.

Following are some common errors you may encounter when using SHELL.

```
SHELL error: swapping to disk
```

This error usually is caused by insufficient disk space. Remember that in addition to the disk space needed for the drawing you are editing, Auto-CAD's temporary files also take up space on the disk.

```
SHELL error: insufficient memory for command
```

Either a program previously used during a SHELL command has not cleared out the environment, or you are trying to load a file that requires more memory than the memory available.

```
Unable to load program: insufficient memory
Program too big to fit in memory
```

You need to modify your ACAD.PGP file and allocate more space for your program.

Tracing and Curing Errors

You are the primary source for error diagnosis and information. Try to duplicate the problem predictably, taking notes about what you are doing. Finding errors in today's complex systems can be like finding a needle in a haystack. Remember that many members of the Autodesk Forum on CompuServe may be able to help you with your error problems.

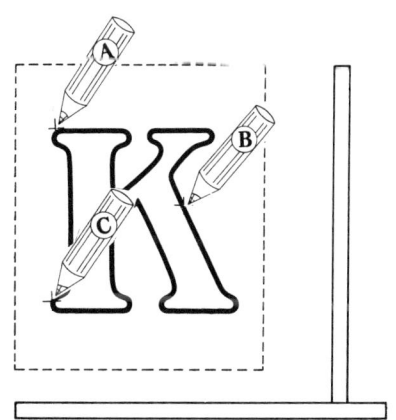

Other Sources of Information

This appendix includes lists of third-party software, AutoCAD users' groups, and a variety of books and periodicals. You can use these lists as a starting point for exploration.

A Listing of Third-party Software

This section lists the software and hardware third-party vendors who were kind enough to respond to our request for a sampling of third-party packages. This is not intended as an evaluation of their product, nor does any firm's omission from this list imply that we have a specific opinion about their product.

These submittals were tremendously helpful in developing Chapter 17, allowing us to provide pointers to you for the evaluation of third-party products. We wish to thank each and every one listed for this help.

We sent letters to a variety of companies representing a cross section (unscientifically) of third-party products. For a more complete listing, get a copy of the Autodesk *Third-Party Applications Catalogue*.

553

Graphic Aids

CAD LETTEREASE
CAD Lettering Systems, Inc.
P.O. Box 850
Oldsmar, FL 33577
(813) 855-2681

A set of custom font files that provide professional quality lettering for use in AutoCAD. Includes a menu and several text-manipulating programs. Each font can be purchased separately, as can the editing routines. Numerous styles are available. The text-editing routines are for kerning letters, changing text, adjusting spacing, two-point justification, placing text on an arc, placing text along a polyline or polyarc, four-point scale/rotation, and three-point rotation. Demonstration diskettes are available, and a complete manual is supplied.

Hardware

CAD-Fax, GammaFax
GammaLink
2452 Embarcadero Way
Palo Alto, CA 94303
(415) 494-7042

This add-on card for PCs lets you send AutoCAD drawings via fax machines, at fax-machine resolution (200 dpi). Uses accompanying software to automatically configure any size drawing to be sent on fax at full drawing scale. Uses HPGL plot files to plot to the fax card. Can serve also as a modem to equally equipped PCs for high-speed data transfer. CAD-Fax works outside AutoCAD after the plot file has been created.

Nth Engine, Nth 3-D Engine, Hydra
Nth Graphics
1807-S. West Braker Lane
Austin, Texas 78758
(512) 832-1944

A set of graphics cards that we call "graphics coprocessors." They are essentially graphics computers in their own right, with accompanying software. Very high-end, high resolution, and very high performance. Includes, among more features than can be listed here: hardware pans and zooms via display-list processing; a birdseye window; zoomslides that allow pan and zoom with mark-up comments (independent of AutoCAD for display); 16 colors from a palette of 4,096; 702-color hardware dithering; plots to a JDL printer without AutoCAD; plus 3-D Engine with 256 colors and—most impressive of all—Hydra software for rendering AutoCAD drawings in 3-D with smooth shading, rotation, and zoom (all very fast).

On a personal note, Nth Graphics were very helpful to us in filling in details about graphics cards. They have excellent products and excellent support. If you are interested in high-performance graphics, we offer this unsolicited recommendation.

SELERIS PC, SEL-NET
Western Automation
1700 N. 55th St.
Boulder, CO 80301
(800) 227-4637

These products are plot buffers that allow AutoCAD plots to be spooled into memory on the card installed in the PC or in a separate external box. A transmission rate of 115K baud from the PC to the buffer, and then of 19.2K baud to the plotter (if your plotter is that fast) is allowed. The plot-spooling software that comes with the hardware will complete sophisticated plot queue management tasks via a pop-up menu from within AutoCAD. The software is memory resident in the plot serving computer. SEL-NET also allows numerous computers to be connected to a single plotter. A variety of memory buffer sizes are available.

Utilities

**Architectural Construction Template,
Plotter Manager, System Manager,
Bill of Materials Reporting System,
Office Furniture System**
Porak Computing Services
2613 Flintridge Drive
Colorado Springs, CO 80907
(303) 593-1187

A wide range of products are available, starting with an architectural template that creates a running account of materials in the project, a plot manager that will plot drawings outside of AutoCAD, a system manager that provides password protection to your computer, a bill-of-materials database manager that is menu driven and compatible with Lotus and dBASE, and an office furniture library, in both 2- and 3-D.

AUTO-DATUM
CADMASTER Incorporated
879 Waterman Avenue
East Providence, RI 02914
(800) 346-0036

An add-on software package accessed via AutoLISP as a DOS executable file. Allows automatic datum-dimensioning of AutoCAD drawings by placing blocks in an AutoCAD drawing and creating dimensions to those blocks from a base dimension line. Adds commands to the AutoCAD menu.

AutoLog
SeCAD Inc.
4707 SW 72 Ave.
Miami, FL 33155
(800) 777-3223

AutoLog is a separate software package that manages your AutoCAD drawings and maintains a database of user information, drawing content, time records, etc. Provides file-standardization capabilities and manages your system through a set of point-and-shoot menus. Numerous database-management capabilities such as editing, sorting, report printouts, file importing, etc. are provided.

AutoManager, AutoSave
CYCO International
1908 Cliff Valley Way
Atlanta, GA 30329
(404) 634-3302

Two programs that read the AutoCAD drawing file directly without AutoCAD. AutoManager lets you view AutoCAD drawings quickly; AutoSave reads corrupted drawing files and repairs them suitably for reading with AutoCAD.

AutoPLOT II
2450 East 7000 South
Salt Lake City, UT 84121
(801) 944-9212

A memory-resident plot spooler that works within AutoCAD and many other programs. It reads from the hard disk after AutoCAD has created a plot file, allowing AutoCAD to be used for editing while it plots in the background.

AutoShapes, Slick, Fsimplex, QuiKey, AutoCALC, MassPlus, AutoESL
CAD Systems Unlimited, Inc.
5201 Great America Parkway
Suite 443
Santa Clara, CA 95054
(408) 562-5745

A set of utilities that allow, in order of the products listed above, the automatic creation of shape and font files from drawings, the viewing of AutoCAD slides without AutoCAD, a mono spaced version of the simplex font style, a LISP program that assigns keystroke macros to AutoCAD commands, a program that allows definition of user coordinate systems independent of AutoCAD's, a program to calculate the area, centroid, moment of inertia, etc. of any two-dimensional object, and a library of electronic shapes.

AutoWord Plus & Art Department
Technical Software, Inc.
28790 Chagrin Blvd.
Cleveland, OH 44121
(216) 765-1133

Text-importing software provides text manipulation for formatting in an AutoCAD drawing. Works independently of AutoCAD and uses a script file to import a DXF text file. Modifies word-processing files so that they can be imported without text formatting characters. Allows right, centered, and left justified text, text style selection, super- and subscripts, underlining, and tabulation (column alignment). Enhanced AutoCAD type fonts are supplied for additional super- and subscript characters. Also allows the use of comma- and field-delimited files.

CLINE I, II, III, Pretty Printer, Interpoly
M. Slinn Engineering Services Inc.
3158 W. 32nd Ave.
Vancouver, B.C. V6L2C1
Canada
(604) 266-5380

CLINE, a program designed to create custom linetypes for use in AutoCAD, uses a combination of its own menu system, AutoLISP, and DOS executable programs that create the lines from within AutoCAD. It requires minor modifications to the AUTOEXEC.BAT and ACAD.PGP files. Pretty Printer configures AutoLISP routines into formats that are more legible to the reader. Also included in the documentation for Pretty Printer is a chart showing group codes for all of AutoCAD's entities. Interpoly, a DOS executable program with AutoLISP assistance, is used to find the centerlines of roads, rivers, and rights-of-way. It will also generate intermediate contours from existing contour indices without entering survey data.

**Duct Size, Shadow, Energy, QHVAC, Fire,
H-S-D-Pipe, Panel, CPM/PERT, Life, AutoSE**
Elite Software Development, Inc.
4444 Carter Creek Parkway
Bryan, TX 77802
(409) 846-2340

Extensive array of specialty programs that work independently of AutoCAD for the purposes of calculating a diverse array of design conditions. In addition, AutoSE is a system-management package for AutoCAD workstations. Demonstration disks are available.

Hatch-Maker
Cantec Software Systems
298 Larch Street
Sudbury, Ontario P3B1M1
Canada
(705) 671-2641

A software package that writes hatch-pattern files using an external program reading a DXF file. It has its own menu system, and uses a standard drawing to create hatch patterns from an AutoCAD drawing.

MiCAD 151, MiGRAPH, ATTREP
MiCAD Systems, Inc.
419 Park Avenue South
New York, NY 10016
(212) 213-9350

MiCAD 151 is a menu system for AEC professionals. Created by MiCAD systems using extensive AutoLISP routines, it has a supplied menu and a symbols library. It also has instructions for customization, which we like.

MiGRAPH is a program for creating graphs of Lotus 1-2-3 data that can be imported into AutoCAD as graphic information. Written in AutoLISP, it reads the DIF file from Lotus and parametrically creates the graph.

ATTREP is a program that prepares reports of AutoCAD attributes. Reports can be imported into the AutoCAD drawing environment as schedules.

PartMASTER 100
Malekko
174 Alexander St. N.W.
Atlanta, GA 30313
(404) 523-0519

A powerful bill-of-materials program for use within AutoCAD. Does not require the use of attributes or DXF files. PMaster uses external master materials and master vendor databases. AutoCAD entities are tagged with a three- or four-digit material code that is assimilated into the bill-of-materials program by PartMaster. Symbol Master is used to convert the user's symbol library by creating new symbol names that can be used in bill-of-materials reports.

Spool-It, Qwik-Change, Cooker 1.0, CAD TIME-CARD
HHS Software
P.O. Box 17905
Memphis, TN 38187-0905
(901) 683-7106

Spool-It is a memory-resident plot spooler, using about 8K of RAM; it supports up to 8 plotting devices, 4 COM ports, 4 LPT ports, and has a spooler user interface for sorting, deleting, or adding to plot queues. Supports AutoCAD's autospool directory.

Quik-Change is a memory-resident text editor for attributes and text via LISP routines.

Cooker 1.0 allows for encryption or decryption of LISP routines. Compresses and removes comments from LISP routines, making them load faster.

CAD Time-Card keeps track of time spent working on an AutoCAD drawing, instead of the time the computer is sitting with the switch on. It is a small TSR and checks for AutoCAD activity.

texCADjr
Creative Technologies, Inc.
4567 Branciforte Drive
Santa Cruz, CA 95065
(408) 426-6806

The texCADjr program creates a typeset format of AutoCAD text fonts. It will do true right justifications with microspacing, variable letter spacing, line leading, adjustable column widths and multiple columns. It requires modification of your ACAD.PGP file. Also available are special fonts for custom font appearance in AutoCAD drawings.

Civil Design Software

ATS-COGO, Auto-Mate, & Autocon
Automated Technical Systems
2127 N. Longmore Street
Chandler, AZ 85224
(602) 899-8714

A coordinate geometry manipulation software package that creates a database from site survey and user input information. It creates data that can be sent to a DXF file and imported into AutoCAD to create 3-D site models.

AutoPROF
ENCAD
201 County Court Blvd., Suite 410
Brampton, Ontario L6w 4L2
Canada
(416) 457-5929

A stand-alone design tool for creating profiles of pipe design. Calculates pipe velocities, pipe sizes, slopes, depths, and flow criteria. Creates a DXF file for use with AutoCAD.

HYDSYS, SANSYS, WATSYS, AutoGRAPHER
KPA CivilSystems Inc.
1005 Cook Street
Victoria, British Columbia V8V3Z6
(604) 381-5955

Programs for the analysis of Water, Sanitary, and Drainage systems that provide data input through AutoGRAPHER into the AutoCAD drawing environment, essentially using AutoCAD to graph the results of the programs. Demonstration disks are available.

LANDIMPROVE
A B Consulting Company, Inc.
3939 N 48th
Lincoln, NB 68504

A full-featured land design set of software for the civil engineering, surveying, and architectural fields. Includes, among others, coordinate geometry, terrain modeling, hydrology, contour mapping, roadway design, and site design. Imports AutoCAD DXF files for design analysis. Has its own graphic representation of 2- and 3-D site images. Uses a floppy disk key for security.

SDRContour and SDRMap
The Lietz Company
9111 Barton, Box 2934
Overland Park, KS 66201
(800) 492-0188

This software works in conjunction with Lietz's surveying equipment to provide a direct input method for the creation of field data based CAD drawings. It can produce DXF files for input to AutoCAD. An easy way to get a field survey turned into an AutoCAD drawing.

terraCADD, COGO A/PLUS, COLINK/PLUS, EARTH/PLUS
Plus III Software, Inc.
One Dunwoody Park
Atlanta, GA 30338
(404) 396-0700

A full-featured land design set of software for the civil engineering, surveying, and architectural fields. Among its features are coordinate geometry, terrain modeling, hydrology, contour mapping, roadway design, and site design. Requires the use of a translation routine to create AutoCAD DXF files. Uses a hardware lock for security.

Menu Systems

AutoMASTER
AutoEase, Inc.
1325 South 800 East, Suite 315
Orem, UT 84058
(801) 224-8833

Architectural template using a task-menu system. The digitizer menu has swapable menu overlays without reconfiguring the menu. Extensive symbols library. Requires its own menu and writes subdirectories to disk. Does not require AUTOEXEC.BAT modifications. Divided into commercial and residential menus; includes landscaping symbols.

AUTOSTEEL
Manson Engineering Services
23 West High Street
Bishopmill, Elgin IV30 2DJ
0343-48384

A set of LISP routines and a menu that create structural steel shapes based on the British Steel Manual or ASTM. Automatically draws sections using parametrics, including centerlines and welds. Requires adjustments to LISP settings, and is bound to a single AutoCAD serial number for copy protection. All LISP routines and menus are customizable, however.

BEAMS and COLUMNS
Computer Derailing Corporation
1310 Industrial Blvd.
Southampton, PA 18966
(215) 355-6003

This menu system for structural steel detailing works inside of AutoCAD. Contains extensive symbols libraries. Primarily for steel detailers and shop drawings. Extensive use of parametric LISP routines is incorporated. A demo is available.

CaddLINK, ElecLINK, MechLINK, VoiceMate
CaddLINK Corporation
3709-A Westerfield Drive, N.E.
Albuquerque, NM 87111
(800) 543-2334

Screen-menu-driven add-on to AutoCAD for creating architectural, electrical, and mechanical drawings. Contains extensive libraries of symbols, uses a task-menu approach, and AutoLISP. Does not require extensive modification of ACAD.LSP or AUTOEXEC.BAT files. Adds its own directory tree to the hard disk. Also market a voice-input hardware system that uses 4 different voice templates to create 64 unique voice-input commands to any DOS-based software package. Requires the use of memory-resident software. Extensive fine-tuning capabilities reduce recognition problems.

COGO-PC Plus, Contour
CIVILSOFT
1592 N. Batavia St., Suite 1A
Orange, CA 92667
(714) 974-1864

This menu system for civil engineers works entirely within AutoCAD. It includes packages for cross sections, profiles, cut-and-fill quantities, road layout, contour, site boundary layout, and field data collection from many brands of data collectors.

DCA CIVIL ENGINEERING SOFTWARE
P.O. Box 955, Proctor Square
Henniker, NH 03242
(603) 428-3199

To our knowledge, the most extensive site design package that works within AutoCAD. Uses numerous LISP routines and menus, with AutoCAD as a background drawing editor. Videotape demos and tutorials are available. Extensively modifies standard AutoCAD settings, and creates its own environment to run within.

LANDCADD INC. (Construction Details, Irrigation Design, Plant Data Base, Site Planning/Landscape Design, E-Z EstimateII, E-Z WORD)
10418 E. Tanglewood Road
Franktown, CO 80116
(303) 688-8160

The granddaddy of the site-planning and landscaping menu systems. There are too many programs to mention here, but if you need it, and it has to do with landscape design and site design, they probably have it. Works within AutoCAD and has extensive libraries. Very nice graphics. We didn't get enough from them to tell you how much modification is required for use with AutoCAD, or whether it can be customized.

PRO-STEEL, PRO-PIPE, PRO-FLOW, PRO-PLANT, PRO-ELEC
Applications Development, Inc.
3300 W. Esplanade S. #207
Metarie, LA 70002
(504) 835-1627

A complete menu system for the design of piping, structural steel, and electrical installations. Extensive symbols library and a video cassette demo are available.

TopDUCT ENGR
3901 Monroe Road
Charlotte, NC 28205
(704) 333-6626

Creates, through a menu-driven set of macros, HVAC drawings for buildings. Requires its own base drawing and drawing standards. Has the ability to complete drawings for HVAC design, including the layout of the architectural elements. Contains an extensive library of symbols. Creates double-line ductwork. Automatic duct size labeling and transition creation. Demo is available.

AutoLISP Aids

BackchAT, AutoMATE 2
Cadro Pty. Ltd.
1 Florizel Street
Burwood, Victoria 3125
Australia
03-299-2921

AutoMATE replaces LISP syntax with syntax more in keeping with Fortran, BASIC, and algebraic conventions, and generates AutoLISP programs and routines in ASCII files. LISP routines are reduced to a streamlined format for fast loading, similar to Kelvination.

Facilities Management

3dISIS
825 Main Street
Kansas City, MO 64105
(816) 221-6311

A 3-D office furnishings library and menu system for use with AutoCAD. Prepares a bill of materials of furniture, manages inventory, and assists in design using a generic library and a vendor library, including furniture from Herman Miller, Steelcase, Stow and Davis, and Knoll.

Archibus & Archibus/FM
Jung/Brannen Research & Development
177 Milk Street
Boston, MA 02109
(617) 482-4886

Archibus/FM is a series of software modules designed to provide the tools required for effective facility management. It uses information provided from AutoCAD, Lotus, and dBASE to create an integrated database for total facilities-management needs. Included are modules for the forecasting of space programming, space design (AutoCAD add-on), furniture and equipment management, and property management.

Symbols Libraries

Architectural Details Library
Laticrete International
1 Laticrete Park North
Bethany, CT 06525
(203) 393-0010

A details library from a tile and concrete products company, free for the asking to AEC professionals. A collection of 26 standard details.

Architectural Library Detail Packages
Matheson Design
P.O. Box 321
Guala, CA 95445
(707) 884-3712

Two sets of architectural detail libraries are available. Each includes its own menu system. A total of 54 details are available, all of which are editable. A demo disk is also available.

KCL Foodservice Equipment Library
Kochman Consultants, Ltd.
9012 N. Waukegan Rd., Box 669
Morton Grove, IL 60053
(312) 470-1195

An ever-growing symbols library of food industry equipment. It contains plan, elevation, and side views of many manufacturers' equipment that can be inserted into AutoCAD drawings.

Companion Software

Kinetic Graphics System
Kinetic Presentations Incorporated
Distillery Commons 250
Louisville, KY 40206-1990
(502) 583-1679

This stand-alone presentation graphics program is a desktop publisher extended into business presentation graphics. Along with the software are support centers that will help you prepare presentations, create slides, overhead transparencies, or laser printed forms, and can also create slides of your AutoCAD drawings. Designed to help you make professional presentations of your work or your design. Service-bureau support is an added bonus.

The SPACE Program
Graphic Systems, Inc.
180 Franklin Street
Cambridge, MA 02139
(617) 492-1148

A program that automatically converts space-planning program information into a design tool format. Measures adjacencies, determines stacking, and creates block diagrams. A tutorial is available. It is really a database approach that interfaces to AutoCAD to graphically represent program development in architecture and interior design.

TOPAS & Supershade
AT&T Graphics Software Labs
10291 N. Meridian, Suite 275
Indianapolis, IN 46290
(317) 844-4364

Too much to mention here. The complete PC-based rendering and animation software package. Rather than tell you everything it will do, read Chapter 15, "Advanced Presentation Techniques," and go see a demonstration of the software. You won't believe your eyes. Special thanks to AT&T and Image Resources for their help with this topic.

Additional Software

DKEY
Digital Mechanics
5347 Arlington Dr. W.
Hanover Park, IL 60103

Smartkey 5.2
Software Research Technologies Inc.
22901 Mill Creek Drive, Suite B
Laguna Hills, CA 92653
(714) 472-0795

AutoCAD Users' Groups

This section contains a partial list of users' groups that specialize in AutoCAD. We have listed only those groups we could verify personally, and only those within the United States or Canada. We can't guarantee that all the information here is accurate (it was, as of our publication date); we apologize in advance for any errors. If you want your users' group to be listed in reprints of this book, please write to the authors, c/o Que Corporation, 11711 N. College Ave., Carmel, IN 46032.

Alabama

Bobby Benson
Birmingham AutoCAD Users' Group
P.O. Box 43462
Birmingham, AL 35243
(205) 995-0190

Arizona

Brian Goelz
AutoCAD Users' Group
CAD Institute
4100 E. Broadway Road, Ste. 150
Phoenix, AZ 85040
(602) 437-0405

California

Lee Walker
Orange County AutoCAD Users' Group
15342 Gemini Lane
Eltoro, CA 92630
(714) 455-1179

Genevieve Katz
East Bay AutoCAD Users' Group
1970 Broadway, Ste. 320
Oakland, CA 94612
(415) 832-2153

Volker Ackermann
Marin County AutoCAD Users' Group
8 West Street
San Rafael, CA 94901
(415) 331-9466

Chuck Handel
AutoCAD Users' Group of Santa Cruz
105 Cooper Street, Suite 206
Santa Cruz, CA 95060
(408) 425-3630

John Weitzel
Sonoma County AutoCAD Users' Group
5003 Rick Drive
Santa Rosa, CA 95403
(415) 777-9144

Christopher DeLucchi
San Diego AutoCAD Users' Group
122 Nardo Avenue
Solana Beach, CA 92075
(619) 755-0854

Colorado

Bernd Hoffmann
N. Colorado AutoCAD Users' Group
636 Powder Horn
Ft. Collins, CO 80526
(303) 229-0314 (h)

Connecticut

Jorge Guillen
Greater Hartford AutoCAD Users' Group
SL/AM Architects
100 Allyn Street, 4th Floor
Hartford, CT 06103
(203) 525-8651

Dan Cummings
Micro Tech Training Center
(203) 234-9490

Delaware

Mel Sloan
Brandwine Area AutoCAD Users' Group
W.L. Gore and Associates Inc.
750 Otts Chapel Rd.
Newark, DE 19714
(302) 368 2575

Florida

Craig Lojewski
Broward County AutoCAD Users' Group
RH Miller and Associates
4800 SW 64th Avenue, Ste. 103
Davie, FL 33314
(305) 791-2900

Tom Kaley
Tampa Bay AutoCAD Users' Group
P.O. Box 12248, Mail Station 15
St. Petersburg, FL 33733
(813) 381-2000

Georgia

James Orrison
Southern Electric Users' Group
Southern Company Services
64A Perimeter Center East BIN 203
Atlanta, GA 30346
(404) 668-2756

William Bland
Macon AutoCAD Users' Group
Architects
348 Cotton Avenue
Macon, GA 31201
(912) 745-4945

Ronald Kolman
Savannah AutoCAD Users' Group
Ronald Kolman Architects
P.O. Box 23192
Savannah, GA 31403
(912) 233-9003

Idaho

Mark Forbord
SE Idaho Area Users' Group
Walker Engineering
1035 Yellowstone Ave.
Pocatello, ID 83201
(208)233-9800

Illinois

Dean Williamson
A.E. Staley
Central Illinois AutoCAD Users' Group
2200 E. Eldorado St.
Decatur, IL 62521
(217) 421-2100

Greg Gooch
John Deere Co.
1600 First Avenue E.
Milan, IL 61264
(309) 756-1445

Indiana

Mark Kitt
Dedicated Registered ACAD Professionals
701 E. South Street
Albion, IN 46701
(219) 693-2167

Rick Oprisu
Indy AutoCAD Users' Group
CAD/CAM Plus, Inc.
122 West Carmel Drive
Carmel, IN 46032
(317) 575-9606

Kansas

Brad Swanson
KC-CAD 417 Rawhide, Suite H
Olathe, KS 66061
(913) 764-2203

Kentucky

Dennis Marshall
Bluegrass AutoCAD Users' Group
Lexington Community College
Cooper Drive, Room 103
Lexington, KY 40506
(606) 257-3650

Greg Heitzman
Kentuckiana AutoCAD Users' Group
Louisville Water Company
435 S. Third Street
Louisville, KY
(502) 569-3600, Ext. 248

Louisiana

Renso Spanoff
Baton Rouge AutoCAD Users' Group
MicroCAD
7290 Exchange Place
Baton Rouge, LA 70806
(504) 387-0303

Maine

Dan Moreno
AutoCAD Users' Group
2 Great Falls Plaza
Auburn, ME 04210
(207) 784-2941

Dick Staples
AutoCAD Users' Group of Maine
East Maine Vo Tech
354 Hogan Road
Bangor, ME 04401
(207) 941-4619

Martha Kleinschmidt
South Maine AutoCAD Users' Groups
Wright-Pierce Engineers
99 Main Street
Popsham, ME 04086
(207) 725-8721

Maryland

David Drazin
CAD/CAM Special Interest Group
Capital PC Users' Group, Inc.
15 Orchard Way, North
Rockville, MD 20854
(301) 279-7593

Mark Glick
Gibraltar Construction
Baltimore Area AutoCAD Users' Group
836 Ritchie Hwy.
Severna Park, MD 21146
(301) 647-8686

Massachusetts

Al Folan
Greater Boston AutoCAD Users' Group
Stone & Webster Engineering
245 Summer St. (4th Floor)
Boston, MA 02107
(617) 589-1535

Michigan

Frank Conner
West Michigan AutoCAD Users' Group
Grand Rapids Junior College
1234 Ball Avenue N.E.
Grand Rapids, MI 49505
(616) 456-4274

Dave Johnson
Iron Mountain AutoCAD Users' Group
M.J. Electric
200 West Frank Pipp Drive
Iron Mountain, MI 49801
(906) 774-8000

Kenneth Hornfeld
Main.Mnu
DiClemente Siegel Engineering, Inc.
22255 Greenfield, Suite 500
Southfield, MI 48075
(313) 275-5226

Minnesota

Wayne Hobbs
Lakes Area AutoCAD Users' Group
HCR121 G
Merrifield, MN 56465
(218) 829-9891

Hani Ayad
AutoCAD.EXE Users' Group
Ellerbee Becket Architects
One Appletree Square
Minneapolis, MN 55425
(612) 853-2104

Missouri

Randy Turner
Pfizer, Inc.
1107 S. 291 Highway
Lee Summit, MO 64081
(816) 524-5580

Keith Wallace or Chris Talbert
Prestress Casting Company
P.O. Box 3499
Springfield, MO 65808
(417) 869-7350

Nebraska

Prof. Leendert Kersten
AutoCAD Users' of Nebraska
3721 Chapin Circle
Lincoln, NE 68506
(402) 472-2384

New Jersey

Richard Finch
South New Jersey AutoCAD Users' Group
49 Park Street
Bordentown, NJ 08505
(609) 298-7449

Robert Weissner
Computer Users' Group
Architects League of Northern NJ
120 North Rt. 17
Paramus, NJ 07652
(201) 599-0030

Mark Meara
Princeton Area AutoCAD Users' Group
CUH2A
600 Alexander Road
Princeton, NJ 08543
(609)452-1212

New York

Rochelle Borgen
Albany AutoCAD Users' Group
40 Colvin Avenue
Albany, NY 12206
(518) 438-6844

Michael Geyer
New York AutoCAD Users' Group
20 W. 20th Street
New York, NY 10011
(212) 691-4722

Bob Schellinger
Rochester Area AutoCAD Users' Group
Olin Corporation
P.O. Box 205
Rochester, NY 14601
(716) 436-3030

North Carolina

Steve Frick
Piedmont AutoCAD Users' Group
Draper Corporation
P.O. Box 16341
Greensboro, NC 27416
(919) 852-4200 ext. 356

David Jerolle
Triangle AutoCAD Group
7416 Chapel Hill Road
Raleigh, NC 27602
(919) 851-3455

North Dakota

David Bauman
Mid-Con AutoCAD Users' Group
616 Main Avenue
Box 44
Fargo, ND 58103
(701) 232-3271

Ohio

Janak Dave
Cincinnati AutoCAD Users' Group
OMI College of Applied Science
2220 Victory Parkway
Cincinnati, OH 45206
(513) 556-6573

Wes Eichelman
Dayton Area AutoCAD Users' Group-DaCad-
6001 B. North Dixie Drive
Dayton, OH 45414
(513) 228-4007

Thomas Altman
Cleveland Computer Aided Design Society
1501 Spring Garden Avenue
Lakewood, OH 44107
(216) 521 2574

Ted Gentsch
Akron Area AutoCAD Users' Group
Linden Industries
4020 Bellaire Lane
Peninsula, OH 44264
(216) 928-4064

Ron Harp
NW Ohio AutoCAD Users' Group
P.O. Box 23332
Toledo, OH 43623
(419) 242-7405

Oklahoma

Dr. Ginger Benedict
AutoCAD Users' Group
East Central University
Ada, OK 74820
(405)332-8000

Chuck Earnhart
AutoCAD ACE Users' Group
AAE, Incorporated
PO Box 32797
Oklahoma City, OK 73123
(405)949-1442

Pennsylvania

Jeff Chambers
Presque Isle AutoCAD Users' Group
Van-Air Systems
2950 Mechanic Street
Lake City, PA 16423
(814) 774-2631

Kenn Anderson
KEYstone ACADemy AuotCAD Users' Group
Keystone Junior College
Box 149
LaPlume, PA 18440
(717) 945-3232

Howard Fulmer
Phila AutoCAD Users' Group
HMF Consulting
161 Jefferson Ct.
Norristown, PA 19401
(215) 275-9866

Al Scheib
Southeast Pennsylvania AutoCAD Users' Group
(717) 872-8167

South Carolina

John Watts
Piedmont AutoCAD Users' Group
Spartanburg Technical College
P.O. Drawer 4386
Spartanburg, SC 29305
(803)591-3674

South Dakota

Jeff Manley
Black Hills Power and Light
P.O. Box 1400
Rapid City, SD 57709
(605) 342-3200

Gene Murphy
Sioux Falls Area AutoCAD Users' Group
Architecture Automated
600 West Avenue N.
Sioux Falls, SD 57104
(605) 336-3722

Tennessee

Barbara Gatlin
Dyersburg Area AutoCAD Users' Group
Dyersburg State Community College
P.O. Box 648
Dyersburg, TN 38025
(901) 285-6910 extension 209

Don Boston
Jackson Area AutoCAD Users' Group
Porter Cable Corporation
Youngs Crossing at Highway 45
Jackson, TN 38305
(901) 668-8600

Joe Cook
Nashville Area AutoCAD Users' Group
120 White Bridge Road
P.O. Box 90285
Nashville, TN 37209
(615) 353-3462

Mike Nichols
NW Tennessee AutoCAD Users' Group
166 Brook Street
Paris, TN 38242
(901) 642-4251

Texas

Clyde Brothers
Brazos Valley AutoCAD Users' Group
Rt. 3 Box 297
College Station, TX 77840
(409) 776-8820

Dan Luce
PRO-CAD Users' Group
Houston Community College
12601 High Star
Houston, TX 77072
(713) 463-0196 (h) or (713) 933-8050 (w)

Mike Salars
Pasadena-Clear Water AutoCAD Users' Group
Dixie Chemical
10701 Bay Area Blvd.
Pasadena, TX 77507
(713) 474-3271

Virginia

Tom Tulloch
Northern Virginia AutoCAD Users' Group
Helbing Lipp, Ltd.
7929 Westpark Drive
McLean, VA 22102
(703) 556-0700

Dale Campbell
Norfolk Area AutoCAD Users' Group
Joe D. Glenn & Associates
P.O. Box 12154, 5 Kroger Exec. Center
Norfolk, VA 23502
(804) 461-9130

Michael Farmer
Central Virginia AutoCAD Users' Group
12343 Sir James Court
Richmond, VA 23233
(804) 360-4764 (h) or (804) 756-7743 (w)

Washington

Dick Vogel
Bellingham Users' Group (BUG)
Western Washington University
Western Washington University,Technology
Bellingham, WA 98225
(206) 676-3380

Dan Flanagan
Seattle Area AutoCAD Users' Group
4301 230th Place S.W.
Mountlake Terrace, WA 98043
(206) 771-5334

Jeff Waymack
Architects/Engineers/Planners Users' Grp.
2102 North 52nd St.
Seattle, WA 98103
(206) 634-0849

West Virginia

Max Dent
Greater Tri-State AutoCAD Users' Group
P.O. Box 53
Scott Depot, WV 25560
(304) 757-9217

Wisconsin

Ron Zenke
Fox Valley Area AutoCAD Users' Group
Fox Valley Tech Institute
1825 North Bluemound Drive
Appleton, WI 54913
(414) 735-2519

David Regge
Apache Stainless Equipment
3103 Baskerville Avenue
Middleton, WI 53562
(414) 887-3721

Gene Roseburg
NorthStar AutoCAD Users' Group
WITI
600 N. Twenty-first St.
Superior, WI 54880
(715) 394-6677

Canada

Randy Russell
107,10945 83rd Street
Edmonton, Alberta
CANADA T5H 1M2
(403) 441-4100 (h)

Peter Varma
New Brunswick Area AutoCAD Users' Group
Engineering Department
Mount Allison University
Sackville, NB
CANADA
(506) 364-2580

Irene Katzighera
S. Winnepeg Technical Center
P.O. Box 145
130 Henlow Bay
Ft. Whyte, Manitoba
CANADA ROG R3Y105
(204) 488-2451

Jamie Monteith
AutoSAR
118 N. Victoria Street
Sarnia, ON
CANADA N7T 5W9
(519) 332-4400

Chris West
Toronto Region AutoCAD Exchange (TRACE)
Berg Chilling Systems
51 Nantucket Blvd.
Scarborough, ON
CANADA M1P 2N6
(416) 755-2225

Bob Tomlinson
Northern Ontario AutoCAD Users' Group
Tomlinson Drafting & Blueprinting
107 Cumberland St. North
Thunderbay, ON
CANADA P7A 4M3
(807) 345-6375

Cathy Hamelin
Vancouver AutoCAD Users' Group
810 West Broadway
Vancouver, BC
CANADA V574C9
(604) 294-1471

A Reading Resource List

This is simply a list of books. It is not a bibliography.

Books on AutoCAD

Using AutoCAD
Brenda L. Fouch
Que Corporation
11711 N. College Ave.
Carmel, IN 46032

Customizing AutoCAD
J. Smith and R. Gesner
New Riders Publishing
P.O. Box 4846
Thousand Oaks, CA 91360

Inside AutoCAD
D. Raker and H. Rice
New Riders Publishing
P.O. Box 4846
Thousand Oaks, CA 91360

AutoCAD Cookbook
Christopher James DeLucchi
John Wiley and Sons, Inc.

AutoLisp in Plain English
George O. Head
Ventana Press
P.O. Box 2468
Chapel Hill, NC 27515

The AutoCAD Database Book
Frederick H. Jones and Lloyd Martin
Ventana Press
P.O. Box 2468
Chapel Hill, NC 27515

The AutoCAD Productivity Book
A. Ted Schaefer and James L. Brittain
Ventana Press
P.O. Box 2468
Chapel Hill, NC 27515

Mastering AutoCAD, 2nd Edition
George Omura
Sybex Inc.
2021 Challenger Drive #100
Alameda, CA 94501

Books on CAD in General

Cad, Drawing, Design, Data Management
E. Lee Kennedy
Whitney Library of Design
Watson-Guptil Publications
A Division of Billboard Publications, Inc.
1515 Broadway
New York, NY 10036

Intelligent Drawings
Terrence G. and Patricia M. Schilling
McGraw Hill Book Co.

General Computer Books

1-2-3 Macro Library, 2nd Edition
David Paul Ewing
Que Corporation
11711 N. College Ave.
Carmel, IN 46032

1-2-3 Command Language
Darien Fenn
Que Corporation
11711 N. College Ave.
Carmel, IN 46032

1-2-3 Tips, Tricks, and Traps, 2nd Edition
Dick Anderson and Douglas Ford Cobb
Que Corporation
11711 N. College Ave.
Carmel, IN 46032

dBASE III Plus Handbook, 2nd Edition
George Tsu-der Chou
Que Corporation
11711 N. College Ave.
Carmel, IN 46032

dBASE III Plus Tips, Tricks, and Traps
George Tsu-der Chou
Que Corporation
11711 N. College Ave.
Carmel, IN 46032

dBASE III Plus Applications Library
Thomas W. Carlton with Charles O. Stewart III
Que Corporation
11711 N. College Ave.
Carmel, IN 46032

dBASE III Plus Made Easy
Miriam Liskin
Osborne McGraw Hill
2600 Tenth Street
Berkley, CA 94710

DOS Programmer's Reference
Terry R. Dettmann
Que Corporation
11711 N. College Ave.
Carmel, IN 46032

Managing Your Hard Disk, 2nd Edition
Don Berliner
Que Corporation
11711 N. College Ave.
Carmel, IN 46032

Using OS/2
Halliday, Minasi, Gobel
Que Corporation
11711 N. College Ave.
Carmel, IN 46032

Peter Norton's DOS Guide
Peter Norton
A Brady Book
Prentice Hall Press
A Division of Simon and Schuster Inc.
Gulf + Western Building
One Gulf + Western Plaza
New York, NY 10023

Inside the IBM PC (Revised)
Peter Norton
A Brady Book
Prentice Hall Press
A Division of Simon and Schuster Inc.
Gulf + Western Building
One Gulf + Western Plaza
New York, NY 10023

Supercharging MS-DOS
Van Wolverton
Microsoft Press
16011 N.E. 36th Way, Box 97017
Redmond, WA 98073-9717

Using Ventura Publisher
Diane Burns, S. Venit and Linda J. Mercer
Que Corporation
11711 N. College Ave.
Carmel, IN 46032

Using WordPerfect 5
Charles O. Stewart III
Que Corporation
11711 N. College Ave.
Carmel, IN 46032

Using WordStar, 2nd Edition
Steve Ditlea
Que Corporation
11711 N. College Ave.
Carmel, IN 46032

Glossary

Included in this glossary are all the terms we could think of that have not been defined explicitly within the text.

Absolute coordinate. The absolute X, Y, Z values of a point's location in the current User Coordinate System, with reference to a specified point in the same UCS.

Aperture. The pixel frame at the intersection of the crosshairs on the AutoCAD screen, when used for selection of an object.

Associative dimension. A dimension whose values are related to specific points in a drawing. By changing the location of the dimension lines, the value of the dimension is updated automatically.

Attribute. A data string stored in association with a block.

Attribute tag. A one-word label for an attribute.

Block. A set of grouped entities bound to the same object in the AutoCAD drawing database.

CAD. An acronym for Computer Aided Design.

Camera. The location from which you are looking at an object in AutoCAD's DVIEW or in AutoShade.

Cartesian coordinate system. A coordinate system that uses three axes (x,y,z) to define the location of a point in space.

Digitizing. The process of using a puck or stylus to enter point data into an electronic drawing.

Elevation. The location of drawing objects with respect to the Z axis.

Entity. A predefined drawing object stored in AutoCAD's database.

Extrusion. An entity's thickness from its X-Y plane of origin along the Z axis of the UCS.

Icon. A graphic image that represents a concept of an activity without the use of text.

Limits. The AutoCAD addressable area that represents a sheet size in real scale.

Mesh. A three-dimensional surface defined by a series of facets that approximate the shape of the surface.

Mouse. A hand-controlled pointing device used to address the screen of a computer.

Nest. In a drawing, a block placed inside another block; in an AutoLISP expression, a list placed inside another list.

Orientation. The location of an object referenced by an expressed angle to another object.

Plan view. The view of the current construction plane from the Z axis.

Point and Shoot. The capability of a program to address its selections of files or programs through the use of the cursor.

Point filter. A technique used in AutoCAD to select one or more of the X,Y,Z coordinates of a point.

Polar coordinate. A coordinate system defined in reference to a specific origin and based on distances and radians from a set of X,Y,Z coordinates.

Polyline (Pline). An entity composed of lines, arcs, and vertices.

Primitive. A simple entity such as a line, circle, arc, ellipse, or polygon.

Properties. Qualities of an entity such as its endpoints, color, linetype, thickness, and elevation.

Prototype drawing. A drawing that is a typical basis for creating new drawings and which contains the desired drawing-setup standards.

Stylus. A hand-held electronic pen.

System variable. A variable that retains standard configurable elements of an AutoCAD drawing.

Target. The location of the point at which you are pointing a camera in AutoCAD's DVIEW command or in AutoShade.

User Coordinate System (UCS). A user-selected coordinate system relative to the working planes of a drawing.

UCS icon. An icon placed by AutoCAD for the purposes of representing the current X-Y axis direction.

Vector. A line with a direction and length that provides the indication of a movement of a point or object through space.

Viewport. A portion of the screen's graphics area defined by a virtual-screen database maintained by AutoCAD. Each viewport has its own virtual screen.

Virtual Screen. The raster image database that represents the entirety of the screen that AutoCAD can display without performing a REGEN.

Wild-card character. A symbol (* or ?) used in file names and/or file extensions to represent a variable character or string of characters.

World Coordinate System (WCS). The base-reference coordinate system defined at the beginning of a drawing edit session in AutoCAD.

Index

! to return variable value, 200
$A1, 197
$B, 197
$I, 197
$P1-$P10, 197
$S, 197
$T1, 197
+ for continuation lines in LISP, 192, 200
; in menu macro, 199
[] to create menu options, 198
\ in menu macro, 199-200
3DFACES, 277

A

acceleration speed, 386
adapters. *See* graphics card (adapters) *and* multiadapter boards
addresses, memory and port, 374, 376
Advanced User Interface (AUI), 27, 29
   mouse use requires, 209
   pull-down menus, 196
   for slide library, 135
AEC. *See also* AutoCAD AEC
AEC Expo, 407
angles, 223
   AutoLISP functions for, 309-310, 313-314
application development for customized use of AutoCAD, rules for, 178-182
architects' standards for project conventions, 118-119

archive files, 94, 164
ASCII characters, extended (high), 66
   batch menu created with, 145-146
ASCII files, scripts as, 216
ASCII format
   contents of files using, 65
   displaying files in, 37
   for files imported to or exported from AutoCAD, 229
Asynchronous Communication Adapter required to run AutoCAD, 27
attributes, 231-235
   AutoCAD, 96, 148
   drawing title, 137
   extraction of from LISP routines, 148
   tags for, 233-234
AutoCAD AEC (Archsoft/Autodesk), 30, 125, 132
   menu system, 185-186, 188-189, 208
AutoCAD Applications Catalog, 407
AutoCAD (Autodesk)
   attributes, 96
      extracting, 148
   automation of, 214-236
   basics, test of knowledge of
      answers, 45-47
      questions, 39-41
   batch file to start, 53
   concepts checklist, 38-39
   configuring, 41
   customization
      assessing need for menu, 187

product developed from, 178, 180-182
rules for, 174, 176-178
with script files and AutoLISP programs, 20, 109
of system variables, prototype-drawing settings, menus, and symbols library, 20
database. *See* database, AutoCAD
desktop publishing software for, 104-105
directory usage, 120-126
enhancements in Release 10
    tilting and rotating the work surface, 276
    User Coordinate System to locate origin point anywhere, 40, 46, 280
errors and solutions, 547-551
executing external programs from within, 40
hardware requirements for, 27
learning more about, 43-44
MS-DOS V4.0 not yet supported for, 90
project-management software output manipulated with, 99-101
Release 9
    menus, 276
    views, 278
return codes, 107
spreadsheet output manipulated by, 97-99
startup from a project subdirectory, 121-122
supplementary software for, 398-409
    disk optimizer, 30
    fonts, 354-356
    hard disk manager, 30
    menus. *See* menus
    text editor, 30
three-dimensional features of, 268-294
word-processing software for, 103
work flow analysis for use of, 188-190
Autodesk (ADESK) Forum, 95
backup program available from, 149
bug testing through, 348
CAD management uses for, 400
CompuServe
    to access, 109-110
keyboard enhancement program available from, 210
menu, 110

product support from, 408
third-party product evaluations from, 405-406
AUTOEXEC.BAT file, 38, 47, 75
disabling, 547
errors with, 548-549
modifications to for AutoCAD, 80, 145-146, 391-393
paths in, 122-124, 435
sample, 435-436
SUBST command in, 125-126
third-party product changes to, 403
variables controlled by, 80-81
AutoFlix (Autodesk), 110, 269, 293
AutoLISP, 296-350
aids from third parties, 402, 564
concepts, 298-305
creating drawings parametrically with, 202-203, 205
data libraries accessed through CompuServe and ADESK Forum, 110
dotted pair
    group code in, 232-233
    periods to create, 303
    value in, 232
execution speed of, 347-348
extended, 348
    not functional with some memory managers on 386 machines, 86
functions, 300. *See also* functions, AutoLISP
    case sensitivity of certain, 304-305
    conditional, 344-347
    data type, 309-312
    entity manipulation, 326-332
    general, 305-308
    input/output, 334-344
    list manipulation, 321-325
    mathematical, 312-315, 319-321
    nil, 302
    quote, 303
    recursive, 302
    subrs as built-in, 302, 304
    table manipulation, 333-334
interpreter, 300, 304
lists in, 299-300

output, 232
for parametrics, 223
pi constant in, 314
responses to commands, samples of, 231-232
special characters
    apostrophe, 303
    backslash to denote control characters, 303
    control, 303-304
    for math functions, 302
    parentheses as list separators (delimiters), 303
    periods to create dotted pairs, 303
    quotation marks to denote a string data type, 303
    semicolon to denote a comment, 303
special conditions, 304
temporary work space used by, 83
AutoLISP programs. *See also* LISP routines
    add-on programs for
        LISPHEAP, 206, 348
        LISPSTACK, 41, 47, 206, 348
    as ASCII file, 37
    atom as basic unit of statement in, 46, 298-299
    to customize AutoCAD, 20
    LISP routines and script files written using, 41, 47
    loading, 41, 47
    shared customized, 116
    spreadsheets to work with data by means of, 98
    word processor to write routines or modify menus in, 41
Auto-Log (SeCAD), 166
AutoManager (Cyco International), 166
Automaster menu system (AUTOEASE), 262
automated drawing routines, 525-541
automation
    factors in determining drawings and tasks for, 13
    selecting processes suitable for, 10, 13-14
Automenu, 146
AutoSAVE (CYCO International), 65
AutoShade, 70, 285-292

.RND files produced by (for AutoFlix movies), 293
camera locations shown by, 285
data libraries accessed through ADESK Forum, 110
fast shade and full shade options, 292
fractals displayed with Mandlebrot option of, 357
light sources used by, 285-292
mouse emulation by digitizer useful with, 71
not suitable for final presentation work, 354
PostScript output of, 367-368
AutoWord, 138
axes, 223

B

backup
    clean, 149-150
    consistent use of system for, 65
    copies of drawings, programs, and operating system, 42
    files overwritten after revisions, 115
    incremental, 131
    LISP routine for, 150-151
    procedures
        batch routine for, 130-131
        described in office manual, 115
    process impeded by too many subdirectories, 52
    programs for, 148-151
    tape units to store, 62
Basic Input/Output System (BIOS), 75
    compatibility problems on clones, 86
    port addresses accessed by, 376
batch files, 33, 435-440
    4.BAT, 437
    8.BAT, 437
    in ACAD.PGP file, 105
    to activate frequently used programs, 53
    AUTOEXEC.BAT. *See* AUTOEXEC.BAT file
    BACKUP.BAT, 130-131
    to change path, 436
    to copy slides, 165

CPY.BAT, 55-56
disk-management, 52
DWGBAK.BAT, 149
for each project, 144-145
to load AutoCAD and redisplay AutoCAD
    directory menu, 436
loading, 145
managed with menus, 144-146, 436-437
M.BAT, 436-438
MOVEARC.BAT, 59-60
nested, problems caused by, 548
written with EDLIN or a word processor, 53
Bernoulli Box, RCD.SYS driver to control, 79
BIGD shading program, 292
blends
    creating, 357
    tweening as three-dimensional, 359
block(s)
    automated drawing affected by, 222-223
    controls, 116
    drawing standardization with, 203-205
    hatch pattern, 258
    INSBLK, 219-220, 525-527
    layers, 192
    listing all of drawing's, 234
    PLOTBLK, 220, 231-233
    title
        coordination, 116
        information stored in predetermined
            locations for, 135
        relationship with sheet border and plot
            area, 133, 178-179
block-management procedures, 116
book
    assumptions about readers of, 4
    audience for, 2
    intended goals of, 5-6
    organization of, 3-4
    reasons for writing, 5
    ways to use, 2-3
border, relationship of title block, plot area, and
    sheet, 133, 178-179
budgetary factors of AutoCAD use, 269-270
buffers
    plot, 386-387
    to set aside RAM, 77
    set to 20 initially for AutoCAD, 77
bulletin boards for CAD management, 400
bump maps, 358
bytes, 372-374

C

CAD habits, 24-48
    bad, 25
        avoiding, 42-43
    good
        comfort with features a factor in
            development of, 26
        developing, 42
CAD LETTEREASE, 254-255
CAD management, 1-2
    advanced techniques for, 142-167
    concerns
        cost savings, 10
        costs for hardware, software, and
            operations, 10
        effects on company management and
            organization, 10
        financial, 10-12
        installation procedures, 10, 14-15
        personnel selection and training, 10, 44
        processes to automate, 10, 13-14
        work flow, 10, 12
    creative, 400-402
    and implementation, 9-11
    manuals to coordinate, 19-20
    overview, 9-23
    procedures, 18-19, 406-407. *See also* data
        management, drawing management, file
        management, job-management tools,
        project management, *and* system
        management
    resources, 407-408
    tools, third-party, 398-409
    training required for, 20-21
CAD publications
    books, 581-582
    CADalyst, 43, 176, 210, 298

Index

CADENCE, 43, 176, 210, 298
CAD TIME-CARD (HHS Software Solutions), 101
calculator software, 101
Carousel, 101
central processing unit (CPU), function of, 68
civil design software, 401, 560-561
CLINE II, 247
CLINE III, 247
Clipper compiler, 96
clock generator chips, 375-376
clock speed, 68, 376
color(s)
   displayable, 70
   palette, 70, 380
   printing, 367-368
   variation of display depending on monitors, 70
command, LISP getenv, 126
COMMAND.COM file (shell program), 37, 76, 106
   to increase environment space, 123
commands and utilities, DOS
   APPEND, 548
   ASSIGN, 126
   BACKUP, 130
   BREAK, 77
   CD, 36, 53
   CHKDSK, 37, 60, 105, 117
   CLS, 54
   COPY, 32, 37, 51
      /V switch to verify copy, 62
      same as AutoCAD COPY command, 107
   DEBUG, 438
   DEL (DELETE), 32, 37, 107
   DIR, 32, 36, 107
      /P switch to pause directories, 36
      /W switch to display full-width listings, 36
   ECHO, 54-55
   ECHO OFF, 38, 54-55, 81
   FILES, 78
   FOR..IN..DO, 59
   FORMAT, 37
      /S switch to copy system files, 37
      /V switch to give disk a volume label, 37
   GOTO, 56
   IF, 56-58
      NOT, 57
   LABEL, 115, 151
   LASTDRIVE, 80
   MORE, 38
   PATH, 38, 76, 80-81, 102
      AUTOEXEC.BAT problems with, 548
      for directory trees, 119, 121-122
      set for AutoCAD, 123-124
   PAUSE, 55
   PROMPT, 38, 82
   RD, 36
   RENAME, 38, 108
   RESTORE, 130
   SET, 80, 82-83
      AUTOEXEC.BAT problems with, 548
      to switch directories in AutoCAD, 121, 125
   SHELL, 76, 123
   SHIFT, 56, 59-60
   SUBST, 125-126
   TYPE, 32, 37, 53-54
   VDISK, 390
commands, AutoCAD
   ARRAY, 40, 45
   ATTDEF, 160
   ATTEXT, 233, 347
   BLOCK, 39, 45
   CANCEL, 199
   CHANGE, 31
   CIRCLE, 200
   COPY, 107
   DRAW, 280
   DTEXT, 40, 46
   DVIEW, 282-285
   DXFOUT, 40
   EDIT, 280
   ELLIPSE, 240
   END, 162, 513
   HATCH, 40
   HIDE, 354
   INSBASE, 158
   INSERT, 217
   LAYER, 39, 224-225

LINE, 240
LINETYPE, 243
LOAD, 158
LTSCALE, 40, 244-245
MOVE, 273
MSLIDE, 147
OOPS, 39
PAN, 41
PEDIT, 40
PLINE, 240
PLOT, 29
POLYGON, 240
PRPLOT, 29
PURGE, 43
REDRAW, 41, 218, 389
REGEN, 218, 389
REVSURF, 291, 357
SAME, 389
SCRIPT, 216
  selection of, 197-198
SET ACAD, 303, 403
SETUP, 132-135
SETVAR, 40-41
SH (SHELL), 31-32, 40, 102, 550
STATUS, 89, 388, 549
STRETCH, 31
STYLE, 39, 45
transparent, 41
UDBASE, 158
UNDO, 40, 45
VIEWPORT, 280
VIEWRES, 278
VPOINT, 278
VSLIDE, 147
WBLOCK, 40, 45, 150
ZOOM, 41
ZOOM ALL, 132
ZOOM DYNAMIC, 40, 45
commands, AutoLISP
  IF, 192
  SETQ, 225
CompuServe
  ADESK (AutoCAD) Forum on, 109-110
  archived files on, 94
  CAD managers recommended to join, 401

computer
  components, 68-70
  reading list, general, 583-585
CONFIG.SYS file
  to customize BIOS, 75-76
  device drivers listed by and installed in, 78, 80
  DEVICE line in, 390, 393
  DOS environment space adjusted with statement in, 123-124
  dummy drive set in, 125
  EMM.SYS file added to, 393
  error messages, 547-548
  LASTDRIVE allocation in, 391
  sample of typical, 76
  third-party product modifications of, 402
Construction Specifications System, 152-155
coordinates
  cartesian, 223
  Z, 279-280
crashes, causes of, 550
Critical-Path Management (CPM), 99-100
  LISP routine for Lotus 1-2-3 to generate data for, 534-538

D

dash-length specification, 241
data
  bits defined, 68
  bus, 374
  exporting, 229-230
    formats for, 228
data management, 21-22, 151
database, AutoCAD (.DXF)
  converted for use in a rendering environment, 359
  set of job management and schedule maintenance tools (run by dBASE) for, 465-516
    to add records to AutoCAD schedule records (SCH_ADD.PRG), 495-498
    to create header for schedule report (SCH_HEAD.PRG), 508-509

Index

to create job time and task report (JOB_TIME.PRG), 483-487
to create summaries for job report (JOB_SUMM.PRG), 476-478
to create temporary databases for totals accumulation (JOB_2A.PRG), 479-482
to create time report header (JOB_HEAD.PRG), 475-476
database structures to accompany, 491
to delete schedule records (SCH_DEL.PRG), 498-501
to edit master data (MASTER.PRG), 487-489
to edit schedules (SCH_EDIT.PRG), 502-505
to export schedule to ASCII file (SCH_EXPT.PRG), 506-508
to import CDF ASCII files from AutoCAD (JOB_IMP.PRG), 469-472
to import CDF schedule files from AutoCAD (SCH_IMP.PRG), 492-494
main (MAIN.PRG), 466-469
to print job history report (JOB_HIST.PRG), 472-475
program controller (PRO_FILE.PRG), 489-490
drawing, 157
software to manipulate output of, 96-97
sorting, 152
as source of information to managers, 22
database-management programs, 96-97
dBASE
features, 96-97
keyword index for LISP routine library, 400
for reports of drawing activity, 148
used with AutoCAD, 227-231
dBASE III Plus to refine AutoCAD databases, 96
dBASE III to run set of job-management tools, 465-516
dealer, reliance on hardware or software, 174
delimiters
defined, 229
parentheses as AutoLISP, 303
desktop publishing software, 104-105
Desqview, 101

device drivers, 78-80
ANSI.SYS, 79, 124, 402
CEMM.SYS, 86
CONFIG.SYS. See CONFIG.SYS file
EMM.SYS, 86
graphics display, 124, 379
HRDDRIVE.SYS, 79
memory management, 389
plotter, 386
port addresses conflict with programs run within AutoCAD, 108
PostScript, 104
QEMM.SYS, 86
RCD.SYS, 79
REMM.SYS, 79
system memory reduced by adding, 124
updates
for each release of AutoCAD, 383
for third-party products, 404
VDISK.SYS, 79, 85-86
dialog boxes accessible with either digitizer or mouse, 29
Digital Equipment VAX, 101
digitizer
capabilities, 70-71
driver to configure AutoCAD for each type of, 41, 46
exchange of data between other devices and, 69
hand-written input using, 395
or mouse required to run AutoCAD, 27
optimal for complex drawing tasks, 27
digitizing to enter data, 28
dip switches, memory card, 389-390, 392-393
Direct Memory Access (DMA) controller, 376
directories
AutoCAD, 120-126
BATCH, 435
creating, 36
DOS, 118-119
errors in changing, 550
logical damage to, 63
MENU1, 145-146
removing, 36
rules for using, 52

switching, 36
tree structure, 119
    sample, 120-121
viewing, 35-36
disk fragmentation, 61
disk optimization program, 30, 117
Disk Optimizer, 30
display
    adapters. *See* graphics card (adapters)
    interlaced/noninterlaced, 381-382
Display Coordinate System (DCS), translating between UCS, WCS, and, 320-321
display list defined, 380
display list processing, 279
    defined, 70
    extended memory used for, 89
    on graphics cards, 380-381
display projectors, 368
DKEY electronic shorthand programs, 102, 210
Dr. Halo, 359
DOS, 51-60
    arguments in command lines, 55
    directory management with, 35-36
    disk drive operations with, 33
    environment size
        increasing, 123
        problems caused by, 549
    file-naming conventions, 127-129
    to handle disk management for AutoCAD, 32
    naming conventions for file extensions, 33-35
    parameters in command lines, replaceable, 55-56
    software companions for, 92-111
    utilities for AutoCAD users, 37-38, 93-95
        BADSEC.ARC, 94
        BC.EXE, 94
        COMSWT.ARC, 94
        DKEY.ARC, 94
        FILL.ARC, 95
        GLOBAL.ARC, 95
        GUDLUK.ARC, 95
        HELP.ARC, 95
        HIDE.ARC, 95
        HOTKEY.ARC, 95
        KEYBUF.COM, 95
        LOC.COM, 95
        MOVE.ARC, 95
        NEWKEY.ARC, 95
        NOTEPAD.COM, 95
        PWORD.ARC, 95
        VDL.ARC, 95
        WAITEX.ARC, 95
        WHATIS.ARC, 95
drafting standards, 119
drawing(s)
    3-D, 268-294
        axonometric drawing as an actual, 284
        management practices for, 271-272
        reasons to use, 270
        requirements for, 270-271
        rules for, 272-279
        slowness of generating, 269, 272
        steps to create, 273-276
    accuracy in, 42
    appearance, macros and routines for enhancing, 238-266
    assembled for editing, 156-157
    assembly, 191
        automated, 217-221
    automated, 359
        assembly, 217-221
        routines for, 525-541
    axonometric, 283-284
    base, shared database procedures for, 116, 156-158
    camera-ready, 265
    capturing, 362
    control sheet, 116
    created from dBASE or Lotus 1-2-3, 228-231
    data extraction from, 189
    database, 157
    detail, stand-alone, 191
    edited by multiple users simultaneously, preventing, 114
    entities automatically with script files, 221-222
    frequent saving of, 42
    importing text to, 541
    incomplete printout of, 29-30

insertion, standardized, 193-194
inventory of equipment or fixtures in, printing, 234-235
isometric, 283-284
lost, causes of, 62
    hardware failure, 64
    improper system management, 64
    media failure, 62-63
management, 18, 113-115, 131-140, 151-156
    linked to project management with menus, 185-186
    LISP routine for, 162-164
master, management of, 116
naming standards, 127-129, 193
numbering, 193
perspective, 283
plot information stored in, 158-161
presentation, 262-263. *See also* renderings
    costs, 355
    hardware to develop, 360
    software to develop, 362
    three-dimensional, 352-369
prototype, 40, 282, 441
revision procedure, 115
sent to a FAX machine, 22
separated from AutoCAD program files, 120
standard, 119
    guidelines for, 135-138
    library, 166
    module sizes for, 135-136
    notation for, 138
standards, 116, 131
    AutoLISP for, 202-203, 205
    blocks for, 203-205
    for drawing reusability, 131, 135-138
    limits, 131-135, 201-202
    menu customization to control and implement, 190-191
    shapes for, 204-205
    tools for developing, 202-205
temporary, RAM disk to store, 393-394
title attributes, 137
viewing, 147
drawing file(s)
    accessing, 147
    annotating, 147-148
    management, 18, 143-167
DSBACKUP+, 130

E

EDLIN
    to create or manipulate text files, 4, 50, 66
    to write batch files, 53
EGA Paint, 359
Enhanced Graphics Adapter (EGA) to run AutoCAD, 27, 69-70, 293
Entity Coordinate System (ECS), 320
equipment schedules extracted from AutoCAD, 22
ergonomics of menu use, 189-190, 209
ERRORLEVEL to reveal errors, 58
errors
    AUTOEXEC.BAT, 548-549
    common to AutoCAD, 547-551
    EREAD, 88
    memory setting, 549-550
    messages for common, 547-548
    SHELL, 550
    tracing, 551
expanded memory, 84
    ACADLIMEM to indicate size of, 393-394
    AutoCAD's use of, 392-394
    configurations of AutoCAD and, 387-389
    dip switches for, 389-390
    management software for
        Enhanced Expanded Memory (EEMS), 86
        Expanded Memory Specification (EMS), 86
        Lotus-Intel Microsoft (LIM), 86
    protected mode to access, 85
    REMM.SYS, 79
    setup rules, 87-88
expansion bus, 68
Extended AutoLISP, 381, 389-390, 392, 394
extended I/O page space, 87, 388
extended memory
    ACADXMEM to indicate size of, 393-394
    AutoCAD's use of, 392-394

configurations of AutoCAD and, 387-389
crashes caused by memory conflicts between programs using, 550
dip switches for, 389-390
display-list processors' use of, 279
protected mode to access, 85, 378
RAM disk created with, 85
REX.SYS driver to use, 79
setup rules, 87-88
status screen to show use of, 89
usable by AutoCAD Release 10 with EXTLISP, 47
extrusions, 277

F

facilities management third-party products, 402, 564
FASTBACK Plus, 130
FAX machine to send drawings from AutoCAD, 22
field defined, 229
file allocation table (FAT)
    logical damage to, 63
    overwritten on RAM disk, 389
    rewritten by optimizer, 61
file extensions, table of typical, 33-35
file log for AutoCAD drawings, 114
file management, 143-147
file, PLOTBLK.DWG drawing, 160-161
file recovery, 65
file-naming conventions, 127-129, 137, 156
files
    archiving, 148-151
    font, 247-248
        .SHP, 248-249, 254
        .SHX, 248, 254
        factors, 248
        instruction codes (special codes), 250-251
        modifying, improving, and creating, 252-254
        opening description, 252
        vector codes, 250-251

formats for exporting and importing
    CDF (Delimited), 228-230, 234
    DIF (Drawing-Interchange File), 234
    DXB (Drawing Interchange Binary), 228-229
    DXF (Drawing Interchange Format), 228-230
    IGES (International Graphic Exchange Standard), 228-229
    SDF (Space Delimited Format), 228-230, 234
shape, 251
standards for erasing, 117
template, 233-234
files, AutoCAD
    ACAD.BAT, 47, 391-393
    ACAD.CFG, 391-392
    ACAD.DWG, 543-546
    ACAD.EXE, 392
    ACAD.LIN, 45, 244-245, 259, 403
    ACAD.LSP, 206, 240
        !ATOMLIST to check variable names in, 349, 403
        third-party products with separate, 403
    ACAD.MNU, 132-134
    ACAD.PAT, 39, 257, 403
    ACAD.PGP (AutoCAD Program Parameter), 39-40, 46
        to accept data from Lotus 1-2-3, 98
        as ASCII file, 37
        batch files in, 105
        DOS shell defined in, 32, 93
        to leave AutoCAD temporarily to run other programs, 105-109
        Slidemanager files placed in, 165
        structure, 105-107
        third-party product changes to, 403
        word processor used from, 66
    overlay (.OVL) and execution (.EXE), used from RAM disk, 388
SETUP.MNU, 132
shaded images created on videotape, prints, and slides from, 292
third-party products may require AutoCAD .DXB or files, LISP

Index

DEFUN C: statement to execute functions at AutoCAD prompt rather than as, 41
filters
   .XY, 284
   .XYZ, 273, 276
financial data extractable from AutoCAD, 22
financial issues concerning CAD, 10-12
fixture schedules extracted from AutoCAD, 22
flag added by microprocessor, 375
floppy disk
   drives, 33
   formats, 63
   rules for handling, 63
font
   character height, determining, 253
   files, 247-256
   monospaced, creating, 252-254
   scale factor of, 252
   third-party, 254-256
   vector, 249
functions, AutoCAD
   STARTUP, 162
functions, AutoLISP. *See also* AutoLISP
   and, 344
   angle, 313
   angtos, 309-310
   append, 321
   assoc, 321-322
   atof, 310
   caar, 322
   cadar, 322
   cadr, 322
   car, 322
   cdar, 322
   cddr, 322
   cdr, 322
   close, 342
   command, 307
   cond, 345
   cons, 323
   defun, 306
   distance, 314
   entdel, 328
   entget, 328
   entmod, 328-329
   entnext, 326-327
   entsel, 326
   entupd, 329-330
   equal, 345-346
   eval, 307-308
   findfile, 340
   float, 311
   getangle, 335
   getcorner, 335-336
   getdist, 336
   getenv, 336-337
   getint, 337
   getkword, 337
   getorient, 337-338
   getpoint, 338
   getreal, 41
   getstring, 338
   getvar, 338-339
   handent, 327
   if, 346
   initget, 339-340
   itoa, 310
   length, 323-324
   list, 323
   load, 305
   member, 324
   menucmd, 342
   nth, 324-325
   open, 340-341
   polar, 314
   prin1, 343
   princ, 343
   print, 343-344
   progn, 308
   prompt, 342-343
   read-line, 341
   rem, 314-315
   setq, 306-307, 331
   ssadd, 332
   ssdel, 332
   ssget, 330-331
   sslength, 331
   ssmemb, 332
   ssname, 331
   strcase, 311

strcat, 311
strlen, 312
subst, 325
substr, 312
tblnext, 333
tblsearch, 334
trans, 320-321
while, 346-347
write-line, 341

G

Gantt techniques, 99
GETKEY.COM machine language program for interactive batch files, 438-440
graphic aids third-party products, 401, 554
graphics card (adapters), 374
    CGA, 379
    display-list-processing, 279, 380-381
    EGA, 27, 69-70, 379
        AutoFlix use of, 293
    guidelines for buying advanced, 383
    multisync monitors work with variety of, 382
    palettes of colors for, 380
    PGA, 379
    software for, 382-383
    VGA, 379

H

halftones
    electrostatic plotters to produce, 384
    laser plotters to produce, 384
    simulating, 264
hard disk
    clearing space on, 60
    damage to, 64
    maintenance procedures, establishing, 117
    optimizers, 30, 61
    partitions, 33
    platens, 64
    required to run AutoCAD, 27

hardware, 67-71
    buying, 171-174
    concepts, advanced, 370-396
    configuration, new hardware and software compatibility with, 172
    input devices, 27-29
    pans and zooms, 381
    required to run AutoCAD, 27, 172
    servicing requirements, 173
    shifts, 15
    third-party sources for, 554-555
    utilities from third parties, 401-402, 404-405, 555-559
hatch patterns
    AutoCAD access to, 257
    cobblestone, 260-261
    defined, 256
    definition, 257
    limits to memory allowed for, 258
    material indication, 257-258
    modifying, improving, and creating, 258-262
    rendering, 262
Hatch-Maker (Cantec Software Systems), 258, 262
Hewlett Packard electrostatic plotter, 384
Hewlett Packard paintjet, 368
hidden lines, removing, 30
hot key defined, 102

I

IBM-compatibility refund guarantee, 173
IBM Professional Graphics Adapter, 70
icon(s)
    accessible with either digitizer or mouse, 29
    camera, 284
    commands, 198-199
    in slide library, 135
    of standard drawing sheet, 194
IGES file, 359
image capturing, 362-363
input-output devices
    for AutoCAD, 27-29
    functions of, 67

Index

for hand-written input, 395
voice-driven, 394
Input/Output (I/O) page space, 83
   extended, 87, 388
   for processing large menus, 388
installation of CAD system, 10, 14
   personnel for, 14-15
   workstation(s) for, 16-17
interrupt(s)
   hardware, 377
   number, 378
   processing, 377-378
   requests defined, 374
   software, 377
interrupt handler, 378

J

job-management tools, 465-516

K

kelvination, 208-209
Kensinger Consulting, 465
kerning, 254-255
keyboard
   ANSI.SYS driver to control, 79-80
   enhancements, 210
   lockups, TSR cause of, 549
keyboard buffer
   expanding, 28, 210
   to store keystrokes while AutoCAD processes commands, 28

L

layer(s)
   for 3-D drawings, 274
   combining purposes of, 152
   control, custom menus for, 191-192
   data sortable, 152
   duplication of, avoiding, 217
   freezing, 274
   line information included in names of, 156
   renaming routine, 441-451
   standard, 192-193
layering system based on construction industry specification system, 152-155
layer-naming conventions, 152-156
LCD panel projectors, 368
library
   project, creating, 164-165
   symbols
      customizing, 20
      digitizers to manipulate, 28
light examples in drawings
   ambient, 287-288
   diffuse, 287, 291
   direct source, 286, 290
   intensity, 287, 290
   point source, 289
   specular component, 287, 291
light, ray tracing to reproduce effects of, 357
line
   color, standardizing, 139
   hidden, 354
   information included in layer names, 156
   patterns, 259-261
   weight
      controlling, 239-240
      standardizing, 139
      standards, 240-241
lines
   dashed, 257
   on top of lines, plotting in color to reveal, 42
linetypes, 239
   alignment changes for, 243
   custom, LISP file for creating, 245-247
   definition, 241-242
   factors, 241
   modifying and improving, 244-245
LISP (LISt Processing) programming language, 298. *See also* AutoLISP
   argument defined, 302
   data type defined, 301

element, 302
entity defined, 301
expression
    defined, 302
    length, 304
file descriptor in, 302
group code defined, 301
list
    defined, 301
    evaluation of parentheses in nested, 299, 304
loop
    defined, 302
    recursive, 302
numbers in
    integer, 301, 304
    real, 301, 304, 309-311
pitfalls of programming in, 315
program defined, 300-301
spaces equivalent to single space in, 304
string
    defined, 301
    evaluation, 304
    null, 302
subroutine defined, 300
symbol
    defined, 301
    evaluation, 304
term definitions, 300-302
values
    bound, 301, 315
    nil, 302
    T, 302
LISP routine(s)
    3-D
        3DARRAY, 277
        3DCIRC, 277
        3DLISP, 277
        3DMESH, 277
        EDGESURF, 277
        PSURF, 277
        PYRAMID, 277
        REVSURF, 278
        RULESURF, 278
        TABSURF, 278
        TUBE, 278
attribute-extraction, 148
to automate drawing assembly and plotting (COMBPLOT.LSP), 218-220
for backups (BACKUP.LSP), 150
to combine drawings for plot (COMBPLOT.LSP), 525-528
to convert drawings from 3-D to 2-D, 271
to convert entities to new layers (CNVRT.LSP), 448-451
to convert nonblocked objects to polylines (LSRPREP.LSP), 411-422
to create a new set of layer names (LYRTBL.LSP), 442-447
to create drawing schedules (SCHED.LSP), 531-534
defined, 300
to develop LISP routines to perform repeated action in drawings (WIDGET.SCR), 528-530
to draw a schedule (SCHED.LSP), 225-227
to extract portion of a drawing (DTL.LSP), 423-427
to generate critical path data (CPM.LSP), 534-540
generic, developing reusable, 176
to import text, 541
indents in, 304
to insert drawing within current drawing (INSDET.LSP), 423, 428-434
to insert base drawing into current drawing, 158
library development, 400
in a macro, 199
to make your own linetypes (LINS.LSP), 245-247
Norton Editor for word processing, 103
pitfalls to avoid in, 315
to plot all current drawings in a plot directory (DPLOT.LSP), 159-161, 453-463
to read file output from database manager and create a drawing, 230
to remove standard layers for notes, title, and dimensions, 193
for text editing on drawings, 138

to track drawings (USER.LSP), 162-164, 509-512
   AutoCAD END command redefined for, 513
   job history report, 514-515
   time/task report, 513-514
long-persistence phosphors, 381
Lotus 1-2-3, 97-98
   AutoCAD used with, 227-231
   critical path generated by, 534-540
   for reports of drawing activity, 148

M

Mace, 30
macros
   to control symbol and function libraries, 28
   defined, 32
   menu. *See* menus, macro
   typing speed versus, 210
management concerns about CAD. *See* CAD management
manuals for CAD management
   office, 114
      for consultant procedures, 116-117
      for drawing management, 115-116
      for file management, 114-115
      for general procedures, 117-118
      for plot procedures, 116
   production, 19
   project, 19
mapping
   bump, 358
   defined, 358
   reflection, 358
   transparencies, 358
math coprocessor
   floating-point calculations handled by, 69
   functions performed by, 375
   required to run AutoCAD on IBM equipment, 27
media failures that cause file loss, 62-63
memory. *See also* expanded memory, extended memory, random access memory (RAM),

and read only memory (ROM)
addressability (real, extended, or expanded), 84
amount, 84
caching, 405
checking available, 549
classification of, 84-85
construction, 84
as factor in computer performance, 84
management, 86-88
   EREAD errors caused by improper, 88
   software in AutoCAD Release 10, 389, 550
   Virtual Control Program Interface standard for, 389
map, 86-87
reserve increased to run programs within AutoCAD, 108
settings, 549-550
type (ROM or RAM), 84
menu standards, coordinating, 116
menus, 184-213
   for 3-D drawings, 271
   accessible with either digitizer or mouse, 29
   for batch files, 144-146
   button
      commands, 198
      reprogramming, 41, 46
      test, 206
   conventions, 199
   customization of, 187
      to control and implement drawing standards, 190-191
      process, 195-201
   defined, 32
   Drawing Setup, 194
   durable, creating templates and protecting, 212
   ergonomics of using, 189-190, 209
   help, 211
   icon, 198-199
   library, combining, 211
   limitations, 195
   macro, 192-193, 195, 199-200, 240, 297, 400

ASMSTFSL 3 sample, 518-521
    icon, 522-524
    SILLS 3 sample, 517-518
    STDSTFSL 3 sample, 521-524
maintenance, 195, 201
Object Snap, 200
OSNAP, 189, 197
outline, 207
plot, 158
for presentation drawing development, 262
pull-down, 197-198
    tablet and screen versus, 209
screen, 41
    bracketed phrases in, 47
    pull-down and tablet versus, 209
size and computer speed, 201
special characters in, 199-200
submenu construction for, 196-197
switching between, 211
systems software, 402, 561-563
tablet, 41
    commands, 198
    pull-down and screen versus, 209
    test, 206
task, 200-201, 211, 262
third-party, 186-187, 205
    kelvination of, 208-209
    pitfalls of, 206
    presentation graphics in, 262
    protection schemes of, 208
    testing and debugging, 206-208
    updates to, 195
tips and tricks, 210-212
work manipulation with, 195-200
microprocessor, 375. *See also* math coprocessor
    families of, 378
    modes
        protected, 378
        real, 378
Microsoft Windows, 101
Microsoft Windows 386, 101
Microsoft Word text format for exporting to AutoCAD, 103
MiGRAPH software for report generation, 98
modeling, three-dimensional, 356
    fractals to produce procedural, 357
    normal, 357
    videotape for, 363
modem (MOdulation-DEModulation)
    ADESK Forum on CompuServe accessed via, 109-110
    exchange of data between other devices and, 69
    external, preferable for use with AutoCAD, 109
monitor
    with Enhanced Graphics Adapter (EGA) to run AutoCAD, 27, 69-70
    genlocking the, 363
    graphics card for, 69
    IBM Personal System/2, 70
    interlaced versus noninterlaced, 70
    large CRT, 368
    modes
        graphics, 379-380
        text, 379
    multisync, 382
    resolution of, 69
mouse
    AUI required for graphics card with, 27
    or digitizer required to run AutoCAD, 27
    disadvantages of using, 29
    exchange of data between other devices and, 69
    menu system used with, 209
movie (.MVI) files, 293
movies from three-dimensional drawing, 352-369. *See also* AutoFlix
    35mm slides to store, 364-367
    storyboards for, 365
MS-DOS
    V4.0, 90
    V4.1, 44
multiadapter boards, 374
MultiMate text format for exporting to AutoCAD, 103
multitasking software, 101-102

Index

N

National Television Standards Committee (NTSC) standard, 362
node space, 83
Norton Commander, 30, 108
    batch file to start, 53
    utilities, 94
Norton Editor, 30, 66, 103, 108
Norton Utilities, 30, 94
    commands added to ACAD.PGP file, 107
numbers
    binary defined, 372
    decimal
        compared with hexadecimal numbers, 373
        defined, 372
        translated with hexadecimal, 373-374
    hexadecimal
        compared with decimal numbers, 373
        defined, 372
        translated to decimal, 373-374
    integer, 224
        in LISP, 301, 304
    real
        entering, 41, 47
        formulas typically create, 224
        in LISP, 301, 304, 309-311
    strings including, 224
numeric keypad, 42

O

offset printing for camera-ready drawings, 265
operating system. *See also* MS-DOS, OS/2, *and* XENIX
    function of, 67
orientation, 223
OS/2
    advantages and disadvantages of, 90

P

parametric engines, 231
parametrics
    AutoLISP commands involving, 223
    components, 223-224
    in creating standard drawings, 202-203
    for schedule routines, 531-534
    WIDGET.SCR routine to develop routines with, 528-530
PC Boss, 30
PC Software Interest Group, 95
PC Week, 94
PC World, 94
PCTOOLS Deluxe, 30, 130
pen-up/pen-down specification, 241
peripheral devices, CPU communication with, 69
Personal Computing, 94
personnel
    acceptance and support of CAD system, 14-15
    shift coordination problems, 15
photo processor to create electronic slides, 367
photoreal images, 355, 367
pin-registered drafting, 156-158
piping, command, 60
pixel
    defined, 69
    magnification, 381
PKPAK utility, 94-95, 130, 150-151
PKZIP utility, 94-95
Plan and Print, 139
planes, 223
plot
    area
        of pen plotter a consideration in purchasing, 385
        relationship of sheet border, title block, and, 133
        standardizing, 135-139
    information stored in drawing, 158-161
    origin
        defined, 30

standardizing, 139
priority request procedure, 116
procedures in office manual, 116
request form, 116-117
resolution, 384-386
rotation, 30
service, 265-266
standard form for, 265
plotter(s), 384
   achieving predictable results from, 132
   basic process for using, 29-30
   buffer, 386-387
   cost, 387
   electrostatic, 384
   exchange of data between other devices and, 69
   language standards
      Digital Microprocessor/Plotting Language (DM/PL), 386
      Hewlett-Packard Graphic Language (HPGL), 386
   laser, 384
   media, standardizing, 139
   paper sizes accepted an important purchase factor with, 385
   pen, 384
      comparing capabilities before purchasing, 385-387
      flatbed versus rollerbed types of, 385
      stepper versus servo motors for, 385
   pens, standardizing, 139
   or printer plotter required to run AutoCAD, 27
   speed, 386
   supplies, 264-265
   transportability of drawings between, 134-135
plotting
   automated, 217-221
   media, 264-265
   standards, 139-140
polylines, 240
port (communication adapter)
   address conflict of programs run within AutoCAD, 108
   defined, 376
   parallel (Centronics), 69
   serial (RS-232), 69
primitives, imaging software to convert AutoCAD, 364
printer plotter
   basic process for using, 29-30
   or plotter required to run AutoCAD, 27
printers
   color, 367-368
   exchange of data between other devices and, 69
   laser, 104
printing
   an incomplete plot, 29-30
   prompts for, 29-30
product developed from AutoCAD customization
   beta test for, 180
   documentation for, 180
   guidelines for, 178-182
Proficient AutoCAD Enhancer (Communication Intelligence Corporation), 395
programmable timer chip, 376
programming
   classes offered by Autodesk, 21
   to customize AutoCAD, 20
project
   closeout procedures, 116
   conventions, 118-119
   data
      components of, 22
      management tasks, 143-144
   numbering system for, 121
Project Evaluation and Review Technique (PERT), 99
project management, 112-140
   3-D and, 269-271
   data, 22, 143-144
   database. See database, AutoCAD (.DXF)
   linked to drawing management with menus, 185-186
   overall procedures, 113-114
   programs, 99-101
project specifications extracted from AutoCAD, 22

projectors to send images from computer to large screen, 368
PROTECT.EXE protection program, 208

Q

quality control procedures, 114

R

radians, 224
RAM disk(s), 390-394
    AutoCAD files used from, 388
    created from extended memory, 85, 388, 391
    directory entries allowed in, 391
    drivers to create, 389
    file allocation table of, 389
    memory use of, 84
    multiple, 80
    setup procedure, 392-394
    size, 390
    temp drawings stored on, 393-394
    VDISK DOS utility to set up, 390
random access memory (RAM), 67
    access times, 77-78
    base memory as first 640K of, 85
    characteristics of, 84
    construction (dynamic, static, or static column), 85
    device driver use of, 78
    for page space in AutoCAD, 83
    set aside in buffers, 77
raster images, 356-357
    required for some electrostatic plotters, 384
raster to create screen images, 380
ray tracing, 357
read only memory (ROM), uses of, 84
record
    defined, 229
    maintenance, 162-164, 270
reflection mapping, 358

registers
    general purpose
        AX, 376
        BX, 376
        CX, 376
        DX, 376
    offset
        BP (Base Pointer), 377
        DI (Destination Index), 377
        IP (Instruction Pointer), 377
        SI (Source Index), 377
        SP (Stack Pointer), 377
    segment
        CS (Code Segment), 376-377
        DS (Data Segment), 377
        ES (Extra Segment), 377
        SS (Segment Stack), 377
renderings. *See also* drawings, presentation
    AutoCAD to develop, 262-263
    electronic slides for, 367
    hatch patterns to enhance, 256
    leaving AutoCAD to simulate reality in, 359-362
    three-dimensional, 352-369
        homemade slides of, 366
        service bureaus to produce, 355
            color printing for, 367-368
            electronic slides for, 367
Renderman interface (Pixar Corporation), 354
resources for CAD management, 407-408
revolved figures, 357
RGB camera, 362

S

scale(s)
    factor, 242
        of fonts, 252
    mixing, 138
    overdrawing a problem with reduced, 42
    standardized for reusable drawings, 137-138
    variable, 194-195
scan rate, 382

scanner input for three-dimensional
    presentation drawings, 362-363
SCO XENIX 386, 101
SCR_ALL.EXE, 149, 161
screen(s). See also monitor
    for halftones, 264
    refreshing, 381-382
    scan rate, 382
    virtual, 380, 388
script (.SCR) files, 216-222
    AutoFlix generation of, 293
    AutoLISP to write, 41, 47
    automated drawing with, 221-222
    COMBPLOT.SCR, 218
    to customize AutoCAD, 20, 109
    loading, 216
    PLOT, 59
    run on multiple drawings in directory with
        SCR_ALL.EXE, 515-516
    STRIP.SCR, 150
scripts defined, 216
section labels
    AUX1, 196
    BUTTON, 196
    ICON, 196
    POPn, 196
    SCREEN, 196-197
    TABLETn, 196
Seleris PC plot buffer (Western Automation),
    386-387
service bureaus, uses of
    for movies of three-dimensional presentation
        drawings, 367
    for photoreal images, 355
shading types
    Gouraud, 358
    Lambert, 358
    Phong, 358
shadow(s)
    casting defined, 358
    showing. See AutoShade
shapes
    automated drawing affected by, 222-223
    to aid drawing standardization, 204-205
    to insert freehand drawings, 239

shareware software for file and drawing
    maintenance, 165-166
sheet divisions, 135-136, 193-194
sheet size, modifications to ACAD.MNU file for
    varying, 133-134
shell program. See COMMAND.COM file (shell
    program) and DOS
Sidekick, 124
slide library, 135
    AutoCAD Support disk program to create,
        147
    for each project, 164-165
    icons created with, 198
    screen or icon menus to access, 147
    SLIDELIB program, 108
Slidemanager version 4.0, 165
slides, three-dimensional presentation images
    output as 35mm, 364-365
    electronic, 367
    homemade, 366
software
    additional, 566
    buying, 171-174
    civil design, 401, 560-561
    companion, 402, 565-566
    third-party add-on, 176-177, 284, 292,
        397-409, 553
space bar preferable to using Enter key, 42
spline curve, 239
spreadsheet programs, 97-99
stack defined, 377
standard symbols, 271
Sun Microsystems 386i, 101
SuperCalc, 97
superimposition, 362-363
Superkey, 124
sweeps
    creating, 357
    tweening as three-dimensional, 359
symbols libraries, 402, 565
system configuration, 75
system management
    basic, 74-91
    improper, 64

T

tablet menu, 28
tape storage, RCD.SYS driver to control, 79
task menuing, 200-201
temp drawing directory size, 388
terminate-and-stay-resident (TSR) software, 101-102
   compatibility issues for third-party products, 403-404
   lockups caused by, 549
   system memory reduced by adding, 124
textures defined, 358
third-party product
   Autodesk Forum best resource for evaluating, 405-406
   information categories, 401-402
   tests, 405
   warranties, support, and service issues, 404-405
throughput defined, 68
time records, 101, 128
time-management software, 99, 101
TOPAS imaging software (AT&T), 360
torus as circle placed on circular sweep, 357
training on AutoCAD, 20-21
transmittal letters, implementation of, 115
transparencies, mapping, 358

U

uninterrupted power supply (UPS) system, 64, 84
User Coordinate System (UCS), 40, 279-280
   configurations, standard
      names and settings for, 282
      saving, 282
   translating between WCS, DCS, and, 320-321
users' groups, AutoCAD, 43
   bug testing through, 348
   CAD managers recommended to join, 401
   Memphis Chapter, 43

addresses and telephone numbers of, 567-581
as way to stay informed, 177
utilities, DOS. *See* DOS

V

variables
   ATTDIA, 206
   ATTMODE, 206
   ATTREQ, 206
   CMDECHO, 206
   DIM, 40, 46
   DRAGMODE, 206
   environment
      ACAD, 82
      ACADCFG, 57, 82-83
      ACADFREERAM, 83
      ACADLIMEM, 83, 88
      ACADXMEM, 83, 88
      LISPHEAP, 83
      LISPSTACK, 83
      setting, 82
   EXPERT, 206
   LTSCALE, 206, 240, 411
   POPUPS, 206
   system
      AXISMODE, 282
      changing all, 40, 46
      GRIDMODE, 282
      read-only, 46
      settings, 282
      SURFTAB1, 291
      SURFTAB2, 291
      UCDFOLLOW, 282
      UCSICON, 282
   TEXTEVAL, 206
   user-definable
      USERI1-4, 206
      USERR1-4, 206
vector
   codes, 250-251
   defined, 356
Ventura Publisher, 71, 104

video input
   camera, genlocking, 363
   for three-dimensional presentation drawings, 362-363
video output (modeling), 363-365
   to a printer or slides, 364
   stages in, 364
videotape for modeling, 363
viewports
   new in Release 10, 279
   viewing objects from multiple, 272, 280-281
view(s)
   FRONT (standard), 280
      coordinates, 278
      developing, 272
   isometric, 283
   LSIDE standard, 280
   PLAN, 273
      standard, 280
   REAR, 282
   RSIDE, 280
Virtual Control Program Interface (VCPI)
   memory management standard, 389
virtual disk. *See* RAM disk
virtual memory, 378
virtual screen, 380, 388
VisiCalc, 97
VoiceMate (CaddLINK Corporation), 394

W

wait states defined, 68
wild cards (* and ?), 37
wire frames, 354
word processor(s), 65-67
   in ASCII or nondocument mode
      for all AutoCAD text editing, 66
      to write AutoLISP routines and modify menus, 41, 46
      to write batch files, 53
   recommendation to use two, 66-67
   as supplemental software for AutoCAD, 30, 103
WordPerfect 4.2, 30

   to capture AutoCAD drawing, 66
   text format for exporting to AutoCAD, 103
WordStar, 30, 66
   batch file to start, 53-54
WordStar 2000, 103
WordStar Professional, 103
work flow
   analysis of AutoCAD use, 188-190
   for projects using CAD, 10, 12
workstation
   considerations for furnishings of, 16
   design, 17
      adjustable monitors, 16
      furniture, lighting, and electrical installations, 17
      table height, 16
   sample, 17
World Coordinate System (WCS), 40
   translating between UCS, DCS, and, 320-321
   UCS set from, 282
WORM (write once read many) drive, 62

X

XENIX, 90

Z

zooms performed by graphics cards, 381

More Computer Knowledge from Que

LOTUS SOFTWARE TITLES

1-2-3 QueCards	21.95
1-2-3 QuickStart	21.95
1-2-3 Quick Reference	6.95
1-2-3 for Business, 2nd Edition	22.95
1-2-3 Command Language	21.95
1-2-3 Macro Library, 2nd Edition	21.95
1-2-3 Tips, Tricks, and Traps, 2nd Edition	21.95
Using 1-2-3, Special Edition	24.95
Using 1-2-3 Workbook and Disk, 2nd Edition	29.95
Using Symphony, 2nd Edition	26.95

DATABASE TITLES

dBASE III Plus Handbook, 2nd Edition	22.95
dBASE IV Handbook, 3rd Edition	23.95
dBASE IV Tips, Tricks, and Traps, 2nd Edition	21.95
dBASE IV QueCards	21.95
dBASE IV Quick Reference	6.95
dBASE IV QuickStart	21.95
dBXL and Quicksilver Programming: Beyond dBASE	24.95
R:BASE Solutions: Applications and Resources	19.95
R:BASE User's Guide, 3rd Edition	19.95
Using Clipper	24.95
Using Reflex	19.95
Using Paradox, 2nd Edition	22.95
Using Q & A, 2nd Edition	21.95

MACINTOSH AND APPLE II TITLES

HyperCard QuickStart: A Graphics Approach	21.95
Using AppleWorks, 2nd Edition	21.95
Using dBASE Mac	19.95
Using Dollars and Sense	19.95
Using Excel	21.95
Using HyperCard: From Home to HyperTalk	24.95
Using Microsoft Word: Macintosh Version	21.95
Using Microsoft Works	19.95
Using WordPerfect: Macintosh Version	19.95

APPLICATIONS SOFTWARE TITLES

CAD and Desktop Publishing Guide	24.95
Smart Tips, Tricks, and Traps	23.95
Using AutoCAD	29.95
Using DacEasy	21.95
Using Dollars and Sense: IBM Version, 2nd Edition	19.95
Using Enable/OA	23.95
Using Excel: IBM Version	24.95
Using Managing Your Money	19.95
Using Quattro	21.95
Using Smart	22.95
Using SuperCalc4	21.95

HARDWARE AND SYSTEMS TITLES

DOS Programmer's Reference	24.95
DOS QueCards	21.95
DOS Tips, Tricks, and Traps	22.95
DOS Workbook and Disk	29.95
IBM PS/2 Handbook	21.95
Managing Your Hard Disk, 2nd Edition	22.95
MS-DOS Quick Reference	6.95
MS-DOS QuickStart	21.95
MS-DOS User's Guide, 3rd Edition	22.95
Networking IBM PCs, 2nd Edition	19.95
Programming with Windows	22.95
Understanding UNIX: A Conceptual Guide, 2nd Edition	21.95
Upgrading and Repairing PCs	24.95
Using Microsoft Windows	19.95
Using OS/2	22.95
Using PC DOS, 2nd Edition	22.95

WORD-PROCESSING AND DESKTOP PUBLISHING TITLES

Microsoft Word Techniques and Applications	19.95
Microsoft Word Tips, Tricks, and Traps	19.95
Using DisplayWrite 4	19.95
Using Microsoft Word, 2nd Edition	21.95
Using MultiMate Advantage, 2nd Edition	19.95
Using PageMaker IBM Version, 2nd Edition	24.95
Using PFS: First Publisher	22.95
Using Sprint	21.95
Using Ventura Publisher, 2nd Edition	24.95
Using WordPerfect, 3rd Edition	21.95
Using WordPerfect 5	24.95
Using WordPerfect 5 Workbook and Disk	29.95
Using WordStar, 2nd Edition	21.95
WordPerfect Macro Library	21.95
WordPerfect QueCards	21.95
WordPerfect Quick Reference	6.95
WordPerfect QuickStart	21.95
WordPerfect Tips, Tricks, and Traps, 2nd Edition	21.95
WordPerfect 5 Workbook and Disk	29.95
Ventura Publisher Tips, Tricks, and Traps	24.95
Ventura Publisher Techniques and Applications	22.95

PROGRAMMING AND TECHNICAL TITLES

Assembly Language Quick Reference	6.95
C Programming Guide, 3rd Edition	24.95
C Quick Reference	6.95
DOS and BIOS Functions Quick Reference	6.95
QuickBASIC Quick Reference	6.95
Turbo Pascal Quick Reference	6.95
Turbo Pascal Tips, Tricks, and Traps	19.95
Using Assembly Language	24.95
Using QuickBASIC 4	19.95
Using Turbo Pascal	21.95
AutoCAD Quick Reference	6.95

Que Order Line: 1-800-428-5331

All prices subject to change without notice. Prices and charges are for domestic orders only.
Non-U.S. prices might be higher.

SELECT QUE BOOKS TO INCREASE YOUR PERSONAL COMPUTER PRODUCTIVITY

Using AutoCAD
by Brenda L. Fouch

AutoCAD is the computer-aided design program that lets you perform complex design and drafting operations on your personal computer. Que's *Using Auto-CAD* is the long-awaited tutorial and desktop reference to the latest version of this popular program, Release 10. This text explains the program's concepts, command structures, and applications, while teaching you the written and unwritten basics of AutoCAD. With *Using AutoCAD*, you will learn how to create, edit, enhance, and plot drawings; customize menus and tablets; and utilize AutoCAD's 3-D capabilities. Picture the power of AutoCAD with *Using AutoCAD*!

Order #92
$29.95 USA
0-88022-288-3, 650 pp.

CAD and Desktop Publishing Guide
Developed by Que Corporation

This book is the ultimate resource for anyone using computer-aided design, desktop publishing, or presentation graphics on a personal computer. The *Guide* is a comprehensive directory to software, hardware, systems, accessories, and services for the three fastest-growing new personal computer technologies. Thousands of listings are included, each with complete product and company information.

Order #864
$24.95 USA
0-880-22-367-7, 400 pp.

Upgrading and Repairing PCs
by Scott Mueller

A comprehensive resource to personal computer upgrade, repair, maintenance, and troubleshooting. All types of IBM computers—from the original PC to the new PS/2 models—are covered, as are major IBM compatibles. You will learn about the components inside your computers, as well as how to use this information to troubleshoot problems and make informed decisions about upgrading.

Order #882
$27.95 USA
0-88022-395-2, 750 pp.

Using Ventura Publisher, 2nd Edition
by Diane Burns, S. Venit, and Linda Mercer

This is a comprehensive text for all levels of Ventura Publisher users. You will learn both program basics and design fundamentals as you progress step-by-step through this informative text. Dozens of detailed example documents are presented, and the new features of Ventura Publisher 2.0—including Professional Extension—are highlighted. Learn how to produce professional publications with *Using Ventura Publisher*, 2nd Edition!

Order #940
$24.95 USA
0-88022-406-1, 800 pp.